BEGINNING

JavaScript®

Fifth Edition

Jeremy McPeak
Paul Wilton

wrox
A Wiley Brand

Beginning JavaScript® 5e

Published by
John Wiley & Sons, Inc.
10475 Crosspoint Boulevard
Indianapolis, IN 46256
www.wiley.com

Copyright © 2015 by John Wiley & Sons, Inc., Indianapolis, Indiana

Published simultaneously in Canada

ISBN: 978-1-118-90333-9
ISBN: 978-1-118-90343-8 (ebk)
ISBN: 978-1-118-90374-2 (ebk)

Manufactured in the United States of America

C10003374_081518

For general information on our other products and services please contact our Customer Care Department within the United States at (877) 762-2974, outside the United States at (317) 572-3993 or fax (317) 572-4002.

Wiley publishes in a variety of print and electronic formats and by print-on-demand. Some material included with standard print versions of this book may not be included in e-books or in print-on-demand. If this book refers to media such as a CD or DVD that is not included in the version you purchased, you may download this material at http://booksupport.wiley.com. For more information about Wiley products, visit www.wiley.com.

Library of Congress Control Number: 2014958440

CREDITS

ABOUT THE AUTHORS

JEREMY McPEAK is a self-taught programmer who began his career by tinkering with websites in 1998. He is the author of JavaScript 24-Hour Trainer (Wiley 2010) and co-author of Professional Ajax, 2nd Edition (Wiley 2007). He also contributes to Tuts+ Code (`http://code.tutsplus.com`), providing articles, video tutorials, and courses for JavaScript, C#, and ASP.NET. He is currently employed by an oil and gas company building in-house conventional and web applications. Jeremy can be contacted via the p2p forums, his website (`http://www.wdonline.com`), and Twitter (@jwmcpeak).

PAUL WILTON started as a Visual Basic applications programmer at the Ministry of Defense in the UK and then found himself pulled into the Net. Having joined an Internet development company, he spent three years helping create Internet solutions. He's now running his own successful and rapidly growing company developing online holiday property reservation systems.

ACKNOWLEDGMENTS

FIRST AND FOREMOST, I want to thank God for the blessings he has bestowed upon me, and thank you, dear reader, for without you this book would not be possible. Also, a huge thank you goes to my wife and family for putting up with me as I spent my available weekend free-time updating this book.

Writing and producing a book requires a lot of people, and I know I cannot name everyone who has had a hand in this project. But a very big thank you goes to Jim Minatel and Robert Elliott for green-lighting this project. Thank you Kelly Talbot for keeping me on track and putting up with me. To the editing team, thank you for making my text look good. And to Russ Mullen, thanks for keeping me honest.

— JEREMY MCPEAK

FIRST, A BIG THANK you to my partner Beci, who, now that the book's finished, will get to see me for more than 10 minutes a week.

I'd also like to say a very big thank you to the editors, who worked very efficiently on getting this book into print.

Thanks also to Jim Minatel for making this book happen.

Many thanks to everyone who's supported and encouraged me over my many years of writing books. Your help will always be remembered.

Finally, pats and treats to my German Shepherd Dog, Katie, who does an excellent job of warding off disturbances from door-to-door salespeople.

— PAUL WILTON

CONTENTS

INTRODUCTION

JAVASCRIPT IS A SCRIPTING LANGUAGE that enables you to enhance static web applications by providing dynamic, personalized, and interactive content. This improves the experience of visitors to your site and makes it more likely that they will visit again. You must have seen the flashy drop-down menus, moving text, and changing content that are now widespread on websites—they are enabled through JavaScript. Supported by all the major browsers, JavaScript is the language of choice on the web. It can even be used outside web applications—to automate administrative tasks, for example.

This book aims to teach you all you need to know to start experimenting with JavaScript: what it is, how it works, and what you can do with it. Starting from the basic syntax, you'll move on to learn how to create powerful web applications. Don't worry if you've never programmed before—this book will teach you all you need to know, step by step. You'll find that JavaScript can be a great introduction to the world of programming: with the knowledge and understanding that you'll gain from this book, you'll be able to move on to learn newer and more advanced technologies in the world of computing.

WHO THIS BOOK IS FOR

To get the most out of this book, you'll need to have an understanding of HTML, CSS, and how to create a static web page. You don't need to have any programming experience.

This book will also suit you if you have some programming experience already and would like to turn your hand to web programming. You will know a fair amount about computing concepts, but maybe not as much about web technologies.

Alternatively, you may have a design background and know relatively little about the web and computing concepts. For you, JavaScript will be a cheap and relatively easy introduction to the world of programming and web application development.

Whoever you are, I hope that this book lives up to your expectations.

WHAT THIS BOOK COVERS

You'll begin by looking at exactly what JavaScript is, and taking your first steps with the underlying language and syntax. You'll learn all the fundamental programming concepts, including data and data types, and structuring your code to make decisions in your programs or to loop over the same piece of code many times.

Once you're comfortable with the basics, you'll move on to one of the key ideas in JavaScript—the object. You'll learn how to take advantage of the objects that are native to the JavaScript language, such as functions, dates, and strings, and find out how these objects enable you to manage complex data and simplify your programs. Next, you'll see how you can use JavaScript to manipulate and detect objects made available to you in the browser and detect the browsers.

From here, you'll move on to more advanced topics, such as writing code to dynamically manipulate elements within a web page and executing code when certain things happen within your page. You'll also learn how to script forms and other controls. Using this knowledge, you can start to create truly professional-looking applications that enable you to interact with the user.

You'll then learn how to store data within the browser and communicate directly with a server. You'll also learn how to write code for the new HTML5 media elements, and write your own custom user interface for them.

You'll explore some of the time saving JavaScript frameworks such as jQuery, Modernizr, Prototype, and MooTools and see how they work and how they can help you create sophisticated JavaScript powered applications.

Finally, you'll look at common syntax and logical errors, how you can spot them, and how to use the JavaScript debuggers for Chrome, Internet Explorer, Firefox, Safari, and Opera to aid you with this task. Also, you need to examine how to handle the errors that slip through the net, and ensure that these do not detract from the experience of the end user of your application.

All the new concepts introduced in this book will be illustrated with practical examples, which enable you to experiment with JavaScript and build on the theory that you have just learned.

You'll find four appendixes at the end of the book. Appendix A provides solutions to the exercises included at the end of most chapters throughout the book. The remaining appendixes contain the reference material that your authors hope you find useful and informational. Appendix B contains the JavaScript language's core reference. Appendix C contains a complete W3C DOM Core reference—as well as information on the HTML DOM and DOM level 2 Event model. Appendix D contains the decimal and hexadecimal character codes for the Latin-1 character set.

WHAT YOU NEED TO USE THIS BOOK

Because JavaScript is a text-based technology, all you really need to create documents containing JavaScript is a text editor. Any will do.

Also, in order to try out the code in this book, you will need a web browser that supports a modern version of JavaScript. Ideally, this means the latest versions of Chrome, Internet Explorer, Firefox, Safari, and Opera. The book has been extensively tested with these browsers. However, the code should work in any modern web browser. Where there are exceptions, they will be clearly noted.

CONVENTIONS

To help you get the most from the text and keep track of what's happening, we've used a number of conventions throughout the book.

TRY IT OUT

The *Try It Out* is an exercise you should work through, following the text in the book.

1. It usually consists of a set of steps.

2. Each step has a number.

3. Follow the steps with your copy of the database.

As you work through each *Try It Out*, the code you've typed will be explained in detail.

> **WARNING** Boxes like this one hold important, not-to-be forgotten information that is directly relevant to the surrounding text.

> **NOTE** *Tips, hints, tricks, and asides to the current discussion are offset and placed in italics like this.*

As for styles in the text:

➤ We *highlight in italic type* new terms and important words when we introduce them.

➤ We show keyboard strokes like this: Ctrl+A.

➤ We show file names, URLs, and code within the text like so: `persistence.properties`.

➤ We present code in two different ways:

```
Important code in code examples is highlighted with a gray background.
The gray highlighting is not used for code that's less important in the present
context, or that has been shown before.
```

SOURCE CODE

As you work through the examples in this book, you may choose either to type in all the code manually or to use the source-code files that accompany the book. All of the source code used in this book is available for download at www.wrox.com. Once at the site, simply locate the book's title (either by using the Search box or by using one of the title lists) and click the Download Code link on the book's detail page to obtain all the source code for the book.

> **NOTE** *Because many books have similar titles, you may find it easiest to search by ISBN; this book's ISBN is 978-1-118-90333-9.*

Once you download the code, just decompress it with your favorite compression tool. Alternately, you can go to the main Wrox code download page at www.wrox.com/dynamic/books/ download.aspx to see the code available for this book and all other Wrox books.

You can also view the examples presented in this book at http://beginningjs.com.

ERRATA

We make every effort to ensure that there are no errors in the text or in the code. However, no one is perfect, and mistakes do occur. If you find an error in one of our books, like a spelling mistake or faulty piece of code, we would be very grateful for your feedback. By sending in errata, you may save another reader hours of frustration, and at the same time you will be helping us provide even higher-quality information.

To find the errata page for this book, go to www.wrox.com and locate the title using the Search box or one of the title lists. Then, on the book details page, click the Book Errata link. On this page you can view all errata that have been submitted for this book and posted by Wrox editors. A complete book list, including links to each book's errata, is also available at www.wrox.com/ misc-pages/booklist.shtml.

If you don't spot "your" error on the Book Errata page, go to www.wrox.com/contact/ techsupport.shtml and complete the form there to send us the error you have found. We'll check the information and, if appropriate, post a message to the book's errata page and fix the problem in subsequent editions of the book.

P2P.WROX.COM

For author and peer discussion, join the P2P forums at p2p.wrox.com. The forums are a web-based system on which you can post messages relating to Wrox books and related technologies and interact with other readers and technology users. The forums offer a subscription feature to e-mail you topics of interest of your choosing when new posts are made to the forums. Wrox authors, editors, other industry experts, and your fellow readers are present on these forums.

At http://p2p.wrox.com you will find a number of different forums that will help you not only as you read this book, but also as you develop your own applications. To join the forums, just follow these steps:

1. Go to p2p.wrox.com and click the Register link.

2. Read the terms of use and click Agree.

3. Complete the required information to join as well as any optional information you wish to provide, and click Submit.

4. You will receive an e-mail with information describing how to verify your account and complete the joining process.

> **NOTE** You can read messages in the forums without joining P2P, but in order to post your own messages, you must join.

Once you join, you can post new messages and respond to messages other users post. You can read messages at any time on the web. If you would like to have new messages from a particular forum e-mailed to you, click the Subscribe to this Forum icon by the forum name in the forum listing.

For more information about how to use the Wrox P2P, be sure to read the P2P FAQs for answers to questions about how the forum software works, as well as many common questions specific to P2P and Wrox books. To read the FAQs, click the FAQ link on any P2P page.

1

Introduction to JavaScript and the Web

WHAT YOU WILL LEARN IN THIS CHAPTER:

- ➤ Adding JavaScript to your web pages
- ➤ Referencing external JavaScript files
- ➤ Changing the background color of a web page

WROX.COM CODE DOWNLOADS FOR THIS CHAPTER

You can find the wrox.com code downloads for this chapter at `http://www.wiley.com/go/ BeginningJavaScript5E` on the Download Code tab. You can also view all of the examples and related files at `http://beginningjs.com`.

In this introductory chapter, you look at what JavaScript is, what it can do for you, and what you need in order to use it. With these foundations in place, you will see throughout the rest of the book how JavaScript can help you to create powerful web applications for your website.

The easiest way to learn something is by actually doing it, so throughout the book you create a number of useful example programs using JavaScript. This process starts in this chapter, by the end of which you will have created your first piece of JavaScript code.

INTRODUCTION TO JAVASCRIPT

In this section you take a brief look at what JavaScript is, where it came from, how it works, and what sorts of useful things you can do with it.

What Is JavaScript?

Having bought this book, you are probably already well aware that JavaScript is some sort of *computer language*, but what is a computer language? Put simply, a computer language is a series of instructions that tell the computer to do something. That something can be one of a wide variety of things, including displaying text, moving an image, or asking the user for information. Normally, the instructions, or what is termed *code*, are *processed* from the top line downward. This simply means that the computer looks at the code you've written, works out what action you want it to take, and then takes that action. The act of processing the code is called *running* or *executing* it.

In natural English, here are instructions, or code, you might write to make a cup of instant coffee:

1. Put coffee crystals in cup.
2. Fill kettle with water.
3. Put kettle on to boil.
4. Has the kettle boiled? If so, then pour water into cup; otherwise, continue to wait.
5. Drink coffee.

You'd start running this code from the first line (instruction 1), and then continue to the next (instruction 2), then the next, and so on until you came to the end. This is pretty much how most computer languages work, JavaScript included. However, on some occasions you might change the flow of execution or even skip over some code, but you see more of this in Chapter 3.

JavaScript is an interpreted language rather than a compiled language. What is meant by the terms *interpreted* and *compiled*?

Well, to let you in on a secret, your computer doesn't really understand JavaScript at all. It needs something to interpret the JavaScript code and convert it into something that it understands; hence it is an *interpreted language*. Computers understand only *machine code*, which is essentially a string of binary numbers (that is, a string of zeros and ones). As the browser goes through the JavaScript, it passes it to a special program called an *interpreter*, which converts the JavaScript to the machine code your computer understands. It's a bit like having a translator translate English to Spanish, for example. The important point to note is that the conversion of the JavaScript happens at the time the code is run; it has to be repeated every time this happens. JavaScript is not the only interpreted language; others exist, including PHP and Ruby.

The alternative *compiled language* is one in which the program code is converted to machine code before it's actually run, and this conversion has to be done only once. The programmer uses a compiler to convert the code that he wrote to machine code, and this machine code is run by the program's user. Compiled languages include C#, Java, and many others. Using a real⊠world analogy, it's a bit like having a Spanish translator verbally tell you in English what a Spanish document says. Unless you change the document, you can use it without retranslation as much as you like.

Perhaps this is a good place to dispel a widespread myth: JavaScript is not the script version of the Java language. In fact, although they share the same name, that's virtually all they do share. Particularly good news is that JavaScript is much, much easier to learn and use than Java. In fact, languages like JavaScript are the easiest of all languages to learn, but they are still surprisingly powerful.

JavaScript and the Web

For most of this book you look at JavaScript code that runs inside a web page loaded into a browser. All you need to create these web pages is a text editor—for example, Windows Notepad—and a web browser, such as Chrome, Firefox, or Internet Explorer (IE), with which you can view your pages. These browsers come equipped with JavaScript interpreters (more commonly known as JavaScript engines).

> **NOTE** *Throughout this book, we use the terms "IE" and "Internet Explorer" interchangeably when referring to Microsoft's Internet Explorer browser.*

In fact, the JavaScript language first became available in Netscape's Navigator 2. Initially, it was called LiveScript, but because Java was the hot technology of the time, Netscape decided that JavaScript sounded more exciting. When JavaScript really took off, Microsoft decided to add its own dialect of JavaScript, called JScript, to Internet Explorer 3.

In 1997, JavaScript was standardized by Ecma International, a membership-based non-profit organization, and renamed to ECMAScript. Today's browser makers look to the ECMAScript standard to implement the JavaScript engines included in their respective browsers, but that doesn't necessarily mean that all browsers support the same features. JavaScript support among today's browsers is certainly more unified than it has ever been, but as you see in future chapters, developers still have to cope with older, and in many cases non-standard, JavaScript implementations.

The ECMAScript standard controls various aspects of the language and helps ensure that different versions of JavaScript are compatible. However, although Ecma sets standards for the actual language, it doesn't specify how it's used in particular hosts. By *host*, we mean hosting environment; in this book, that is the web browser. Other hosting environments include PDF files, web servers, and many, many other places. In this book, we discuss only its use within the web browser. The organization that sets the standards for web pages is the World Wide Web Consortium (W3C). It not only sets standards for HTML and CSS, but also for how JavaScript interacts with web pages inside a web browser. You learn much more about this in later chapters of the book. Initially, you'll look at the essentials of JavaScript before the more advanced stuff. In the appendices of this book, you'll find useful guides to the JavaScript language and how it interacts with the web browser.

The majority of the web pages containing JavaScript that you create in this book can be stored on your hard drive and loaded directly into your browser from the hard drive itself, just as you'd load any normal file (such as a text file). However, this is not how web pages are loaded when you browse websites on the Internet. The Internet is really just one great big network connecting computers. Access to websites is a special service provided by particular computers on the Internet; the computers providing this service are known as *web servers*.

Basically, the job of a web server is to hold lots of web pages on its hard drive. When a browser, usually on a different computer, requests a web page contained on that web server, the web server loads it from its own hard drive and then passes the page back to the requesting computer via a special communications protocol called *Hypertext Transfer Protocol (HTTP)*. The computer running the web browser that makes the request is known as the *client*. Think of the client/server relationship as a bit like a customer/shopkeeper relationship. The customer goes into a shop and says, "Give me one of those." The shopkeeper serves the customer by reaching for the item requested and passing it back to the customer. In a web situation, the client machine running the web browser is like the customer, and the web server providing the page requested is like the shopkeeper.

When you type an address into the web browser, how does it know which web server to get the page from? Well, just as shops have addresses, say, 45 Central Avenue, Sometownsville, so do web servers. Web servers don't have street names; instead, they have *Internet protocol (IP) addresses*, which uniquely identify them on the Internet. These consist of four sets of numbers, separated by dots (for example, `127.0.0.1`).

If you've ever surfed the Net, you're probably wondering what on earth we're talking about. Surely web servers have nice `www.somewebsite.com` names, not IP addresses? In fact, the `www.somewebsite.com` name is the "friendly" name for the actual IP address; it's a whole lot easier for us humans to remember. On the Internet, the friendly name is converted to the actual IP address by computers called *domain name servers*, which your Internet service provider will have set up for you.

What Can JavaScript Do for Me?

JavaScript is primarily used to interact with users. That's a rather broad statement, so let's break "interact with users" into two categories: user input validation and enhancement.

JavaScript was originally created for validating form input. For example, if you had a form that takes a user's credit card details in preparation for on online purchase of goods, you'd want to make sure he had actually filled in those details before you sent the goods. You might also want to check that the data being entered is of the correct type, such as a number for his age rather than text.

Thanks to the advances made in today's JavaScript engines, JavaScript is used for much, much more than input⊠related tasks. In fact, advanced JavaScript⊠driven applications can be created that rival the speed and functionality of conventional desktop applications. Examples of such applications include Google Maps, Google Calendar, and even full⊠fledged productivity software such as Microsoft's Office Web Apps. These applications provide a real service. In most of these applications, JavaScript only powers the user interface, with the actual data processing being done on the server. But even then, JavaScript could be used on the server if used with a JavaScript⊠based processing engine (one such environment is called Node).

Tools Needed to Create JavaScript Web Applications

The great news is that learning JavaScript requires no expensive software purchases; you can learn JavaScript for free on any PC or Mac. This section discusses what tools are available and how to obtain them.

Development Tools

All that you need to get started writing JavaScript code for web applications is a simple text editor, such as Notepad for Windows or TextEdit for Mac OS X. You can also use one of the many advanced text editors that provide line numbering, color coding, search and replace, and so on. Here are just a few:

➤ **Notepad2 (Windows):** `www.flos freeware.ch/notepad2.html`

➤ **WebMatrix (Windows):** `www.microsoft.com/web/webmatrix/`

➤ **Brackets (Cross Platform):** `brackets.io`

➤ **Sublime Text (Cross Platform):** `www.sublimetext.com`

Sublime Text is not free software, but it does have a time limited evaluation. If you try it and like it, please support the developers of that application.

You might also prefer a proper HTML editor; you'll need one that enables you to edit the HTML source code, because that's where you need to add your JavaScript. A number of very good tools specifically aimed at developing web based applications, such as Adobe's Dreamweaver, are also available. However, this book concentrates on JavaScript rather than any specific development tool. When it comes to learning the basics, it's often best to write the code by hand rather than rely on a tool to do it for you. This helps you understand the fundamentals of the language before you attempt the more advanced logic that is beyond a tool's capability. When you have a good understanding of the basics, you can use tools as timesavers so that you can spend time on the more advanced and more interesting coding.

Once you become more proficient, you may find that a web page editor makes life easier by inclusion of features such as checking the validity of your code, color coding important JavaScript words, and making it easier to view your pages before loading them into a web browser. Many other, equally good, free web page editors are available. A Google search on web editing software will bring back a long list of software you can use.

As you write web applications of increasing complexity, you'll find useful tools that help you spot and solve errors. Errors in code are what programmers call bugs, though when our programs go wrong, we prefer to call them "unexpected additional features." Very useful in solving bugs are development tools called debuggers. Debuggers let you monitor what is happening in your code as it's running. In Chapter 18, you take an in depth look at bugs and debugger development tools.

Web Browsers

In addition to software that lets you edit web pages, you'll also need a browser to view your web pages. It's best to develop your JavaScript code on the sorts of browsers you expect visitors to use to access your website. You see later in the chapter that although browsers are much more standards based, differences exist in how they view web pages and treat JavaScript code. All the examples provided in this book have been tested on Chrome, IE9 11, Firefox, Safari, and Opera. Wherever a piece of code does not work on any of these browsers, a note to this effect is made in the text.

If you're running Windows, you'll almost certainly have IE installed. If not, a trip to `windows.microsoft.com/en us/internet explorer/download ie` will get you the latest version for your version of Windows.

You can find Chrome at www.google.com/chrome, and you can download Firefox at www.getfirefox.com.

By default, most browsers have JavaScript support enabled, but it is possible to disable this functionality in all browsers except Firefox. So before you start on your first JavaScript examples in the next section, you should check to make sure JavaScript is enabled in your browser.

To do this in Chrome, you want to modify the JavaScript settings in Content Settings, as shown in Figure 1-1. You can access these settings by navigating to chrome://settings/content or by following these instructions:

1. Go to the Settings option in the menu.

2. Click the "Show advanced settings…" link.

3. Under Privacy, click the "Content settings…" button.

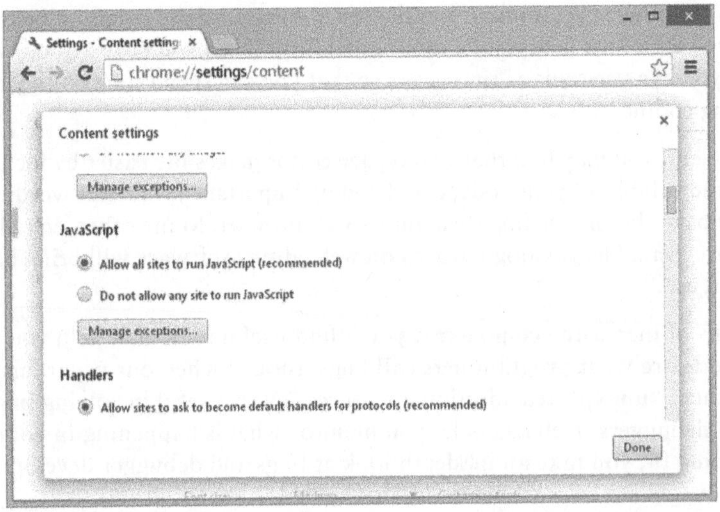

FIGURE 1-1

It is harder to turn off scripting in Internet Explorer. Choose Internet Options from the menu (the gear icon in the upper⊠right corner), click the Security tab, and check whether the Internet or Local intranet options have custom security settings. If either of them does, click the Custom Level button and scroll down to the Scripting section. Check that Active Scripting is set to Enable.

A final point to note is how to open the code examples in your browser. For this book, you simply need to open the file on your hard drive in which an example is stored. You can do this in a number of ways, but the easiest is to just double⊠click the file.

WHERE DO MY SCRIPTS GO?

Inserting JavaScript into a web page is much like inserting any other HTML content; you use tags to mark the start and end of your script code. The element you use to do this is `<script/>`. This tells the browser that the following chunk of text, bounded by the closing `</script>` tag, is not HTML to be displayed, but rather script code to be processed. The chunk of code surrounded by the `<script>` and `</script>` tags is called a *script block*. Here's an example:

```
<script>
    // JavaScript goes here
</script>
```

Basically, when the browser spots `<script>` tags, instead of trying to display the contained text to the user, it uses the browser's JavaScript engine to run the code's instructions. Of course, the code might give instructions about changes to the way the page is displayed or what is shown in the page, but the text of the code itself is never shown to the user.

You can put the `<script/>` element inside the header (between the `<head>` and `</head>` tags) or inside the body (between the `<body>` and `</body>` tags) of the HTML page. However, although you can put them outside these areas—for example, before the `<html>` tag or after the `</html>` tag—this is not permitted in the web standards and so is considered bad practice. Today's JavaScript developers typically add their `<script/>` elements directly before the `</body>` tag.

The `<script/>` element has a `type` attribute that tells the browser what type of text is contained within the element. For JavaScript, the best practice is to omit the `type` attribute (browsers automatically assume that any `<script/>` element without a `type` attribute is JavaScript). We used to always set the `type` attribute to `text/javascript`, but with the introduction of the HTML5 specification, it is no longer considered good practice to do so. Only include the `type` attribute if the `<script/>` element contains something other than JavaScript.

> **NOTE** The `<script/>` element can be used for more than just JavaScript. Some JavaScript-based templating engines use `<script/>` elements to contain snippets of HTML.

Linking to an External JavaScript File

The `<script/>` element has another arrow in its quiver: the capability to specify that the JavaScript code is not inside the web page, but inside a separate file. You should give any external files the file extension `.js`. Though it's not compulsory, it does make it easier for you to work out what is contained in each of your files.

To link to an external JavaScript file, you need to create a `<script/>` element as described earlier and use its `src` attribute to specify the location of the external file. For example, imagine you've created a file called `MyCommonFunctions.js` to which you want to link, and the file is in the same directory as your web page. The `<script/>` element would look like this:

```
<script src="MyCommonFunctions.js"></script>
```

The web browser will read this code and include the file contents as part of your web page. When linking to external files, you must not put any code within the opening and closing `<script>` tags; for example, the following would be invalid:

```
<script src="MyCommonFunctions.js">
var myVariable;
if ( myVariable == 1 ) {
    // do something
}
</script>
```

It's important to note that an opening `<script>` tag must be accompanied by a closing `</script>` tag. You cannot use the self⊠closing syntax found in XML. Therefore, the following is invalid:

```
<script src="MyCommonFunctions.js" />
```

Generally, you use the `<script/>` element to load local files (those on the same computer as the web page itself). However, you can load external files from a web server by specifying the web address of the file. For example, if your file was called `MyCommonFunctions.js` and was loaded on a web server with the domain name `www.mysite.com`, the `<script/>` element would look like this:

```
<script src="http://www.mysite.com/MyCommonFunctions.js"></script>
```

Linking to an external file is common when incorporating well⊠known JavaScript libraries into a web page. The servers hosting these libraries are referred to as *Content Delivery Networks*, or CDNs. CDNs are relatively safe, but beware of linking to external files if they are controlled by other people. It would give those people the ability to control and change your web page, so you need to be very sure you trust them!

Advantages of Using an External File

The biggest advantage of external files is code reuse. Say you write a complex bit of JavaScript that performs a general function you might need in lots of pages. If you include the code inline (within the web page rather than via an external file), you need to cut and paste the code into each web page that uses it. This is fine as long as you never need to change the code, but the reality is you probably will need to change or improve the code at some point. If you've cut and pasted the code to 30 different web pages, you'll need to update it in 30 different places. Quite a headache! By using one external file and including it in all the pages that need it, you need to update the code only once and all the 30 pages are updated instantly. So much easier!

Another advantage of using external files is that the browser will cache them, much as it does with images shared between pages. If your files are large, this could save download time and also reduce bandwidth usage.

YOUR FIRST SIMPLE JAVASCRIPT PROGRAM

Enough talk about the subject of JavaScript; let's write some! We'll start with a simple example that changes the background color of the web page.

TRY IT OUT   Painting the Page Red

This is a simple example of using JavaScript to change the background color of the browser. In your text editor, type the following:

```
<!DOCTYPE html>

<html lang="en">
    <head>
        <meta charset="utf-8" />
        <title>Chapter 1, Example 1</title>
    </head>
    <body bgcolor="white">
        <p>Paragraph 1</p>
        <script>
            document.bgColor = "red";
        </script>
    </body>
</html>
```

Save the page as `ch1_example1.html` to a convenient place on your hard drive, and load it into your web browser. You should see a red web page with the text `Paragraph 1` in the top⊠left corner. But wait—don't you set the `<body>` tag's `BGCOLOR` attribute to white? Okay, let's look at what's going on here.

The page is contained within `<html>` and `</html>` tags. This block contains a `<body>` element. When you define the opening `<body>` tag, you use HTML to set the page's background color to white:

```
<body bgcolor="white">
```

Then you let the browser know that your next lines of code are JavaScript code by using the `<script>` start tag:

```
<script>
```

Everything from here until the close tag, `</script>`, is JavaScript and is treated as such by the browser. Within this script block, you use JavaScript to set the document's background color to red:

```
document.bgColor = "red";
```

What you might call the *page* is known as the *document* for the purpose of scripting in a web page. The document has lots of properties, including its background color, `bgColor`. You can reference properties of the document by writing `document`, followed by a dot, followed by the property name. Don't worry about the use of `document` at the moment; you look at it in greater depth later in the book.

Note that the preceding line of code is an example of a JavaScript *statement*. Every line of code between the `<script>` and `</script>` tags is called a statement, although some statements may run on to more than one line.

You'll also see that there's a semicolon (;) at the end of the line. You use a semicolon in JavaScript to indicate the end of a statement. In practice, JavaScript is very relaxed about the need for semicolons, and when you start a new line, JavaScript will usually be able to work out whether you mean to start a new line of code. However, for good coding practice, you should use a semicolon at the end of statements of code, and a single JavaScript statement should fit onto one line rather than continue on to two or more lines. Moreover, you'll find some situations in which you must include a semicolon, which you'll come to later in the book.

Finally, to tell the browser to stop interpreting your text as JavaScript and start interpreting it as HTML, you use the script close tag:

```
</script>
```

You've now looked at how the code works, but you haven't looked at the order in which it works. When the browser loads in the web page, the browser goes through it, rendering it tag by tag from top to bottom of the page. This process is called *parsing*. The web browser starts at the top of the page and works its way down to the bottom of the page. The browser comes to the `<body>` tag first and sets the document's background to white. Then it continues parsing the page. When it comes to the JavaScript code, it is instructed to change the document's background to red.

WRITING MORE JAVASCRIPT

The first example let you dip your toes into the JavaScript waters. We'll write a few more JavaScript programs to demonstrate the web page flow and one of the many ways to display a result in the browser.

TRY IT OUT   Way Things Flow

Let's extend the previous example to demonstrate the parsing of a web page in action. Type the following into your text editor:

```
<!DOCTYPE html>

<html lang="en">
    <head>
        <meta charset="utf-8" />
        <title>Chapter 1, Example 2</title>
    </head>
    <body bgcolor="white">
        <p>Paragraph 1</p>
        <script>
            // script block 1
```

```
        alert("First Script Block");
    </script>
    <p>Paragraph 2</p>
    <script>
        // script block 2
                    document.bgColor = "red";
                    alert("Second Script Block");
    </script>
    <p>Paragraph 3</p>
    </body>
</html>
```

Save the file to your hard drive as ch1 _ example2.html and then load it into your browser. When you load the page, you should see the first paragraph, Paragraph 1, followed by a message box displayed by the first script block. The browser halts its parsing until you click the OK button. As you see in

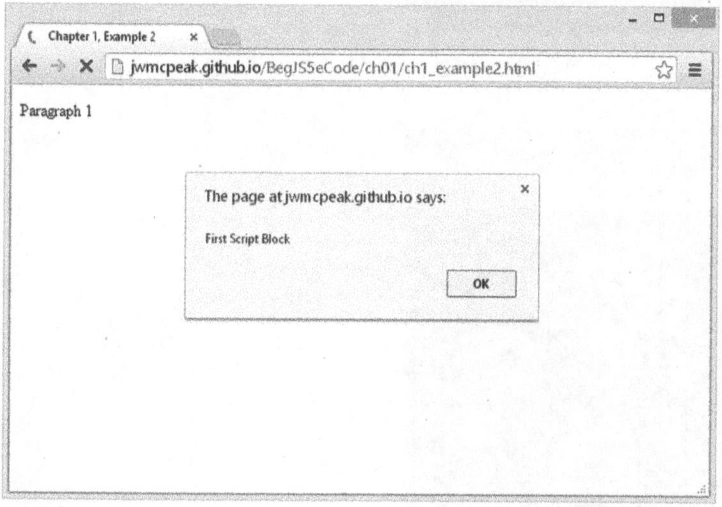

FIGURE 1-2

Figure 1-2, the page background is white, as set in the <body> tag, and only the first paragraph is displayed.

Click the OK button, and the parsing continues. The browser displays the second paragraph, and the second script block is reached, which changes the background color to red. Another message box is displayed by the second script block, as shown in Figure 1-3.

Click OK, and again the parsing continues, with the third paragraph, Paragraph 3, being displayed. The web page is complete, as shown in Figure 1-4.

The first part of the page is the same as in our earlier example. The background color for the page is set to white in the definition of the <body> tag, and then a paragraph is written to the page:

```
<body bgcolor="white">
        <p>Paragraph 1</p>
```

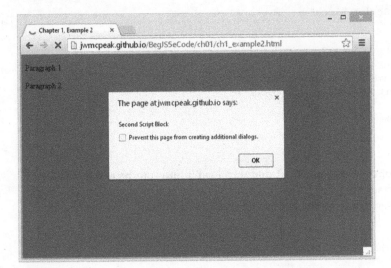

FIGURE 1-3

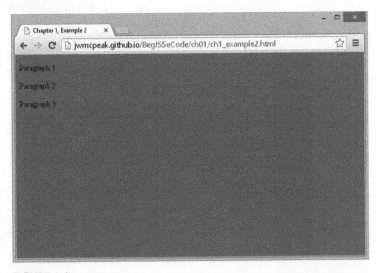

FIGURE 1-4

The first new section is contained in the first script block:

```
<script>
    // script block 1
    alert("First Script Block");
</script>
```

This script block contains two lines, both of which are new to you. The first line

```
// Script block 1
```

is just a *comment*, solely for your benefit. The browser recognizes anything on a line after a double forward slash (//) to be a comment and does not do anything with it. It is useful for you as a programmer because you can add explanations to your code that make it easier to remember what you were doing when you come back to your code later.

The alert() function in the second line of code is also new to you. Before learning what it does, you need to know what a *function* is.

Functions are defined more fully in Chapter 4, but for now you need only think of them as pieces of JavaScript code that you can use to do certain tasks. If you have a background in math, you may already have some idea of what a function is: it takes some information, processes it, and gives you a result. A function makes life easier for you as a programmer because you don't have to think about how the function does the task—you can just concentrate on when you want the task done.

In particular, the alert() function enables you to alert or inform the user about something by displaying a message box. The message to be given in the message box is specified inside the parentheses of the alert() function and is known as the function's *parameter*.

The message box displayed by the alert() function is *modal*. This is an important concept, which you'll come across again. It simply means that the message box won't go away until the user closes it by clicking the OK button. In fact, parsing of the page stops at the line where the alert() function is used and doesn't restart until the user closes the message box. This is quite useful for this example, because it enables you to demonstrate the results of what has been parsed so far: The page color has been set to white, and the first paragraph has been displayed.

When you click OK, the browser carries on parsing down the page through the following lines:

```
<p>Paragraph 2</p>
<script>
    // script block 2
    document.bgColor = "red";
    alert("Second Script Block");
</script>
```

The second paragraph is displayed, and the second block of JavaScript is run. The first line of the script block code is another comment, so the browser ignores this. You saw the second line of the script code in the previous example—it changes the background color of the page to red. The third line of code is the alert() function, which displays the second message box. Parsing is brought to a halt until you close the message box by clicking OK.

When you close the message box, the browser moves on to the next lines of code in the page, displaying the third paragraph and, finally, ending the web page:

```
    <p>Paragraph 3</p>
  </body>
</html>
```

Another important point raised by this example is the difference between setting properties of the page, such as background color, via HTML and doing the same thing using JavaScript. The method of setting properties using HTML is *static*: A value can be set only once and never changed again by means of HTML. Setting properties using JavaScript enables you to dynamically change their values. The term *dynamic* refers to something that can be changed and whose value or appearance is not set in stone.

This example is just that, an example. In practice, if you want the page's background to be red, simply set the background color with CSS (don't use the bgcolor attribute in practice). Where you want to use JavaScript is where you want to add some sort of intelligence or logic to the page. For example, if the user's screen resolution is particularly low, you might want to change what's displayed on the page, and you can do that with JavaScript.

TRY IT OUT Displaying Results in a Web Page

In this final example, you discover how to write information directly to a web page using JavaScript. This proves more useful when you're writing the results of a calculation or text you've created using JavaScript, as you see in the next chapter. For now, you'll just write "Hello World!" to a blank page using JavaScript:

```html
<!DOCTYPE html>

<html lang="en">
    <head>
        <meta charset="utf-8" />
        <title>Chapter 1, Example 3</title>
    </head>
    <body>
        <p id="results"></p>
        <script>
            document.getElementById("results").innerHTML = "Hello World!";
        </script>
    </body>
</html>
```

Save the page as ch1_example3.html to a convenient place on your hard drive. Now load it into your web browser and you'll see Hello World! in the page. Although it would be easier to use HTML to do the same thing, this technique will prove useful in later chapters.

The first part of the page is the same as in our earlier examples, but things start to change when you reach this line:

```html
<p id="results"></p>
```

You'll notice the <p/> element has been given an ID using the id attribute. This ID must be unique in the web page, because it is used by JavaScript to identify the specific HTML element in the following line:

```javascript
document.getElementById("results").innerHTML = "Hello World!";
```

Don't worry if this seems complex at the moment; you learn more about how this works in later chapters. Basically, the code is saying, "Get me the element with the ID of `results` and set the HTML inside that element to Hello World!"

It's important in that the code accessing the paragraph is after the actual `<p/>` element. Otherwise, the code would be attempting to access a paragraph before it existed in the page and would throw an error.

A BRIEF LOOK AT BROWSERS AND COMPATIBILITY PROBLEMS

In the preceding example you saw that by using JavaScript you can change a web page's `document` background color using the `bgColor` property of the `document`. The example worked regardless of what browser you used because they all support a `document` with a `bgColor` property. You can say that the example is *cross⬛browser compatible*. However, it's not always the case that the property or language feature available in one browser will be available in another browser. This is even sometimes the case between versions of the same browser.

One of the main headaches involved in creating web⬛based JavaScript is the differences between different web browsers, the level of HTML and CSS they support, and the functionality their JavaScript engines can handle. Each new release of any browser sees new and exciting features added to its HTML, CSS, and JavaScript support. The good news is that to a much greater extent than ever before, browser creators are complying with standards set by organizations such as Ecma and the W3C.

Which browsers you want to support really comes down to the browsers you think the majority of your website's visitors—that is, your *user base*—will be using. This book is aimed at standards⬛compliant browsers, such as Chrome, IE9+, Firefox, Safari, and Opera.

If you want your website to be professional, you need to somehow deal with older browsers. You could make sure your code is backward compatible—that is, it only uses features available in older browsers. However, you may decide that it's simply not worth limiting yourself to the features of older browsers. In this case you need to make sure your pages degrade gracefully. In other words, make sure that although your pages won't work in older browsers, they will fail in a way that means the user is either never aware of the failure or is alerted to the fact that certain features on the website are not compatible with his or her browser. The alternative to degrading gracefully is for your code to raise lots of error messages, cause strange results to be displayed on the page, and generally make you look like an idiot who doesn't know what he's doing!

So how do you make your web pages degrade gracefully? You can do this by using JavaScript to determine which browser the web page is running in after it has been partially or completely loaded. You can use this information to determine what scripts to run or even to redirect the user to another page written to make best use of her particular browser. In later chapters, you see how to find out what features the browser supports and take appropriate action so that your pages work acceptably on as many browsers as possible.

SUMMARY

At this point, you should have a feel for what JavaScript is and what it can do. In particular, this brief introduction covered the following:

➤ You looked into the process the browser follows when interpreting your web page. It goes through the page element by element (parsing) and acts upon your HTML tags and JavaScript code as it comes to them.

➤ Unlike many programming languages, JavaScript requires just a text editor to start creating code. Something like Windows Notepad is fine for getting started, though more extensive tools will prove valuable once you get more experience.

➤ JavaScript code is embedded into the web page itself, along with the HTML. Its existence is marked out by the use of `<script/>` elements. As with HTML, the script executes from the top of the page and works down to the bottom, interpreting and executing the code statement by statement.

2

Data Types and Variables

WHAT YOU WILL LEARN IN THIS CHAPTER:

➤ Representing data in code

➤ Storing data in memory

➤ Making calculations

➤ Converting data

WROX.COM CODE DOWNLOADS FOR THIS CHAPTER

You can find the wrox.com code downloads for this chapter at http://www.wiley.com/go/
BeginningJavaScript5E on the Download Code tab. You can also view all of the examples
and related files at http://beginningjs.com.

One of the main uses of computers is to process and display information. By processing, we
mean the information is modified, interpreted, or filtered in some way by the computer. For
example, on an online banking website, a customer may request details of all money paid out
from his account in the past month. Here the computer would retrieve the information, filter
out any information not related to payments made in the past month, and then display what's
left in a web page. In some situations, information is processed without being displayed, and
at other times, information is obtained directly without being processed. For example, in
a banking environment, regular payments may be processed and transferred electronically
without any human interaction or display.

In computing, information is referred to as *data*. Data comes in all sorts of forms, such as
numbers, text, dates, and times, to mention just a few. In this chapter, you look specifically
at how JavaScript handles data such as numbers and text. An understanding of how data is
handled is fundamental to any programming language.

In this chapter you start by looking at the various types of data JavaScript can process. Then
you look at how you can store this data in the computer's memory so you can use it again and
again in the code. Finally, you see how to use JavaScript to manipulate and process the data.

TYPES OF DATA IN JAVASCRIPT

Data can come in many different forms, or *types*. You'll recognize some of the data types that JavaScript handles from the world outside of programming—for example, numbers and text. Other data types are a little more abstract and are used to make programming easier; one example is the object data type, which you won't see in detail until Chapter 5.

Some programming languages are strongly typed. In these languages, whenever you use a piece of data, you need to explicitly state what sort of data you are dealing with, and use of that data must follow strict rules applicable to its type. For example, in a strongly typed language you can't add a number and a word.

JavaScript, on the other hand, is a weakly typed language and a lot more forgiving about how you use different types of data. When you deal with data, you often don't need to specify type; JavaScript will work that out for itself. Furthermore, when you are using different types of data at the same time, JavaScript will work out behind the scenes what it is you're trying to do.

Given how easygoing JavaScript is about data, why talk about data types at all? Why not just cut to the chase and start using data without worrying about its type?

First of all, although JavaScript is very good at working out what data it's dealing with, on occasion it'll get things wrong or at least not do what you want it to do. In these situations, you need to make it explicit to JavaScript what sort of data type you intended and how it should be used. To do that, you first need to know a little bit about data types.

A second reason is that data types enable you to use data effectively in your code. The things that you can do with data and the results you'll get depend on the type of data being used, even if you don't explicitly specify what type it is. For example, although trying to multiply two numbers makes sense, doing the same thing with text doesn't. Also, the result of adding numbers is very different from the result of adding text. With numbers you get the sum, but with text you get one big piece of text consisting of the other pieces joined together.

Let's take a brief look at some of the more commonly used data types: numerical, text, and boolean. You see how to use them later in the chapter.

Numerical Data

Numerical data comes in two forms:

➤ Whole numbers, such as 145, which are also known as *integers*. These numbers can be positive or negative and can span a very wide range in JavaScript: -2^{53} to 2^{53}.

➤ Fractional numbers, such as 1.234, which are also known as *floating-point* numbers. Like integers, they can be positive or negative, and they also have a massive range.

In simple terms, unless you're writing specialized scientific applications, you're not going to face problems with the size of numbers available in JavaScript. Also, although you can treat integers and floating-point numbers differently when it comes to storing them, JavaScript actually treats them both as floating-point numbers. It kindly hides the detail from you so you generally don't need to worry about it. One exception is when you want an integer but you have a floating-point number, in which case you'll round the number to make it an integer. You take a look at rounding numbers later in this chapter.

Text Data

Another term for one or more characters of text is a *string*. You tell JavaScript that text is to be treated as text and not as code simply by enclosing it inside quotation marks ("). For example, "Hello World" and "A" are examples of strings that JavaScript will recognize. You can also use the single quotation marks ('), so 'Hello World' and 'A' are also examples of strings that JavaScript will recognize. However, you must end the string with the same quotation mark that you started it with. Therefore, "A' is not a valid JavaScript string, and neither is 'Hello World".

What if you want a string with a single quotation mark in the middle, say a string like Peter O'Toole? If you enclose it in double quotes, you'll be fine, so "Peter O'Toole" is recognized by JavaScript. However, 'Peter O'Toole' will produce an error. This is because JavaScript thinks that your text string is Peter O (that is, it treats the middle single quote as marking the end of the string) and falls over wondering what the Toole' is.

Another way around this is to tell JavaScript that the middle ' is part of the text and is not indicating the end of the string. You do this by using the backslash character (\), which has special meaning in JavaScript and is referred to as an *escape character*. The backslash tells the browser that the next character is not the end of the string, but part of the text. So 'Peter O\'Toole' will work as planned.

What if you want to use a double quote inside a string enclosed in double quotes? Well, everything just said about the single quote still applies. So 'Hello "Paul"' works, but "Hello "Paul"" won't. However, "Hello \"Paul\"" will work.

JavaScript has a lot of other special characters, which can't be typed in but can be represented using the escape character in conjunction with other characters to create *escape sequences*. These work much the same as in HTML. For example, more than one space in a row is ignored in HTML, so a space is represented by the term . Similarly, in JavaScript you'll find instances where you can't use a character directly but must use an escape sequence. The following table details some of the more useful escape sequences.

ESCAPE SEQUENCES	CHARACTER REPRESENTED
\b	Backspace
\f	Form feed
\n	New line
\r	Carriage return
\t	Tab
\'	Single quote
\"	Double quote
\\	Backslash
\x*NN*	*NN* is a hexadecimal number that identifies a character in the Latin-1 character set.

The least obvious of these is the last, which represents individual characters by their character number in the Latin-1 character set rather than by their normal appearance. Let's pick an example: Say you wanted to include the copyright symbol (©) in your string. What would your string need to look like? The answer is `"\xA9 Paul Wilton"`.

Similarly, you can refer to characters using their Unicode escape sequence. These are written \u*NNNN*, where *NNNN* refers to the Unicode number for that particular character. For example, to refer to the copyright symbol using this method, you use the string `\u00A9`.

Boolean Data

The use of yes or no, positive or negative, and true or false is commonplace in the physical world. The idea of true and false is also fundamental to digital computers; they don't understand maybes, only true and false. In fact, the concept of "yes or no" is so useful it has its own data type in JavaScript: the *boolean* data type. The boolean type has two possible values: `true` for yes and `false` for no.

The purpose of boolean data in JavaScript is just the same as in the world outside programming: it enables you to answer questions and make decisions based on the answer. For example, if you are asked, "Is this book about JavaScript?" you would hopefully answer, "Yes it is," or you might also say, "That's true." Similarly, you might say, "If it's false that the subject of the book is JavaScript, then put it down." Here you have a boolean logic statement (named after its inventor George Boole), which asks a question and then does something based on whether the answer is true or false. In JavaScript, you can use the same sort of boolean logic to give your programs decision-making abilities. You take a more detailed look at boolean logic in the next chapter.

VARIABLES—STORING DATA IN MEMORY

Data can be stored either permanently or temporarily.

You will want to keep important data, such as the details of a person's bank account, in a permanent store. For example, when Ms. Bloggs takes ten dollars or pounds or euros out of her account, you want to deduct the money from her account and keep a permanent record of the new balance. Information like this might be stored in something called a *database*.

However, in other cases you don't want to permanently store data, but simply want to keep a temporary note of it. Let's look at an example. Say Ms. Bloggs has a loan from BigBank Inc., and she wants to find out how much is still outstanding on this loan. She goes to the online banking page for loans and clicks a link to find out how much she owes. This is data that will be stored permanently somewhere. However, suppose you also provide a facility for increasing loan repayments to pay off the loan early. If Ms. Bloggs enters an increased repayment amount into the text box on the web page, you might want to show how much sooner the loan will be paid. This will involve a few possibly complex calculations, so to make it easier, you want to write code that calculates the result in several stages, storing the result at each stage as you go along, before providing a final result. After you've done the calculation and displayed the results, there's no need to permanently store the results for each stage, so rather than use a database, you need to use something called a *variable*. Why is it called a variable? Well, perhaps because a variable can be used to store temporary data that can be altered, or varied.

Another bonus of variables is that unlike permanent storage, which might be saved to disk or magnetic tape, variables are held in the computer's memory. This means that it is much, much faster to store and retrieve the data.

So what makes variables good places for temporarily storing your data? Well, variables have a limited lifetime. When your visitors close the page or move to a new one, your variables are lost, unless you take some steps to save them somewhere.

You give each variable a name so that you can refer to it elsewhere in your code. These names must follow certain rules.

As with much of JavaScript code, variable names are case sensitive. For example, `myVariable` is not the same as `myvariable`. You'll find that this is a very easy way for errors to slip into your code, even when you become an expert at JavaScript.

Also, you can't use certain names and characters for your variable names. Names you can't use are called *reserved* words. Reserved words are words that JavaScript keeps for its own use (for example, the word `var` or the word `with`). Certain characters are also forbidden in variable names: for example, the ampersand (`&`) and the percent sign (`%`). You are allowed to use numbers in your variable names, but the names must not begin with numbers. So `101myVariable` is not okay, but `myVariable101` is. Let's look at some more examples.

Invalid names include:

➤   `with`

➤   `99variables`

➤   `my%Variable`

➤   `theGood&theBad`

Valid names include:

➤   `myVariable99`

➤   `myPercent_Variable`

➤   `the_Good_and_the_Bad`

You may want to use a naming convention for your variables (for example, one that describes what sort of data you plan to hold in the variable). You can notate your variables in lots of different ways—none are right or wrong, but it's best to stick with one of them.

Today, the convention most JavaScript developers use is to simply give their variables descriptive names. For example, a variable for a person's first name would be called `firstName`; his account number would be `accountNumber`. However, as long as the names you use make sense and are used consistently, it really doesn't matter what convention you choose.

Creating Variables and Giving Them Values

Before you can use a variable, you should declare its existence to the JavaScript engine using the `var` keyword. This warns the engine that it needs to reserve some memory in which to store your data later. To declare a new variable called `myFirstVariable`, write the following:

```
var myFirstVariable;
```

Note that the semicolon at the end of the line is not part of the variable name, but instead is used to indicate to JavaScript the end of a statement. This line is an example of a JavaScript statement.

Once declared, you can use a variable to store any type of data. As mentioned earlier, many other programming languages (called strongly typed languages) require you to declare not only the variable, but also the type of data that will be stored, such as numbers or text. However, JavaScript is a weakly typed language; you don't need to limit yourself to what type of data a variable can hold.

You put data into your variables, a process called *assigning values* to your variables, by using the equals sign (=). For example, if you want your variable named `myFirstVariable` to hold the number 101, you would write this:

```
myFirstVariable = 101;
```

The equals sign has a special name when used to assign values to a variable; it's called the *assignment operator*.

TRY IT OUT Declaring Variables

Let's look at an example in which a variable is declared, store some data in it, and finally, access its contents. You'll also see that variables can hold any type of data, and that the type of data being held can be changed. For example, you can start by storing text and then change to storing numbers without JavaScript having any problems. Type the following code into your text editor and save it as `ch2_example1.html`:

```html
<!DOCTYPE html>

<html lang="en">
<head>
    <title>Chapter 2, Example 1</title>
</head>
<body>
    <script>
        var myFirstVariable;

        myFirstVariable = "Hello";
        alert(myFirstVariable);

        myFirstVariable = 54321;
        alert(myFirstVariable);
    </script>
</body>
</html>
```

As soon as you load this into your web browser, it should show an `alert` box with "Hello" in it, as shown in Figure 2-1. This is the content of the variable `myFirstVariable` at that point in the code.

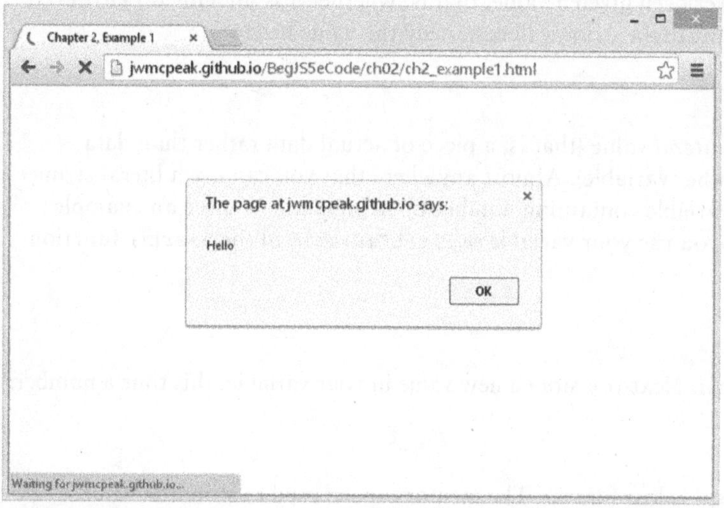

FIGURE 2-1

Click OK and another `alert` box appears with 54321 in it, as shown in Figure 2-2. This is the new value you assigned to the variable `myFirstVariable`.

Within the script block, you first declare your variable:

```
var myFirstVariable;
```

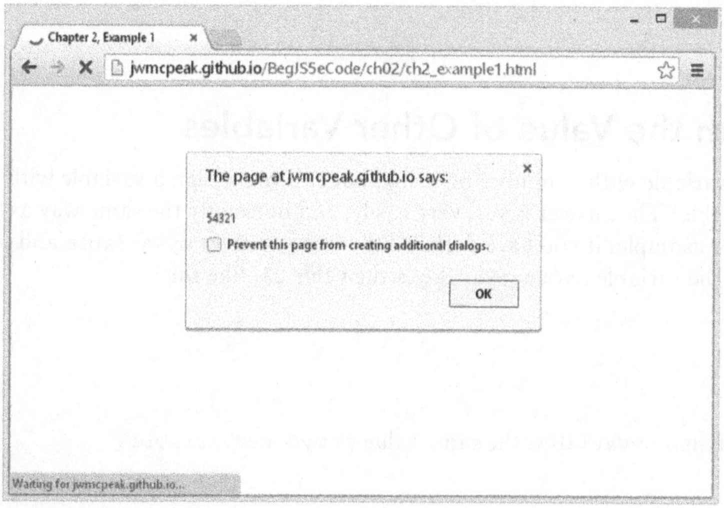

FIGURE 2-2

Currently, its value is the undefined value because you've declared only its existence to the JavaScript engine, not any actual data. It may sound odd, but undefined is an actual primitive value in JavaScript, and it enables you to do comparisons. (For example, you can check to see whether a variable contains an actual value or whether it has not yet been given a value, that is, whether it is undefined.) However, in the next line you assign myFirstVariable a string value, namely the value Hello:

```
myFirstVariable = "Hello";
```

Here you have assigned the variable a *literal* value (that is, a piece of actual data rather than data obtained by a calculation or from another variable). Almost anywhere that you can use a literal string or number, you can replace it with a variable containing number or string data. You see an example of this in the next line of code, where you use your variable myFirstVariable in the alert() function that you saw in the previous chapter:

```
alert(myFirstVariable);
```

This causes the first alert box to appear. Next you store a new value in your variable, this time a number:

```
myFirstVariable = 54321;
```

The previous value of myFirstVariable is lost forever. The memory space used to store the value is freed up automatically by JavaScript in a process called *garbage collection*. Whenever JavaScript detects that the contents of a variable are no longer usable, such as when you allocate a new value, it performs the garbage collection process and makes the memory available. Without this automatic garbage collection process, more and more of the computer's memory would be consumed, until eventually the computer would run out and the system would grind to a halt. However, garbage collection is not always as efficient as it should be and may not occur until another page is loaded.

Just to prove that the new value has been stored, use the alert() function again to display the variable's new contents:

```
alert(myFirstVariable);
```

Assigning Variables with the Value of Other Variables

You've seen that you can assign a variable with a number or string, but can you assign a variable with the data stored inside another variable? The answer is yes, very easily, and in exactly the same way as giving a variable a literal value. For example, if you have declared the two variables myVariable and myOtherVariable and have given the variable myOtherVariable the value 22, like this:

```
var myVariable;
var myOtherVariable;
myOtherVariable = 22;
```

you can use the following line to assign myVariable the same value as myOtherVariable (that is, 22):

```
myVariable = myOtherVariable;
```

TRY IT OUT **Assigning Variables the Values of Other Variables**

Let's look at another example, this time assigning variables the values of other variables.

1. Type the following code into your text editor and save it as ch2_example2.html:

```
<!DOCTYPE html>

<html lang="en">
<head>
    <title>Chapter 2, Example 2</title>
</head>
<body>
    <script>
        var string1 = "Hello";
        var string2 = "Goodbye";

        alert(string1);
        alert(string2);

        string2 = string1;

        alert(string1);
        alert(string2);

        string1 = "Now for something different";

        alert(string1);
        alert(string2);
    </script>
</body>
<html>
```

2. Load the page into your browser, and you'll see a series of six alert boxes appear.

3. Click OK on each alert box to see the next alert. The first two show the values of string1 and string2—Hello and Goodbye, respectively. Then you assign string2 the value that's in string1. The next two alert boxes show the contents of string1 and string2; this time both are Hello.

4. Finally, you change the value of string1. Note that the value of string2 remains unaffected. The final two alert boxes show the new value of string1 (Now for something different) and the unchanged value of string2 (Hello).

The first thing you do in the script block is declare your two variables: string1 and string2. However, notice that you have assigned them values at the same time that you have declared them. This is a shortcut, called *initializing*, that saves you typing too much code:

```
var string1 ="Hello";
var string2 = "Goodbye";
```

Note that you can use this shortcut with all data types, not just strings. In the next two lines you use the alert() function to show the current value of each variable to the user:

```
alert(string1);
alert(string2);
```

Then you assign `string2` the value that's contained in `string1`. To prove that the assignment has really worked, you again use the `alert()` function to show the user the contents of each variable:

```
string2 = string1;

alert(string1);
alert(string2);
```

Next, you set `string1` to a new value:

```
string1 = "Now for something different";
```

This leaves `string2` with its current value, demonstrating that `string2` has its own copy of the data assigned to it from `string1` in the previous step. You see in later chapters that this is not always the case. However, as a general rule, basic data types, such as text and numbers, are always copied when assigned, whereas more complex data types, like the objects you come across in Chapter 5, are actually shared and not copied. For example, if you have a variable with the string `Hello` and assign five other variables the value of this variable, you now have the original data and five independent copies of the data. However, if it was an object rather than a string and you did the same thing, you'd find you still have only one copy of the data, but that six variables share it. Changing the data using any of the six variable names would change it for all the variables.

Finally, you use the `alert()` function to show the current values of each variable:

```
alert(string1);
alert(string2);
```

USING DATA—CALCULATIONS AND BASIC STRING MANIPULATION

You've seen how to declare variables and how they can store information, but so far you haven't done anything really useful with this knowledge—so just why would you want to use variables at all?

What variables enable you to do is temporarily hold information that you can use for processing in mathematical calculations, in building up text messages, or in processing words that the user has entered. Variables are a little bit like the Memory Store button on the average pocket calculator. Say you were adding up your finances. You might first add up all the money you needed to spend, and then store it in temporary memory. After you had added up all your money coming in, you could deduct the amount stored in the memory to figure out how much would be left over. You can use variables in a similar way: You can first gain the necessary user input and store it in variables, and then you can do your calculations using the values obtained.

In this section you see how you can put the values stored in variables to good use in both number-crunching and text-based operations.

Numerical Calculations

JavaScript has a range of basic mathematical capabilities, such as addition, subtraction, multiplication, and division. Each of the basic math functions is represented by a symbol: plus

(+), minus (–), star (*), and forward slash (/), respectively. These symbols are called *operators* because they operate on the values you give them. In other words, they perform some calculation or operation and return a result. You can use the results of these calculations almost anywhere you'd use a number or a variable.

Imagine you were calculating the total value of items on a shopping list. You could write this calculation as follows:

Total cost of shopping = 10 + 5 + 5

Or, if you actually calculate the sum, it's:

Total cost of shopping = 20

Now let's see how to do this in JavaScript. In actual fact, it is very similar except that you need to use a variable to store the final total:

```
var totalCostOfShopping;
totalCostOfShopping = 10 + 5 + 5;
alert(totalCostOfShopping);
```

First, you declare a variable, `totalCostOfShopping`, to hold the total cost.

In the second line, you have the code `10 + 5 + 5`. This piece of code is known as an *expression*. When you assign the variable `totalCostOfShopping` the value of this expression, JavaScript automatically calculates the value of the expression (20) and stores it in the variable. Notice that the equals sign tells JavaScript to store the results of the calculation in the `totalCostOfShopping` variable. This is called *assigning* the value of the calculation to the variable, which is why the single equals sign (=) is called the *assignment operator*.

Finally, you display the value of the variable in an `alert` box.

The operators for subtraction and multiplication work in exactly the same way. Division is a little different.

TRY IT OUT   Calculations

Let's take a look at an example using the division operator to see how it works.

1. Enter the following code and save it as `ch2_example3.html`:

```
<!DOCTYPE html>

<html lang="en">
<head>
    <title>Chapter 2, Example 3</title>
</head>
<body>
    <script>
        var firstNumber = 15;
        var secondNumber = 10;
        var answer;
        answer = 15 / 10;
```

```
            alert(answer);

            alert(15 / 10);

            answer = firstNumber / secondNumber;
            alert(answer);
        </script>
    </body>
</html>
```

2. Load this into your web browser. You should see a succession of three `alert` boxes, each containing the value `1.5`. These values are the results of three calculations.

3. The first thing you do in the script block is declare your three variables and assign the first two of them values that you'll be using later:

```
var firstNumber = 15;
var secondNumber = 10;
var answer;
```

4. Next, you set the answer variable to the results of the calculation of the expression `15/10`. You show the value of this variable in an `alert` box:

```
answer = 15 / 10;
alert(answer);
```

This example demonstrates one way of doing the calculation, but in reality you'd almost never do it this way.

To demonstrate that you can use expressions in places you'd use numbers or variables, you show the results of the calculation of `15/10` directly by including it in the `alert()` function:

```
alert(15 / 10);
```

Finally, you do the same calculation, but this time using the two variables: `firstNumber`, which was set to `15`, and `secondNumber`, which was set to `10`. You have the expression `firstNumber / secondNumber`, the result of which you store in your answer variable. Then, to prove it has all worked, you show the value contained in answer by using your friend the `alert()` function:

```
answer = firstNumber / secondNumber;
alert(answer);
```

You'll do most calculations the third way (that is, using variables, or numbers and variables, and storing the result in another variable). The reason for this is that if the calculation used literal values (actual values, such as 15 / 10), then you might as well program in the result of the calculation, rather than force JavaScript to calculate it for you. For example, rather than writing `15 / 10`, you might as well just write `1.5`. After all, the more calculations you force JavaScript to do, the slower it will be, though admittedly just one calculation won't tax it too much.

Another reason for using the result rather than the calculation is that it makes code more readable. Which would you prefer to read in code: `1.5 * 45 - 56 / 67 + 2.567` or `69.231`? Still better, a variable named, for example, `pricePerKG`, makes code even easier to understand for someone not familiar with it.

Increment and Decrement Operators

A number of operations using the math operators are so commonly used that they have been given their own operators. The two you'll be looking at here are the *increment* and *decrement* operators, which are represented by two plus signs (++) and two minus signs (--), respectively. Basically, all they do is increase or decrease a variable's value by one. You could use the normal + and - operators to do this, for example:

```
myVariable = myVariable + 1;
myVariable = myVariable - 1;
```

> **NOTE** *You can assign a variable a new value that is the result of an expression involving its previous value.*

However, using the increment and decrement operators shortens this to:

```
myVariable++;
myVariable--;
```

The result is the same—the value of `myVariable` is increased or decreased by one—but the code is shorter. When you are familiar with the syntax, this becomes very clear and easy to read.

Right now, you may well be thinking that these operators sound as useful as a poke in the eye. However, in Chapter 3, when you look at how you can run the same code a number of times, you'll see that these operators are very useful and widely used. In fact, the ++ operator is so widely used it has a computer language named after it: C++. The joke here is that C++ is one up from C. (Well, that's programmer humor for you!)

As well as placing the ++ or -- after the variable, you can also place it before, like so:

```
++myVariable;
--myVariable;
```

When the ++ and -- are used on their own, as they usually are, it makes no difference where they are placed, but it is possible to use the ++ and -- operators in an expression along with other operators. For example:

```
myVar = myNumber++ - 20;
```

This code takes 20 away from `myNumber` and then increments the variable `myNumber` by one before assigning the result to the variable `myVar`. If instead you place the ++ before and prefix it like this:

```
myVar = ++myNumber - 20;
```

`myNumber` is first incremented by one, and then `myNumber` has 20 subtracted from it. It's a subtle difference, but in some situations a very important one. Take the following code:

```
myNumber = 1;
myVar = (myNumber++ * 10 + 1);
```

What value will myVar contain? Well, because the ++ is postfixed (it's after the myNumber variable), it will be incremented afterward. So the equation reads: Multiply myNumber by 10 plus 1 and then increment myNumber by one.

```
myVar = 1 * 10 + 1 = 11
```

Then add 1 to myNumber to get 12, but do this after the value 11 has been assigned to myVar. Now take a look at the following code:

```
myNumber = 1;
myVar = ++myNumber * 10 + 1;
```

This time myNumber is incremented by one first, then times 10 and plus 1:

```
myVar = 2 * 10 + 1 = 21
```

As you can imagine, such subtlety can easily be overlooked and lead to bugs in code; therefore, it's usually best to avoid this syntax.

Before going on, this seems to be a good place to introduce another operator: +=. You can use this operator as a shortcut for increasing the value held by a variable by a set amount. For example,

```
myVar += 6;
```

does exactly the same thing as:

```
myVar = myVar + 6;
```

You can also do the same thing for subtraction and multiplication, as shown here:

```
myVar -= 6;
myVar *= 6;
```

which is equivalent to:

```
myVar = myVar - 6;
myVar = myVar * 6;
```

Operator Precedence

You've seen that symbols that perform some function—like +, which adds two numbers, and –, which subtracts one number from another—are called operators. Unlike people, not all operators are created equal; some have a higher *precedence*—that is, they get dealt with sooner. A quick look at a simple example will help demonstrate this point:

```
var myVariable;

myVariable = 1 + 1 * 2;

alert(myVariable);
```

If you were to type this, what result would you expect the alert box to show as the value of myVariable? You might expect that because 1 + 1 = 2 and 2 * 2 = 4, the answer is 4. Actually, you'll find that the alert box shows 3 as the value stored in myVariable as a result of the calculation. So what gives? Doesn't JavaScript add up right?

Well, you probably already know the reason from your understanding of mathematics. The way JavaScript does the calculation is to first calculate 1 * 2 = 2, and then use this result in the addition, so that JavaScript finishes off with 1 + 2 = 3.

Why? Because * has a higher precedence than +. The = symbol, also an operator (called the assignment operator), has the lowest precedence—it always gets left until last.

The + and – operators have an equal precedence, so which one gets done first? Well, JavaScript works from left to right, so if operators with equal precedence exist in a calculation, they get calculated in the order in which they appear when going from left to right. The same applies to * and /, which are also of equal precedence.

TRY IT OUT   Fahrenheit to Centigrade

Take a look at a slightly more complex example—a Fahrenheit to centigrade converter. (Centigrade is another name for the Celsius temperature scale.) Type this code and save it as ch2_example4.html:

```
<!DOCTYPE html>

<html lang="en">
<head>
    <title>Chapter 2, Example 4</title>
</head>
<body>
    <script>
        // Equation is °C = 5/9 (°F - 32).
        var degFahren = prompt("Enter the degrees in Fahrenheit",50);
        var degCent;

        degCent = 5/9 * (degFahren - 32);

        alert(degCent);
    </script>
</body>
</html>
```

If you load the page into your browser, you should see a prompt box, like that shown in Figure 2-3, that asks you to enter the degrees in Fahrenheit to be converted. The value 50 is already filled in by default.

If you leave it at 50 and click OK, an alert box with the number 10 in it appears. This represents 50 degrees Fahrenheit converted to centigrade.

Reload the page and try changing the value in the prompt box to see what results you get. For example, change the value to 32 and reload the page. This time you should see 0 appear in the box.

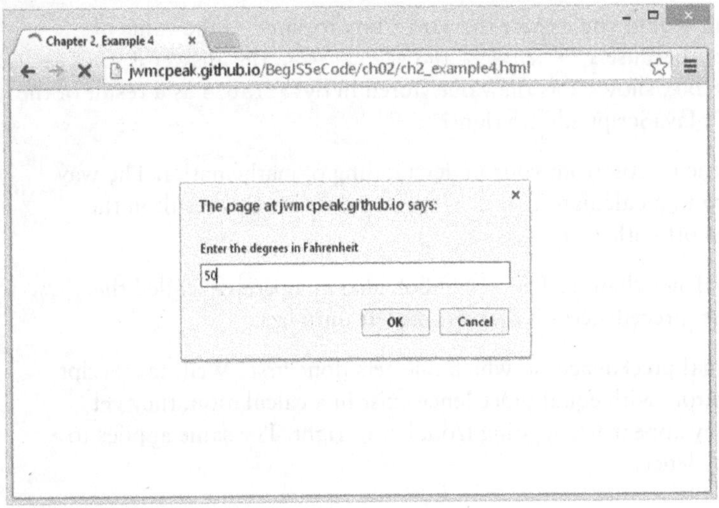

FIGURE 2-3

Because it's still a fairly simple example, there's no checking of data input, so it'll let you enter abc as the degrees Fahrenheit. Later, in the "Data Type Conversion" section of this chapter, you see how to spot invalid characters posing as numeric data.

<hr>

TRY IT OUT Security Issues with Internet Explorer

When loading the page to Internet Explorer (IE), you may see the security warning issue shown in Figure 2-4, and the prompt window doesn't appear.

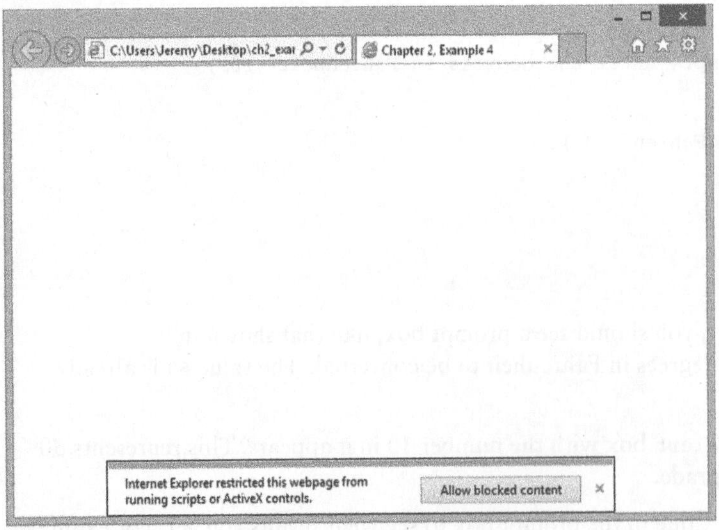

FIGURE 2-4

If it does you'll need to change IE's security settings to allow active content from your computer. To do this:

1. Open IE and select the "Internet options" menu from the Tools menu, as shown in Figure 2-5.

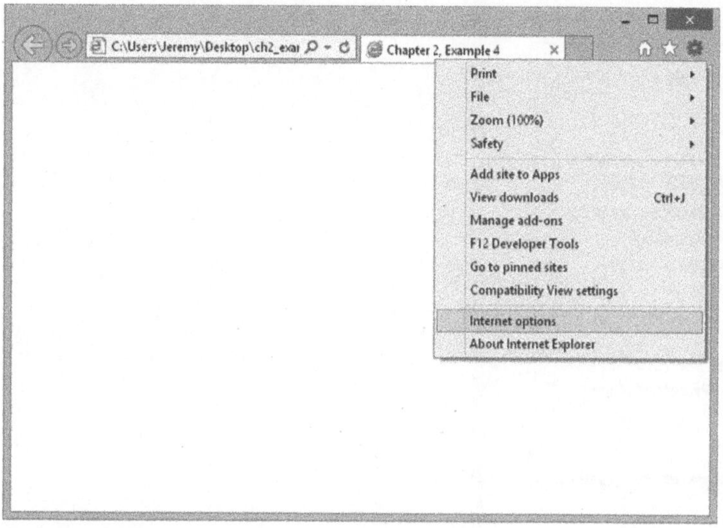

FIGURE 2-5

2. Click the Advanced tab and then scroll down to the Security section. Check the "Allow active content to run in files on My Computer" option, as shown in Figure 2-6.

3. Click the OK button on the Internet Options dialog box and close Internet Explorer. Open Example 4 from the "Fahrenheit to Centigrade" Try It Out again, and the example will now work.

The first line of the script block is a comment, because it starts with two forward slashes (`//`). It contains the equation for converting Fahrenheit temperatures to centigrade and is in the example code solely for reference:

```
// Equation is °C - 5/9 (°F - 32).
```

Your task is to represent this equation in JavaScript code. You start by declaring your variables, `degFahren` and `degCent`:

```
var degFahren - prompt("Enter the degrees in Fahrenheit",50);
var degCent;
```

Instead of initializing the `degFahren` variable to a literal value, you get a value from the user using the `prompt()` function. The `prompt()` function works in a similar way to an `alert()` function, except that as well as displaying a message, it also contains a text box in which the user can enter a value. It is this value that will be stored inside the `degFahren` variable. The value returned is a text string, but this will be implicitly converted by JavaScript to a number when you use it as a number, as discussed in the section "Data Type Conversion" later in this chapter.

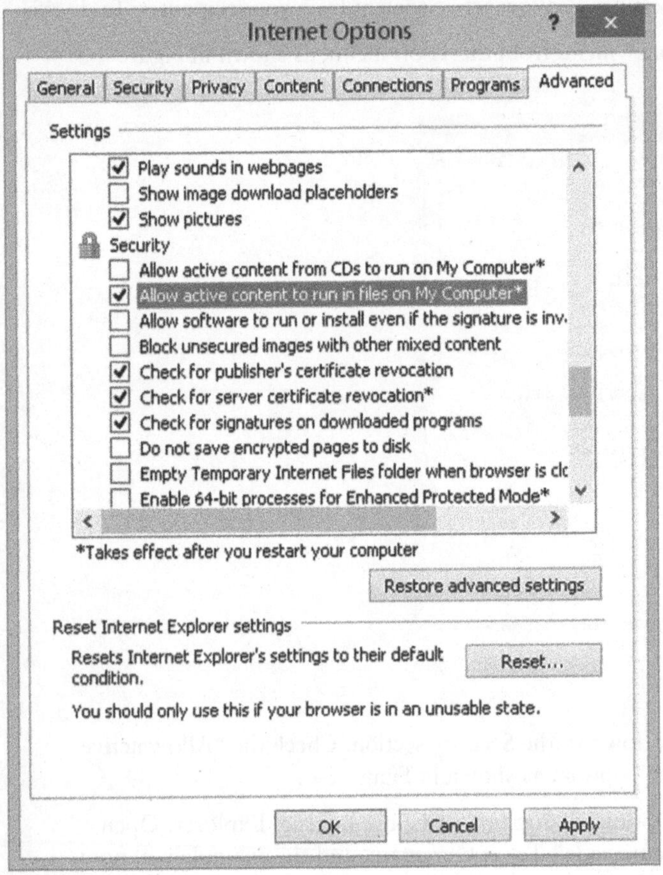

FIGURE 2-6

You pass two pieces of information to the prompt() function:

➤ The text to be displayed—usually a question that prompts the user for input

➤ The default value that is contained in the input box when the prompt dialog box first appears

These two pieces of information must be specified in the given order and separated by a comma. If you don't want a default value to be contained in the input box when the prompt box opens, use an empty string ("") for the second piece of information.

As you can see in the preceding code, the text is "Enter the degrees in Fahrenheit," and the default value in the input box is 50.

Next in the script block comes the equation represented in JavaScript. You store the result of the equation in the degCent variable. You can see that the JavaScript looks very much like the equation you have in the comment, except you use degFahren instead of °F, and degCent rather than °C:

```
degCent = 5/9 * (degFahren - 32);
```

The calculation of the expression on the right-hand side of the equals sign raises a number of important points. First, just as in math, the JavaScript equation is read from left to right, at least for the basic math functions like +, -, and so on. Secondly, as you saw earlier, just as there is precedence in math, there is precedence in JavaScript.

Starting from the left, first JavaScript works out 5/9 = .5556 (approximately). Then it comes to the multiplication, but wait... the last bit of your equation, degFahren - 32, is in parentheses. This raises the order of precedence and causes JavaScript to calculate the result of degFahren - 32 before doing the multiplication. For example, when degFahren is set to 50, (degFahren - 32) = (50 - 32) = 18. Now JavaScript does the multiplication, .5556 * 18, which is approximately 10.

What if you didn't use the parentheses? Then your code would be:

```
degCent = 5/9 * degFahren - 32;
```

The calculation of 5/9 remains the same, but then JavaScript would have calculated the multiplication, 5/9 * degFahren. This is because the multiplication takes precedence over the subtraction. When degFahren is 50, this equates to 5/9 * 50 = 27.7778. Finally, JavaScript would have subtracted the 32, leaving the result as -4.2221; not the answer you want!

Finally, in your script block, you display the answer using the alert() function:

```
alert(degCent);
```

That concludes a brief look at basic calculations with JavaScript. However, in Chapter 5 you look at the Math object, which enables you to do more complex calculations.

Basic String Operations

In an earlier section, you looked at the text or string data type, as well as numerical data. Just as numerical data has associated operators, strings have operators too. This section introduces some basic string manipulation techniques using such operators. Strings are covered in more depth in Chapter 5, and advanced string handling is covered in Chapter 6.

One thing you'll find yourself doing again and again in JavaScript is joining two strings to make one string—a process termed *concatenation*. For example, you may want to concatenate the two strings "Hello " and "Paul" to make the string "Hello Paul". So how do you concatenate? Easy! Use the + operator. Recall that when applied to numbers, the + operator adds them up, but when used in the context of two strings, it joins them:

```
var concatString = "Hello " + "Paul";
```

The string now stored in the variable concatString is "Hello Paul". Notice that the last character of the string "Hello" is a space—if you left this out, your concatenated string would be "HelloPaul".

TRY IT OUT Concatenating Strings

Let's look at an example using the + operator for string concatenation.

1. Type the following code and save it as ch2_example5.html:

```
<!DOCTYPE html>

<html lang="en">
<head>
    <title>Chapter 2, Example 5</title>
</head>
<body>
    <script>
        var greetingString = "Hello";
        var myName = prompt("Please enter your name", "");
        var concatString;

        document.write(greetingString + " " + myName + "<br/>");

        concatString = greetingString + " " + myName;

        document.write(concatString);
    </script>
</body>
</html>
```

2. If you load it into your web browser, you should see a prompt box asking for your name.

3. Enter your name and click OK. You should see a greeting and your name displayed twice on the web page.

You start the script block by declaring three variables. You set the first variable, greetingString, to a string value. The second variable, myName, is assigned to whatever is entered by the user in the prompt box. You do not initialize the third variable, concatString, here. It will be used to store the result of the concatenation that you'll do later in the code.

```
var greetingString = "Hello";
var myName = prompt("Please enter your name", "");
var concatString;
```

In the previous chapter, you saw how the web page was represented by the concept of a document and that it had a number of different properties, such as bgColor. You can also use document to write text and HTML directly into the page itself. You do this by using the word document, followed by a dot, and then write(). You then use document.write() much as you do the alert() function, in that you put the text that you want displayed in the web page inside the parentheses following the word write. Don't worry too much about this here, though, because it is all explained in detail in later chapters. However, you now make use of document.write() in your code to write the result of an expression to the page:

```
document.write(greetingString + " " + myName + "<br/>");
```

The expression written to the page is the concatenation of the value of the `greetingString` variable, a space (`" "`), the value of the `myName` variable, and the HTML `<br/>` element, which causes a line break. For example, if you enter `Jeremy` into the prompt box, the value of this expression will be as follows:

```
Hello Jeremy<br/>
```

In the next line of code is a similar expression. This time it is just the concatenation of the value in the variable `greetingString`, a space, and the value in the variable `myName`. You store the result of this expression in the variable `concatString`. Finally, you write the contents of the variable `concatString` to the page using `document.write()`:

```
concatString = greetingString + " " + myName;
document.write(concatString);
```

Mixing Numbers and Strings

What if you want to mix text and numbers in an expression? A prime example of this would be in the temperature converter you saw earlier. In the example, you just display the number without telling the user what it actually means. What you really want to do is display the number with descriptive text wrapped around it, such as "The value converted to degrees centigrade is 10."

Mixing numbers and text is actually very easy. You can simply join them using the + operator. JavaScript is intelligent enough to know that when both a string and a number are involved, you're not trying to do numerical calculations, but rather that you want to treat the number as a string and join it to the text. For example, to join the text `My age is` and the number 101, you could simply do the following:

```
alert("My age is " + 101);
```

This would produce an `alert` box with "My age is 101" inside it.

TRY IT OUT **Making the Temperature Converter User-Friendly**

You can try out this technique of concatenating strings and numbers in the temperature-converter example. You output some explanatory text, along with the result of the conversion calculation. The changes that you need to make are very small, so load `ch2 _ example4.html` into your text editor and change the following line. Then save it as `ch2 _ example6.html`.

```
<!DOCTYPE html>

<html lang="en">
<head>
    <title>Chapter 2, Example 6</title>
</head>
<body>
    <script>
        // Equation is °C = 5/9 (°F - 32).
        var degFahren = prompt("Enter the degrees in Fahrenheit",50);
```

```
        var degCent;

        degCent = 5/9 * (degFahren - 32);

        alert(degFahren + "\xB0 Fahrenheit is " + degCent + "\xB0 centigrade");
    </script>
</body>
</html>
```

Load the page into your web browser. Click OK in the prompt box to submit the value 50, and this time you should see the box shown in Figure 2-7.

This example is identical to ch2_example4.html, except for one line:

```
    alert(degFahren + "\xB0 Fahrenheit is " + degCent + "\xB0 centigrade");
```

So we will just look at this line here. You can see that the alert() function contains an expression. Let's look at that expression more closely.

First is the variable degFahren, which contains numerical data. You concatenate that to the string "\xB0 Fahrenheit is ". JavaScript realizes that because you are adding a number and a string, you want to join them into one string rather than trying to take their sum, and so it automatically converts the number contained in degFahren to a string. You next concatenate this string to the variable degCent, containing numerical data. Again JavaScript converts the value of this variable to a string. Finally, you concatenate to the string "\xB0 centigrade".

The page at jwmcpeak.github.io says:

50° Fahrenheit is 10° centigrade

☐ Prevent this page from creating additional dialogs.

OK

FIGURE 2-7

Note also the escape sequence used to insert the degree character into the strings. You'll remember from earlier in the chapter that you can use \xNN to insert special characters not available to type in directly. (NN is a hexadecimal number representing a character from the Latin-1 character table.) So when JavaScript spots \xB0 in a string, instead of showing those characters it does a lookup to see what character is represented by B0 and shows that instead.

Something to be aware of when using special characters is that they are not necessarily cross-platform–compatible. Although you can use \xNN for a certain character on a Windows computer, you may find you need to use a different character on a Mac or a Unix machine.

You look at more string manipulation techniques in Chapter 5—you see how to search strings and insert characters in the middle of them, and in Chapter 6 you see some very sophisticated string techniques.

DATA TYPE CONVERSION

As you've seen, if you add a string and a number, JavaScript makes the sensible choice and converts the number to a string, then concatenates the two. Usually, JavaScript has enough sense to make data type conversions like this whenever it needs to, but in some situations you need to convert the type of a piece of data yourself. For example, you may be given a piece of string data that you want to think of as a number. This is especially likely if you are using forms to collect data from the user. Any values input by the user are treated as strings, even though they may contain numerical data, such as the user's age.

Why is changing the type of the data so important? Consider a situation in which you collect two numbers from the user using a form and want to calculate their sum. The two numbers are available to you as strings, for example "22" and "15". When you try to calculate the sum of these values using "22" + "15" you get the result "2215", because JavaScript thinks you are trying to concatenate two strings rather than trying to find the sum of two numbers. To add to the possible confusion, the order also makes a difference. So:

```
1 + 2 + "abc"
```

results in a string containing "3abc", whereas:

```
"abc" + 1 + 2
```

would result in the string containing "abc12".

In this section you look at two conversion functions that convert strings to numbers: `parseInt()` and `parseFloat()`.

Let's take `parseInt()` first. This function takes a string and converts it to an integer. The name is a little confusing at first—why `parseInt()` rather than `convertToInt()`? The main reason for the name comes from the way that the function works. It actually goes through (that is, parses) each character of the string you ask it to convert and sees if it's a valid number. If it is valid, `parseInt()` uses it to build up the number; if it is not valid, the command simply stops converting and returns the number it has converted so far.

For example, if your code is `parseInt("123")`, JavaScript will convert the string "123" to the number 123. For the code `parseInt("123abc")`, JavaScript will also return the number 123. When the JavaScript engine gets to the letter a, it assumes the number has ended and gives 123 as the integer version of the string "123abc".

The `parseFloat()` function works in the same way as `parseInt()`, except that it returns floating-point numbers—fractional numbers—and that a decimal point in the string, which it is converting, is considered to be part of the allowable number.

TRY IT OUT Converting Strings to Numbers

Let's look at an example using `parseInt()` and `parseFloat()`. Enter the following code and save it as ch2_example7.html:

```html
<!DOCTYPE html>

<html lang="en">
<head>
    <title>Chapter 2, Example 7</title>
</head>
```

```
<body>
    <script>
        var myString = "56.02 degrees centigrade";
        var myInt;
        var myFloat;

        document.write("\"" + myString + "\" is " + parseInt(myString, 10) +
            " as an integer" + "<br/>");

        myInt = parseInt(myString, 10);
        document.write("\"" + myString +
            "\" when converted to an integer equals " + myInt + "<br/>");

        myFloat = parseFloat(myString);
        document.write("\"" + myString +
            "\" when converted to a floating point number equals " + myFloat);
    </script>
</body>
</html>
```

Load it into your browser, and you'll see three lines written in the web page, as shown in Figure 2-8.

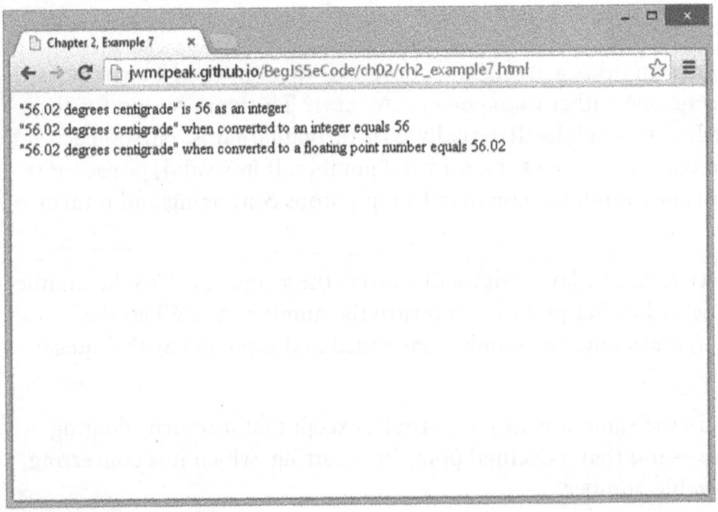

FIGURE 2-8

Your first task in the script block is to declare some variables. The variable myString is declared and initialized to the string you want to convert. You could just as easily have used the string directly in this example rather than storing it in a variable, but in practice you'll find that you use variables more often than literal values. You also declare the variables myInt and myFloat, which will hold the converted numbers:

```
var myString = "56.02 degrees centigrade";
var myInt;
var myFloat;
```

Next, you write to the page the converted integer value of myString displayed inside a user-friendly sentence you build up using string concatenation. Notice that you use the escape sequence \" to display quotes (") around the string you are converting:

```
document.write("\"" + myString + "\" is " + parseInt(myString, 10) +
    " as an integer" + "<br/>");
```

As you can see, you can use parseInt() and parseFloat() in the same places you would use a number itself or a variable containing a number. In fact, in this line the JavaScript engine is doing two conversions. First, it converts myString to an integer, because that's what you asked for by using parseInt(). Then it automatically converts that integer number back to a string, so it can be concatenated with the other strings to make up your sentence. Also note that only the 56 part of the myString variable's value is considered a valid number when you're dealing with integers. Anything after the 6 is considered invalid and is ignored.

Notice the second value, the number 10, that is passed to parseInt(). This is called the radix, and it determines how the string is parsed into a number. By passing the number 10, you tell the parseInt() function to convert the number using the Base 10 number system. Base 10 is our common number system, but you can use parseInt() to convert numbers to binary (Base 2), hex (Base 16), and other number systems. For example, parseInt(10, 2) converts the number 10 using the binary number system, resulting in the number 2. Always specify the radix! Without it, JavaScript guesses what number system to use, and you could encounter unexpected results.

Next, you do the same conversion of myString using parseInt(), but this time you store the result in the myInt variable. On the following line you use the result in some text you display to the user:

```
myInt = parseInt(myString, 10);
document.write("\"" + myString +
    "\" when converted to an integer equals " + myInt + "<br/>");
```

Again, though myInt holds a number, the JavaScript interpreter knows that +, when a string and a number are involved, means you want the myInt value converted to a string and concatenated to the rest of the string so it can be displayed.

Finally, you use parseFloat() to convert the string in myString to a floating-point number, which you store in the variable myFloat. This time the decimal point is considered to be a valid part of the number, so it's anything after the 2 that is ignored. Again you use document.write() to write the result to the web page inside a user-friendly string:

```
myFloat = parseFloat(myString);
document.write("\"" + myString +
    "\" when converted to a floating point number equals " + myFloat);
```

Dealing with Strings That Won't Convert

Some strings simply are not convertible to numbers, such as strings that don't contain any numerical data. What happens if you try to convert these strings? As a little experiment, try changing the preceding example so that myString holds something that is not convertible. For example, change the line

```
var myString = "56.02 degrees centigrade";
```

to

```
var myString = "I'm a name not a number";
```

Now reload the page in your browser and you should see what's shown in Figure 2-9.

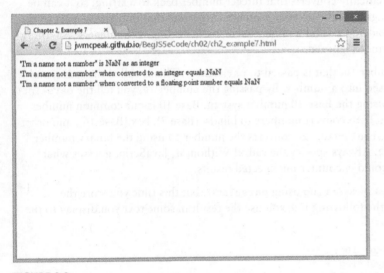

FIGURE 2-9

You can see that in the place of the numbers you got before, you get NaN. What sort of number is that? Well, it's *Not a Number* at all!

If you use parseInt() or parseFloat() with any string that is empty or does not start with at least one valid digit, you get NaN, meaning Not a Number.

NaN is actually a special value in JavaScript. It has its own function, isNaN(), which checks whether something is NaN or not. For example,

```
myVar1 = isNaN("Hello");
```

will store the value true in the variable myVar1, because "Hello" is not a number, whereas

```
myVar2 = isNaN("34");
```

will store the value false in the variable myVar2, because 34 can be converted successfully from a string to a number by the isNaN() function.

In later chapters you see how you can use the isNaN() function to check the validity of strings as numbers, something that proves invaluable when dealing with user input.

ARRAYS

Now we're going to look at a new concept—something called an *array*. An array is similar to a normal variable, in that you can use it to hold any type of data. However, it has one important difference, which you see in this section.

As you have already seen, a normal variable can only hold one piece of data at a time. For example, you can set myVariable to be equal to 25 like so:

```
myVariable = 25;
```

and then go and set it to something else, say 35:

```
myVariable = 35;
```

However, when you set the variable to 35, the first value of 25 is lost. The variable myVariable now holds just the number 35.

The following table illustrates the variable:

VARIABLE NAME	VALUE
myVariable	35

The difference between such a normal variable and an array is that an array can hold *more than one* item of data at the same time. For example, you could use an array with the name myArray to store both the numbers 25 and 35. Each place where a piece of data can be stored in an array is called an *element*.

How do you distinguish between these two pieces of data in an array? You give each piece of data an *index* value. To refer to that piece of data, you enclose its index value in square brackets after the name of the array. For example, an array called myArray containing the data 25 and 35 could be illustrated using the following table:

ELEMENTNAME	VALUE
myArray[0]	25
myArray[1]	35

Notice that the index values start at 0 and not 1. Why is this? Surely 1 makes more sense—after all, we humans tend to say the first item of data, followed by the second item, and so on. Computers start from 0, and think of the first item as the zero item, the second as the first item, and so on. Confusing, but you'll soon get used to this.

Arrays can be very useful because you can store as many (within the limits of the language, which specifies a maximum of two to the power of 32 elements) or as few items of data in an array as you want. Also, you don't have to say up front how many pieces of data you want to store in an array.

So how do you create an array? This is slightly different from declaring a normal variable. To create a new array, you need to declare a variable name and tell JavaScript that you want it to be a new array using the new keyword and the Array() function. For example, you could define the array myArray like this:

```
var myArray = new Array();
```

Note that, as with everything in JavaScript, the code is case-sensitive, so if you type array() rather than Array(), the code won't work. Using the new operator is explained in Chapter 5.

Today's JavaScript developers create arrays like this:

```
var myArray = [];
```

This uses an *array literal* to create the array. It is functionally the same as using new Array(), but it requires less typing. There is no right or wrong way to create an array, but for the remainder of this book, we use the array literal to create arrays.

As with normal variables, you can also declare your variable first, and then tell JavaScript you want it to be an array. For example:

```
var myArray;
myArray = [];
```

You have seen how to declare a new array, but how do you store your pieces of data inside it? You can do this when you define your array by including your data inside the square brackets, with each piece of data separated by a comma. For example:

```
var myArray = ["Paul",345,"John",112,"Bob",99];
```

Here the first item of data, "Paul", will be put in the array with an index of 0. The next piece of data, 345, will be put in the array with an index of 1, and so on. This means that the element with the name myArray[0] contains the value "Paul", the element with the name myArray[1] contains the value 345, and so on.

You don't have to provide an array's data when you first create the array. For example, you could also write the preceding line like this:

```
var myArray = [];
myArray[0] = "Paul";
myArray[1] = 345;
myArray[2] = "John";
myArray[3] = 112;
myArray[4] = "Bob";
myArray[5] = 99;
```

You use each element name as you would a variable, assigning them with values. You learn this method of declaring the values of array elements in the following "Try It Out" section.

Obviously, in this example the first way of defining the data items is much easier. However, there will be situations in which you want to change the data stored in a particular element in an array after the data items have been declared. In that case you will have to use the latter method of defining the values of the array elements.

You'll also spot from the preceding example that you can store different data types in the same array. JavaScript is very flexible as to what you can put in an array and where you can put it.

TRY IT OUT An Array

In this example, you create an array to hold some names, and you use the second method described in the preceding section to store these pieces of data in the array. You then display the data to the user. Type this code and save it as ch2 _ example8.html:

```
<!DOCTYPE html>

<html lang="en">
<head>
    <title>Chapter 2, Example 8</title>
</head>
<body>
    <script>
        var myArray = [];
        myArray[0] = "Jeremy";
        myArray[1] = "Paul";
        myArray[2] = "John";

        document.write("myArray[0] = " + myArray[0] + "<br/>");
        document.write("myArray[2] = " + myArray[2] + "<br/>");
        document.write("myArray[1] = " + myArray[1] + "<br/>");

        myArray[1] = "Mike";
        document.write("myArray[1] changed to " + myArray[1]);
    </script>
</body>
</html>
```

If you load this into your web browser, you should see a web page that looks something like the one shown in Figure 2-10.

The first task in the script block is to declare a variable and initialize it as an array:

```
var myArray = [];
```

Now that you have your array defined, you can store some data in it. Each time you store an item of data with a new index, JavaScript automatically creates a new storage space for it. Remember that the first element will be at myArray[0].

Take each addition to the array in turn and see what's happening. Before you add anything, your array is empty. Then you add an array element with the following line:

```
myArray[0] = "Jeremy";
```

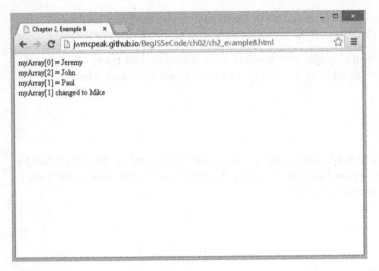

FIGURE 2-10

Your array now looks like this:

INDEX	DATA STORED
0	Jeremy

Then you add another element to the array, this time with an index of 1:

```
myArray[1] = "Paul";
```

Your array now looks like this:

INDEX	DATA STORED
0	Jeremy
1	Paul

Finally, you add another element to the array with an index of 2:

```
myArray[2] = "John";
```

Your array now looks like this:

INDEX	DATA STORED
0	Jeremy
1	Paul
2	John

Next, you use a series of `document.write()` functions to insert the values that each element of the array contains into the web page. Here the array is out of order just to demonstrate that you can access it that way:

```
document.write("myArray[0] = " + myArray[0] + "<br/>");
document.write("myArray[2] = " + myArray[2] + "<br/>");
document.write("myArray[1] = " + myArray[1] + "<br/>");
```

You can treat each particular position in an array as if it's a standard variable, so you can use it to do calculations, transfer its value to another variable or array, and so on. However, if you try to access the data inside an array position before you have defined it, you'll get `undefined` as a value.

Finally, you changed the value of the second array position to `"Mike"`. You could have changed it to a number because, just as with normal variables, you can store any data type at any time in each individual data position in an array:

```
myArray[1] = "Mike";
```

Now your array's contents look like this:

INDEX	DATA STORED
0	Jeremy
1	Mike
2	John

Just to show that the change you made has worked, you use `document.write()` to display the second element's value:

```
document.write("myArray[1] changed to " + myArray[1]);
```

A Multi-Dimensional Array

Suppose you want to store a company's personnel information in an array. You might have data such as names, ages, addresses, and so on. One way to create such an array would be to store the information sequentially—the first name in the first element of the array, then the corresponding age in the next element, the address in the third, the next name in the fourth element, and so on. Your array could look something like this:

INDEX	DATA STORED
0	Name1
1	Age1
2	Address1

continues

(continued)

INDEX	DATA STORED
3	Name2
4	Age2
5	Address2
6	Name3
7	Age3
8	Address3

This would work, but there is a neater solution: using a *multi-dimensional array*. Up to now you have been using single-dimension arrays. In these arrays each element is specified by just one index—that is, one dimension. So, taking the preceding example, you can see Name1 is at index 0, Age1 is at index 1, and so on.

A multi-dimensional array is one with two or more indexes for each element. For example, this is how your personnel array could look as a two-dimensional array:

INDEX	0	1	2
0	Name1	Name2	Name3
1	Age1	Age2	Age3
2	Address1	Address2	Address3

You see how to create such multi-dimensional arrays in the following "Try It Out" section.

TRY IT OUT A Two-Dimensional Array

This example illustrates how you can create such a multi-dimensional array in JavaScript code and how you can access the elements of this array. Type this code and save it as ch2 _ example9.html:

```
<!DOCTYPE html>

<html lang="en">
<head>
    <title>Chapter 2, Example 9</title>
</head>
<body>
    <script>
        var personnel = [];

        personnel[0] = [];
        personnel[0][0] = "Name0";
        personnel[0][1] = "Age0";
```

```
            personnel[0][2] - "Address0";

            personnel[1] - [];
            personnel[1][0] - "Name1";
            personnel[1][1] - "Age1";
            personnel[1][2] - "Address1";

            personnel[2] - [];
            personnel[2][0] - "Name2";
            personnel[2][1] - "Age2";
            personnel[2][2] - "Address2";

            document.write("Name : " + personnel[1][0] + "<br/>");
            document.write("Age : " + personnel[1][1] + "<br/>");
            document.write("Address : " + personnel[1][2]);
        </script>
    </body>
    </html>
```

If you load it into your web browser, you'll see three lines written into the page, which represent the name, age, and address of the person whose details are stored in the personnel[1] element of the array, as shown in Figure 2-11.

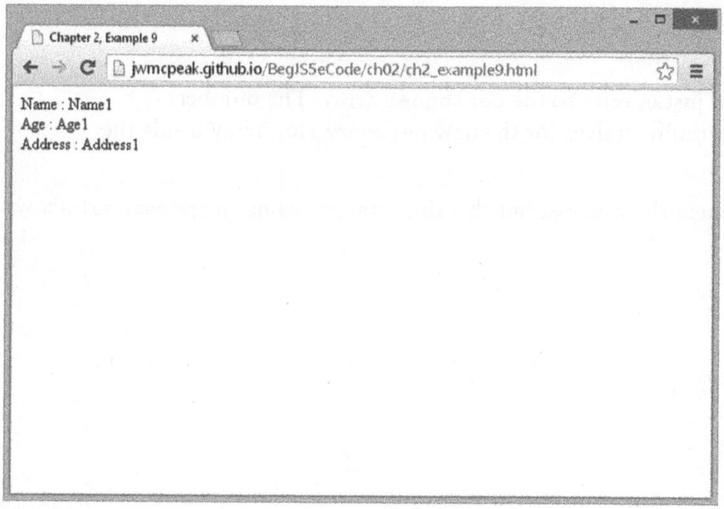

```
Chapter 2, Example 9

jwmcpeak.github.io/BegJS5eCode/ch02/ch2_example9.html

Name : Name1
Age : Age1
Address : Address1
```

FIGURE 2-11

The first thing to do in this script block is declare a variable, personnel, and tell JavaScript that you want it to be a new array:

```
var personnel - [];
```

Then you do something new; you tell JavaScript you want index 0 of the personnel array, that is, the element personnel[0], to be another new array:

```
personnel[0] - [];
```

So what's going on? Well, the truth is that JavaScript doesn't actually support multi-dimensional arrays, only single ones. However, JavaScript enables you to fake multi-dimensional arrays by creating an array inside another array. So what the preceding line is doing is creating a new array inside the element with index 0 of your `personnel` array.

In the next three lines, you put values into the newly created `personnel[0]` array. JavaScript makes it easy to do this: You just state the name of the array, `personnel[0]`, followed by another index in square brackets. The first index (0) belongs to the `personnel` array; the second index belongs to the `personnel[0]` array:

```
personnel[0][0] = "Name0";
personnel[0][1] = "Age0";
personnel[0][2] = "Address0";
```

After these lines of code, your array looks like this:

INDEX	0
0	Name0
1	Age0
2	Address0

The numbers at the top, at the moment just 0, refer to the `personnel` array. The numbers going down the side, 0, 1, and 2, are actually indices for the new `personnel[0]` array inside the `personnel` array.

For the second person's details, you repeat the process, but this time you are using the `personnel` array element with index 1:

```
personnel[1] = [];
personnel[1][0] = "Name1";
personnel[1][1] = "Age1";
personnel[1][2] = "Address1";
```

Now your array looks like this:

INDEX	0	1
0	Name0	Name1
1	Age0	Age1
2	Address0	Address1

You create a third person's details in the next few lines. You are now using the element with index 2 inside the `personnel` array to create a new array:

```
personnel[2] = [];
personnel[2][0] = "Name2";
personnel[2][1] = "Age2";
personnel[2][2] = "Address2";
```

The array now looks like this:

INDEX	0	1	2
0	Name0	Name1	Name2
1	Age0	Age1	Age2
2	Address0	Address1	Address2

You have now finished creating your multi-dimensional array. You end the script block by accessing the data for the second person (Name1, Age1, Address1) and displaying it in the page by using document.write(). As you can see, accessing the data is very much the same as storing it. You can use the multi-dimensional array anywhere you would use a normal variable or single-dimension array.

```
document.write("Name : " + personnel[1][0] + "<br/>");
document.write("Age : " + personnel[1][1] + "<br/>");
document.write("Address : " + personnel[1][2]);
```

Try changing the document.write() commands so that they display the first person's details. The code would look like this:

```
document.write("Name : " + personnel[0][0] + "<br/>");
document.write("Age : " + personnel[0][1] + "<br/>");
document.write("Address : " + personnel[0][2]);
```

It's possible to create multi-dimensional arrays of three, four, or even a hundred dimensions, but things can start to get very confusing, and you'll find that you rarely, if ever, need more than two dimensions. To give you an idea, here's how to declare and access a five-dimensional array:

```
var myArray = [];
myArray[0] = [];
myArray[0][0] = [];
myArray[0][0][0] = [];
myArray[0][0][0][0] = [];

myArray[0][0][0][0][0] = "This is getting out of hand";

document.write(myArray[0][0][0][0][0]);
```

That's it for arrays for now, but you return to them in Chapter 5, where you'll find out something shocking about them. You also learn about some of their more advanced features.

SUMMARY

In this chapter you have built up knowledge of the fundamentals of JavaScript's data types and variables and how to use them in operations. In particular, you saw that:

➤ JavaScript supports a number of types of data, such as numbers, text, and booleans.

➤ Text is represented by strings of characters and is surrounded by quotes. You must match the quotes surrounding strings. Escape characters enable you to include characters in your string that cannot be typed.

➤ Variables are JavaScript's means of storing data, such as numbers and text, in memory so that they can be used again and again in your code.

➤ Variable names must not include certain illegal characters, like the percent sign (%) and the ampersand (&), or be a reserved word, like `with`.

➤ Before you can give a value to a variable, you must declare its existence to the JavaScript interpreter.

➤ JavaScript has the four basic math operators, represented by the symbols plus (+), minus (−), star (*), and forward slash (/). To assign values of a calculation to a variable, you use the equals sign (=), termed the assignment operator.

➤ Operators have different levels of precedence, so multiplication and division will be calculated before addition and subtraction.

➤ Strings can be joined, or concatenated, to produce one big string by means of the + operator. When numbers and strings are concatenated with the + operator, JavaScript automatically converts the number into a string.

➤ Although JavaScript's automatic data conversion suits us most of the time, on some occasions you need to force the conversion of data. You saw how `parseInt()` and `parseFloat()` can be used to convert strings to numbers. Attempting to convert strings that won't convert will result in `NaN` (Not a Number) being returned.

➤ Arrays are a special type of variable that can hold more than one piece of data. The data is inserted and accessed by means of a unique index number.

EXERCISES

You can find suggested solutions to these questions in Appendix A.

1. Write a JavaScript program to convert degrees centigrade into degrees Fahrenheit, and to write the result to the page in a descriptive sentence. The JavaScript equation for Fahrenheit to centigrade is as follows:

```
degFahren = 9 / 5 * degCent + 32
```

2. The following code uses the `prompt()` function to get two numbers from the user. It then adds those two numbers and writes the result to the page:

```
<!DOCTYPE html>

<html lang="en">
<head>
    <title>Chapter 2, Question 2</title>
</head>
<body>

<script>
    var firstNumber = prompt("Enter the first number","");
    var secondNumber = prompt("Enter the second number","");
    var theTotal = firstNumber + secondNumber;

    document.write(firstNumber + " added to " + secondNumber +
        " equals " + theTotal);
</script>
</body>
</html>
```

However, if you try out the code, you'll discover that it doesn't work. Why not? Change the code so that it does work.

3

Decisions and Loops

WHAT YOU WILL LEARN IN THIS CHAPTER:

- ➤ Comparing number and string values
- ➤ Making decisions with the if, else, and switch statements
- ➤ Repeating code for as long as a condition is true

WROX.COM CODE DOWNLOADS FOR THIS CHAPTER

You can find the wrox.com code downloads for this chapter at http://www.wiley.com/go/ BeginningJavaScript5E on the Download Code tab. You can also view all of the examples and related files at http://beginningjs.com.

So far, you've seen how to use JavaScript to get user input, perform calculations and tasks with that input, and write the results to a web page. However, a pocket calculator can do all this, so what is it that makes computers different? That is to say, what gives computers the appearance of having intelligence? The answer is the capability to make decisions based on information gathered.

How will decision-making help you in creating websites? In the preceding chapter you wrote some code that converted temperature in degrees Fahrenheit to centigrade. You obtained the degrees Fahrenheit from the user using the prompt() function. This worked fine if the user entered a valid number, such as 50. If, however, the user entered something invalid for the Fahrenheit temperature, such as the string aaa, you would find that your code no longer works as expected. Now, if you had some decision-making capabilities in your program, you could check to see if what the user has entered is valid. If it is, you can do the calculation, and if it isn't, you can tell the user why and ask him to enter a valid number.

Validation of user input is probably one of the most common uses of decision making in JavaScript, but it's far from being the only use.

In this chapter you look at how decision making is implemented in JavaScript and how you can use it to make your code smarter.

DECISION MAKING—THE IF AND SWITCH STATEMENTS

All programming languages enable you to make decisions—that is, they enable the program to follow a certain course of action depending on whether a particular *condition* is met. This is what gives programming languages their intelligence.

Conditions are comparisons between variables and data, such as the following:

➤ Is *A* bigger than *B*?

➤ Is *X* equal to *Y*?

➤ Is *M* not equal to *N*?

For example, if the variable `today` held the day of the week on which you are reading this chapter, the condition would be this:

Is `today` equal to Friday?

You'll notice that all of these questions have a yes or no answer—that is, they are boolean-based and can only evaluate to `true` or `false`. How do you use this to create decision-making capabilities in your code? You get the browser to test for whether the condition is `true`. If (and only if) it is `true`, you execute a particular section of code.

Look at another example. Recall from Chapter 1 the natural English instructions used to demonstrate how code flows. One of these instructions for making a cup of coffee is:

Has the kettle boiled? If so, then pour water into cup; otherwise, continue to wait.

This is an example of making a decision. The condition in this instruction is "Has the kettle boiled?" It has a `true` or `false` answer. If the answer is `true`, you pour the water into the cup. If it isn't `true`, you continue to wait.

In JavaScript, you can change the flow of the code's execution depending on whether a condition is `true` or `false`, using an `if` statement or a `switch` statement. You look at these shortly, but first we need to introduce some new operators that are essential for the definition of conditions—*comparison operators*.

Comparison Operators

In Chapter 2 you saw how mathematical functions, such as addition and division, were represented by symbols, such as plus (+) and forward slash (/), called operators. You also saw that if you want to give a variable a value, you can assign to it a value or the result of a calculation using the equals sign (=), termed the assignment operator.

Decision making also has its own operators, which enable you to test conditions. Comparison operators, just like the mathematical operators you saw in the preceding chapter, have a left-hand side (LHS) and a right-hand side (RHS), and the comparison is made between the two. The technical terms for these are the *left operand* and the *right operand*. For example, the less-than operator, with the symbol <, is a comparison operator. You could write 23 < 45, which translates as "Is 23 less than 45?" Here, the answer would be true (see Figure 3-1).

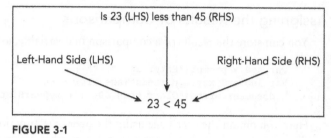

Is 23 (LHS) less than 45 (RHS)

Left-Hand Side (LHS)   Right-Hand Side (RHS)

23 < 45

FIGURE 3-1

Other comparison operators exist, the more useful of which are summarized in the following table:

OPERATOR SYMBOL	PURPOSE
==	Tests if LHS is equal to RHS
<	Tests if LHS is less than RHS
>	Tests if LHS is greater than RHS
<=	Tests if LHS is less than or equal to RHS
>=	Tests if LHS is greater than or equal to RHS
!=	Tests if LHS is not equal to RHS

You see these comparison operators in use in the next section when you look at the if statement.

Precedence

Recall from Chapter 2 that operators have an order of precedence. This applies also to the comparison operators. The == and != comparison operators have the lowest order of precedence, and the rest of the comparison operators, <, >, <=, and >=, have an equal precedence.

All of these comparison operators have a precedence that is below arithmetic operators, such as +, −, *, and /. This means that if you make a comparison such as 3 * 5 > 2 * 5, the multiplication calculations are worked out first, before their results are compared. However, in these circumstances, it's both safer and clearer if you wrap the calculations on either side inside parentheses; for example, (3 * 5) > (2 * 5). As a general rule, it's a good idea to use parentheses to ensure that the precedence is clear, or you may find yourself surprised by the outcome.

Assignment versus Comparison

One very important point to mention is the ease with which the assignment operator (=) and the comparison operator (==) can be mixed up. Remember that the = operator assigns a value to a variable and that the == operator compares the value of two variables. Even when you have this idea clear, it's amazingly easy to put one equals sign where you meant to put two.

Assigning the Results of Comparisons

You can store the results of a comparison in a variable, as shown in the following example:

```
var age = prompt("Enter age:", "");
var isOverSixty = parseInt(age, 10) > 60;
  document.write("Older than 60: " + isOverSixty);
```

Here you obtain the user's age using the prompt() function. This returns, as a string, whatever value the user enters. You then convert that to a number using the parseInt() function you saw in the previous chapter and use the greater-than operator to see if it's greater than 60. The result (either true or false) of the comparison will be stored in the variable isOverSixty.

If the user enters 35, the document.write() on the final line will write this to the page:

```
Older than 60: false
```

If the user enters 61, this will be displayed:

```
Older than 60: true
```

The if Statement

The if statement is one you'll find yourself using in almost every program that is more than a couple of lines long. It works very much as it does in the English language. For example, you might say in English, "If the room temperature is more than 80 degrees Fahrenheit, then I'll turn the air conditioning on." In JavaScript, this would translate into something like this:

```
if (roomTemperature > 80) {
    roomTemperature = roomTemperature - 10;
}
```

How does this work? See Figure 3-2.

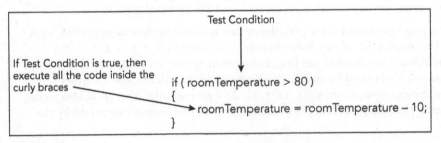

FIGURE 3-2

Notice that the test condition is placed in parentheses and follows the if keyword. Also, note that there is no semicolon at the end of this line. The code to be executed if the condition is true is placed in curly braces on the line after the condition, and each of these lines of code does end with a semicolon.

The curly braces, {}, have a special purpose in JavaScript: They mark out a *block* of code. Marking out lines of code as belonging to a single block means that JavaScript will treat them all as one piece of code. If the condition of an `if` statement is `true`, JavaScript executes the next line or block of code following the `if` statement. In the preceding example, the block of code has only one statement, so we could equally as well have written this:

```
if (roomTemperature > 80)
    roomTemperature = roomTemperature - 10;
```

However, if you have a number of lines of code that you want to execute, you need the braces to mark them out as a single block of code. For example, a modified version of the example with three statements of code would have to include the braces:

```
if (roomTemperature > 80) {
    roomTemperature = roomTemperature - 10;
    alert("It's getting hot in here");
    alert("Air conditioning switched on");
}
```

A particularly easy mistake to make is to forget the braces when marking out a block of code to be executed. Instead of the code in the block being executed when the condition is true, you'll find that *only the first line* after the `if` statement is executed. However, the other lines will always be executed regardless of the outcome of the test condition. To avoid mistakes like these, it's a good idea to always use braces, even where there is only one statement. If you get into this habit, you'll be less likely to leave them out when they are actually needed.

TRY IT OUT   The if Statement

Let's return to the temperature converter example from Chapter 2 and add some decision-making functionality.

1. Enter the following code and save it as `ch3_example1.html`:

```
<!DOCTYPE html>

<html lang="en">
<head>
    <title>Chapter 3, Example 1</title>
</head>
<body>
    <script>
        var degFahren = parseInt(prompt("Enter the degrees Fahrenheit", 32), 10);
        var degCent = 5/9 * (degFahren - 32);

        document.write(degFahren + "\xB0 Fahrenheit is " + degCent +
            "\xB0 centigrade<br />");

        if (degCent < 0) {
            document.write("That's below the freezing point of water");
        }

        if (degCent == 100)
```

```
            document.write("That's the boiling point of water");
    </script>
</body>
</html>
```

2. Load the page into your browser and enter 32 into the prompt box for the Fahrenheit value to be converted. With a value of 32, neither of the if statement's conditions will be true, so the only line written in the page will be that shown in Figure 3-3.

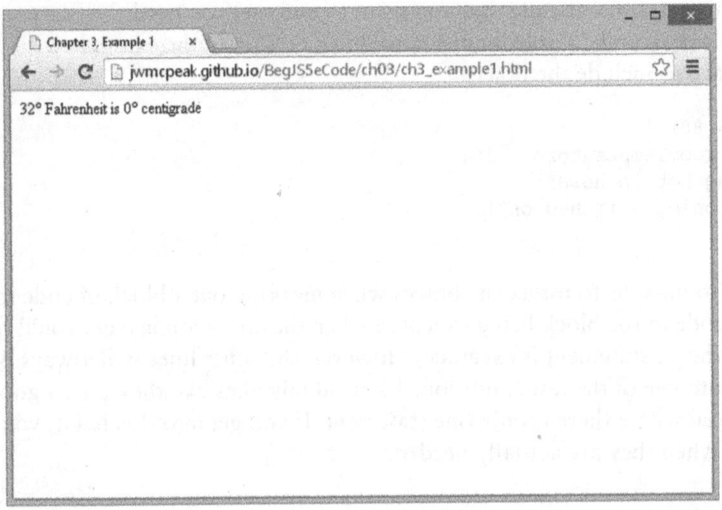

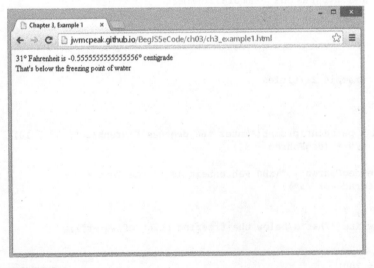

FIGURE 3-3

3. Now reload the page and enter 31 for the Fahrenheit value. This time you'll see two lines in the page, as shown in Figure 3-4.

FIGURE 3-4

4. Finally, reload the page again, but this time, enter 212 in the prompt box. The two lines shown in Figure 3-5 will appear in the page.

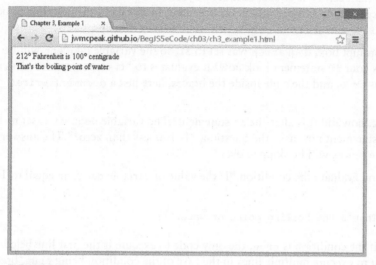

FIGURE 3-5

The first part of the script block in this page is similar to the example ch2 _ example4.html in Chapter 2. You declare two variables, degFahren and degCent. The variable degFahren is given an initial value obtained from the user with the prompt() function. Note the prompt() function returns a string value, which you then convert to a numeric value using the parseInt() function. The variable degCent is initialized to the result of the calculation 5/9 * (degFahren - 32), which is the Fahrenheit-to-centigrade conversion calculation:

```
var degFahren = parseInt(prompt("Enter the degrees Fahrenheit", 32), 10);
var degCent = 5/9 * (degFahren - 32);
```

Then you write the result of your calculation to the page:

```
document.write(degFahren + "\xB0 Fahrenheit is " + degCent +
    "\xB0 centigrade<br />");
```

Now comes the new code; the first of two if statements:

```
if (degCent < 0) {
    document.write("That's below the freezing point of water");
}
```

This if statement has the condition that asks, "Is the value of the variable degCent less than zero?" If the answer is yes (true), the code inside the curly braces executes. In this case, you write a sentence to the page using document.write(). If the answer is no (false), the processing moves on to the next line after the closing brace. Also worth noting is the fact that the code inside the if statement's opening brace is indented. This is not necessary, but it is a good practice to get into because it makes your code much easier to read.

When trying out the example, you started by entering 32, so that degFahren will be initialized to 32. In this case the calculation degCent = 5/9 * (degFahren − 32) will set degCent to 0. So the answer to the question "Is degCent less than zero?" is false, because degCent is equal to zero, not less than zero. The code inside the curly braces will be skipped and never executed. In this case, the next line to be executed will be the second if statement's condition, which we'll discuss shortly.

When you entered 31 in the prompt box, degFahren was set to 31, so the variable degCent will be −0.55555555556. So how does your if statement look now? It evaluates to "Is −0.55555555556 less than zero?" The answer this time is true, and the code inside the braces, here just a document.write() statement, executes.

Finally, when you entered 212, how did this alter the if statement? The variable degCent is set to 100 by the calculation, so the if statement now asks the question, "Is 100 less than zero?" The answer is false, and the code inside the braces will be skipped over.

In the second if statement, you evaluate the condition "Is the value of variable degCent equal to 100?":

```
if (degCent == 100)
    document.write("That's the boiling point of water");
```

There are no braces here, so if the condition is true, the only code to execute is the first line below the if statement. When you want to execute multiple lines in the case of the condition being true, braces are required.

You saw that when degFahren is 32, degCent will be 0. So your if statement will be "Is 0 equal to 100?" The answer is clearly false, and the code won't execute. Again, when you set degFahren to 31, degCent will be calculated to be -0.55555555556; "Is −0.55555555556 equal to 100?" is also false, and the code won't execute.

Finally, when degFahren is set to 212, degCent will be 100. This time the if statement is "Is 100 equal to 100?" and the answer is true, so the document.write() statement executes.

As you have seen already, one of the most common errors in JavaScript, even for experts, is using one equals sign for evaluating, rather than the necessary two. Take a look at the following code extract:

```
if (degCent = 100)
    document.write("That's the boiling point of water");
```

This condition will always evaluate to true, and the code below the if statement will always execute. Worse still, your variable degCent will be set to 100. Why? Because a single equals sign assigns values to a variable; only a double equals sign compares values. The reason an assignment always evaluates to true is that the result of the assignment expression is the value of the right-hand side expression and this is the number 100, which is then implicitly converted to a boolean and any number besides 0 and NaN converts to true.

Logical Operators

You should have a general idea of how to use conditions in if statements now, but how do you use a condition such as "Is degFahren greater than zero but less than 100?" You have two conditions to test here. You need to test whether degFahren is greater than zero *and* whether degFahren is less than 100.

JavaScript enables you to use such multiple conditions. To do this, you need to learn about three more operators: the logical operators AND, OR, and NOT. The symbols for these are listed in the following table:

OPERATOR	SYMBOL
AND	&&
OR	||
NOT	!

Notice that the AND and OR operators are *two* symbols repeated: && and | |. If you type just one symbol, & or |, strange things will happen because these are special operators called *bitwise operators* used in binary operations—for logical operations you must always use two.

After you've learned about the three logical operators, you take a look at how to use them in if statements, with plenty of practical examples. So if it seems a bit confusing on first read, don't panic. All will become clear. Let's look at how each of these works, starting with the AND operator.

AND

Recall that we talked about the left-hand side (LHS) and the right-hand side (RHS) of the operator. The same is true with the AND operator. However, now the LHS and RHS of the condition are boolean values (usually the result of a condition).

The AND operator works very much as it does in English. For example, you might say, "If I feel cold *and* I have a coat, then I'll put my coat on." Here, the left-hand side of the "and" word is "Do I feel cold?" and this can be evaluated as true or false. The right-hand side is "Do I have a coat?" which again is evaluated to either true or false. If the left-hand side is true (I am cold) *and* the right-hand side is true (I do have a coat), then you put your coat on.

This is very similar to how the AND operator works in JavaScript. The AND operator actually produces a result, just as adding two numbers produces a result. However, the AND operator takes two boolean values (on its LHS and RHS) and results in another boolean value. If the LHS and RHS conditions evaluate to true, the result will be true. In any other circumstance, the result will be false.

Following is a *truth table* of possible evaluations of left-hand sides and right-hand sides and the result when AND is used:

LEFT-HAND SIDE	RIGHT-HAND SIDE	RESULT
true	true	true
false	true	false
true	false	false
false	false	false

Although the table is, strictly speaking, true, it's worth noting that JavaScript doesn't like doing unnecessary work. Well, who does! If the left-hand side is false, even if the right-hand side does evaluate to `true`, it won't make any difference to the final result—it'll still be `false`. So to avoid wasting time, if the left-hand side is `false`, JavaScript doesn't even bother checking the right-hand side and just returns a result of `false`.

OR

Just like AND, OR also works much as it does in English. For example, you might say that if it is raining *or* if it is snowing, then you'll take an umbrella. If either of the conditions "it is raining" or "it is snowing" is true, you will take an umbrella.

Again, just like AND, the OR operator acts on two boolean values (one from its left-hand side and one from its right-hand side) and returns another boolean value. If the left-hand side evaluates to `true` or the right-hand side evaluates to `true`, the result returned is `true`. Otherwise, the result is `false`. The following table shows the possible results:

LEFT-HAND SIDE	RIGHT-HAND SIDE	RESULT
true	true	true
false	true	true
true	false	true
false	false	false

As with the AND operator, JavaScript likes to avoid doing things that make no difference to the final result. If the left-hand side is `true`, then whether the right-hand side is `true` or `false` makes no difference to the final result—it'll still be `true`. So, to avoid work, if the left-hand side is `true`, the right-hand side is not evaluated, and JavaScript simply returns `true`. The end result is the same—the only difference is in how JavaScript arrives at the conclusion. However, it does mean you should not rely on the right-hand side of the OR operator to be executed.

NOT

In English, we might say, "If I'm *not* hot, then I'll eat soup." The condition being evaluated is whether we're hot. The result is true or false, but in this example we act (eat soup) if the result is false.

However, JavaScript is used to executing code only if a condition is `true`. So if you want a `false` condition to cause code to execute, you need to switch that `false` value to `true` (and any `true` value to `false`). That way you can trick JavaScript into executing code after a `false` condition.

You do this using the NOT operator. This operator reverses the logic of a result; it takes one boolean value and changes it to the other boolean value. So it changes `true` to `false` and `false` to `true`. This is sometimes called *negation*.

To use the NOT operator, you put the condition you want reversed in parentheses and put the `!` symbol in front of the parentheses. For example:

```
if (!(degCent < 100)) {
    // Some code
}
```

Any code within the braces will be executed only if the condition degCent < 100 is false. The following table details the possible results when using NOT:

RIGHT-HAND SIDE	RESULT
true	false
false	true

Multiple Conditions Inside an if Statement

The previous section started by asking how you could use the condition "Is degFahren greater than zero but less than 100?" One way of doing this would be to use two if statements, one nested inside another. *Nested* simply means that there is an outer if statement, and inside this is an inner if statement. If the condition for the outer if statement is true, then (and only then) will the nested inner if statement's condition be tested.

Using nested if statements, your code would be:

```
if (degCent < 100) {
    if (degCent > 0) {
        document.write("degCent is between 0 and 100");
    }
}
```

This would work, but it's a little verbose and can be quite confusing. JavaScript offers a better alternative—using multiple conditions inside the condition part of the if statement. The multiple conditions are strung together with the logical operators you just looked at. So the preceding code could be rewritten like this:

```
if (degCent > 0 && degCent < 100) {
    document.write("degCent is between 0 and 100");
}
```

The if statement's condition first evaluates whether degCent is greater than zero. If that is true, the code goes on to evaluate whether degCent is less than 100. Only if both of these conditions are true will the document.write() code line execute.

TRY IT OUT Multiple Conditions

This example demonstrates multi-condition if statements using the AND, OR, and NOT operators. Type the following code, and save it as ch3_example2.html:

```
<!DOCTYPE html>

<html lang="en">
<head>
    <title>Chapter 3, Example 2</title>
</head>
```

```
<body>
    <script>
        var myAge = parseInt( prompt("Enter your age", 30), 10 );

        if (myAge >= 0 && myAge <= 10) {
            document.write("myAge is between 0 and 10<br />");
        }

        if ( !(myAge >= 0 && myAge <= 10) ) {
            document.write("myAge is NOT between 0 and 10<br />");
        }

        if ( myAge >= 80 || myAge <= 10 ) {
            document.write("myAge is 80 or above OR 10 or below<br />");
        }

        if ( (myAge >= 30 && myAge <= 39) || (myAge >= 80 && myAge <= 89) ) {
            document.write("myAge is between 30 and 39 or myAge is " +
                            "between 80 and 89");
        }
    </script>
</body>
</html>
```

When you load it into your browser, a prompt box should appear. Enter the value 30, then press Return, and the lines shown in Figure 3-6 are written to the web page.

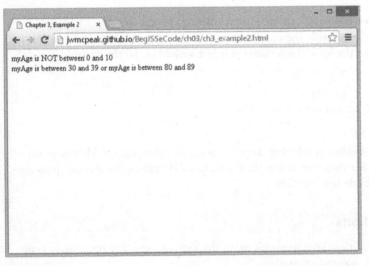

FIGURE 3-6

The script block starts by defining the variable myAge and initializing it to the value entered by the user in the prompt box and converted to a number:

```
var myAge = parseInt( prompt("Enter your age", 30), 10 );
```

After this are four if statements, each using multiple conditions. You look at each in detail in turn.

The easiest way to work out what multiple conditions are doing is to split them up into smaller pieces and then evaluate the combined result. In this example you have entered the value 30, which has been stored in the variable myAge. You'll substitute this value into the conditions to see how they work.

Here's the first if statement:

```
if (myAge >= 0 && myAge <= 10) {
    document.write("myAge is between 0 and 10<br />");
}
```

The first if statement is asking the question, "Is myAge between 0 and 10?" You'll take the LHS of the condition first, substituting your particular value for myAge. The LHS asks, "Is 30 greater than or equal to 0?" The answer is true. The question posed by the RHS condition is "Is 30 less than or equal to 10?" The answer is false. These two halves of the condition are joined using &&, which indicates the AND operator. Using the AND results table shown earlier, you can see that if LHS is true and RHS is false, you have an overall result of false. So the end result of the condition for the if statement is false, and the code inside the braces won't execute.

Let's move on to the second if statement:

```
if ( !(myAge >= 0 && myAge <= 10) ) {
    document.write("myAge is NOT between 0 and 10<br />");
}
```

The second if statement is posing the question, "Is myAge not between 0 and 10?" Its condition is similar to that of the first if statement, but with one small difference: You have enclosed the condition inside parentheses and put the NOT operator (!) in front.

The part of the condition inside the parentheses is evaluated and, as before, produces the same result—false. However, the NOT operator reverses the result and makes it true. Because the if statement's condition is true, the code inside the braces *will* execute this time, causing a document.write() to write a response to the page.

What about the third if statement?

```
if ( myAge >= 80 || myAge <= 10 ) {
    document.write("myAge is 80 or above OR 10 or below<br />");
}
```

The third if statement asks, "Is myAge greater than or equal to 80, or less than or equal to 10?" Taking the LHS condition first—"Is 30 greater than or equal to 80?"—the answer is false. The answer to the RHS condition—"Is 30 less than or equal to 10?"—is again false. These two halves of the condition are combined using ||, which indicates the OR operator. Looking at the OR result table earlier in this section, you see that false OR false produces a result of false. So again the if statement's condition evaluates to false, and the code within the curly braces does not execute.

The final if statement is a little more complex:

```
if ( (myAge >= 30 && myAge <= 39) || (myAge >= 80 && myAge <= 89) ) {
    document.write("myAge is between 30 and 39 or myAge is between 80 and 89");
}
```

It asks the question, "Is myAge between 30 and 39 or between 80 and 89?" Let's break down the condition into its component parts. There is a left-hand-side and a right-hand-side condition, combined by means of an OR operator. However, the LHS and RHS themselves have an LHS and RHS each, which are combined using AND operators. Notice how parentheses are used to tell JavaScript which parts of the condition to evaluate first, just as you would do with numbers in a mathematical calculation.

Let's look at the LHS of the condition first, namely (myAge >= 30 && myAge <= 39). By putting the condition into parentheses, you ensure that it's treated as a single condition; no matter how many conditions are inside the parentheses, it only produces a single result, either true or false. Breaking down the conditions in the parentheses, you have "Is 30 greater than or equal to 30?" with a result of true, and "Is 30 less than or equal to 39?" again with a result of true. From the AND table, you know true AND true produces a result of true.

Now let's look at the RHS of the condition, namely (myAge >= 80 && myAge <= 89). Again breaking down the condition, you see that the LHS asks, "Is 30 greater than or equal to 80?" which gives a false result, and the RHS asks, "Is 30 less than or equal to 89?" which gives a true result. You know that false AND true gives a false result.

Now you can think of your if statement's condition as looking like (true || false). Looking at the OR results table, you can see that true OR false gives a result of true, so the code within the braces following the if statement will execute, and a line will be written to the page.

However, remember that JavaScript does not evaluate conditions where they won't affect the final result, and the preceding condition is one of those situations. The LHS of the condition evaluated to true. After that, it does not matter if the RHS of the condition is true or false because only one of the conditions in an OR operation needs to be true for a result of true. Thus JavaScript does not actually evaluate the RHS of the condition. We did so simply for demonstration purposes.

As you have seen, the easiest way to approach understanding or creating multiple conditions is to break them down into the smallest logical chunks. You'll find that with experience, you will do this almost without thinking, unless you have a particularly tricky condition to evaluate.

Although using multiple conditions is often better than using multiple if statements, sometimes it makes your code harder to read and therefore harder to understand and debug. It's possible to have 10, 20, or more than 100 conditions inside your if statement, but can you imagine trying to read an if statement with even 10 conditions? If you feel that your multiple conditions are getting too complex, break them down into smaller logical chunks.

For example, imagine you want to execute some code if myAge is in the ranges 30–39, 80–89, or 100–115, using different code in each case. You could write the statement like so:

```
if ( (myAge >= 30 && myAge <= 39) || (myAge >= 80 && myAge <= 89) ||
      (myAge >= 100 && myAge <= 115) ) {
    document.write("myAge is between 30 and 39 " +
                   "or myAge is between 80 " +
                   "and 89 or myAge is between 100 and 115");
}
```

There's nothing wrong with this, but it is starting to get a little long and difficult to read. Instead, you could create another if statement for the code executed for the 100–115 range.

else and else if

Imagine a situation where you want some code to execute if a certain condition is true and some other code to execute if it is false. You can achieve this by having two `if` statements, as shown in the following example:

```
if (myAge >= 0 && myAge <= 10) {
    document.write("myAge is between 0 and 10");
}

if ( !(myAge >= 0 && myAge <= 10) ) {
    document.write("myAge is NOT between 0 and 10");
}
```

The first `if` statement tests whether `myAge` is between 0 and 10, and the second for the situation where `myAge` is not between 0 and 10. However, JavaScript provides an easier way of achieving this: with an `else` statement. Again, the use of the word `else` is similar to its use in the English language. You might say, "If it is raining, I will take an umbrella; otherwise I will take a sun hat." In JavaScript you can say `if` the condition is `true`, then execute one block of code; `else` execute an alternative block. Rewriting the preceding code using this technique, you would have the following:

```
if (myAge >= 0 && myAge <= 10) {
    document.write("myAge is between 0 and 10");
} else {
    document.write("myAge is NOT between 0 and 10");
}
```

Writing the code like this makes it simpler and therefore easier to read. Plus it also saves JavaScript from testing a condition to which you already know the answer.

You could also include another `if` statement with the `else` statement. For example:

```
if (myAge >= 0 && myAge <= 10) {
    document.write("myAge is between 0 and 10");
} else if ( (myAge >= 30 && myAge <= 39) || (myAge >= 80 && myAge <= 89) ){
    document.write("myAge is between 30 and 39 " +
                   "or myAge is between 80 and 89");
} else {
    document.write("myAge is NOT between 0 and 10, " +
                   "nor is it between 30 and 39, nor " +
                   "is it between 80 and 89");
}
```

The first `if` statement checks whether `myAge` is between 0 and 10 and executes some code if that's true. If it's `false`, an `else if` statement checks if `myAge` is between 30 and 39 or 80 and 89, and executes some other code if either of those conditions is `true`. Failing that, you have a final `else` statement, which catches the situation in which the value of `myAge` did not trigger `true` in any of the earlier `if` conditions.

When using `if` and `else if`, you need to be extra careful with your curly braces to ensure that the `if` and `else if` statements start and stop where you expect, and you don't end up with an `else` that doesn't belong to the right `if`. This is quite tricky to describe with words—it's easier to see what we mean with an example:

```
if (myAge >= 0 && myAge <= 10) {
document.write("myAge is between 0 and 10");
if (myAge == 5){
document.write("You're 5 years old");
}
}else{
document.write("myAge is NOT between 0 and 10");
}
```

Notice that we haven't indented the code. Although this does not matter to JavaScript, it does make the code more difficult for humans to read and hides the missing curly brace that should be before the final `else` statement.

Correctly formatted and with the missing bracket inserted, the code looks like this:

```
if (myAge >= 0 && myAge <= 10) {
    document.write("myAge is between 0 and 10<br />");
    if (myAge == 5) {
        document.write("You're 5 years old");
    }
} else {
    document.write("myAge is NOT between 0 and 10");
}
```

As you can see, the code is working now; it is also a lot easier to see which code is part of which `if` block.

Comparing Strings

Up to this point, you have been looking exclusively at using comparison operators with numbers. However, they work just as well with strings. All that's been said and done with numbers applies to strings, but with one important difference. You are now comparing data alphabetically rather than numerically, so you have a few traps to watch out for.

In the following code, you compare the variable `myName`, which contains the string `"Paul"`, with the string literal `"Paul"`:

```
var myName = "Paul";
if (myName == "Paul") {
    alert("myName is Paul");
}
```

How does JavaScript deal with this? Well, it goes through each letter in turn on the LHS and checks it with the letter in the same position on the RHS to see if it's actually the same. If at any point it finds a difference, it stops, and the result is `false`. If, after having checked each letter in turn all the way to the end, it confirms that they are all the same, it returns `true`. The condition in the preceding `if` statement will return `true`, so you'll see an `alert` box.

However, string comparison in JavaScript is case sensitive. So `"P"` is not the same as `"p"`. Taking the preceding example, but changing the variable `myName` to `"paul"`, you find that the condition is `false` and the code inside the `if` statement does not execute:

```
var myName = "paul";
if (myName == "Paul"){
    alert("myName is Paul");
}
```

The `>=`, `>`, `<=`, and `<` operators work with strings as well as with numbers, but again it is an alphabetical comparison. So `"A"` < `"B"` is `true`, because A comes before B in the alphabet. However, JavaScript's case sensitivity comes into play again. `"A"` < `"B"` is `true`, but `"a"` < `"B"` is `false`. Why? Because uppercase letters are treated as always coming *before* lowercase letters. Why is this? Each letter has a code number in the ASCII and Unicode character sets, and the code numbers for uppercase letters are lower than the code numbers for lowercase letters. This is something to watch out for when writing your own code.

The simplest way to avoid confusion with different cases is to convert both strings to either uppercase or lowercase before you compare them. You can do this easily using the `toUpperCase()` or `toLowerCase()` function, which you learn about in Chapter 5.

The switch Statement

You saw earlier how the `if` and `else if` statements could be used for checking various conditions; if the first condition is not valid, then another is checked, and another, and so on. However, when you want to check the value of a particular variable for a large number of possible values, there is a more efficient alternative, namely the `switch` statement. The structure of the `switch` statement is given in Figure 3-7.

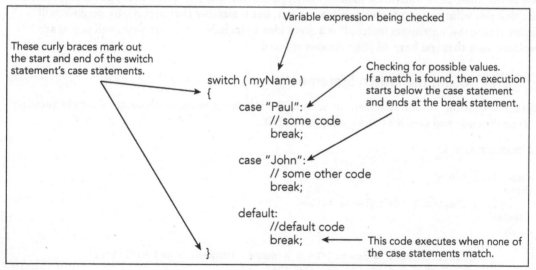

FIGURE 3-7

The best way to think of the switch statement is "Switch to the code where the case matches." The switch statement has four important elements:

➤ The test expression

➤ The case statements

➤ The break statements

➤ The default statement

The test expression is given in the parentheses following the switch keyword. In the previous example, you are testing using the variable myName. Inside the parentheses, however, you could have any valid expression.

Next come the case statements. The case statements do the condition checking. To indicate which case statements belong to your switch statement, you must put them inside the curly braces following the test expression. Each case statement specifies a value, for example "Paul". The case statement then acts like if (myName == "Paul"). If the variable myName did contain the value "Paul", execution would commence from the code starting below the case "Paul" statement and would continue to the end of the switch statement. This example has only two case statements, but you can have as many as you like.

In most cases, you want only the block of code directly underneath the relevant case statement to execute, not *all* the code below the relevant case statement, including any other case statements. To achieve this, you put a break statement at the end of the code that you want executed. This tells JavaScript to stop executing at that point and leave the switch statement.

Finally, you have the default case, which (as the name suggests) is the code that will execute when none of the other case statements match. The default statement is optional; if you have no default code that you want to execute, you can leave it out, but remember that in this case no code will execute if no case statements match. It is a good idea to include a default case, unless you are absolutely sure that you have all your options covered.

TRY IT OUT Using the switch Statement

Let's take a look at the switch statement in action. The following example illustrates a simple guessing game. Type the code and save it as ch3 _ example3.html.

```
<!DOCTYPE html>

<html lang="en">
<head>
    <title>Chapter 3, Example 3</title>
</head>
<body>
    <script>
        var secretNumber = prompt("Pick a number between 1 and 5:", "");
        secretNumber = parseInt(secretNumber, 10);

        switch (secretNumber) {
```

```
        case 1:
            document.write("Too low!");
            break;

        case 2:
            document.write("Too low!");
            break;

        case 3:
            document.write("You guessed the secret number!");
            break;

        case 4:
            document.write("Too high!");
            break;

        case 5:
            document.write("Too high!");
            break;

        default:
            document.write("You did not enter a number between 1 and 5.");
            break;
        }

        document.write("<br />Execution continues here");
    </script>
  </body>
</html>
```

Load this into your browser and enter, for example, the value 1 in the prompt box. You should then see something like what is shown in Figure 3-8.

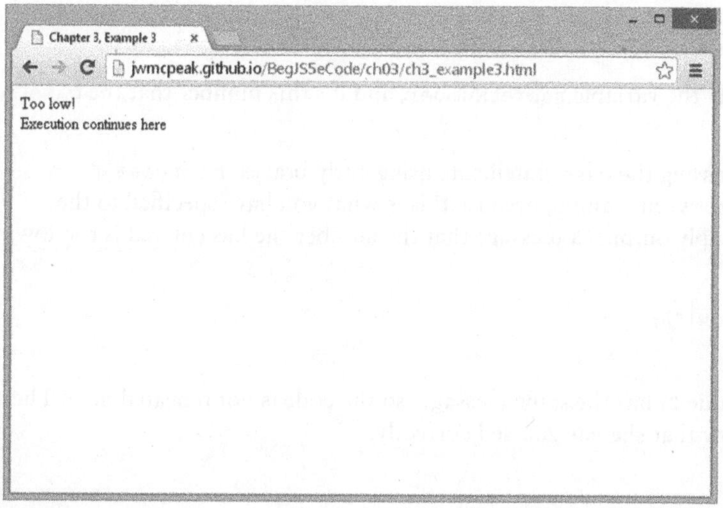

FIGURE 3-8

If, on the other hand, you enter the value 3, you should see a friendly message letting you know that you guessed the secret number correctly, as shown in Figure 3-9.

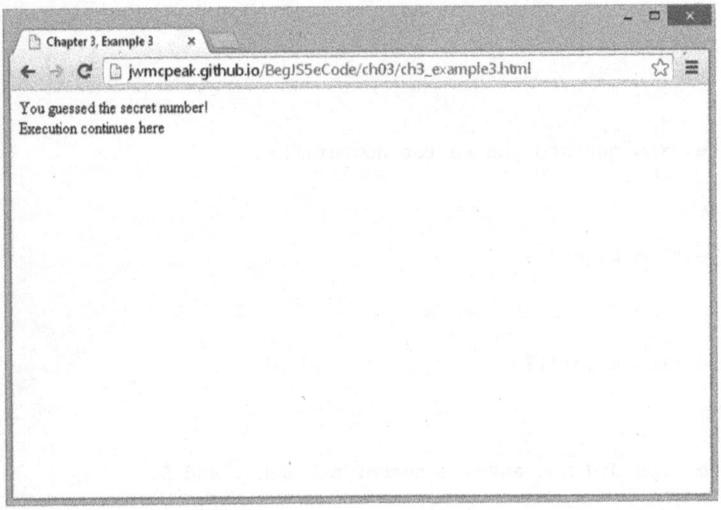

FIGURE 3-9

First you declare the variable `secretNumber` and set it to the value entered by the user via the prompt box. Note that you use the `parseInt()` function to convert the string that is returned from `prompt()` to an integer value:

```
var secretNumber = prompt("Pick a number between 1 and 5:", "");
secretNumber = parseInt(secretNumber, 10);
```

Next you create the start of the `switch` statement:

```
switch (secretNumber) {
```

The expression in parentheses is simply the variable `secretNumber`, and it's this number that the `case` statements will be compared against.

You specify the block of code encompassing the `case` statements using curly braces. Each `case` statement checks one of the numbers between 1 and 5, because this is what you have specified to the user that she should enter. The first simply outputs a message that the number she has entered is too low:

```
case 1:
    document.write("Too low!");
    break;
```

The second `case` statement, for the value 2, has the same message, so the code is not repeated here. The third `case` statement lets the user know that she has guessed correctly:

```
case 3:
    document.write("You guessed the secret number!");
    break;
```

Finally, the fourth and fifth `case` statements output a message that the number the user has entered is too high:

```
case 4:
    document.write("Too high!");
    break;
```

You do need to add a `default` case in this example, because the user might very well (despite the instructions) enter a number that is not between 1 and 5, or even perhaps a letter. In this case, you add a message to let the user know that there is a problem:

```
default:
    document.write("You did not enter a number between 1 and 5.");
    break;
```

A `default` statement is also very useful for picking up bugs—if you have coded some of the `case` statements incorrectly, you will pick that up very quickly if you see the `default` code being run when it shouldn't be.

Finally, you have added the closing brace indicating the end of the `switch` statement. After this you output a line to indicate where the execution continues:

```
}
    document.write("<br />Execution continues here");
```

Note that each `case` statement ends with a `break` statement. This is important to ensure that execution of the code moves to the line after the end of the `switch` statement. If you forget to include this, you could end up executing the code for each `case` following the `case` that matches.

Executing the Same Code for Different Cases

You may have spotted a problem with the `switch` statement in this example—you want to execute the same code if the user enters a 1 or a 2, and the same code for a 4 or a 5. However, to achieve this, you have had to repeat the code in each case. What you want is an easier way of getting JavaScript to execute the same code for different cases. Well, that's easy! Simply change the code so that it looks like this:

```
switch (secretNumber) {
    case 1:
    case 2:
        document.write("Too low!");
        break;

    case 3:
        document.write("You guessed the secret number!");
        break;

    case 4:
    case 5:
        document.write("Too high!");
```

```
    break;

default:
    document.write("You did not enter a number between 1 and 5.");
    break;
}
```

If you load this into your browser and experiment with entering some different numbers, you should see that it behaves exactly like the previous code.

Here, you are making use of the fact that if there is no break statement underneath the code for a certain case statement, execution will continue through each following case statement until a break statement or the end of the switch is reached. Think of it as a sort of free fall through the switch statement until you hit the break statement.

If the case statement for the value 1 is matched, execution simply continues until the break statement under case 2, so effectively you can execute the same code for both cases. The same technique is used for the case statements with values 4 and 5.

LOOPING—THE FOR AND WHILE STATEMENTS

Looping means repeating a block of code when a condition is true. This is achieved in JavaScript with the use of two statements: the while statement and the for statement. You'll be looking at these shortly, but why would you want to repeat blocks of code anyway?

Well, take the situation where you have a series of results, say the average temperature for each month in a year, and you want to plot these on a graph. The code needed for plotting each point will most likely be the same. So, rather than write the code 12 times (once for each point), it's much easier to execute the same code 12 times by using the next item of data in the series. This is where the for statement would come in handy, because you know how many times you want the code to execute.

In another situation, you might want to repeat the same piece of code when a certain condition is true, for example, while the user keeps clicking a Start Again button. In this situation, the while statement would be very useful.

The for Loop

The for statement enables you to repeat a block of code a certain number of times. The syntax is illustrated in Figure 3-10.

Let's look at the makeup of a for statement. You can see from Figure 3-10 that, just like the if and switch statements, the for statement also has its logic inside parentheses. However, this time that logic is split into three parts, each part separated by a semicolon. For example, in Figure 3-10 you have the following:

```
(var loopCounter = 1; loopCounter <= 3; loopCounter++)
```

The first part of the for statement's logic is the *initialization* part of the for statement. To keep track of how many times you have looped through the code, you need a variable to keep count. It's in the initialization part that you initialize variables. In the example, you have declared `loopCounter` and set it to the value of 1. This part is only executed once during the execution of the loops, unlike the other parts. You don't need to declare the variable if it was declared earlier in the code:

```
var loopCounter;
for (loopCounter = 1; loopCounter <= 3; loopCounter++)
```

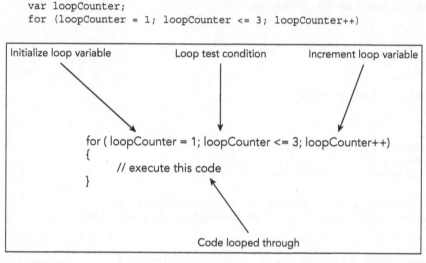

FIGURE 3-10

Following the semicolon, you have the *test condition* part of the for statement. The code inside the for statement will keep executing for as long as this test condition evaluates to true. After the code is looped through each time, this condition is tested. In Figure 3-10, you execute for as long as `loopCounter` is less than or equal to 3. The number of times a loop is performed is often called the number of *iterations*.

Finally, you have the *increment* part of the for loop, where variables in your loop's test condition have their values incremented. Here you can see that `loopCounter` is incremented by one by means of the ++ operator you saw in Chapter 2. Again, this part of the for statement is repeated with every loop of the code. Although we call it the increment part, it can actually be used to decrease, or *decrement*, the value—for example, if you wanted to count down from the top element in an array to the first.

After the for statement comes the block of code that will be executed repeatedly, as long as the test condition is true. This block of code is contained within curly braces. If the condition is never true, even at the first test of the loop condition, the code inside the for loop will be skipped over and never executed.

Putting all this together, how does the for loop work?

1. Execute initialization part of the for statement.

2. Check the test condition. If true, continue; if not, exit the for statement.

3. Execute code in the block after the for statement.

4. Execute the increment part of the for statement.

5. Repeat steps 2 through 4 until the test condition is false.

TRY IT OUT **Converting a Series of Fahrenheit Values**

Let's change the temperature converter so that it converts a series of values, stored in an array, from Fahrenheit to centigrade. You will be using the for statement to go through each element of the array. Type the following code and save it as ch3 _ example4.html:

```
<!DOCTYPE html>

<html lang="en">
<head>
    <title>Chapter 3, Example 4</title>
</head>
<body>
    <script>
        var degFahren = [212, 32, -459.15];
        var degCent = [];
        var loopCounter;

        for (loopCounter = 0; loopCounter <= 2; loopCounter++) {
            degCent[loopCounter] = 5/9 * (degFahren[loopCounter] - 32);
        }

        for (loopCounter = 2; loopCounter >= 0; loopCounter--) {
            document.write("Value " + loopCounter +
                            " was " + degFahren[loopCounter] +
                            " degrees Fahrenheit");

            document.write(" which is " + degCent[loopCounter] +
                            " degrees centigrade<br />");
        }
    </script>
</body>
</html>
```

On loading this into your browser, you'll see a series of three lines in the page, containing the results of converting your array of Fahrenheit values into centigrade (as shown in Figure 3-11).

The first task is to declare the variables you are going to use. First, you declare and initialize degFahren to contain an array of three values: 212, 32, and –459.15. Next, you declare degCent as an empty array. Finally, you declare loopCounter and will use it to keep track of which array index you are accessing during your looping:

```
var degFahren = [212, 32, -459.15];
var degCent = [];
var loopCounter;
```

Following this comes your first for loop:

```
for (loopCounter = 0; loopCounter <= 2; loopCounter++) {
    degCent[loopCounter] = 5/9 * (degFahren[loopCounter] - 32);
}
```

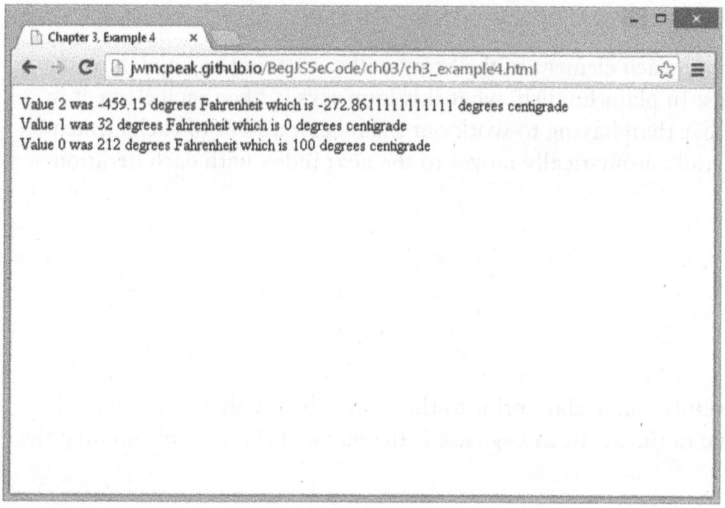

Value 2 was -459.15 degrees Fahrenheit which is -272.8611111111111 degrees centigrade
Value 1 was 32 degrees Fahrenheit which is 0 degrees centigrade
Value 0 was 212 degrees Fahrenheit which is 100 degrees centigrade

FIGURE 3-11

In the first line, you start by initializing the loopCounter to 0. Then the for loop's test condition, loopCounter <= 2, is checked. If this condition is true, the loop executes for the first time. After the code inside the curly braces has executed, the incrementing part of the for loop, loopCounter++, will be executed, and then the test condition will be re-evaluated. If it's still true, another execution of the loop code is performed. This continues until the for loop's test condition evaluates to false, at which point looping will end, and the first statement after the closing curly brace will be executed.

The code inside the curly braces is the equation you saw in earlier examples, only this time you are placing its result into the degCent array, with the index being the value of loopCounter.

In the second for loop, you write the results contained in the degCent array to the screen:

```
for (loopCounter = 2; loopCounter >= 0; loopCounter--) {
    document.write("Value " + loopCounter +
                    " was " + degFahren[loopCounter] +
                    " degrees Fahrenheit");

    document.write(" which is " + degCent[loopCounter] +
                    " degrees centigrade<br />");
}
```

This time you're counting *down* from 2 to 0. The variable loopCounter is initialized to 2, and the loop condition remains true until loopCounter is less than 0. This time loopCounter is actually decremented each time rather than incremented, by means of loopCounter--. Again, loopCounter is serving a dual purpose: It keeps count of how many loops you have done and also provides the index position in the array.

> **NOTE** *In these examples, you've used whole numbers in your loops. However, there is no reason why you can't use fractional numbers, although it's much less common to do so.*

The for . . . in Loop

This loop enables you to loop through each element in the array without having to know how many elements the array actually contains. In plain English, what this loop says is "For each element in the array, execute some code." Rather than having to work out the index number of each element, the for...in loop does it for you and automatically moves to the next index with each iteration (loop through).

Its syntax for use with arrays is:

```
for (index in arrayName) {
    //some code
}
```

In this code extract, index is a variable you declare prior to the loop, which will automatically be populated with the next index value in the array. arrayName is the name of the variable holding the array you want to loop through.

Let's look at an example to make things clearer. You define an array and initialize it with three values:

```
var myArray = ["Paul","Paula","Pauline"];
```

To access each element using a conventional for loop, you'd write this:

```
for (var loopCounter = 0; loopCounter < 3; loopCounter++) {
    document.write(myArray[loopCounter]);
}
```

To do exactly the same thing with the for . . . in loop, you write this:

```
for (var elementIndex in myArray) {
    document.write(myArray[elementIndex]);
}
```

As you can see, the code in the second example is a little clearer, as well as shorter. Both methods work equally well and will iterate three times. However, if you increase the size of the array, for example, by adding the element myArray[3] = "Philip", the first method will still loop only through the first three elements in the array, whereas the second method will loop through all four elements.

The while Loop

Whereas the for loop is used for looping a certain number of times, the while loop enables you to test a condition and keep on looping while it's true. The for loop is useful when you know how many times you need to loop; for example, when you are looping through an array that you know has a certain number of elements. The while loop is more useful when you don't know how many times you'll need to loop. For example, if you are looping through an array of temperature values and want to continue looping when the temperature value contained in the array element is less than 100, you will need to use the while statement.

Let's take a look at the structure of the while statement, as illustrated in Figure 3-12.

You can see that the while loop has fewer parts to it than the for loop. The while loop consists of a condition which, if it evaluates to true, causes the block of code inside the curly braces to execute once; then the condition is re-evaluated. If it's still true, the code is executed again, the condition is re-evaluated, and so on until the condition evaluates to false.

One thing to watch out for is that if the condition is false to start with, the while loop never executes. For example:

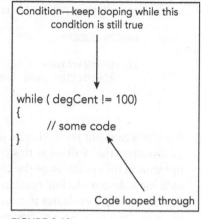

```
while ( degCent != 100)
{
    // some code
}
```

Condition—keep looping while this condition is still true

Code looped through

FIGURE 3-12

```
var degCent = 100;

while (degCent != 100) {
    // some code
}
```

Here, the loop will run if degCent does not equal 100. However, because degCent is 100, the condition is false, and the code never executes.

In practice you would normally expect the loop to execute once; whether it executes again will depend on what the code inside the loop has done to variables involved in the loop condition. For example:

```
var degCent = [];
degFahren = [34, 123, 212];
var loopCounter = 0;
while (loopCounter < 3) {
    degCent[loopCounter] = 5/9 * (degFahren[loopCounter] - 32);
    loopCounter++;
}
```

The loop will execute so long as loopCounter is less than 3. It's the code inside the loop (loopCounter++;) that increments loopCounter and will eventually cause loopCounter < 3 to be false so that the loop stops. Execution will then continue on the first line after the closing brace of the while statement.

Something to watch out for is the *infinite loop*—a loop that will never end. Suppose you forgot to include the loopCounter++; line in the code. Leaving this line out would mean that loopCounter will remain at 0, so the condition (loopCounter < 3) will always be true, and the loop will continue until the user gets bored and cross, and shuts down her browser. However, it is an easy mistake to make, and one that JavaScript won't warn you about.

It's not just missing lines that can cause infinite loops, but also mistakes inside the loop's code. For example:

```
var testVariable = 0;
while (testVariable <= 10) {
```

```
        alert("Test Variable is " + testVariable);

        testVariable++;

        if (testVariable = 10) {
            alert("The last loop");
        }
    }
```

See if you can spot the deliberate mistake that leads to an infinite loop—yes, it's the if statement that will cause this code to go on forever. Instead of using == as the comparison operator in the condition of the if statement, you put =, so testVariable is set to 10 again in each loop, despite the line testVariable++. This means that at the start of each loop, the test condition always evaluates to true, because 10 is less than or equal to 10. Put the extra = in to make if (testVariable == 10), and everything is fine.

The do . . . while loop

With the while loop, you saw that the code inside the loop only executes if the condition is true; if it's false, the code never executes, and execution instead moves to the first line after the while loop. However, there may be times when you want the code in the while loop to execute at least once, regardless of whether the condition in the while statement evaluates to true. It might even be that some code inside the while loop needs to be executed before you can test the while statement's condition. It's situations like this for which the do. . .while loop is ideal.

Look at an example in which you want to get the user's age via a prompt box. You want to show the prompt box but also make sure that what the user has entered is a number:

```
    var userAge;

    do {
        userAge = prompt("Please enter your age","")
    } while (isNaN(userAge) == true);
```

The code line within the loop:

```
    userAge = prompt("Please enter your age","")
```

will be executed regardless of the while statement's condition. This is because the condition is not checked *until* one loop has been executed. If the condition is true, the code is looped through again. If it's false, looping stops.

Note that within the while statement's condition, you are using the isNaN() function that you saw in Chapter 2. This checks whether the userAge variable's value is NaN (Not a Number). If it is not a number, the condition returns a value of true; otherwise, it returns false. As you can see from the example, it enables you to test the user input to ensure the right data has been entered. The user might lie about his age, but at least you know he entered a number!

The do. . .while loop is fairly rare; there's not much you can't do without it, so it's best avoided unless really necessary.

The break and continue Statements

You met the break statement earlier when you looked at the switch statement. Its function inside a switch statement is to stop code execution and move execution to the next line of code after the closing curly brace of the switch statement. However, you can also use the break statement as part of the for and while loops when you want to exit the loop prematurely. For example, suppose you're looping through an array, as you did in the temperature conversion example, and you hit an invalid value. In this situation, you might want to stop the code in its tracks, notify the user that the data is invalid, and leave the loop. This is one situation where the break statement comes in handy.

Let's see how you could change the example where you converted a series of Fahrenheit values (ch3 _ example4.html) so that if you hit a value that's not a number you stop the loop and let the user know about the invalid data:

```
<script>
var degFahren = [212, "string data", -459.67];
var degCent = [];
var loopCounter;

for (loopCounter = 0; loopCounter <= 2; loopCounter++) {
    if (isNaN(degFahren[loopCounter])) {
            alert("Data '" + degFahren[loopCounter] + "' at array index " +
                    loopCounter + " is invalid");
            break;
    }

    degCent[loopCounter] = 5/9 * (degFahren[loopCounter] - 32);
}
```

You have changed the initialization of the degFahren array so that it now contains some invalid data. Then, inside the for loop, you add an if statement to check whether the data in the degFahren array is not a number. You do this by means of the isNaN() function; it returns true if the value passed to it in the parentheses, here degFahren[loopCounter], is not a number. If the value is not a number, you tell the user where in the array you have the invalid data. Then you break out of the for loop altogether, using the break statement, and code execution continues on the first line after the end of the for statement.

That's the break statement, but what about continue? The continue statement is similar to break in that it stops the execution of a loop at the point where it is found, but instead of leaving the loop, it starts execution at the next iteration, starting with the for or while statement's condition being re-evaluated, just as if the last line of the loop's code had been reached.

In the break example, it was all or nothing—if even one piece of data was invalid, you broke out of the loop. It might be better if you tried to convert all the values in degFahren, but if you hit an invalid item of data in the array, you notify the user and continue with the next item, rather than giving up as the break statement example does:

```
if (isNaN(degFahren[loopCounter])) {
    alert("Data '" + degFahren[loopCounter] + "' at array index " +
            loopCounter + " is invalid");
    continue;
}
```

Just change the break statement to a continue. You will still get a message about the invalid data, but the third value will also be converted.

SUMMARY

In this chapter you continued your look at the core of the JavaScript language and its syntax.

The chapter looked at the following:

➤ **Decision making with the if and switch statements:** The ability to make decisions is essentially what gives the code its "intelligence." Based on whether a condition is true or false, you can decide on a course of action to follow.

➤ **Comparison operators:** The comparison operators compare the value on the left of the operator (left-hand side, LHS) with the value on the right of the operator (right-hand side, RHS) and return a boolean value. Here is a list of the main comparison operators:

> ➤ == means "is the LHS equal to the RHS?"
>
> ➤ != means "is the LHS not equal to the RHS?"
>
> ➤ <= means "is the LHS less than or equal to the RHS?"
>
> ➤ >= means "is the LHS greater than or equal to the RHS?"
>
> ➤ < means "is the LHS less than the RHS?"
>
> ➤ > means "is the LHS greater than the RHS?"

➤ **The if statement:** Using the if statement, you can choose to execute a block of code (defined by being in curly braces) when a condition is true. The if statement has a test condition, specified in parentheses. If this condition evaluates to true, the code after the if statement will execute.

➤ **The else statement:** If you want code to execute when the if statement is false, you can use the else statement that appears after the if statement.

➤ **Logical operators:** To combine conditions, you can use the three logical operators: AND, OR, and NOT, represented by &&, ||, and !, respectively:

> ➤ The AND operator returns true only if both sides of the expression are true.
>
> ➤ The OR operator returns true when either one or both sides of an expression are true.
>
> ➤ The NOT operator reverses the logic of an expression.

➤ **The switch statement:** This compares the result of an expression with a series of possible cases and is similar in effect to a multiple if statement.

➤ **Looping with for, for...in, while, and do...while:** It's often necessary to repeat a block of code a number of times, something JavaScript enables by looping.

> ➤ **The for loop:** Useful for looping through code a certain number of times, the for loop consists of three parts: the initialization, test condition, and increment parts.

Looping continues while the test condition is `true`. Each loop executes the block of code and then executes the increment part of the `for` loop before re-evaluating the test condition to see if the results of incrementing have changed it.

➤ **The `for...in` loop:** This is useful when you want to loop through an array without knowing the number of elements in the array. JavaScript works this out for you so that no elements are missed.

➤ **The `while` loop:** This is useful for looping through some code for as long as a test condition remains `true`. It consists of a test condition and the block of code that's executed only if the condition is `true`. If the condition is never `true`, the code never executes.

➤ **The `do...while` loop:** This is similar to a `while` loop, except that it executes the code once and then keeps executing the code as long as the test condition remains `true`.

➤ `break` **and** `continue` **statements:** Sometimes you have a good reason to break out of a loop prematurely, in which case you need to use the `break` statement. On hitting a `break` statement, code execution stops for the block of code marked out by the curly braces and starts immediately after the closing brace. The `continue` statement is similar to `break`, except that when code execution stops at that point in the loop, the loop is not broken out of but instead continues as if the end of that reiteration had been reached.

EXERCISES

You can find suggested solutions to these questions in Appendix A.

1. A junior programmer comes to you with some code that appears not to work. Can you spot where he went wrong? Give him a hand and correct the mistakes.

```
var userAge = prompt("Please enter your age");

if (userAge = 0) {;
    alert("So you're a baby!");
} else if ( userAge < 0 | userAge > 200)
    alert("I think you may be lying about your age");
else {
    alert("That's a good age");
}
```

2. Using `document.write()`, write code that displays the results of the 12 times table. Its output should be the results of the calculations.

```
12 * 1 = 12
12 * 2 = 24
12 * 3 = 36
...
12 * 11 = 132
12 * 12 = 144
```

4

Functions and Scope

WHAT YOU WILL LEARN IN THIS CHAPTER:

➤ Creating your own functions

➤ Identifying, creating, and using global and local variables

➤ Using functions as a value

WROX.COM CODE DOWNLOADS FOR THIS CHAPTER

You can find the wrox.com code downloads for this chapter at http://www.wiley.com/go/
BeginningJavaScript5E on the Download Code tab. You can also view all of the examples
and related files at http://beginningjs.com.

A function is something that performs a particular task. Take a pocket calculator as an
example. It performs lots of basic calculations, such as addition and subtraction. However,
many also have function keys that perform more complex operations. For example, some
calculators have a button for calculating the square root of a number, and others even provide
statistical functions, such as the calculation of an average. Most of these functions could be
done with the basic mathematical operations of add, subtract, multiply, and divide, but that
might take a lot of steps—it's much simpler for the user if she only needs to press one button.
All she needs to do is provide the data—numbers in this case—and the function key does
the rest.

Functions in JavaScript work a little like the function buttons on a pocket calculator: They
encapsulate a block of code that performs a certain task. Over the course of the book so far,
you have come across a number of handy built-in functions that perform a certain task, such
as the parseInt() and parseFloat() functions, which convert strings to numbers, and the
isNaN() function, which tells you whether a particular value can be converted to a number.
Some of these functions return data, such as parseInt(), which returns an integer number;

others simply perform an action but return no data. You'll also notice that some functions can be passed data, whereas others cannot. For example, the isNaN() function needs to be passed some data, which it checks to see if it is NaN. The data that a function requires to be passed are known as its *parameter(s)*.

As you work your way through the book, you'll be coming across many more useful built-in functions, but wouldn't it be great to be able to write your own functions? After you've worked out, written, and debugged a block of code to perform a certain task, it would be nice to be able to call it again and again when you need it. JavaScript enables us to do just that, and this is what you'll be concentrating on in this section.

CREATING YOUR OWN FUNCTIONS

Creating and using your own functions is very simple. Figure 4-1 shows an example of a function declaration.

You've probably already realized what this function does and how the code works. Yes, it's the infamous Fahrenheit-to-centigrade conversion code again.

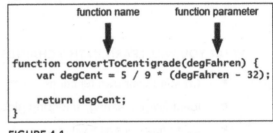

FIGURE 4-1

Each function you define in JavaScript must be given a unique name for that particular page. The name comes immediately after the function keyword. To make life easier for yourself, try using meaningful names so that when you see them being used later in your code, you'll know exactly what they do. For example, a function that takes as its parameters someone's birthday and today's date and returns the person's age could be called getAge(). However, the names you can use are limited, much as variable names are. For example, you can't use words reserved by JavaScript, so you can't call your function if() or while().

The parameters for the function are given in parentheses after the function's name. A parameter is just an item of data that the function needs to be given in order to do its job. Usually, not passing the required parameters will result in an error. A function can have zero or more parameters, though even if it has no parameters, you must still put the open and close parentheses after its name. For example, the top of your function definition must look like the following:

```
function myNoParamFunction()
```

You then write the code, which the function will execute when called on to do so. All the function code must be put in a block with a pair of curly braces.

Functions also enable you to return a value from a function to the code that called it. You use the return statement to return a value. In the example function given earlier, you return the value of the variable degCent, which you have just calculated. You don't have to return a value if you don't want to, but it's important to note that every function returns a value even if you don't use the return statement. Functions that do not explicitly return a value—that is, return a value with the return statement—return undefined.

When JavaScript comes across a `return` statement in a function, it treats it a bit like a `break` statement in a `for` loop—it exits the function, returning any value specified after the `return` keyword.

You'll probably find it useful to build up a "library" of functions that you use frequently in JavaScript code, which you can reference in your pages.

Having created your functions, how do you use them? Unlike the code you've seen so far, which executes when JavaScript reaches that line, functions only execute if you ask them to, which is termed *calling* or *invoking* the function. You call a function by writing its name at the point where you want it to be called and making sure that you pass any parameters it needs, separated by commas. For example:

```
myTemp = convertToCentigrade(212);
```

This line calls the `convertToCentigrade()` function you saw earlier, passing 212 as the parameter and storing the `return` value from the function (that is, 100) in the `myTemp` variable.

Have a go at creating your own functions now, taking a closer look at how parameters are passed. Parameter passing can be a bit confusing, so you'll first create a simple function that takes just one parameter (the user's name) and writes it to the page in a friendly welcome string. First, you need to think of a name for your function. A short but descriptive name is `writeUserWelcome()`. Now you need to define what parameters the function expects to be passed. There's only one parameter—the username. Defining parameters is a little like defining variables—you need to stick to the same rules for naming, so that means no spaces, special characters, or reserved words. Let's call your parameter `userName`. You need to add it inside parentheses to the end of the function name (note that you don't put a semicolon at the end of the line):

```
function writeUserWelcome(userName)
```

Okay, now you have defined your function name and its parameters; all that's left is to create the function body—that is, the code that will be executed when the function is called. You mark out this part of the function by wrapping it in curly braces:

```
function writeUserWelcome(userName) {
    document.write("Welcome to my website " + userName + "<br />");
    document.write("Hope you enjoy it!");
}
```

The code is simple enough; you write out a message to the web page using `document.write()`. You can see that `userName` is used just as you'd use any normal variable; in fact, it's best to think of parameters as normal variables. The value that the parameter has will be that specified by the JavaScript code where the function was called.

Let's see how you would call this function:

```
writeUserWelcome("Paul");
```

Simple, really—just write the name of the function you want to call, and then in parentheses add the data to be passed to each of the parameters, here just one piece. When the code in the function is executed, the variable userName, used in the body of the function code, will contain the text "Paul".

Suppose you wanted to pass two parameters to your function—what would you need to change? Well, first you'd have to alter the function definition. Imagine that the second parameter will hold the user's age—you could call it userAge because that makes it pretty clear what the parameter's data represents. Here is the new code:

```
function writeUserWelcome(userName, userAge) {
    document.write("Welcome to my website" + userName + "<br />");
    document.write("Hope you enjoy it<br />");
    document.write("Your age is " + userAge);
}
```

You've added a line to the body of the function that uses the parameter you have added. To call the function, you'd write the following:

```
writeUserWelcome("Paul",31);
```

The second parameter is a number, so there is no need for quotes around it. Here the userName parameter will be Paul, and the second parameter, userAge, will be 31.

TRY IT OUT   Fahrenheit to Centigrade Function

Let's rewrite the temperature converter page using functions. You can cut and paste most of this code from ch3_example4.html—the parts that have changed have been highlighted. When you've finished, save it as ch4_example1.html.

```
<!DOCTYPE html>

<html lang="en">
<head>
    <title>Chapter 4, Example 1</title>
</head>
<body>
    <script>
        function convertToCentigrade(degFahren) {
            var degCent = 5 / 9 * (degFahren - 32);

            return degCent;
        }

        var degFahren = [212, 32, -459.15];
        var degCent = [];
        var loopCounter;

        for (loopCounter = 0; loopCounter <= 2; loopCounter++) {
            degCent[loopCounter] = convertToCentigrade(degFahren[loopCounter]);
        }

        for (loopCounter = 2; loopCounter >= 0; loopCounter--) {
```

```
        document.write("Value " + loopCounter +
                    " was " + degFahren[loopCounter] +
                    " degrees Fahrenheit");

        document.write(" which is " + degCent[loopCounter] +
                    " degrees centigrade<br />");
    }
  </script>
 </body>
</html>
```

When you load this page into your browser, you should see exactly the same results that you had with ch3_example4.html.

At the top of the script block you declare your convertToCentigrade() function. You saw this function earlier:

```
function convertToCentigrade(degFahren) {
   var degCent = 5/9 * (degFahren - 32);

   return degCent;
}
```

If you're using a number of separate script blocks in a page, it's very important that the function be defined before any script calls it. If you have a number of functions, you may want to put them all in their own script file and load it before all other scripts. That way you know where to find all your functions, and you can be sure that they have been declared before they have been used.

You should be pretty familiar with how the code in the function works. You declare a variable degCent, do your calculation, and then return degCent back to the calling code. The function's parameter is degFahren, which provides the information the calculation needs.

Following the function declaration is the code that executes when the page loads. First you define the variables you need, and then you have the two loops that calculate and then output the results. This is mostly the same as before, apart from the first for loop:

```
for (loopCounter = 0; loopCounter <= 2; loopCounter++) {
    degCent[loopCounter] = convertToCentigrade(degFahren[loopCounter]);
}
```

The code inside the first for loop puts the value returned by the function convertToCentigrade() into the degCent array.

There is a subtle point to the code in this example. Notice that you declare the variable degCent within your function convertToCentigrade(), and you also declare it as an array after the function definition.

Surely this isn't allowed?

Well, this leads neatly to the next topic of this chapter—scope.

SCOPE AND LIFETIME

What is meant by *scope*? Well, put simply, it's the scope or extent of a variable's or function's availability—which parts of your code can access a variable and the data it contains. Scope is important to any programming language—even more so in JavaScript—so it's imperative that you understand how scope works in JavaScript.

Global Scope

Any variables or functions declared outside of a function will be available to all JavaScript code on the page, whether that code is inside a function or otherwise—we call this *global scope*. Look at the following example:

```
var degFahren = 12;

function convertToCentigrade() {
    var degCent = 5/9 * (degFahren - 32);

    return degCent;
}
```

In this code, the degFahren variable is a global variable because it is created outside of a function, and because it is global, it can be used anywhere in the page. The convertToCentigrade() function accesses the degFahren variable, using it as part of the calculation to convert Fahrenheit to centigrade.

This also means you can change the value of a global variable, and the following code does just that:

```
var degFahren = 12;

function convertToCentigrade() {
    degFahren = 20;
    var degCent = 5/9 * (degFahren - 32);

    return degCent;
}
```

This new line of code changes the value of degFahren to 20; so the original value of 12 is no longer used in the calculation. This change in value isn't seen only inside of the convertToCentigrade() function. The degFahren variable is a global variable, and thus its value is 20 everywhere it is used.

Additionally, the covertToCentigrade() function is a global function because it is defined outside of another function (yes, you can create a function within a function ... funception!), and they too can be accessed anywhere in the page.

In practice, you want to avoid creating global variables and functions because they can be easily and unintentionally modified. You can use some tricks to avoid globals, and you will see them throughout this book, but they all boil down to creating variables and functions in functional scope.

Functional Scope

Variables and functions declared inside a function are visible *only* inside that function—no code outside the function can access them. For example, consider our standard convertToCentigrade() function:

```
function convertToCentigrade(degFahren) {
    var degCent = 5/9 * (degFahren - 32);

    return degCent;
}
```

The degCent variable is defined inside the convertToCentigrade() function. Therefore, it can only be accessed from within convertToCentigrade(). This is commonly referred to as *functional* or *local scope*, and degCent is commonly called a *local variable*.

Function parameters are similar to variables; they have local scope, and thus can only be accessed from within the function. So in the case of the previous convertToCentigrade() function, degFahren and degCent are local variables.

So what happens when the code inside a function ends and execution returns to the point at which the code was called? Do the variables defined within the function retain their value when you call the function the next time?

The answer is no: Variables not only have the scope property—where they are visible—but they also have a *lifetime*. When the function finishes executing, the variables in that function die and their values are lost, unless you return one of them to the calling code. Every so often JavaScript performs garbage collection (which we talked about in Chapter 2), whereby it scans through the code and sees if any variables are no longer in use; if so, the data they hold are freed from memory to make way for the data of other variables.

Identifier Lookup

What happens if you use the same variable name for both a global and local variable? JavaScript handles this seemingly catastrophic event with a process called *identifier lookup*. An *identifier* is simply the name you give a variable or function. So, identifier lookup is the process that the JavaScript engine uses to find a variable or function with a given name. Consider the following code:

```
var degCent = 10;

function convertToCentigrade(degFahren) {
    var degCent = 5/9 * (degFahren - 32);

    return degCent;
}
```

This code contains two degCent variables: One is global, and the other is local to convertToCentigrade(). When you execute the function, the JavaScript engine creates the local degCent variable and assigns it the result of the Fahrenheit-to-centigrade conversion—the global degCent variable is left alone and still contains 10. But what value does the return statement return: the global or local degCent?

The JavaScript engine begins the identifier lookup process in the current level of scope. Therefore, it starts looking within the functional scope of convertToCentigrade() for a variable or function with the name degCent, it finds the local variable, and uses its value in the return statement.

But if degCent was not created within convertToCentigrade(), the JavaScript engine would then look in the next level of scope—the global scope in this case—for the degCent identifier. It would find the global variable and use its value.

So now that you understand how scope works, revisit Example 1 in the "Fahrenheit to Centigrade Function" Try It Out. Even though it has two degCent variables—one global and one local to convertToCentigrade()—the code executes without a problem. Inside the function, the local degCent variable takes precedence over the global. And outside of the function, the local variable is no longer in scope; therefore, the global degCent is used.

Although it's perfectly valid to use the same identifier for global and local variables, it is highly recommended that you avoid doing so. It adds extra, and often unnecessary, complexity and confusion to your code. It can also make it easier to introduce bugs that are difficult to find and fix. Imagine that, within a function, you modified a local variable when you meant to modify a global variable. That is a bug, and if you replicated it in many other functions, you will spend precious time finding and fixing those errors.

FUNCTIONS AS VALUES

JavaScript is a powerful language, and a lot of that power comes from functions. Unlike many other languages, functions are *first-class citizens* in JavaScript; in other words, we can treat functions just like any other type of value. For example, let's take the convertToCentigrade() function and assign it to a variable:

```
function convertToCentigrade(degFahren) {
    var degCent = 5/9 * (degFahren - 32);

    return degCent;
}

var myFunction = convertToCentigrade;
```

This code assigns the convertToCentigrade() function to the myFunction variable, but look closely at the right-hand side of the assignment—the opening and closing parentheses are missing at the end of the convertToCentigrade identifier. It looks a lot like a variable!

In this statement, we are not executing convertToCentigrade(); we are referring to the actual function itself. This means that we now have two ways of executing the same function. We can call it normally by executing convertToCentigrade(), or we can execute myFunction(), like this:

```
var degCent = myFunction(75); // 23.88888889
var degCent2 = convertToCentigrade(75); // 23.88888889
```

This also means we can pass a function to another function's parameter. Take a look at the following code:

```
function doSomething(fn) {
    fn("Hello, World");
}

doSomething(alert);
```

This code defines a function called doSomething(), and it has a single parameter called fn. Inside the function, the fn variable is used as a function; it's executed by using the fn identifier followed by a pair of parentheses. The final line of code executes the doSomething() function and passes the alert function as the parameter. When this code executes, an alert box displays the message "Hello, World".

TRY IT OUT   Passing Functions

Let's rewrite the temperature converter page to use more functions. You can cut and paste some of the code from ch4_example1.html, but the majority of this example will be new code. When you've finished, save it as ch4_example2.html.

```
<!DOCTYPE html>

<html lang="en">
<head>
    <title>Chapter 4, Example 2</title>
</head>
<body>
        <script>
        function toCentigrade(degFahren) {
            var degCent = 5 / 9 * (degFahren - 32);

            document.write(degFahren + " Fahrenheit is " +
                        degCent + " Celsius.<br/>");
        }

        function toFahrenheit(degCent) {
            var degFahren = 9 / 5 * degCent + 32;

            document.write(degCent + " Celsius is " +
                        degFahren + " Fahrenheit.<br/>");
        }

        function convert(converter, temperature) {
            converter(temperature);
        }

        convert(toFahrenheit, 23);
        convert(toCentigrade, 75);
    </script>
</body>
</html>
```

When you load this page into your browser, you should see the results shown in Figure 4-2.

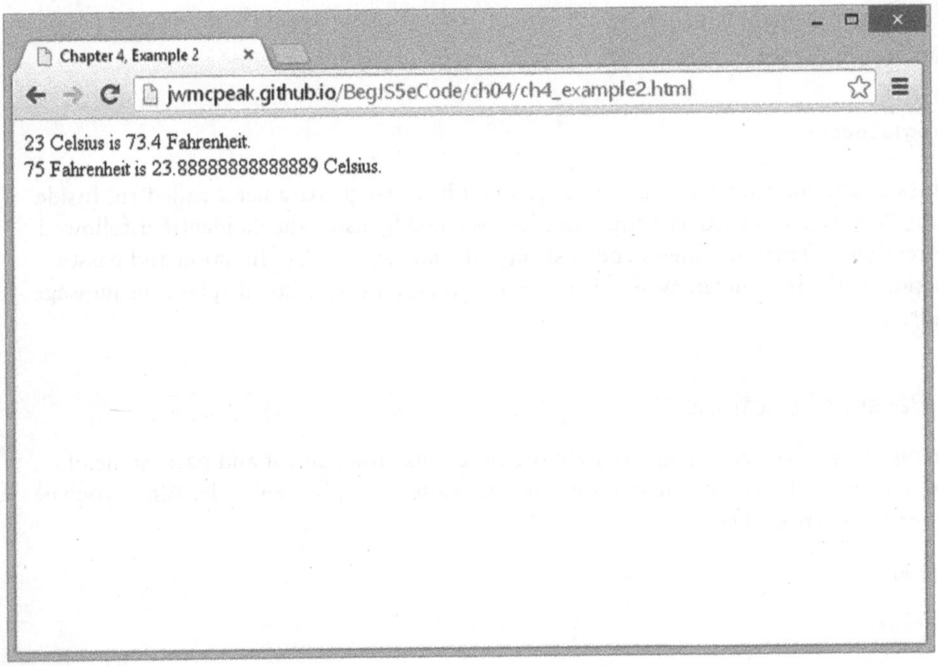

```
Chapter 4, Example 2        ×

←  →  C   🗋 jwmcpeak.github.io/BegJS5eCode/ch04/ch4_example2.html          ☆  ≡

23 Celsius is 73.4 Fahrenheit.
75 Fahrenheit is 23.88888888888889 Celsius.
```

FIGURE 4-2

At the top of the script block is the `toCentigrade()` function. It is somewhat similar to the `convertToCentigrade()` function from `ch4_example1.html`; instead of returning the converted value, it simply writes the conversion information to the document:

```
function toCentigrade(degFahren) {
    var degCent = 5 / 9 * (degFahren - 32);

    document.write(degFahren + " Fahrenheit is " +
                   degCent + " Celsius.<br/>");
}
```

The next function, `toFahrenheit()`, is similar to `toCentigrade()` except that it converts the supplied value to Fahrenheit. It then writes the conversion information to the document:

```
function toFahrenheit(degCent) {
    var degFahren = 9 / 5 * degCent + 32;

    document.write(degCent + " Celsius is " +
                   degFahren + " Fahrenheit.<br/>");
}
```

Admittedly, you could use these functions as is without any problem, but that wouldn't result in a very interesting example. Instead, the third function, convert(), will be used to execute toCentigrade() and toFahrenheit():

```
function convert(converter, temperature) {
    return converter(temperature);
}
```

This function takes the first parameter, converter, and uses it as a function. The second parameter, temperature, is then passed to converter() to perform the conversion and write the results to the document.

The final two lines of code use convert() and pass it the appropriate converter function and temperature value:

```
convert(toFahrenheit, 23);
convert(toCentigrade, 75);
```

Although this is certainly a more complex solution to a relatively simple problem, it demonstrates the fact that functions are values in JavaScript. We can assign them to variables and pass them to other functions. This is an extremely important concept to understand, and you'll see why in Chapter 10 when you learn about events.

SUMMARY

In this chapter you concluded your look at the core of the JavaScript language and its syntax. Everything from now on builds on these foundations, and with the less interesting syntax under your belt, you can move on to more interesting things in the remainder of the book.

The chapter looked at the following:

> **Functions are reusable bits of code.** JavaScript has a lot of built-in functions that provide programmers services, such as converting a string to a number. However, JavaScript also enables you to define and use your own functions using the function keyword. Functions can have zero or more parameters passed to them and can return a value if you so wish.

> **Variable scope and lifetime:** Variables declared outside a function are available globally—that is, anywhere in the page. Any variables defined inside a function are private to that function and can't be accessed outside of it. Variables have a lifetime, the length of which depends on where the variable was declared. If it's a global variable, its lifetime is that of the page—while the page is loaded in the browser, the variable remains alive. For variables defined in a function, the lifetime is limited to the execution of that function. When the function is finished executing, the variables die, and their values are lost. If the function is called again later in the code, the variables will be empty.

> **Identifier lookup:** When you use a variable or function, the JavaScript engine goes through the identifier lookup process to find the value associated with the identifier.

> **Functions are first-class citizens in JavaScript.** You can assign functions to variables and pass them to other functions.

EXERCISES

You can find suggested solutions to these questions in Appendix A.

1. Change the code of Question 2 from Chapter 3 so that it's a function that takes as parameters the times table required and the values at which it should start and end. For example, you might try the 4 times table displayed starting with 4 * 4 and ending at 4 * 9.

2. Modify the code of Question 1 to request the times table to be displayed from the user; the code should continue to request and display times tables until the user enters -1. Additionally, do a check to make sure that the user is entering a valid number; if the number is not valid, ask the user to re-enter it.

5

JavaScript—An Object-Based Language

WHAT YOU WILL LEARN IN THIS CHAPTER:

➤ Using JavaScript's built-in objects to work with complex data

➤ Creating custom objects to represent complex ideas and data

➤ Defining custom reference types

WROX.COM CODE DOWNLOADS FOR THIS CHAPTER

You can find the wrox.com code downloads for this chapter at http://www.wiley.com/go/
BeginningJavaScript5E on the Download Code tab. You can also view all of the examples
and related files at http://beginningjs.com.

In this chapter, you look at a concept that is central to JavaScript, namely *objects*. But what
are objects, and why are they useful?

First, we have to break it to you: You have been using objects throughout this book (for
example, an array is an object). JavaScript is an object-based language, and therefore most of
what you do involves manipulating objects. You'll see that when you make full use of these
objects, the range of things you can do with JavaScript expands immensely.

We'll start this chapter by taking a look at the idea of what objects are and why they are
important. We'll move on to what kinds of objects are used in JavaScript, how to create them
and use them, and how they simplify many programming tasks for you. Finally, you'll see in
more detail some of the most useful objects that JavaScript provides and how to use these in
practical situations.

Not only does the JavaScript language consist of a number of these things called objects (which
are also called *native JavaScript objects*), but also the browser itself is modeled as a collection
of objects available for your use. You learn about these objects in particular in Chapter 8.

OBJECT-BASED PROGRAMMING

Object-based programming is a slightly scarier way of saying "programming using objects." But what are these objects that you will be programming with? Where are they and how and why would you want to program with them? In this section, you look at the answers to these questions, both in general programming terms and more specifically within JavaScript.

What Are Objects?

To start the introduction to objects, let's think about what is meant by an object in the "real world" outside computing. The world is composed of things, or objects, such as tables, chairs, and cars (to name just a few!). Let's take a car as an example, to explore what an object really is.

How would you define the car? You might say it's a blue car with four-wheel drive. You might specify the speed at which it's traveling. When you do this, you are specifying *properties* of the object. For example, the car has a color property, which in this instance has the value blue.

How do you use the car? You turn the ignition key, press the gas pedal, beep the horn, change the gear (that is, choose between 1, 2, 3, 4, and reverse on a manual car, or drive and reverse on an automatic), and so on. When you do this, you are using *methods* of the object.

You can think of methods as being a bit like functions. Sometimes, you may need to use some information with the method, or pass it a parameter, to get it to work. For example, when you use the changing-gears method, you need to say which gear you want to change to. Other methods may pass information back to the owner. For example, the dipstick method will tell the owner how much oil is left in the car.

Sometimes using one or more of the methods may change one or more of the object's properties. For example, using the accelerator method will probably change the car's speed property. Other properties can't be changed: for example, the body-shape property of the car (unless you hit a brick wall with the speed property at 100 miles per hour!).

You could say that the car is defined by its collection of methods and properties. In object-based programming, the idea is to model real-world situations by objects, which are defined by their methods and properties.

Objects in JavaScript

You should now have a basic idea of what an object is—a "thing" with methods and properties. But how do you use this concept in JavaScript?

In the previous chapters you have (for the most part) been dealing with *primitive* data (that is, you've been working with actual data). This type of data is not too complex and is fairly easy to deal with. However, not all information is as simple as primitive data. Let's look at an example to clarify things a little.

Suppose you had written a web application that displayed timetable information for buses or trains. Once the user has selected a journey, you might want to let him know how long that journey will take. To do that, you need to subtract the arrival time from the departure time.

However, that's not quite as simple as it may appear at first glance. For example, consider a departure time of 14:53 (for 2:53 p.m.) and an arrival time of 15:10 (for 3:10 p.m.). If you tell JavaScript to evaluate the expression 15.10–14.53, you get the result 0.57, which is 57 minutes. However, you know that the real difference in time is 17 minutes. Using the normal mathematical operators on times doesn't work!

What would you need to do to calculate the difference between these two times? You would first need to separate the hours from the minutes in each time. Then, to get the difference in minutes between the two times, you would need to check whether the minutes of the arrival time were greater than the minutes of the departure. If so, you could simply subtract the departure time minutes from the arrival time minutes. If not, you'd need to add 60 to the arrival time minutes and subtract one from the arrival time hours to compensate, before taking the departure time minutes from the arrival time minutes. You'd then need to subtract the departure time hours from the arrival time hours, before putting the minutes and hours that you have arrived at back together.

This would work okay so long as the two times were in the same day. It wouldn't work, for example, with the times 23:45 and 04:32.

This way of working out the time difference obviously has its problems, but it also seems very complex. Is there an easier way to deal with more complex data such as times and dates?

This is where objects come in. You can define your departure and arrival times as Date objects. Because they are Date objects, they come with a variety of properties and methods that you can use when you need to manipulate or calculate times. For example, you can use the getTime() method to get the number of milliseconds between the time in the Date object and January 1, 1970, 00:00:00. Once you have these millisecond values for the arrival and departure times, you can simply subtract one from the other and store the result in another Date object. To retrieve the hours and minutes of this time, you simply use the getHours() and getMinutes() methods of the Date object. You see more examples of this later in the chapter.

The Date object is not the only type of object that JavaScript has to offer. Another object type was introduced in Chapter 2, but to keep things simple, we didn't tell you what it was at the time: the Array object. Recall that an array is a way of holding a number of pieces of data at the same time.

Array objects have a property called length that tells you how many pieces of data, or rather how many elements, the array holds. They also have a number of methods. One example is the sort() method, which you can use to sort the elements within the array into alphabetical order.

You should now have an idea why objects are useful in JavaScript. You have seen the Date and Array objects, but JavaScript makes available many other types of objects so that you can achieve more with your code. These include the Math and String objects, which we talk more about later in the chapter.

Using JavaScript Objects

Now that you have seen the *why* of JavaScript objects, you need to look at the *what* and the *how*.

Each of JavaScript's objects has a collection of related properties and methods that you can use to manipulate a certain kind of data. For example, the Array object consists of methods to manipulate arrays and properties to find out information from them. In most cases, to make use of these methods and properties, you need to define your data as one of these objects. In other words, you need to create an object.

In this section, you look at how to go about creating an object and, having done that, how you use its properties and methods.

Creating an Object

To create many types of objects, you use the new operator. The following statement creates a Date object:

```
var myDate = new Date();
```

The first half of the statement is familiar to you. You use the var keyword to define a variable called myDate. This variable is initialized, using the equals sign assignment operator (=), to the right-hand side of the statement.

The right-hand side of the statement consists of two parts. First you have the operator new. This tells JavaScript that you want to create a new object. Next you have Date(). This is the *constructor* for a Date object. It's a function that tells JavaScript what type of object you want to create. Most objects have constructors like this. For example, the Array object has the Array() constructor (but remember, we typically don't use it in favor of the literal []). The only exception you see in this book is the Math object, and this is explained in a later part of the chapter.

Because a constructor is a function, you can pass parameters to the constructor to add data to your object. For example, the following code creates a Date object containing the date 1 January 2014:

```
var myDate = new Date("1 Jan 2014");
```

How object data is stored in variables differs from how primitive data, such as text and numbers, is stored. (Primitive data is the most basic data possible in JavaScript.) With primitive data, the variable holds the data's actual value. For example:

```
var myNumber = 23;
```

This code means that the variable myNumber holds the data 23. However, variables assigned to objects don't hold the actual data, but rather a *reference* to the memory address where the data can be found. This doesn't mean you can get hold of the memory address—this is something only JavaScript has details of and keeps to itself in the background. All you need to remember is that when you say that a variable references an object, you mean it references a memory address. This is shown in the following example:

```
var myArrayRef = [0, 1, 2];
var mySecondArrayRef = myArrayRef;
myArrayRef[0] = 100;
alert(mySecondArrayRef[0]);
```

First you set the myArrayRef variable to reference the new array object, and then you set mySecondArrayRef to the same reference—for example, now mySecondArrayRef is set to reference the same array object. So when you set the first element of the array to 100, as shown here:

```
myArrayRef[0] = 100;
```

and display the contents of the first element of the array referenced in `mySecondArrayRef` as follows:

```
alert(mySecondArrayRef[0]);
```

you'll see it has also magically changed to 100! However, as you now know, it's not magic; it's because both variables reference the same array object—when it comes to objects, it's a reference to the object and not the object itself that is stored in a variable. When you did the assignment, it didn't make a copy of the array object, it simply copied the reference. Contrast that with the following:

```
var myVariable = "ABC";
var mySecondVariable = myVariable;
myVariable = "DEF";
alert(mySecondVariable);
```

In this case you're dealing with a string, which is a primitive data type, as are numbers. This time the actual values are stored in the variable, so when you do this:

```
var mySecondVariable = myVariable;
```

`mySecondVariable` gets its own separate copy of the data in `myVariable`. So the alert at the end will still show `mySecondVariable` as holding `"ABC"`.

To summarize this section, you create JavaScript objects using the following basic syntax:

```
var myVariable = new ConstructorName(optional parameters);
```

Using an Object's Properties

Accessing the values contained in an object's properties is very simple. You write the name of the variable containing (or referencing) your object, followed by a dot, and then the name of the object's property.

For example, if you defined an `Array` object contained in the variable `myArray`, you could access its `length` property like this:

```
myArray.length
```

But what can you do with this property now that you have it? You can use it as you would any other piece of data and store it in a variable:

```
var myVariable = myArray.length;
```

Or you can show it to the user:

```
alert(myArray.length);
```

In some cases, you can even change the value of the property, like this:

```
myArray.length = 12;
```

However, unlike variables, some properties are read-only—you can get information from them, but you can't *change* information inside them.

Calling an Object's Methods

Methods are very much like functions in that they can be used to perform useful tasks, such as getting the hours from a particular date or generating a random number. Again like functions, some methods return a value, such as a Date object's getHours() method, whereas others perform a task, but return no data, such as an Array object's sort() method.

Using the methods of an object is very similar to using properties, in that you put the object's variable name first, then a dot, and then the name of the method. For example, to sort the elements of an Array in the variable myArray, you can use the following code:

```
myArray.sort();
```

Just as with functions, you can pass parameters to some methods by placing the parameters between the parentheses following the method's name. However, whether or not a method takes parameters, you must still put parentheses after the method's name, just as you did with functions. As a general rule, anywhere you can use a function, you can use a method of an object.

Primitives and Objects

You should now have a good idea about the difference between primitive data, such as numbers and strings, and object data, such as Dates and Arrays. However, as was mentioned earlier, there is also a String object. Where does this fit in?

In fact, there are String, Number, and Boolean objects corresponding to the string, number, and boolean primitive data types. For example, to create a String object containing the text "I'm a String object" you can use the following code:

```
var myString = new String("I'm a String object");
```

String objects have the length property just as Array objects do. This returns the number of characters in the String object. For example,

```
var lengthOfString = myString.length;
```

would store the value 19 in the variable lengthOfString (remember that spaces are referred to as characters, too).

But what if you had declared a primitive string called mySecondString holding the text "I'm a primitive string" like this:

```
var mySecondString = "I'm a primitive string";
```

and wanted to know how many characters could be found in this primitive string?

This is where JavaScript helps you out. Recall from previous chapters that JavaScript can handle the conversion of one data type to another automatically. For example, if you tried to add a string primitive to a number primitive, like this:

```
theResult = "23" + 23;
```

JavaScript would assume that you want to treat the number as a string and concatenate the two together, the number being converted to text automatically. The variable theResult would contain "2323"—the concatenation of 23 and 23, and not the sum of 23 and 23, which would be 46.

The same applies to objects. If you declare a primitive string and then treat it as an object, such as by trying to access one of its methods or properties, JavaScript will know that the operation you're trying to do won't work. The operation will only work with an object; for example, it would be valid with a String object. In this case, JavaScript converts the plaintext string into a temporary String object, just for that operation, and destroys the object when it's finished the operation.

So, for your primitive string mySecondString, you can use the length property of the String object to find out the number of characters it contains. For example:

```
var lengthOfSecondString = mySecondString.length;
```

This would store the data 22 in the variable lengthOfSecondString.

The same ideas expressed here are also true for number and boolean primitives and their corresponding Number and Boolean objects. However, these objects are not used very often, so we will not be discussing them further in this book.

JAVASCRIPT'S NATIVE OBJECT TYPES

So far, you have just been looking at what objects are, how to create them, and how to use them. Now take a look at some of the more useful objects that are native to JavaScript—that is, those that are built into the JavaScript language.

You won't be looking at all of the native JavaScript objects, just some of the more commonly used ones, namely the String object, the Math object, the Array object, and the Date object.

String Objects

Like most objects, String objects need to be created before they can be used. To create a String object, you can write this:

```
var string1 = new String("Hello");
var string2 = new String(123);
var string3 = new String(123.456);
```

However, as you have seen, you can also declare a string primitive and use it as if it were a String object, letting JavaScript do the conversion to an object for you behind the scenes. For example:

```
var string1 = "Hello";
```

Using this technique is preferable. The advantages to doing it this way are that there is no need to create a String object itself, and you avoid the troubles with comparing string objects. When you try to compare string objects with primitive string values, the actual values are compared, but with String objects, the object references are compared.

The String object has a vast number of methods and properties. In this section, you look only at some of the less complex and more commonly used methods. However, in Chapter 6 you look at some of the trickier but very powerful methods associated with strings and the regular expression object (RegExp). Regular expressions provide a very powerful means of searching strings for patterns of characters. For example, if you want to find "Paul" where it exists as a whole word in the string "Pauline, Paul, Paula", you need to use regular expressions. However, they can be a little tricky to use, so we won't discuss them further in this chapter—we want to save some fun for later!

With most of the String object's methods, it helps to remember that a string is just a series of individual characters and that, as with arrays, each character has a position, or index. Also as with arrays, the first position, or index, is labeled 0 and not 1. So, for example, the string "Hello World" has the character positions shown in the following table:

CHARACTER INDEX	0	1	2	3	4	5	6	7	8	9	10
Character	H	e	l	l	o		W	o	r	l	d

The length Property

The length property simply returns the number of characters in the string. For example,

```
var myName = "Jeremy";
document.write(myName.length);
```

will write the length of the string "Jeremy" (that is, 6) to the page.

Finding a String Inside Another String—The indexOf() and lastIndexOf() Methods

The methods indexOf() and lastIndexOf() are used for searching for the occurrence of one string inside another. A string contained inside another is usually termed a *substring*. They are useful when you have a string of information but only want a small part of it. For example, in the trivia quiz, when someone enters a text answer, you want to check if certain keywords are present within the string.

Both indexOf() and lastIndexOf() take two parameters:

➤ The string you want to find

➤ The character position you want to start searching from (optional)

Character positions start at 0. If you don't include the second parameter, searching starts from the beginning of the string.

The return value of indexOf() and lastIndexOf() is the character position in the string at which the substring was found. Again, it's zero-based, so if the substring is found at the start of the string, then 0 is returned. If there is no match, the value -1 is returned.

For example, to search for the substring `"Jeremy"` in the string `"Hello jeremy. How are you Jeremy"`, you can use the following code:

```
var myString = "Hello jeremy. How are you Jeremy";
var foundAtPosition = myString.indexOf("Jeremy");

alert(foundAtPosition);
```

This code should result in a message box containing the number 26, which is the character position of `"Jeremy"`. You might be wondering why it's 26, which clearly refers to the second `"Jeremy"` in the string, rather than 6 for the first `"jeremy"`.

This is due to case sensitivity. JavaScript takes case sensitivity very seriously, both in its syntax and when making comparisons. If you type `IndexOf()` instead of `indexOf()`, JavaScript will complain. Similarly, `"jeremy"` is not the same as `"Jeremy"`. Remember that mistakes with case are very common and so easy to make, even for experts, and it's best to be very aware of case when programming.

You've seen `indexOf()` in action, but how does `lastIndexOf()` differ? Well, whereas `indexOf()` starts searching from the beginning of the string, or the position you specified in the second parameter, and works toward the end, `lastIndexOf()` starts at the end of the string, or the position you specified, and works toward the beginning of the string. Let's modify the previous example to the following code:

```
var myString = "Hello Jeremy. How are you Jeremy";

var foundAtPosition = myString.indexOf("Jeremy");
alert(foundAtPosition);

foundAtPosition = myString.lastIndexOf("Jeremy");
alert(foundAtPosition);
```

First, notice the string value assigned to `myString`; both instances of `"Jeremy"` now begin with a capital letter. The first `alert` box displays the result of 6 because that is the position of the first occurrence of `"Jeremy"`. The second `alert` box displays 26 because `lastIndexOf()` starts searching at the end of the string, and the position of the first occurrence of `"Jeremy"` from the end of the string is 26.

TRY IT OUT Counting Occurrences of Substrings

In this example, you look at how to use the "start character position" parameter of `indexOf()`. Here you will count how many times the word Wrox appears in the string:

```
<!DOCTYPE html>

<html lang="en">
<head>
    <title>Chapter 5, Example 1</title>
</head>
<body>
    <script>
```

```
                var myString = "Welcome to Wrox books. " +
                              "The Wrox website is www.wrox.com. " +
                              "Visit the Wrox website today. Thanks for buying Wrox";

                var foundAtPosition = 0;
                var wroxCount = 0;

                while (foundAtPosition != -1) {
                    foundAtPosition = myString.indexOf("Wrox", foundAtPosition);

                    if (foundAtPosition != -1) {
                        wroxCount++;
                        foundAtPosition++;
                    }
                }

                document.write("There are " + wroxCount + " occurrences of the word Wrox");
            </script>
    </body>
    </html>
```

Save this example as ch5 _ example1.html. When you load the page into your browser, you should see the following sentence: There are 4 occurrences of the word Wrox.

At the top of the script block, you built up a string inside the variable myString, which you then want to search for the occurrence of the word Wrox. You also define two variables: wroxCount will contain the number of times Wrox is found in the string, and foundAtPosition will contain the position in the string of the current occurrence of the substring Wrox.

You then used a while loop, which continues looping all the while you are finding the word Wrox in the string—that is, while the variable foundAtPosition is not equal to -1. Inside the while loop, you have this line:

```
    foundAtPosition = myString.indexOf("Wrox", foundAtPosition);
```

Here you search for the next occurrence of the substring Wrox in the string myString. How do you make sure that you get the next occurrence? You use the variable foundAtPosition to give you the starting position of your search, because this contains the index after the index position of the last occurrence of the substring Wrox. You assign the variable foundAtPosition to the result of your search, the index position of the next occurrence of the substring Wrox.

Each time Wrox is found (that is, each time foundAtPosition is not -1) you increase the variable wroxCount, which counts how many times you have found the substring, and you increase foundAtPosition so that you continue the search at the next position in the string:

```
    if (foundAtPosition != -1) {
        wroxCount++;
        foundAtPosition++;
    }
```

Finally, you document.write() the value of the variable wroxCount to the page.

Chapter 3 talked about the danger of infinite loops, and you can see that there is a danger of one here. If `foundAtPosition++` were removed, you'd keep searching from the same starting point and never move to find the next occurrence of the word `Wrox`.

The `indexOf()` and `lastIndexOf()` methods are more useful when coupled with the `substr()` and `substring()` methods, which you look at in the next section. Using a combination of these methods enables you to cut substrings out of a string.

Copying Part of a String—The substr() and substring() Methods

If you wanted to cut out part of a string and assign that cut-out part to another variable or use it in an expression, you would use the `substr()` and `substring()` methods. Both methods provide the same end result—that is, a part of a string—but they differ in the parameters they require.

The method `substring()` accepts two parameters: the character start position and the position after the last character desired in the substring. The second parameter is optional; if you don't include it, all characters from the start position to the end of the string are included.

For example, if your string is `"JavaScript"` and you want just the text `"Java"`, you could call the method like so:

```
var myString = "JavaScript";
var mySubString = myString.substring(0,4);
alert(mySubString);
```

The character positions for the string `"JavaScript"` are:

CHARACTER POSITION	0	1	2	3	4	5	6	7	8	9
Character	J	a	v	a	S	c	r	i	p	t

Like `substring()`, the method `substr()` again takes two parameters, the first being the start position of the first character you want included in your substring. However, this time the second parameter specifies the length of the string of characters that you want to cut out of the longer string. For example, you could rewrite the preceding code like this:

```
var myString = "JavaScript";
var mySubString = myString.substr(0,4);
alert(mySubString);
```

As with the `substring()` method, the second parameter is optional. If you don't include it, all the characters from the start position onward will be included.

> **NOTE** The `substring()` method was introduced long before `substr()`. Most of the time, you will use the `substr()` method.

Let's look at the use of the `substr()` and `lastIndexOf()` methods together. Later in the book, you see how you can retrieve the file path and name of the currently loaded web page. However, there is no way of retrieving the filename alone. So if, for example, your file is `http://mywebsite/temp/myfile.html`, you may need to extract the `myfile.html` part. This is where `substr()` and `lastIndexOf()` are useful:

```
var fileName = window.location.href;
fileName = fileName.substr(fileName.lastIndexOf("/") + 1);
document.write("The file name of this page is " + fileName);
```

The first line sets the variable `fileName` to the current file path and name, such as /mywebsite/temp/myfile.html. Don't worry about understanding this line right now; you'll see it later.

The second line is where the interesting action is. You can see that this code uses the return value of the `lastIndexOf()` method as a parameter for another method, something that's perfectly correct and very useful. The goal in using `fileName.lastIndexOf("/")` is to find the position of the final forward slash (/), which will be the last character before the name of the file. You add one to this value, because you don't want to include that character, and then pass this new value to the `substr()` method. There's no second parameter here (the length), because you don't know it. As a result, `substr()` will return all the characters right to the end of the string, which is what you want.

> **NOTE** This example retrieves the name of the page on the local machine, because you're not accessing the page from a web server. However, don't let this mislead you into thinking that accessing files on a local hard drive from a web page is something you'll be able to do with JavaScript alone. To protect users from malicious hackers, JavaScript's access to the user's system, such as access to files, is very limited. You learn more about this later in the book.

Converting Case—The toLowerCase() and toUpperCase() Methods

If you want to change the case of a string (for example, to remove case sensitivity when comparing strings), you need the `toLowerCase()` and `toUpperCase()` methods. It's not hard to guess what these two methods do. Both of them return a string that is the value of the string in the `String` object, but with its case converted to either upper or lower depending on the method invoked. Any non-alphabetical characters remain unchanged by these functions.

In the following example, you can see that by changing the case of both strings you can compare them without case sensitivity being an issue:

```
var myString = "I Don't Care About Case";

if (myString.toLowerCase() == "i don't care about case") {
    alert("Who cares about case?");
}
```

Even though `toLowerCase()` and `toUpperCase()` don't take any parameters, you must remember to put the two empty parentheses—that is, `()`—at the end, if you want to call a method.

Selecting a Single Character from a String—The charAt() and charCodeAt() Methods

If you want to find out information about a single character within a string, you need the `charAt()` and `charCodeAt()` methods. These methods can be very useful for checking the validity of user input, something you see more of in Chapter 11 when you look at HTML forms.

The `charAt()` method accepts one parameter: the index position of the character you want in the string. It then returns that character. `charAt()` treats the positions of the string characters as starting at 0, so the first character is at index 0, the second at index 1, and so on.

For example, to find the last character in a string, you could use this code:

```
var myString = prompt("Enter some text", "Hello World!");
var theLastChar = myString.charAt(myString.length - 1);
document.write("The last character is " + theLastChar);
```

In the first line, you prompt the user for a string, with the default of `"Hello World!"`, and store this string in the variable `myString`.

In the next line, you use the `charAt()` method to retrieve the last character in the string. You use the index position of `(myString.length - 1)`. Why? Let's take the string `"Hello World!"` as an example. The `length` of this string is 12, but the last character position is 11 because the indexing starts at 0. Therefore, you need to subtract one from the length of the string to get the last character's position.

In the final line, you write the last character in the string to the page.

The `charCodeAt()` method is similar in use to the `charAt()` method, but instead of returning the character itself, it returns a number that represents the decimal character code for that character in the Unicode character set. Recall that computers only understand numbers—to the computer, all your strings are just numeric data. When you request text rather than numbers, the computer does a conversion based on its internal understanding of each number and provides the respective character.

For example, to find the character code of the first character in a string, you could write this:

```
var myString = prompt("Enter some text", "Hello World!");
var theFirstCharCode = myString.charCodeAt(0);
document.write("The first character code is " + theFirstCharCode);
```

This will get the character code for the character at index position 0 in the string given by the user, and write it out to the page.

Character codes go in order, so, for example, the letter A has the code 65, B 66, and so on. Lowercase letters start at 97 (a is 97, b is 98, and so on). Digits go from 48 (for the number 0) to 57 (for the number 9). You can use this information for various purposes, as you see in the next example.

TRY IT OUT | Checking a Character's Case

This is an example that detects the type of the character at the start of a given string—that is, whether the character is uppercase, lowercase, numeric, or other:

```
<!DOCTYPE html>

<html lang="en">
<head>
    <title>Chapter 5, Example 2</title>
</head>
<body>
    <script>
        function checkCharType(charToCheck) {
            var returnValue = "O";
            var charCode = charToCheck.charCodeAt(0);

            if (charCode >= "A".charCodeAt(0) && charCode <= "Z".charCodeAt(0)) {
                returnValue = "U";
            } else if (charCode >= "a".charCodeAt(0) &&
                        charCode <= "z".charCodeAt(0)) {
                returnValue = "L";
            } else if (charCode >= "0".charCodeAt(0) &&
                        charCode <= "9".charCodeAt(0)) {
                returnValue = "N";
            }

            return returnValue;
        }

        var myString = prompt("Enter some text", "Hello World!");

        switch (checkCharType(myString)) {
            case "U":
                document.write("First character was upper case");
                break;
            case "L":
                document.write("First character was lower case");
                break;
            case "N":
                document.write("First character was a number");
                break;
            default:
                document.write("First character was not a character or a number");
        }
    </script>
</body>
</html>
```

Type the code and save it as `ch5_example2.html`. When you load the page into your browser, you will be prompted for a string. A message will then be written to the page informing you of the type of the first character that you entered—whether it is uppercase, lowercase, a number, or something else, such as a punctuation mark.

To start with, you define a function `checkCharType()`. You start this function by declaring the variable `returnValue` and initializing it to the character `"O"` to indicate it's some other character than a lowercase letter, uppercase letter, or numerical character:

```
function checkCharType(charToCheck) {
    var returnValue = "O";
```

You use this variable as the value to be returned at the end of the function, indicating the type of character. It will take the values U for uppercase, L for lowercase, N for number, and O for other.

The next line in the function uses the `charCodeAt()` method to get the character code of the first character in the string stored in `charToCheck`, which is the function's only parameter. The character code is stored in the variable `charCode`:

```
var charCode = charToCheck.charCodeAt(0);
```

In the following lines, you have a series of `if` statements, which check within what range of values the character code falls. You know that if it falls between the character codes for A and Z, it's uppercase, and so you assign the variable `returnValue` the value U. If the character code falls between the character codes for a and z, it's lowercase, and so you assign the value L to the variable `returnValue`. If the character code falls between the character codes for 0 and 9, it's a number, and you assign the value N to the variable `returnValue`. If the value falls into none of these ranges, the variable retains its initialization value of O for other, and you don't have to do anything.

```
if (charCode >= "A".charCodeAt(0) && charCode <= "Z".charCodeAt(0)) {
    returnValue = "U";
} else if (charCode >= "a".charCodeAt(0) &&
            charCode <= "z".charCodeAt(0)) {
    returnValue = "L";
} else if (charCode >= "0".charCodeAt(0) &&
            charCode <= "9".charCodeAt(0)) {
    returnValue = "N";
}
```

This probably seems a bit weird at first, so let's see what JavaScript is doing with your code. When you write

```
"A".charCodeAt(0)
```

it appears that you are trying to use a method of the `String` object on a string literal, which is the same as a primitive string in that it's just characters and not an object. However, JavaScript realizes what you are doing and does the necessary conversion of literal character `"A"` into a temporary `String` object containing `"A"`. Then, and only then, does JavaScript perform the `charCodeAt()` method on the `String` object it has created in the background. When it has finished, the `String` object is disposed of. Basically, this is a shorthand way of writing the following:

```
var myChar = new String("A");
myChar.charCodeAt(0);
```

In either case, the first (and, in this string, the only) character's code is returned to you. For example, `"A".charCodeAt(0)` will return the number 65.

Finally, you come to the end of the function and return the returnValue variable to where the function was called:

```
    return returnValue;
}
```

You might wonder why you bother using the variable returnValue at all, instead of just returning its value. For example, you could write the code as follows:

```
if (charCode >= "A".charCodeAt(0) && charCode <= "Z".charCodeAt(0)) {
    return "U";
} else if (charCode >= "a".charCodeAt(0) &&
            charCode <= "z".charCodeAt(0)) {
    return "L";
} else if (charCode >= "0".charCodeAt(0) &&
            charCode <= "9".charCodeAt(0)) {
    return "N";
}

return "O";
```

This would work fine, so why not do it this way? The disadvantage of this way is that it's difficult to follow the flow of execution of the function, which is not that bad in a small function like this, but can get tricky in bigger functions. With the original code you always know exactly where the function execution stops: It stops at the end with the only return statement. The version of the function just shown finishes when any of the return statements is reached, so there are four possible places where the function might end.

The next chunk of code checks that the function works. You first use the variable myString, initialized to "Hello World!" or whatever the user enters into the prompt box, as your test string.

```
var myString = prompt("Enter some text", "Hello World!");
```

Next, the switch statement uses the checkCharType() function that you defined earlier in its comparison expression. Depending on what is returned by the function, one of the case statements will execute and let the user know what the character type was:

```
switch (checkCharType(myString)) {
    case "U":
        document.write("First character was upper case");
        break;
    case "L":
        document.write("First character was lower case");
        break;
    case "N":
        document.write("First character was a number");
        break;
    default:
        document.write("First character was not a character or a number");
}
```

That completes the example, but before moving on, it's worth noting that this example is just that—an example of using `charCodeAt()`. In practice, it would be much easier to just write

```
if (char >= "A" && char <= "Z")
```

rather than

```
if (charCode >= "A".charCodeAt(0) && charCode <= "Z".charCodeAt(0))
```

which you have used here.

Converting Character Codes to a String—The fromCharCode() Method

You can think of the method `fromCharCode()` as the opposite of `charCodeAt()`, in that you pass it a series of comma-separated numbers representing character codes, and it converts them to a single string.

However, the `fromCharCode()` method is unusual in that it's a *static* method—you don't need to have created a `String` object to use it with; it's always available to you.

For example, the following lines put the string `"ABC"` into the variable `myString`:

```
var myString = String.fromCharCode(65,66,67);
```

The `fromCharCode()` method can be very useful when used with variables. For example, to build up a string consisting of all the uppercase letters of the alphabet, you could use the following code:

```
var myString = "";
var charCode;

for (charCode = 65; charCode <= 90; charCode++) {
    myString = myString + String.fromCharCode(charCode);
}

document.write(myString);
```

You use the `for` loop to select each character from A to Z in turn and concatenate this to `myString`. Note that although this is fine as an example, it is more efficient and less memory-hungry to simply write this instead:

```
var myString = "ABCDEFGHIJKLMNOPQRSTUVWXYZ";
```

Removing Leading and Trailing Whitespace—The trim() Method

When working with user-provided data, you're never guaranteed that the users input their data exactly how you want them to. Therefore, it's always best to assume user input is incorrect, and it's your job to make it correct.

The process of scrubbing data is dependent on the specific needs of your application, but you'll commonly want to trim the whitespace from the start and end of the string. For this, `String` objects have the `trim()` method. It returns a new string with all leading and trailing whitespace removed. For example:

```
var name = prompt("Please enter your name");
name = name.trim();

alert("Hello, " + name);
```

This code prompts users to enter their name. You then trim their input of whitespace and use the resulting value in a greeting that is displayed in an `alert` box. So, if the user entered "   Jim", he'd still only see "Hello, Jim" in the `alert` box because you trimmed his input.

Array Objects

You saw how to create and use arrays in Chapter 2, and this chapter mentioned earlier that they are actually objects.

In addition to storing data, `Array` objects provide a number of useful properties and methods you can use to manipulate the data in the array and find out information such as the size of the array.

Again, this is not an exhaustive look at every property and method of `Array` objects, but rather just some of the more useful ones.

Finding Out How Many Elements Are in an Array—The length Property

The `length` property gives you the number of elements within an array. Sometimes you know exactly how long the array is, but in some situations you may have been adding new elements to an array with no easy way of keeping track of how many have been added.

You can use the `length` property to find the index of the last element in the array. This is illustrated in the following example:

```
var names = [];

names[0] = "Paul";
names[1] = "Jeremy";
names[11] = "Nick";

document.write("The last name is " + names[names.length - 1]);
```

> **NOTE** Note that you have inserted data in the elements with index positions 0, 1, and 11. The array index starts at 0, so the last element is at index `length` - 1, which is 11, rather than the value of the `length` property, which is 12.

Another situation in which the `length` property proves useful is where a JavaScript method returns an array it has built itself. For example, in the next chapter, you see that the `string` object has the `split()` method, which splits text into pieces and passes back the result as an `Array` object. Because

JavaScript created the array, there is no way for you to know, without the `length` property, what the index is of the last element in the array.

Adding Elements—The push() Method

You'll find that `Array` objects have many useful methods, but you will probably use the `push()` method more than any other. Its purpose is simple—add elements to the array—and it lets you do so without needing to specify an index, like this:

```
var names = [];
names.push("Jeremy");
names.push("Paul");
```

Its usage is simple—simply pass the value you want to add to the array, and that value will be pushed to the end of the array. So in the previous `names` array, `"Jeremy"` and `"Paul"` are in index positions of `0` and `1`, respectively.

Joining Arrays—The concat() Method

If you want to take two separate arrays and join them into one big array, you can use the `Array` object's `concat()` method. The `concat()` method returns a new array, which is the combination of the two arrays: the elements of the first array, then the elements of the second array. To do this, you use the method on your first array and pass the name of the second array as its parameter.

For example, say you have two arrays, `names` and `ages`, and separately they look like the following tables:

names array			
ELEMENT INDEX	0	1	2
VALUE	Paul	Jeremy	Nick

ages array			
ELEMENT INDEX	0	1	2
VALUE	31	30	31

If you combine them using `names.concat(ages)`, you will get an array like the one in the following table:

ELEMENT INDEX	0	1	2	3	4	5
VALUE	Paul	Jeremy	Nick	31	30	31

In the following code, this is exactly what you are doing:

```
var names = [ "Paul", "Jeremy", "Nick" ];
var ages = [ 31, 30, 31 ];

var concatArray = names.concat(ages);
```

It's also possible to combine two arrays into one but assign the new array to the name of the existing first array, using `names = names.concat(ages)`.

If you were to use `ages.concat(names)`, what would be the difference? Well, as you can see in the following table, the difference is that now the `ages` array elements are first, and the elements from the `names` array are concatenated on the end:

ELEMENT INDEX	0	1	2	3	4	5
VALUE	31	30	31	Paul	Jeremy	Nick

Copying Part of an Array—The slice() Method

When you just want to copy a portion of an array, you can use the `slice()` method. Using the `slice()` method, you can slice out a portion of the array and assign it to a new variable name. The `slice()` method has two parameters:

➤ The index of the first element you want copied

➤ The index of the element marking the end of the portion you are slicing out (optional)

Just as with string copying with `substring()`, the start point is included in the copy, but the end point is not. Again, if you don't include the second parameter, all elements from the start index onward are copied.

Suppose you have the array names shown in the following table:

INDEX	0	1	2	3	4
VALUE	Paul	Sarah	Jeremy	Adam	Bob

If you want to create a new array with elements 1, `Sarah`, and 2, `Jeremy`, you would specify a start index of 1 and an end index of 3. The code would look something like this:

```
var names = [ "Paul", "Sarah", "Jeremy", "Adam", "Bob" ];
var slicedArray = names.slice(1,3);
```

When JavaScript copies the array, it copies the new elements to an array in which they have indexes 0 and 1, not their old indexes of 1 and 2.

After slicing, the `slicedArray` looks like the following table:

INDEX	0	1
VALUE	Sarah	Jeremy

The first array, names, is unaffected by the slicing.

Converting an Array into a Single String—The join() Method

The `join()` method concatenates all the elements in an array and returns them as a string. It also enables you to specify any characters you want to insert *between* elements as they are joined together. The method has only one parameter, and that's the string you want between elements.

An example will help explain things. Imagine that you have your weekly shopping list stored in an array, which looks something like this:

INDEX	0	1	2	3	4
VALUE	Eggs	Milk	Potatoes	Cereal	Banana

Now you want to write out your shopping list to the page using `document.write()`. You want each item to be on a different line, and you can do this by using the `<br />` tag between each element in the array. The `<br/>` tag is an HTML line break, a visual carriage return for breaking text into different lines. First, you need to declare your array:

```
var myShopping = [ "Eggs", "Milk", "Potatoes", "Cereal", "Banana" ];
```

Next, convert the array into one string with the `join()` method:

```
var myShoppingList = myShopping.join("<br />");
```

Now the variable `myShoppingList` will hold the following text:

```
"Eggs<br />Milk<br />Potatoes<br />Cereal<br />Banana"
```

which you can write out to the page with `document.write()`:

```
document.write(myShoppingList);
```

The shopping list will appear in the page with each item on a new line, as shown in Figure 5-1.

Putting Your Array in Order—The sort() Method

If you have an array that contains similar data, such as a list of names or a list of ages, you may want to put them in alphabetical or numerical order. This is something that the `sort()` method makes very easy. In the following code, you define your array and then put it in ascending alphabetical order using `names.sort()`. Finally, you output it so that you can see that it's in order:

```
var names = [ "Paul", "Sarah", "Jeremy", "Adam", "Bob" ];

names.sort();

document.write("Now the names again in order <br />");

for (var index = 0; index < names.length; index++) {
    document.write(names[index] + "<br />");
}
```

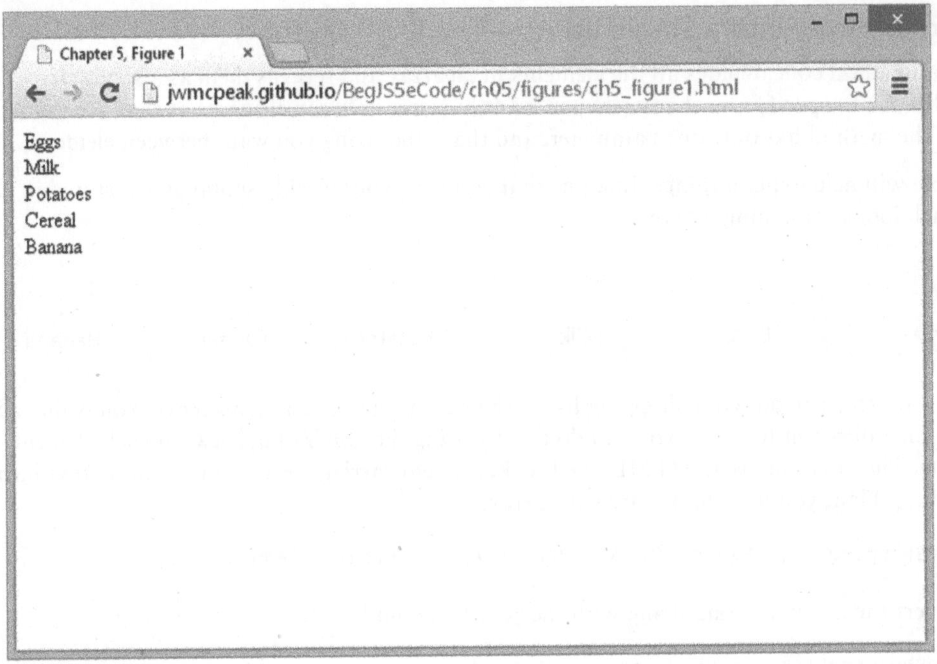

FIGURE 5-1

Don't forget that the sorting is case sensitive, so Paul will come before paul. Remember that JavaScript stores letters encoded in their equivalent Unicode number, and that sorting is done based on Unicode numbers rather than actual letters. It just happens that Unicode numbers match the order in the alphabet. However, lowercase letters are given a different sequence of numbers, which come after the uppercase letters. So the array with elements Adam, adam, Zoë, zoë, will be sorted to the order Adam, Zoë, adam, zoë.

Note that in your for statement you've used the Array object's length property in the condition statement, rather than inserting the length of the array (5), like this:

```
for (var index = 0; index < 5; index++)
```

Why do this? After all, you know in advance that you have five elements in the array. Well, what would happen if you altered the number of elements in the array by adding two more names?

```
var names = [ "Paul", "Sarah", "Jeremy", "Adam", "Bob", "Karen", "Steve" ];
```

If you had inserted 5 rather than names.length, your loop code wouldn't work as you want it to. It wouldn't display the last two elements unless you changed the condition part of the for loop to 7. By using the length property, you've made life easier, because now there is no need to change code elsewhere if you add array elements.

Okay, you've put things in ascending order, but what if you wanted descending order? That is where the reverse() method comes in.

Putting Your Array into Reverse Order—The reverse() Method

The next method for the `Array` object is the `reverse()` method, which, no prizes for guessing, reverses the order of the array so that the elements at the back are moved to the front. Let's take the shopping list again as an example:

INDEX	0	1	2	3	4
VALUE	Eggs	Milk	Potatoes	Cereal	Banana

If you use the `reverse()` method

```
var myShopping = [ "Eggs", "Milk", "Potatoes", "Cereal", "Banana" ];
myShopping.reverse();
```

you get

INDEX	0	1	2	3	4
VALUE	Banana	Cereal	Potatoes	Milk	Eggs

To prove this, you could write it to the page with the `join()` method you saw earlier.

```
var myShoppingList = myShopping.join("<br />")
document.write(myShoppingList);
```

TRY IT OUT   Sorting an Array

When used in conjunction with the `sort()` method, the `reverse()` method can be used to sort an array so that its elements appear in reverse alphabetical or numerical order. This is shown in the following example:

```
<!DOCTYPE html>

<html lang="en">
<head>
    <title>Chapter 5, Example 3</title>
</head>
<body>
    <script>
        var myShopping = ["Eggs", "Milk", "Potatoes", "Cereal", "Banana"];

        var ord = prompt("Enter 1 for alphabetical order, " +
                    "and -1 for reverse order", 1);

        if (ord == 1) {
            myShopping.sort();
            document.write(myShopping.join("<br />"));
        } else if (ord == -1) {
            myShopping.sort();
```

```
            myShopping.reverse();
            document.write(myShopping.join("<br />"));
        } else {
            document.write("That is not a valid input");
        }
    </script>
</body>
</html>
```

Save the example as ch5_example3.html. When you load this into your browser, you will be asked to enter some input depending on whether you want the array to be ordered in forward or backward order. If you enter 1, the array will be displayed in forward order. If you enter –1, the array will be displayed in reverse order. If you enter neither of these values, you will be told that your input was invalid.

At the top of the script block, you define the array containing your shopping list. Next you define the variable ord to be the value entered by the user in a prompt box:

```
var ord = prompt("Enter 1 for alphabetical order, " +
                "and -1 for reverse order", 1);
```

This value is used in the conditions of the if statements that follow. The first if checks whether the value of ord is 1—that is, whether the user wants the array in alphabetical order. If so, the following code is executed:

```
myShopping.sort();
document.write(myShopping.join("<br />"));
```

The array is sorted and then displayed to the user on separate lines using the join() method. Next, in the else if statement, you check whether the value of ord is -1—that is, whether the user wants the array in reverse alphabetical order. If so, the following code is executed:

```
myShopping.sort();
myShopping.reverse();
document.write(myShopping.join("<br />"));
```

Here, you sort the array before reversing its order. Again the array is displayed to the user by means of the join() method.

Finally, if ord has neither the value 1 nor the value -1, you tell the user that his input was invalid:

```
document.write("That is not a valid input");
```

Finding Array Elements—The indexOf() and lastIndexOf() Methods

As you can probably guess, the Array object's indexOf() and lastIndexOf() methods behave similarly to the String object's methods—they return the index of an item's first and last occurrence in an array. Consider the following code:

```
var colors = [ "red", "blue", "green", "blue" ];

alert(colors.indexOf("red"));
alert(colors.lastIndexOf("blue"));
```

The first line of code creates an array called colors. It has four elements (two of which are blue). The second line alerts 0 to the user, because red is the first element of the array. The third line returns the value of 3 because the lastIndexOf() method begins its search at the very end of the array.

Both the indexOf() and lastIndexOf() methods return -1 if the provided value cannot be found in the array.

Iterating through an Array without Loops

The remaining five methods are called iterative methods because they iterate, or loop, through the array. In addition, these methods execute a function that you define on every element while they iterate through the array. The function these methods use must follow one rule—it must accept three arguments like the following code:

```
function functionName(value, index, array) {
    // do something here
}
```

When executed, JavaScript passes three arguments to your function. The first is the value of the element, the second is the index of the element, and the third is the array itself. These three parameters enable you to perform just about any operation or comparison you might need in relation to the array and its elements.

Testing Each Element—The every(), some(), and filter() Methods

Let's look at the every() and some() methods first. These are testing methods. The every() method tests whether all elements in the array pass the test in your function. Consider the following code:

```
var numbers = [ 1, 2, 3, 4, 5 ];

function isLessThan3(value, index, array) {
    var returnValue = false;

    if (value < 3) {
        returnValue = true;
    }

    return returnValue;
}

alert(numbers.every(isLessThan3));
```

The first line shows the creation of an array called numbers; its elements hold the values 1 through 5. The next line defines the isLessThan3() function. It accepts the three mandatory arguments and determines if the value of each element is less than 3. The last line alerts the outcome of the every() test. Because not every value in the array is less than 3, the result of the every() test is false.

Contrast this with the some() method. Unlike every(), the some() test only cares if some of the elements pass the test in your function. Using the same numbers array and isLessThan3() function, consider this line of code:

```
alert(numbers.some(isLessThan3));
```

The result is true because some of the elements in the array are less than 3. It's easy to keep these two methods straight. Just remember the every() method returns true if, and only if, all elements in the array pass the test in your function; the some() method returns true if, and only if, some of the elements in the array pass your function's test.

Let's assume you want to retrieve the elements that have a value less than 3. You already know some elements meet this criterion, but how do you identify those elements and retrieve them? This is where the filter() method becomes useful.

The filter() method executes your function on every element in the array, and if your function returns true for a particular element, that element is added to a new array that the filter() method returns. Keeping that in mind, look at the following code:

```
var numbers = [ 1, 2, 3, 4, 5 ];

function isLessThan3 (value, index, array) {
    var returnValue = false;

    if (value < 3) {
        returnValue = true;
    }

    return returnValue;
}

if (numbers.some(isLessThan3)) {
    var result = numbers.filter(isLessThan3);
    alert("These numbers are less than 3: " + result);
}
```

This code redefines the numbers array and the isLessThan3 function used in previous examples. The highlighted code determines if any elements in the numbers array contain a value less than 3, and if so, calls the filter() method to place those elements into a new array. The result of this code is shown in Figure 5-2.

Operating on Elements—The forEach() and map() Methods

The final two methods are the forEach() and map() methods. Unlike the previous iterative methods, these two methods do not test each element in the array with your function; instead, the function you write should perform some kind of operation that uses the element in some way. Look at the following code:

```
var numbers = [ 1, 2, 3, 4, 5 ];

for (var i = 0; i < numbers.length; i++) {
    var result = numbers[i] * 2;
    alert(result);
}
```

As a programmer, you'll often see and use this type of code. It defines an array and loops through it in order to perform some kind of operation on each element. In this case, the value of each element is doubled, and the result is shown in an alert box to the user.

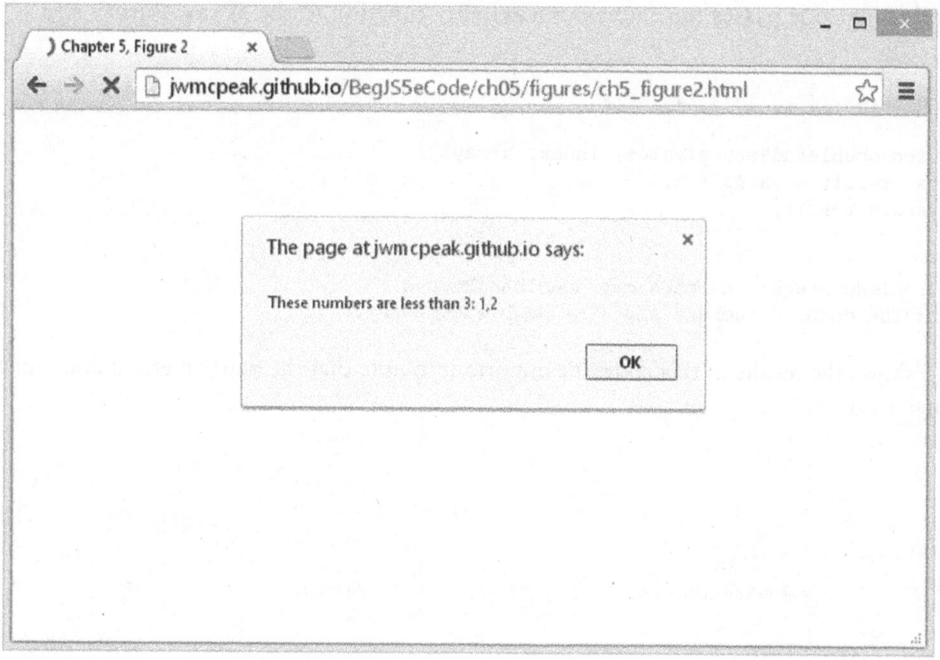

FIGURE 5-2

This code can be rewritten to use the `forEach()` method. As its name implies, it does something *for each* element in the array. All you need to do is write a function to double a given value and output the result in an `alert` box, like this:

```
var numbers = [ 1, 2, 3, 4, 5 ];

function doubleAndAlert(value, index, array) {
    var result = value * 2;
    alert(result);
}

numbers.forEach(doubleAndAlert);
```

Notice that the `doubleAndAlert()` function doesn't return a value like the testing methods. It cannot return a value; its only purpose is to perform an operation on every element in the array. This is useful in many cases, but you'll want to use the `map()` method when you need to store the results of the function.

The premise of the `map()` method is similar to that of `forEach()`. It executes a given function on every element in an array, but it also returns a new array that contains the results of the function.

Let's modify the previous example and write a new function called `doubleAndReturn()`. It will still double each element in the array, but it will return the doubled value instead of alerting it. The following code passes the `doubleAndReturn()` function to the `Array` object's `map()` method:

```
var numbers = [ 1, 2, 3, 4, 5 ];

function doubleAndReturn(value, index, array) {
    var result = value * 2;
    return result;
}

var doubledNumbers = numbers.map(doubleAndReturn);
alert("The doubled numbers are: " + doubledNumbers);
```

Figure 5-3 shows the results of this code. It's important to note that the `map()` method does not alter the original array.

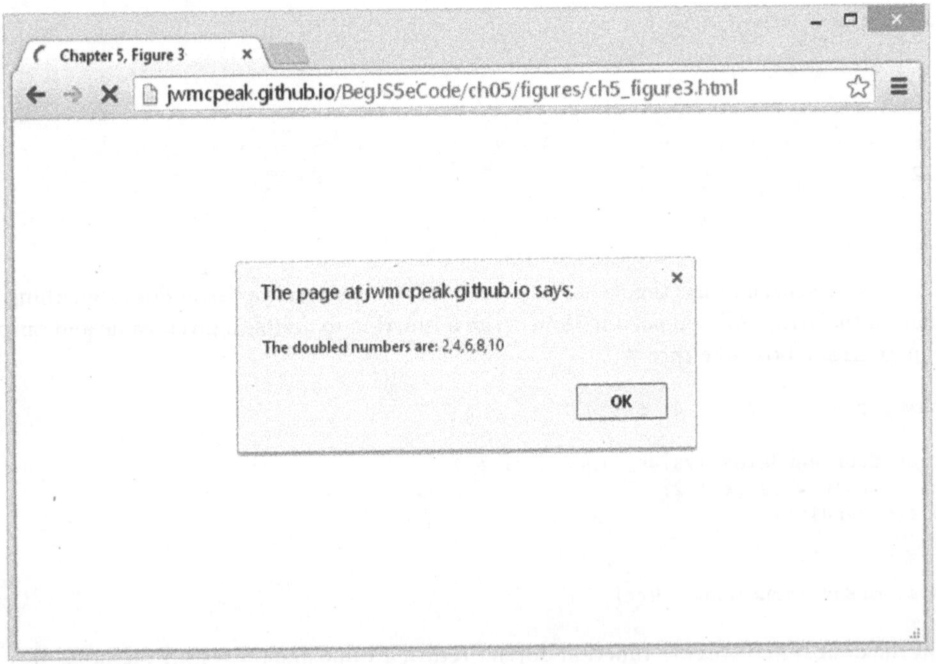

FIGURE 5-3

The Math Object

The `Math` object provides a number of useful mathematical functions and number manipulation methods. You take a look at some of them here, but you'll find the rest described in detail at the Mozilla Developer Network: `https://developer.mozilla.org/en-US/docs/Web/JavaScript/Reference/Global_Objects/Math`.

The Math object is a little unusual in that JavaScript creates it for you automatically. There's no need to declare a variable as a Math object or define a new Math object before being able to use it, making it a little bit easier to use.

The properties of the Math object include some useful math constants, such as the PI property (giving the value 3.14159 and so on). You access these properties, as usual, by placing a dot after the object name (Math) and then writing the property name. For example, to calculate the area of a circle, you can use the following code:

```
var radius = prompt("Give the radius of the circle", "");
var area = Math.PI * radius * radius;
document.write("The area is " + area);
```

The methods of the Math object include some operations that are impossible, or complex, to perform using the standard mathematical operators (+, −, *, and /). For example, the cos() method returns the cosine of the value passed as a parameter. You look at a few of these methods now.

The abs() Method

The abs() method returns the absolute value of the number passed as its parameter. Essentially, this means that it returns the positive value of the number. So -1 is returned as 1, -4 as 4, and so on. However, 1 would be returned as 1 because it's already positive.

For example, the following code writes the number 101 to the page:

```
var myNumber = -101;
document.write(Math.abs(myNumber));
```

Finding the Largest and Smallest Numbers—The min() and max() Methods

Let's say you have two numbers, and you want to find either the largest or smallest of the two. To aid you in this task, the Math object provides the min() and max() methods. These methods both accept at least two arguments, all of which must obviously be numbers. Look at this example code:

```
var max = Math.max(21,22); // result is 22
var min = Math.min(30.1, 30.2); // result is 30.1
```

The min() method returns the number with the lowest value, and max() returns the number with the highest value. The numbers you pass to these two methods can be whole or floating-point numbers.

> **NOTE** The max() and min() methods can accept many numbers; you're not limited to two.

Rounding Numbers

The Math object provides a few methods to round numbers, each with its own specific purpose.

The ceil() Method

The ceil() method always rounds a number up to the next largest whole number or integer. So 10.01 becomes 11, and –9.99 becomes –9 (because –9 is greater than –10). The ceil() method has just one parameter, namely the number you want rounded up.

Using ceil() is different from using the parseInt() function you saw in Chapter 2, because parseInt() simply chops off any numbers after the decimal point to leave a whole number, whereas ceil() rounds the number up.

For example, the following code writes two lines in the page, the first containing the number 102 and the second containing the number 101:

```
var myNumber = 101.01;
document.write(Math.ceil(myNumber) + "<br />");
document.write(parseInt(myNumber, 10));
```

The floor() Method

Like the ceil() method, the floor() method removes any numbers after the decimal point, and returns a whole number or integer. The difference is that floor() always rounds the number down. So if you pass 10.01 you will be returned 10, and if you pass –9.99 you will see –10 returned.

The round() Method

The round() method is very similar to ceil() and floor(), except that instead of always rounding up or always rounding down, it rounds up only if the decimal part is .5 or greater, and rounds down otherwise.

For example:

```
var myNumber = 44.5;
document.write(Math.round(myNumber) + "<br />");

myNumber = 44.49;
document.write(Math.round(myNumber));
```

This code would write the numbers 45 and 44 to the page.

Summary of Rounding Methods

As you have seen, the ceil(), floor(), and round() methods all remove the numbers after a decimal point and return just a whole number. However, which whole number they return depends on the method used: floor() returns the lowest, ceil() the highest, and round() the nearest equivalent integer. This can be a little confusing, so the following is a table of values and what whole number would be returned if these values were passed to the parseInt() function, and ceil(), floor(), and round() methods:

PARAMETER	PARSEINT() RETURNS	CEIL() RETURNS	FLOOR() RETURNS	ROUND() RETURNS
10.25	10	11	10	10
10.75	10	11	10	11
10.5	10	11	10	11
−10.25	−10	−10	−11	−10
−10.75	−10	−10	−11	−11
−10.5	−10	−10	−11	−10

> **NOTE** *Remember that* `parseInt()` *is a native JavaScript function, not a method of the* `Math` *object, like the other methods presented in this table.*

TRY IT OUT   Rounding Methods Results Calculator

If you're still not sure about rounding numbers, this example should help. Here, you look at a calculator that gets a number from the user, and then writes out what the result would be when you pass that number to parseInt(), ceil(), floor(), and round():

```
<!DOCTYPE html>

<html lang="en">
<head>
    <title>Chapter 5, Example 4</title>
</head>
<body>
    <script>
    var myNumber = prompt("Enter the number to be rounded","");

        document.write("<h3>The number you entered was " + myNumber +
                    "</h3>");

        document.write("<p>The rounding results for this number are</p>");
        document.write("<table width='150' border='1'>");
        document.write("<tr><th>Method</th><th>Result</th></tr>");

        document.write("<tr><td>parseInt()</td><td>" +
                    parseInt(myNumber, 10) + "</td></tr>");

        document.write("<tr><td>ceil()</td><td>" + Math.ceil(myNumber) +
                    "</td></tr>");

        document.write("<tr><td>floor()</td><td>"+ Math.floor(myNumber) +
```

```
                              "</td></tr>");

            document.write("<tr><td>round()</td><td>" + Math.round(myNumber) +
                              "</td></tr>");

            document.write("</table>");
        </script>
    </body>
</html>
```

Save this as `ch5_example4.html` and load it into a web browser. In the prompt box, enter a number (for example, `12.354`), and click OK. The results of this number being passed to `parseInt()`, `ceil()`, `floor()`, and `round()` will be displayed in the page formatted inside a table, as shown in Figure 5-4.

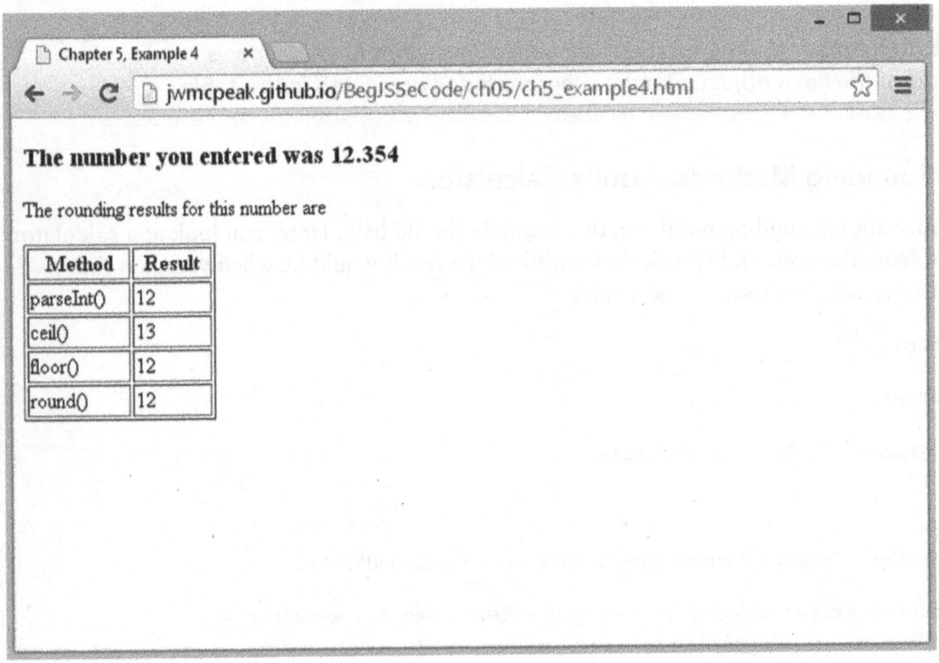

The number you entered was 12.354

The rounding results for this number are

Method	Result
parseInt()	12
ceil()	13
floor()	12
round()	12

FIGURE 5-4

The first task is to get the number to be rounded from the user:

```
var myNumber = prompt("Enter the number to be rounded","");
```

Then you write out the number and some descriptive text:

```
document.write("<h3>The number you entered was " + myNumber + "</h3>");
document.write("<p>The rounding results for this number are</p>");
```

Notice how this time some HTML tags for formatting have been included—the main header being in `<h3>` tags, and the description of what the table means being inside a paragraph `<p>` tag.

Next you create the table of results:

```
document.write("<table width='150' border='1'>");
document.write("<tr><th>Method</th><th>Result</th></tr>");

document.write("<tr><td>parseInt()</td><td>" +
            parseInt(myNumber, 10) + "</td></tr>");

document.write("<tr><td>ceil()</td><td>" + Math.ceil(myNumber) +
            "</td></tr>");

document.write("<tr><td>floor()</td><td>"+ Math.floor(myNumber) +
            "</td></tr>");

document.write("<tr><td>round()</td><td>" + Math.round(myNumber) +
            "</td></tr>");

document.write("</table>");
```

You create the table header first before actually displaying the results of each rounding function on a separate row. The principles are the same as with HTML in a page: You must make sure your tag's syntax is valid or otherwise things will appear strange or not appear at all.

Each row follows the same principle but uses a different rounding function. Let's look at the first row, which displays the results of parseInt():

```
document.write("<tr><td>parseInt()</td><td>" +
            parseInt(myNumber, 10) + "</td></tr>");
```

Inside the string to be written out to the page, you start by creating the table row with the <tr> tag. Then you create a table cell with a <td> tag and insert the name of the method from which the results are being displayed on this row. Then you close the cell with </td> and open a new one with <td>. Inside this next cell you are placing the actual results of the parseInt() function. Although a number is returned by parseInt(), because you are concatenating it to a string, JavaScript automatically converts the number returned by parseInt() into a string before concatenating. All this happens in the background without you needing to do a thing. Finally, you close the cell and the row with </td></tr>.

The random() Method

The random() method returns a random floating-point number in the range between 0 and 1, where 0 is included and 1 is not. This can be very useful for displaying random banner images or for writing a JavaScript game.

Let's look at how you would mimic the roll of a single die. In the following page, 10 random numbers are written to the page. Click the browser's Refresh button to get another set of random numbers.

```
<!DOCTYPE html>

<html lang="en">
<body>
    <script>
```

```
        var diceThrow;

        for (var throwCount = 0; throwCount < 10; throwCount++) {
            diceThrow = (Math.floor(Math.random() * 6) + 1);
            document.write(diceThrow + "<br>");
        }
    </script>
</body>
</html>
```

You want `diceThrow` to be between 1 and 6. The `random()` function returns a floating-point number between 0 and just under 1. By multiplying this number by 6, you get a number between 0 and just under 6. Then by adding 1, you get a number between 1 and just under 7. By using `floor()` to always round it down to the next lowest whole number, you can ensure that you'll end up with a number between 1 and 6.

If you wanted a random number between 1 and 100, you would just change the code so that `Math.random()` is multiplied by 100 rather than 6.

The pow() Method

The `pow()` method raises a number to a specified power. It takes two parameters, the first being the number you want raised to a power, and the second being the power itself. For example, to raise 2 to the power of 8 (that is, to calculate 2 * 2 * 2 * 2 * 2 * 2 * 2 * 2), you would write `Math.pow(2,8)`—the result being 256. Unlike some of the other mathematical methods, like `sin()`, `cos()`, and `acos()`, which are not commonly used in web programming unless it's a scientific application you're writing, the `pow()` method can often prove very useful.

TRY IT OUT Using pow()

In this example, you write a function using `pow()`, which fixes the number of decimal places in a number:

```
<!DOCTYPE html>

<html lang="en">
<head>
    <title>Chapter <5, Example 5</title>
</head>
<body>
    <script>
        function fix(fixNumber, decimalPlaces) {
            var div = Math.pow(10, decimalPlaces);
            fixNumber = Math.round(fixNumber * div) / div;
            return fixNumber;
        }

        var number1 = prompt("Enter the number with decimal places you " +
                             "want to fix", "");

        var number2 = prompt("How many decimal places do you want?", "");

        document.write(number1 + " fixed to " + number2 + " decimal places is: ");
        document.write(fix(number1, number2));
```

```
        </script>
    </body>
    </html>
```

Save the page as `ch5_example5.html`. When you load the page into your browser, you will be presented with two prompt boxes. In the first, enter the number for which you want to fix the number of decimal places (for example, 2.2345). In the second, enter the number of decimal places you want fixed (for example, 2). Then the result of fixing the number you have entered to the number of decimal places you have chosen will be written to the page, as shown in Figure 5-5. For the example numbers, this will be 2.23.

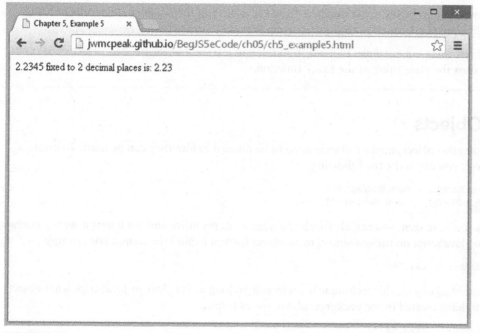

FIGURE 5-5

You first define the function `fix()`. This function will fix its `fixNumber` parameter to a maximum of its `decimalPlaces` parameter's number of digits after the decimal place. For example, fixing 34.76459 to a maximum of three decimal places will return 34.765.

The first line of code in the function sets the variable `div` to the number 10 raised to the power of the number of decimal places you want:

```
function fix(fixNumber, decimalPlaces) {
    var div = Math.pow(10,decimalPlaces);
```

Then, in the next line, you calculate the new number:

```
fixNumber = Math.round(fixNumber * div) / div;
```

What the code `Math.round(fixNumber * div)` does is move the decimal point in the number that you are converting to after the point in the number that you want to keep. So for `2.2345`, if you want to keep two decimal places, you convert it to `223.45`. The `Math.round()` method rounds this number to the nearest integer (in this case `223`) and so removes any undesired decimal part.

You then convert this number back into the fraction it should be, but of course only the fractional part you want is left. You do this by dividing by the same number (`div`) that you multiplied by. In this example, you divide `223` by `100`, which leaves `2.23`. This is `2.2345` fixed to two decimal places. This value is returned to the calling code in the line:

```
    return fixNumber;
}
```

Next, you use two prompt boxes to get numbers from the user. You then display the results of using these numbers in your `fix()` function to the user using `document.write()`.

This example is just that—an example. In a few minutes, you learn about the `Number` object's `toFixed()` method, which does the same thing as the `fix()` function.

Number Objects

As with the `String` object, `Number` objects need to be created before they can be used. To create a `Number` object, you can write the following:

```
var firstNumber = new Number(123);
var secondNumber = new Number('123');
```

However, as you have seen, you can also declare a number as primitive and use it as if it were a `Number` object, letting JavaScript do the conversion to an object for you behind the scenes. For example:

```
var myNumber = 123.765;
```

As with the `String` object, this technique is preferable so long as it's clear to JavaScript what object you expect to have created in the background. So, for example,

```
var myNumber = "123.567";
```

will lead JavaScript to assume, quite rightly, that it's a string, and any attempts to use the `Number` object's methods will fail.

You look at just the `toFixed()` method of the `Number` object because that's the most useful method for regular use.

The toFixed() Method

The `toFixed()` method cuts a number off after a certain point. Let's say you want to display a price after sales tax. If your price is $9.99 and sales tax is 7.5 percent, that means the after-tax cost will be $10.73925. Well, this is rather an odd amount for a money transaction—what you really want to do is fix the number to no more than two decimal places. Let's create an example:

```
var itemCost = 9.99;
var itemCostAfterTax = 9.99 * 1.075;

document.write("Item cost is $" + itemCostAfterTax + "<br />");

itemCostAfterTax = itemCostAfterTax.toFixed(2);

document.write("Item cost fixed to 2 decimal places is " +
               "$" + itemCostAfterTax);
```

The first `document.write()` outputs the following to the page:

```
Item cost is $10.73925
```

However, this is not the format you want; instead you want two decimal places, so on the next line, enter this:

```
itemCostAfterTax = itemCostAfterTax.toFixed(2);
```

You use the `toFixed()` method of the `Number` object to fix the number variable that `itemCostAfterTax` holds to two decimal places. The method's only parameter is the number of decimal places you want your number fixed to. This line means that the next `document.write` displays this:

```
Item cost fixed to 2 decimal places is $10.74
```

The first thing you might wonder is why 10.74 and not 10.73? Well, the `toFixed()` method doesn't just chop off the digits not required; it also rounds up or down. In this case, the number was 10.739, which rounds up to 10.74. If it'd been 10.732, it would have been rounded down to 10.73.

Note that you can only fix a number from 0 to 20 decimal places.

Date Objects

The `Date` object handles everything to do with date and time in JavaScript. Using it, you can find out the current date and time, store your own dates and times, do calculations with these dates, and convert the dates into strings.

The `Date` object has a lot of methods and can be a little tricky to use, which is why Chapter 7 is dedicated to the date, time, and timers in JavaScript. However, in this section you focus on how to create a `Date` object and some of its more commonly used methods.

Creating a Date Object

You can declare and initialize a `Date` object in four ways. In the first method, you simply declare a new `Date` object without initializing its value. In this case, the date and time value will be set to the current date and time on the PC on which the script is run:

```
var theDate1 = new Date();
```

Secondly, you can define a `Date` object by passing the number of milliseconds since January 1, 1970, at 00:00:00 GMT. In the following example, the date is 31 January 2000 00:20:00 GMT (that is, 20 minutes past midnight):

```
var theDate2 = new Date(949278000000);
```

It's unlikely that you'll be using this way of defining a `Date` object very often, but this is how JavaScript actually stores the dates. The other formats for giving a date are simply for convenience.

The third way for you to declare a `Date` object is to pass a string representing a date, or a date and time. In the following example, you have `"31 January 2014"`:

```
var theDate3 = new Date("31 January 2014");
```

However, you could have written `31 Jan 2014`, `Jan 31 2014`, or any of a number of valid variations you'd commonly expect when writing down a date normally—if in doubt, try it out.

If you are writing your web pages for an international audience, you need to be aware of the different ways of specifying dates. In the United Kingdom and many other places, the standard is day, month, year, whereas in the United States the standard is month, day, year. This can cause problems if you specify only numbers—JavaScript may think you're referring to a day when you mean a month.

In the fourth and final way of defining a `Date` object, you initialize it by passing the following parameters separated by commas: year, month, day, hours, minutes, seconds, and milliseconds. For example:

```
var theDate4 = new Date(2014,0,31,15,35,20,20);
```

> **TIP** *It's very easy to make a mistake when specifying a month using either the third or fourth method of declaring a `Date` object. The easiest way to avoid such headaches is to always use the name of the month where possible. That way there can be no confusion.*

This date is actually 31 January 2014 at 15:35:20 and 20 milliseconds. You can specify just the date part if you want and ignore the time. Something to be aware of is that in this instance January is month 0, not month 1, as you'd expect, and December is month 11.

Getting Date Values

It's all very nice having stored a date, but how do you get the information out again? Well, you just use the `get` methods. These are summarized in the following table:

METHOD	RETURNS
getDate()	The day of the month
getDay()	The day of the week as an integer, with Sunday as 0, Monday as 1, and so on
getMonth()	The month as an integer, with January as 0, February as 1, and so on
getFullYear()	The year as a four-digit number
toDateString()	Returns the full date based on the current time zone as a human-readable string, for example, "Wed 31 Dec 2003"

For example, if you want to get the month in `ourDateObj`, you can simply write the following:

```
theMonth = myDateObject.getMonth();
```

All the methods work in a very similar way, and all values returned are based on local time, meaning time local to the machine on which the code is running. It's also possible to use Universal Time, previously known as GMT, which we discuss in Chapter 7.

TRY IT OUT   Using the Date Object to Retrieve the Current Date

In this example, you use the `get date type` methods you have been looking at to write the current day, month, and year to a web page:

```html
<!DOCTYPE html>

<html lang="en">
<head>
    <title>Chapter 5, Example 6</title>
</head>
<body>
    <script>
        var months = ["January", "February", "March", "April", "May",
                      "June", "July", "August", "September",
                      "October", "November", "December"];

        var dateNow = new Date();
        var yearNow = dateNow.getFullYear();
        var monthNow = months[dateNow.getMonth()];
        var dayNow = dateNow.getDate();
        var daySuffix;

        switch (dayNow) {
            case 1:
            case 21:
            case 31:
                daySuffix = "st";
                break;
            case 2:
            case 22:
                daySuffix = "nd";
                break;
            case 3:
            case 23:
                daySuffix = "rd";
                break;
            default:
                daySuffix = "th";
                break;
        }

        document.write("It is the " + dayNow + daySuffix + " day ");
        document.write("in the month of " + monthNow);
        document.write(" in the year " + yearNow);
    </script>
</body>
</html>
```

Save the code as `ch5_example6.html`. When you load the page in your browser, you should see a correctly formatted sentence telling you the current date.

The first thing you do in the code is declare an array and populate it with the months of a year. Why do this? Well, there is no method of the `Date` object that'll give you the month by name instead of as a number. However, this poses no problem; you just declare an array of months and use the month number as the array index to select the correct month name:

```
var months = ["January", "February", "March", "April", "May", "June", "July",
              "August", "September", "October", "November", "December"];
```

Next you create a new `Date` object, and by not initializing it with your own value, you allow it to initialize itself to the current date and time:

```
var dateNow = new Date();
```

Following this you set the `yearNow` variable to the current year, as returned by the `getFullYear()` method:

```
var yearNow = dateNow.getFullYear();
```

You then populate your `monthNow` variable with the value contained in the array element with an index of the number returned by `getMonth()`. Remember that `getMonth()` returns the month as an integer value, starting with 0 for January—this is a bonus because arrays also start at 0, so no adjustment is needed to find the correct array element:

```
var monthNow = months[dateNow.getMonth()];
```

Finally, you put the current day of the month into the variable `dayNow`:

```
var dayNow = dateNow.getDate();
```

Next you use a `switch` statement, which you learned about in Chapter 3. This is a useful technique for adding the correct suffix to the date that you already have. After all, your application will look more professional if you can say `"it is the 1st day"`, rather than `"it is the 1 day"`. This is a little tricky, however, because the suffix you want to add depends on the number that precedes it. So, for the first, twenty-first, and thirty-first days of the month, you have this:

```
switch (dayNow) {
    case 1:
    case 21:
    case 31:
        daySuffix = "st";
        break;
```

For the second and twenty-second days, you have this:

```
    case 2:
    case 22:
        daySuffix = "nd";
        break;
```

and for the third and twenty-third days, you have this:

```
case 3:
case 23:
    daySuffix = "rd";
    break;
```

Finally, you need the `default` case for everything else. As you will have guessed by now, this is simply `"th"`:

```
default:
    daySuffix = "th";
    break;
}
```

In the final lines you simply write the information to the HTML page, using `document.write()`.

Setting Date Values

To change part of the date in a `Date` object, you have a group of `set` functions, which pretty much replicate the `get` functions described earlier, except that you are setting, not getting, the values. These functions are summarized in the following table:

METHOD	DESCRIPTION
setDate()	The date of the month is passed in as the parameter to set the date.
setMonth()	The month of the year is passed in as an integer parameter, where 0 is January, 1 is February, and so on.
setFullYear()	This sets the year to the four-digit integer number passed in as a parameter.

> **NOTE** Note that for security reasons, there is no way for web-based JavaScript to change the current date and time on a user's computer.

So, to change the year to 2016, the code would be as follows:

```
myDateObject.setFullYear(2016);
```

Setting the date and month to the 27th of February looks like this:

```
myDateObject.setDate(27);
myDateObject.setMonth(1);
```

One minor point to note here is that there is no direct equivalent of the `getDay()` method. After the year, date, and month have been defined, the day is automatically set for you.

Calculations and Dates

Take a look at the following code:

```
var myDate = new Date("1 Jan 2010");
myDate.setDate(32);
document.write(myDate);
```

Surely there is some error—since when has January had 32 days? The answer is that of course it doesn't, and JavaScript knows that. Instead JavaScript sets the date to 32 days from the first of January—that is, it sets it to the 1st of February.

The same also applies to the setMonth() method. If you set it to a value greater than 11, the date automatically rolls over to the next year. So if you use setMonth(12), that will set the date to January of the next year, and similarly setMonth(13) is February of the next year.

How can you use this feature of setDate() and setMonth() to your advantage? Well, let's say you want to find out what date it will be 28 days from now. Given that different months have different numbers of days and that you could roll over to a different year, it's not as simple a task as it might first seem. Or at least that would be the case if it were not for setDate(). The code to achieve this task is as follows:

```
var nowDate = new Date();
var currentDay = nowDate.getDate();
nowDate.setDate(currentDay + 28);
```

First you get the current system date by setting the nowDate variable to a new Date object with no initialization value. In the next line, you put the current day of the month into a variable called currentDay. Why? Well, when you use setDate() and pass it a value outside of the maximum number of days for that month, it starts from the first of the month and counts that many days forward. So, if today's date is January 15 and you use setDate(28), it's not 28 days from the 15th of January, but 28 days from the 1st of January. What you want is 28 days from the current date, so you need to add the current date to the number of days ahead you want. So you want setDate(15 + 28). In the third line, you set the date to the current date, plus 28 days. You stored the current day of the month in currentDay, so now you just add 28 to that to move 28 days ahead.

If you want the date 28 days prior to the current date, you just pass the current date minus 28. Note that this will most often be a negative number. You need to change only one line, and that's the third one, which you change to the following:

```
nowDate.setDate(currentDay - 28);
```

You can use exactly the same principles for setMonth() as you have used for setDate().

Getting Time Values

The methods you use to retrieve the individual pieces of time data work much like the get methods for date values. The methods you use here are:

> getHours()

> getMinutes()

➤ getSeconds()

➤ getMilliseconds()

➤ toTimeString()

These methods return, respectively, the hours, minutes, seconds, milliseconds, and full time of the specified Date object, where the time is based on the 24-hour clock: 0 for midnight and 23 for 11 p.m. The last method is similar to the toDateString() method in that it returns an easily readable string, except that in this case it contains the time (for example, "13:03:51 UTC").

TRY IT OUT Writing the Current Time into a Web Page

Let's look at an example that writes out the current time to the page:

```
<!DOCTYPE html>

<html lang="en">
<head>
    <title>Chapter 5, Example 7</title>
</head>
<body>
    <script>
        var greeting;

        var nowDate = new Date();
        var nowHour = nowDate.getHours();
        var nowMinute = nowDate.getMinutes();
        var nowSecond = nowDate.getSeconds();

        if (nowMinute < 10) {
            nowMinute = "0" + nowMinute;
        }

        if (nowSecond < 10) {
            nowSecond = "0" + nowSecond;
        }

        if (nowHour < 12) {
            greeting = "Good Morning";
        } else if (nowHour < 17) {
            greeting = "Good Afternoon";
        } else {
            greeting = "Good Evening";
        }

        document.write("<h4>" + greeting + " and welcome to my website</h4>");
        document.write("According to your clock the time is ");
        document.write(nowHour + ":" + nowMinute + ":" + nowSecond);
    </script>
</body>
</html>
```

Save this page as `ch5_example7.html`. When you load it into a web browser, it writes a greeting based on the time of day as well as the current time, as shown in Figure 5-6.

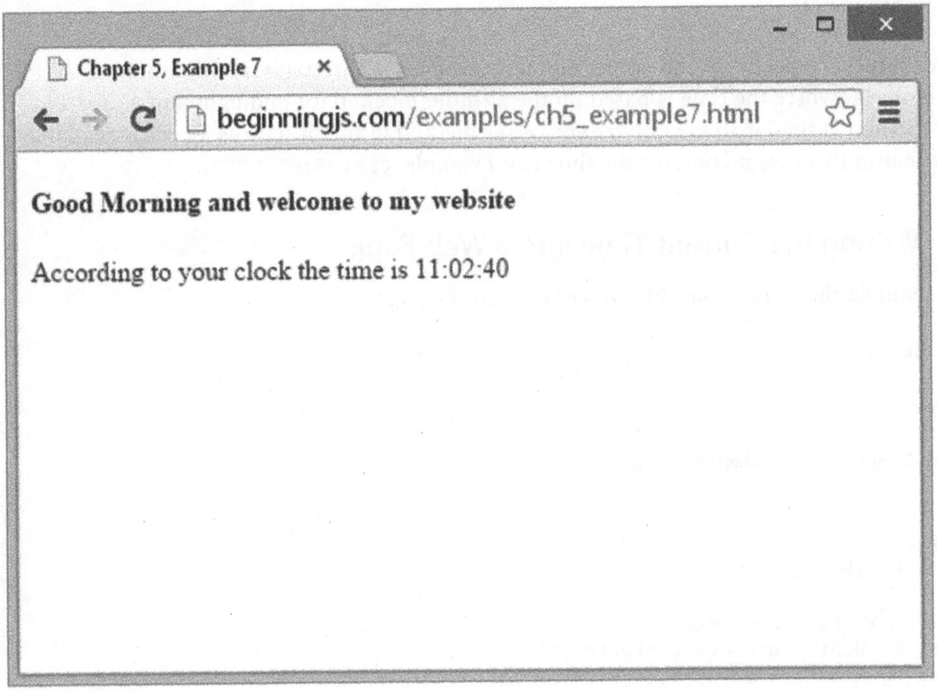

FIGURE 5-6

The first two lines of code declare two variables—`greeting` and `nowDate`:

```
var greeting;
var nowDate = new Date();
```

The `greeting` variable will be used shortly to store the welcome message on the website, whether this is `"Good Morning"`, `"Good Afternoon"`, or `"Good Evening"`. The `nowDate` variable is initialized to a new `Date` object. Note that the constructor for the `Date` object is empty, so JavaScript will store the current date and time in it.

Next, you get the information on the current time from `nowDate` and store it in various variables. You can see that getting time data is very similar to getting date data, just using different methods:

```
var nowHour = nowDate.getHours();
var nowMinute = nowDate.getMinutes();
var nowSecond = nowDate.getSeconds();
```

You may wonder why the following lines are included in the example:

```
if (nowMinute < 10) {
    nowMinute = "0" + nowMinute;
```

```
    }

    if (nowSecond < 10) {
        nowSecond = "0" + nowSecond;
    }
```

These lines are there just for formatting reasons. If the time is nine minutes past 10, then you expect to see something like 10:09. You don't expect 10:9, which is what you would get if you used the getMinutes() method without adding the extra zero. The same goes for seconds. If you're just using the data in calculations, you don't need to worry about formatting issues—you do here because you're inserting the time the code executed into the web page.

Next, in a series of if statements, you decide (based on the time of day) which greeting to create for displaying to the user:

```
    if (nowHour < 12) {
        greeting = "Good Morning";
    } else if (nowHour < 17) {
        greeting = "Good Afternoon";
    } else {
        greeting = "Good Evening";
    }
```

Finally, you write out the greeting and the current time to the page:

```
    document.write("<h4>" + greeting + " and welcome to my website</h4>");
    document.write("According to your clock the time is ");
    document.write(nowHour + ":" + nowMinute + ":" + nowSecond);
```

Setting Time Values

When you want to set the time in your Date objects, you have a series of methods similar to those used for getting the time:

➤ setHours()

➤ setMinutes()

➤ setSeconds()

➤ setMilliseconds()

These work much like the methods you use to set the date, in that if you set any of the time parameters to an illegal value, JavaScript assumes you mean the next or previous time boundary. If it's 9:57 and you set minutes to 64, the time will be set to 10:04—that is, 64 minutes from 9:00.

This is demonstrated in the following code:

```
    var nowDate = new Date();
    nowDate.setHours(9);
    nowDate.setMinutes(57);
```

```
alert(nowDate);

nowDate.setMinutes(64);
alert(nowDate);
```

First you declare the nowDate variable and assign it to a new Date object, which will contain the current date and time. In the following two lines, you set the hours to 9 and the minutes to 57. You show the date and time using an alert box, which should show a time of 9:57. The minutes are then set to 64 and again an alert box is used to show the date and time to the user. Now the minutes have rolled over the hour so the time shown should be 10:04.

If the hours were set to 23 instead of 9, setting the minutes to 64 would not just move the time to another hour, but also cause the day to change to the next date.

CREATING YOUR OWN CUSTOM OBJECTS

We've spent a lot of time discussing objects built into JavaScript, but JavaScript's real power comes from the fact that you can create your own objects to represent complex data. For example, imagine that you need to represent an individual person in your code. You could simply use two variables for an individual person's first name and last name, like this:

```
var firstName = "John";
var lastName = "Doe";
```

But what if you needed to represent multiple people? Creating two variables for every person would get unwieldy very quickly, and keeping track of every variable for every person would cause headaches for even the best programmers in the world. Instead, you could create an object to represent each individual person. Each of these objects would contain the necessary information that makes one person unique from other (such as a person's first and last names).

To create an object in JavaScript, simply use the new operator in conjunction with the Object constructor, like this:

```
var johnDoe = new Object();
```

But like arrays, JavaScript provides a literal syntax to signify an object: a pair of curly braces ({}). So you can rewrite the previous code like this:

```
var johnDoe = {};
```

Today's JavaScript developers favor this literal syntax instead of calling the Object constructor.

Once you have an object, you can begin to populate it with properties. It is similar to creating a variable, except you do not use the var keyword. Simply use the name of the object, followed by a dot, then the name of the property, and assign it a value. For example:

```
johnDoe.firstName = "John";
johnDoe.lastName = "Doe";
```

These two lines of code create the firstName and lastName properties on the johnDoe object and assign their respective values. JavaScript does not check if these properties exist before they're created; it simply creates them. This free property creation might sound great (and it is!), but it does have drawbacks. The primary issue is that JavaScript won't tell you if you accidentally misspell a property name; it'll just create a new property with the misspelled name, something that can make it difficult to track bugs. So always be careful when creating properties.

You can assign methods in the same way, except you assign a function instead of another type of value, like this:

```
johnDoe.greet = function()  {
    alert("My name is " + this.firstName + " " + this.lastName;
};
```

This code creates a method called greet(), which simply alerts a greeting. A few important things are important to note in this code.

First, notice there is no name between function and (). A function that has no name is called an *anonymous function*. Anonymous functions, in and of themselves, are a syntax error unless you assign that function to a variable. Once you assign an anonymous function to a variable, that function's name becomes the name of the variable. So you can execute the anonymous function assigned to johnDoe.greet like this:

```
johnDoe.greet();
```

Next, notice the use of this inside of the function: this.firstName and this.lastName. In JavaScript, this is a special variable that refers to the current object—the johnDoe object in this case. It literally means "this object." So you could rewrite greet() like the following:

```
johnDoe.greet = function()  {
    alert("My name is " + johnDoe.firstName + " " + johnDoe.lastName;
};
```

However, you won't always have the name of object to use in place of this. Therefore, it is preferred to refer to the current object inside of a method by using this rather than the actual name of the object.

The full code for creating this johnDoe object looks like this:

```
var johnDoe = {};

johnDoe.firstName = "John";
johnDoe.lastName = "Doe";
johnDoe.greet = function()  {
    alert("My name is " + johnDoe.firstName + " " + johnDoe.lastName;
};
```

This is perfectly valid JavaScript, but it takes four statements to create the complete object. These four statements can be reduced to one statement by defining the entire object using literal notation. Admittedly, it will look a little weird at first, but you'll soon get used to it:

```
var johnDoe = {
    firstName : "John",
    lastName : "Doe",
```

```
    greet : function() {
        alert("My name is " +
        this.firstName + " " +
        this.lastName;
    }
};
```

Take a moment and study this code. First, notice this code uses curly braces to enclose the entire object. Then notice that each property and method is defined by specifying the name of the property/method, followed by a colon, and then its value. So, assigning the `firstName` property looks like this:

```
firstName : "John"
```

There is no equal sign used here. In object literal notation, the colon sets the value of the property.

Finally, notice that each property and method definition is separated by a comma—very much like how you separate individual elements in an array literal.

TRY IT OUT   Using Object Literals

It is very important for you to understand object literals—they are used extremely liberally by JavaScript developers. Let's look at an example that uses a function to create a custom object:

```
<!DOCTYPE html>

<html lang="en">
<head>
    <title>Chapter 5, Example 8</title>
</head>
<body>
    <script>
        function createPerson(firstName, lastName) {
            return {
                firstName: firstName,
                lastName: lastName,
                getFullName: function() {
                    return this.firstName + " " + this.lastName
                },
                greet: function(person) {
                    alert("Hello, " + person.getFullName() +
                        ". I'm " + this.getFullName());
                }
            };
        }

        var johnDoe = createPerson("John", "Doe");
        var janeDoe = createPerson("Jane", "Doe");

        johnDoe.greet(janeDoe);
    </script>
</body>
</html>
```

Save this page as ch5_example8.html. When you load the page into a web browser, it displays the message: "Hello, Jane Doe. I'm John Doe".

First, this code creates a function called createPerson() that accepts a person's first and last names as parameters. This function creates an object with the person's first and last names using object literal notation:

```
function createPerson(firstName, lastName) {
    return {
```

The first property created is the firstName property, and it is assigned the value of the firstName parameter:

```
        firstName: firstName,
```

Next is the lastName property, which receives its value from the createPerson() function's lastName parameter:

```
        lastName: lastName,
```

Then a method called getFullName() is created. Its purpose is to return the first and last name of the person to the caller:

```
        getFullName: function() {
            return this.firstName + " " + this.lastName
        },
```

This method uses the this variable to access this object's firstName and lastName properties. Note that the this variable is the only way to retrieve these properties—the object doesn't have a name; it is an anonymous object that is created and then returned to the caller.

The final method of this object is greet(). It accepts another person object as a parameter and uses its getFullName() in order to greet that person:

```
        greet: function(person) {
            alert("Hello, " + person.getFullName() +
                ". I'm " + this.getFullName());
        }
    };
}
```

The next two lines create two objects two represent two individual people:

```
var johnDoe = createPerson("John", "Doe");
var janeDoe = createPerson("Jane", "Doe");
```

Notice the absence of the new keyword. The createPerson() function is not a constructor function (you learn how to write constructor functions later). It's simply a function that creates and returns an object.

Finally, John Doe greets Jane Doe by calling the greet() method and passing the janeDoe object to it:

```
johnDoe.greet(janeDoe);
```

CREATING NEW TYPES OF OBJECTS (REFERENCE TYPES)

This section's focus is on some advanced stuff. It's not essential stuff, so you may want to move on and come back to it later.

You've seen that JavaScript provides a number of objects built into the language and ready for us to use. You've also built custom objects that you can use to represent more complex data, but JavaScript also enables you to create your own type of objects. For example, you created an object that represented an individual person, but you can also create an object that is a Person object.

It's a bit like a house that's built already and you can just move on in. However, what if you want to create your own house, to design it for your own specific needs? In that case you'll use an architect to create technical drawings and plans that provide the template for the new house—the builders use the plans to tell them how to create the house.

So what does any of this have to do with JavaScript and objects? Well, JavaScript enables you to be an architect and create the templates for your own objects to your own specification, to fit your specific needs. Going back to the person object example, JavaScript doesn't come with built-in person objects, so you'd have to design your own.

Just as a builder of a house needs an architect's plans to know what to build and how it should be laid out, you need to provide blueprints telling JavaScript how your object should look. You somewhat did this with the createPerson() function in ch5_example8.html, but you only created plain objects with custom properties and methods—you didn't create an actual Person object.

But JavaScript supports the definition of *reference types*. Reference types are essentially templates for an object, as the architect's drawings are the template used to build a house. Before you can use your new object type, you need to define it along with its methods and properties. The important distinction is that when you define your reference type, no object based on that type is created. It's only when you create an instance of your reference type using the new keyword that an object of that type, based on your blueprint or prototype, is created.

Before you start, an important distinction must be made. Many developers refer to reference types as classes and use the two terms interchangeably. Although this is correct for many object-oriented languages such as Java, C#, and C++, it is not correct for JavaScript. JavaScript does not yet support a class construct, although the next version of JavaScript will provide formal classes. JavaScript does, however, fully support the logical equivalent, reference types.

It's also important to point out that the built-in objects discussed thus far in this chapter are also reference types. String, Array, Number, Date, and even Object are all reference types, and the objects you created are instances of these types.

A reference type consists of three things:

➤ A constructor

➤ Method definitions

➤ Properties

A constructor is a function that is called every time one of your objects based on this reference type is created. It's useful when you want to initialize properties or the object in some way. You need to create a constructor even if you don't pass any parameters to it or if it contains no code. (In that case it'd just be an empty definition.) As with all functions, a constructor can have zero or more parameters.

You've created objects to represent individual people. Next you create a simple reference, called `Person`, to do the same thing—except that these objects will be actual `Person` objects.

Defining a Reference Type

The first thing you need to do is create the constructor, which is shown here:

```
function Person(firstName, lastName) {
    this.firstName = firstName;
    this.lastName = lastName;
}
```

Your first thought might be that what you have here is simply a function, and you'd be right. It's not until you start defining the properties and methods that it becomes something more than a function. This is in contrast to some programming languages, which have a more formal way of defining types.

> **NOTE** Typically, a reference type is defined with an uppercase letter. Doing so makes it easy to differentiate a function from a reference type easily and quickly.

Inside the function, notice the use of the `this` variable. Once again, it literally means "this object," and it is the only way to access the object that is being created. So to create the `firstName` and `lastName` properties, you write the following code:

```
this.firstName = firstName;
this.lastName = lastName;
```

Now you need to define `getFullName()` and `greet()` methods. You can define them inside of the constructor, but it is more efficient to define them on `Person`'s prototype, like this:

```
Person.prototype.getFullName = function() {
    return this.firstName + " " + this.lastName;
};

Person.prototype.greet = function(person) {
    alert("Hello, " + person.getFullName() +
        ". I'm " + this.getFullName());
};
```

The first thing you notice is `Person.prototype`. Remember from Chapter 4 that functions are objects in JavaScript, and in this chapter you learned that objects have properties and methods. So it's easy to assume that functions have properties and methods.

Every function object has a `prototype` property, but it is only useful for constructor functions. You can think of the `Person.prototype` property as an actual prototype for `Person` objects. Any properties and methods you assign to `Person.prototype` are usable on all `Person` objects. In fact, they're more than usable—they're shared!

The functions assigned to `Person.prototype.getFullName` and `Person.prototype.greet` are shared between all objects, or instances, of `Person`. This means that the function object of one `Person` object's `getFullName` is the exact same function object on another `Person` object's `getFullName`. To express that in code:

```
var areSame = person1.getFullName == person2.getFullName; // true
```

But why were `firstName` and `lastName` assigned in the constructor instead of `Person.prototype`? The `firstName` and `lastName` properties are called *instance data*. Instance data is unique to each individual object, or instance. So because `firstName` and `lastName` are instance data, we define them in the constructor—they shouldn't be shared between all `Person` objects.

Creating and Using Reference Type Instances

You create instances of your reference type in the same way you created instances of JavaScript's built-in types: using the `new` keyword. So to create a new instance of `Person`, you'd write this:

```
var johnDoe = new Person("John", "Doe");
var janeDoe = new Person("Jane", "Doe");
```

Here, as with a `Date` object, you have created two new objects and stored them in variables, `johnDoe` and `janeDoe`, but this time it's a new object based on the `Person` type.

> **NOTE** The use of the `new` keyword is very important when creating an object with a constructor. The browser does not throw an error if you do not use the `new` keyword, but your script will not work correctly. Instead of creating a new object, you actually add properties to the global `window` object. The problems caused by not using the `new` keyword can be hard to diagnose, so make sure you specify the `new` keyword when creating objects with a constructor.

You use these objects just like you did in `ch5_example8.html`. In the following code, Jane Doe greets John Doe:

```
janeDoe.greet(johnDoe);
```

Even though `getFullName()` and `greet()` are defined on `Person.prototype`, you still call them like normal methods. JavaScript is intelligent enough to look at `Person.prototype` for those methods.

Now for the million dollar question: Why define a reference type instead of creating plain, but custom, objects? It's a valid question. Both the objects created in `ch5 _ example8.html` and from the `Person` constructor serve the same purpose: to represent an individual person. The main difference is how the objects are created. Objects created from a constructor typically consume less of the computer's memory than literal objects.

Frankly, it's a question you don't have to worry about at this point in time. It's more important to know how to create objects than using the correct approach. So practice both methods; create your own custom objects and reference types!

SUMMARY

In this chapter you've taken a look at the concept of objects and seen how vital they are to an understanding of JavaScript, which represents virtually everything with objects. You also looked at some of the various native reference types that the JavaScript language provides to add to its functionality.

You saw that:

➤ JavaScript is object-based—it represents things, such as strings, dates, and arrays, using the concept of objects.

➤ Objects have properties and methods. For example, an Array object has the length property and the sort() method.

➤ To create a new object, you simply write new ObjectType(). You can choose to initialize an object when you create it.

➤ To set an object's property value or get that value, you simply write objectName .objectProperty.

➤ Calling the methods of an object is similar to calling functions. Parameters may be passed, and return values may be passed back. Accessing the methods of an object is identical to accessing a property, except that you must remember to add parentheses at the end, even when it has no parameters. For example, you would write objectName.objectMethod().

➤ The string type provides lots of handy functionality for text and gives you ways of finding out how long the text is, searching for text inside the string, and selecting parts of the text.

➤ The Math type is created automatically and provides a number of mathematical properties and methods. For example, to obtain a random number between 0 and 1, you use the method Math.random().

➤ The Array type provides ways of manipulating arrays. Some of the things you can do are find the length of an array, sort its elements, and join two arrays together.

➤ The Date type provides a way of storing, calculating with, and later accessing dates and times.

➤ JavaScript lets you create your own custom objects, giving them the properties and methods that you want them to have.

➤ JavaScript enables you to create your own types of objects using reference types. These can be used to model real-world situations and for making code easier to create and more maintainable, though they do require extra effort at the start.

EXERCISES

You can find suggested solutions to these questions in Appendix A.

1. Using the `Date` type, calculate the date 12 months from now and write this into a web page.

2. Obtain a list of names from the user, storing each name entered in an array. Keep getting another name until the user enters nothing. Sort the names in ascending order and then write them out to the page, with each name on its own line.

3. `ch5_example8.html` uses a function to create objects using literal notation. Modify this example to use the `Person` data type.

6

String Manipulation

WHAT YOU WILL LEARN IN THIS CHAPTER:

➤   Using the String object's advanced methods to manipulate strings

➤   Matching substrings follow a specific pattern

➤   Validating useful pieces of information, such as telephone numbers, e-mail addresses, and postal codes

WROX.COM CODE DOWNLOADS FOR THIS CHAPTER

You can find the wrox.com code downloads for this chapter at http://www.wiley.com/go/ BeginningJavaScript5E on the Download Code tab. You can also view all of the examples and related files at http://beginningjs.com.

In Chapter 5 you looked at the String object, which is one of the native objects that JavaScript makes available to you. You saw a number of its properties and methods, including the following:

➤   length—The length of the string in characters

➤   charAt() and charCodeAt()—The methods for returning the character or character code at a certain position in the string

➤   indexOf() and lastIndexOf()—The methods that allow you to search a string for the existence of another string and that return the character position of the string if found

➤   substr() and substring()—The methods that return just a portion of a string

➤   toUpperCase() and toLowerCase()—The methods that return a string converted to upper- or lowercase

In this chapter you look at four new methods of the String object, namely split(), match(), replace(), and search(). The last three, in particular, give you some very powerful text-manipulation functionality. However, to make full use of this functionality, you need to learn about a slightly more complex subject.

The methods split(), match(), replace(), and search() can all make use of *regular expressions*, something JavaScript wraps up in an object called the RegExp object. Regular expressions enable you to define a pattern of characters, which you can use for text searching or replacement. Say, for example, that you have a string in which you want to replace all single quotes enclosing text with double quotes. This may seem easy—just search the string for ' and replace it with "—but what if the string is Bob O'Hara said "Hello"? You would not want to replace the single-quote character in O'Hara. You can perform this text replacement without regular expressions, but it would take more than the two lines of code needed if you do use regular expressions.

Although split(), match(), replace(), and search() are at their most powerful with regular expressions, they can also be used with just plaintext. You take a look at how they work in this simpler context first, to become familiar with the methods.

ADDITIONAL STRING METHODS

In this section you take a look at the split(), replace(), search(), and match() methods, and see how they work without regular expressions.

The split() Method

The String object's split() method splits a single string into an array of substrings. Where the string is split is determined by the separation parameter that you pass to the method. This parameter is simply a character or text string.

For example, to split the string "A,B,C" so that you have an array populated with the letters between the commas, the code would be as follows:

```
var myString = "A,B,C";
var myTextArray = myString.split(",");
```

JavaScript creates an array with three elements. In the first element it puts everything from the start of the string myString up to the first comma. In the second element it puts everything from after the first comma to before the second comma. Finally, in the third element it puts everything from after the second comma to the end of the string. So, your array myTextArray will look like this:

```
A  B  C
```

If, however, your string were "A,B,C," JavaScript would split it into four elements, the last element containing everything from the last comma to the end of the string; in other words, the last string would be an empty string:

```
A  B  C
```

This is something that can catch you off guard if you're not aware of it.

TRY IT OUT Reversing the Order of Text

Let's create a short example using the `split()` method, in which you reverse the lines written in a `<textarea>` element:

```
<!DOCTYPE html>

<html lang="en">
<head>
    <title>Chapter 6, Example 1</title>
</head>
    <body>
        <script>
            var values = prompt("Please enter a set of comma separated values.",
                "Apples,Oranges,Bananas");

            function splitAndReverseText(csv) {
                var parts = csv.split(",");
                parts.reverse();

                var reversedString = parts.join(",");

                alert(reversedString);
            }

            splitAndReverseText(values);
        </script>
    </body>
</html>
```

Save this as `ch6_example1.html` and load it into your browser. Use the default value in the prompt box, click OK, and you should see the screen shown in Figure 6-1.

Try other comma-separated values to test it further.

The key to how this code works is the function `splitAndReverseText()`. It accepts a string value that should contain one or more commas. You start by splitting the value contained within `csv` using the `split()` method and putting the resulting array inside the `parts` variable:

```
function splitAndReverseText(csv) {
    var parts = csv.split(",");
```

This uses a comma as the separator. You then reverse the array of string parts using the `Array` object's `reverse()` method:

```
    parts.reverse();
```

With the array now reversed, it's just a simple matter of creating the new string. You can easily accomplish this with the `Array` object's `join()` method:

```
    var reversedString = parts.join(",");
```

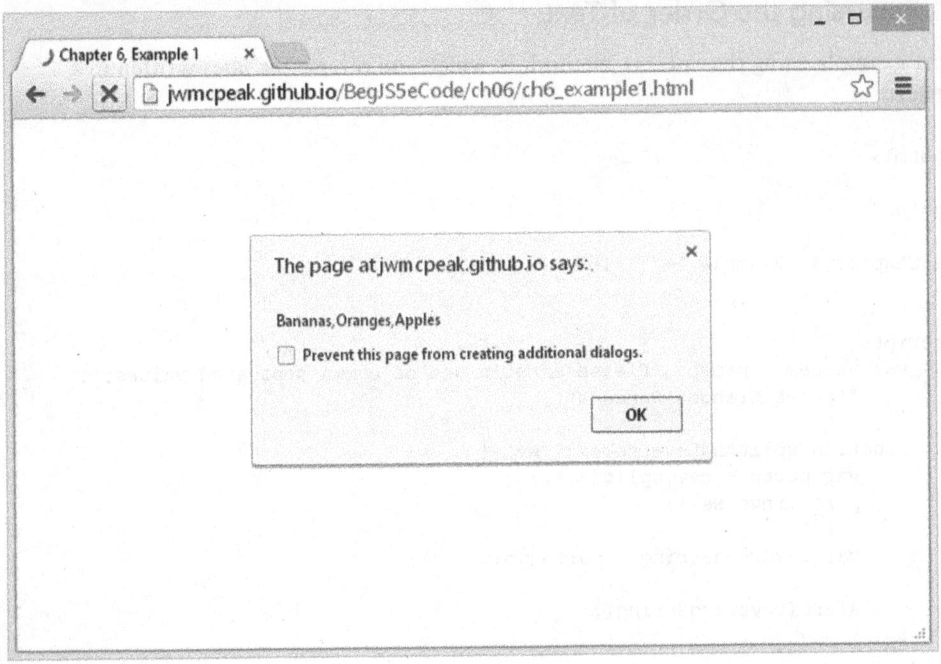

FIGURE 6-1

Remember from Chapter 5 that the `join()` method converts an array into a string, separating each element with the specified separator.

Finally, you display the new string in an `alert` box:

```
        alert(reversedString);
    }
```

After you've looked at regular expressions, you'll revisit the `split()` method.

The replace() Method

The `replace()` method searches a string for occurrences of a substring. Where it finds a match for this substring, it replaces the substring with a third string that you specify.

Let's look at an example. Say you have a string with the word May in it, as shown in the following:

```
    var myString = "The event will be in May, the 21st of June";
```

Now, say you want to replace May with June. You can use the replace() method like so:

```
Var myCleanedUpString = myString.replace("May", "June");
```

The value of myString will not be changed. Instead, the replace() method returns the value of myString but with May replaced with June. You assign this returned string to the variable myCleanedUpString, which will contain the corrected text:

```
"The event will be in June, the 21st of June"
```

The search() Method

The search() method enables you to search a string for a particular piece of text. If the text is found, the character position at which it was found is returned; otherwise, -1 is returned. The method takes only one parameter, namely the text you want to search for.

When used with plaintext, the search() method provides no real benefit over methods like indexOf(), which you've already seen. However, you see later that the power of this method becomes apparent when you use regular expressions.

In the following example, you want to find out if the word Java is contained within the string called myString:

```
var myString = "Beginning JavaScript, Beginning Java, " +
               "Professional JavaScript";

alert(myString.search("Java"));
```

The alert box that occurs will show the value 10, which is the character position of the J in the first occurrence of Java, as part of the word JavaScript.

The match() Method

The match() method is very similar to the search() method, except that instead of returning the position at which a match was found, it returns an array. Each element of the array contains the text of each match that is found.

Although you can use plaintext with the match() method, it would be completely pointless to do so. For example, take a look at the following:

```
var myString = "1997, 1998, 1999, 2000, 2000, 2001, 2002";
myMatchArray = myString.match("2000");
alert(myMatchArray.length);
```

This code results in myMatchArray holding an element containing the value 2000.
Given that you already know your search string is 2000, you can see it's been a pretty pointless exercise.

However, the `match()` method makes a lot more sense when you use it with regular expressions. Then you might search for all years in the twenty-first century—that is, those beginning with 2. In this case, your array would contain the values 2000, 2000, 2001, and 2002, which is much more useful information!

REGULAR EXPRESSIONS

Before you look at the `split()`, `match()`, `search()`, and `replace()` methods of the `String` object again, you need to look at regular expressions and the `RegExp` object. Regular expressions provide a means of defining a pattern of characters, which you can then use to split, search for, or replace characters in a string when they fit the defined pattern.

JavaScript's regular expression syntax borrows heavily from the regular expression syntax of Perl, another scripting language. Most modern programming languages support regular expressions, as do lots of applications, such as WebMatrix, Sublime Text, and Dreamweaver, in which the Find facility allows regular expressions to be used. You'll find that your regular expression knowledge will prove useful even outside JavaScript.

Regular expressions in JavaScript are used through the `RegExp` object, which is a native JavaScript object, as are `String`, `Array`, and so on. You have two ways of creating a new `RegExp` object. The easier is with a regular expression literal, such as the following:

```
var myRegExp = /\b'|'\b/;
```

The forward slashes (/) mark the start and end of the regular expression. This is a special syntax that tells JavaScript that the code is a regular expression, much as quote marks define a string's start and end. Don't worry about the actual expression's syntax yet (the `\b'|'\b`)—that is explained in detail shortly.

Alternatively, you could use the `RegExp` object's constructor function `RegExp()` and type the following:

```
var myRegExp = new RegExp("\\b'|'\\b");
```

Either way of specifying a regular expression is fine, though the former method is a shorter, more efficient one for JavaScript to use and therefore is generally preferred. For much of the remainder of the chapter, you use the first method. The main reason for using the second method is that it allows the regular expression to be determined at run time (as the code is executing and not when you are writing the code). This is useful if, for example, you want to base the regular expression on user input.

Once you get familiar with regular expressions, you will come back to the second way of defining them, using the `RegExp()` constructor. As you can see, the syntax of regular expressions is slightly different with the second method, so we'll return to this subject later.

Although you'll be concentrating on the use of the `RegExp` object as a parameter for the `String` object's `split()`, `replace()`, `match()`, and `search()` methods, the `RegExp` object does have its own methods and properties. For example, the `test()` method enables you to test to see if the string passed to it as a parameter contains a pattern matching the one defined in the `RegExp` object. You see the `test()` method in use in an example shortly.

Simple Regular Expressions

Defining patterns of characters using regular expression syntax can get fairly complex. In this section you explore just the basics of regular expression patterns. The best way to do this is through examples.

Let's start by looking at an example in which you want to do a simple text replacement using the `replace()` method and a regular expression. Imagine you have the following string:

```
var myString = "Paul, Paula, Pauline, paul, Paul";
```

and you want to replace any occurrence of the name "Paul" with "Ringo."

Well, the pattern of text you need to look for is simply `Paul`. Representing this as a regular expression, you just have this:

```
var myRegExp = /Paul/;
```

As you saw earlier, the forward-slash characters mark the start and end of the regular expression. Now let's use this expression with the `replace()` method:

```
myString = myString.replace(myRegExp, "Ringo");
```

You can see that the `replace()` method takes two parameters: the `RegExp` object that defines the pattern to be searched and replaced, and the replacement text.

If you put this all together in an example, you have the following:

```
<!DOCTYPE html>

<html lang="en">
<head>
    <title>Chapter 6, Figure 2</title>
</head>
<body>
    <script>
        var myString = "Paul, Paula, Pauline, paul, Paul";
        var myRegExp = /Paul/;

        myString = myString.replace(myRegExp, "Ringo");
        alert(myString);
    </script>
</body>
</html>
```

You can save and run this code. You will see the screen shown in Figure 6-2.

You can see that this has replaced the first occurrence of `Paul` in your string. But what if you wanted all the occurrences of `Paul` in the string to be replaced? The two at the far end of the string are still there, so what happened?

By default, the `RegExp` object looks only for the first matching pattern, in this case the first `Paul`, and then stops. This is a common and important behavior for `RegExp` objects. Regular expressions tend to start at one end of a string and look through the characters until the first complete match is found, then stop.

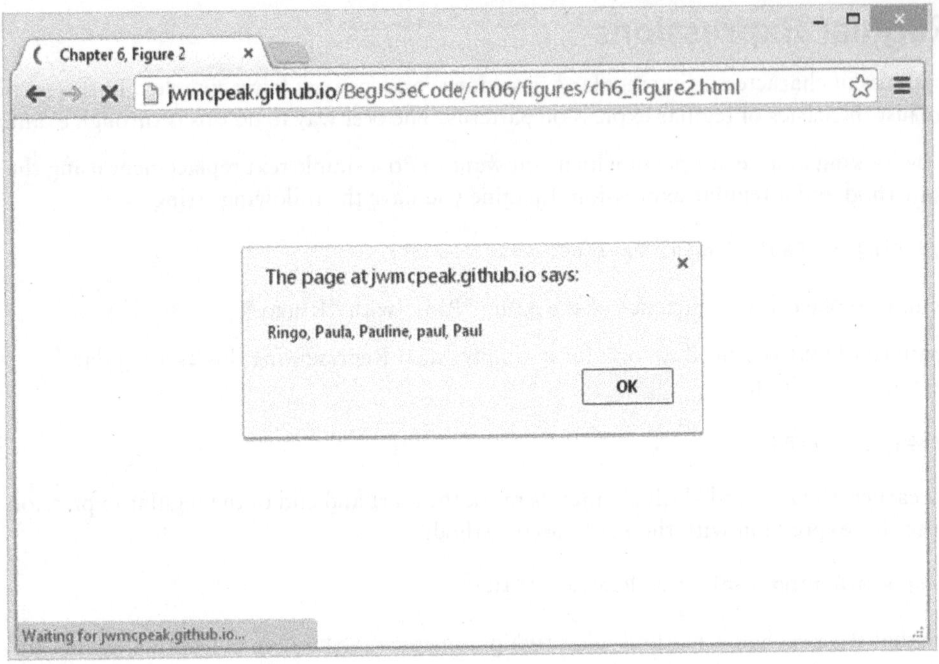

FIGURE 6-2

What you want is a global match, which is a search for all possible matches to be made and replaced. To help you out, the `RegExp` object has three attributes you can define, as listed in the following table:

ATTRIBUTE CHARACTER	DESCRIPTION
G	Global match. This looks for all matches of the pattern rather than stopping after the first match is found.
I	Pattern is case-insensitive. For example, `Paul` and `paul` are considered the same pattern of characters.
M	Multi-line flag. This specifies that the special characters ^ and $ can match the beginning and the end of lines as well as the beginning and end of the string.

You learn more about these attribute characters later in the chapter.

If you change the `RegExp` object in the code to the following, a global case-insensitive match will be made:

```
var myRegExp = /Paul/gi;
```

Running the code now produces the result shown in Figure 6-3.

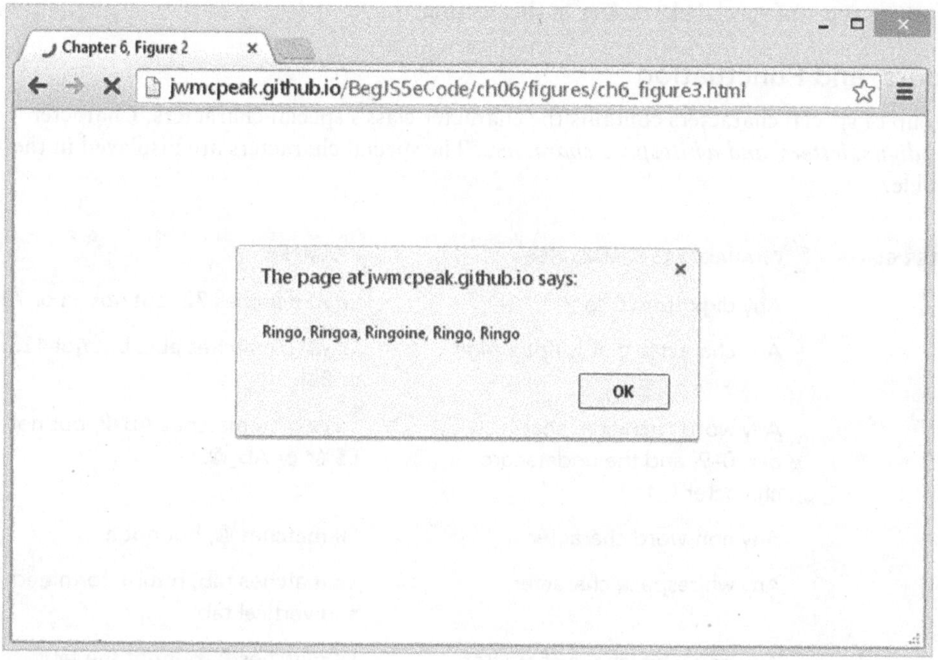

FIGURE 6-3

This looks as if it has all gone horribly wrong. The regular expression has matched the Paul substrings at the start and the end of the string, and the penultimate paul, just as you wanted. However, the Paul substrings inside Pauline and Paula have also been replaced.

The RegExp object has done its job correctly. You asked for all patterns of the characters Paul to be replaced and that's what you got. What you actually meant was for all occurrences of Paul, when it's a single word and not part of another word, such as Paula, to be replaced. The key to making regular expressions work is to define exactly the pattern of characters you mean, so that only that pattern can match and no other. So let's do that.

1. You want paul or Paul to be replaced.

2. You don't want it replaced when it's actually part of another word, as in Pauline.

How do you specify this second condition? How do you know when the word is joined to other characters, rather than just joined to spaces or punctuation or the start or end of the string?

To see how you can achieve the desired result with regular expressions, you need to enlist the help of regular expression special characters. You look at these in the next section, by the end of which you should be able to solve the problem.

Regular Expressions: Special Characters

You look at three types of special characters in this section.

Text, Numbers, and Punctuation

The first group of special characters contains the character class's special characters. Character class means *digits, letters, and whitespace characters*. The special characters are displayed in the following table:

CHARACTER CLASS	CHARACTERS IT MATCHES	EXAMPLE
\d	Any digit from 0 to 9	\d\d matches 72, but not aa or 7a.
\D	Any character that is not a digit	\D\D\D matches abc, but not 123 or 8ef.
\w	Any word character; that is, A–Z, a–z, 0–9, and the underscore character (_)	\w\w\w\w matches Ab_2, but not £$%* or Ab_@.
\W	Any non-word character	\W matches @, but not a.
\s	Any whitespace character	\s matches tab, return, formfeed, and vertical tab.
\S	Any non-whitespace character	\S matches A, but not the tab character.
.	Any single character other than the newline character (\n)	. matches a or 4 or @.
[...]	Any one of the characters between the brackets [a-z] matches any character in the range a to z	[abc] matches a or b or c, but nothing else.
[^...]	Any one character, but not one of those inside the brackets	[^abc] matches any character except a or b or c. [^a-z] matches any character that is not in the range a to z.

Note that uppercase and lowercase characters mean very different things, so you need to be extra careful with case when using regular expressions.

Let's look at an example. To match a telephone number in the format 1-800-888-5474, the regular expression would be as follows:

```
\d-\d\d\d-\d\d\d-\d\d\d\d
```

You can see that there's a lot of repetition of characters here, which makes the expression quite unwieldy. To make this simpler, regular expressions have a way of defining repetition. You see this a little later in the chapter, but first let's look at another example.

TRY IT OUT Checking a Passphrase for Alphanumeric Characters

You use what you've learned so far about regular expressions in a full example in which you check that a passphrase contains only letters and numbers—that is, alphanumeric characters, not punctuation or symbols like @, %, and so on:

```
<!DOCTYPE html>

<html lang="en">
<head>
    <title>Chapter 6, Example 2</title>
</head>
<body>
    <script>
        var input = prompt("Please enter a pass phrase.", "");

        function isValid (text) {
            var myRegExp = /[^a-z\d ]/i;
            return !(myRegExp.test(text));
        }

        if (isValid(input)) {
            alert("Your passphrase contains only valid characters");
        } else {
            alert("Your passphrase contains one or more invalid characters");
        }
    </script>
</body>
</html>
```

Save the page as ch6_example2.html, and then load it into your browser. Type just letters, numbers, and spaces into the prompt box, click OK, and you'll be told that the phrase contains valid characters. Try putting punctuation or special characters like @, ^, $, and so on into the text box, and you'll be informed that your passphrase is invalid.

Let's start by looking at the isValid() function. As its name implies, it checks the validity of the passphrase:

```
function isValid(text) {
    var myRegExp = /[^a-z\d ]/i;
    return !(myRegExp.test(text));
}
```

The function takes just one parameter: the text you want to validate. You then declare a variable, myRegExp, and set it to a new regular expression, which implicitly creates a new RegExp object.

The regular expression itself is fairly simple, but first think about what pattern you are looking for. What you want to find out is whether your passphrase string contains any characters that are not letters between A and Z or between a and z, numbers between 0 and 9, or spaces. Let's see how this translates into a regular expression:

1. You use square brackets with the ^ symbol:

```
[^]
```

This means you want to match any character that is not one of the characters specified inside the square brackets.

2. You add a-z, which specifies any character in the range a through z:

```
[^a-z]
```

So far, your regular expression matches any character that is not between a and z. Note that, because you added the i to the end of the expression definition, you've made the pattern case-insensitive. So your regular expression actually matches any character not between A and Z or a and z.

3. You add \d to indicate any digit character, or any character between 0 and 9:

```
[^a-z\d]
```

4. Your expression matches any character that is not between a and z, A and Z, or 0 and 9. You decide that a space is valid, so you add that inside the square brackets:

```
[^a-z\d ]
```

Putting this all together, you have a regular expression that matches any character that is not a letter, a digit, or a space.

5. On the second and final line of the function, you use the RegExp object's test() method to return a value:

```
return !(myRegExp.test(text));
```

The test() method of the RegExp object checks the string passed as its parameter to see if the characters specified by the regular expression syntax match anything inside the string. If they do, true is returned; if not, false is returned. Your regular expression matches the first invalid character found, so if you get a result of true, you have an invalid passphrase. However, it's a bit illogical for an is_valid function to return true when it's invalid, so you reverse the result returned by adding the NOT operator (!).

Previously you saw the two-line validity-checker function using regular expressions. Just to show how much more coding is required to do the same thing without regular expressions, here is a second function that does the same thing as isValid() but without regular expressions:

```
function isValid2(text) {
    var returnValue = true;
    var validChars = "abcdefghijklmnopqrstuvwxyz1234567890 ";

    for (var charIndex = 0; charIndex < text.length;charIndex++) {
        if (validChars.indexOf(text.charAt(charIndex).toLowerCase()) < 0) {
            returnValue = false;
            break;
        }
    }
    return returnValue;
}
```

This is probably as small as the non-regular expression version can be, and yet it's still several lines longer than `isValid()`.

The principle of this function is similar to that of the regular expression version. You have a variable, `validChars`, which contains all the characters you consider to be valid. You then use the `charAt()` method in a `for` loop to get each character in the passphrase string and check whether it exists in your `validChars` string. If it doesn't, you know you have an invalid character.

In this example, the non-regular expression version of the function is 10 lines, but with a more complex problem you could find it takes 20 or 30 lines to do the same thing a regular expression can do in just a few.

Back to your actual code: you use an `if...else` statement to display the appropriate message to the user. If the passphrase is valid, an `alert` box tells the user that all is fine:

```
if (isValid(input)) {
    alert("Your passphrase contains only valid characters");
}
```

If it isn't, another `alert` box tells users that their text was invalid:

```
else {
    alert("Your passphrase contains one or more invalid characters");
}
```

Repetition Characters

Regular expressions include something called repetition characters, which are a means of specifying how many of the last item or character you want to match. This proves very useful, for example, if you want to specify a phone number that repeats a character a specific number of times. The following table lists some of the most common repetition characters and what they do:

SPECIAL CHARACTER	MEANING	EXAMPLE
{n}	Match n of the previous item.	x{2} matches xx.
{n,}	Match n or more of the previous item.	x{2,} matches xx, xxx, xxxx, xxxxx, and so on.
{n,m}	Match at least n and at most m of the previous item.	x{2,4} matches xx, xxx, and xxxx.
?	Match the previous item zero or one time.	x? matches nothing or x.
+	Match the previous item one or more times.	x+ matches x, xx, xxx, xxxx, xxxxx, and so on.
*	Match the previous item zero or more times.	x* matches nothing, or x, xx, xxx, xxxx, and so on.

You saw earlier that to match a telephone number in the format 1-800-888-5474, the regular expression would be \d-\d\d\d-\d\d\d-\d\d\d\d. Let's see how this would be simplified with the use of the repetition characters.

The pattern you're looking for starts with one digit followed by a dash, so you need the following:

```
\d-
```

Next are three digits followed by a dash. This time you can use the repetition special characters— \d{3} will match exactly three \d, which is the any-digit character:

```
\d-\d{3}-
```

Next, you have three digits followed by a dash again, so now your regular expression looks like this:

```
\d-\d{3}-\d{3}-
```

Finally, the last part of the expression is four digits, which is \d{4}:

```
\d-\d{3}-\d{3}-\d{4}
```

You'd declare this regular expression like this:

```
var myRegExp = /\d-\d{3}-\d{3}-\d{4}/
```

Remember that the first / and last / tell JavaScript that what is in between those characters is a regular expression. JavaScript creates a RegExp object based on this regular expression.

As another example, what if you have the string Paul Paula Pauline, and you want to replace Paul and Paula with George? To do this, you would need a regular expression that matches both Paul and Paula.

Let's break this down. You know you want the characters Paul, so your regular expression starts as:

```
Paul
```

Now you also want to match Paula, but if you make your expression Paula, this will exclude a match on Paul. This is where the special character ? comes in. It enables you to specify that the previous character is optional—it must appear zero (not at all) or one time. So, the solution is:

```
Paula?
```

which you'd declare as:

```
var myRegExp = /Paula?/
```

Position Characters

The third group of special characters includes those that enable you to specify either where the match should start or end or what will be on either side of the character pattern. For example, you might want your pattern to exist at the start or end of a string or line, or you might want it to be between two words. The following table lists some of the most common position characters and what they do:

POSITION CHARACTER	DESCRIPTION
^	The pattern must be at the start of the string, or if it's a multi-line string, then at the beginning of a line. For multi-line text (a string that contains carriage returns), you need to set the multi-line flag when defining the regular expression using /myreg ex/m. Note that this is only applicable to IE 5.5 and later and NN 6 and later.
$	The pattern must be at the end of the string, or if it's a multi-line string, then at the end of a line. For multi-line text (a string that contains carriage returns), you need to set the multi-line flag when defining the regular expression using /myreg ex/m. Note that this is only applicable to IE 5.5 and later and NN 6 and later.
\b	This matches a word boundary, which is essentially the point between a word character and a non-word character.
\B	This matches a position that's not a word boundary.

For example, if you wanted to make sure your pattern was at the start of a line, you would type the following:

```
^myPattern
```

This would match an occurrence of myPattern if it was at the beginning of a line.

To match the same pattern, but at the end of a line, you would type the following:

```
myPattern$
```

The word-boundary special characters \b and \B can cause confusion, because they do not match characters but the positions between characters.

Imagine you had the string "Hello world!, let's look at boundaries said 007." defined in the code as follows:

```
var myString = "Hello world!, let's look at boundaries said 007.";
```

To make the word boundaries (that is, the boundaries between the words) of this string stand out, let's convert them to the | character:

```
var myRegExp = /\b/g;
myString = myString.replace(myRegExp, "|");
alert(myString);
```

You've replaced all the word boundaries, \b, with a |, and your message box looks like the one in Figure 6-4.

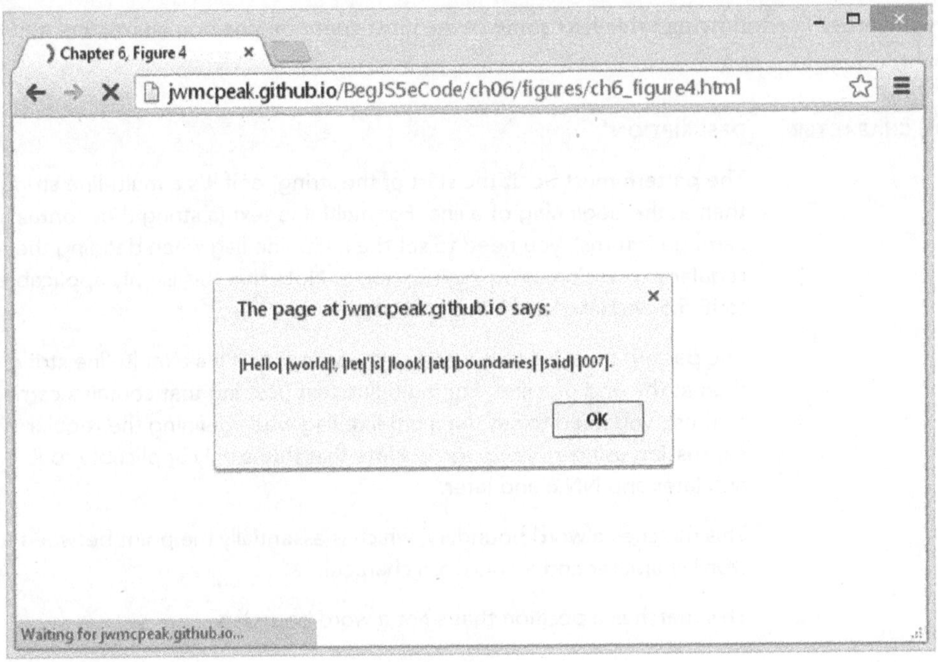

FIGURE 6-4

You can see that the position between any word character (letters, numbers, or the underscore character) and any non-word character is a word boundary. You'll also notice that the boundary between the start or end of the string and a word character is considered to be a word boundary. The end of this string is a full stop. So the boundary between the full stop and the end of the string is a non-word boundary, and therefore no | has been inserted.

If you change the regular expression in the example, so that it replaces non-word boundaries as follows:

```
var myRegExp = /\B/g;
```

you get the result shown in Figure 6-5.

Now the position between a letter, number, or underscore and another letter, number, or underscore is considered a non-word boundary and is replaced by an | in the example. However, what is slightly confusing is that the boundary between two non-word characters, such as an exclamation mark and a comma, is also considered a non-word boundary. If you think about it, it actually does make sense, but it's easy to forget when creating regular expressions.

You'll remember this example from when you started looking at regular expressions:

```
<!DOCTYPE html>

<html lang="en">
<head>
```

```
        <title>Chapter 6, Figure 2</title>
    </head>
    <body>
        <script>
            var myString = "Paul, Paula, Pauline, paul, Paul";
            var myRegExp = /Paul/gi;

            myString = myString.replace(myRegExp, "Ringo");
            alert(myString);
        </script>
    </body>
</html>
```

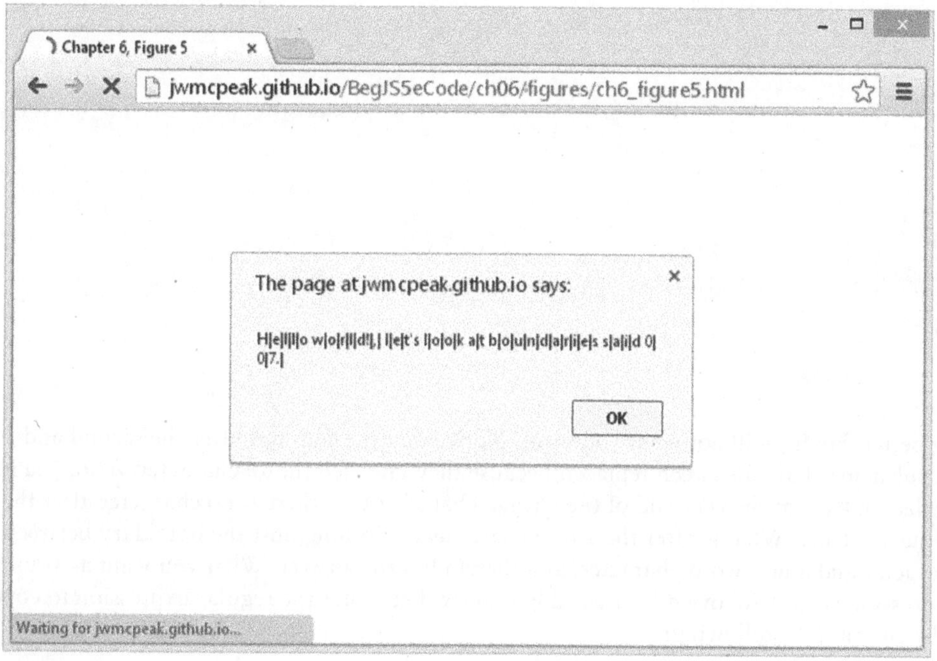

FIGURE 6-5

You used this code to convert all instances of Paul or paul to Ringo.

However, you found that this code actually converts all instances of Paul to Ringo, even when the word Paul is inside another word.

One way to solve this problem would be to replace the string Paul only where it is followed by a non-word character. The special character for non-word characters is \W, so you need to alter the regular expression to the following:

```
    var myRegExp = /Paul\W/gi;
```

This gives the result shown in Figure 6-6.

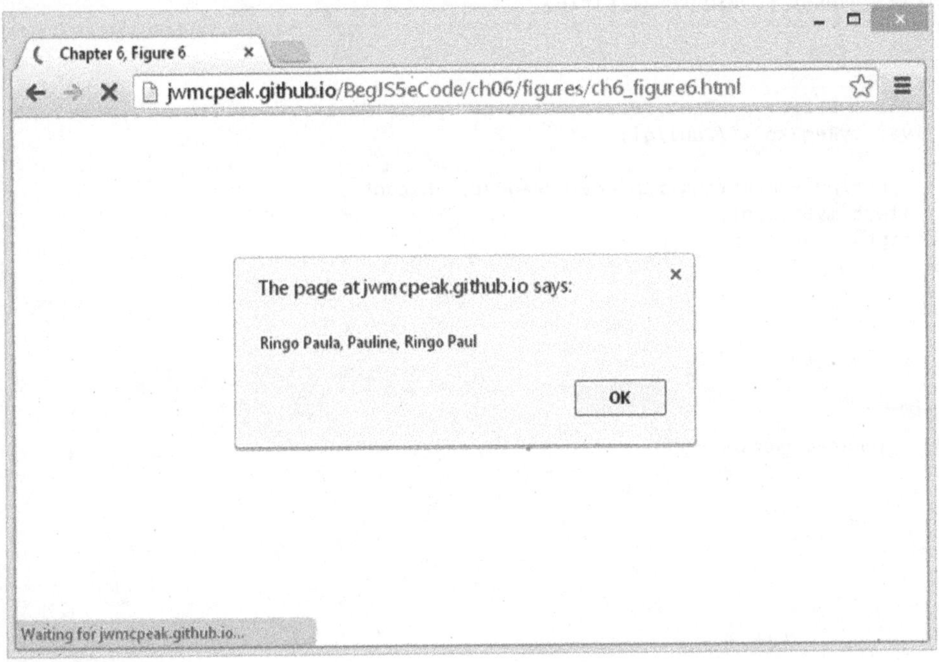

FIGURE 6-6

It's getting better, but it's still not what you want. Notice that the commas after the second and third `Paul` substrings have also been replaced because they matched the `\W` character. Also, you're still not replacing `Paul` at the very end of the string. That's because there is no character after the letter l in the last `Paul`. What is after the l in the last `Paul`? Nothing, just the boundary between a word character and a non-word character, and therein lies the answer. What you want as your regular expression is `Paul` followed by a word boundary. Let's alter the regular expression to cope with that by entering the following:

```
var myRegExp = /Paul\b/gi;
```

Now you get the result you want, as shown in Figure 6-7.

At last you've got it right, and this example is finished.

Covering All Eventualities

Perhaps the trickiest thing about a regular expression is making sure it covers all eventualities. In the previous example your regular expression works with the string as defined, but does it work with the following?

```
var myString = "Paul, Paula, Pauline, paul, Paul, JeanPaul";
```

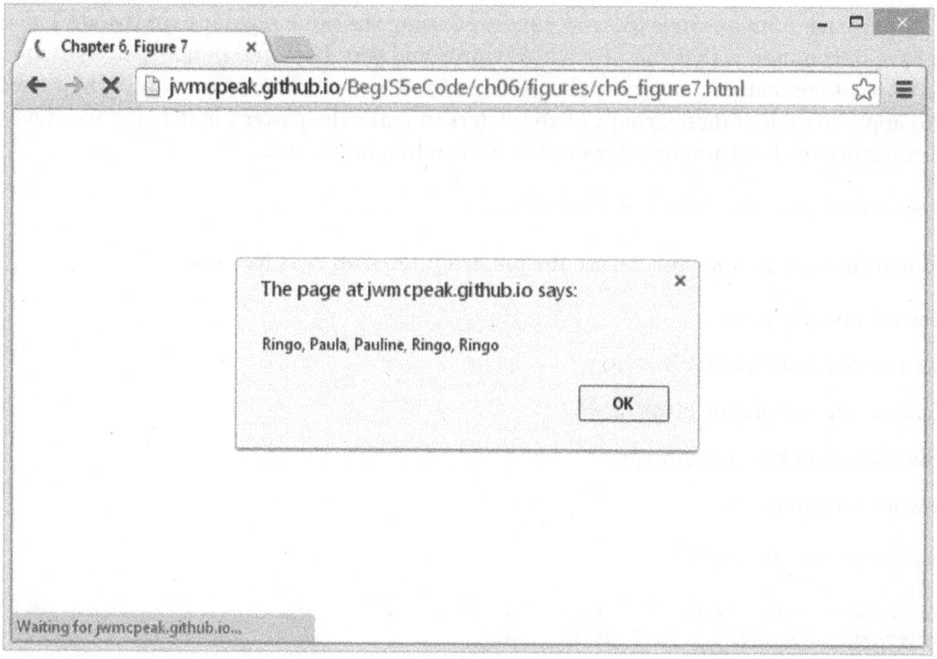

FIGURE 6-7

Here the `Paul` substring in `JeanPaul` will be changed to `Ringo`. You really only want to convert the substring `Paul` where it is on its own, with a word boundary on either side. If you change your regular expression code to:

```
var myRegExp = /\bPaul\b/gi;
```

you have your final answer and can be sure only `Paul` or `paul` will ever be matched.

Grouping Regular Expressions

The final topic under regular expressions, before you look at examples using the `match()`, `replace()`, and `search()` methods, is how you can group expressions. In fact, it's quite easy. If you want a number of expressions to be treated as a single group, you just enclose them in parentheses, for example, `/(\d\d)/`. Parentheses in regular expressions are special characters that group together character patterns and are not themselves part of the characters to be matched.

Why would you want to do this? Well, by grouping characters into patterns, you can use the special repetition characters to apply to the whole group of characters, rather than just one.

Let's take the following string defined in `myString` as an example:

```
var myString = "JavaScript, VBScript and PHP";
```

How could you match both JavaScript and VBScript using the same regular expression? The only thing they have in common is that they are whole words and they both end in Script. Well, an easy way would be to use parentheses to group the patterns Java and VB. Then you can use the ? special character to apply to each of these groups of characters to make the pattern match any word having zero or one instance of the characters Java or VB, and ending in Script:

```
var myRegExp = /\b(VB)?(Java)?Script\b/gi;
```

Breaking down this expression, you can see the pattern it requires is as follows:

1. **A word boundary:** \b
2. **Zero or one instance of VB:** (VB)?
3. **Zero or one instance of Java:** (Java)?
4. **The characters** Script: Script
5. **A word boundary:** \b

Putting these together, you get this:

```
var myString = "JavaScript, VBScript and PHP";
var myRegExp = /\b(VB)?(Java)?Script\b/gi;
myString = myString.replace(myRegExp, "xxxx");
alert(myString);
```

The output of this code is shown in Figure 6-8.

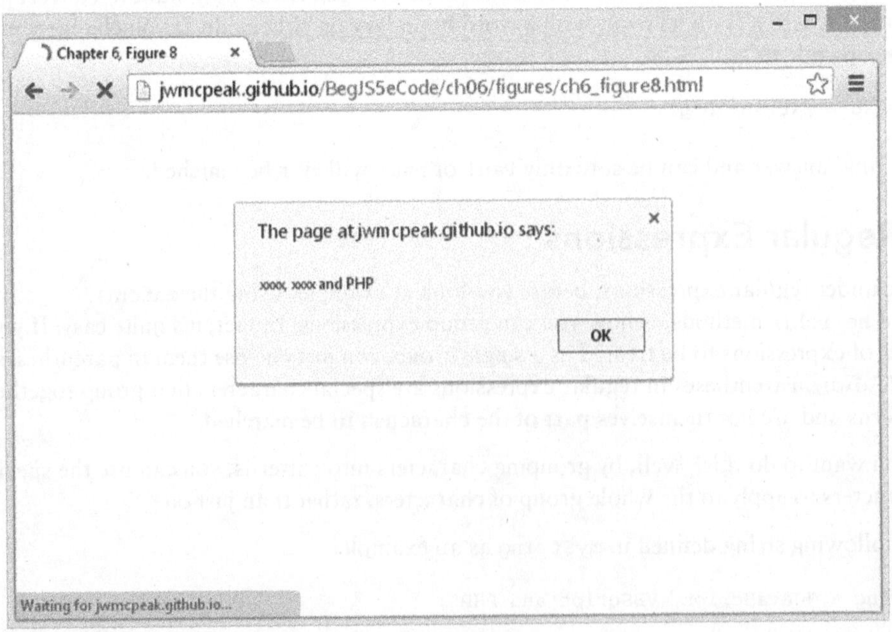

FIGURE: 6-8

If you look back at the special repetition characters table, you'll see that they apply to the item preceding them. This can be a character, or, where they have been grouped by means of parentheses, the previous group of characters.

However, there is a potential problem with the regular expression you just defined. As well as matching VBScript and JavaScript, it also matches VBJavaScript. This is clearly not exactly what you meant.

To get around this you need to make use of both grouping and the special character |, which is the alternation character. It has an or-like meaning, similar to || in if statements, and will match the characters on either side of itself.

Let's think about the problem again. You want the pattern to match VBScript or JavaScript. Clearly they have the Script part in common. So what you want is a new word starting with Java or starting with VB; either way, it must end in Script.

First, you know that the word must start with a word boundary:

```
\b
```

Next you know that you want either VB or Java to be at the start of the word. You've just seen that in regular expressions | provides the "or" you need, so in regular expression syntax you want the following:

```
\b(VB|Java)
```

This matches the pattern VB or Java. Now you can just add the Script part:

```
\b(VB|Java)Script\b
```

Your final code looks like this:

```
var myString = "JavaScript, VBScript and Perl";
var myRegExp = /\b(VB|Java)Script\b/gi;
myString = myString.replace(myRegExp, "xxxx");
alert(myString);
```

Reusing Groups of Characters

You can reuse the pattern specified by a group of characters later on in the regular expression. To refer to a previous group of characters, you just type \ and a number indicating the order of the group. For example, you can refer to the first group as \1, the second as \2, and so on.

Let's look at an example. Say you have a list of numbers in a string, with each number separated by a comma. For whatever reason, you are not allowed to have two instances of the same number in a row, so although

```
009,007,001,002,004,003
```

would be okay, the following:

```
007,007,001,002,002,003
```

would not be valid, because you have 007 and 002 repeated after themselves.

How can you find instances of repeated digits and replace them with the word ERROR? You need to use the ability to refer to groups in regular expressions.

First, let's define the string as follows:

```
var myString = "007,007,001,002,002,003,002,004";
```

Now you know you need to search for a series of one or more number characters. In regular expressions the \d specifies any digit character, and + means one or more of the previous character. So far, that gives you this regular expression:

```
\d+
```

You want to match a series of digits followed by a comma, so you just add the comma:

```
\d+,
```

This will match any series of digits followed by a comma, but how do you search for any series of digits followed by a comma, then followed again by the same series of digits? Because the digits could be any digits, you can't add them directly into the expression like so:

```
\d+,007
```

This would not work with the 002 repeat. What you need to do is put the first series of digits in a group; then you can specify that you want to match that group of digits again. You can do this with \1, which says, "Match the characters found in the first group defined using parentheses." Put all this together, and you have the following:

```
(\d+),\1
```

This defines a group whose pattern of characters is one or more digit characters. This group must be followed by a comma and then by the same pattern of characters as in the first group. Put this into some JavaScript, and you have the following:

```
var myString = "007,007,001,002,002,003,002,004";
var myRegExp = /(\d+),\1/g;
myString = myString.replace(myRegExp, "ERROR");
alert(myString);
```

The alert box will show this message:

```
ERROR,1,ERROR,003,002,004
```

That completes your brief look at regular expression syntax. Because regular expressions can get a little complex, it's often a good idea to start simple and build them up slowly, as in the previous example. In fact, most regular expressions are just too hard to get right in one step—at least for us mere mortals without a brain the size of a planet.

If it's still looking a bit strange and confusing, don't panic. In the next sections, you look at the String object's split(), replace(), search(), and match() methods with plenty more examples of regular expression syntax.

THE STRING OBJECT

The main functions making use of regular expressions are the String object's split(), replace(), search(), and match() methods. You've already seen their syntax, so in this section you concentrate on their use with regular expressions and at the same time learn more about regular expression syntax and usage.

The split() Method

You've seen that the split() method enables you to split a string into various pieces, with the split being made at the character or characters specified as a parameter. The result of this method is an array with each element containing one of the split pieces. For example, the following string:

```
var myListString = "apple, banana, peach, orange"
```

could be split into an array in which each element contains a different fruit, like this:

```
var myFruitArray = myListString.split(", ");
```

How about if your string is this instead?

```
var myListString = "apple, 0.99, banana, 0.50, peach, 0.25, orange, 0.75";
```

The string could, for example, contain both the names and prices of the fruit. How could you split the string, but retrieve only the names of the fruit and not the prices? You could do it without regular expressions, but it would take many lines of code. With regular expressions you can use the same code and just amend the split() method's parameter.

TRY IT OUT Splitting the Fruit String

Let's create an example that solves the problem just described—it must split your string, but include only the fruit names, not the prices:

```
<!DOCTYPE html>

<html lang="en">
<head>
    <title>Chapter 6, Example 3</title>
</head>
<body>
    <script>
        var myListString = "apple, 0.99, banana, 0.50, peach, 0.25, orange, 0.75";
        var theRegExp = /[^a-z]+/i;
        var myFruitArray = myListString.split(theRegExp);

        document.write(myFruitArray.join("<br />"));
    </script>
</body>
</html>
```

Save the file as ch6_example3.html and load it in your browser. You should see the four fruits from your string written out to the page, with each fruit on a separate line.

Within the script block, first you have your string with fruit names and prices:

```
var myListString = "apple, 0.99, banana, 0.50, peach, 0.25, orange, 0.75";
```

How do you split it in such a way that only the fruit names are included? Your first thought might be to use the comma as the split() method's parameter, but of course that means you end up with the prices. What you have to ask is, "What is it that's between the items I want?" Or in other words, what is between the fruit names that you can use to define your split? The answer is that various characters are between the names of the fruit, such as a comma, a space, numbers, a full stop, more numbers, and finally another comma. What is it that these things have in common and makes them different from the fruit names that you want? What they have in common is that none of them are letters from a through z. If you say "Split the string at the point where there is a group of characters that are not between a and z," then you get the result you want. Now you know what you need to create your regular expression.

You know that what you want is not the letters a through z, so you start with this:

```
[^a-z]
```

The ^ says "Match any character that does not match those specified inside the square brackets." In this case you've specified a range of characters not to be matched—all the characters between a and z. As specified, this expression will match only one character, whereas you want to split wherever there is a single group of one or more characters that are not between a and z. To do this you need to add the + special repetition character, which says "Match one or more of the preceding character or group specified":

```
[^a-z]+
```

The final result is this:

```
var theRegExp = /[^a-z]+/i
```

The / and / characters mark the start and end of the regular expression whose RegExp object is stored as a reference in the variable theRegExp. You add the i on the end to make the match case-insensitive.

Don't panic if creating regular expressions seems like a frustrating and less-than-obvious process. At first, it takes a lot of trial and error to get it right, but as you get more experienced, you'll find creating them becomes much easier and will enable you to do things that without regular expressions would be either very awkward or virtually impossible.

In the next line of script you pass the RegExp object to the split() method, which uses it to decide where to split the string:

```
var myFruitArray = myListString.split(theRegExp);
```

After the split, the variable myFruitArray will contain an Array with each element containing the fruit name, as shown here:

ARRAY ELEMENT INDEX	0	1	2	3
Element value	apple	banana	peach	orange

You then join the string together again using the `Array` object's `join()` methods, which you saw in Chapter 4:

```
document.write(myFruitArray.join("<br />"))
```

The replace() Method

You've already looked at the syntax and usage of the `replace()` method. However, something unique to the `replace()` method is its ability to replace text based on the groups matched in the regular expression. You do this using the $ sign and the group's number. Each group in a regular expression is given a number from 1 to 99; any groups greater than 99 are not accessible. To refer to a group, you write $ followed by the group's position. For example, if you had the following:

```
var myRegExp = /(\d)(\W)/g;
```

then $1 refers to the group(\d), and $2 refers to the group (\W). You've also set the global flag g to ensure that all matching patterns are replaced—not just the first one.

You can see this more clearly in the next example. Say you have the following string:

```
var myString = "2012, 2013, 2014";
```

If you wanted to change this to `"the year 2012, the year 2013, the year 2014"`, how could you do it with regular expressions?

First, you need to work out the pattern as a regular expression, in this case four digits:

```
var myRegExp = /\d{4}/g;
```

But given that the year is different every time, how can you substitute the year value into the replaced string?

Well, you change your regular expression so that it's inside a group, as follows:

```
var myRegExp = /(\d{4})/g;
```

Now you can use the group, which has group number 1, inside the replacement string like this:

```
myString = myString.replace(myRegExp, "the year $1");
```

The variable `myString` now contains the required string
`"the year 2012, the year 2013, the year 2014"`.

Let's look at another example in which you want to convert single quotes in text to double quotes. Your test string is this:

```
He then said 'My Name is O'Connerly, yes that's right, O'Connerly'.
```

One problem that the test string makes clear is that you want to replace the single-quote mark with a double only where it is used in pairs around speech, not when it is acting as an apostrophe, such as in the word that's, or when it's part of someone's name, such as in O'Connerly.

Let's start by defining the regular expression. First, you know that it must include a single quote, as shown in the following code:

```
var myRegExp = /'/;
```

However, as it is this would replace every single quote, which is not what you want.

Looking at the text, you should also notice that quotes are always at the start or end of a word—that is, at a boundary. On first glance it might be easy to assume that it would be a word boundary. However, don't forget that the ' is a non-word character, so the boundary will be between it and another non-word character, such as a space. So the boundary will be a non-word boundary or, in other words, \B.

Therefore, the character pattern you are looking for is either a non-word boundary followed by a single quote or a single quote followed by a non-word boundary. The key is the "or," for which you use | in regular expressions. This leaves your regular expression as the following:

```
var myRegExp = /\B'|'\B/g;
```

This will match the pattern on the left of the | or the character pattern on the right. You want to replace all the single quotes with double quotes, so the g has been added at the end, indicating that a global match should take place.

TRY IT OUT   Replacing Single Quotes with Double Quotes

Let's look at an example using the regular expression just defined:

```
<!DOCTYPE html>

<html lang="en">
<head>
    <title>Chapter 6, Example 4</title>
</head>
<body>
    <script>
        var text = "He then said 'My Name is O'Connerly, yes " +
                   "that's right, O'Connerly'";

        document.write("Original: " + text + "<br/>");

        var myRegExp = /\B'|'\B/g;
        text = text.replace(myRegExp, '"');

        document.write("Corrected: " + text);
    </script>
</body>
</html>
```

Save the page as ch6 _ example4.html. Load the page into your browser and you should see what is shown in Figure 6-9.

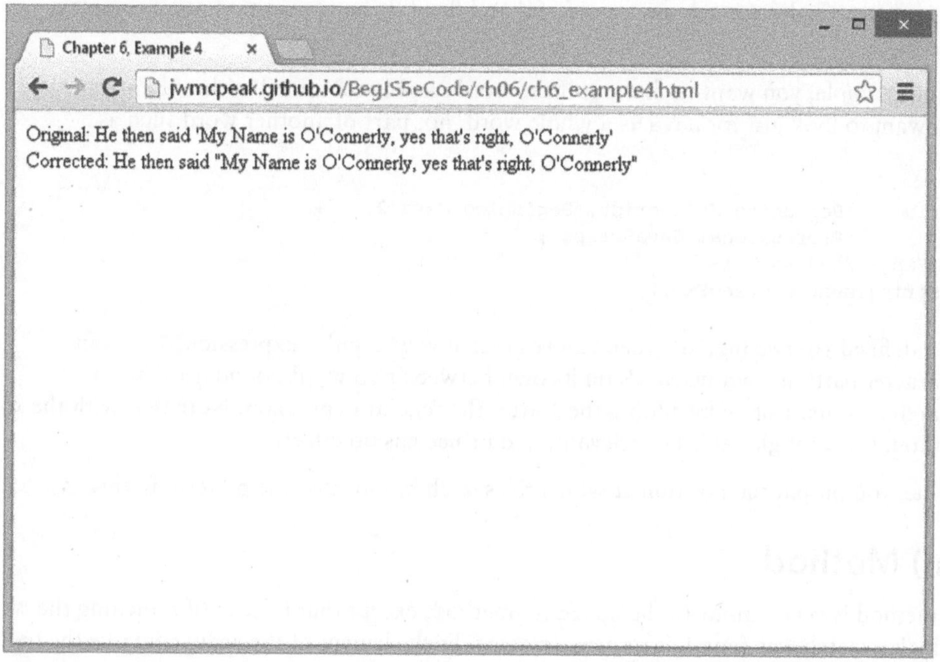

FIGURE 6-9

You can see that by using regular expressions, you have completed a task in a couple of lines of simple code. Without regular expressions, it would probably take four or five times that amount.

The workhorses of this code are two simple lines:

```
var myRegExp = /\B'|'\B/g;
text = text.replace(myRegExp, '"');
```

You define your regular expression (as discussed previously), which matches any non-word boundary followed by a single quote or any single quote followed by a non-word boundary. For example, 'H will match, as will H', but O'R won't, because the quote is between two word boundaries. Don't forget that a word boundary is the position between the start or end of a word and a non-word character, such as a space or punctuation mark.

The second line of code uses the replace() method to do the character pattern search and replace, and assigns the new value to the text variable.

The search() Method

The search() method enables you to search a string for a pattern of characters. If the pattern is found, the character position at which it was found is returned; otherwise, -1 is returned. The method takes only one parameter, the RegExp object you have created.

Although for basic searches the indexOf() method is fine, if you want more complex searches, such as a search for a pattern of any digits or one in which a word must be in between a certain boundary, search() provides a much more powerful and flexible, but sometimes more complex, approach.

In the following example, you want to find out if the word Java is contained within the string. However, you want to look just for Java as a whole word, not part of another word such as JavaScript:

```
var myString = "Beginning JavaScript, Beginning Java 2, " +
               "Professional JavaScript";
var myRegExp = /\bJava\b/i;
alert(myString.search(myRegExp));
```

First, you have defined your string, and then you've created your regular expression. You want to find the character pattern Java when it's on its own between two word boundaries. You've made your search case-insensitive by adding the i after the regular expression. Note that with the search() method, the g for global is not relevant, and its use has no effect.

On the final line, you output the position at which the search has located the pattern, in this case 32.

The match() Method

The match() method is very similar to the search() method, except that instead of returning the position at which a match was found, it returns an array. Each element of the array contains the text of a match made.

For example, if you had the string:

```
var myString = "The years were 2012, 2013 and 2014";
```

and wanted to extract the years from this string, you could do so using the match() method. To match each year, you are looking for four digits in between word boundaries. This requirement translates to the following regular expression:

```
var myRegExp = /\b\d{4}\b/g;
```

You want to match all the years, so the g has been added to the end for a global search.

To do the match and store the results, you use the match() method and store the Array object it returns in a variable:

```
var resultsArray = myString.match(myRegExp);
```

To prove it has worked, let's use some code to output each item in the array. You've added an if statement to double-check that the results array actually contains an array. If no matches were made, the results array will contain null—doing if (resultsArray) will return true if the variable has a value and not null:

```
if (resultsArray) {
  for (var index = 0; index < resultsArray.length; index++) {
```

```
        alert(resultsArray[index]);
    }
}
```

This would result in three `alert` boxes containing the numbers 2012, 2013, and 2014.

TRY IT OUT Splitting HTML

In this example, you want to take a string of HTML and split it into its component parts. For example, you want the HTML `<p>Hello</p>` to become an array, with the elements having the following contents:

| `<p>` | Hello | `</p>` |

```html
<!DOCTYPE html>

<html lang="en">
<head>
    <title>Chapter 6, Example 5</title>
</head>
    <body>
        <div id="output"></div>
        <script>
            var html = "<h2>Hello World!</h2>" +
                "<p>We love JavaScript!</p>";

            var regex = /<[^>\r\n]+>|[^<>\r\n]+/g;
            var results = html.match(regex);

            document.getElementById("output").innerText = results.join("\r\n");
        </script>
    </body>
</html>
```

Save this file as `ch6_example5.html`. When you load the page into your browser you'll see that the string of HTML is split, with each element's tags and content displayed on separate lines, as shown in Figure 6-10.

Once again, the code that makes all of this work consists of just a few lines. You first create a `RegExp` object and initialize it to your regular expression:

```
var regex = /<[^>\r\n]+>|[^<>\r\n]+/g;
```

Let's break it down to see what pattern you're trying to match. First, note that the pattern is broken up by an alternation symbol: |. This means that you want the pattern on the left or the right of this symbol. Look at these patterns separately. On the left, you have the following:

➤   The pattern must start with a `<`.

➤   In `[^>\r\n]` +, you specify that you want one or more of any character except the `>` or a `\r` (carriage return) or a `\n` (linefeed).

➤   `>` specifies that the pattern must end with a `>`.

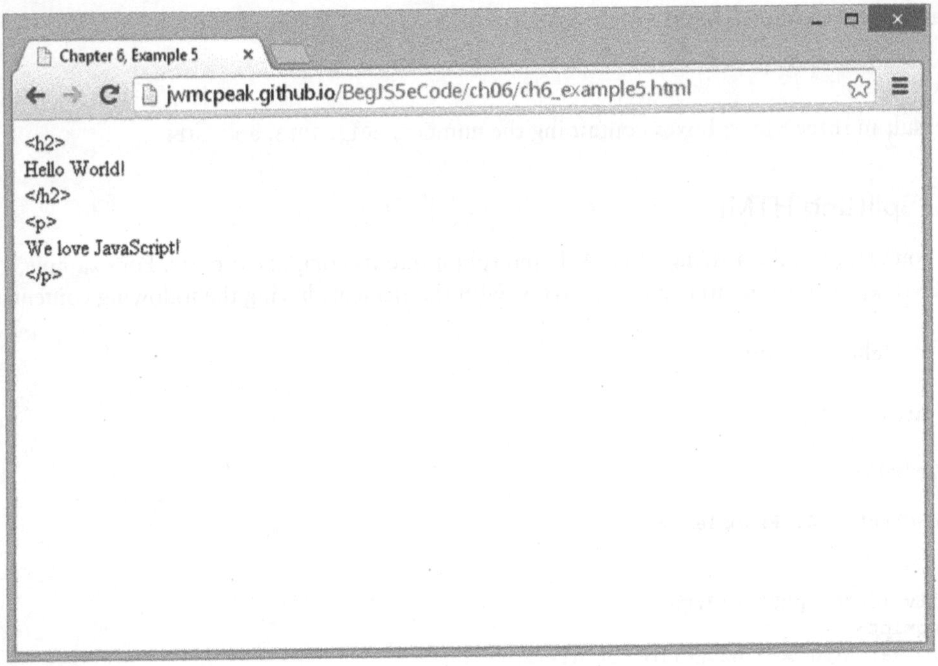

FIGURE 6-10

On the right, you have only the following:

➤ `[^<>\r\n]+` specifies that the pattern is one or more of any character, so long as that character is not a `<`, `>`, `\r`, or `\n`. This will match plaintext.

After the regular expression definition you have a g, which specifies that this is a global match.

So the `<[^>\r\n]+>` regular expression will match any start or close tags, such as `<p>` or `</p>`. The alternative pattern is `[^<>\r\n]+`, which will match any character pattern that is not an opening or closing tag.

In the following line, you assign the `results` variable to the `Array` object returned by the `match()` method:

```
var results = html.match(regex);
```

The remainder of the code populates a `<div/>` element with the split HTML:

```
document.getElementById("output").innerText = results.join("\r\n");
```

This code uses features you haven't yet seen. It essentially retrieves the element that has an id value of `output`; this is the `<div/>` element at the top of the body. The `innerText` property enables you to set the text inside of the `<div/>` element. You learn more in later chapters.

You then use the `Array` object's `join()` method to join all the array's elements into one string with each element separated by a `\r\n` character, so that each tag or piece of text goes on a separate line.

USING THE REGEXP OBJECT'S CONSTRUCTOR

So far you've been creating RegExp objects using the / and / characters to define the start and end of the regular expression, as shown in the following example:

```
var myRegExp = /[a-z]/;
```

Although this is the generally preferred method, it was briefly mentioned that a RegExp object can also be created by means of the RegExp() constructor. You might use the first way most of the time. However, on some occasions the second way of creating a RegExp object is necessary (for example, when a regular expression is to be constructed from user input).

As an example, the preceding regular expression could equally well be defined as:

```
var myRegExp = new RegExp("[a-z]");
```

Here you pass the regular expression as a string parameter to the RegExp() constructor function.

A very important difference when you are using this method is in how you use special regular expression characters, such as \b, that have a backward slash in front of them. The problem is that the backward slash indicates an escape character in JavaScript strings—for example, you may use \b, which means a backspace. To differentiate between \b meaning a backspace in a string and the \b special character in a regular expression, you have to put another backward slash in front of the regular expression special character. So \b becomes \\b when you mean the regular expression \b that matches a word boundary, rather than a backspace character.

For example, say you have defined your RegExp object using the following:

```
var myRegExp = /\b/;
```

To declare it using the RegExp() constructor, you would need to write this:

```
var myRegExp = new RegExp("\\b");
```

and not this:

```
var myRegExp = new RegExp("\b");
```

All special regular expression characters, such as \w, \b, \d, and so on, must have an extra \ in front when you create them using RegExp().

When you define regular expressions with the / and / method, after the final / you could add the special flags m, g, and i to indicate that the pattern matching should be multi-line, global, or case-insensitive, respectively. When using the RegExp() constructor, how can you do the same thing?

Easy. The optional second parameter of the RegExp() constructor takes the flags that specify a global or case-insensitive match. For example, this will do a global case-insensitive pattern match:

```
var myRegExp = new RegExp("hello\\b","gi");
```

You can specify just one of the flags if you want—such as the following:

```
var myRegExp = new RegExp("hello\\b","i");
```

or

```
var myRegExp = new RegExp("hello\\b","g");
```

TRY IT OUT   Form Validation Module

In this Try It Out, you create a set of useful JavaScript functions that use regular expressions to validate the following:

➤   Telephone numbers

➤   Postal codes

➤   E-mail addresses

The validation only checks the format. So, for example, it can't check that the telephone number actually exists, only that it would be valid if it did.

First is the .js code file with the input validation code. Please note that the lines of code in the following block are too wide for the book—make sure each regular expression is contained on one line:

```
function isValidTelephoneNumber(telephoneNumber) {
    var telRegExp = /^(\+\d{1,3} ?)?(\(\d{1,5}\)|\d{1,5})
        ?\d{3}?\d{0,7}( (x|xtn|ext|extn|pax|pbx|extension)?\.? ?\d{2-5})?$/i;
    return telRegExp.test(telephoneNumber);
}

function isValidPostalCode(postalCode) {
    var pcodeRegExp = /^(\d{5}(-\d{4})?|([a-z] [a-z] ?\d\d?|[a-z{2}\d[a-z])
        ?\d[a-z] [a-z])$/i;
    return pcodeRegExp.test(postalCode);
}

function isValidEmail(emailAddress) {
    var emailRegExp = /^((([^<>()[\]\\.,;:@"\x00-\x20\x7F]|\\.)+|(""("([^\x0A\x0D"\\]
        |\\\\)+""")))@(([a-z]|#\d+?)([a-z0-9-]|#\d+?)*([a-z0-9]
        |#\d+?)\.)+([a-z]{2,4})$/i;
    return emailRegExp.test(emailAddress);
}
```

Save this as ch6 _ example6.js.

To test the code, you need a simple page:

```
<!DOCTYPE html>

<html lang="en">
```

```
<head>
    <title>Chapter 6, Example 6</title>
</head>
    <body>
        <script src="ch6_example6.js"></script>
        <script>
            var phoneNumber = prompt("Please enter a phone number.", "");

            if (isValidTelephoneNumber(phoneNumber)) {
                alert("Valid Phone Number");
            } else {
                alert("Invalid Phone Number");
            }

            var postalCode = prompt("Please enter a postal code.", "");

            if (isValidPostalCode(postalCode)) {
                alert("Valid Postal Code");
            } else {
                alert("Invalid Postal Code");
            }

            var email = prompt("Please enter an email address.", "");

            if (isValidEmail(email)) {
                alert("Valid Email Address");
            } else {
                alert("Invalid Email Address");
            }
        </script>
    </body>
</html>
```

Save this as `ch6_example6.html` and load it into your browser, and you'll be prompted to enter a phone number. Enter a valid telephone number (for example, +1 (123) 123 4567), and you'll see a message that states whether or not the phone number is valid.

You'll then be prompted to enter a postal code and an e-mail. Enter those values to test those functions. This is pretty basic, but it's sufficient for testing your code.

The actual code is very simple, but the regular expressions are tricky to create, so let's look at those in depth starting with telephone number validation.

Telephone Number Validation

Telephone numbers are more of a challenge to validate. The problems are:

➤ Phone numbers differ from country to country.

➤ A valid number can be entered in different ways (for example, with or without the national or international code).

For this regular expression, you need to specify more than just the valid characters; you also need to specify the format of the data. For example, all of the following are valid:

> +1 (123) 123 4567
>
> +1123123 456
>
> +44 (123) 123 4567
>
> +44 (123) 123 4567 ext 123
>
> +44 20 7893 4567

The variations that your regular expression needs to deal with (optionally separated by spaces) are shown in the following table:

The international number	"+" followed by one to three digits (optional)
The local area code	Two to five digits, sometimes in parentheses (compulsory)
The actual subscriber number	Three to 10 digits, sometimes with spaces (compulsory)
An extension number	Two to five digits, preceded by x, xtn, extn, pax, pbx, or extension, and sometimes in parentheses

Obviously, this won't work in some countries, which is something you'd need to deal with based on where your customers and partners would be. The following regular expression is rather complex (its length meant it had to be split across two lines; make sure you type it in on one line):

```
^(\+\d{1,3} ?)?(\(\d{1,5}\)|\d{1,5}) ?\d{3} ?\d{0,7}
( (x|xtn|ext|extn|pax|pbx|extension)?\.? ?\d{2-5})?$
```

You will need to set the case-insensitive flag with this, as well as the explicit capture option. Although this seems complex, if broken down, it's quite straightforward.

Let's start with the pattern that matches an international dialing code:

```
(\+\d{1,3} ?)?
```

So far, you're matching a plus sign (\+) followed by one to three digits (\d{1,3}) and an optional space (?). Remember that because the + character is a special character, you add a \ character in front of it to specify that you mean an actual + character. The characters are wrapped inside parentheses to specify a group of characters. You allow an optional space and match this entire group of characters zero or one time, as indicated by the ? character after the closing parenthesis of the group.

Next is the pattern to match an area code:

```
(\(\d{1,5}\)|\d{1,5})
```

This pattern is contained in parentheses, which designate it as a group of characters, and matches either one to five digits in parentheses ((\(\d{1,5}\))) or just one to five digits (\d{1,5}). Again, because the parenthesis characters are special characters in regular expression syntax and you want to match actual parentheses, you need the \ character in front of them. Also note the use of the pipe symbol (|), which means "OR" or "match either of these two patterns."

Next, let's match the subscriber number:

```
?\d{3,4} ?\d{0,7}
```

> **NOTE** The initial space and ? mean "match zero or one space." This is followed by three or four digits (\d{3,4})—although U.S. numbers always have three digits, UK numbers often have four. Then there's another "zero or one space," and, finally, between zero and seven digits (\d{0,7}).

Finally, add the part to cope with an optional extension number:

```
( (x|xtn|ext|extn|extension)?\.? ?\d{2-5})?
```

This group is optional because its parentheses are followed by a question mark. The group itself checks for a space, optionally followed by x, ext, xtn, extn, or extension, followed by zero or one period (note the \ character, because . is a special character in regular expression syntax), followed by zero or one space, followed by between two and five digits. Putting these four patterns together, you can construct the entire regular expression, apart from the surrounding syntax. The regular expression starts with ^ and ends with $. The ^ character specifies that the pattern must be matched at the beginning of the string, and the $ character specifies that the pattern must be matched at the end of the string. This means that the string must match the pattern completely; it cannot contain any other characters before or after the pattern that is matched.

Therefore, with the regular expression explained, let's look once again at the isValidTelephoneNumber() function in ch6_example6.js:

```
function isValidTelephoneNumber(telephoneNumber) {
    var telRegExp = /^(\+\d{1,3} ?)?(\(\d{1,5}\)|\d{1,5}) ?\d{3}
        ?\d{0,7}( (x|xtn|ext|extn|pax|pbx|extension)?\.? ?\d{2-5})?$/i;
    return telRegExp.test( telephoneNumber );
}
```

Note in this case that it is important to set the case-insensitive flag by adding an i on the end of the expression definition; otherwise, the regular expression could fail to match the ext parts. Please also note that the regular expression itself must be on one line in your code—it's shown in multiple lines here due to the page-width restrictions of this book.

Validating a Postal Code

We just about managed to check worldwide telephone numbers, but doing the same for postal codes would be something of a major challenge. Instead, you'll create a function that only checks for

U.S. ZIP codes and UK postcodes. If you needed to check for other countries, the code would need modifying. You may find that checking more than one or two postal codes in one regular expression begins to get unmanageable, and it may well be easier to have an individual regular expression for each country's postal code you need to check. For this purpose though, let's combine the regular expression for the United Kingdom and the United States:

```
^(\d{5}(-\d{4})?|[a-z][a-z]?\d\d? ?\d[a-z][a-z])$
```

This is actually in two parts. The first part checks for ZIP codes, and the second part checks for UK postcodes. Start by looking at the ZIP code part.

ZIP codes can be represented in one of two formats: as five digits (12345), or five digits followed by a dash and four digits (12345-1234). The ZIP code regular expression to match these is as follows:

```
\d{5}(-\d{4})?
```

This matches five digits, followed by an optional non-capturing group that matches a dash, followed by four digits.

For a regular expression that covers UK postcodes, let's consider their various formats. UK postcode formats are one or two letters followed by either one or two digits, followed by an optional space, followed by a digit, and then two letters. Additionally, some central London postcodes look like SE2V 3ER, with a letter at the end of the first part. Currently, only some of those postcodes start with SE, WC, and W, but that may change. Valid examples of UK postcodes include: CH3 9DR, PR29 1XX, M27 1AE, WC1V 2ER, and C27 3AH.

Based on this, the required pattern is as follows:

```
([a-z][a-z]?\d\d?|[a-z]{2}\d[a-z]) ?\d[a-z][a-z]
```

These two patterns are combined using the | character to "match one or the other" and grouped using parentheses. You then add the ^ character at the start and the $ character at the end of the pattern to be sure that the only information in the string is the postal code. Although postal codes should be uppercase, it is still valid for them to be lowercase, so you also set the case-insensitive option as follows when you use the regular expression:

```
^(\d{5}(-\d{4})?|([a-z][a-z]?\d\d?|[a-z]{2}\d[a-z]) ?\d[a-z][a-z])$
```

Just for reference, let's look once again at the isValidPostalCode() function:

```
function isValidPostalCode(postalCode) {
    var pcodeRegExp = /^(\d{5}(-\d{4})?|([a-z][a-z]?\d\d?|[a-z]{2}\d[a-z])
        ?\d[a-z][a-z])$/i;
    return pcodeRegExp.test( postalCode );
}
```

Again, remember that the regular expression must be on one line in your code.

Validating an E-mail Address

Before working on a regular expression to match e-mail addresses, you need to look at the types of valid e-mail addresses you can have. For example:

➤ `someone@mailserver.com`

➤ `someone@mailserver.info`

➤ `someone.something@mailserver.com`

➤ `someone.something@subdomain.mailserver.com`

➤ `someone@mailserver.co.uk`

➤ `someone@subdomain.mailserver.co.uk`

➤ `someone.something@mailserver.co.uk`

➤ `someone@mailserver.org.uk`

➤ `some.one@subdomain.mailserver.org.uk`

Also, if you examine the SMTP RFC (`http://www.ietf.org/rfc/rfc0821.txt`), you can have the following:

➤ `someone@123.113.209.32`

➤ `"""Paul Wilton"""@somedomain.com`

That's quite a list, and it contains many variations to cope with. It's best to start by breaking it down. First, note that the latter two versions are exceptionally rare and not provided for in the regular expression you'll create.

Second, you need to break up the e-mail address into separate parts. Let's look at the part after the @ symbol first.

Validating a Domain Name

Everything has become more complicated since Unicode domain names have been allowed. However, the e-mail RFC still doesn't allow these, so let's stick with the traditional definition of how a domain can be described using ASCII. A domain name consists of a dot-separated list of words, with the last word being between two and four characters long. It was often the case that if a two-letter country word was used, there would be at least two parts to the domain name before it: a grouping domain (.co, .ac, and so on) and a specific domain name. However, with the advent of the .tv names, this is no longer the case. You could make this very specific and provide for the allowed top-level domains (TLDs), but that would make the regular expression very large, and it would be more productive to perform a DNS lookup instead.

Each part of a domain name must follow certain rules. It can contain any letter or number or a hyphen, but it must start with a letter. The exception is that, at any point in the domain name, you can use a #, followed by a number, which represents the ASCII code for that letter, or in Unicode, the 16-bit Unicode value. Knowing this, let's begin to build up the regular expression, first with the name part, assuming that the case-insensitive flag will be set later in the code:

```
([a-z]|#\d+)([a-z0-9-]|#\d+)*([a-z0-9]|#\d+)
```

This breaks the domain into three parts. The RFC doesn't specify how many digits can be contained here, so neither will we. The first part must only contain an ASCII letter; the second must contain zero or more of a letter, number, or hyphen; and the third must contain either a letter or number. The top-level domain has more restrictions, as shown here:

```
[a-z]{2,4}
```

This restricts you to a two-, three-, or four-letter top-level domain. So, putting it all together, with the periods you end up with this:

```
^((([a-z]|#\d+?)([a-z0-9-]|#\d+?)*([a-z0-9]|#\d+?)\.)+([a-z]{2,4})$
```

Again, the domain name is anchored at the beginning and end of the string. The first thing is to add an extra group to allow one or more name. portions and then anchor a two- to four-letter domain name at the end in its own group. We have also made most of the wildcards lazy. Because much of the pattern is similar, it makes sense to do this; otherwise, it would require too much backtracking. However, we have left the second group with a "greedy" wildcard: It will match as much as it can, up until it reaches a character that does not match. Then it will only backtrack one position to attempt the third group match. This is more resource-efficient than a lazy match is in this case, because it could be constantly going forward to attempt the match. One backtrack per name is an acceptable amount of extra processing.

Validating a Person's Address

You can now attempt to validate the part before the @ sign. The RFC specifies that it can contain any ASCII character with a code in the range from 33 to 126. You are assuming that you are matching against ASCII only, so you can assume that the engine will match against only 128 characters. This being the case, it is simpler to just exclude the required values as follows:

```
[^<>()\[\],;:@"\x00-\x20\x7F]+
```

Using this, you're saying that you allow any number of characters, as long as none of them are those contained within the square brackets. The square bracket and backslash characters ([,], and \) have to be escaped. However, the RFC allows for other kinds of matches.

Validating the Complete Address

Now that you have seen all the previous sections, you can build up a regular expression for the entire e-mail address. First, here's everything up to and including the @ sign:

```
^(([^<>()\[\],;:@"\x00-\x20\x7F]|\\.)+@
```

That was straightforward. Now for the domain name part:

```
^([^<>()\[\],;:@"\x00-\x20\x7F]|\\.)+@(([a-z]|#\d+?)([a-z0-9-]
|#\d+?)*([a-z0-9]|#\d+?)\.)+([a-z]{2,4})$
```

We've had to put it on two lines to fit this book's page width, but in your code this must all be on one line.

Finally, here's the `isValidEmail()` function for reference:

```
function isValidEmail(emailAddress) {
    var emailRegExp =
        /^(([^<>()\[\]\\.,;:@"\x00-\x20\x7F]|\\.)+|(""("([^\x0A\x0D"\\]|\\\\)+""))
        @(([a-z]|#\d+?)([a-z0-9-]|#\d+?)*([a-z0-9]|#\d+?)\.)
        +([a-z]{2,4})$/i;
    return emailRegExp.test( emailAddress );
}
```

Again, note the regular expression must all be on one line in your code.

SUMMARY

In this chapter you've looked at some more advanced methods of the String object and how you can optimize their use with regular expressions.

To recap, the chapter covered the following points:

➤ The split() method splits a single string into an array of strings. You pass a string or a regular expression to the method that determines where the split occurs.

➤ The replace() method enables you to replace a pattern of characters with another pattern that you specify as a second parameter.

➤ The search() method returns the character position of the first pattern matching the one given as a parameter.

➤ The match() method matches patterns, returning the text of the matches in an array.

➤ Regular expressions enable you to define a pattern of characters that you want to match. Using this pattern, you can perform splits, searches, text replacement, and matches on strings.

➤ In JavaScript, the regular expressions are in the form of a RegExp object. You can create a RegExp object using either myRegExp = /myRegularExpression/ or myRegExp = new RegExp("myRegularExpression"). The second form requires that certain special characters that normally have a single \ in front now have two.

➤ The g and i characters at the end of a regular expression (as in, for example, myRegExp = / Pattern/gi;) ensure that a global and case-insensitive match is made.

➤ As well as specifying actual characters, regular expressions have certain groups of special characters that allow any of certain groups of characters, such as digits, words, or non-word characters, to be matched.

➤ You can also use special characters to specify pattern or character repetition. Additionally, you can specify what the pattern boundaries must be—for example, at the beginning or end of the string, or next to a word or non-word boundary.

➤ Finally, you can define groups of characters that can be used later in the regular expression or in the results of using the expression with the `replace()` method.

In the next chapter, you take a look at using and manipulating dates and times using JavaScript, and time conversion between different world time zones. Also covered is how to create a timer that executes code at regular intervals after the page is loaded.

EXERCISES

You can find suggested solutions to these questions in Appendix A.

1. What problem does the following code solve?

```
var myString = "This sentence has has a fault and and we need to fix it."
var myRegExp = /(\b\w+\b) \1/g;
myString = myString.replace(myRegExp,"$1");
```

Now imagine that you change that code, so that you create the `RegExp` object like this:

```
var myRegExp = new RegExp("(\b\w+\b) \1");
```

Why would this not work, and how could you rectify the problem?

2. Write a regular expression that finds all of the occurrences of the word "a" in the following sentence and replaces them with "the":

"a dog walked in off a street and ordered a finest beer"

The sentence should become:

"the dog walked in off the street and ordered the finest beer"

3. Imagine you have a website with a message board. Write a regular expression that would remove barred words. (You can make up your own words!)

7

Date, Time, and Timers

WHAT YOU WILL LEARN IN THIS CHAPTER:

➤ Retrieving specific date and time information from a Date object

➤ Modifying the date and time of a Date object

➤ Delaying the execution of a function

➤ Executing a function at a set interval of time

Chapter 5 discussed that the concepts of date and time are embodied in JavaScript through the Date object. You looked at some of the properties and methods of the Date object, including the following:

➤ The methods getDate(), getDay(), getMonth(), and getFullYear() enable you to retrieve date values from inside a Date object.

➤ The setDate(), setMonth(), and setFullYear() methods enable you to set the date values of an existing Date object.

➤ The getHours(), getMinutes(), getSeconds(), and getMilliseconds() methods retrieve the time values in a Date object.

➤ The setHours(), setMinutes(), setSeconds(), and setMilliseconds() methods enable you to set the time values of an existing Date object.

One thing not covered in that chapter is the idea that the time depends on your location around the world. In this chapter you correct that omission by looking at date and time in relation to *world time.*

For example, imagine you have a chat room on your website and want to organize a chat for a certain date and time. Simply stating 15:30 is not good enough if your website attracts international visitors. The time 15:30 could be Eastern Standard Time, Pacific Standard Time, the time in the United Kingdom, or even the time in Kuala Lumpur. You could, of course, say 15:30 EST and let your visitors work out what that means, but even that isn't foolproof. There is an EST in Australia as well as in the United States. Wouldn't it be great if you could automatically convert the time to the user's time zone? In this chapter, you see how.

In addition to looking at world time, you also look at how to create a *timer* in a web page. You'll see that by using the timer you can trigger code, either at regular intervals or just once (for example, five seconds after the page has loaded). You'll see how you can use timers to add a real-time clock to a web page. Timers can also be useful for creating animations or special effects in your web applications, which you explore in later chapters.

WORLD TIME

The concept of *now* means the same point in time everywhere in the world. However, when that point in time is represented by numbers, those numbers differ depending on where you are. What is needed is a standard number to represent that moment in time. This is achieved through Coordinated Universal Time (UTC), which is an international basis of civil and scientific time and was implemented in 1964. It was previously known as GMT (Greenwich Mean Time), and, indeed, at 0:00 UTC it is midnight in Greenwich, London.

The following table shows local times around the world at 0:00 UTC time:

SAN FRANCISCO	NEW YORK (EST)	GREENWICH, LONDON	BERLIN, GERMANY	TOKYO, JAPAN
4:00 pm	7:00 pm	0:00 (midnight)	1:00 am	9:00 am

> **NOTE**   Note that the times given are winter times—no daylight savings hours are taken into account.

The support for UTC in JavaScript comes from a number of methods of the Date object that are similar to those you have already seen. For each of the set-date and get-date–type methods you've seen so far, there is a UTC equivalent. For example, setHours() sets the local hour in a Date object, and setUTCHours() does the same thing for UTC time. You look at these methods in more detail in the next section.

In addition, three more methods of the Date object involve world time.

You have the methods toUTCString() and toLocaleString(), which return the date and time stored in the Date object as a string based on either UTC or local time. Most modern browsers also have these additional methods: toLocaleTimeString(), toTimeString(), toLocaleDateString(), and toDateString().

If you simply want to find out the difference in minutes between the current locale's time and UTC, you can use the getTimezoneOffset() method. If the time zone is behind UTC, such as in the United States, it will return a positive number. If the time zone is ahead, such as in Australia or Japan, it will return a negative number.

TRY IT OUT   The World Time Method of the Date Object

In the following code you use the `toLocaleString()`, `toUTCString()`, `getTimezoneOffset()`, `toLocaleTimeString()`, `toTimeString()`, `toLocaleDateString()`, and `toDateString()` methods and write their values out to the page:

```
<!DOCTYPE html>

<html lang="en">
<head>
    <title>Chapter 7, Example 1</title>
</head>
<body>
    <script>
        var localTime = new Date();

        var html = "<p>UTC Time is " + localTime.toUTCString() + "</p>";
        html += "Local Time is " + localTime.toLocaleString() + "</p>";

        html += "<p>Time Zone Offset is " +
                  localTime.getTimezoneOffset() + "</p>";

        html += "<p>Using toLocalTimeString() gives: " +
                  localTime.toLocaleTimeString() + "</p>";

        html += "<p>Using toTimeString() gives: " +
                  localTime.toTimeString() + "</p>";

        html += "<p>Using toLocaleDateString() gives: " +
                  localTime.toLocaleDateString() + "</p>";

        html += "<p>Using toDateString() gives: : " +
                  localTime.toDateString() + "</p>";

        document.write(html);
    </script>
</body>
</html>
```

Save this as `ch7_example1.html` and load it into your browser. What you see, of course, depends on which time zone your computer is set to, but your browser should show something similar to Figure 7-1.

Here the computer's time is set to 09:28:318 PM on March 30, 2014, in America's Eastern Daylight Time (for example, New York).

So how does this work? At the top of the page's script block, you have just:

```
var localTime = new Date();
```

This creates a new `Date` object and initializes it to the current date and time based on the client computer's clock. (Note that the `Date` object simply stores the number of milliseconds between the date and time on your computer's clock and midnight UTC on January 1, 1970.)

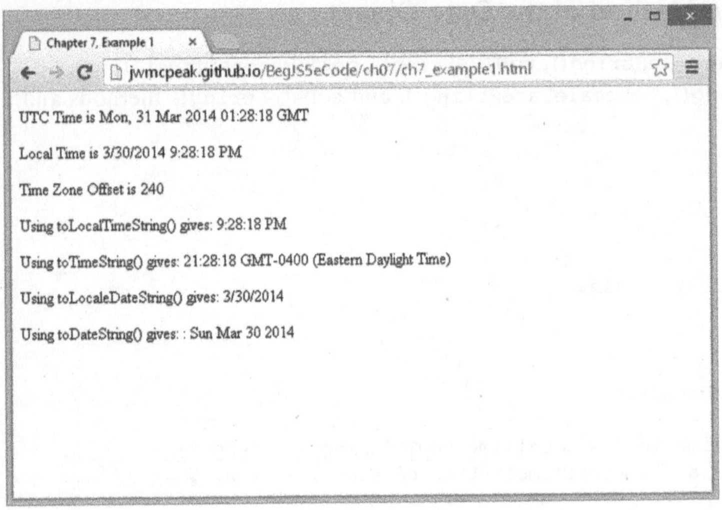

FIGURE 7-1

Within the rest of the script block, you obtain the results from various time and date functions. The results are stored in variable `html`, and this is then displayed in the page.

In the following line, you store the string returned by the `toUTCString()` method in the `html` variable:

```
var html = "<p>UTC Time is " + localTime.toUTCString() + "</p>";
```

This converts the date and time stored inside the `localTime` `Date` object to the equivalent UTC date and time.

Then the following line stores a string with the local date and time value:

```
html += "Local Time is " + localTime.toLocaleString() + "</p>";
```

Because this time is just based on the user's clock, the string returned by this method also adjusts for daylight savings time (as long as the clock adjusts for it).

Next, this code stores a string with the difference, in minutes, between the local time zone's time and that of UTC:

```
html += "<p>Time Zone Offset is " + localTime.getTimezoneOffset() + "</p>";
```

You may notice in Figure 7-1 that the difference between New York time and UTC time is written to be 240 minutes, or 4 hours. Yet in the previous table, you saw that New York time is 5 hours behind UTC. So what is happening?

Well, in New York on March 30, daylight savings hours are in use. Whereas in the summer it's 8:00 p.m. in New York when it's 0:00 UTC, in the winter it's 7:00 p.m. in New York when it's 0:00 UTC. Therefore, in the summer the `getTimezoneOffset()` method returns 240, whereas in the winter the `getTimezoneOffset()` method returns 300.

To illustrate this, compare Figure 7-1 to Figure 7-2, where the date on the computer's clock has been advanced to December, which is in the winter when daylight savings is not in effect.

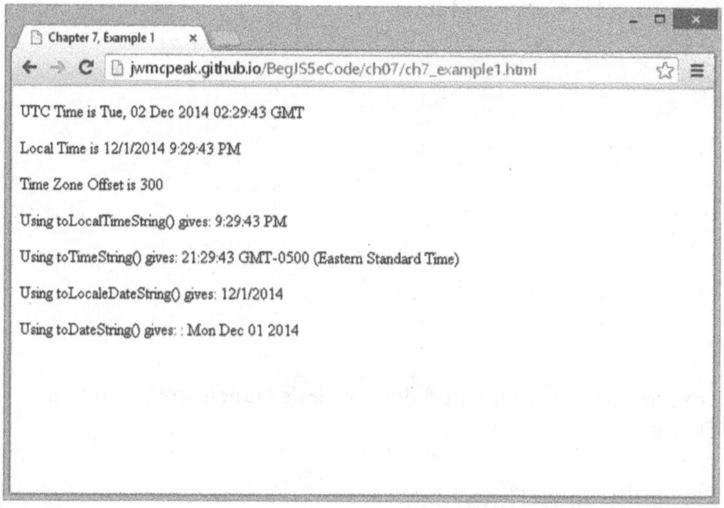

Chapter 7, Example 1

jwmcpeak.github.io/BegJS5eCode/ch07/ch7_example1.html

UTC Time is Tue, 02 Dec 2014 02:29:43 GMT

Local Time is 12/1/2014 9:29:43 PM

Time Zone Offset is 300

Using toLocalTimeString() gives: 9:29:43 PM

Using toTimeString() gives: 21:29:43 GMT-0500 (Eastern Standard Time)

Using toLocaleDateString() gives: 12/1/2014

Using toDateString() gives: : Mon Dec 01 2014

FIGURE 7-2

The next two methods are `toLocaleTimeString()` and `toTimeString()`, as follows:

```
html += "<p>Using toLocalTimeString() gives: " +
        localTime.toLocalTimeString() + "</p>";

html += "<p>Using toTimeString() gives: " +
        localTime.toTimeString() + "</p>";
```

These methods display just the time part of the date and time held in the Date object. The `toLocaleTimeString()` method displays the time as specified by the user on his computer. The second method displays the time but also gives an indication of the time zone (in the example, EST for Eastern Standard Time in America).

The final two methods display the date part of the date and time. The `toLocaleDateString()` displays the date in the format the user has specified on his computer. On Windows operating systems, this is set in the regional settings of the PC's Control Panel. However, because it relies on the user's PC setup, the look of the date varies from computer to computer. The `toDateString()` method displays the current date contained in the PC date in a standard format.

Of course, this example relies on the fact that the user's clock is set correctly, not something you can be 100 percent sure of—it's amazing how many users have their local time zone settings set completely wrong.

Setting and Getting a Date Object's UTC Date and Time

When you create a new Date object, you can either initialize it with a value or let JavaScript set it to the current date and time. Either way, JavaScript assumes you are setting the *local* time values. If you want to specify UTC time, you need to use the `setUTC` type methods, such as `setUTCHours()`.

Following are the seven methods for setting UTC date and time:

➤ `setUTCDate()`

➤ `setUTCFullYear()`

➤ `setUTCHours()`

➤ `setUTCMilliseconds()`

➤ `setUTCMinutes()`

➤ `setUTCMonth()`

➤ `setUTCSeconds()`

The names pretty much give away exactly what each method does, so let's launch straight into a simple example, which sets the UTC time.

TRY IT OUT Working with UTC Date and Time

Let's look at a quick example. Open your text editor and type the following:

```
<!DOCTYPE html>

<html lang="en">
<head>
    <title>Chapter 7, Example 2</title>
</head>
<body>
    <script>
        var myDate = new Date();
        myDate.setUTCHours(12);
        myDate.setUTCMinutes(0);
        myDate.setUTCSeconds(0);

        var html = "<p>" + myDate.toUTCString() + "</p>";
        html += "<p>" + myDate.toLocaleString() + "</p>";

        document.write(html);
    </script>
</body>
</html>
```

Save this as `ch7_example2.html`. When you load it in your browser, you should see something like what is shown in Figure 7-3 in your web page, although the actual date will depend on the current date and where you are in the world.

You might want to change your computer's time zone and time of year to see how it varies in different regions and with daylight savings changes. In Windows you can make the changes by opening the Control Panel and then double-clicking the Date/Time icon.

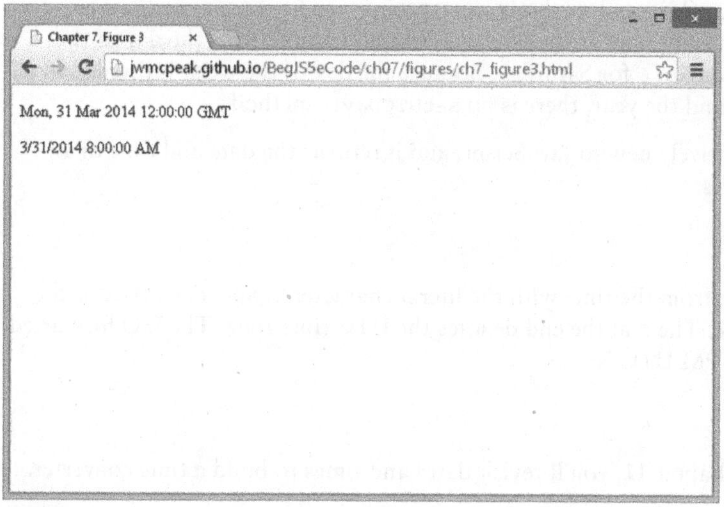

FIGURE 7-3

So how does this example work? You declare a variable, myDate, and set it to a new Date object. Because you haven't initialized the Date object to any value, it contains the local current date and time.

Then, using the setUTC methods, you set the hours, minutes, and seconds so that the time is 12:00:00 UTC (midday, not midnight).

Now, when you write out the value of myDate as a UTC string, you get 12:00:00 and today's date. When you write out the value of the Date object as a local string, you get today's date and a time that is the UTC time 12:00:00 converted to the equivalent local time. The local values you'll see, of course, depend on your time zone. For example, New Yorkers will see 08:00:00 during the summer and 07:00:00 during the winter because of daylight savings. In the United Kingdom, in the winter you'll see 12:00:00, but in the summer you'll see 13:00:00.

For getting UTC dates and times, you have the same functions you would use for setting UTC dates and times, except that this time, for example, it's getUTCHours(), not setUTCHours():

➤ getUTCDate()

➤ getUTCDay()

➤ getUTCFullYear()

➤ getUTCHours()

➤ getUTCMilliseconds()

➤ getUTCMinutes()

➤ getUTCMonth()

➤ getUTCSeconds()

➤ toISOString()

Notice that this time you have two additional methods, getUTCDay() and toISOString(). The getUTCDay() method works in the same way as the getDay() method and returns the day of the week as a number, from 0 for Sunday to 6 for Saturday. Because the day of the week is decided by the day of the month, the month, and the year, there is no setUTCDay() method.

The toISOString() method is relatively new to JavaScript, and it returns the date and time in an ISO-formatted string. The format is:

```
YYYY-MM-DDTHH:mm:ss.sssZ
```

The ISO format separates the date from the time with the literal character T. So YYYY-MM-DD is the date, and HH:mm:ss.sss is the time. The Z at the end denotes the UTC time zone. The ISO formatted string for March 30, 2014 at 3:10 PM UTC is:

```
2014-03-30T15:10:00Z
```

When you learn about forms in Chapter 11, you'll revisit dates and times to build a time converter.

TIMERS IN A WEB PAGE

You can create two types of timers: one-shot timers and continually firing timers. The one-shot timer triggers just once after a certain period of time, and the second type of timer continually triggers at set intervals. You investigate each of these types of timers in the next two sections.

Within reasonable limits, you can have as many timers as you want and can set them going at any point in your code, such as when the user clicks a button. Common uses for timers include animating elements, creating advertisement banner pictures that change at regular intervals, and displaying the changing time in a web page.

One-Shot Timer

Setting a one-shot timer is very easy; you just use the setTimeout() function:

```
var timerId = setTimeout(yourFunction, millisecondsDelay)
```

The setTimeout() method takes two parameters. The first is a function you want executed, and the second is the delay, in milliseconds (thousandths of a second), until the code is executed.

The method returns a value (an integer), which is the timer's unique ID. If you decide later that you want to stop the timer firing, you use this ID to tell JavaScript which timer you are referring to.

TRY IT OUT Delaying a Message

In this example, you set a timer that fires three seconds after the page has loaded:

```
<!DOCTYPE html>

<html lang="en">
<head>
```

```
        <title>Chapter 7, Example 3</title>
    </head>
        <body>
            <script>
                function doThisLater() {
                    alert("Time's up!");
                }

                setTimeout(doThisLater, 3000);
            </script>
        </body>
    </html>
```

Save this file as ch7_example3.html, and load it into your browser.

This page displays a message box three seconds after the browser executes the JavaScript code in the body of the page. Let's look at that code starting with the doThisLater() function:

```
function doThisLater() {
    alert("Time's up!");
}
```

This function, when called, simply displays a message in an alert box. You delay the call of this function by using setTimeout():

```
    setTimeout(doThisLater, 3000);
```

Take note how doThisLater() is passed to setTimeout()—the parentheses are omitted. You do not want to call doThisLater() here; you simply want to refer to the function object.

The second parameter tells JavaScript to execute doThisLater() after 3,000 milliseconds, or 3 seconds, have passed.

It's important to note that setting a timer does not stop the script from continuing to execute. The timer runs in the background and fires when its time is up. In the meantime the page runs as usual, and any script after you start the timer's countdown will run immediately. So, in this example, the alert box telling you that the timer has been set appears immediately after the code setting the timer has been executed.

What if you decided that you wanted to stop the timer before it fired?

To clear a timer you use the clearTimeout() function. This takes just one parameter: the unique timer ID returned by the setTimeout() function.

TRY IT OUT   Stopping a Timer

In this example, you'll alter the preceding example and provide a button that you can click to stop the timer:

```
<!DOCTYPE html>

<html lang="en">
```

```
<head>
    <title>Chapter 7, Example 4</title>
</head>
    <body>
        <script>
            function doThisLater() {
                alert("Time's up!");
            }

            var timerId = setTimeout(doThisLater, 3000);

            clearTimeout(timerId);
        </script>
    </body>
</html>
```

Save this as ch7_example4.html and load it into your browser. You will not see an alert box displaying the Time's up! message because you called clearTimeout() and passed the timer ID before the timeout could expire.

Setting a Timer that Fires at Regular Intervals

The setInterval() and clearInterval() functions work similarly to setTimeout() and clearTimeout(), except that the timer fires continually at regular intervals rather than just once.

The setInterval() function takes the same parameters as setTimeout(), except that the second parameter now specifies the interval, in milliseconds, between each firing of the timer, rather than just the length of time before the timer fires.

For example, to set a timer that fires the function myFunction() every five seconds, the code would be as follows:

```
var myTimerID = setInterval(myFunction,5000);
```

As with setTimeout(), the setInterval() method returns a unique timer ID that you'll need if you want to clear the timer with clearInterval(), which works identically to clearTimeout(). So to stop the timer started in the preceding code, you would use the following:

```
clearInterval(myTimerID);
```

TRY IT OUT A Counting Clock

In this example, you write a simple page that displays the current date and time. That's not very exciting, so you'll also make it update every second:

```
<!DOCTYPE html>

<html lang="en">
<head>
```

```
        <title>Chapter 7, Example 5</title>
    </head>
        <body>
            <div id="output"></div>
            <script>
                function updateTime() {
                    document.getElementById("output").innerHTML = new Date();
                }

                setInterval(updateTime, 1000);
            </script>
        </body>
    </html>
```

Save this file as ch7_example5.html, and load it into your browser.

In the body of this page is a <div /> element, and its id attribute has the value of output:

```
<div id="output"></div>
```

The updated date and time will be displayed inside this element, and the contents of this element are updated by the updateTime() function:

```
function updateTime() {
    document.getElementById("output").innerText = new Date();
}
```

This function uses the document.getElementById() method to retrieve the aforementioned <div/> element, and it uses the innerText property to set the element's text to a new Date object. When displayed in the browser, JavaScript converts the Date object to a human-readable string containing both the date and time.

To change the date and time, you use the setInterval() function, passing it a reference to the updateTime() function, and setting it to execute every second (1,000 milliseconds). This, in turn, changes the text inside of the <div/> element, thus showing the current date and time every second.

That completes your look at this example and also your introduction to timers. You use the setInterval() and clearInterval() functions in later chapters.

SUMMARY

You started the chapter by looking at Coordinated Universal Time (UTC), which is an international standard time. You then looked at how to create timers in web pages.

The particular points covered were the following:

➤   The Date object enables you to set and get UTC time in a way similar to setting a Date object's local time by using methods (such as setUTCHours() and getUTCHours()) for setting and getting UTC hours with similar methods for months, years, minutes, seconds, and so on.

➤ A useful tool in international time conversion is the `getTimezoneOffset()` method, which returns the difference, in minutes, between the user's local time and UTC. One pitfall of this is that you are assuming the user has correctly set his time zone on his computer. If not, `getTimezoneOffset()` is rendered useless, as will be any local date and time methods if the user's clock is incorrectly set.

➤ Using the `setTimeout()` method, you found you could start a timer that would fire just once after a certain number of milliseconds. `setTimeout()` takes two parameters: The first is the function you want executed, and the second is the delay before that code is executed. It returns a value, the unique timer ID that you can use if you later want to reference the timer; for example, to stop it before it fires, you use the `clearTimeout()` method.

➤ To create a timer that fires at regular intervals, you used the `setInterval()` method, which works in the same way as `setTimeout()`, except that it keeps firing unless the user leaves the page or you call the `clearInterval()` method.

In the next chapter, you turn your attention to the web browser itself and, particularly, the various objects that it makes available for your JavaScript programming. You see that the use of browser objects is key to creating powerful web pages.

EXERCISES

You can find suggested solutions to these questions in Appendix A.

1. Create a page that gets the user's date of birth. Then, using that information, tell her on what day of the week she was born.

2. Create a web page similar to Example 5 in the "A Counting Clock" Try It Out, but make it display only the hour, minutes, and seconds.

8

Programming the Browser

WHAT YOU WILL LEARN IN THIS CHAPTER:

- ➤ Working with the browser's native window object
- ➤ Sending the browser to a URL
- ➤ Manipulating images after they are loaded in the page
- ➤ Retrieving the browser's current geographical position
- ➤ Detecting the user's browser

WROX.COM CODE DOWNLOADS FOR THIS CHAPTER

You can find the wrox.com code downloads for this chapter at http://www.wiley.com/go/
BeginningJavaScript5E on the Download Code tab. You can also view all of the examples
and related files at http://beginningjs.com.

Over the past few chapters, you've examined the core JavaScript language. You've seen how to
work with variables and data, perform operations on that data, make decisions in your code,
loop repeatedly over the same section of code, and even how to write your own functions. You
moved on to learn how JavaScript is an object-based language, and you saw how to work with
the native JavaScript objects. However, you are not interested only in the language itself; you
want to find out how to write scripts for the web browser. Using this ability, you can start to
create more impressive web pages.

Not only is JavaScript object-based, but the browser is also made up of objects. When
JavaScript is running in the browser, you can access the browser's objects in exactly the same
way that you used JavaScript's native objects. But what kinds of objects does the browser
provide?

The browser makes available a remarkable number of objects. For example, there is a window
object corresponding to the window of the browser. You have already been using two methods

of this object, namely the alert() and prompt() methods. For simplicity, we previously referred to these as functions, but they are, in fact, methods of the browser's window object.

Another object made available by the browser is the page itself, represented by the document object. Again, you have already used methods and properties of this object. Recall from previous chapters that you used the document object's write() method to write information to the page.

A variety of other objects exist, representative of the HTML you write in the page. For example, there is an img object for each <img/> element that you use to insert an image into your document.

The collection of objects that the browser makes available to you for use with JavaScript is generally called the *browser object model* (BOM).

> **NOTE** *You will often see this termed the document object model (DOM); it is incorrect to do so. Throughout this book, we'll use the term DOM to refer to the W3C's standard document object model, which is discussed in the next chapter.*

All this added functionality of JavaScript comes with a potential downside: There is no standard BOM implementation (although some attempt is being made with the HTML5 specification). Which collections of objects are made available to you is highly dependent on the brand and version of the browser that you are using. Some objects are made available in some browsers and not in others, whereas other objects have different properties and methods in different browsers. The good news is that browser makers typically do not change much of their browser's BOM, because doing so would create a rift in interoperability. This means if you stick to the core functionality of the BOM (the common objects in all browsers), your code is more likely to work between the different browsers and versions. This chapter's focus is the BOM core functionality. You can achieve a lot in JavaScript by just sticking to the core.

INTRODUCTION TO THE BROWSER'S OBJECTS

This section introduces the objects of the BOM that are common to all browsers.

In Chapter 5, you saw that JavaScript has a number of native objects that you can access and use. Most of the objects are those that you need to create yourself, such as the String and Date objects. Others, such as the Math object, exist without you needing to create them and are ready for use immediately when the page starts loading.

When JavaScript is running in a web page, it has access to a large number of other objects made available by the web browser. Like the Math object, these are created for you rather than your needing to create them explicitly. As mentioned, the objects, their methods, properties, and events are all mapped out in the BOM.

The BOM is very large and potentially overwhelming at first. However, you'll find that initially you won't be using more than 10 percent of the available objects, methods, and properties in the BOM. You start in this chapter by looking at the more commonly used parts of the BOM, as shown in Figure 8-1. These parts of the BOM are, to a certain extent, common across all browsers. Later chapters build on this so that by the end of the book you'll be able to really make the BOM work for you.

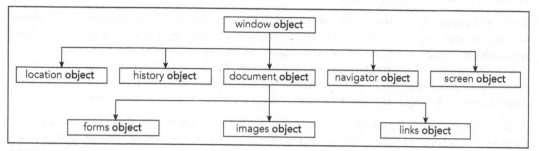

FIGURE 8-1

The BOM has a hierarchy. At the very top of this hierarchy is the window object. You can think of this as representing the frame of the browser and everything associated with it, such as the scrollbars, navigator bar icons, and so on.

Contained inside the window frame is the page. The page is represented in the BOM by the document object. You can see these two objects represented in Figure 8-2.

Now let's look at each of these objects in more detail.

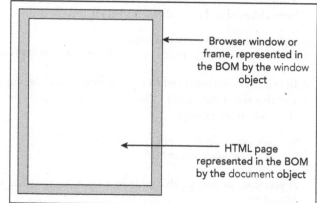

FIGURE 8-2

The window Object

The window object represents the browser's frame or window, in which your web page is contained. To some extent, it also represents the browser itself and includes a number of properties that are there simply because they don't fit anywhere else. For example, via the properties of the window object, you can find out what browser is running, the pages the user has visited, the size of the browser window, the size of the user's screen, and much more. You can also use the window object to access and change the text in the browser's status bar, change the page that is loaded, and even open new windows.

The window object is a *global object*, which means you don't need to use its name to access its properties and methods. In fact, the global functions and variables (the ones accessible for you to script anywhere in a page) are all created as properties of the global object. For example, the alert() function you have been using since the beginning of the book is, in fact, the alert() method of the window object. Although you have been using this simply as this:

```
alert("Hello!");
```

You could write this with the same, exact results:

```
window.alert("Hello!");
```

However, because the window object is the global object, it is perfectly correct to use the first version.

Some of the properties of the window object are themselves objects. Those common to all browsers include the document, navigator, history, screen, and location objects. The document object represents your page, the history object contains the history of pages visited by the user, the navigator object holds information about the browser, the screen object contains information about the display capabilities of the client, and the location object contains details on the current page's location. You look at these important objects individually later in the chapter.

At this point it's worth highlighting the fact that, within a web page, you shouldn't use names for your functions or variables that conflict with names of BOM objects or their properties and methods. If you do, you may not get an error, but instead get unexpected results. For example, the following code declares a variable named history, and tries to use the history property of the window object to go back to the previous page. This, however, won't work because history has been changed to hold a different value:

```
var history = "Hello, BOM!";
window.history.back(); // error; string objects don't have a back() method
```

In this situation you need to use a different variable name. This happens because any function or variable you define within the global scope actually gets appended to the window object. Look at this code as an example:

```
var myVariable = "Hello, World!";
alert(window.myVariable);
```

If you were to execute this code in a browser, the alert window would display the message "Hello, World."

As with all the BOM objects, you can look at lots of properties and methods for the window object. However, in this chapter you concentrate on the history, location, navigator, screen, and document properties. All five of these properties contain objects (the history, location, navigator, screen, and document objects), each with its own properties and methods. In the next few pages, you look at each of these objects in turn and find out how they can help you make full use of the BOM.

The history Object

The history object keeps track of each page that the user visits. This list of pages is commonly called the *history stack* for the browser. It enables the user to click the browser's Back and Forward buttons to revisit pages. You have access to this object via the window object's history property.

Like the native JavaScript Array type, the history object has a length property. You can use this to find out how many pages are in the history stack.

As you might expect, the history object has the back() and forward() methods. When they are called, the location of the page currently loaded in the browser is changed to the previous or next page that the user has visited.

The `history` object also has the `go()` method. This takes one parameter that specifies how far forward or backward in the history stack you want to go. For example, if you wanted to return the user to the page before the previous page, you'd write this:

```
history.go(-2);
```

To go forward three pages, you'd write this:

```
history.go(3);.
```

Note that `go(-1)` and `back()` are equivalent, as are `go(1)` and `forward()`.

The location Object

The `location` object contains lots of potentially useful information about the current page's location. Not only does it contain the uniform resource locator (URL) for the page, but also the server hosting the page, the port number of the server connection, and the protocol used. This information is made available through the `location` object's `href`, `hostname`, `port`, and `protocol` properties. However, many of these values are only really relevant when you are loading the page from a server and not, as you are doing in the present examples, loading the page directly from a local hard drive.

In addition to retrieving the current page's location, you can use the methods of the `location` object to change the location and refresh the current page.

You can navigate to another page in two ways. You can either set the `location` object's `href` property to point to another page, or you can use the `location` object's `replace()` method. The effect of the two is the same; the page changes location. However, they differ in that the `replace()` method removes the current page from the history stack and replaces it with the new page you are moving to, whereas using the `href` property simply adds the new page to the top of the history stack. This means that if the `replace()` method has been used and the user clicks the Back button in the browser, the user can't go back to the original page loaded. If the `href` property has been used, the user can use the Back button as normal.

For example, to replace the current page with a new page called `myPage.html`, you'd use the `replace()` method and write the following:

```
location.replace("myPage.html");
```

This loads `myPage.html` and replaces any occurrence of the current page in the history stack with `myPage.html`.

To load the same page and to add it to the history of pages navigated to, you use the `href` property:

```
location.href = "myPage.html";
```

This adds the currently loaded page to the history. In both of the preceding cases, `window` is in front of the expression, but because the `window` object is global throughout the page, you could have written one of the following:

```
location.replace("myPage.html");
location.href = "myPage.html";
```

The navigator Object

The navigator object is another object that is a property of window and is available in all browsers. Its name is more historical than descriptive. Perhaps a better name would be the "browser object," because the navigator object contains lots of information about the browser and the operating system in which it's running.

Historically, the most common use of the navigator object is for handling browser differences. Using its properties, you can find out which browser, version, and operating system the user has. You can then act on that information and make sure your code works only in browsers that support it. This is referred to as *browser sniffing*, and though it has its uses, it does have limitations.

A better alternative to browser sniffing is *feature detection*, the act of determining if a browser supports a particular feature. We won't go into these subjects here; later sections of this chapter are devoted to browser sniffing and feature detection.

The geolocation Object

The HTML5 specification adds the geolocation property to navigator. Its purpose is simple: to enable developers to obtain and use the position of the device or computer. That sounds like a scary proposition, but users must give permission for that information to be retrieved and used.

At the heart of the geolocation object is its getCurrentPosition() method. When you call this method, you must pass it a *callback function*, which is a function that executes when getCurrentPosition() successfully completes its work. In Chapter 4, you learned that functions are values. You can assign them to variables and pass them to other functions, and the latter is what you do with the getCurrentPosition() method. For example:

```
function success(position) {
    alert("I have you now!");
}

navigator.geolocation.getCurrentPosition(success);
```

In this code, success() is the callback function that executes when navigator.geolocation .getCurrentPosition() determines the computer's or device's location. The parameter, position, is an object that contains the Earthly position and altitude of the computer or device, and you can retrieve these pieces of information through its coords property, like this:

```
function success(position) {
    var latitude = position.coords.latitude;
    var longitude = position.coords.longitude;
    var altitude = position.coords.altitude;
    var speed = position.coords.speed;
}
```

The latitude, longitude, and altitude properties are self-explanatory; they are simply numeric values representing the latitude, longitude, and altitude of the device or computer, respectively. The speed property retrieves the speed, or rather the velocity, of the device/computer in meters per second.

If you need to retrieve more than one of these values, it makes sense to assign `position.coords` to a variable and then use the variable to retrieve the positional values. For example:

```
function success(position) {
    var crds = position.coords;

    var latitude = crds.latitude;
    var longitude = crds.longitude;
    var altitude = crds.altitude;
    var speed = crds.speed;
}
```

This reduces the amount of code you have to type. It also has the advantage of reducing the size of your code, resulting in a slightly faster download time.

The `getCurrentPosition()` method accepts a second parameter, another callback function that executes when an error occurs:

```
function geoError(errorObj) {
    alert("Uh oh, something went wrong");
}

navigator.geolocation.getCurrentPosition(success, geoError);
```

The error callback function has a single parameter that represents the reason for `getCurrentPosition()`'s failure. It is an object containing two properties. The first, `code`, is a numeric value indicating the reason of failure. The following table lists the possible values and their meanings:

VALUE	DESCRIPTION
1	Failure occurred because the page did not have permission to acquire the position of the device/computer.
2	An internal error occurred.
3	The time allowed to retrieve the device's/computer's position was reached before the position was obtained.

The second property is called `message`; it's a human-readable message that describes the error.

TRY IT OUT   Using Geolocation

In this example, you use the `geolocation` object to retrieve the latitude and longitude of the device/computer:

```
<!DOCTYPE html>

<html lang="en">
<head>
    <title>Chapter 8, Example 1</title>
</head>
    <body>
        <script>
            function geoSuccess(position) {
```

```
            var coords = position.coords;
            var latitude = coords.latitude;
            var longitude = coords.longitude;

            var message = "You're at " + latitude + ", " + longitude

            alert(message);
        }
        function geoError(errorObj) {
            alert(errorObj.message);
        }

        navigator.geolocation.getCurrentPosition(geoSuccess, geoError);
    </script>
  </body>
</html>
```

Save the page as ch8_example1.html and load it into your browser.

The page requires the user's consent in order to retrieve his or her geographical position. So the first thing you will see is a prompt asking you to allow or deny the page permission to retrieve that information. Every browser displays this request differently; Figure 8-3 is Chrome's request.

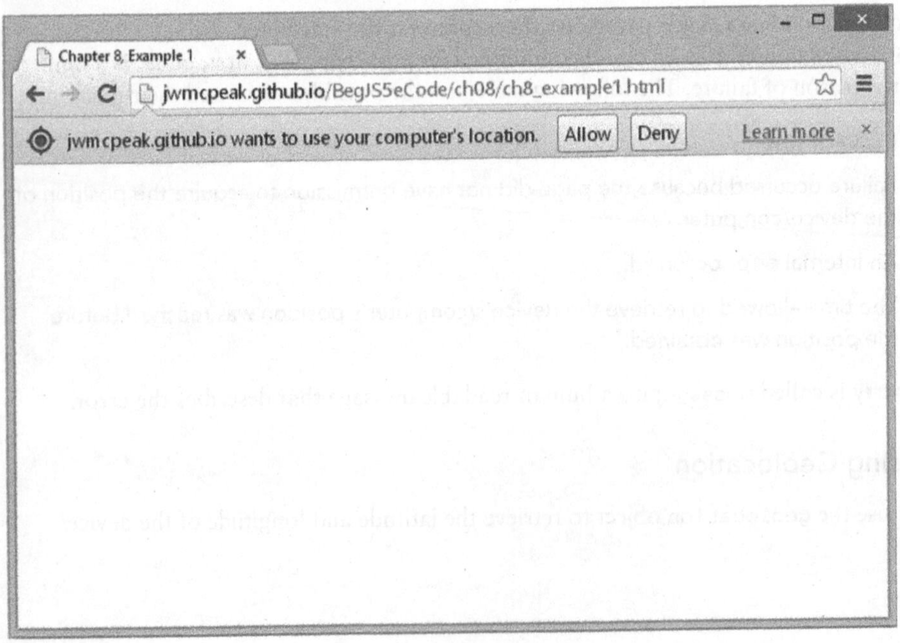

FIGURE 8-3

If you allow the page to access your position, you'll see the latitude and longitude of your device or computer displayed in an alert box. If you choose to deny access, you'll see a message similar to that shown in Figure 8-4.

Two functions in this page are responsible for the aforementioned behavior. The first function, geoSuccess(), is the callback function that executes when the browser can successfully retrieve your device's/computer's position:

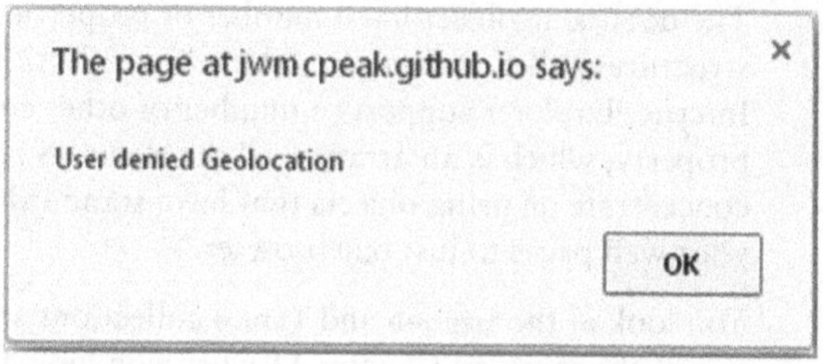

```
function geoSuccess(position) {
    var coords = position.coords;
    var latitude = coords.latitude;
    var longitude = coords.longitude;
```

The page at jwm cpeak.github.io says:

User denied Geolocation

OK

FIGURE 8-4

The first statement in this function stores position.coords in the coords variable to access the positional information with fewer keystrokes. The second and third statements retrieve the latitude and longitude, respectively.

Now that you have the latitude and longitude, you assemble a message that contains this information and display it to the user:

```
    var message = "You're at " + latitude + ", " + longitude

    alert(message);
}
```

If you denied the page access to your position, or if the browser cannot obtain your position, the geoError() callback function executes:

```
function geoError(errorObj) {
    alert(errorObj.message);
}
```

This simple function simply uses the error object's message property to tell the user why getCurrentPosition() failed.

The screen Object

The screen object property of the window object contains a lot of information about the display capabilities of the client machine. Its properties include the height and width properties, which indicate the vertical and horizontal range of the screen, respectively, in pixels.

Another property of the screen object, which you use in an example later, is the colorDepth property. This tells you the number of bits used for colors on the client's screen.

The document Object

Along with the window object, the document object is probably one of the most important and commonly used objects in the BOM. Via this object you can gain access to the HTML elements, their properties, and their methods inside your page.

This chapter concentrates on the basic properties and methods that are common to all browsers. More advanced manipulation of the document object is covered in Chapter 9.

The document object has a number of properties associated with it, which are also array-like structures called *collections*. The main collections are the forms, images, and links collections. Internet Explorer supports a number of other collection properties, such as the all collection property, which is an array of all the elements represented by objects in the page. However, you'll concentrate on using objects that have standard cross-browser support, so that you are not limiting your web pages to just one browser.

You look at the images and links collections shortly. A third collection, the forms collection, is one of the topics of Chapter 11 when you look at forms in web browsers. First, though, you look at a nice, simple example of how to use the document object's methods and properties.

Using the document Object

You've already come across some of the document object's properties and methods—for example, the write() method and the bgColor property.

TRY IT OUT Setting Colors According to the User's Screen Color Depth

In this example, you set the background color of the page according to how many colors the user's screen supports. This is termed *screen color depth*. If the user has a display that supports just two colors (black and white), there's no point in you setting the background color to bright red. You accommodate different depths by using JavaScript to set a color the user can actually see.

```html
<!DOCTYPE html>

<html lang="en">
<head>
    <title>Chapter 8, Example 2</title>
</head>
    <body>
        <script>
            var colorDepth = window.screen.colorDepth;

            switch (colorDepth) {
                case 1:
                case 4:
                    document.bgColor = "white";
                    break;
                case 8:
                case 15:
                case 16:
                    document.bgColor = "blue";
                    break;
                case 24:
                case 32:
                    document.bgColor = "skyblue";
                    break;
                default:
                    document.bgColor = "white";
```

```
        }
        document.write("Your screen supports " + colorDepth +
                       "bit color");
    </script>
  </body>
</html>
```

Save the page as `ch8_example2.html`. When you load it into your browser, the background color of the page will be determined by your current screen color depth. Also, a message in the page will tell you what the color depth currently is.

You can test that the code is working properly by changing the colors supported by your screen. By refreshing the browser, you can see what difference this makes to the color of the page.

> **NOTE** *In Firefox, Safari, and Chrome browsers, it's necessary to shut down and restart the browser to observe any effect.*

As you saw earlier, the `window` object has the `screen` object property. One of the properties of this object is the `colorDepth` property, which returns a value of 1, 4, 8, 15, 16, 24, or 32. This represents the number of bits assigned to each pixel on your screen. (A *pixel* is just one of the many dots that make up your screen.) To work out how many colors you have, you just calculate the value of 2 to the power of the `colorDepth` property. For example, a `colorDepth` of 1 means that two colors are available, a `colorDepth` of 8 means that 256 colors are available, and so on. Currently, most people have a screen color depth of at least 8, but usually 24 or 32.

The first task of the script block is to set the color of the background of the page based on the number of colors the user can actually see. You do this in a big `switch` statement. The condition that is checked for in the `switch` statement is the value of the `colorDepth` variable, which is set to `window.screen.colorDepth`:

```
var colorDepth = window.screen.colorDepth;

switch (colorDepth) {
```

You don't need to set a different color for each `colorDepth` possible, because many of them are similar when it comes to general web use. Instead, you set the same background color for different, but similar, `colorDepth` values. For a `colorDepth` of 1 or 4, you set the background to white. You do this by declaring the `case 1:` statement, but you don't give it any code. If the `colorDepth` matches this `case` statement, it will fall through to the `case 4:` statement below it, where you do set the background color to white. You then call a `break` statement, so that the case matching will not fall any further through the `switch` statement:

```
case 1:
case 4:
    document.bgColor = "white";
    break;
```

You do the same with `colorDepth` values of 8, 15, and 16, setting the background color to blue as follows:

```
case 8:
case 15:
case 16:
    document.bgColor = "blue";
    break;
```

Finally, you do the same for `colorDepth` values of 24 and 32, setting the background color to sky blue:

```
case 24:
case 32:
    document.bgColor = "skyblue";
    break;
```

You end the `switch` statement with a `default` case, just in case the other `case` statements did not match. In this `default` case, you again set the background color to white:

```
default:
    document.bgColor = "white";
}
```

In the next bit of script, you use the `document` object's `write()` method, something you've been using in these examples for a while now. You use it to write to the document—that is, the page—the number of bits at which the color depth is currently set, as follows:

```
document.write("Your screen supports " + colorDepth +
               "bit color")
```

You've already been using the `document` object in the examples throughout the book. You used its `bgColor` property in Chapter 1 to change the background color of the page, and you've also made good use of its `write()` method in the examples to write HTML and text out to the page.

Now let's look at some of the slightly more complex properties of the `document` object. These properties have in common the fact that they all contain collections. The first one you look at is a collection containing an object for each image in the page.

The images Collection

As you know, you can insert an image into an HTML page using the following tag:

```
<img alt="USA" name="myImage" src="usa.gif" />
```

The browser makes this image available for you to manipulate with JavaScript by creating an `img` object for it with the name `myImage`. In fact, each image on your page has an `img` object created for it.

Each of the `img` objects in a page is stored in the `images` collection, which is a property of the `document` object. You use this, and other collections, as you would an array. The first image on the page is found in the element `document.images[0]`, the second in `document.images[1]`, and so on.

If you want to, you can assign a variable to reference an `img` object in the `images` collection. It can make code easier to type and read. For example, the following code assigns a reference to the `img` object at index position 1 to the `myImage2` variable:

```
var myImage2 = document.images[1];
```

Now you can write `myImage2` instead of `document.images[1]` in your code, with exactly the same effect.

Because the `document.images` property is a collection, it has properties similar to the native JavaScript `Array` type, such as the `length` property. For example, if you want to know how many images are on the page, the code `document.images.length` will tell you.

TRY IT OUT   Image Selection

The `img` object itself has a number of useful properties. The most important of these is its `src` property. By changing this, you can change the image that's loaded. This example demonstrates this:

```
<!DOCTYPE html>

<html lang="en">
<head>
    <title>Chapter 8, Example 3</title>
</head>
<body>
    <img src="" width="200" height="150" alt="My Image" />
    <script>
        var myImages = [
            "usa.gif",
            "canada.gif",
            "jamaica.gif",
            "mexico.gif"
        ];

        var imgIndex = prompt("Enter a number from 0 to 3", "");

        document.images[0].src = myImages[imgIndex];
    </script>
</body>
</html>
```

Save this as `ch8_example3.html`. You will also need four image files, called `usa.gif`, `canada.gif`, `jamaica.gif`, and `mexico.gif`. You can create these images yourself or obtain the ones provided with the code download for the book.

A prompt box asks you to enter a number from 0 to 3 when this page loads into the browser. A different image is displayed depending on the number you enter.

At the top of the page you have your HTML `<img/>` element. Notice that the `src` attribute is left empty:

```
<img src="" width="200" height="150" alt="My Image" />
```

Next you come to the script block where the image to be displayed is decided. On the first line, you define an array containing a list of image sources. In this example, the images are in the same directory as the HTML file, so a path is not specified. If yours are not, make sure you enter the full path (for example, `C:\myImages\mexico.gif`).

Then you ask the user for a number from 0 to 3, which will be used as the array index to access the image source in the `myImages` array:

```
var imgIndex = prompt("Enter a number from 0 to 3","");
```

Finally, you set the `src` property of the `img` object to the source text inside the `myImages` array element with the index number provided by the user:

```
document.images[0].src = myImages[imgIndex];
```

Don't forget that when you write `document.images[0]`, you are accessing the `img` object stored in the `images` collection. It's an index position of 0, because it's the first (and only) image on this page.

The links Collection

For each hyperlink element `<a/>` defined with an `href` attribute, the browser creates an a object. The most important property of the a object is the `href` property, corresponding to the `href` attribute of the tag. Using this, you can find out where the link points to, and you can change this even after the page has loaded.

The collection of all a objects in a page is contained within the `links` collection, much as the `img` objects are contained in the `images` collection, as you saw earlier.

DETERMINING THE USER'S BROWSER

Many browsers, versions of those browsers, and operating systems are out there on the Internet, each with its own version of the BOM, its own set of features, and its own particular quirks. It's therefore important that you make sure your pages will work correctly on all browsers, or at least *degrade gracefully*, such as by displaying a message suggesting that the user upgrade his or her browser.

You have two ways to test if the browser can execute your code: *feature detection* and *browser sniffing*. They share a similar end goal (to execute code for a given browser), but they are used for different purposes.

Feature Detection

Not all browsers support the same features (although today's modern browsers do a very good job of it). When we say "feature," we're not referring to tabbed browsing, download managers, and so on. We mean features that we, as JavaScript developers, can access and use in our code.

Feature detection is the process of determining if a browser supports a given feature, and it is the preferred method of browser detection. It requires little maintenance, and it is used to execute code across all browsers that implement (or don't implement) a specific feature.

For example, all modern browsers support `navigator.geolocation`. You can use it in your page, and visitors using those browsers will not experience any issues. However, visitors using Internet Explorer 8 would experience script errors because IE8 does not support geolocation.

This is a common problem because even the latest versions of browsers don't always support the same features, but you can avoid these types of issues with feature detection. The pattern is simple: Check if the feature exists, and only use the feature if it does. Therefore, all you need is an `if` statement, like this:

```
if (navigator.geolocation) {
    // use geolocation
}
```

Whoa! Wait a minute! This code uses `navigator.geolocation` as the `if` statement's condition! Isn't the `if` statement supposed to work on `true` or `false` values? Yes, but JavaScript can treat any value as `true` or `false`. We call these *truthy* and *falsey*. They aren't true boolean values, but they evaluate to `true` and `false` when used in a conditional statement.

Here's how this works; the following values are falsey:

- ➤ `0`
- ➤ `""` (an empty string)
- ➤ `null`
- ➤ `undefined`
- ➤ `[]` (an empty array)
- ➤ `false`

Just about everything else is truthy.

In browsers that don't support geolocation, `navigator.geolocation` is `undefined` and is therefore falsey.

We know that this can be confusing, and it can add some ambiguity to your code. So many JavaScript developers like to avoid using truthy/falsey statements, and opt for a clearer comparison by using the `typeof` operator, like this:

```
if (typeof navigator.geolocation != "undefined") {
    // use geolocation
}
```

The `typeof` operator returns a string that tells you the type of a value or object. In this code, the `typeof` operator is used on `navigator.geolocation`. In browsers that support geolocation, the type is `"object"`; in browsers that don't, it's `"undefined"`.

You can use the `typeof` operator on any object or value. Refer to the following table for the possible values returned by `typeof`:

STATEMENT	RESULT
typeof 1	number
typeof "hello"	string
typeof true	boolean
typeof [] (or any array)	object
typeof {} (or any object)	object
typeof undefined	undefined
typeof null	object

TRY IT OUT Using Feature Detection

In this example, you modify ch8_example1.html and ensure that the page works in browsers that do not support geolocation.

```
<!DOCTYPE html>

<html lang="en">
<head>
    <title>Chapter 8, Example 4</title>
</head>
    <body>
        <script>
            function geoSuccess(position) {
                var coords = position.coords;
                var latitude = coords.latitude;
                var longitude = coords.longitude;

                var message = "You're at " + latitude + ", " + longitude

                alert(message);
            }

            function geoError(errorObj) {
                alert(errorObj.message);
            }

            if (typeof navigator.geolocation != "undefined") {
                navigator.geolocation.getCurrentPosition(geoSuccess, geoError);
            } else {
                alert("This page uses geolocation, and your " +
                      "browser doesn't support it.");
            }
        </script>
    </body>
</html>
```

Save this example as ch8_example4.html.

The key difference in this example is the `if ... else` statement at the bottom of the JavaScript code:

```
if (typeof navigator.geolocation != "undefined") {
    navigator.geolocation.getCurrentPosition(geoSuccess, geoError);
} else {
    alert("This page uses geolocation, and your " +
        "browser doesn't support it.");
}
```

Here, you use the `typeof` operator on `navigator.geolocation` to determine if the browser supports that feature. If it does, the `getCurrentPosition()` method is called.

If the browser doesn't support geolocation, the code displays a message to the user stating that his or her browser doesn't support the necessary feature. If you had attempted to use geolocation without ensuring that the browser supports it, the browser would throw an error.

Feature detection is extremely useful, and it enables you to isolate browsers based on the features they do or don't support. But browser makers are not perfect, and they sometimes release a version of a browser that exhibits unique and quirky behavior. In these cases, you need to isolate an individual browser, and feature detection rarely gives you that fine level of control.

Browser Sniffing

First, let us reiterate this point: Most of the time, you want to use feature detection. Browser sniffing has many drawbacks, one of which is that some less common browsers may falsely identify themselves as a more common browser. Another problem is that browser sniffing relies on the browser's *user-agent string*, which is a string that identifies the browser, and browser makers can drastically change the user-agent string between different versions (you see an example of this later). You should use the techniques contained in this section only when you need to target a single browser for its own quirky behavior.

The `navigator` object exposes two properties that are useful in identifying a browser: `appName` and `userAgent`. The `appName` property returns the model of the browser, such as "Microsoft Internet Explorer" for IE or "Netscape" for Firefox, Chrome, and Safari.

The `userAgent` property returns a string containing various bits of information, such as the browser version, operating system, and browser model. However, the value returned by this property varies from browser to browser, so you have to be very, very careful when using it. For example, the browser's version is embedded in different locations of the string.

TRY IT OUT Checking for and Dealing with Different Browsers

In this example, you create a page that uses the aforementioned properties to discover the client's browser and browser version. The page can then take action based on the client's specifications.

```
<!DOCTYPE html>

<html lang="en">
<head>
    <title>Chapter 8, Example 5</title>
</head>
<body>
```

```
<script>
    function getBrowserName() {
        var lsBrowser = navigator.userAgent;

        if (lsBrowser.indexOf("MSIE") >= 0) {
            return "MSIE";
        } else if (lsBrowser.indexOf("Firefox") >= 0) {
            return "Firefox";
        } else if (lsBrowser.indexOf("Chrome") >= 0) {
            return "Chrome";
        } else if (lsBrowser.indexOf("Safari") >= 0) {
            return "Safari";
        } else if (lsBrowser.indexOf("Opera") >= 0) {
            return "Opera";
        } else {
            return "UNKNOWN";
        }
    }

    function getBrowserVersion() {
        var ua = navigator.userAgent;
        var browser = getBrowserName();
        var findIndex = ua.indexOf(browser) + browser.length + 1;
        var browserVersion = parseFloat(
            ua.substring(findIndex, findIndex + 3));

        return browserVersion;
    }

    var browserName = getBrowserName();
    var browserVersion = getBrowserVersion();

    if (browserName == "MSIE") {
        if (browserVersion < 9) {
            document.write("Your version of IE is too old");
        } else {
            document.write("Your version of IE is fully supported");
        }
    } else if (browserName == "Firefox") {
        document.write("Firefox is fully supported");
    } else if (browserName == "Safari") {
        document.write("Safari is fully supported");
    } else if (browserName == "Chrome") {
        document.write("Chrome is fully supported");
    } else if (browserName == "Opera") {
        document.write("Opera is fully supported");
    } else {
        document.write("Sorry this browser version is not supported");
    }
</script>
</body>
</html>
```

Save this file as ch8_example5.html.

If the browser is Firefox, IE9 or 10, Safari, Chrome, or Opera, a message appears telling users that the browser is supported. If it's an earlier version of IE, the user sees a message telling him or her the version of that browser is not supported.

If it's not one of those browsers (including IE11+), the user sees a message saying the browser is unsupported.

At the top of the script block are two important functions. The getBrowserName() function finds out the name of the browser and the getBrowserVersion() function finds out the browser version.

The key to the browser-checking code is the value returned by the navigator.userAgent property. Here are a few example user-agent strings from current browsers:

1. `Mozilla/5.0 (Windows NT 6.3; WOW64; Trident/7.0; .NET4.0E; .NET4.0C; .NET CLR 3.5.30729; .NET CLR 2.0.50727; .NET CLR 3.0.30729; rv:11.0) like Gecko`

2. `Mozilla/5.0 (compatible; MSIE 10.0; Windows NT 6.3; WOW64; Trident/7.0; .NET4.0E; .NET4.0C; .NET CLR 3.5.30729; .NET CLR 2.0.50727; .NET CLR 3.0.30729)`

3. `Mozilla/5.0 (Windows NT 6.3; WOW64) AppleWebKit/537.36 (KHTML, like Gecko) Chrome/34.0.1847.131 Safari/537.36`

4. `Mozilla/5.0 (Windows NT 6.3; WOW64; rv:32.0) Gecko/20100101 Firefox/32.0`

Here each line of the userAgent strings has been numbered. Looking closely at each line, it's not hard to guess which browser each agent string relates to. In order:

1. Microsoft IE11
2. Microsoft IE10
3. Chrome 34.0.1847.131
4. Firefox 32

Using this information, let's start on the first function, getBrowserName(). First you get the name of the browser, as found in navigator.userAgent, and store it in the variable lsBrowser:

```
function getBrowserName() {
    var lsBrowser = navigator.userAgent;
```

The string returned by this property tends to be quite long and does vary. However, by checking for the existence of certain keywords, such as MSIE or Firefox, you can usually determine the browser name. Start with the following lines:

```
if (lsBrowser.indexOf("MSIE") >= 0) {
    return "MSIE";
}
```

These lines search the lsBrowser string for MSIE. If the indexOf value of this substring is 0 or greater, you know you have found it, and so you set the return value to MSIE.

The following else if statement does the same, except that it is modified for Firefox:

```
else if (lsBrowser.indexOf("Firefox") >= 0) {
    return "Firefox";
}
```

This principle carries on for another three if statements, in which you also check for Chrome, Safari, and Opera. If you have a browser you want to check for, this is the place to add its if statement. Just view the string it returns in navigator.userAgent and look for its name or something that uniquely identifies it.

If none of the if statements match, you return UNKNOWN as the browser name:

```
else {
    return "UNKNOWN";
}
```

Now turn to the final function, getBrowserVersion().

The browser version details often appear in the userAgent string right after the name of the browser. For these reasons, your first task in the function is to find out which browser you are dealing with. You declare and initialize the browser variable to the name of the browser, using the getBrowserName() function you just wrote:

```
function getBrowserVersion() {
    var ua = navigator.userAgent;
    var browser = getBrowserName();
```

If the browser is MSIE (Internet Explorer), you need to use the userAgent property again. Under IE, the userAgent property always contains MSIE followed by the browser version. So what you need to do is search for MSIE, and then get the number following that.

You set findIndex to the character position of the browser name plus the length of the name, plus one. Doing this ensures you to get the character after the name and just before the version number. browserVersion is set to the floating-point value of that number, which you obtain using the substring() method. This selects the characters starting at findIndex and ending with the one before findIndex, plus three. This ensures that you just select three characters for the version number:

```
var findIndex = ua.indexOf(browser) + browser.length + 1;
var browserVersion = parseFloat(ua.substring(findIndex, findIndex + 3));
```

If you look back to the userAgent strings, you see that IE10's is similar to this:

```
Mozilla/5.0 (compatible; MSIE 10.0; Windows NT 6.3; WOW64; Trident/7.0)
```

So findIndex will be set to the character index of the number 10 following the browser name. browserVersion will be set to three characters from and including the 10, giving the version number as 10.0.

At the end of the function, you return browserVersion to the calling code, as shown here:

```
    return browserVersion;
}
```

You've seen the supporting functions, but how do you make use of them? Well, in the following code you obtain two bits of information—browser name and version—and use these to filter which browser the user is running:

```
var browserName = getBrowserName();
var browserVersion = getBrowserVersion();

if (browserName == "MSIE") {
```

```
    if (browserVersion < 9) {
        document.write("Your version of Internet Explorer is too old");
    } else {
        document.write("Your version of Internet Explorer is fully supported");
    }
}
```

The first of the `if` statements is shown in the preceding code and checks to see if the user has IE. If true, it then checks to see if the version is lower than 9. If it is, the user sees the message stating his or her browser is too old. If it is 9 or 10, the message tells the user that his or her browser is fully supported. Something goes wrong with this code with IE11, and you'll find out what that is shortly.

You do this again for Firefox, Chrome, Safari, and Opera. The versions of these browsers aren't checked in this example, but you can do so if you want to:

```
else if (browserName == "Firefox") {
    document.write("Firefox is fully supported");
} else if (browserName == "Safari") {
    document.write("Safari is fully supported");
} else if (browserName == "Chrome") {
    document.write("Chrome is fully supported");
} else if (browserName == "Opera") {
    document.write("Opera is fully supported");
} else {
    document.write("Sorry this browser version is not supported.");
}
```

On the final part of the `if` statements is the `else` statement that covers all other browsers and tells the user the browser is not supported.

If you run this page in IE11, you'll see the message "Sorry this browser version is not supported." At first glance, this appears to be an error, but look at IE11's user-agent string:

```
Mozilla/5.0 (Windows NT 6.3; WOW64; Trident/7.0; rv:11.0) like Gecko
```

There is no mention of MSIE anywhere, but for those versed in the browser maker's code words, we know that Trident is Microsoft's rendering engine and the version is 11.0. Microsoft had very good reasons for changing its user-agent string with version 11, but this just drives the point home: You cannot rely on browser sniffing beyond targeting a single browser.

SUMMARY

You've covered a lot in this chapter, but now you have all the grounding you need to move on to more useful things, such as interacting with the page and forms and handling user input.

➤ You turned your attention to the browser, the environment in which JavaScript exists. Just as JavaScript has native objects, so do web browsers. The objects within the web browser, and the hierarchy in which they are organized, are described by something called the browser object model (BOM). This is essentially a map of a browser's objects. Using it, you can navigate your way around each of the objects made available by the browser, together with their properties, methods, and events.

➤ The first of the main objects you looked at was the window object. This sits at the very top of the BOM's hierarchy. The window object contains a number of important sub-objects, including the location object, the navigator object, the history object, the screen object, and the document object.

➤ The location object contains information about the current page's location, such as its filename, the server hosting the page, and the protocol used. Each of these is a property of the location object. Some properties are read-only, but others, such as the href property, not only enable you to find the location of the page, but can be changed so that you can navigate the page to a new location.

➤ The history object is a record of all the pages the user has visited since opening his or her browser. Sometimes pages are not noted (for example, when the location object's replace() method is used for navigation). You can move the browser forward and backward in the history stack and discover what pages the user has visited.

➤ The navigator object represents the browser itself and contains useful details of what type of browser, version, and operating system the user has. These details enable you to write pages dealing with various types of browsers, even where they may be incompatible.

➤ The screen object contains information about the display capabilities of the user's computer.

➤ The document object is one of the most important objects. It's an object representation of your page and contains all the elements, also represented by objects, within that page. The differences between the various browsers are particularly prominent here, but similarities exist between the browsers that enable you to write cross-browser code.

➤ The document object contains three properties that are actually collections. These are the links, images, and forms collections. Each contains all the objects created by the <a/>, <img/>, and <form/> elements on the page, and it's a way of accessing those elements.

➤ The images collection contains an img object for each <img/> element on the page. You found that even after the page has loaded, you can change the properties of images. For example, you can make the image change when clicked. The same principles for using the images collection apply to the links collection.

➤ Finally, you looked at how you can check what type of browser the user has, thereby giving you the power to use new features without causing errors in older browsers. You also learned how to sniff the browser with the navigator object's appName and userAgent properties, and how unreliable that information can be.

That's it for this chapter. In the next chapter, you move on to the more exciting document object model, where you can access and manipulate the elements in your page.

EXERCISES

You can find suggested solutions to these questions in Appendix A.

1. Create two pages, one called `legacy.html` and the other called `modern.html`. Each page should have a heading telling you what page is loaded. For example:

   ```
   <h2>Welcome to the Legacy page. You need to upgrade!</h2>
   ```

   Using feature detection and the `location` object, send browsers that do not support geolocation to `legacy.html`; send browsers that do support geolocation to `modern.html`.

2. Modify Example 3 from the "Image Selection" Try It Out to display one of the four images randomly. Hint: refer to Chapter 5 and the `Math.random()` method.

9

DOM Scripting

WHAT YOU WILL LEARN IN THIS CHAPTER:

- ➤ Finding elements in the page
- ➤ Creating and inserting elements into the page dynamically
- ➤ Navigating the web page, travelling from one element to another
- ➤ Changing elements' style after they are loaded in the page
- ➤ Animating elements by manipulating their positioning

WROX.COM CODE DOWNLOADS FOR THIS CHAPTER

You can find the wrox.com code downloads for this chapter at `http://www.wiley.com/go/ BeginningJavaScript5E` on the Download Code tab. You can also view all of the examples and related files at `http://beginningjs.com`.

JavaScript's primary role in web development is to interact with the user, to add some kind of behavior to your web page. JavaScript enables you to completely change all aspects of a web page after it's loaded in the browser. What gives JavaScript this power over a web page is the *document object model* (DOM), a tree-like representation of the web page.

The DOM is one of the most misunderstood standards set forth by the World Wide Web Consortium (W3C), a body of developers who recommend standards for browser makers and web developers to follow. The DOM gives developers a way of representing everything on a web page so that it is accessible via a common set of properties and methods in JavaScript. By everything, we mean *everything*. You can literally change anything on the page: the graphics, tables, forms, style, and even text itself by altering a relevant DOM property with JavaScript.

The DOM should not be confused with the browser object model (BOM) that was introduced in Chapter 8. You'll see the differences between the two in detail shortly. For now, though, think of the BOM as a browser-dependent representation of every feature of the browser, from the browser buttons, URL address line, and title bar to the browser window controls, as well as parts of the web page, too. The DOM, however, deals only with the contents of the browser window or web page (in other words, the HTML document). It makes the document available in such a way that any browser can use exactly the same code to access and manipulate the content of the document. To summarize, the BOM gives you access to the browser and some of the document, whereas the DOM gives you access to all of the document, but *only* the document.

The great thing about the DOM is that it is browser- and platform-independent. This means that developers can write JavaScript code that dynamically updates the page, and that will work on any DOM-compliant browser without any tweaking. You should not need to code for different browsers or take excessive care when coding.

The DOM achieves this independence by representing the contents of the page as a generic tree structure. Whereas in the BOM you might expect to access something by looking up a property relevant to that part of the browser and adjusting it, the DOM requires navigation through its representation of the page through nodes and properties that are not specific to the browser. You explore this structure a little later.

However, to use the DOM standard, ultimately developers require browsers that completely implement the standard, something that no browser does 100 percent efficiently, unfortunately. To make matters worse, no one browser implements the exact same DOM features that other browsers support, but don't be scared off yet. All modern browsers support many of the same features outlined by the DOM standard.

To provide a true perspective on how the DOM fits in, we need to take a brief look at its relationship with some of the other currently existing web standards. We should also talk about why there is more than one version of the DOM standard, as well as different sections within the standard itself. After understanding the relationships, you can look at using JavaScript to navigate the DOM and to dynamically change a web page's content in more than one browser. The following items are on your agenda:

- ➤ The HTML and ECMAScript standards
- ➤ The DOM standards
- ➤ Manipulating the DOM
- ➤ Writing cross-browser JavaScript

> **NOTE** *Remember that the examples within this chapter are targeted only at the DOM (with very few exceptions) and will be supported by modern browsers (IE 9+, Chrome, Firefox, Opera, and Safari). Legacy browsers (IE8 and below, earlier versions of Chrome, and similar early browsers) may or may not support them.*

THE WEB STANDARDS

When Tim Berners-Lee created HTML in 1991, he probably had little idea that this technology for marking up scientific papers via a set of tags for his own global hypertext project, known as the World Wide Web, would, within a matter of years, become a battleground between the two giants of the software business of the mid-1990s. HTML was a simple derivation from the meta-language Standard Generalized Markup Language (SGML) that had been kicking around academic institutions for decades. Its purpose was to preserve the structure of the documents created with it. HTML depends on a protocol, HyperText Transfer Protocol (HTTP), to transmit documents back and forth between the resource and the viewer (for example, the server and the client computer). These two technologies formed the foundation of the web, and it quickly became obvious in the early 1990s that there needed to be some sort of policing of both specifications to ensure a common implementation of HTML and HTTP so that communications could be conducted worldwide.

In 1994, Tim founded the World Wide Web Consortium (W3C), a body that set out to oversee the technical evolution of the web. It has three main aims:

> ➤ To provide universal access, so that anybody can use the web

> ➤ To develop a software environment to allow users to make use of the web

> ➤ To guide the development of the web, taking into consideration the legal, social, and commercial issues that arise

Each new version of a specification of a web technology has to be carefully vetted by W3C before it can become a standard. The HTML and HTTP specifications are subject to this process, and each new set of updates to these specifications yields a new version of the standard. Each standard has to go through a working draft, a candidate recommendation, and a proposed recommendation stage before it can be considered a fully operational standard. At each stage of the process, members of the W3C consortium vote on which amendments to make, or even on whether to cancel the standard completely and send it back to square one.

It sounds like a very painful and laborious method of creating a standard format, and not something you'd think of as spearheading the cutting edge of technical revolution. Indeed, the software companies of the mid-1990s found the processes involved too slow, so they set the tone by implementing new innovations themselves and then submitting them to the standards body for approval. Netscape started by introducing new elements in its browser, such as the <font /> element, to add presentational content to the web pages. This proved popular, so Netscape added a whole raft of elements that enabled users to alter aspects of presentation and style on web pages. Indeed, JavaScript itself was such an innovation from Netscape.

When Microsoft entered the fray, it was playing catch up for the first two iterations of its Internet Explorer browser. However, with Internet Explorer 3 in 1996, Microsoft established a roughly equal set of features to compete with Netscape and so was able to add its own browser-specific elements. Very quickly, the web polarized between these two browsers, and pages viewable on one browser quite often wouldn't work on another. One problem was that Microsoft had used its much stronger position in the market to give away its browser for free, whereas Netscape still needed to sell its own browser because it couldn't afford to freely distribute its flagship product. To maintain a competitive position, Netscape needed to offer new features to make the user want to purchase its browser rather than use the free Microsoft browser.

Things came to a head with both companies' version 4 browsers, which introduced dynamic page functionality. Unfortunately, Netscape did this by the means of a `<layer />` element, whereas Microsoft chose to implement it via scripting language properties and methods. The W3C needed to take a firm stand here, because one of its three principal aims had been compromised: that of universal access. How could access be universal if users needed a specific vendor's browser to view a particular set of pages? They decided on a solution that used existing standard HTML elements and cascading style sheets, both of which had been adopted as part of the Microsoft solution. As a result, Microsoft gained a dominant position in the browser war, and it held that position for many years. Today, Microsoft's Internet Explorer is still the dominant browser, but it has lost a lot of its market share to Chrome and Firefox.

With a relatively stable version of the HTML standard in place with version 4.01, which boasts a set of features that will take any browser manufacturer a long time to implement completely, attention was turned to other areas of the web. A new set of standards was introduced in the late 1990s to govern the means of presenting HTML (style sheets) and the representation of the HTML document in script (the DOM). Other standards emerged, such as Extensible Markup Language (XML), which offers a common format for representing data in a way that preserves its structure.

The W3C website (www.w3.org) has a huge number of standards in varying stages of creation. Not all of these standards concern us, and not all of the ones that concern us can be found at this website. However, the vast majority of standards that do concern us can be found there.

You're going to take a brief look now at the technologies and standards that have an impact on JavaScript and find out a little background information about each. Some of the technologies may be unfamiliar, but you need to be aware of their existence at the very least.

HTML

The HTML standard is maintained by W3C. This standard might seem fairly straightforward, given that each version should have introduced just a few new elements, but in reality the life of the standards body was vastly complicated by the browser wars. The 1.0 and 2.0 versions of HTML were simple, small documents, but when the W3C came to debate HTML version 3.0, they found that much of the new functionality it was discussing had already been superseded by new additions (such as the `<applet />` and `<style />` elements) to the version 3.0 browser's appletstyle. Version 3.0 was discarded, and a new version, 3.2, became the standard.

However, a lot of the features that went into HTML 3.2 had been introduced at the behest of the browser manufacturers and ran contrary to the spirit of HTML, which was intended solely to define structure. The new features, stemming from the `<font />` element, just confused the issue and added unnecessary presentational features to HTML. These features really became redundant with the introduction of style sheets. So suddenly, in the version 3 browsers, there were three distinct ways to define the style of an item of text. Which was the correct way? And if all three ways were used, which style did the text ultimately assume? Version 4.0 of the HTML standard was left with the job of unmuddling this chaotic mess and designated a lot of elements for deprecation (removal) in the next version of the standards. It was the largest version of the standard so far and included features that linked it to style sheets and the DOM, and also added facilities for the visually impaired and other unfairly neglected minority interest areas.

In 2004, the W3C was focusing on XHTML 2.0, a specification that many, and perhaps most, in the web development community thought to be the wrong direction for the web. So another body, the Web Hypertext Application Technology Working Group (WHATWG) started working on HTML5. In 2009, the W3C officially dropped XHTML 2.0, and today the W3C and the WHATWG work together on developing HTML5.

HTML5 introduces many new features. First are new elements that identify a page's navigation, header, and footer with the `<nav />`, `<header />`, and `<footer />` elements. It also adds `<audio />` and `<video />` elements to replace `<object />`. HTML5 also removes elements like `<font />` and `<center />`, elements that are purely used for presentation purposes. HTML5 also defines native support for drag and drop, geolocation, storage, and much more.

> **NOTE** The HTML5 specification is not completely finalized, but many of its individual features are said to be complete. As a result, you'll find many features implemented in today's modern browsers. You can visit the W3C website at `http://www.w3.org/TR/html5/` or the WHATWG living standard at `http://html.spec.whatwg.org/multipage/` if you want to read the actual specifications.

ECMAScript

JavaScript itself followed a trajectory similar to that of HTML. It was first used in Netscape Navigator and then added to Internet Explorer. The Internet Explorer version of JavaScript was christened JScript and wasn't far removed from the version of JavaScript found in Netscape Navigator. However, once again, there were differences between the two implementations and a lot of care had to be taken in writing script for both browsers.

Oddly enough, it was left to the European Computer Manufacturers Association (ECMA) to propose a standard specification for JavaScript. This didn't appear until a few versions of JavaScript had already been released. Unlike HTML, which had been developed from the start with the W3C consortium, JavaScript was a proprietary creation. This is the reason that it is governed by a different standards body. Microsoft and Netscape both agreed to use ECMA as the standards vehicle/debating forum, because of its reputation for fast-tracking standards and perhaps also because of its perceived neutrality. The name ECMAScript was chosen so as not to be biased toward either vendor's creation and also because the "Java" part of JavaScript was a trademark of Sun licensed to Netscape. The standard, named ECMA-262, laid down a specification that was roughly equivalent to the JavaScript 1.1 specification.

That said, the ECMAScript standard covers only core JavaScript features, such as the primitive data types of numbers, strings, and booleans, native objects like the `Date`, `Array`, and `Math` objects, and the procedural statements like `for` and `while` loops, and `if` and `else` conditionals. It makes no reference to client-side objects or collections, such as `window`, `document`, `forms`, `links`, and `images`.

So, although the standard helps to make core programming tasks compatible when both JavaScript and JScript comply with it, it is of no use in making the scripting of client-side objects compatible between the main browsers. Some incompatibilities remain.

All current implementations of JavaScript are expected to conform to the current ECMAScript standard, which is ECMAScript edition 5, published in December 2009.

Although there used to be quite a few irregularities between the different dialects of JavaScript, they're now similar enough to be considered the same language. This is a good example of how standards have provided a uniform language across browser implementations, although a debate that is similar to the one that took place over HTML still rages to a lesser degree over JavaScript.

It's now time for you to consider the document object model itself.

THE DOCUMENT OBJECT MODEL

The document object model (DOM) is, as previously mentioned, a way of representing the document independent of browser type. It allows a developer to access the document via a common set of objects, properties, methods, and events, and to alter the contents of the web page dynamically using scripts.

You should be aware that some small variations are usually added to the DOM by the browser vendor. So, to guarantee that you don't fall afoul of a particular implementation, the W3C has provided a generic set of objects, properties, and methods that should be available in all browsers, in the form of the DOM standard.

The DOM Standard

We haven't talked about the DOM standard so far, and for a particular reason: It's not the easiest standard to follow. Supporting a generic set of properties and methods has proved to be a very complex task, and the DOM standard has been broken down into separate levels and sections to deal with the different areas. The different levels of the standard are all at differing stages of completion.

Level 0

Level 0 is a bit of a misnomer, because there wasn't really a level 0 of the standard. This term in fact refers to the "old way" of doing things—the methods implemented by the browser vendors before the DOM standard. Someone mentioning level 0 properties is referring to a more linear notation of accessing properties and methods. For example, typically you'd reference items on a form with the following code:

```
document.forms[0].elements[1].value = "button1";
```

We're not going to cover such properties and methods in this chapter, because they have been superseded by newer methods.

Level 1

Level 1 is the first version of the standard. It is split into two sections: One is defined as core (objects, properties, and methods that can apply to both XML and HTML) and the other as HTML

(HTML-specific objects, properties, and methods). The first section deals with how to go about navigating and manipulating the structure of the document. The objects, properties, and methods in this section are very abstract. The second section deals with HTML only and offers a set of objects corresponding to all the HTML elements. This chapter mainly deals with the second section—level 1 of the standard.

In 2000, level 1 was revamped and corrected, though it only made it to a working draft and not to a full W3C recommendation.

Level 2

Level 2 is complete and many of the properties, methods, and events have been implemented by today's browsers. It has sections that add specifications for events and style sheets to the specifications for core and HTML-specific properties and events. (It also provides sections on views and traversal ranges, neither of which is covered in this book; you can find more information at www.w3.org/TR/2000/PR-DOM-Level-2-Views-20000927/ and www.w3.org/TR/2000/PR-DOM-Level-2-Traversal-Range-20000927/.)

Level 3

Level 3 achieved recommendation status in 2004. It is intended to resolve a lot of the complications that still exist in the event model in level 2 of the standard, and adds support for XML features, such as content models and being able to save the DOM as an XML document.

Level 4

In May 2014, DOM level 4 reached candidate recommendation status. It consolidates DOM level 3 with several independent components. At the time of this writing, no modern browser supports DOM level 4, although that will change in the future.

Browser Compliance with the Standards

Almost no browser has 100 percent compliance with any standard. Therefore, there is no guarantee that all the objects, properties, and methods of the DOM standard will be available in a given version of a browser. However, all modern browsers do a very good job of supporting the standard DOM. The only browsers you truly have to watch out for are IE8 and below.

Much of the material in the DOM standard has only recently been clarified, and a lot of DOM features and support have been added to only the latest browser versions. For this reason, examples in this chapter will be guaranteed to work on only the latest versions of IE, Chrome, Firefox, Opera, and Safari. Although cross-browser scripting is a realistic goal, backward-compatible support isn't at all.

Although the standards might still not be fully implemented, they do give you an idea as to how a particular property or method should be implemented, and provide a guideline for all browser manufacturers to agree to work toward in later versions of their browsers. The DOM doesn't introduce any new HTML elements or style sheet properties to achieve its ends. The idea of the DOM is to make use of the existing technologies, and quite often the existing properties and methods of one or other of the browsers.

Differences between the DOM and the BOM

As mentioned earlier, two main differences exist between the document object model and the browser object model. However, complicating the issue is the fact that a BOM is sometimes referred to under the name DOM. Look out for this in any literature on the subject.

➤ First, the DOM covers only the document of the web page, whereas the BOM offers scripting access to all areas of the browsers, from the buttons to the title bar, including some parts of the page.

➤ Second, the BOM is unique to a particular browser. This makes sense if you think about it: you can't expect to standardize browsers, because they have to offer competitive features. Therefore, you need a different set of properties and methods and even objects to be able to manipulate them with JavaScript.

Representing the HTML Document as a Tree Structure

Because HTML is standardized so that web pages can contain only the standard features supported in the language, such as forms, tables, images, and the like, a common method of accessing these features is needed. This is where the DOM comes in. It provides a uniform representation of the HTML document, and it does this by representing the entire HTML document/web page as a *tree structure*.

In fact, it is possible to represent any HTML as a tree structure, and for best results, the HTML document should be well formed. Browsers tolerate, to a greater or lesser extent, quirks such as unclosed tags, or HTML form controls not being enclosed within a <form/> element; however, for the structure of the HTML document to be accurately depicted, you need to be able to always predict the structure of the document. The ability to access elements via the DOM depends on the ability to represent the page as a hierarchy.

What Is a Tree Structure?

If you're not familiar with the concept of trees, don't worry. They're just a diagrammatic means of representing a hierarchical structure.

Let's consider the example of a book with several chapters. If instructed to, you could find the third line on page 543 after a little searching. If an updated edition of the book were printed with extra chapters, more likely than not you'd fail to find the same text if you followed those same instructions. However, if the instructions were changed to, say, "Find the chapter on still-life painting, the section on using watercolors, and the paragraph on positioning light sources," you'd be able to find that even in a reprinted edition with extra pages and chapters, albeit with perhaps a little more effort than the first request required.

Books aren't particularly dynamic examples, but given something like a web page, where the information could be changed daily, or even hourly, can you see why it would be of more use to give the second set of directions than the first? The same principle applies with the DOM. Navigating the DOM in a hierarchical fashion, rather than in a strictly linear way, makes much more sense. When you treat the DOM as a tree, it becomes easy to navigate the page in this fashion. Consider how you locate files on your computer. The file/folder manager (Windows Explorer in Windows, Finder in Mac OS, and so on) creates a tree view of folders through which you can drill down. Instead of looking for a file alphabetically, you locate it by going into a particular folder.

The rules for creating trees are simple. You start at the top of the tree with the document and the element that contains all other elements in the page. The document is the *root node*. A *node* is just a point on the tree representing a particular element or attribute of an element, or even the text that an element contains. The root node contains all other nodes, such as the DTD declaration and the root element (the HTML or XML element that contains all other elements). The

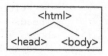

FIGURE 9-1

root element should always be the <html/> element in an HTML document. Underneath the root element are the HTML elements that the root element contains. Typically, an HTML page will have <head/> and <body/> elements inside the <html/> element. These elements are represented as nodes underneath the root element's node, which itself is underneath the root node at the top of the tree (see Figure 9-1).

The two nodes representing the <head/> and <body/> elements are examples of *child nodes*, and the <html/> element's node above them is a *parent node*. Because the <head/> and <body/> elements are both child nodes of the <html/> element, they both go on the same level underneath the parent node <html/> element. The <head/> and <body/> elements in turn contain other child nodes/HTML elements, which will appear at a level underneath their nodes. So child nodes can also be parent nodes. Each time you encounter a set of HTML elements within another element, they each form a separate node at the same level on the tree. The easiest way of explaining this clearly is with an example.

An Example HTML Page

Let's consider a basic HTML page such as this:

```
<!DOCTYPE html>

<html lang="en">
<head>
</head>
<body>
    <h1>My Heading</h1>
    <p>This is some text in a paragraph.</p>
</body>
</html>
```

The <html/> element contains <head/> and <body/> elements. The <body/> element contains an <h1/> element and a <p/> element. The <h1/> element contains the text My Heading. When you reach an item, such as text, an image, or an element, that contains no others, the tree structure will terminate at that node. Such a node is termed a *leaf node*. You then continue to the <p/> node, which contains some text, which is also a node in the document. You can depict this with the tree structure shown in Figure 9-2.

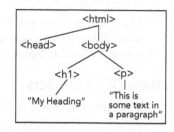

FIGURE 9-2

Simple, eh? This example is almost too straightforward, so let's move on to a slightly more complex one that involves a table as well:

```
<!DOCTYPE html>

<html lang="en">
<head>
```

```
        <title>This is a test page</title>
    </head>
    <body>
        <span>Below is a table</span>
        <table>
            <tr>
                <td>Row 1 Cell 1</td>
                <td>Row 1 Cell 2</td>
            </tr>
        </table>
    </body>
</html>
```

There is nothing out of the ordinary here; the document contains a table with two rows with two cells in each row. You can once again represent the hierarchical structure of your page (for example, the fact that the `<html/>` element contains a `<head/>` and a `<body/>` element, and that the `<head/>` element contains a `<title/>` element, and so on) using your tree structure, as shown in Figure 9-3.

The top level of the tree is simple enough; the `<html/>` element contains `<head/>` and `<body/>` elements. The `<head/>` element in turn contains a `<title/>` element and the `<title/>` element contains some text. This text node is a child node that terminates the branch (a leaf node). You

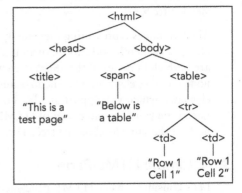

FIGURE 9-3

can then go back to the next node, the `<body/>` element node, and go down that branch. Here you have two elements contained within the `<body/>` element: the `<span/>` and `<table/>` elements. Although the `<span/>` element contains only text and terminates there, the `<table/>` element contains one row (`<tr/>`), and it contains two table cell (`<td/>`) elements. Only then do you get to the bottom of the tree with the text contained in each table cell. Your tree is now a complete representation of your HTML code.

The Core DOM Objects

What you have seen so far has been highly theoretical, so let's get a little more practical now.

The DOM provides you with a concrete set of objects, properties, and methods that you can access through JavaScript to navigate the tree structure of the DOM. Let's start with the set of objects, within the DOM, that is used to represent the nodes (elements, attributes, or text) on your tree.

Base DOM Objects

Three objects, shown in the following table, are known as the base DOM objects.

OBJECT	DESCRIPTION
Node	Each node in the document has its own Node object.
NodeList	This is a list of Node objects.
NamedNodeMap	This provides access by name rather than by index to all the Node objects.

This is where the DOM differs from the BOM quite extensively. The BOM objects have names that relate to a specific part of the browser, such as the `window` object, or the `forms` and `images` collections. As mentioned earlier, to be able to navigate in the web page as though it were a tree, you have to do it abstractly. You can have no prior knowledge of the structure of the page; everything ultimately is just a node. To move around from HTML element to HTML element, or element to attribute, you have to go from node to node. This also means you can add, replace, or remove parts of your web page without affecting the structure as a whole, because you're just changing nodes. This is why you have three rather obscure-sounding objects that represent your tree structure.

I've already mentioned that the top of your tree structure is the root node, and that the root node contains the DTD and root element. Therefore, you need more than just these three objects to represent your document. In fact, there are different objects to represent the different types of nodes on the tree.

High-Level DOM Objects

Because everything in the DOM is a node, it's no wonder that nodes come in a variety of types. Is the node an element, an attribute, or just plaintext? The `Node` object has different objects to represent each possible type of node. The following is a complete list of all the different node type objects that can be accessed via the DOM. A lot of them won't concern you in this book, because they're better suited for XML documents and not HTML documents, but you should notice that your three main types of nodes, namely element, attribute, and text, are all covered.

OBJECT	DESCRIPTION
Document	The root node of the document
DocumentType	The DTD or schema type of the XML document
DocumentFragment	A temporary storage space for parts of the document
EntityReference	A reference to an entity in the XML document
Element	An element in the document
Attr	An attribute of an element in the document
ProcessingInstruction	A processing instruction
Comment	A comment in an XML document or HTML document
Text	Text that must form a child node of an element
CDATASection	A CDATA section within the XML document
Entity	An unparsed entity in the DTD
Notation	A notation declared within a DTD

We won't go over most of these objects in this chapter.

Each of these objects inherits all the properties and methods of the Node object, but also has some properties and methods of its own. You look at some examples in the next section.

DOM Objects and Their Properties and Methods

If you tried to look at the properties and methods of all the objects in the DOM, it would take up half the book. Instead you're going to actively consider only three of the objects, namely the Node object, the Element object, and the Document object. This is all you'll need to be able to create, amend, and navigate your tree structure. Also, you're not going to spend ages trawling through each of the properties and methods of these objects, but rather look only at some of the most useful properties and methods and use them to achieve specific ends.

> **NOTE** Appendix C contains a relatively complete reference to the DOM, its objects, and their properties.

The Document Object and its Methods

The Document reference type exposes various properties and methods that are very helpful to someone scripting the DOM. Its methods enable you to find individual or groups of elements and create new elements, attributes, and text nodes. Any DOM scripter should know these methods and properties, because they're used quite frequently.

The Document object's methods are probably the most important methods you'll learn. Although many tools are at your disposal, the Document object's methods let you find, create, and delete elements in your page.

Finding Elements or an Element

Let's say you have an HTML web page—how do you go about getting back a particular element on the page in script? The Document reference type exposes the following methods to perform this task.

METHODS OF THE DOCUMENT OBJECT	DESCRIPTION
getElementById(idValue)	Returns a reference (a node) of an element, when supplied with the value of the id attribute of that element
getElementsByTagName(tagName)	Returns a reference (a node list) to a set of elements that have the same tag as the one supplied in the argument
querySelector(cssSelector)	Returns a reference (a node) of the first element that matches the given CSS selector
querySelectorAll(cssSelector)	Returns a reference (a node list) to a set of elements that match the given CSS selector

The first of these methods, getElementById(), requires you to ensure that every element you want to quickly access in the page uses an id attribute, otherwise a null value (a word indicating a missing or unknown value) will be returned by your method. Let's go back to the first example and add some id attributes to the elements.

```
<!DOCTYPE html>

<html lang="en">
<head>
</head>
<body>
    <h1 id="heading1">My Heading</h1>
    <p id="paragraph1">This is some text in a paragraph.</p>
</body>
</html>
```

Now you can use the getElementById() method to return a reference to any of the HTML elements with id attributes on your page. For example, if you add the following code in the highlighted section, you can find and reference the <h1/> element:

```
<!DOCTYPE html>

<html lang="en">
<head>
</head>
<body>
    <h1 id="heading1">My Heading</h1>
    <p id="paragraph1">This is some text in a paragraph.</p>
    <script>
        alert(document.getElementById("heading1"));
    </script>
</body>
</html>
```

Figure 9-4 shows the result of this code in Firefox.

> **NOTE** HTMLHeadingElement *is an object of the HTML DOM. All HTML elements have a corresponding reference type in the DOM. See Appendix C for more objects of the HTML DOM.*

You might have been expecting it to return something along the lines of <h1/> or <h1 id="heading1">, but all it's actually returning is a reference to the <h1/> element. This reference to the <h1/> element is more useful though, because you can use it to alter attributes of the element, such as by changing the color or size. You can do this via the style object:

```
<!DOCTYPE html>

<html lang="en">
```

```
<head>
</head>
<body>
    <h1 id="heading1">My Heading</h1>
    <p id="paragraph1">This is some text in a paragraph.</p>

    <script>
        var h1Element = document.getElementById("heading1");
        h1Element.style.color = "red";
    </script>
</body>
</html>
```

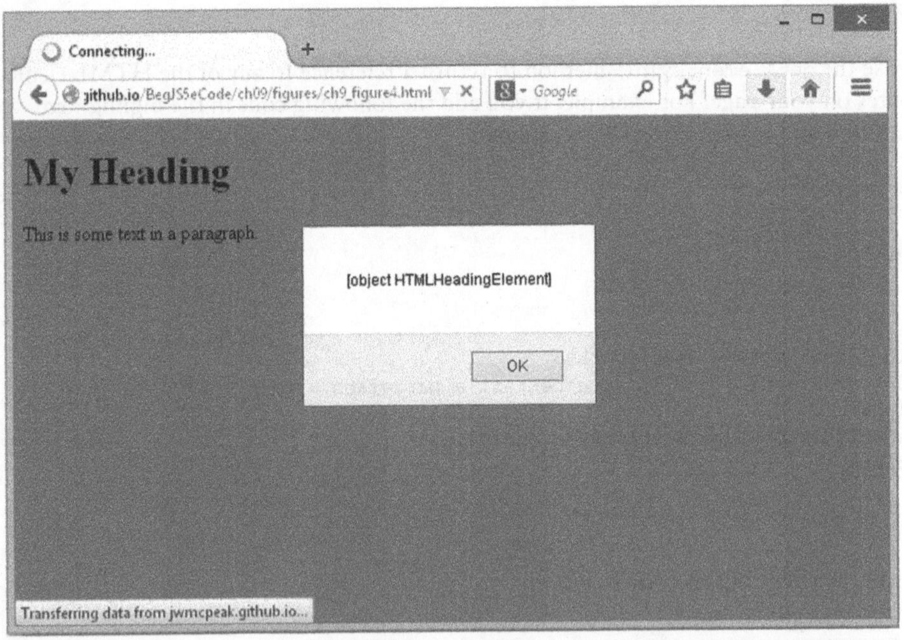

FIGURE 9-4

If you display this in the browser, you see that you can directly influence the attributes of the <h1/> element in script, as you have done here by changing its text color to red.

> **NOTE** The style *object points to the style attribute of an element; it enables you to change the CSS style assigned to an element. The* style *object is covered later in the chapter.*

The second method, getElementsByTagName(), works in the same way, but, as its name implies, it can return more than one element. If you were to go back to the example HTML document with the table and use this method to return the table cells (<td/>) in your code, you would get a node list containing a total of four tables. You'd still have only one object returned, but this object would be a collection of elements. Remember that collections are array-like structures, so specify the index number for the specific element you want from the collection. You can use the square brackets if you want; another alternative is to use the item() method of the NodeList object, like this:

```
<!DOCTYPE html>

<html lang="en">
<head>
    <title>This is a test page</title>
</head>
<body>
    <span>Below is a table</span>
    <table>
        <tr>
            <td>Row 1 Cell 1</td>
            <td>Row 1 Cell 2</td>
        </tr>
    </table>
    <script>
        var tdElement = document.getElementsByTagName("td").item(0);
        tdElement.style.color = "red";
    </script>
</body>
</html>
```

If you ran this example, once again using the style object, it would alter the style of the contents of the first cell in the table. If you wanted to change the color of all the cells in this way, you could loop through the node list, like this:

```
<script>
    var tdElements = document.getElementsByTagName("td");
    var length = tdElements.length;

    for (var i = 0; i < length; i++) {
        tdElements[i].style.color = "red";
    }
</script>
```

One thing to note about the getElementsByTagName() method is that it takes the element names within quotation marks and without the angle brackets (<>) that normally surround tags.

The third method, querySelector(), retrieves the first element that matches the provided CSS selector. This is a convenient way of retrieving an element that does not have an id attribute (if it does have an id attribute, you want to use getElementById()).

For example, consider the following HTML:

```
<p class="sub-title">This is a <span>special</span> paragraph element
    that contains <span>some text</span></p>.
```

Using the `querySelector()` method, you can retrieve the first `<span/>` element in this HTML with the following code:

```
var firstSpan = document.querySelector(".sub-title span");
```

The provided CSS selector matches all `<span/>` elements contained within a parent element with a CSS class of `sub-title`. This HTML contains two such `<span/>` elements, but `querySelector()` only returns the first: the `<span/>` element containing the text "special." Just as with the previous examples, you can modify the element's text color with its `style` property:

```
<script>
    var firstSpan = document.querySelector(".sub-title span");
    firstSpan.style.color = "red";
</script>
```

If you wanted to retrieve all of the `<span/>` elements in this HTML, you want to use the fourth method, `querySelectorAll()`, like this:

```
var spans = document.querySelectorAll(".sub-title span");
```

And just as with the `getElementsByTagName()` example, you can use a loop and modify all the elements contained within the spans `NodeList`:

```
<script>
    var spans = document.querySelectorAll(".sub-title span");
    var length = spans.length;

    for (var i = 0; i < length; i++) {
        spans[i].style.color = "red";
    }
</script>
```

> **NOTE** The `querySelector()` and `querySelectorAll()` methods aren't actually part of the DOM standard. They're defined within the W3C's Selectors API, which is one of the components to be consolidated with DOM level 3 into DOM level 4. You can use these methods on `Element` objects, too.

Creating Elements and Text

The `Document` object also boasts some methods for creating elements and text, shown in the following table.

METHODS OF THE DOCUMENT OBJECT	DESCRIPTION
createElement(elementName)	Creates an element node with the specified tag name. Returns the created element
createTextNode(text)	Creates and returns a text node with the supplied text

The following code demonstrates the use of these methods:

```
var pElement = document.createElement("p");
var text = document.createTextNode("This is some text.");
```

This code creates a `<p/>` element and stores its reference in the pElement variable. It then creates a text node containing the text This is some text. and stores its reference in the text variable.

It's not enough to create nodes, however; you have to add them to the document. We'll discuss how to do this in just a bit.

Property of the Document Object: Getting the Document's Root Element

You now have a reference to individual elements on the page, but what about the tree structure mentioned earlier? The tree structure encompasses all the elements and nodes on the page and gives them a hierarchical structure. If you want to reference that structure, you need a particular property of the document object that returns the outermost element of your document. In HTML, this should always be the `<html/>` element. The property that returns this element is documentElement, as shown in the following table.

PROPERTY OF THE DOCUMENT OBJECT	DESCRIPTION
documentElement	Returns a reference to the outermost element of the document (the root element; for example, `<html/>`)

You can use documentElement as follows. If you go back to the simple HTML page, you can transfer your entire DOM into one variable like this:

```
<!DOCTYPE html>

<html lang="en">
<head>
    <title></title>
</head>
<body>
    <h1 id="heading1">My Heading</h1>
    <p id="paragraph1">This is some text in a paragraph</p>
    <script>
        var container = document.documentElement;
    </script>
</body>
</html>
```

The variable `container` now contains the root element, which is `<html/>`. The `documentElement` property returned a reference to this element in the form of an object, an `Element` object to be precise. The `Element` object has its own set of properties and methods. If you want to use them, you can refer to them by using the variable name, followed by the method or property name:

```
container.elementObjectProperty
```

Fortunately, the `Element` object has only one property.

The Element Object

The `Element` object is quite simple, especially compared to the `Node` object (which you are introduced to later). It exposes only a handful of *members* (properties and methods).

MEMBER NAME	DESCRIPTION
`tagName`	Gets the element's tag name
`getAttribute()`	Gets the value of an attribute
`setAttribute()`	Sets an attribute with a specified value
`removeAttribute()`	Removes a specific attribute and its value from the element

Getting the Element's Tag Name: The tagName Property

The sole property of the `Element` object is a reference to the tag name of the element: the `tagName` property.

In the previous example, the variable `container` contained the `<html/>` element. Add the following highlighted line, which makes use of the `tagName` property:

```
<!DOCTYPE html>

<html lang="en">
<head>
    <title></title>
</head>
<body>
    <h1 id="heading1">My Heading</h1>
    <p id="paragraph1">This is some text in a paragraph</p>
    <script>
        var container = document.documentElement;
        alert(container.tagName);
    </script>
</body>
</html>
```

This code will now return proof that your variable `container` holds the outermost element, and by implication all other elements within it (see Figure 9-5).

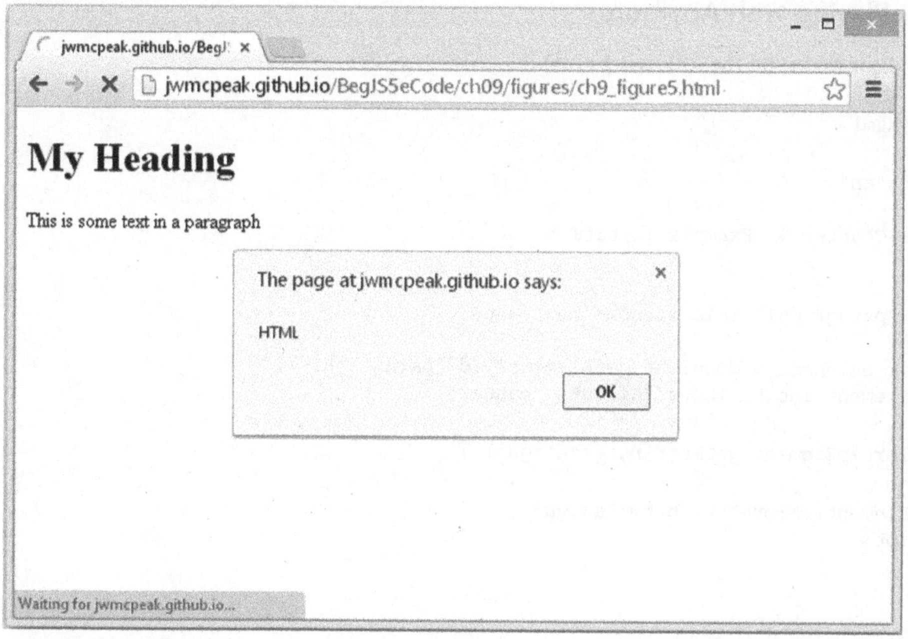

FIGURE 9-5

Methods of the Element Object: Getting and Setting Attributes

If you want to set any element attributes, other than the `style` attribute, you should use the DOM-specific methods of the `Element` object.

The three methods you can use to return and alter the contents of an HTML element's attributes are `getAttribute()`, `setAttribute()`, and `removeAttribute()`, as shown in the following table.

METHODS OF THE ELEMENT OBJECT	DESCRIPTION
`getAttribute(attributeName)`	Returns the value of the supplied attribute Returns `null` or an empty string if the attribute does not exist
`setAttribute(attributeName, value)`	Sets the value of an attribute
`removeAttribute(attributeName)`	Removes the value of an attribute and replaces it with the default value

Let's take a quick look at how these methods work now.

TRY IT OUT   Playing with Attributes

Open your text editor and type the following code:

```
<!DOCTYPE html>

<html lang="en">
<head>
    <title>Chapter 9, Example 1</title>
</head>
<body>
    <p id="paragraph1">This is some text.</p>
    <script>
        var pElement = document.getElementById("paragraph1");
        pElement.setAttribute("align", "center");

        alert(pElement.getAttribute("align"));

        pElement.removeAttribute("align");
    </script>
</body>
</html>
```

Save this as ch9_example1.html and open it in a browser. You'll see the text of the <p/> element in the center of the screen and an alert box displaying the text center (Figure 9-6).

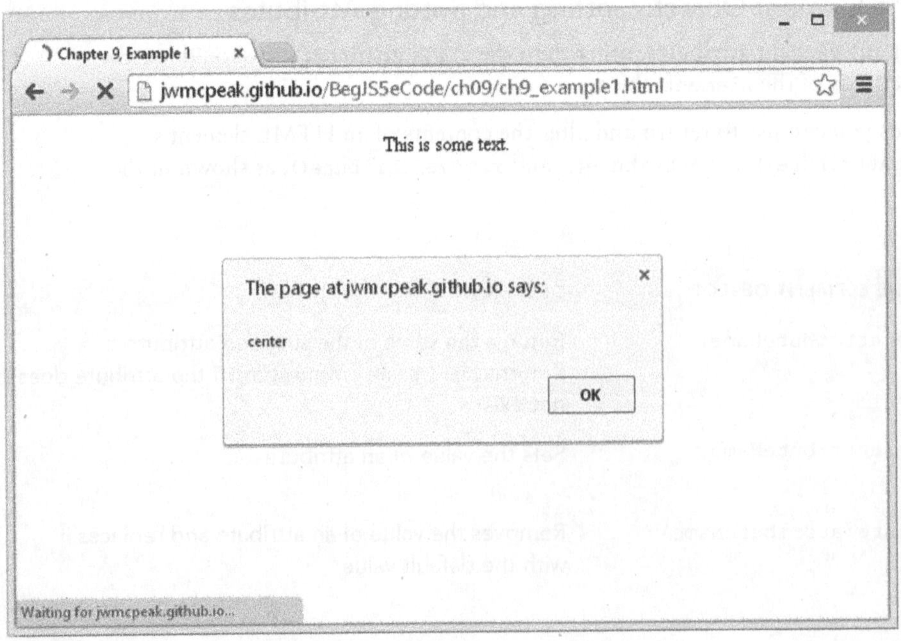

FIGURE 9-6

When you click the OK button, you'll see the text become left-aligned (Figure 9-7).

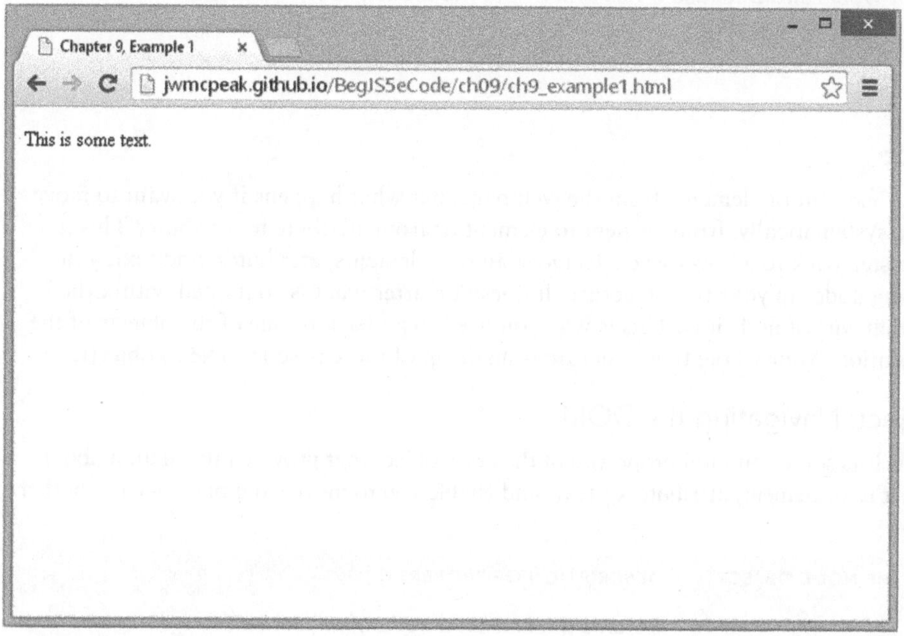

FIGURE 9-7

This HTML page contains one `<p/>` element with an `id` value of `paragraph1`. You use this value in the JavaScript code to find the element node and store its reference in the `pElement` variable with the `getElementById()` method:

```
var pElement = document.getElementById("paragraph1");
```

Now that you have a reference to the element, you use the `setAttribute()` method to set the `align` attribute to `center`:

```
pElement.setAttribute("align", "center");
```

The result of this code moves the text to the center of the browser's window.

You then use the `getAttribute()` method to get the `align` attribute's value and display it in an `alert` box:

```
alert(pElement.getAttribute("align"));
```

This code displays the value `"center"` in the `alert` box.

Finally, you remove the `align` attribute with the `removeAttribute()` method, effectively making the text left-aligned.

> **NOTE** Strictly speaking, the `align` attribute is deprecated, but you used it because it works and because it has one of the most easily demonstrable visual effects on a web page.

The Node Object

You now have your element or elements from the web page, but what happens if you want to move through your page systematically, from element to element or from attribute to attribute? This is where you need to step back to a lower level. To move among elements, attributes, and text, you have to move among nodes in your tree structure. It doesn't matter what is contained within the node, or rather, what sort of node it is. This is why you need to go back to one of the objects of the core DOM specification. Your whole tree structure is made up of these base-level Node objects.

The Node Object: Navigating the DOM

The following table lists some common properties of the Node object that provide information about the node, whether it is an element, attribute, or text, and enable you to move from one node to another.

PROPERTIES OF THE NODE OBJECT	DESCRIPTION OF PROPERTY
`firstChild`	Returns the first child node of an element
`lastChild`	Returns the last child node of an element
`previousSibling`	Returns the previous child node of an element at the same level as the current child node
`nextSibling`	Returns the next child node of an element at the same level as the current child node
`ownerDocument`	Returns the root node of the document that contains the node (note this is not available in IE 5 or 5.5)
`parentNode`	Returns the element that contains the current node in the tree structure
`nodeName`	Returns the name of the node
`nodeType`	Returns the type of the node as a number
`nodeValue`	Gets or sets the value of the node in plaintext format

Let's take a quick look at how some of these properties work. Consider this familiar example:

```
<!DOCTYPE html>

<html lang="en">
<head>
```

```
    <title></title>
</head>
<body>
    <h1 id="heading1">My Heading</h1>
    <p id="paragraph1">This is some text in a paragraph</p>

    <script>
        var h1Element = document.getElementById("heading1");
        h1Element.style.color = "red";
    </script>
</body>
</html>
```

You can now use h1Element to navigate your tree structure and make whatever changes you desire. The following code uses h1Element as a starting point to find the <p/> element and change its text color:

```
<!DOCTYPE html>

<html lang="en">
<head>
    <title></title>
</head>
<body>
    <h1 id="heading1">My Heading</h1>
    <p id="paragraph1">This is some text in a paragraph</p>
    <script>
        var h1Element = document.getElementById("heading1");
        h1Element.style.color = "red";

        var pElement;

        if (h1Element.nextSibling.nodeType == 1) {
            pElement = h1Element.nextSibling;
        } else {
            pElement = h1Element.nextSibling.nextSibling;
        }
        pElement.style.color = "red";
    </script>
</body>
</html>
```

This code demonstrates a fundamental difference between the DOM present in modern browsers and that in older versions of IE. The DOM in modern browsers treats everything as a node in the DOM tree, including the whitespace between elements. On the other hand, older versions of IE strip out this whitespace. So to locate the <p/> element in the previous example, a sibling to the <h1/> element, you must check the next sibling's nodeType property. An element's node type is 1 (text nodes are 3). If the nextSibling's nodeType is 1, you assign that sibling's reference to pElement. If not, you get the next sibling (the <p/> element) of h1Element's sibling (the whitespace text node).

In effect, you are navigating through the tree structure as shown in Figure 9-8.

The same principles also work in reverse. You can go back and change the code to navigate from the <p/> element to the <h1/> element:

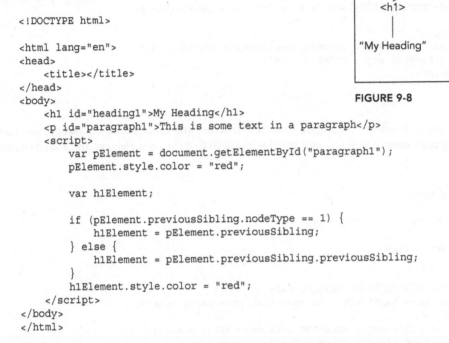

FIGURE 9-8

```
<!DOCTYPE html>

<html lang="en">
<head>
    <title></title>
</head>
<body>
    <h1 id="heading1">My Heading</h1>
    <p id="paragraph1">This is some text in a paragraph</p>
    <script>
        var pElement = document.getElementById("paragraph1");
        pElement.style.color = "red";

        var h1Element;

        if (pElement.previousSibling.nodeType == 1) {
            h1Element = pElement.previousSibling;
        } else {
            h1Element = pElement.previousSibling.previousSibling;
        }
        h1Element.style.color = "red";
    </script>
</body>
</html>
```

What you're doing here is the exact opposite; you find the <p/> by passing the value of its id attribute to the getElementById() method and storing the returned element reference to the pElement variable. You then find the correct previous sibling so that your code works in all browsers, and you change its text color to red.

TRY IT OUT   Navigating Your HTML Document Using the DOM

Up until now, you've been cheating, because you haven't truly navigated your HTML document. You've just used document.getElementById() to return an element and navigated to different nodes from there. Now let's use the documentElement property of the document object and do this properly. You'll start at the top of your tree and move down through the child nodes to get at those elements; then you'll navigate through your child nodes and change the properties in the same way as before.

Type the following into your text editor:

```
<!DOCTYPE html>

<html lang="en">
<head>
    <title>Chapter 9, Example 2</title>
</head>
<body>
    <h1 id="heading1">My Heading</h1>
```

```html
    <p id="paragraph1">This is some text in a paragraph</p>

    <script>
        var htmlElement; // htmlElement stores reference to <html>
        var headElement; // headingElement stores reference to <head>
        var bodyElement; // bodyElement stores reference to <body>
        var h1Element; // h1Element stores reference to <h1>
        var pElement; // pElement stores reference to <p>

        htmlElement = document.documentElement;
        headElement = htmlElement.firstChild;

        alert(headElement.tagName);

        if (headElement.nextSibling.nodeType == 3) {
            bodyElement = headElement.nextSibling.nextSibling;
        } else {
            bodyElement = headElement.nextSibling;
        }

        alert(bodyElement.tagName);

        if (bodyElement.firstChild.nodeType == 3) {
            h1Element = bodyElement.firstChild.nextSibling;
        } else {
            h1Element = bodyElement.firstChild;
        }

        alert(h1Element.tagName);
        h1Element.style.fontFamily = "Arial";

        if (h1Element.nextSibling.nodeType == 3) {
            pElement = h1Element.nextSibling.nextSibling;
        } else {
            pElement = h1Element.nextSibling;
        }

        alert(pElement.tagName);
        pElement.style.fontFamily = "Arial";

        if (pElement.previousSibling.nodeType == 3) {
            h1Element = pElement.previousSibling.previousSibling;
        } else {
            h1Element = pElement.previousSibling;
        }

        h1Element.style.fontFamily = "Courier";
    </script>
</body>
</html>
```

Save this as ch9_example2.html and open it in your browser.

Click OK in each of the message boxes until you see the page shown in Figure 9-9 (unfortunately, IE does not render the style changes until all alert boxes have been opened and closed).

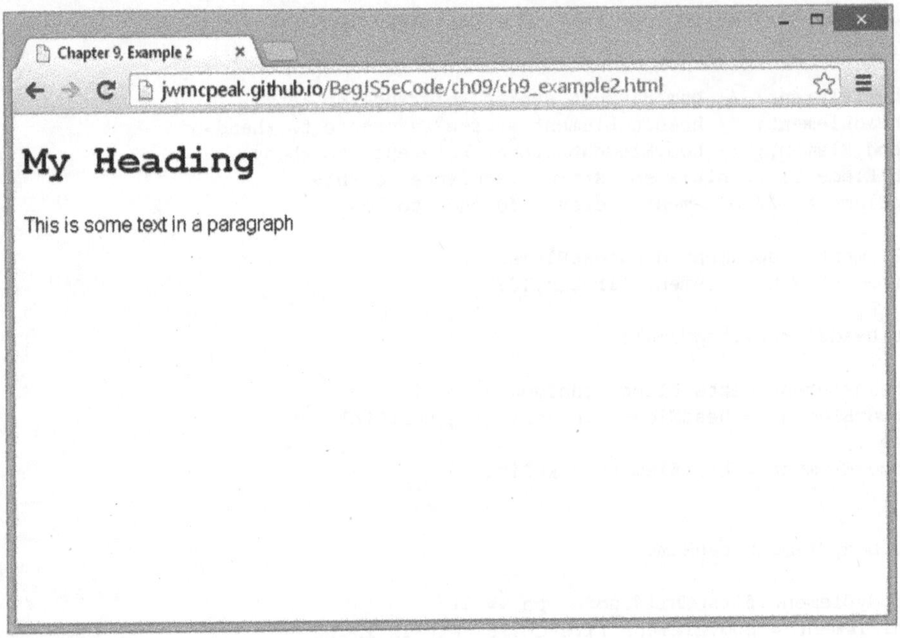

FIGURE 9-9

You've hopefully made this example very transparent by adding several alerts to demonstrate where you are along each section of the tree. You've also named the variables with their various elements, to give a clearer idea of what is stored in each variable. (You could just as easily have named them a, b, c, d, and e, so don't think you need to be bound by this naming convention.)

You start at the top of the script block by retrieving the whole document using the documentElement property:

```
var htmlElement = document.documentElement;
```

The root element is the <html/> element, hence the name of your first variable. Now if you refer to your tree, you'll see that the HTML element must have two child nodes: one containing the <head/> element and the other containing the <body/> element. You start by moving to the <head/> element. You get there using the firstChild property of the Node object, which contains your <html/> element. You use your first alert to demonstrate that this is true:

```
alert(headingElement.tagName);
```

Your <body/> element is your next sibling across from the <head/> element, so you navigate across by creating a variable that is the next sibling from the <head/> element:

```
if (headingElement.nextSibling.nodeType == 3) {
    bodyElement = headingElement.nextSibling.nextSibling;
} else {
```

```
        bodyElement = headingElement.nextSibling;
    }

    alert(bodyElement.tagName);
```

Here you check to see what the nodeType of the nextSibling of headingElement is. If it returns 3, (nodeType 3 is a text node), you set bodyElement to be the nextSibling of the nextSibling of headingElement; otherwise, you just set it to be the nextSibling of headingElement.

You use an alert to prove that you are now at the <body/> element:

```
    alert(bodyElement.tagName);
```

The <body/> element in this page also has two children, the <h1/> and <p/> elements. Using the firstChild property, you move down to the <h1/> element. Again you check whether the child node is whitespace for standard-compliant browsers. You use an alert again to show that you have arrived at <h1/>:

```
    if (bodyElement.firstChild.nodeType == 3) {
        h1Element = bodyElement.firstChild.nextSibling;
    } else {
        h1Element = bodyElement.firstChild;
    }

    alert(h1Element.tagName);
```

After the third alert, the style will be altered on your first element, changing the font to Arial:

```
    h1Element.style.fontFamily = "Arial";
```

You then navigate across to the <p/> element using the nextSibling property, again checking for whitespace:

```
    if (h1Element.nextSibling.nodeType == 3) {
        pElement = h1Element.nextSibling.nextSibling;
    } else {
        pElement = h1Element.nextSibling;
    }

    alert(pElement.tagName);
```

You change the <p/> element's font to Arial also:

```
    pElement.style.fontFamily = "Arial";
```

Finally, you use the previousSibling property to move back in your tree to the <h1/> element and this time change the font to Courier:

```
    if (pElement.previousSibling.nodeType == 3) {
        h1Element = pElement.previousSibling.previousSibling;
    } else {
        h1Element = pElement.previousSibling;
    }

    h1Element.style.fontFamily = "Courier";
```

This is a fairly easy example to follow because you're using the same tree structure you created with diagrams, but it does show how the DOM effectively creates this hierarchy and that you can move around within it using script.

Methods of the Node Object

Whereas the `Node` object's properties enable you to navigate the DOM, its methods provide the completely different ability to add and remove nodes from the DOM, thus fundamentally altering the structure of the HTML document. The following table lists these methods.

METHODS OF NODE OBJECTS	DESCRIPTION
`appendChild(newNode)`	Adds a new `Node` object to the end of the list of child nodes. This method returns the appended node.
`cloneNode(cloneChildren)`	Returns a duplicate of the current node. It accepts a boolean value. If the value is `true`, the method clones the current node and all child nodes. If the value is `false`, only the current node is cloned and child nodes are left out of the clone.
`hasChildNodes()`	Returns `true` if a node has any child nodes and `false` if not
`insertBefore(newNode, referenceNode)`	Inserts a new `Node` object into the list of child nodes before the node stipulated by `referenceNode`. Returns the inserted node
`removeChild(childNode)`	Removes a child node from a list of child nodes of the `Node` object. Returns the removed node

TRY IT OUT   Creating HTML Elements and Text with DOM Methods

In this Try It Out you create a web page with just paragraph `<p/>` and heading `<h1/>` elements, but instead of HTML you'll use the DOM properties and methods to place these elements on the web page. Start up your preferred text editor and type the following:

```
<!DOCTYPE html>

<html lang="en">
<head>
    <title>Chapter 9, Example 3</title>
</head>
<body>
    <script>
        var newText = document.createTextNode("My Heading");
```

```
            var newElem = document.createElement("h1");

            newElem.appendChild(newText);
            document.body.appendChild(newElem);

            newText = document.createTextNode("This is some text in a paragraph");
            newElem = document.createElement("p");

            newElem.appendChild(newText);
            document.body.appendChild(newElem);
        </script>
    </body>
    </html>
```

Save this page as ch9 _ example3.html and open it in a browser (Figure 9-10).

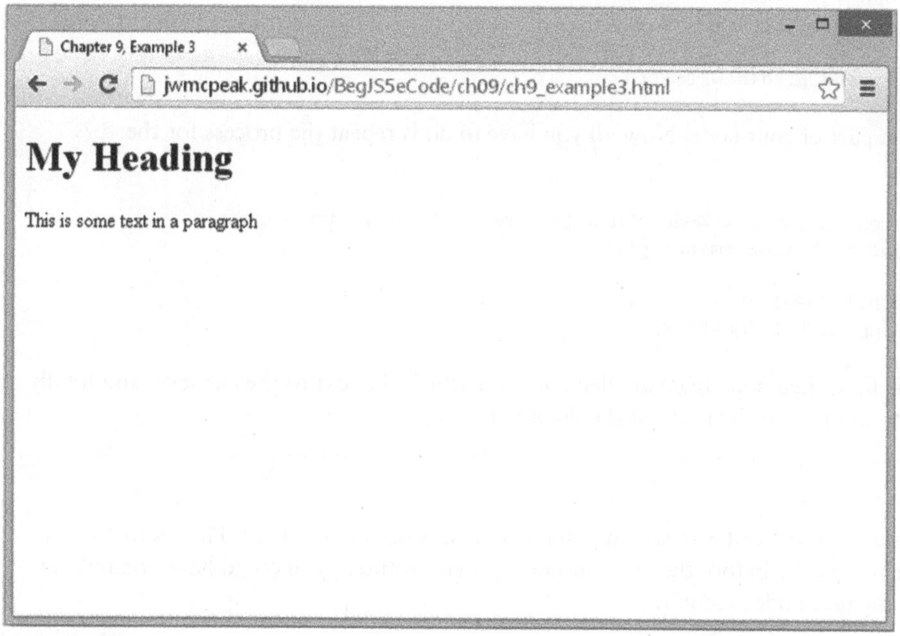

FIGURE 9-10

It all looks a bit dull and tedious, doesn't it? And yes, you could have done this much more simply with HTML. That isn't the point, though. The idea is that you use DOM properties and methods, accessed with JavaScript, to insert these elements. The first two lines of the script block are used to define the variables in your script, which are initialized to hold the text you want to insert into the page and the HTML element you want to insert:

```
    var newText = document.createTextNode("My Heading");
    var newElem = document.createElement("h1");
```

You start at the bottom of your tree first, by creating a text node with the `createTextNode()` method. Then use the `createElement()` method to create an HTML heading.

At this point, the two variables are entirely separate from each other. You have a text node, and you have an `<h1/>` element, but they're not connected. The next line enables you to attach the text node to your HTML element. You reference the HTML element you have created with the variable name `newElem`, use the `appendChild()` method of your node, and supply the contents of the `newText` variable you created earlier as a parameter:

```
newElem.appendChild(newText);
```

Let's recap. You created a text node and stored it in the `newText` variable. You created an `<h1/>` element and stored it in the `newElem` variable. Then you appended the text node as a child node to the `<h1/>` element. That still leaves you with a problem: You've created an element with a value, but the element isn't part of your document. You need to attach the entirety of what you've created so far to the document body. Again, you can do this with the `appendChild()` method, but this time call it on the `document.body` object (which, too, is a `Node`):

```
document.body.appendChild(newElem);
```

This completes the first part of your code. Now all you have to do is repeat the process for the `<p/>` element:

```
newText = document.createTextNode("This is some text in a paragraph");
newElem = document.createElement("p");

newElem.appendChild(newText);
document.body.appendChild(newElem);
```

You create a text node first; then you create an element. You attach the text to the element, and finally you attach the element and text to the body of the document.

It's important to note that the order in which you create nodes does not matter. This example had you create the text nodes before the element nodes; if you wanted, you could have created the elements first and the text nodes second.

However, the order in which you append nodes is very important for performance reasons. Updating the DOM can be an expensive process, and performance can suffer if you make many changes to the DOM. For example, this example updated the DOM only two times by appending the completed elements to the document's body. It would require four updates if you appended the element to the document's body and then appended the text node to the element. As a rule of thumb, only append completed element nodes (that is, the element, its attributes, and any text) to the document whenever you can.

Now that you can navigate and make changes to the DOM, let's look further into manipulating DOM nodes.

MANIPULATING THE DOM

DOM scripting is the manipulation of an HTML page after it's loaded into the browser. Up to this point, you've examined the properties and methods of the basic DOM objects and learned how to traverse the DOM through JavaScript.

Throughout the previous section, you saw some examples of manipulating the DOM; more specifically, you saw that you can change the color and font family of text contained within an element. In this section, you expand on that knowledge.

Accessing Elements

As you saw in the previous section, the DOM holds the tools you need to find and access HTML elements; you used the `getElementById()` method quite frequently, and through examples you saw how easy it was to find specific elements in the page.

When scripting the DOM, chances are you have a pretty good idea of what elements you want to manipulate. The easiest ways to find those elements are with the `getElementById()`, `querySelector()`, and `querySelectorAll()` methods. If an element has an `id` attribute, use `getElementById()` because it is the fastest way to find an element in the page. Otherwise, you'll need to use the `querySelector()` and `querySelectorAll()` methods.

Changing Appearances

Probably the most common DOM manipulation is to change the way an element looks. Such a change can create an interactive experience for visitors to your website and can even be used to alert them to important information or that an action is required by them. Changing the way an element looks consists almost exclusively of changing CSS properties for an HTML element. You can do this two ways through JavaScript:

➤ Change each CSS property with the `style` property.

➤ Change the value of the element's `class` attribute.

Using the style Property

To change specific CSS properties, you must look to the `style` property. All browsers implement this object, which maps directly to the element's `style` attribute. This object contains CSS properties, and by using it you can change any CSS property that the browser supports. You've already seen the `style` property in use, but here's a quick refresher:

```
element.style.cssProperty = value;
```

The CSS property names generally match those used in a CSS style sheet; therefore, changing the text color of an element requires the use of the `color` property, like this:

```
var divAdvert = document.getElementById("divAdvert");
divAdvert.style.color = "blue";
```

In some cases, however, the property name is a little different from the one seen in a CSS file. CSS properties that contain a hyphen (-) are a perfect example of this exception. In the case of these properties, you remove the hyphen and capitalize the first letter of the word that follows the hyphen. The following code shows the incorrect and correct ways to do this:

```
divAdvert.style.background-color = "gray";  // wrong

divAdvert.style.backgroundColor = "gray";  // correct
```

You can also use the `style` object to retrieve styles that have previously been declared. However, if the `style` property you try to retrieve has not been set with the `style` attribute (inline styles) or with the `style` object, you will not retrieve the property's value. Consider the following HTML containing a style sheet and `<div/>` element:

```
<style>
#divAdvert {
    background-color: gray;
}
</style>

<div id="divAdvert" style="color: green">I am an advertisement.</div>
```

When the browser renders this element, it will have green text on a gray background. If you had used the `style` object to retrieve the value of both the `background-color` and `color` properties, you'd get the following mixed results:

```
var divAdvert = document.getElementById("divAdvert");
alert(divAdvert.style.backgroundColor);  // alerts an empty string
alert(divAdvert.style.color);  // alerts green
```

You get these results because the `style` object maps directly to the `style` attribute of the element. If the style declaration is set in a `<style/>` element, or in an external style sheet, you cannot retrieve that property's value with the `style` object.

TRY IT OUT   Using the style Object

Let's look at a simple example of changing the appearance of some text by using the `style` object. Type the following code:

```
<!DOCTYPE html>

<html lang="en">
<head>
    <title>Chapter 9, Example 4</title>
    <style>
        #divAdvert {
            font: 12pt arial;
        }
    </style>

</head>
```

```
<body>
    <div id="divAdvert">
        Here is an advertisement.
    </div>

    <script>
        var divAdvert = document.getElementById("divAdvert");
        divAdvert.style.fontStyle = "italic";
        divAdvert.style.textDecoration = "underline";
    </script>

</body>
</html>
```

Save this as ch9_example4.html. When you run this in your browser, you should see a single line of text that is italicized and underlined, as shown in Figure 9-11.

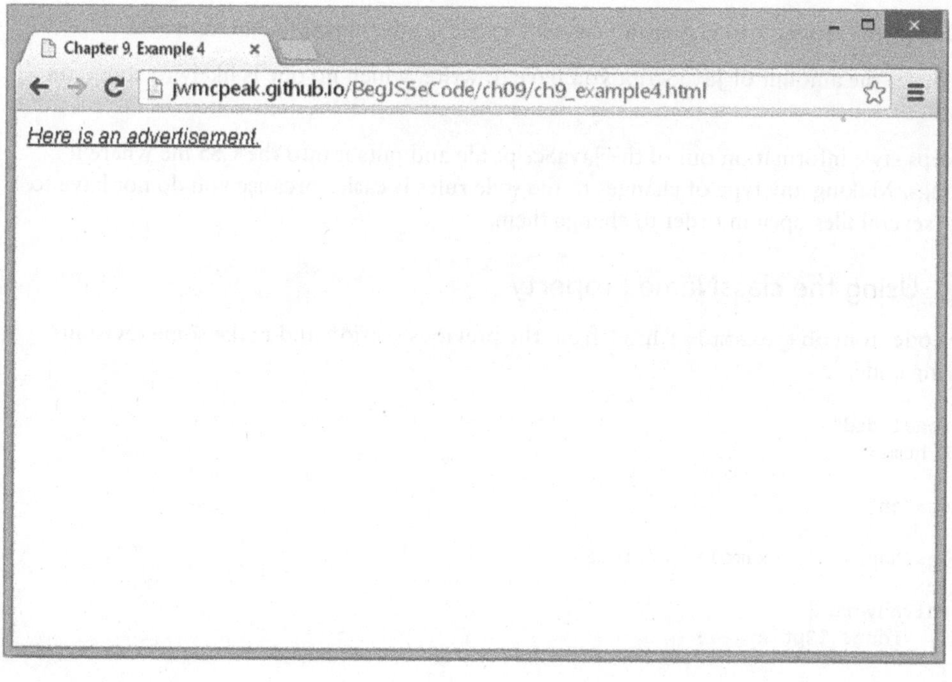

FIGURE 9-11

In the page's body, a `<div/>` element is defined with an id of `divAdvert`. The `<script/>` element appears after the `<div/>`, and it contains the following JavaScript code:

```
var divAdvert = document.getElementById("divAdvert");
divAdvert.style.fontStyle = "italic";
divAdvert.style.textDecoration = "underline";
```

Before you can do anything to the `<div/>` element, you must first retrieve it. You do this simply by using the `getElementById()` method. Now that you have the element, you manipulate its style by first italicizing the text with the `fontStyle` property. Next, you underline the text by using the `textDecoration` property and assigning its value to `underline`.

It's very important that the `<div id="divAdvert"/>` element is loaded into the browser before you retrieve it with `getElementById()`. This is why the `<script/>` element appears after `<div id="divAdvert"/>`. By the time the browser loads and executes the JavaScript code, the `<div/>` element is loaded into the DOM.

Changing the class Attribute

You can assign a CSS class to elements by using the element's `class` attribute. This attribute is exposed in the DOM by the `className` property and can be changed through JavaScript to associate a different style rule with the element:

```
element.className = sNewClassName;
```

Using the `className` property to change an element's style is advantageous in two ways:

➤ It reduces the amount of JavaScript you have to write, which no one is likely to complain about.

➤ It keeps style information out of the JavaScript file and puts it into the CSS file where it belongs. Making any type of changes to the style rules is easier because you do not have to have several files open in order to change them.

TRY IT OUT Using the className Property

Let's revisit the code from `ch9_example4.html` from the previous section and make some revisions. Type the following code:

```
-transitional.dtd">
<!DOCTYPE html>

<html lang="en">
<head>
    <title>Chapter 9, Example 5</title>
    <style>
        #divAdvert {
            font: 12pt arial;
        }

        .new-style {
            font-style: italic;
            text-decoration: underline;
        }
    </style>

</head>
<body>
    <div id="divAdvert">
```

```
                Here is an advertisement.
        </div>

        <script>
            var divAdvert = document.getElementById("divAdvert");
            divAdvert.className = "new-style";
        </script>

    </body>
    </html>
```

Save this as `ch9_example5.html`.

Two key differences exist between `ch9_example4.html` and `ch9_example5.html`. The first is the addition of a CSS class called `new-style`:

```
.newStyle {
    font-style: italic;
    text-decoration: underline;
}
```

This class contains style declarations to specify italicized and underlined text.

The second change is in the JavaScript itself:

```
        var divAdvert = document.getElementById("divAdvert");
        divAdvert.className = "new-style";
}
```

The first statement retrieves the `<div/>` element by using the `getElementById()` method. The second statement changes the `className` property to the value `new-style`. With this line, the `divAdvert` element takes on a new style rule and the browser changes the way it looks.

> **NOTE** *Although it wasn't demonstrated here, the HTML* `class` *attribute, and thus the* `className` *property, can contain multiple CSS class names. You see more about multiple class names in Chapter 16.*

Positioning and Moving Content

Changing the appearance of an element is an important pattern in DOM scripting, and it finds its place in many scripts. However, there is more to DOM scripting than just changing the way content appears on the page; you can also change the position of an element with JavaScript.

Moving content with JavaScript is just as easy as using the `style` object. You use the `position` property to change the type of position desired, and by using the `left` and `top` properties, you can position the element:

```
var divAdvert = document.getElementById("divAdvert");

divAdvert.style.position = "absolute";
```

```
divAdvert.style.left = "100px"; // set the left position
divAdvert.style.top = "100px";  // set the right position
```

This code first retrieves the `divAdvert` element. Then it sets the element's position to absolute and moves the element 100 pixels from the left and top edges. Notice the addition of px to the value assigned to the positions. You must specify a unit when assigning a positional value; otherwise, the browser will not position the element.

> **NOTE** *Positioning elements requires the position of absolute or relative.*

Example: Animated Advertisement

Perhaps the most creative use of DOM scripting is in animating content on the page. You can perform a variety of animations: you can fade text elements or images in and out, give them a swipe animation (making it look like as if they are wiped onto the page), and animate them to move around on the page.

Animation can give important information the flair it needs to be easily recognized by your reader, as well as adding a "that's cool" factor. Performing animation with JavaScript follows the same principles of any other type of animation: You make seemingly insignificant changes one at a time in a sequential order until you reach the end of the animation. Essentially, with any animation, you have the following requisites:

1. The starting state
2. The movement toward the final goal
3. The end state; stopping the animation

Animating an absolutely positioned element, as you're going to do in this section, is no different. First, with CSS, position the element at the start location. Then perform the animation up until you reach the end point, which signals the end of the animation.

In this section, you learn how to animate content to bounce back and forth between two points. To do this, you need one important piece of information: the content's current location.

Are We There Yet?

The DOM in modern browsers exposes the `offsetTop` and `offsetLeft` properties of an HTML element object. These two properties return the calculated position relative to the element's parent element: `offsetTop` tells you the top location, and `offsetLeft` tells you the left position. The values returned by these properties are numerical values, so you can easily check to see where your element currently is in the animation. For example:

```
var endPointX = 394;

if (element.offsetLeft < endPointX) {
    // continue animation
}
```

The preceding code specifies the end point (in this case, 394) and assigns it to the endPointX variable. You can then check to see if the element's offsetLeft value is currently less than that of the end point. If it is, you can continue the animation. This example brings us to the next topic in content movement: performing the animation.

Performing the Animation

To perform an animation, you need to modify the top and left properties of the style object incrementally and quickly. You do this with periodic function execution until it's time to end the animation. To do this, use one of two methods of the window object: setTimeout() or setInterval(). This example uses the setInterval() method to periodically move an element.

TRY IT OUT Animating Content

This page moves an element across the page from right to left. Open your text editor and type the following:

```
<!DOCTYPE html>

<html lang="en">
<head>
    <title>Chapter 9, Example 6</title>
    <style>
        #divAdvert {
            position: absolute;
            font: 12px Arial;
            top: 4px;
            left: 0px;
        }
    </style>
</head>
<body>
    <div id="divAdvert">
        Here is an advertisement.
    </div>

    <script>
        var switchDirection = false;

        function doAnimation() {
            var divAdvert = document.getElementById("divAdvert");
            var currentLeft = divAdvert.offsetLeft;
            var newLocation;

            if (!switchDirection) {
                newLocation = currentLeft + 2;

                if (currentLeft >= 400) {
                    switchDirection = true;
                }
```

```
            } else {
                newLocation = currentLeft - 2;

                if (currentLeft <= 0) {
                    switchDirection = false;
                }
            }
        }

        divAdvert.style.left = newLocation + "px";
    }

    setInterval(doAnimation, 10);
    </script>

</body>
</html>
```

Save this page as `ch9_example6.html` and load it into your browser. When you load the page into the browser, the content should start moving from left to right, starting at the left edge of the viewport. When the content reaches a left position of 400 pixels, the content switches directions and begins to move back toward the left edge. This animation is continuous, so it should bounce between the two points (0 and 400) perpetually.

Inside the body of the page is a `<div/>` element. This element has an `id` of `divAdvert` so that you can retrieve it with the `getElementById()` method, because this is the element you want to animate:

```
<div id="divAdvert">
    Here is an advertisement.
</div>
```

This element has no `style` attributes because all the style information is inside the style sheet located in the head of the page. In the style sheet, you define a starting point for this `<div/>`. You want the animation to go first from left to right, and you want it to start at the left edge of the browser:

```
#divAdvert {
    position: absolute;
    font: 12pt arial;
    top: 4px;
    left: 0px;
}
```

The first style declaration positions the element absolutely, and the second specifies the font as 12-point Arial. The next declaration positions the element four pixels from the top of the browser's viewport. Setting the top position away from the topmost edge makes the text a little easier to read. Finally, the last line positions the `divAdvert` element along the left edge of the viewport with the `left` property.

Within the script block is a global variable called `switchDirection`:

```
var switchDirection = false;
```

This variable keeps track of the direction in which the content is currently going. If `switchDirection` is `false`, the content is moving from left to right, which is the default. If `switchDirection` is `true`, the content is moving from right to left.

Next in the script block is the doAnimation() function, which performs the animation:

```
function doAnimation() {
    var divAdvert = document.getElementById("divAdvert");
    var currentLeft = divAdvert.offsetLeft;
    var newLocation;
```

First, you retrieve the divAdvert element with the getElementById() method; you also retrieve the offsetLeft property and assign its value to the currentLeft variable. You use this variable to check the content's current position. Next, create a variable called newLocation that will contain the new left position, but before you assign its value you need to know the direction in which the content is moving:

```
    if (!switchDirection) {
        newLocation = currentLeft + 2;

        if (currentLeft >= 400) {
            switchDirection = true;
        }
    }
```

First, check the direction by checking the switchDirection variable. Remember, if it is false, the animation is moving from left to right; so assign newLocation to contain the content's current position and add 2, thus moving the content two pixels to the right.

You then need to check if the content has reached the left position of 400 pixels. If it has, you need to switch the direction of the animation, and you do this by changing switchDirection to true. So the next time doAnimation() runs, it will begin to move the content from right to left.

The code to move the element in this new direction is similar to the previous code, except for a few key differences:

```
    else {
        newLocation = currentLeft - 2;

        if (currentLeft <= 0) {
            switchDirection = false;
        }
    }
```

The first difference is the value assigned to newLocation; instead of adding 2 to the current location, you subtract 2, thus moving the content two pixels to the left. Next, check if currentLeft is less than or equal to 0. If it is, you know you've reached the ending point of the right-to-left movement and need to switch directions again by assigning switchDirection to be false.

Finally, set the new position of the content:

```
    divAdvert.style.left = newLocation + "px";
}
```

This final line of the function sets the element's left property to the value stored in the newLocation variable plus the string "px".

To run the animation, use setInterval() to continuously execute doAnimation(). The following code runs doAnimation() every 10 milliseconds:

```
setInterval(doAnimation, 10);
```

At this speed, the content moves at a pace that is easily seen by those viewing the page. If you want to speed up or slow down the animation, simply change how often the setInterval() function calls doAnimation() by changing the second parameter.

What have you seen so far? Well, you've seen the DOM hierarchy and how it represents the HTML document as a tree-like structure. You navigated through the different parts of it via DOM objects (the Node objects) and their properties, and you changed the properties of objects, thus altering the content of the web page. This leaves just one area of the DOM to cover: the event model. You learn about events in the next chapter.

SUMMARY

This chapter has featured quite a few diversions and digressions, but these were necessary to demonstrate the position and importance of the document object model in JavaScript.

This chapter covered the following points:

➤ It started by outlining two of the main standards—HTML and ECMAScript—and examined the relationships between them. You saw that a common aim emerging from these standards was to provide guidelines for coding HTML web pages. Those guidelines in turn benefited the document object model, making it possible to access and manipulate any item on the web page using script if web pages were coded according to those guidelines.

➤ You examined the document object model and saw that it offered a browser-independent means of accessing the items on a web page, and that it resolved some of the problems that dogged older browsers. You saw how the DOM represents the HTML document as a tree structure and how it is possible for you to navigate through the tree to different elements and use the properties and methods it exposes to access the different parts of the web page.

➤ The DOM lets you change a page after it is loaded into the browser, and you can perform a variety of user interface tricks to add some flair to your page.

➤ You learned how to change a tag's style by using the style and className properties.

➤ You also learned the basics of animation and made text bounce back and forth between two points.

EXERCISES

You can find suggested solutions to these questions in Appendix A.

1. Here's some HTML code that creates a table. Re-create this table using only JavaScript and the core DOM objects to generate the HTML. Test your code in all browsers available to you to make sure it works in them. Hint: Comment each line as you write it to keep track of where you are in the tree structure, and create a new variable for every element on the page (for example, not just one for each of the TD cells but nine variables).

```
<table>
    <tr>
        <td>Car</td>
        <td>Top Speed</td>
        <td>Price</td>
    </tr>
    <tr>
        <td>Chevrolet</td>
        <td>120mph</td>
        <td>$10,000</td>
    </tr>
    <tr>
        <td>Pontiac</td>
        <td>140mph</td>
        <td>$20,000</td>
    </tr>
</table>
```

2. Modify `ch9_example6.html` from the "Animating Content" Try It Out so that the amount of pixels moved in either direction is controlled by a global variable. Call it `direction`. Remove the `switchDirection` variable, and change the code to use the new `direction` variable to determine when the animation should change directions.

10

Events

WHAT YOU WILL LEARN IN THIS CHAPTER:

➤ Connecting your code to events to respond to user actions

➤ Writing standards-compliant, event-driven code

➤ Writing event code for older versions of Internet Explorer

➤ Handling the difference between standards-compliant and old-IE event models

➤ Dragging and dropping content with HTML5's native drag-and-drop capabilities

➤ Animating elements by manipulating their positioning

WROX.COM CODE DOWNLOADS FOR THIS CHAPTER

You can find the wrox.com code downloads for this chapter at http://www.wiley.com/go/BeginningJavaScript5E on the Download Code tab. You can also view all of the examples and related files at http://beginningjs.com.

There's no doubt that JavaScript is a useful tool in web programming. You've seen how to dynamically create, remove, and manipulate HTML in the page, and in the coming chapters, you learn how to process user input and send data to the server.

Although these capabilities are very important in today's web programming, perhaps the most important concept you'll learn and use is that of *events*. In the real world, an event is, put simply, something that happens. For example, a ringing telephone is an event. If you are expecting a friend or colleague to call, you usually want to do something: Answer the call.

In programming, events are very similar to a telephone call. Something in the page will happen, and if it's something you are expecting, you can respond to it. For example, the user clicking the page, pressing a key on the keyboard, or moving the mouse pointer over some text all cause events to occur. Another example, which is used quite frequently, is the load event for the page: The window raises (or fires) a notification when the page is completely loaded in the browser.

Why should you be interested in events?

Take as an example the situation in which you want to make a menu pop up when the user clicks anywhere in your web page. Assuming that you can write a function that will make the pop-up menu appear, how do you know *when* to make it appear, or in other words, *when* to call the function? You somehow need to intercept the event of the user clicking in the document, and make sure your function is called when that event occurs.

To do this, you need to use something called an *event handler*, or *listener*. You associate this with the code that you want to execute when the event occurs. This provides you with a way of intercepting events and making your code execute when they have occurred. You will find that adding an event handler to your code is often known as "connecting your code to the event." It's a bit like setting an alarm clock—you set the clock to make a ringing noise when a certain event happens. With alarm clocks, the event is when a certain time is reached.

TYPES OF EVENTS

Web development, especially when it comes to JavaScript, is primarily *event-driven*, meaning that the flow of the program is controlled by events. In other words, a large portion of your JavaScript code usually only executes when an event occurs, and you can listen for many events.

Take a moment and think about how you interact with a web page. On a computer or laptop, you move your mouse around the page, perhaps you select text that you want to copy and paste into your note-taking program, and you definitely click things (like links). On touch-based devices, you tap items in the page. And on all web-enabled devices, you fill out forms by typing keys on the keyboard. Virtually everything you do triggers an event, and a lot of the time, you want to write code that reacts to some of those events.

Following is a list of the many types of events that you can listen for and react to:

➤ **Mouse events:** These occur when the user does something with the mouse, such as moving the cursor, clicking, double-clicking, dragging, and so on.

➤ **Keyboard events:** These occur when keys on the keyboard are pressed or depressed. Though commonly used in conjunction with forms, keyboard events occur every time the user presses or depresses a key.

➤ **Progression events:** These are more generic events that occur at different stages of an object. For example, when the document loads.

➤ **Form events:** These occur when something in the form changes.

➤ **Mutation events:** These occur when DOM nodes are modified.

➤ **Touch events:** These occur when the user touches the sensor.

➤ **Error events:** These occur when an error occurs.

The most common user-based events are mouse events, and rightly so. The primary way users interact with their computers is with the mouse, but that's starting to change as more and more people own touch-enabled devices.

The main focus of this chapter is to teach you how to listen for events, and it does so primarily with mouse events. In the next chapter, you use some keyboard events to interact with forms.

CONNECTING CODE TO EVENTS

Browsers have been around for quite some time, and as you can guess, the way in which we listen for events has evolved over the years. But even with the many changes the JavaScript community has seen over the years, the old ways of listening for events are still supported and useful in certain situations.

Chapter 5 introduced objects defined by their methods and properties. However, objects also have events associated with them. This was not mentioned before, because native JavaScript objects do not have these events, but the objects of the browser object model (BOM) and document object model (DOM) do.

You can connect your code to an event in three ways:

➤ Assigning HTML attributes

➤ Assigning an object's special properties

➤ Calling an object's special methods

Handling Events via HTML Attributes

In this section you create a simple HTML page with a single hyperlink, given by the element `<a/>`. Associated with this element is the a object, and one of the events the a object has is the `click` event. The `click` event fires, not surprisingly, when the user clicks the hyperlink. Feel free to follow along; open your text editor and type the following:

```
<!DOCTYPE html>

<html lang="en">
<head>
    <title>Connecting Events Using HTML Attributes</title>
</head>
<body>
    <a href="somepage.html">Click Me</a>
</body>
</html>
```

As it stands, this page does nothing a normal hyperlink doesn't do. You click it, and it navigates the window to another page, called `somepage.html`, which would need to be created. There's been no event handler added to the link—yet!

As mentioned earlier, one way of connecting the event to your code is to add it directly to the opening tag of the element object whose event you are capturing. In this case, it's the `click` event of the a object, as defined by the `<a/>` element. On clicking the link, you want to capture the event and connect it to your code. You need to add the event handler, in this case onclick, as an attribute to the opening <a> tag. You set the value of the attribute to the code you want to execute when the event occurs.

Rewrite the opening <a> tag to do this as follows:

```
<a href="somepage.html" onclick="alert('You clicked?')">Click Me</a>
```

This code adds onclick="alert('You Clicked?')" to the definition of the opening <a> tag. Now, when the link is clicked, you see an alert box. After this, the hyperlink does its usual stuff and takes you to the page defined in the href attribute.

This is fine if you have only one line of code to connect to the event handler, but what if you want a number of lines to execute when the link is clicked?

Well, all you need to do is define the function you want to execute and call it in the onclick code. Do that now:

```
<!DOCTYPE html>

<html lang="en">
<head>
    <title>Connecting Events Using HTML Attributes</title>
</head>
<body>
    <a href="somepage.html" onclick="return linkClick()">Click Me</a>
    <script>
        function linkClick()        {
            alert("You Clicked?");
            return true;
        }
    </script>
</body>
</html>
```

Within the script block, you have created a standard function. The onclick attribute is now connected to some code that calls the function linkClick(). Therefore, when the user clicks the hyperlink, this function will be executed.

You'll also see that the function returns a value, true in this case. Also, where you define your onclick attribute, you return the return value of the function by using the return statement before the function name. Why do this?

The value returned by onclick="return linkClick()" is used by JavaScript to decide whether the normal action of the link—that is, going to a new page—should occur. If you return true, the action continues, and you go to somepage.html. If you return false, the normal chain of events (that is, going to somepage.html) does not happen. You say that the action associated with the event is canceled. Try changing the function to this:

```
function linkClick() {
    alert("This link is going nowhere");
    return false;
}
```

Now you'll find that you just get a message, and no attempt is made to go to somepage.html.

> **NOTE** *Not all objects and their events make use of the return value, so sometimes it's redundant.*

Some events are not directly linked with the user's actions as such. For example, the window object has the load event, which fires when a page is loaded, and the unload event, which fires when the page is unloaded (that is, when the user either closes the browser or moves to another page).

Event handlers for the window object actually go inside the opening <body> tag. For example, to add an event handler for the load and unload events, you'd write the following:

```
<body onload="myOnLoadfunction()" onunload="myOnUnloadFunction()">
```

TRY IT OUT Displaying Random Images with HTML Attribute Event Handlers

In this Try It Out, you connect to an image's click event to randomly change the image loaded in a page. Open your editor and type in the following code:

```
<!DOCTYPE html>

<html lang="en">
<head>
    <title>Chapter 10: Example 1</title>
</head>
<body>
    <img src="usa.gif" onclick="changeImg(this)" />
    <img src="mexico.gif" onclick="changeImg(this)" />

    <script>
        var myImages = [
            "usa.gif",
            "canada.gif",
            "jamaica.gif",
            "mexico.gif"
        ];

        function changeImg(that) {
            var newImgNumber = Math.round(Math.random() * 3);

            while (that.src.indexOf(myImages[newImgNumber]) != -1) {
                newImgNumber = Math.round(Math.random() * 3);
            }

            that.src = myImages[newImgNumber];
        }
    </script>
</body>
</html>
```

Save the page as ch10_example1.html. You will need four image files for the example, which you can create or retrieve from the code download available with this book.

Load the page into your browser. You should see a page like that shown in Figure 10-1.

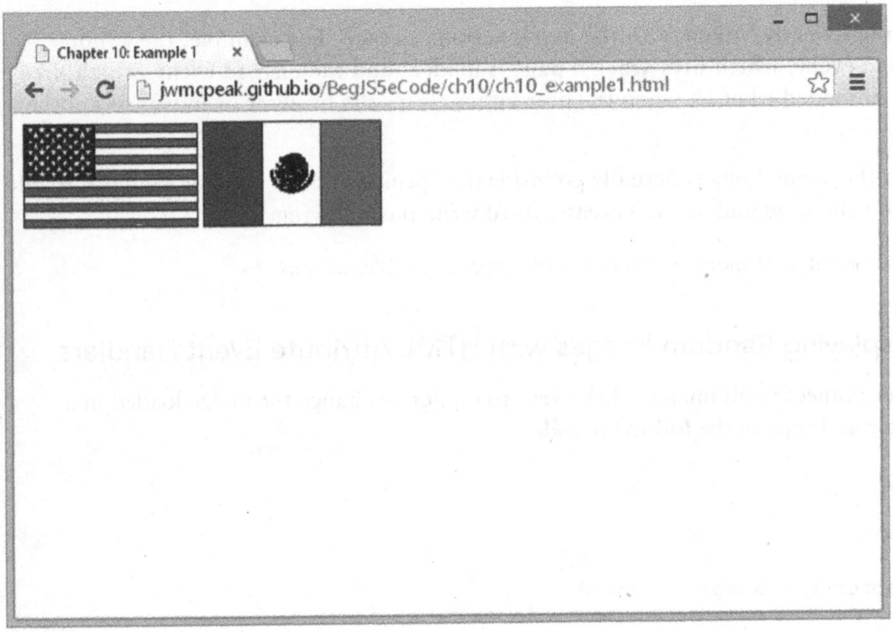

FIGURE 10-1

If you click an image, you'll see it change to a different image, which is selected randomly.

The first line in the script block at the top of the page defines a variable with page-level scope. This is an array that contains your list of image sources:

```
var myImages = [
    "usa.gif",
    "canada.gif",
    "jamaica.gif",
    "mexico.gif"
];
```

Next you have the changeImg() function, which will be connected to the onclick event handler of the <img/> elements defined in the page. You are using the same function for the onclick event handlers of both images, and indeed, can connect one function to as many event handlers as you like. This function accepts one parameter called that. It is called that because you pass the this keyword to the function, which gives you immediate access to the img object you click. You can actually name the parameter whatever you want, but most developers use the word "that" when it references this.

In the first line of the function, you set the `newImgNumber` variable to a random integer between 0 and 3:

```
function changeImg(that) {
    var newImgNumber = Math.round(Math.random() * 3);
```

The `Math.random()` method provides a random number between 0 and 1, and you multiply that by three to get a number between 0 and 3. This number is rounded to the nearest whole number (0, 1, 2, or 3) by means of `Math.round()`. This integer provides the index for the image `src` that you will select from the `myImages` array.

The next lines are a `while` loop, the purpose of which is to ensure that you don't select the same image as the current one. If the string contained in `myImages[newImgNumber]` is found inside the `src` property of the current image, you know it's the same and that you need to get another random number. You keep looping until you get a new image, at which point `myImages[newImgNumber]` will not be found in the existing `src`, and -1 will be returned by the `indexOf()` method, breaking out of the loop:

```
while (that.src.indexOf(myImages[newImgNumber]) != -1) {
    newImgNumber = Math.round(Math.random() * 3);
}
```

Next, you set the `src` property of the `img` object to the new value contained in your `myImages` array:

```
    that.src = myImages[newImgNumber];
}
```

You connect the `onclick` event of the first `<img/>` element to the `changeImg()` function:

```
<img src="usa.gif" onclick="changeImg(this)" />
```

And now to the second `<img/>` element:

```
<img src="mexico.gif" onclick="changeImg(this)" />
```

Passing `this` in the `changeImg()` function gives the function direct access to this `<img/>` element's corresponding object. When you pass `this` to an HTML element's attribute event handler, the corresponding object of that element is passed to the function. It's a nice, clean way of accessing the element's object in your JavaScript code.

This example had you pass `this` as an argument to the function handling the element's `click` event. This is a simple and easy way of accessing the element that received the event, but there's a far more useful object you can pass: an `Event` object that contains all the information about the event.

Passing the `Event` object is very simple to do; simply pass `event` instead of `this`. For example, in the following code the `<p/>` element will raise a `dblclick` event:

```
<p ondblclick="handle(event)">Paragraph</p>

<script>
```

```
function handle(e) {
    alert(e.type);
}
</script>
```

Notice that event is passed to the handle() function in the ondblclick attribute. This event variable is special in that it is not defined anywhere; instead, it is an argument used only with event handlers that are connected through HTML attributes. It passes a reference to the current event object when the event fires.

If you ran the previous example, it would just tell you what kind of event raised your event-handling function. This might seem self-evident in the preceding example, but if you had included the following extra lines of code, any one of three elements could have raised the function:

```
<p ondblclick="handle(event)">Paragraph</p>
<h1 onclick="handle(event)">Heading 1</h1>
<span onmouseover="handle(event)">Special Text</span>

<script>
function handle(e) {
    alert(e.type);
}
</script>
```

This makes the code much more useful. In general, you will use relatively few event handlers to deal with any number of events, and you can use the event properties as a filter to determine what type of event happened and what HTML element triggered it, so that you can treat each event differently.

In the following example, you see that you can take different courses of action depending on what type of event is returned:

```
<p ondblclick="handle(event)">Paragraph</p>
<h1 onclick="handle(event)">Heading 1</h1>
<span onmouseover="handle(event)">Special Text</span>

<script>
function handle(e) {
    if (e.type == "mouseover") {
        alert("You moved over the Special Text");
    }
}
</script>
```

This code uses the type property to determine what type of event occurred. If users move their mouse cursor over the <span/> element, an alert box tells them so.

You learn a lot more about the Event object later in the chapter, but for now, just know that it exposes a property called target. This is the *target* of the event, the element object that received the event. With this information, you can rewrite ch10_example1.html to use the more versatile Event object.

TRY IT OUT | Displaying Random Images with Object Property Event Handlers and the Event Object

In this Try It Out, you rewrite ch10_example1.html to use the Event object instead of this. Type in the following code:

```
<!DOCTYPE html>

<html lang="en">
<head>
    <title>Chapter 10: Example 2</title>
</head>
<body>
    <img src="usa.gif" onclick="changeImg(event)" />
    <img src="mexico.gif" onclick="changeImg(event)" />

    <script>
        var myImages = [
            "usa.gif",
            "canada.gif",
            "jamaica.gif",
            "mexico.gif"
        ];

        function changeImg(e) {
            var el = e.target;
            var newImgNumber = Math.round(Math.random() * 3);

            while (el.src.indexOf(myImages[newImgNumber]) != -1) {
                newImgNumber = Math.round(Math.random() * 3);
            }

            el.src = myImages[newImgNumber];
        }
    </script>
</body>
</html>
```

Save the page as ch10_example2.html. Load the page into your browser, and you will see a page similar to ch10_example1.html. Click an image, and you'll see it change to a random picture.

The code for this page is almost identical to ch10_example1.html. This new version just has a few changes.

The first two changes are in the onclick event handlers of the <img/> elements. Instead of passing this to changeImg(), you pass event.

The next change is in the changeImg() declaration:

```
function changeImg(e) {
```

The parameter name is now e, meaning event. Keep in mind that it doesn't matter what you call this parameter, but the general convention is to use e.

When the browser calls this function, it will pass an `Event` object as the e parameter, and you can retrieve the img element object that received the event by using e.target:

```
var el = e.target;
```

You assign this object to a variable called el (short for element), and you use it in the while loop:

```
while (el.src.indexOf(myImages[newImgNumber]) != -1) {
    newImgNumber = Math.round(Math.random() * 3);
}
```

You also use it to assign its src property in the last line of the function:

```
el.src = myImages[newImgNumber];
```

The changes made to changeImg() are minimal, and though it does require just a little bit more code, it is much more versatile, as you learn later in the chapter.

Using the HTML attribute event handlers is an easy way to connect your JavaScript code to an element's events, but they have some downsides:

➤ Your HTML and JavaScript are mixed together. This makes it more difficult to maintain and find and fix bugs.

➤ You can't remove an event handler without changing the HTML.

➤ You can only set up event handlers for elements that appear in your HTML code, as opposed to elements you create dynamically (like, for example, when you create an element using `document.createElement()`).

These issues, however, are solved with an object's event handler properties.

Handling Events via Object Properties

With this method, you first need to define the function that will be executed when the event occurs. Then you need to set that object's event handler property to the function you defined.

This is illustrated in the following example. Open your editor and type in the following code:

```
<!DOCTYPE html>

<html lang="en">
<head>
    <title>Chapter 10, Example 3</title>
</head>
<body>
    <a id="someLink" href="somepage.html">
        Click Me
    </a>
    <script>
        function linkClick() {
```

```
            alert("This link is going nowhere");
            return false;
        }

        document.getElementById("someLink").onclick = linkClick;
    </script>
</body>
</html>
```

Save this as ch10_example3.html.

First, you have the <a/> element, whose object's event you are connecting to. You'll notice there is no mention of the event handler or the function within the attributes of the tag, but do notice that it now has an id attribute. This is so that you can easily find the element in the document with the getElementById() method.

Next, you define the function linkClick(), much as you did previously. As before, you can return a value indicating whether you want the normal action of that object to happen.

The connection is made between the object's event and the function on the final lines of script, as shown in the following code:

```
document.getElementById("someLink").onclick = linkClick;
```

As you learned in the previous chapter, the getElementById() method finds the element with the given id and returns the a object. You set this object's onclick property to reference your function—this makes the connection between the object's event handler and your function. Note that no parentheses are added after the function name. You are assigning the linkClick function object to the element's onclick property, not executing linkClick() and assigning its return value to onclick.

Take a moment and look back at ch10_example2.html. When you listened for the click event using the onclick attribute, you had complete control over how changeImg() was called; you simply called the function and passed it the event object.

But that's now an issue. Look again at the onclick property assignment:

```
document.getElementById("someLink").onclick = linkClick;
```

You no longer control how the event handler function is executed; the browser executes the function for you. How then do you attain a reference to the Event? When an event triggers and an event handler executes, the browser automatically passes an Event object to the handler function.

> **TRY IT OUT** Displaying Random Images with Object Property Event Handlers

In this Try It Out, you rewrite ch10_example2.html to use the onclick property of the img objects. Type in the following code:

```
<!DOCTYPE html>

<html lang="en">
```

```
<head>
    <title>Chapter 10: Example 4</title>
</head>
<body>
    <img id="img0" src="usa.gif" />
    <img id="img1" src="mexico.gif" />

    <script>
        var myImages = [
            "usa.gif",
            "canada.gif",
            "jamaica.gif",
            "mexico.gif"
        ];

        function changeImg(e) {
            var el = e.target;
            var newImgNumber = Math.round(Math.random() * 3);

            while (el.src.indexOf(myImages[newImgNumber]) != -1) {
                newImgNumber = Math.round(Math.random() * 3);
            }

            el.src = myImages[newImgNumber];
        }

        document.getElementById("img0").onclick = changeImg;
        document.getElementById("img1").onclick = changeImg;
    </script>
</body>
</html>
```

Save the page as `ch10_example4.html`. Load the page into your browser, and you will see a page similar to `ch10_example2.html`. Click an image, and you'll see it change to a random picture.

The code for this page is almost identical to `ch10_example2.html`. The first changes are in the `<img>` tags. They no longer have `onclick` attributes, and they now have `id` attributes. The first image has an `id` of `img0`, and the second is `img1`. These elements have an `id` so that you can reference them in your JavaScript code.

The only other changes are the final two lines of JavaScript code:

```
document.getElementById("img0").onclick = changeImg;
document.getElementById("img1").onclick = changeImg;
```

You use `document.getElementById()` to retrieve the two `img` objects from the DOM and assign their `onclick` properties, thus setting up the `changeImg()` functions to handle the `click` events on both `img` objects.

Removing an event handler is rather trivial. Simply assign `null` to the event handler property, like this:

```
img1.onclick = null;
```

By assigning null, you have overwritten the previous value contained by the property, and that introduces the main problem with these types of event handlers: you can assign only one function to handle a given event. For example:

```
img2.onclick = functionOne;
img2.onclick = functionTwo;
```

The first line of this code assigns a function called functionOne() to an element's onclick property. The second line, however, overwrites the value of img2.onclick by assigning it a new value. So, when the user clicks img2, only functionTwo() executes. That behavior is fine if it's what you actually want, but more often than not, you want both functionOne() and functionTwo() to execute when img2 is clicked.

You can do that thanks to the standard DOM event model.

THE STANDARD EVENT MODEL

Up until this point, you've been working with nonstandard techniques for listening for events. Yes, they work in every browser, but that support exists primarily for backward compatibility. They are not guaranteed to work in future browser versions.

First, some history. The two major browsers in the late 1990s were Internet Explorer 4 and Netscape 4—the first browser war. Not surprisingly, both browser vendors implemented vastly different DOMs and event models, fragmenting the web into two groups: websites that catered to Netscape only, and websites that catered to IE only. Very few developers chose the frustrating task of cross-browser development.

Obviously, a need for a standard grew from this fragmentation and frustration. So the W3C introduced the DOM standard, which grew into DOM level 2, which included a standard event model.

The DOM standard defines an object called EventTarget. Its purpose is to define a standard way of adding and removing listeners for an event on the target. Every element node in the DOM is an EventTarget, and as such, you can dynamically add and remove event listeners for a given element.

The standard also describes an Event object that provides information about the element that has generated an event and enables you to retrieve it in script. It provides a set of guidelines for a standard way of determining what generated an event, what type of event it was, and when and where the event occurred. If you want to make it available in script, it must be passed as a parameter to the function connected to the event handler.

> **NOTE** *Older versions of Internet Explorer (8 and below) do not implement the DOM event model. The code in this section only works with modern browsers: IE9+, Chrome, Firefox, Opera, and Safari.*

Connecting Code to Events—The Standard Way

The EventTarget object defines two methods for adding and removing event listeners (remember that an EventTarget is an element). The first method, addEventListener(), registers an event listener on the target on which it's called. You call it on a target/element object, as you see in the following example. Type in the following code:

```
<!DOCTYPE html>

<html lang="en">
<head>
    <title>Chapter 10, Example 5</title>
</head>
<body>
    <a id="someLink" href="somepage.html">
        Click Me
    </a>
    <script>
        var link = document.getElementById("someLink");

        link.addEventListener("click", function (e) {
            alert("This link is going nowhere");

            e.preventDefault();
        });
    </script>
</body>
</html>
```

Save this as ch10_example5.html. This is a re-creation of ch10_example3.html, but it uses the standard event model *application programming interface* (API), which is a set of objects, properties, and methods, to register an event listener and prevent the default action of a link from occurring.

The first line of JavaScript retrieves the element that has an id of someLink, and stores it in the link variable. You then call the addEventListener() method and pass it two arguments. The first is the name of the event without the "on" prefix. In this example, an event listener is registered for the click event.

The second argument is the function that executes when the event occurs. The previous code uses an anonymous function, a common pattern that you'll see very often, but it's more useful to pass a declared function, like this:

```
function linkClick() {
    alert("This link is going nowhere");
    e.preventDefault();
}

link.addEventListener("click", linkClick);
```

Using a declared function lets you reuse it for multiple event listeners, as you see in the next exercise. But first, notice that linkClick() no longer returns false; instead, it calls the preventDefault() method on the Event object. This is the standard way that you prevent the default action from occurring.

TRY IT OUT **Displaying Random Images with Standard Event Handlers**

In this Try It Out, you rewrite ch10_example4.html to use the standard DOM event model. Type in the following code:

```
<!DOCTYPE html>

<html lang="en">
<head>
    <title>Chapter 10: Example 6</title>
</head>
<body>
    <img id="img0" src="usa.gif" />
    <img id="img1" src="mexico.gif" />

    <script>
        var myImages = [
            "usa.gif",
            "canada.gif",
            "jamaica.gif",
            "mexico.gif"
        ];

        function changeImg(e) {
            var el = e.target;
            var newImgNumber = Math.round(Math.random() * 3);

            while (el.src.indexOf(myImages[newImgNumber]) != -1) {
                newImgNumber = Math.round(Math.random() * 3);
            }

            el.src = myImages[newImgNumber];
        }

        document.getElementById("img0").addEventListener("click", changeImg);
        document.getElementById("img1").addEventListener("click", changeImg);
    </script>
</body>
</html>
```

Save the page as ch10_example6.html. Load the page into your browser, and you will see the familiar page from the previous examples. Click an image, and you'll see it change to a random picture.

The only changes from ch10_example4.html are the final two lines of JavaScript:

```
document.getElementById("img0").addEventListener("click", changeImg);
document.getElementById("img1").addEventListener("click", changeImg);
```

Instead of using each element object's onclick property, you register the click event handler using addEventListener().

Using a declared function is also useful because it enables you to unregister an event listener with the removeEventListener() method:

```
elementObj.removeEventListener("click", elementObjClick);
```

When you remove an event listener, you must provide the *same exact* information that you called addEventListener() with; this includes not only the same name of the event, but the same function object that you passed to addEventListener().

The beauty of the standard DOM event model is that you can register multiple event listeners for a single event on a single element. This is extremely useful when you need to listen for the same event on an element with different and unrelated functions. To do this, simply call addEventListener() as many times as you need to, like this:

```
elementObj.addEventListener("click", handlerOne);
elementObj.addEventListener("click", handlerTwo);
elementObj.addEventListener("click", handlerThree);
```

This code registers three listeners for the click event on the element referenced by elementObj. As you may suspect, these listeners execute in the order in which they were registered. So, when you click elementObj, handlerOne() executes first, handlerTwo() executes second, and handlerThree() executes third.

TRY IT OUT Adding and Removing Multiple Event Listeners

In this Try It Out, you practice registering multiple event listeners for a single element, and you remove those listeners when a condition is met. Type in the following code:

```
<!DOCTYPE html>

<html lang="en">
<head>
    <title>Chapter 10: Example 7</title>
</head>
<body>
    <img id="img0" src="usa.gif" />
    <div id="status"></div>

    <script>
        var myImages = [
            "usa.gif",
            "canada.gif",
            "jamaica.gif",
            "mexico.gif"
        ];

        function changeImg(e) {
            var el = e.target;
            var newImgNumber = Math.round(Math.random() * 3);

            while (el.src.indexOf(myImages[newImgNumber]) != -1) {
                newImgNumber = Math.round(Math.random() * 3);
```

```
                }

            el.src = myImages[newImgNumber];
        }

        function updateStatus(e) {
            var el = e.target;
            var status = document.getElementById("status");

            status.innerHTML = "The image changed to " + el.src;

            if (el.src.indexOf("mexico") > -1) {
                el.removeEventListener("click", changeImg);
                el.removeEventListener("click", updateStatus);
            }
        }

        var imgObj = document.getElementById("img0");

        imgObj.addEventListener("click", changeImg);
        imgObj.addEventListener("click", updateStatus);
    </script>
    </body>
    </html>
```

Save the page as `ch10_example7.html`. Load the page into your browser, and you will see a page with a single image. Click the image, and it will change to a random picture. You'll also see the text of the `<div/>` element change to contain the URL of the new picture, as shown in Figure 10-2.

This code is reminiscent of the past few examples; so, let's just focus on what's different. First, the HTML:

```
<img id="img0" src="usa.gif" />
<div id="status"></div>
```

Instead of two image elements, this HTML defines a single `<img/>` element with an `id` of `img0` and a `<div/>` element whose `id` is `status`. The contents of the `<div/>` element will change when the user clicks the image.

There's a new function called `updateStatus()`, and its purpose is to update the text inside `<div id="status"/>`. The first two lines of this function acquire references to the event target (the image) and `<div/>` element:

```
function updateStatus(e) {
    var el = e.target;
    var status = document.getElementById("status");
```

The next line of code changes the text of the `status` element:

```
status.innerHTML = "The image changed to " + el.src;
```

Element objects have an `innerHTML` property that lets you set the contents of the element to whatever value you assign to it. In this code, you change the `<div/>` element's contents to contain the URL of the picture currently displayed in the browser.

To add some variety, the next few lines of code remove the image's click event listeners if the Mexico flag is displayed in the browser:

```
if (el.src.indexOf("mexico") > -1) {
    el.removeEventListener("click", changeImg);
    el.removeEventListener("click", updateStatus);
    }
}
```

The `if` statement uses the `indexOf()` method on the image's `src` to determine if the Mexico flag is currently displayed. If so, you remove the image's two event listeners using the `removeEventListener()` method. We have yet to discuss the code for registering these `click` event listeners, but you pass the same information to `removeEventListener()` that you pass to `addEventListener()`. If you don't, you won't remove the event listeners.

The final lines of code set up the event listeners:

```
var imgObj = document.getElementById("img0");

imgObj.addEventListener("click", changeImg);
imgObj.addEventListener("click", updateStatus);
```

The first line retrieves the `<img id="img0" />` element, and you register the `click` event handlers by calling `addEventListener()` and passing `click` for the event and the two functions, `changeImg()` and `updateStatus()`, respectively.

It's important to remember that when you register multiple event handlers on a single element, the listening functions execute in the order in which you registered them. In this example, you registered a listener with `changeImg()` before a listener with `updateStatus()`. This is ideal because you want the status to display the URL of the image after you change it. If you had registered `updateStatus()` before `changeImg()`, the status would update before the image, thus displaying incorrect information.

Using Event Data

The standard outlines several properties of the `Event` object that offer information about that event: what element it happened at, what type of event took place, and what time it occurred. These are all pieces of data offered by the `Event` object. The following table lists the properties outlined in the specification.

PROPERTIES OF THE EVENT OBJECT	DESCRIPTION
`bubbles`	Indicates whether an event can *bubble*—passing control from one element to another starting from the event target and bubbling up the hierarchy
`cancelable`	Indicates whether an event can have its default action canceled
`currentTarget`	Identifies the current target for the event as the event traverses the DOM
`defaultPrevented`	Indicates whether or not `preventDefault()` has been called on the event
`eventPhase`	Indicates which phase of the event flow an event is in
`target`	Indicates which element caused the event; in the DOM event model, text nodes are a possible target of an event
`timestamp`	Indicates at what time the event occurred
`type`	Indicates the name of the event

Secondly, the DOM event model introduces a `MouseEvent` object, which deals with events generated specifically by the mouse. This is useful because you might need more specific information about the event, such as the position in pixels of the cursor, or the element the mouse has come from. The following table lists some of the `MouseEvent` object's properties:

PROPERTIES OF THE MOUSEEVENT OBJECT	DESCRIPTION
altKey	Indicates whether the Alt key was pressed when the event was generated
button	Indicates which button on the mouse was pressed
clientX	Indicates where in the browser window, in horizontal coordinates, the mouse pointer was when the event was generated
clientY	Indicates where in the browser window, in vertical coordinates, the mouse pointer was when the event was generated
ctrlKey	Indicates whether the Ctrl key was pressed when the event was generated
metaKey	Indicates whether the meta key was pressed when the event was generated
relatedTarget	Used to identify a secondary event target. For mouseover events, this property references the element at which the mouse pointer exited. For mouseout events, this property references the element at which the mouse pointer entered
screenX	Indicates the horizontal coordinates relative to the origin in the screen
screenY	Indicates the vertical coordinates relative to the origin in the screen
shiftKey	Indicates whether the Shift key was pressed when the event was generated

Although any event might create an Event object, only a select set of events can generate a MouseEvent object. On the occurrence of a MouseEvent event, you'd be able to access properties from the Event object and the MouseEvent object. With a non-mouse event, none of the MouseEvent object properties in the preceding table would be available. The following mouse events can create a MouseEvent object:

➤ click occurs when a mouse button is clicked (pressed and released) with the pointer over an element or text.

➤ mousedown occurs when a mouse button is pressed with the pointer over an element or text.

➤ mouseup occurs when a mouse button is released with the pointer over an element or text.

➤ mouseover occurs when a mouse button is moved onto an element or text.

➤ mousemove occurs when a mouse button is moved and it is already on top of an element or text.

➤ mouseout occurs when a mouse button is moved out and away from an element or text.

Unlike MouseEvent, the current DOM specification does not define a KeyboardEvent object for keyboard-related events (although one will be defined in the next version, DOM level 3). You can, however, still access information about keyboard-related events with the properties listed in the following table.

PROPERTIES OF THE KEYBOARDEVENT OBJECT	DESCRIPTION
altKey	Indicates whether the Alt key was pressed when the event was generated
charCode	Used for the keypress event. The Unicode reference number of the key
ctrlKey	Indicates whether the Ctrl key was pressed when the event was generated
keyCode	A system- and browser-dependent numerical code identifying the pressed key
metaKey	Indicates whether the meta key was pressed when the event was generated
shiftKey	Indicates whether the Shift key was pressed when the event was generated

TRY IT OUT Using the DOM Event Model

In this Try It Out, you take a quick look at an example that uses some properties of the MouseEvent object.

Open a text editor and type the following:

```
<!DOCTYPE html>

<html lang="en">
<head>
    <title>Chapter 10: Example 8</title>
    <style>
        .underline {
            color: red;
            text-decoration: underline;
        }
    </style>


</head>
<body>
    <p>This is paragraph 1.</p>
    <p>This is paragraph 2.</p>
```

```
        <p>This is paragraph 3.</p>

    <script>
        function handleEvent(e) {
            var target = e.target;
            var type = e.type;

            if (target.tagName == "P") {
                if (type == "mouseover") {
                    target.className = "underline";
                } else if (type == "mouseout") {
                    target.className = "";
                }
            }

            if (type == "click") {
                alert("You clicked the mouse button at the X:"
                    + e.clientX + " and Y:" + e.clientY + " coordinates");
            }
        }

        document.addEventListener("mouseover", handleEvent);
        document.addEventListener("mouseout", handleEvent);
        document.addEventListener("click", handleEvent);
    </script>

</body>
</html>
```

Save this as ch10_example8.html and run it in your browser. When you move your mouse over one of the paragraphs, you'll notice its text changes color to red and it becomes underlined. Click anywhere in the page, and you'll see an alert box like Figure 10-3.

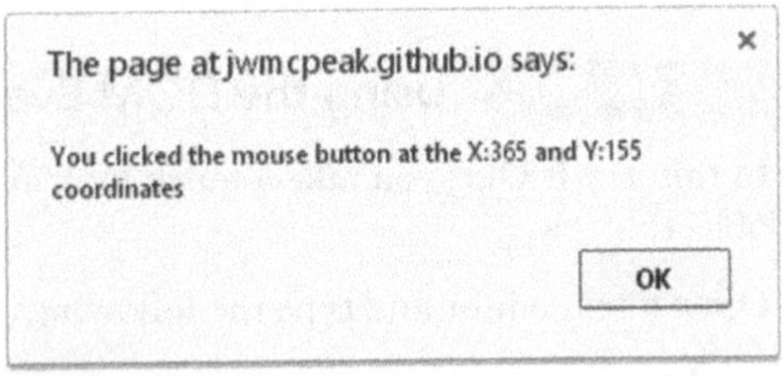

Now click OK, move the pointer in the browser window, and click again. A different result appears.

This example is consistent with the event-handling behavior: The browser waits for an event, and every

---

The page at jwmcpeak.github.io says: ✕

You clicked the mouse button at the X:365 and Y:155
coordinates

                                              [OK]

FIGURE 10-3

---

time that event occurs it calls the corresponding function. It will continue to wait for the event until you exit the browser or that particular web page. In this example, you assign event handlers for the mouseover, mouseout, and click events on the document object:

```
document.addEventListener("mouseover", handleEvent);
document.addEventListener("mouseout", handleEvent);
document.addEventListener("click", handleEvent);
```

One function, handleEvent(), handles all three of these events.

Whenever any of these events fire, the handleClick() function is raised and a new MouseEvent object is generated. Remember that MouseEvent objects give you access to Event object properties as well as MouseEvent object properties, and you use some of them in this example.

The function accepts the MouseEvent object and assigns it the reference e:

```
function handleEvent(e) {
    var target = e.target;
    var type = e.type;

    if (target.tagName == "P") {
```

Inside the function, the first thing you do is initialize the target and type variables with the target and type event properties, respectively. These are convenience variables to make accessing that information easier. You then check if the event target (the element that caused the event) has a tagName of P. If the target is a paragraph element, the next bit of information you need to find is what kind of event took place by using the type variable:

```
if (type == "mouseover") {
    target.className = "underline";
} else if (type == "mouseout") {
    target.className = "";
}
}
```

If the event is a mouseover, the paragraph's CSS class is assigned the underline class defined in the page's style sheet. If the event type is mouseout, the element's className property is cleared, which returns the text to its original style. This style-changing code runs only if the element that caused the event is a paragraph element.

Next, the function determines if the user clicked his mouse by again checking the type variable:

```
if (type == "click") {
    alert("You clicked the mouse button at the X:"
        + e.clientX + " and Y:" + e.clientY + " coordinates");
}
```

If the user did indeed click somewhere in the page, you use the alert() method to display the contents of the clientX and clientY properties of the MouseEvent object on the screen.

The MouseEvent object supplied to this function is overwritten and re-created every time you generate an event, so the next time you click the mouse or move the pointer, it creates a new MouseEvent object containing the coordinates for the x and y positions and the information on the element that caused the event to fire.

Let's look at another example.

TRY IT OUT A Crude Tab Strip

In this Try It Out, you will write a functional, yet flawed, tab strip using the mouseover, mouseout, and click events. Open your text editor and type the following:

```
<!DOCTYPE html>

<html lang="en">
<head>
```

```
    <title>Chapter 10: Example 9</title>
    <style>
        .tabStrip {
            background-color: #E4E2D5;
            padding: 3px;
            height: 22px;
        }

        .tabStrip div {
            float: left;
            font: 14px arial;
            cursor: pointer;
        }

        .tabStrip-tab {
            padding: 3px;
        }

        .tabStrip-tab-hover {
            border: 1px solid #316AC5;
            background-color: #C1D2EE;
            padding: 2px;
        }

        .tabStrip-tab-click {
            border: 1px solid #facc5a;
            background-color: #f9e391;
            padding: 2px;
        }
    </style>
</head>
<body>
    <div class="tabStrip">
        <div data-tab-number="1" class="tabStrip-tab">Tab 1</div>
        <div data-tab-number="2" class="tabStrip-tab">Tab 2</div>
        <div data-tab-number="3" class="tabStrip-tab">Tab 3</div>
    </div>
    <div id="descContainer"></div>

    <script>
        function handleEvent(e) {
            var target = e.target;

            switch (e.type) {
                case "mouseover":
                    if (target.className == "tabStrip-tab") {
                        target.className = "tabStrip-tab-hover";
                    }
                    break;
                case "mouseout":
                    if (target.className == "tabStrip-tab-hover") {
                        target.className = "tabStrip-tab";
                    }
                    break;
                case "click":
```

```
                    if (target.className == "tabStrip-tab-hover") {
                        target.className = "tabStrip-tab-click";
                        var num = target.getAttribute("data-tab-number");

                        showDescription(num);
                    }
                    break;
            }
        }

        function showDescription(num) {
            var text = "Description for Tab " + num;

            descContainer.innerHTML = text;
        }

        document.addEventListener("mouseover", handleEvent);
        document.addEventListener("mouseout", handleEvent);
        document.addEventListener("click", handleEvent);
    </script>
</body>
</html>
```

Save this file as ch10_example9.html. Open it in your browser, and when you move your mouse pointer over a tab, its style changes to a blue background with a darker blue border. When you click a tab, its style changes yet again to make the tab's background color a light orange with a darker orange border color. Also, when you click a tab, text is added to the page. For example, clicking tab 3 results in the text "Description for Tab 3" being added to the page.

Take a look at the HTML in the body, and its style, first:

```
<div class="tabStrip">
    <div data-tab-number="1" class="tabStrip-tab">Tab 1</div>
    <div data-tab-number="2" class="tabStrip-tab">Tab 2</div>
    <div data-tab-number="3" class="tabStrip-tab">Tab 3</div>
</div>
<div id="descContainer"></div>
```

The first `<div/>` element has a CSS class of `tabStrip`. The three `<div/>` elements contained within it represent three tabs. Each tab `<div/>` element has a numeric value assigned to its `data-tab-number` attribute, and a CSS class of `tabStrip-tab`.

The tab strip `<div/>` element has a sibling `<div/>` element with an `id` value of `descContainer`. It doesn't contain any children, and it doesn't have a CSS class associated with it.

In this example, the tab strip is visually set apart from the rest of the page by giving it a gray background:

```
.tabStrip {
    background-color: #E4E2D5;
    padding: 3px;
    height: 22px;
}
```

It's given an actual height of 28 pixels (height + top padding + bottom padding). This height and padding vertically centers the tab <div/> elements within the tab strip.

The tabs have several CSS rules to define the way they are rendered in the browser because they have three states: normal, hover, and click. Despite these three states, they are still tabs and thus share some visual characteristics. The first rule dictates these shared properties:

```
.tabStrip div {
    float: left;
    font: 14px arial;
    cursor: pointer;
}
```

The selector tells the browser to apply these properties to all <div/> elements inside the tab strip. The elements are set to float left to give them an inline appearance (<div/> elements are block elements, and appear on a new line by default).

The next rule, the tabStrip-tab class, defines the normal state:

```
.tabStrip-tab {
    padding: 3px;
}
```

All this rule adds is a padding of three pixels on all sides of the element. Next is the hover state, as defined by the tabStrip-tab-hover class:

```
.tabStrip-tab-hover {
    border: 1px solid #316AC5;
    background-color: #C1D2EE;
    padding: 2px;
}
```

This rule reduces the padding to two pixels, adds a one-pixel-wide border, and changes the background color to a shade of blue. Borders, like padding, add to the actual dimensions of an element; reducing the padding while adding a border keeps the element in a hover state, the same height and width as it was in the normal state.

The final rule declares the tabStrip-tab-click class:

```
.tabStrip-tab-click {
    border: 1px solid #facc5a;
    background-color: #f9e391;
    padding: 2px;
}
```

This class is similar to the hover class; the only difference is the dark orange border color and light orange background color.

Now let's look at the JavaScript code that performs the magic. The code consists of the handleEvent() function, which is registered as the document object's mouseover, mouseout, and click event listeners:

```
document.addEventListener("mouseover", handleEvent);
document.addEventListener("mouseout", handleEvent);
document.addEventListener("click", handleEvent);
```

The function begins by declaring a variable called `target`, which is initialized with the event object's `target` property:

```
function handleEvent(e) {
    var target = e.target;
```

Now you need to determine what type of event took place and make the appropriate changes to the DOM. A `switch` statement works well here, and you use the event object's `type` property as the switch expression:

```
switch (e.type) {
    case "mouseover":
        if (target.className == "tabStrip-tab") {
            target.className = "tabStrip-tab-hover";
        }
        break;
```

First, check for the `mouseover` event. If the element that caused the event has a class name of `tabStrip-tab`, a tab in its normal state, change the element's `className` property to `tabStrip-tab-hover`. In doing so, the tab is now in the hover state.

If a `mouseout` event occurred, you also need to make changes to the DOM:

```
case "mouseout":
    if (target.className == "tabStrip-tab-hover") {
        target.className = "tabStrip-tab";
    }
    break;
```

This code changes the tab's `className` property to `tabStrip-tab` (the normal state) only when the tab in which the mouse pointer exited is in the hover state.

The last event you need to look for is the `click` event, so check for it now with the following code:

```
case "click":
    if (target.className == "tabStrip-tab-hover") {
        target.className = "tabStrip-tab-click";
```

This code changes the tab element's `className` to `tabStrip-tab-click`, thus putting it into the click state.

Next, you need to add the tab's description to the page, and you start this process by getting the tab's number from the `<div/>` element's `data-tab-number` attribute. You use the `getAttribute()` method to retrieve this value:

```
        var num = target.getAttribute("data-tab-number");

        showDescription(num);
    }
    break;
}
}
```

Now that you have the tab's number, you pass it to the showDescription() function:

```
function showDescription(num) {
    var descContainer = document.getElementById("descContainer");
```

The tabs' descriptions are added to the <div/> element with an id of descContainer, so as this code shows, you first retrieve that element using the getElementById() method.

The descriptions are dynamically created by this function, so now you need to build the description text and display that text in the descContainer element. First, create a string containing the description for the tab. In this example, the description is simple and includes the tab's number:

```
var text = "Description for Tab " + num;
```

Then add the text to the description element by using its innerHTML property:

```
descContainer.innerHTML = text;
}
```

One problem that has plagued the web is the lack of compatibility between the major browsers. Today's modern browsers do a very good job of implementing the standard DOM, but older browsers, specifically IE8 and below, only partially support the DOM standard. Despite the lack of support for the DOM standard in these old browsers, you can still acquire the same useful information on a given event with old-IE's event model.

EVENT HANDLING IN OLD VERSIONS OF INTERNET EXPLORER

Old-IE's event model incorporates the use of a global event object (it is a property of the window object), and one such object exists for each open browser window. The browser updates the event object every time the user causes an event to occur, and it provides information similar to that of the standard DOM Event object.

> **NOTE** To be clear, the information in this section applies to IE8 and below. We will refer to these old browsers as "old-IE." IE9 and later implement the standard DOM event model. Thankfully, old-IE's usage continues to dwindle with each passing year.

Accessing the event Object

Because the event object is a property of window, it is very simple to access:

```
<p ondblclick="handle()">Paragraph</p>

<script>
```

```
function handle() {
    alert(event.type);
}
</script>
```

This code assigns the `handle()` function to handle the `<p/>` element's `dblclick` event. When the function executes, it gets the type of event that caused the `handle()` function's execution. Because the event object is global, there is no need to pass the object to the handling function like the DOM event model. Also note that like other properties of the `window` object, it's not required that you precede the event object with `window`.

> **NOTE** Even though you don't have to pass `event` to an event handler, you still want to do so in order to support both old-IE and modern browsers.

The same holds true when you assign event handlers through JavaScript using object properties:

```
<p id="p">Paragraph</p>
<h1 id="h1">Heading 1</h1>
<span id="span">Special Text</span>

<script>
function handle() {
    if (event.type == "mouseover") {
        alert("You moved over the Special Text");
    }
}

document.getElementById("p").ondblclick = handle;
document.getElementById("h1").onclick = handle;
document.getElementById("span").onmouseover = handle;
</script>
```

Old-IE does not support `addEventListener()` and `removeEventListener()`, but it does implement two similar methods: `attachEvent()` and `detachEvent()`. Rewrite Example 5 using old-IE's event API:

```
<!DOCTYPE html>

<html lang="en">
<head>
    <title>Chapter 10, Example 10</title>
</head>
<body>
    <a id="someLink" href="somepage.html">
        Click Me
    </a>
    <script>
        var link = document.getElementById("someLink");

        function linkClick(e) {
```

```
            alert("This link is going nowhere");

            e.returnValue = false;
        }

        link.attachEvent("onclick", linkClick);
    </script>
    </body>
    </html>
```

Save this as ch10 _ example10.html.

Let's first look at the call to attachEvent(). The overall pattern is the same as addEventListener() (and thus removeEventListener()); you pass the event you want to listen for and the function to execute when the event occurs. But as you'll notice from this code, the event names are prefixed with "on".

The second argument is the function that executes when the event occurs. Notice, though, that the linkClick() function defines a parameter called e. When you register an event handler with attachEvent(), old-IE passes the event object to the handling function.

Also notice that linkClick() does not return false or call preventDefault(). Instead, old-IE's event object has a property called returnValue, and setting it to false achieves the same result.

Using Event Data

Unsurprisingly, IE's event object provides some different properties from the DOM standard's Event and MouseEvent objects, although they typically provide you with similar data.

The following table lists some of the properties of IE's event object.

PROPERTIES OF THE EVENT OBJECT	DESCRIPTION
altKey	Indicates whether the Alt key was pressed when the event was generated
button	Indicates which button on the mouse was pressed
cancelBubble	Gets or sets whether the current event should bubble up the hierarchy of event handlers
clientX	Indicates where in the browser window, in horizontal coordinates, the mouse pointer was when the event was generated
clientY	Indicates where in the browser window, in vertical coordinates, the mouse pointer was when the event was generated
ctrlKey	Indicates whether the Ctrl key was pressed when the event was generated
fromElement	Gets the element object the mouse pointer is exiting

keyCode	Gets the Unicode keycode associated with the key that caused the event
returnValue	Gets or sets the return value from the event
screenX	Indicates where in the browser window, in horizontal coordinates relative to the origin in the screen coordinates, the mouse pointer was when the event was generated
screenY	Indicates where in the browser window, in vertical coordinates relative to the origin in the screen coordinates, the mouse pointer was when the event was generated
shiftKey	Indicates whether the Shift key was pressed when the event was generated
srcElement	Gets the element object that caused the event
toElement	Gets the element object that the mouse pointer is entering
type	Retrieves the event's name

Let's revisit some previous examples and make them work exclusively in old-IE.

TRY IT OUT Adding and Removing Multiple Event Handlers in Old-IE

In this Try It Out, you rewrite ch10_example7.html to use old-IE's attachEvent() and detachEvent() methods. Type in the following code:

```
<!DOCTYPE html>

<html lang="en">
<head>
    <title>Chapter 10: Example 11</title>
</head>
<body>
    <img id="img0" src="usa.gif" />
    <div id="status"></div>

    <script>
        var myImages = [
            "usa.gif",
            "canada.gif",
            "jamaica.gif",
            "mexico.gif"
        ];

        function changeImg(e) {
            var el = e.srcElement;
```

```
                var newImgNumber = Math.round(Math.random() * 3);

                while (el.src.indexOf(myImages[newImgNumber]) != -1) {
                    newImgNumber = Math.round(Math.random() * 3);
                }

                el.src = myImages[newImgNumber];
            }

        function updateStatus(e) {
            var el = e.srcElement;
            var status = document.getElementById("status");

            status.innerHTML = "The image changed to " + el.src;

            if (el.src.indexOf("mexico") > -1) {
                el.detachEvent("onclick", changeImg);
                el.detachEvent("onclick", updateStatus);
            }
        }

        var imgObj = document.getElementById("img0");

        imgObj.attachEvent("onclick", updateStatus);
        imgObj.attachEvent("onclick", changeImg);
    </script>
  </body>
</html>
```

Save the page as ch10_example11.html. Load the page into your browser, and you will see it behave like ch10_example7.html. Clicking the image results in it changing to a random picture, and the text of the <div/> element changes to contain the URL of the new picture.

Let's jump right to the code, which is mostly the same as ch10_example7.html. The first big difference is how you register the event handlers for the image object. Instead of using addEventListener(), you use old-IE's attachEvent() method:

```
        imgObj.attachEvent("onclick", updateStatus);
        imgObj.attachEvent("onclick", changeImg);
```

But there's another big difference here. Unlike the standard addEventListener(), the handlers registered with attachEvent() execute in reverse order. So, you register the handler with the updateStatus() function before registering with changeImg().

The next change is in the first statement of the changeImg() function. You want to retrieve the element that received the event, and old-IE's event object gives you that information with the srcElement property:

```
    function changeImg(e) {
        var el = e.srcElement;
```

The rest of the function is left unchanged.

You want to do the same thing in the `updateStatus()` function, so you change the first statement to use old-IE's `srcElement` property as well:

```
function updateStatus(e) {
    var el = e.srcElement;
```

After you retrieve the status element and set its `innerHTML`, you then want to remove the event handlers if the Mexico flag is displayed. You do this with the `detachEvent()` method:

```
if (el.src.indexOf("mexico") > -1) {
    el.detachEvent("onclick", changeImg);
    el.detachEvent("onclick", updateStatus);
}
```

Here, the order in which you call `detachEvent()` doesn't matter. It will simply remove the event handler from the element.

Next, you rewrite Example 8 to use old-IE's event model.

TRY IT OUT **Using the IE Event Model**

In this Try It Out, you use the old-IE's event model. Open your text editor and type the following. Feel free to copy and paste the elements within the body and the style sheet from `ch10_example8.html`.

```
<!DOCTYPE html>

<html lang="en">
<head>
    <title>Chapter 10: Example 12</title>
    <style>
        .underline {
            color: red;
            text-decoration: underline;
        }
    </style>
</head>
<body>
    <p>This is paragraph 1.</p>
    <p>This is paragraph 2.</p>
    <p>This is paragraph 3.</p>

    <script>
        function handleEvent(e) {
            var target = e.srcElement;
            var type = e.type;

            if (target.tagName == "P") {
                if (type == "mouseover") {
                    target.className = "underline";
                } else if (type == "mouseout") {
                    target.className = "";
```

```
        }
    }

    if (type == "click") {
        alert("You clicked the mouse button at the X:"
            + e.clientX + " and Y:" + e.clientY + " coordinates");
    }
}

document.attachEvent("onmouseover", handleEvent);
document.attachEvent("onmouseout", handleEvent);
document.attachEvent("onclick", handleEvent);
    </script>
</body>
</html>
```

Save this as ch10_example12.html, and load it into old-IE. It'll look and behave exactly like Example 8; the paragraph text will change to red and have an underline as you move your mouse pointer over the paragraphs. When your mouse pointer leaves a paragraph, the text returns to the original state. When you click your mouse, an alert box tells you the coordinates of where your mouse pointer was when you clicked.

You assign the handleEvent() function to handle the mouseover, mouseout, and click events on the document object:

```
document.attachEvent("onmouseover", handleEvent);
document.attachEvent("onmouseout", handleEvent);
document.attachEvent("onclick", handleEvent);
```

When you cause any of these events to fire, the browser updates the event object and calls the handleEvent() function:

```
function handleEvent(e) {
    var target = e.srcElement;
    var type = e.type;
```

First, you want to get the target of the event (or in old-IE speak, the source element), so initialize the target variable with the event object's srcElement property and the type variable with the event object's type property.

Next, you check if the event target has a tagName of P. If so, you determine what kind of event took place by using the type variable:

```
    if (target.tagName == "P") {
        if (type == "mouseover") {
            target.className = "underline";
        } else if (type == "mouseout") {
            target.className = "";
        }
    }
```

For mouseover events, you change the paragraph's CSS class to underline. If the event type is mouseout, the element's className property is set to an empty string—returning the text to its original style.

Before moving on, notice the name of these events: mouseover and mouseout. Like the standard DOM, old-IE's type property returns the name of the event without the "on" prefix. So even though you register the event handlers with onmouseover, onmouseout, and onclick, the type property will return mouseover, mouseout, and click, respectively.

The next bit of code displays the mouse pointer's location if the mouse button was clicked:

```
if (type == "click") {
    alert("You clicked the mouse button at the X:"
        + e.clientX + " and Y:" + e.clientY + " coordinates");
}
}
```

If you compare Example 8 with Example 12, you will notice the two primary differences are how the event handlers are registered, and how to retrieve the element that caused the event to occur. Most everything else is shared between the standard DOM event model and IE's event model.

Now let's look at Example 9 through the prism of old-IE.

TRY IT OUT **A Crude Tab Strip for Old-IE**

In this Try It Out, you will rewrite ch10_example9.html to use old-IE's event model. Open your text editor and type the following, or you can copy ch10_example9.html and change the highlighted lines of code:

```
<!DOCTYPE html>

<html lang="en">
<head>
    <title>Chapter 10: Example 13</title>
    <style>
        .tabStrip {
            background-color: #E4E2D5;
            padding: 3px;
            height: 22px;
        }

        .tabStrip div {
            float: left;
            font: 14px arial;
            cursor: pointer;
        }

        .tabStrip-tab {
            padding: 3px;
        }

        .tabStrip-tab-hover {
            border: 1px solid #316AC5;
            background-color: #C1D2EE;
            padding: 2px;
```

```
            }
        .tabStrip-tab-click {
            border: 1px solid #facc5a;
            background-color: #f9e391;
            padding: 2px;
        }
    </style>
</head>
<body>
    <div class="tabStrip">
        <div data-tab-number="1" class="tabStrip-tab">Tab 1</div>
        <div data-tab-number="2" class="tabStrip-tab">Tab 2</div>
        <div data-tab-number="3" class="tabStrip-tab">Tab 3</div>
    </div>
    <div id="descContainer"></div>

    <script>
        function handleEvent(e) {
            var target = e.srcElement;

            switch (e.type) {
                case "mouseover":
                    if (target.className == "tabStrip-tab") {
                        target.className = "tabStrip-tab-hover";
                    }
                    break;
                case "mouseout":
                    if (target.className == "tabStrip-tab-hover") {
                        target.className = "tabStrip-tab";
                    }
                    break;
                case "click":
                    if (target.className == "tabStrip-tab-hover") {
                        target.className = "tabStrip-tab-click";
                        var num = target.getAttribute("data-tab-number");

                        showDescription(num);
                    }
                    break;
            }
        }

        function showDescription(num) {
            var text = "Description for Tab " + num;

            descContainer.innerHTML = text;
        }

        document.attachEvent("onmouseover", handleEvent);
        document.attachEvent("onmouseout", handleEvent);
        document.attachEvent("onclick", handleEvent);
    </script>
</body>
</html>
```

Save this file as `ch10_example13.html`. Open it in your browser, and you'll see it work exactly like `ch10_example9.html`. When you move your mouse pointer over a tab, its style changes to a blue background with a darker blue border. When you click a tab, its style changes yet again and adds the tab's description to the page.

Four things are different in this version of the tab script. The first three are how you register the event handlers:

```
document.attachEvent("onmouseover", handleEvent);
document.attachEvent("onmouseout", handleEvent);
document.attachEvent("onclick", handleEvent);
```

Instead of using `addEventListener()`, you use old-IE's `attachEvent()` method to register the event handlers.

The next and last modification is the first statement of `handleEvent()`:

```
function handleEvent(e) {
    var target = e.srcElement;
```

As in the previous examples, you use the event object's `srcElement` property to retrieve the event target. The rest of the function remains unchanged.

In the next section, you learn how to handle the fundamental differences between both event models and to write cross-browser DHTML code.

WRITING CROSS-BROWSER CODE

By now you've written two versions of multiple examples: one for standards-compliant browsers and one for old-IE. In the real world, creating separate versions of websites is rarely considered best practice, and it's much, much easier to write a cross-browser version of the web page. In this section, you use the knowledge you've gained of the DOM, the standard DOM event model, and old-IE's event model to write cross-browser code.

The trick to cross-browser JavaScript is to create a unified API that hides the complexity of working with different browser implementations. For example, to register a new event listener, you need to do three things:

➤ Check if the browser supports the standard DOM event model.

➤ If so, use `addEventListener()`.

➤ If not, use `attachEvent()`.

Using the technique of feature detection, which you learned about in Chapter 8, you can easily determine if the browser supports `addEventListener()`. Simply check to see if it exists, like this:

```
if (typeof addEventListener != "undefined") {
    // use addEventListener()
```

```
    } else {
        // use attachEvent()
    }
```

When writing cross-browser JavaScript, you always want to check for standards compliance first because some browsers may support both options. For example, IE9 and IE10 support both `addEventListener()` and `attachEvent()`. If you check for `attachEvent()` instead of `addEventListener()`, like this:

```
// wrong! Do not do!
if (typeof attachEvent != "undefined") {
    // use attachEvent
} else {
    // use addEventListener
}
```

IE9 and IE10 will use `attachEvent()` instead of `addEventListener()`. We know that `attachEvent()` exhibits different behavior than `addEventListener()`, and as such, we want to avoid that behavior as much as possible. Plus, we always want to use standards-compliant code because it is guaranteed to work in every standards-compliant browser.

The previous example uses the `typeof` operator to determine if the `addEventListener()` method is not undefined, but you can simplify the code by using `addEventListener` as a truthy or falsy value, like this:

```
if (addEventListener) {
    // use addEventListener()
} else {
    // use attachEvent()
}
```

Whether you use the `typeof` operator or truthy/falsy values, either approach will give you the same results. Just keep in mind that you want to be consistent as you write your code. If you use `typeof`, use it for all of your feature-detection code.

So with this in mind, you can write a function like this:

```
function addListener(obj, type, fn) {
    if (obj.addEventListener) {
        obj.addEventListener(type, fn)
    } else {
        obj.attachEvent("on" + type, fn);
    }
}
```

Let's break down this code. Here, you define a function called `addListener()`. It has three parameters—the object to register the event listener on, the event type, and the function to execute when the event fires:

```
function addListener(obj, type, fn) {
```

The first thing you do inside this function is to check if the given object has an `addEventListener()` method:

```
if (obj.addEventListener) {
    obj.addEventListener(type, fn)
}
```

If `addEventListener()` exists, you call it and pass the `type` and `fn` parameters to it. But if `addEventListener()` doesn't exist, you want to call `attachEvent()`:

```
    else {
        obj.attachEvent("on" + type, fn);
    }
}
```

Here, you append on to the value contained within the `type` variable. This way, you can pass the standard name of the event, such as `click`, to the `addListener()` function, and it'll work with both standards-compliant browsers and old-IE.

To use this function, you'd call it like this:

```
addListener(elementObj, "click", eventHandler);
```

Assuming `elementObj` is an element object and `eventHandler()` is a function, you'd successfully register an event listener/handler for standards-compliant browsers and old-IE.

Following the pattern used in the `addListener()` function, you can write an event utility object that makes it easier to write cross-browser, event-driven code. An event utility object should provide the capability to add and remove listeners, as well as get the event target.

TRY IT OUT A Cross-Browser Event Utility

In this Try It Out, you will write a utility to make it easier to write cross-browser code. Open your text editor and type the following:

```
var evt = {
    addListener: function(obj, type, fn) {
        if (obj.addEventListener) {
            obj.addEventListener(type, fn);
        } else {
            obj.attachEvent("on" + type, fn);
        }
    },
    removeListener: function(obj, type, fn) {
        if (obj.removeEventListener) {
            obj.removeEventListener(type, fn);
        } else {
            obj.detachEvent("on" + type, fn);
        }
    },
    getTarget: function(e) {
        if (e.target) {
```

```
            return e.target;
        }

        return e.srcElement;
    },
    preventDefault: function(e) {
        if (e.preventDefault) {
            e.preventDefault();
        } else {
            e.returnValue = false;
        }
    }
};
```

Save it as event-utility.js.

Using object literal notation, you create an object called evt. Its purpose is to make it easier to write cross-browser code:

```
var evt = {
```

The first method you write is the addListener() method, and it is exactly the same as the addListener() function you previously wrote:

```
addListener: function(obj, type, fn) {
    if (obj.addEventListener) {
        obj.addEventListener(type, fn);
    } else {
        obj.attachEvent("on" + type, fn);
    }
},
```

If the browser supports addEventListener(), it uses the method to register an event listener. Otherwise, the browser calls attachEvent().

The next method is removeListener(). As its name implies, it removes a listener that was added previously to an object:

```
removeListener: function(obj, type, fn) {
    if (obj.removeEventListener) {
        obj.removeEventListener(type, fn);
    } else {
        obj.detachEvent("on" + type, fn);
    }
},
```

The code is almost identical to addListener() except for a few key changes. First, it checks if the given object has a removeEventListener() method, and if so, it calls removeEventListener(). If not, it assumes the browser is old-IE and calls detachEvent().

The third method, getTarget(), is responsible for getting the event target from the event object:

```
getTarget: function(e) {
    if (e.target) {
        return e.target;
```

```
        }
        return e.srcElement;
    }
};
```

It follows the same pattern used in `addListener()` and `removeListener()`; it uses the `target` property as a truthy/falsy value to determine if the browser supports the standard API. If `target` is supported, it is returned. Otherwise, the function returns the element object contained within `srcElement`.

The fourth and final method is `preventDefault()`. The purpose of this method is to prevent the default action of the event that took place (if such an action exists). It first checks for standards compliance by determining if the supplied event object has a `preventDefault()` method. If so, it calls the method; otherwise, it sets the event object's `returnValue` to false.

Before moving on, it's important to realize that this event utility object is based on an assumption: If the browser doesn't support the standard event model, it must be old-IE. Although this is a safe assumption to make, it is not always 100 percent correct. Some old mobile browsers do not support either the standard event model or old-IE's event model. However, as Windows, Android, and iOS mobile devices continue to gain market share, these old, non-compliant mobile browsers are vanishing from the market. In most cases, it's safe to ignore them.

Now that you have a utility for making it easier to write cross-browser, event-driven code, let's revisit the previous examples and put it to use.

Start by modifying Example 10. Here's the revised code:

```html
<!DOCTYPE html>

<html lang="en">
<head>
    <title>Chapter 10, Example 14</title>
</head>
<body>
    <a id="someLink" href="somepage.html">
        Click Me
    </a>

    <script src="event-utility.js"></script>
    <script>
        var link = document.getElementById("someLink");

        function linkClick(e) {
            alert("This link is going nowhere");

            evt.preventDefault(e);
        }

        evt.addListener(link, "click", linkClick);
    </script>
</body>
</html>
```

Save this as `ch10_example14.html`.

The highlighted lines of code are the only changes. First, you include event-utility.js. The code in this example assumes the file is in the same directory as ch10_example14.html:

```
<script src="event-utility.js"></script>
```

You then register the event listener using evt.addListener():

```
evt.addListener(link, "click", linkClick);
```

You pass it the element object you want to register the listener on, the name of the event you want to listen for, and the function to execute when the event occurs.

The final change is inside the linkClick() function. You want to prevent the browser from navigating to somepage.html, so you call your event utility's preventDefault() method and pass it the event object. Now, when you click the link, the browser will stay on the same page.

TRY IT OUT Adding and Removing Multiple Event Handlers

In this Try It Out, you rewrite ch10_example11.html and use your event utility object to add and remove event listeners/handlers. You can write it from scratch, or you can copy and paste from ch10_example11 .html. The highlighted lines indicate what changed in this example.

```
<!DOCTYPE html>

<html lang="en">
<head>
    <title>Chapter 10: Example 15</title>
</head>
<body>
    <img id="img0" src="usa.gif" />
    <div id="status"></div>

    <script src="event-utility.js"></script>
    <script>
        var myImages = [
            "usa.gif",
            "canada.gif",
            "jamaica.gif",
            "mexico.gif"
        ];

        function changeImg(e) {
            var el = evt.getTarget(e);
            var newImgNumber = Math.round(Math.random() * 3);

            while (el.src.indexOf(myImages[newImgNumber]) != -1) {
                newImgNumber = Math.round(Math.random() * 3);
            }

            el.src = myImages[newImgNumber];
        }

        function updateStatus(e) {
```

```
            var el = evt.getTarget(e);
            var status = document.getElementById("status");

            status.innerHTML = "The image changed to " + el.src;

            if (el.src.indexOf("mexico") > -1) {
                evt.removeListener(el, "click", changeImg);
                evt.removeListener(el, "click", updateStatus);
            }
        }

        var imgObj = document.getElementById("img0");

        evt.addListener(imgObj, "click", changeImg);
        evt.addListener(imgObj, "click", updateStatus);
    </script>
</body>
</html>
```

Save the page as ch10_example15.html. Load the page into your browser, and you will see it behave like ch10_example11.html. Clicking the image results in it changing to a random picture, and the text of the <div/> element changes to contain the URL of the new picture.

You've seen this code a few times now, so the pertinent changes are highlighted. First, you want to include your event-utility.js file.

The next change is how you register the event listeners for the image object. Using your event utility's addListener() method, you pass it the image object, event name, and the function:

```
    evt.addListener(imgObj, "click", changeImg);
    evt.addListener(imgObj, "click", updateStatus);
```

In the changeImg() and updateStatus() functions, you change their first lines to retrieve the event target to use your new getTarget() method:

```
    var el = evt.getTarget(e);
```

Then inside updateStatus(), you modify the code inside the if statement to use your new removeListener() method:

```
    if (el.src.indexOf("mexico") > -1) {
        evt.removeListener(el, "click", changeImg);
        evt.removeListener(el, "click", updateStatus);
    }
```

There is, however, an issue with this new version: In old-IE, the event listeners execute in reverse order. This is a problem, but one you'll fix at the very end of this chapter.

Next, you rewrite Example 12 to use your new evt object.

TRY IT OUT Using the Event Models of Differing Browsers

In this Try It Out, you will rewrite `ch10_example12.html` using your event utility. Open your text editor and type the following. Feel free to copy and paste the elements within the body and the style sheet from `ch10_example12.html`.

```html
<!DOCTYPE html>

<html lang="en">
<head>
    <title>Chapter 10: Example 16</title>
    <style>
        .underline {
            color: red;
            text-decoration: underline;
        }
    </style>
</head>
<body>
    <p>This is paragraph 1.</p>
    <p>This is paragraph 2.</p>
    <p>This is paragraph 3.</p>

    <script src="event-utility.js"></script>
    <script>
        function handleEvent(e) {
            var target = evt.getTarget(e);
            var type = e.type;

            if (target.tagName == "P") {
                if (type == "mouseover") {
                    target.className = "underline";
                } else if (type == "mouseout") {
                    target.className = "";
                }
            }

            if (type == "click") {
                alert("You clicked the mouse button at the X:"
                    + e.clientX + " and Y:" + e.clientY + " coordinates");
            }
        }

        evt.addListener(document, "mouseover", handleEvent);
        evt.addListener(document, "mouseout", handleEvent);
        evt.addListener(document, "click", handleEvent);
    </script>
</body>
</html>
```

Save this as `ch10_example16.html`, and load it into different browsers (preferably a standards-compliant browser and old-IE, if you have access to one). It'll look and behave exactly like `ch10_example12.html`; the paragraph text will change to red and have an underline as you move your mouse pointer over the paragraphs. When your mouse pointer leaves a paragraph, the text returns to the original state. When you click your mouse, an `alert` box tells you the coordinates of where your mouse pointer was when you clicked.

Once again, the majority of code is left untouched with only five lines of code having changes. First, you want to include the event-utility.js file using a `<script/>` element:

```
<script src="event-utility.js"></script>
```

Next, you register the `mouseover`, `mouseout`, and `click` event listeners using your `evt.addListener()` method:

```
evt.addListener(document, "mouseover", handleEvent);
evt.addListener(document, "mouseout", handleEvent);
evt.addListener(document, "click", handleEvent);
```

And finally, you change the first line of the `handleEvent()` function:

```
function handleEvent(e) {
    var target = evt.getTarget(e);
```

Instead of using any browser-specific code, you use `evt.getTarget()` to retrieve the element object that received the event.

Now let's look at `ch10_example13.html` and use the evt object.

TRY IT OUT   A Crude Tab Strip for All Browsers

In this Try It Out, you will rewrite `ch10_example13.html` using your cross-browser event utility. Open your text editor and type the following, or you can copy `ch10_example13.html` and change the highlighted lines of code:

```
<!DOCTYPE html>

<html lang="en">
<head>
    <title>Chapter 10: Example 17</title>
    <style>
        .tabStrip {
            background-color: #E4E2D5;
            padding: 3px;
            height: 22px;
        }

        .tabStrip div {
            float: left;
            font: 14px arial;
            cursor: pointer;
        }

        .tabStrip-tab {
            padding: 3px;
```

```
            }

        .tabStrip-tab-hover {
            border: 1px solid #316AC5;
            background-color: #C1D2EE;
            padding: 2px;
        }

        .tabStrip-tab-click {
            border: 1px solid #facc5a;
            background-color: #f9e391;
            padding: 2px;
        }
    </style>
</head>
<body>
    <div class="tabStrip">
        <div data-tab-number="1" class="tabStrip-tab">Tab 1</div>
        <div data-tab-number="2" class="tabStrip-tab">Tab 2</div>
        <div data-tab-number="3" class="tabStrip-tab">Tab 3</div>
    </div>
    <div id="descContainer"></div>

    <script src="event-utility.js"></script>
    <script>
        function handleEvent(e) {
            var target = evt.getTarget(e);

            switch (e.type) {
                case "mouseover":
                    if (target.className == "tabStrip-tab") {
                        target.className = "tabStrip-tab-hover";
                    }
                    break;
                case "mouseout":
                    if (target.className == "tabStrip-tab-hover") {
                        target.className = "tabStrip-tab";
                    }
                    break;
                case "click":
                    if (target.className == "tabStrip-tab-hover") {
                        target.className = "tabStrip-tab-click";
                        var num = target.getAttribute("data-tab-number");

                        showDescription(num);
                    }
                    break;
            }
        }

        function showDescription(num) {
            var descContainer = document.getElementById("descContainer");

            var text = "Description for Tab " + num;

            descContainer.innerHTML = text;
```

```
        }
    evt.addListener(document, "mouseover", handleEvent);
    evt.addListener(document, "mouseout", handleEvent);
    evt.addListener(document, "click", handleEvent);
    </script>
  </body>
</html>
```

Save this file as `ch10_example17.html`. Open it in multiple browsers, and you'll see it work exactly like Example 13.

The code is mostly unchanged; this new version changes only five lines of code. As with the past two examples, you need to include the file containing your evt object:

```
<script src="event-utility.js"></script>
```

Next, you register the event listeners on the document object for the click, mouseover, and mouseout events using the evt object's addListener() method:

```
evt.addListener(document, "mouseover", handleEvent);
evt.addListener(document, "mouseout", handleEvent);
evt.addListener(document, "click", handleEvent);
```

And finally, you change the first line of the handleEvent() function:

```
function handleEvent(e) {
    var target = evt.getTarget(e);
```

Instead of directly using the standard or old-IE's target and srcElement properties, you use evt.getTarget() to retrieve the element object that received the event.

Thankfully with each passing year, the importance of cross-browser JavaScript diminishes as old-IE continues to lose market share. IE8 is currently the most popular version of old-IE, and the number of people using that browser is dwindling. Whether or not you need to support old-IE is determined by your target audience, and only you can decide if you need to put forth the effort of supporting it.

The past few sections have been rather repetitive, but understanding events and how they work is absolutely vital in JavaScript development. Much of the code you write will be in reaction to an event occurring within the page.

Additionally, you'll find that more events are added to browsers as they implement new features—for example, the new HTML5 Drag and Drop API.

NATIVE DRAG AND DROP

Dragging and dropping objects within a web page has been the Holy Grail of JavaScript development, and rightly so—the system we spend the majority of our time with, our computer's/device's operating system, has always provided that functionality.

Unfortunately, true drag-and-drop support has been elusive in web development, although some JavaScript libraries came close. Though they enabled us to drag and drop elements within the web page, they were limited by the capabilities, or lack of in this case, exposed by the browser; interacting with dropped objects from the operating system was impossible.

But HTML5 changes that. For browsers that support it, you can now incorporate true drag-and-drop capabilities within your web pages thanks to HTML5's Drag and Drop API. Not only can you move elements around the page by dragging and dropping them, but the API enables you to drag objects from the operating system, like files, and drop them in your page.

> **NOTE** *Native drag and drop is only supported in IE10+, Chrome, Firefox, Opera, and Safari.*

Making Content Draggable

HTML5 makes it easy to create draggable content. By simply adding the draggable attribute to an element and setting it to true, you tell the browser that the element can be used for drag and drop:

```
<div draggable="true">Draggable Content</div>
```

In most browsers, images, links, and selected text are draggable by default. Figure 10-4 shows some selected text being dragged in Chrome.

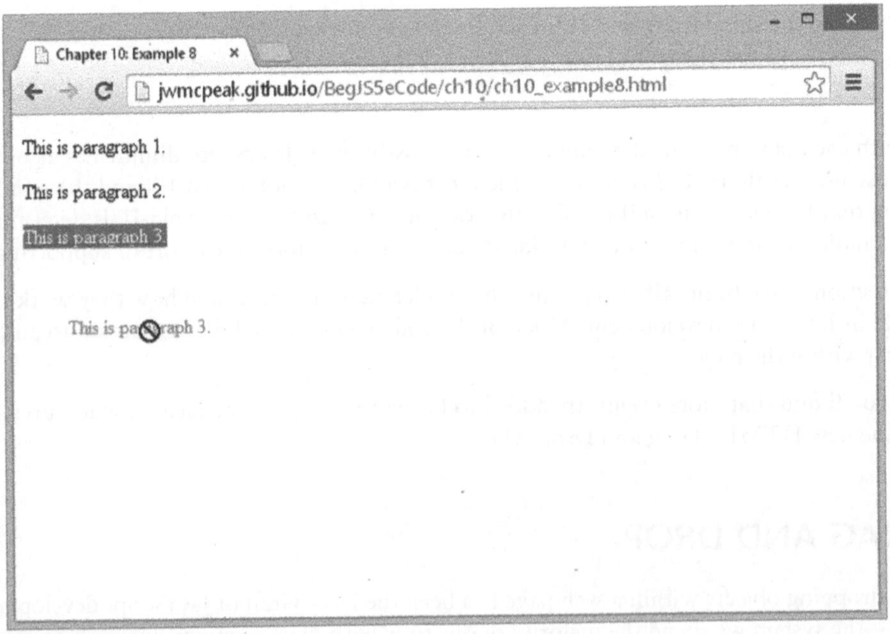

FIGURE 10-4

Three events are related to the source of the drag—that is, the element that is being dragged. The following table lists them.

DRAG SOURCE EVENTS	DESCRIPTION
dragstart	Fires on the element when a drag is started. This does not fire when dragging an object from the filesystem
drag	Fires continuously while the object is dragged
dragend	Fires when the drag operation is complete, regardless of whether the object was dropped. This does not fire when dragging an object from the filesystem

To perform a drag-and-drop operation, the only event you need to listen for is dragstart, but that doesn't mean the drag and dragend events are not useful. You can use them to add extra functionality and/or visual cues to enhance the user's experience.

Creating a Drop Target

If you are dragging objects, chances are very good that you need some place to drop them—a drop target. There aren't special attributes or HTML to signify an element as a drop target. Instead, you listen for one or multiple events on the element serving as the drop target.

One of them is the dragenter event. This event fires when the mouse cursor enters the target while dragging an object. For example:

```
<!DOCTYPE html>

<html lang="en">
<head>
    <title>Chapter 10: Example 18</title>
    <style>
        .drop-zone {
            width: 300px;
            padding: 20px;
            border: 2px dashed #000;
        }
    </style>
</head>
<body>
    <div id="dropZone" class="drop-zone">Drop Zone!</div>
    <div id="dropStatus"></div>

    <script>
        function handleDragEnter(e) {
            dropStatus.innerHTML = "You're dragging something!";
        }

        var dropZone = document.getElementById("dropZone");
```

```
            var dropStatus = document.getElementById("dropStatus");

            dropZone.addEventListener("dragenter", handleDragEnter);
        </script>
    </body>
    </html>
```

Save this file as ch10_example18.html. Open it and you'll see something like Figure 10-5.

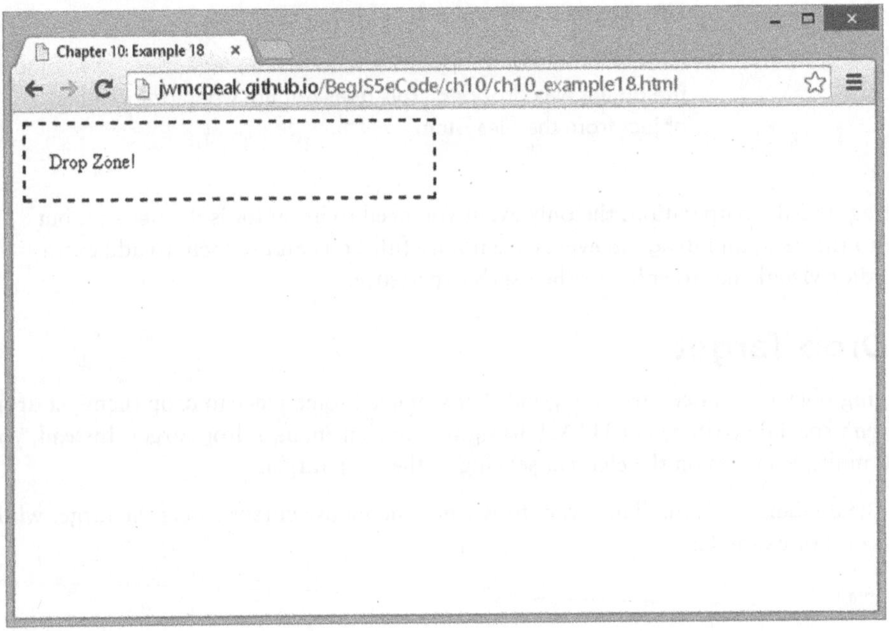

FIGURE 10-5

Drag anything to the target. It can be selected text, a file on your computer, and so on. As your mouse pointer enters the target, you'll see the text You're dragging something! appear on the page. Figure 10-6 shows text being dragged over the drop zone in Chrome.

In this page, a <div/> element is used as the drop zone:

```
<div id="dropZone" class="drop-zone">Drop Zone!</div>
```

It has an id of dropZone and has the CSS class of drop-zone. The CSS is unimportant from a functional standpoint, but it does add visual clarity because it defines the area in which you can drop something.

The important stuff is in the JavaScript. First, you retrieve the drop target element by using the document.getElementById() method and listen for its dragenter event. You also retrieve the <div/> element with an id of dropStatus. You'll use it to display status messages during the drag operation:

```
var dropZone = document.getElementById("dropZone");
var dropStatus = document.getElementById("dropStatus");

dropZone.addEventListener("dragenter", handleDragEnter);
```

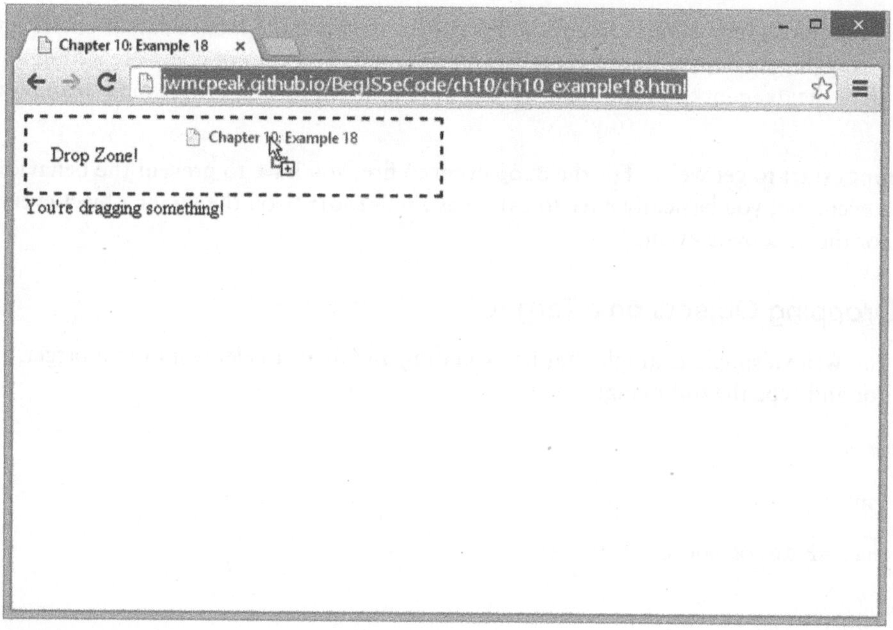

FIGURE 10-6

This event fires only when you are dragging something and the mouse cursor enters the target. When this happens, the handleDragEnter() function executes:

```
function handleDragEnter(e) {
    dropStatus.innerHTML = "You're dragging something!";
}
```

This simple function changes the status element's contents to state, You're dragging something!

The dragenter event is one of four events you can listen for on the target element. The following table lists them.

DRAG SOURCE EVENTS	DESCRIPTION
dragenter	Fires when the mouse is first moved over the target element while dragging
dragover	Fires on the target as the mouse moves over an element while dragging
dragleave	Fires on the target when the mouse leaves the target while dragging
drop	Fires on the target when the drop (the user releases the mouse button) occurs

The `dragenter` event looks important; after all, it lets you know when the mouse cursor enters the drop zone while dragging an object. But in actuality, it's optional. You cannot complete a drag-and-drop operation with the `dragenter` event. Instead, you have to listen for the drop zone's `dragover` event.

This is where things start to get weird. For the `drop` event to fire, you have to prevent the behavior of the `dragover` event. So, you basically have to call `preventDefault()` on the `Event` object every time you listen for the `dragover` event.

TRY IT OUT   Dropping Objects on a Target

In this Try It Out, you write a simple example that lets you drag and drop an element onto a target. Open your text editor and type the following:

```html
<!DOCTYPE html>

<html lang="en">
<head>
    <title>Chapter 10: Example 19</title>
    <style>
        .box {
            width: 100px;
            height: 100px;
        }

        .red {
            background-color: red;
        }

        .drop-zone {
            width: 300px;
            padding: 20px;
            border: 2px dashed #000;
        }
    </style>
</head>
<body>
    <div draggable="true" class="box red"></div>
    <div id="dropZone" class="drop-zone">Drop Zone!</div>
    <div id="dropStatus"></div>

    <script>
        function dragDropHandler(e) {
            e.preventDefault();

            if (e.type == "dragover") {
                dropStatus.innerHTML = "You're dragging over the drop zone!";
            } else {
                dropStatus.innerHTML = "You dropped something!";
            }
        }

        var dropZone = document.getElementById("dropZone");
```

```
        var dropStatus = document.getElementById("dropStatus");

        dropZone.addEventListener("dragover", dragDropHandler);
        dropZone.addEventListener("drop", dragDropHandler);
    </script>
</body>
</html>
```

Save this file as `ch10_example19.html`, and open it. Your web page will look like Figure 10-7.

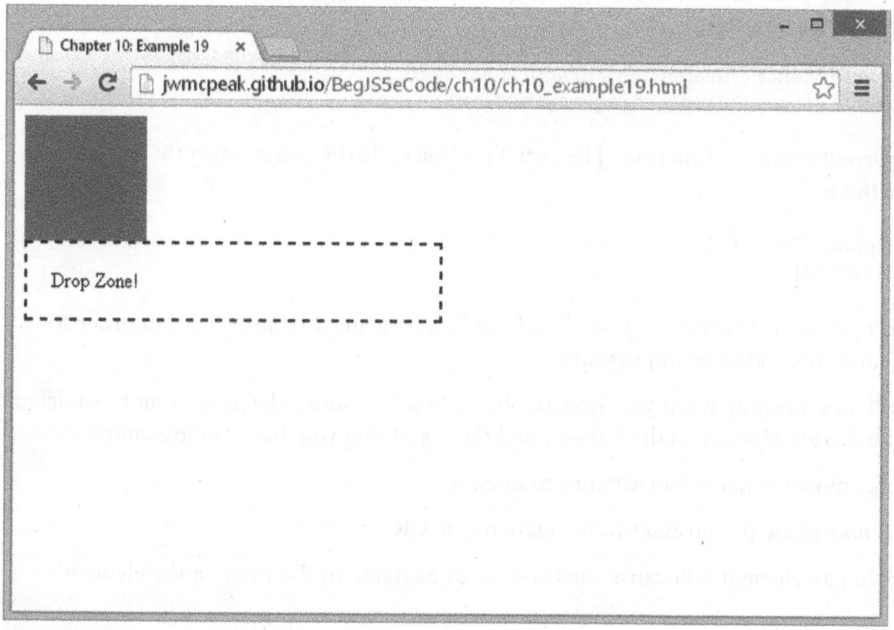

FIGURE 10-7

Drag the red box over the target element, and you'll see the text of the status element change to `You're dragging over the drop zone!` Drop the element in the drop zone, and the status text will change to `You dropped something!`

There is one exception, however: Firefox will not let you drag the red box, but it will let you drop objects from other sources (such as text, files on the filesystem, and so on). We'll explain why later.

The CSS of this example defines three classes. You've already seen the drop-zone class, and the box and red classes are extremely simple:

```
.box {
    width: 100px;
    height: 100px;
}
.red {
    background-color: red;
}
```

The box class sets the element's width and height properties to 100 pixels, and red gives the element a background color of red. These are arbitrary values meant to only give the draggable element some visibility.

Next, the HTML. The only new element in this HTML document is a draggable <div/> element:

```
<div draggable="true" class="box red"></div>
```

To make it draggable, you set the draggable attribute to true, and you apply the box and red CSS classes to make it easier to drag and drop.

But as with Example 18, the good stuff is in the JavaScript. First, you register listeners for the dropZone's dragover and drop events:

```
dropZone.addEventListener("dragover", dragDropHandler);
dropZone.addEventListener("drop", dragDropHandler);
```

Let's look at the dragDropHandler() function. The very first line calls the Event object's preventDefault() method:

```
function dragDropHandler(e) {
    e.preventDefault();
```

This is crucial for two reasons. First, the dragover's default behavior must be prevented in order for the drop event to fire (and that's kind of important).

Second, the browser will do something when you drop an object. In other words, the drop event has a default behavior, but the exact behavior depends on the browser and the object that you drop. Some examples are:

➤ For a file or image, most browsers will attempt to open it.

➤ Dropping a URL may cause the browser to navigate to the URL.

➤ In Firefox, dropping an element will cause the browser to navigate to the value in the element's id attribute.

Therefore, you want to prevent the drop event's default behavior in most cases.

After preventing the default behavior, the dragDropHandler() function changes the content of the dropStatus element based on the type of event:

```
if (e.type == "dragover") {
    dropStatus.innerHTML = "You're dragging over the drop zone!";
} else {
    dropStatus.innerHTML = "You dropped something!";
}
}
```

For the dragover event, it simply states that you are dragging over the target element; otherwise, the function knows that you dropped something and tells you so.

Frustratingly, native drag and drop doesn't work exactly the same in all modern browsers. The aforementioned partial list of the browsers' default behavior for the drop event is just one thing JavaScript developers have to contend with.

But also remember that Example 19 doesn't completely work in Firefox. Although it is frustrating that JavaScript developers have to cope with inconsistent implementations, Firefox's drag-and-drop implementation, whether it's right or wrong, does make some sense in this regard. As we try to drag the red box, we haven't told the browser what we're transferring.

Transferring Data

When you think about it, a drag-and-drop operation is the transference of data. For example, when you drag a file on your filesystem from one folder to another, you are transferring the data (the file) between the two folder locations. When dragging text from one application to another, you are transferring the textual data between the two applications.

Drag and drop in the browser follows a similar concept. When starting a drag, you need to tell the browser what you plan to transfer, and when you drop the object, you need to specify how that data transfers from the source to the target.

The drag-and-drop specification defines a `DataTransfer` object that is used to hold the data that is being dragged during a drag-and-drop operation. You access this object with the `Event` object's `dataTransfer` property. You set data with the `DataTransfer` object's `setData()` method in the `dragstart` event handler, and you read that data in the `drop` event handler with the `getData()` method.

To make Example 19 work in Firefox, you need to handle the `dragstart` event and use the `DataTransfer` object's `setData()` method. The following adds the necessary code:

```
<!DOCTYPE html>

<html lang="en">
<head>
    <title>Chapter 10: Example 20</title>
    <style>
        .box {
            width: 100px;
            height: 100px;
        }

        .red {
            background-color: red;
        }

        .drop-zone {
            width: 300px;
            padding: 20px;
            border: 2px dashed #000;
        }
    </style>
</head>
<body>
    <div draggable="true" class="box red"></div>
    <div id="dropZone" class="drop-zone">Drop Zone!</div>
    <div id="dropStatus"></div>

    <script>
```

```
            function dragStartHandler(e) {
                e.dataTransfer.setData("text", "Drag and Drop!");
            }

            function dragDropHandler(e) {
                e.preventDefault();

                if (e.type == "dragover") {
                    dropStatus.innerHTML = "You're dragging over the " +
                                            "drop zone!";
                } else {
                    dropStatus.innerHTML = e.dataTransfer.getData("text");
                }
            }

            var dragBox = document.querySelector("[draggable]");
            var dropZone = document.getElementById("dropZone");
            var dropStatus = document.getElementById("dropStatus");

            dragBox.addEventListener("dragstart", dragStartHandler);
            dropZone.addEventListener("dragover", dragDropHandler);
            dropZone.addEventListener("drop", dragDropHandler);
        </script>
    </body>
    </html>
```

Save this file as `ch10_example20.html`, and open it in Firefox. Now drag the red box to the target, and you'll see that it behaves similarly to `ch10_example19.html` in all browsers (Firefox included).

Let's focus only on the new lines of code. First, you store the draggable box in the `dragBox` variable by using `document.querySelector()` and passing the attribute selector of "`[draggable]`":

```
        var dragBox = document.querySelector("[draggable]");
```

Next, you register an event listener for the `dragstart` event on the `dragBox` object:

```
        dragBox.addEventListener("dragstart", dragStartHandler);
```

The `dragStartHandler()` function executes when you start a drag operation on the `dragBox` object. This function makes use of the `DataTransfer` object's `setData()` method to hold data for the drag-and-drop operation:

```
        function dragStartHandler(e) {
            e.dataTransfer.setData("text", "Drag and Drop!");
        }
```

The `setData()` function accepts two arguments: the type of data to store and the actual data. The only data types supported by all browsers are "`text`" and "`url`"; therefore, this function stores the textual data of `Drag and Drop!`

> **NOTE** *Most browsers support other data types, such as MIME types (for example, text/plain, text/html, and so on). IE10 and IE11, however, only support text and url.*

The last new/changed line is in the `dragDropHandler()` function. Instead of displaying an arbitrary string value in the status element when the `drop` event fires, you retrieve the data from the `dataTransfer` object by using the `getData()` method:

```
dropStatus.innerHTML = e.dataTransfer.getData("text");
```

The `getData()` method accepts only one argument: the data type you used when calling `setData()`. Therefore, this code retrieves the value of `Drag and Drop!` and uses it as the inner HTML of the status element.

TRY IT OUT Full Drag and Drop

In this Try It Out, you apply everything you've learned about native drag and drop and write a page that lets you drag and drop elements between two drop targets.

Open your text editor and type the following:

```html
<!DOCTYPE html>

<html lang="en">
<head>
    <title>Chapter 10: Example 21</title>
    <style>
        [data-drop-target] {
            height: 400px;
            width: 200px;
            margin: 2px;
            background-color: gainsboro;
            float: left;
        }

        .drag-enter {
            border: 2px dashed #000;
        }

        .box {
            width: 200px;
            height: 200px;
        }

        .navy {
            background-color: navy;
        }

        .red {
            background-color: red;
        }
    </style>
</head>
<body>
    <div data-drop-target="true">
        <div id="box1" draggable="true" class="box navy"></div>
        <div id="box2" draggable="true" class="box red"></div>
    </div>
```

```
        <div data-drop-target="true"></div>

    <script>
        function handleDragStart(e) {
            e.dataTransfer.setData("text", this.id);
        }

        function handleDragEnterLeave(e) {
            if (e.type == "dragenter") {
                this.className = "drag-enter";
            } else {
                this.className = "";
            }
        }

        function handleOverDrop(e) {
            e.preventDefault();

            if (e.type != "drop") {
                return;
            }

            var draggedId = e.dataTransfer.getData("text");
            var draggedEl = document.getElementById(draggedId);

            if (draggedEl.parentNode == this) {
                return;
            }

            draggedEl.parentNode.removeChild(draggedEl);

            this.appendChild(draggedEl);
            this.className = "";
        }

        var draggable = document.querySelectorAll("[draggable]");
        var targets = document.querySelectorAll("[data-drop-target]");

        for (var i = 0; i < draggable.length; i++) {
            draggable[i].addEventListener("dragstart", handleDragStart);
        }

        for (i = 0; i < targets.length; i++) {
            targets[i].addEventListener("dragover", handleOverDrop);
            targets[i].addEventListener("drop", handleOverDrop);
            targets[i].addEventListener("dragenter", handleDragEnterLeave);
            targets[i].addEventListener("dragleave", handleDragEnterLeave);
        }
    </script>
</body>
</html>
```

Save this file as ch10_example21.html and open it in your modern browser of choice. You'll see a page that consists of two columns. On the left, a blue box sits on top of a red one, and on the right is a solid grayish rectangle, as shown in Figure 10-8.

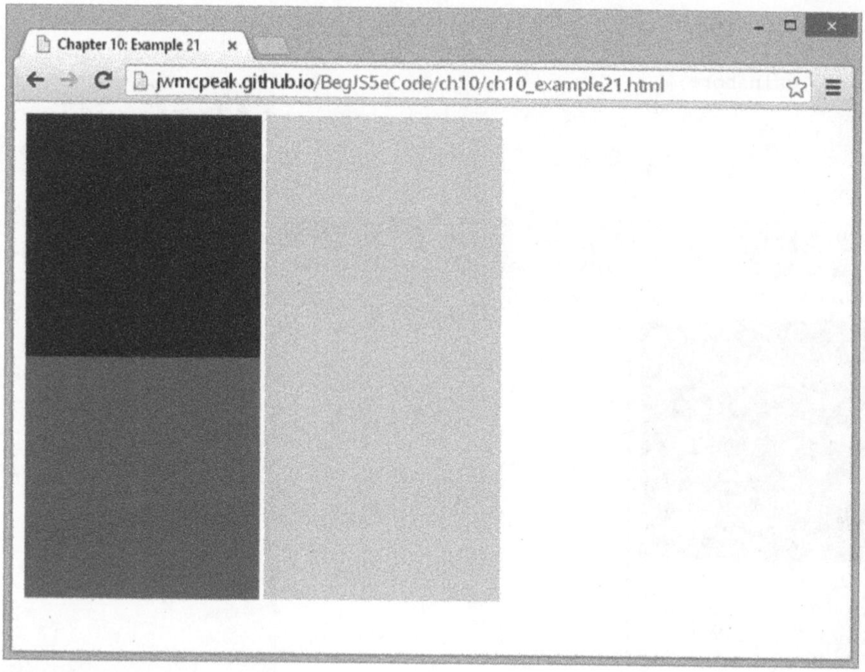

FIGURE 10-8

The grayish areas are drop targets, and the blue and red boxes are draggable objects. Drag the blue box to the empty drop target, and you'll see a dashed border appear around the target (Figure 10-9).

Drop the blue box on that target, and you'll see it move from the left target to the right. Now drag the boxes between the two drop targets to see the full effect.

Let's start with the HTML. A drop target in this example is an element identified with the `data-drop-target` attribute set to `true`. This example consists of two drop targets, although you can easily add more:

```
<div data-drop-target="true">
    <div id="box1" draggable="true" class="box navy"></div>
    <div id="box2" draggable="true" class="box red"></div>
</div>
<div data-drop-target="true"></div>
```

The first drop target contains two draggable `<div/>` elements, and they each have an `id` attribute. Other than their `id` values, the only difference is their CSS. Both use the `box` CSS class, but one also uses the `navy` CSS class, whereas the other uses the `red` class.

Speaking of CSS, let's look at the styles defined in the style sheet. The first rule matches all elements that have a `data-drop-target` attribute:

```
[data-drop-target] {
    height: 400px;
```

```
        width: 200px;
        margin: 2px;
        background-color: gainsboro;
        float: left;
    }
```

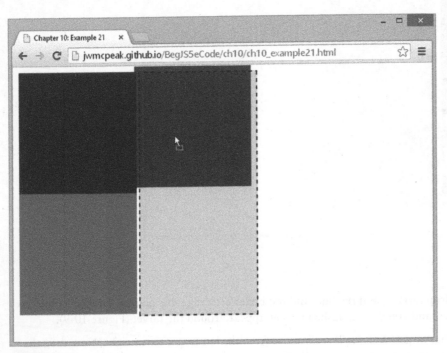

FIGURE 10-9

The height and width are set to accommodate two draggable boxes at a time. A margin of two pixels gives just enough space between the drop target elements to visually separate them. A background color makes them easily distinguishable between the page's background, and they each float left.

The next rule also applies to drop targets:

```
    .drag-enter {
        border: 2px dashed #000;
    }
```

The drag-enter class is used as a visual cue. As you drag an object over a drop target element, this drag-enter class is applied to the element. This isn't necessary for the drag-and-drop operation to complete, but it does enhance the user's experience.

The final set of CSS rules is used for the draggable elements:

```
    .box {
        width: 200px;
```

```
    height: 200px;
}

.navy {
    background-color: navy;
}

.red {
    background-color: red;
}
```

Each draggable element uses the box class to set its height and width. The navy and red classes are used in conjunction with the box class to give the element a background color of navy or red, respectively.

As for the JavaScript, you first retrieve two groups of elements—those that are draggable and those that are drop targets:

```
var draggable = document.querySelectorAll("[draggable]");
var targets = document.querySelectorAll("[data-drop-target]");
```

So using the document.querySelectorAll() method, you retrieve both groups of elements with their respective [draggable] and [data-drop-target] CSS selectors and assign them to the draggable and targets variables.

Next, you want to register the dragstart event listeners on the draggable elements:

```
for (var i = 0; i < draggable.length; i++) {
    draggable[i].addEventListener("dragstart", handleDragStart);
}
```

Using a for loop, you iterate over the draggable collection and call the addEventListener() method on each draggable object, passing dragstart as the event and the handleDragStart() function object as the handler.

You then want to use a similar process on the target elements:

```
for (i = 0; i < targets.length; i++) {
    targets[i].addEventListener("dragover", handleOverDrop);
    targets[i].addEventListener("drop", handleOverDrop);
    targets[i].addEventListener("dragenter", handleDragEnterLeave);
    targets[i].addEventListener("dragleave", handleDragEnterLeave);
}
```

By using another for loop, you loop through the targets collection and register event handlers for the dragover, drop, dragenter, and dragleave events. Two functions are used to handle these four events: the handleOverDrop() function handles the dragover and drop events, and handleDragEnterLeave() handles dragenter and dragleave.

The first function, handleDragStart(), contains just a single line of code:

```
function handleDragStart(e) {
    e.dataTransfer.setData("text", this.id);
}
```

Its purpose is simple: to store the id of the draggable element. Notice the use of this in this.id. When you register an event listener, the handler function executes within the context of the element object the event fired on. In this case, the dragstart event fired on one of the draggable elements; so, this refers to that element. In other words, this is the same as e.target.

The next function is handleDragEnterLeave(), and as mentioned earlier, it executes when the dragenter and dragleave events fire on a drop target:

```
function handleDragEnterLeave(e) {
    if (e.type == "dragenter") {
        this.className = "drag-enter";
    } else {
        this.className = "";
    }
}
```

The first line of this function checks the type of event that occurred. If the event is dragenter, the CSS class of the drop target element is set to drag-enter (once again, notice this is used instead of e.target—it's much easier to type). If the event isn't dragenter, the element's CSS class is set to an empty string, thus removing the drag-enter class.

The final function, handleOverDrop(), performs the real magic of the drag-and-drop operation. This function handles both the dragover and drop events and should therefore prevent the default action from occurring. Thus, the first line of the function calls e.preventDefault():

```
function handleOverDrop(e) {
    e.preventDefault();
```

This is all that is needed for the dragover event. So, if the event isn't a drop event, the function simply exits:

```
if (e.type != "drop") {
    return;
}
```

If it is a drop event, the function continues on and retrieves the draggable element's id from the DataTransfer object:

```
var draggedId = e.dataTransfer.getData("text");
var draggedEl = document.getElementById(draggedId);
```

And with this id, you retrieve the draggable element's object with document.getElementById() and store it in the draggedEl variable.

You have two options when it comes to dropping one of the draggable boxes: you can either drop it in the target it's currently in, or you can drop it in another target. If dropped in its current location, there's nothing left to do except reset the target's CSS class. This is easy enough to check; simply use the element's parentNode property:

```
if (draggedEl.parentNode == this) {
    this.className = "";
    return;
}
```

If the dragged element's parent node is the target drop zone, you set the `className` property to an empty string and exit the function using the `return` statement. Otherwise, you want to move the dragged element node from its old parent/drop target to its new parent/drop target:

```
draggedEl.parentNode.removeChild(draggedEl);

this.appendChild(draggedEl);
```

This is a simple process, as you can see. To remove the draggable element from its current parent, you retrieve its `parentNode` and call the `removeChild()` method. The `removeChild()` method doesn't delete the node; it simply removes it so that you can append it to another node in the DOM.

With the dragged element moved from one drop target to another, the drag-and-drop operation is complete, and you set the drop target element's CSS class to an empty string:

```
this.className = "";
```

This visually resets the drop target, giving users a visual cue that the drag-and-drop operation is complete.

A web page is an interactive environment. Users are busy clicking, typing, dragging, and doing other things. As such, events are an extremely important matter for web developers. Not only are events how we respond and interact with the user, they also enable us to execute code when specific things happen in the page. In later chapters, you see examples of such and use events to respond to an object's action, rather than a user's action.

SUMMARY

You've covered a lot in this chapter, but now you have a solid basis on how to work with and handle events in the browsers that are currently in use on the web. You even know the difference between the standard DOM event model and old-IE's event model, and you wrote an event utility that makes writing cross-browser JavaScript relatively simple.

This chapter covered the following points:

➤   You saw that HTML elements have events as well as methods and properties. You handle these events in JavaScript by using event handlers, which you connect to code that you want to have executed when the event occurs. The events available for use depend on the object you are dealing with.

➤   You can connect a function to an element's event handler using the element's "on" attributes. But you also learned that doing so mixes your HTML and JavaScript, and this approach should be avoided most of the time.

➤   Events can be handled by using an object's "on" properties, which is a better solution than the HTML attributes, but still has its own issues.

➤   The standard DOM event model is supported by all modern browsers, and it provides the best way to connect your code to events.

➤ You learned about the standard Event object and how it provides a lot of information about the event that occurred, including the type of event and the element that received the event.

➤ You learned about old-IE's proprietary event model, how to connect events with attachEvent(), and how to access old-IE's event object.

➤ Some differences exist between the standard DOM event model and the old-IE event model. You learned the key differences and wrote a simple cross-browser event utility.

➤ Some events have a default action that occurs when the event fires, and you can prevent that action with the standard Event object's preventDefault() method and old-IE's returnValue property.

➤ Modern browsers support native drag-and-drop capabilities, and you can write code that takes advantage of this new feature.

➤ In some instances, such as for the document object, a second way of connecting event handlers to code is necessary. Setting the object's property with the name of the event handler to your function produces the same effect as if you did it using the event handler as an attribute.

➤ In some instances, returning values from event functions enables you to cancel the action associated with the event. For example, to stop a clicked link from navigating to a page, you return false from the event handler's code.

That's it for this chapter. In the next chapter, you move on to form scripting, where you can add various controls to your page to help you gather information from the user.

EXERCISES

You can find suggested solutions to these questions in Appendix A.

1. Add a method to the event utility object called isOldIE() that returns a boolean value indicating whether or not the browser is old-IE.

2. Example 15 exhibits some behavior inconsistencies between standards-compliant browsers and old-IE. Remember that the event handlers execute in reverse order in old-IE. Modify this example to use the new isOldIE() method so that you can write specific code for old-IE and standards-compliant browsers (Hint: you will call the addListener() method four times).

3. Example 17 had you write a cross-browser tab script, but as you probably noticed, it behaves peculiarly. The basic idea is there, but the tabs remain active as you click another tab. Modify the script so that only one tab is active at a time.

11

HTML Forms: Interacting with the User

WHAT YOU WILL LEARN IN THIS CHAPTER:

➤ Scripting text, password, text area, and hidden form controls

➤ Writing code for select, check box, and radio button form controls

➤ Using JavaScript to interact with new HTML5 form controls

WROX.COM CODE DOWNLOADS FOR THIS CHAPTER

You can find the wrox.com code downloads for this chapter at http://www.wiley.com/go/ BeginningJavaScript5E on the Download Code tab. You can also view all of the examples and related files at http://beginningjs.com.

Web pages would be very boring if you could not interact with or obtain information from the user, such as text, numbers, or dates. Luckily, with JavaScript this is possible. You can use this information within the web page, or you can post it to the web server where you can manipulate it and store it in a database if you wish. This chapter concentrates on using the information within the web browser, which is called *client-side processing*.

You're quite accustomed to various user interface elements. For example, every operating system has a number of standard elements, such as buttons you can click; lists, drop-down list boxes, and radio buttons you can select from; and boxes you can check. These elements are the means by which you now interface with applications. The good news is that you can include many of these types of elements in your web page—and even better, it's very easy to do so. When you have such an element—say, a button—inside your page, you can then tie code to its events. For example, when the button is clicked, you can fire off a JavaScript function you created.

All of the HTML elements used for interaction should be placed inside an HTML form. Let's start by taking a look at HTML forms and how you interact with them in JavaScript.

HTML FORMS

Forms provide you with a way of grouping together HTML interaction elements with a common purpose. For example, a form may contain elements that enable the input of a user's data for registering on a website. Another form may contain elements that enable the user to ask for a car insurance quote. It's possible to have a number of separate forms in a single page. You don't need to worry about pages containing multiple forms until you have to submit information to a web server—then you need to be aware that the information from only one of the forms on a page can be submitted to the server at one time.

To create a form, use the `<form>` and `</form>` tags to declare where it starts and where it ends. The `<form/>` element has a number of attributes, such as the `action` attribute, which determines where the form is submitted; the `method` attribute, which determines how the information is submitted; and the `target` attribute, which determines the frame to which the response to the form is loaded.

Generally speaking, for client-side scripting where you have no intention of submitting information to a server, these attributes are not necessary. For now the only attribute you need to set in the `<form/>` element is the `name` attribute, so that you can reference the form.

So, to create a blank form, the tags required would look something like this:

```
<form name="myForm">
</form>
```

You won't be surprised to hear that these tags create an `HtmlFormElement` object, which you can use to access the form. You can access this object in two ways.

First, you can access the object directly using its name—in this case `document.myForm`. Alternatively, you can access the object through the `document` object's `forms` collection property. Remember that Chapter 8 included a discussion of the `document` object's `images` collection and how you can manipulate it like any other array. The same applies to the `forms` collection, except that instead of each element in the collection holding an `HtmlImageElement` object, it now holds an `HtmlFormElement` (hereby called simply `Form`) object. For example, if it's the first form in the page, you reference it using `document.forms[0]`.

> **NOTE**   *Of course, you can also access a form using the* `document` *`.getElementById()` and `document.querySelector()` methods.*

Many of the attributes of the `<form/>` element can be accessed as properties of the `HtmlFormElement` object. In particular, the `name` property mirrors the `name` attribute of the `<form/>` element.

TRY IT OUT The forms Collection

In this Try It Out, you'll use the forms collection to access each of three Form objects and show the value of their name properties in a message box. Open your text editor and type the following:

```
<!DOCTYPE html>

<html lang="en">
<head>
    <title>Chapter 11: Example 1</title>
</head>
<body>
    <form action="" name="form1">
        <p>
            This is inside form1.
        </p>
    </form>
    <form action="" name="form2">
        <p>
            This is inside form2
        </p>
    </form>
    <form action="" name="form3">
        <p>
            This is inside form3
        </p>
    </form>
    <script>
        var numberForms = document.forms.length;
        for (var index = 0; index < numberForms; index++) {
            alert(document.forms[index].name);
        }
    </script>
</body>
</html>
```

Save this as ch11_example1.html. When you load it into your browser, you should see an alert box display the name of the first form. Click the OK button to display the next form's name, and then click OK a third time to display the third and final form's name.

Within the body of the page you define three forms. You give each form a name and a paragraph of text.

In the JavaScript code, you loop through the forms collection. Just like any other JavaScript array, the forms collection has a length property, which you can use to determine how many times you need to loop. Actually, because you know how many forms you have, you can just write the number in. However, this example uses the length property, because that makes it easier to add to the collection without having to change the code. Generalizing your code like this is a good practice to get into.

The code starts by getting the number of Form objects within the forms collection and storing that number in the variable numberForms:

```
var numberForms = document.forms.length;
```

Next you define the for loop:

```
for (var formIndex = 0; formIndex < numberForms; formIndex++) {
    alert(document.forms[formIndex].name);
}
```

Remember that because the indexes for arrays start at 0, your loop needs to go from an index of 0 to an index of numberForms - 1. You enable this by initializing the index variable to 0, and setting the condition of the for loop to index < numberForms.

Within the for loop's code, you pass the index of the form you want (that is, index) to document .forms[], which gives you the Form object at that index in the forms collection. To access the Form object's name property, you put a dot at the end of the name of the property, name.

TRADITIONAL FORM OBJECT PROPERTIES AND METHODS

The HTML form controls commonly found in forms, which you look at in more detail shortly, also have corresponding objects. One way to access these is through the elements property of the Form object, another collection. The elements collection contains all the objects corresponding to the HTML interaction elements within the form, with the exception of the little-used <input type="image"/> element. As you see later, this property is very useful for looping through each of the elements in a form. For example, you can loop through each element to check that it contains valid data prior to submitting a form.

Being a collection, the elements property of the Form object has the length property, which tells you how many elements are in the form. The Form object also has the length property, which also gives you the number of elements in the form. Which of these you use is up to you because both do the same job, although writing myForm.length is shorter, and therefore quicker to type and less lengthy to look at in code, than myForm.elements.length.

When you submit data from a form to a server, you normally use the Submit button, which you will come to shortly. However, the Form object also has the submit() method, which does nearly the same thing.

> **NOTE** The submit() method submits the form, but it does not fire the submit event of the Form object; thus, submit event listeners are not called when submitting the form with submit().

Recall that in Chapter 10 you learned that you can affect whether the normal course of events continues or is canceled. You saw, for example, that calling preventDefault() in a hyperlink's click event handler causes the link's navigation to be canceled. Well, the same principle applies to the Form object's submit event, which fires when the user submits the form. By calling preventDefault(), the submission is canceled. This makes the submit event handler's code a great place to do form validation—that is, to check that what the user has entered into the form is valid. For example, if you ask for the users' ages and they enter mind your own business, you can spot that this is text rather than a valid number and stop them from continuing.

In addition to there being a Reset button, which is discussed later in the chapter, the Form object has the reset() method, which clears the form, or restores default values if these exist.

Creating blank forms is not exactly exciting or useful, so now let's turn our attention to the HTML elements that provide interaction functionality inside forms.

HTML Elements in Forms

About ten elements are commonly found within <form/> elements. The most useful are shown in Figures 11-1, 11-2, 11-3, and 11-4, ordered into general types. Each type name is given and, in parentheses, the HTML needed to create it, though note this is not the full HTML but only a portion. The new HTML5 form controls are not listed here; you examine them later in the chapter.

As you can see, most form elements are created by means of the <input/> element. One of the <input/> element's attributes is the type attribute. It's this attribute that decides which of the form elements this element will be. Examples of values for this attribute include button (to create a button) and text (to create a text box).

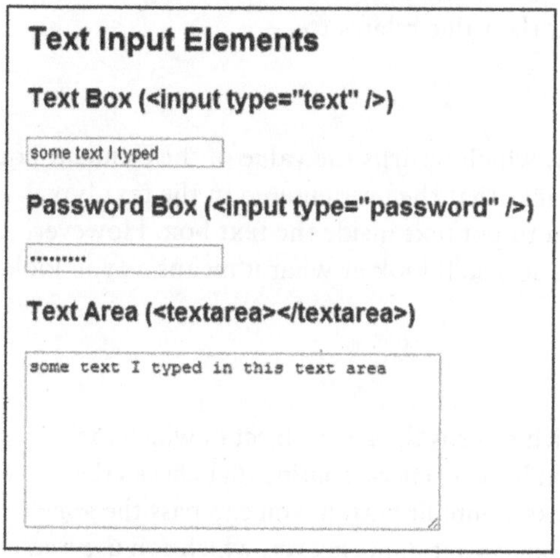

Text Input Elements

Text Box (<input type="text" />)

some text I typed

Password Box (<input type="password" />)

••••••••

Text Area (<textarea></textarea>)

some text I typed in this text area

FIGURE 11-1

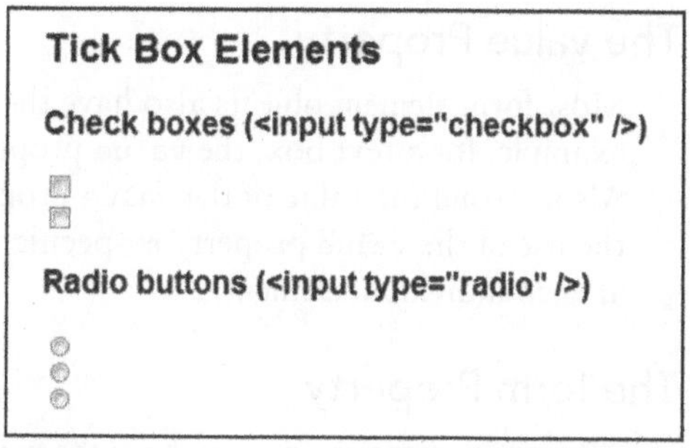

Tick Box Elements

Check boxes (<input type="checkbox" />)

☐
☐

Radio buttons (<input type="radio" />)

○
○
○

FIGURE 11-2

Select Elements

Drop Down List (<select><option></option></select>)

First List Item ▼

List Box (<select size="4"><option></option></select>)

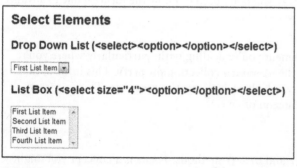
First List Item
Second List Item
Third List Item
Fourth List Item

FIGURE 11-3

Buttons

Standard Button (<input type="button" />)

Button

Submit Button (<input type="submit" />)

Submit

Reset Button (<input type="reset" />)

Reset

FIGURE 11-4

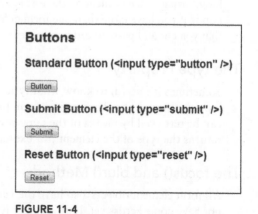

Each form element inside the web page is made available to you as—yes, you guessed it—an object. As with all the other objects you have seen, each element's object has its own set of distinctive properties, methods, and events. You'll be taking a look at each form element in turn and how to use its particular properties, methods, and events, but before you do that, let's look at properties and methods that the objects of the form elements have in common.

Common Properties and Methods

Because most form elements are created by the `<input/>` element, it would be correct to guess that all form elements share several properties and methods in common.

Here are a few.

The name Property

One property that all the objects of the form elements have in common is the name property. You can use the value of this property to reference that particular element in your script. Also, if you are sending the information in the form to a server, the element's name property is sent along with any value of the form element, so that the server knows what the value relates to.

The value Property

Most form element objects also have the value property, which returns the value of the element. For example, for a text box, the value property returns the text that the user entered in the text box. Also, setting the value of the value property enables you to put text inside the text box. However, the use of the value property is specific to each element, so you'll look at what it means as you look at each individual element.

The form Property

All form element objects also have the form property, which returns the Form object in which the element is contained. This can be useful in cases where you have a generic routine that checks the validity of data in a form. For example, when the user clicks a Submit button, you can pass the Form object referenced by the form property of the Submit button to your data checker, which can use it to loop through each element on the form in turn, checking that the data in the element is valid. This is handy if you have more than one form defined on the page or where you have a generic data checker that you cut and paste to different pages—this way you don't need to know the form's name in advance.

The type Property

Sometimes it's useful to know what type of element you're dealing with, particularly where you're looping through the elements in a form using the elements collection property. This information can be retrieved by means of the type property, which each element's object has. This property returns the type of the element (for example, button or text).

The focus() and blur() Methods

All form element objects also have the focus() and blur() methods. *Focus* is a concept you might not have come across yet. If an element is the center of the focus, any key presses made by the user are passed directly to that element. For example, if a text box has focus, pressing keys will enter values into the text box. Also, if a button has the focus, pressing the Enter key causes the button's `onclick` event handler code to fire, just as if a user had clicked the button with his mouse.

The user can set which element currently has the focus by clicking it or by using the Tab key to select it. However, you as the programmer can also decide which element has the focus by using the form element's object's `focus()` method. For example, if you have a text box for the user to enter his age and he enters an invalid value, such as a letter rather than a number, you can tell him that his input is invalid and send him back to that text box to correct his mistake.

Blur, which perhaps could be better called "lost focus," is the opposite of focus. If you want to remove a form element from being the focus of the user's attention, you can use the `blur()` method. When used with a form element, the `blur()` method usually results in the focus shifting to the page containing the form.

In addition to the `focus()` and `blur()` methods, all the form element's objects have the `onfocus` and `onblur` event handlers. These are fired, as you'd expect, when an element gets or loses the focus, respectively, due to user action or the `focus()` and `blur()` methods. The `onblur` event handler can be a good place to check the validity of data in the element that has just lost the focus. If the data is invalid, you can set the focus back to the element and let the user know why the data he entered is wrong.

> **NOTE** Remember that the `submit()` method behaves differently than `focus()` and `blur()` in that it does not fire the `submit` event.

One thing to be careful of is using the `focus()` and `blur()` methods in the `focus` or `blur` event listener code. There is the danger of an infinite loop occurring. For example, consider two elements, each of whose `focus` events passes the focus to the other element. Then, if one element gets the focus, its `focus` event will pass the focus to the second element, whose `focus` event will pass the focus back to the first element, and so on until the only way out is to close the browser down. This is not likely to please your users!

Also be very wary of using the `focus()` and `blur()` methods to put focus back in a problem field if that field or others depend on some of the user's input. For example, say you have two text boxes: one in which you want users to enter their city and the other in which you want them to enter their state. Also say that the input into the state text box is checked to make sure that the specified city is in that state. If the state does not contain the city, you put the focus back on the state text box so that the user can change the name of the state. However, if the user actually input the wrong city name and the right state name, she may not be able to go back to the city text box to rectify the problem.

Button Elements

We're starting our look at form elements with the standard button element because it's probably the most commonly used and is fairly simple. The HTML element to create a button is `<input/>`. For example, to create a button called `myButton`, which has the words "Click Me" on its face, the `<input/>` element would need to be as follows:

```
<input type="button" name="myButton" value="Click Me" />
```

The type attribute is set to button, and the value attribute is set to the text you want to appear on the face of the button. You can leave the value attribute off, but you'll end up with a blank button, which will leave your users guessing as to its purpose.

This element creates an associated HTMLInputElement object (in fact, all <input/> elements create HTMLInputElement objects); in this example it is called myButton. This object has all the common properties and methods described earlier, including the value property. This property enables you to change the text on the button face using JavaScript, though this is probably not something you'll need to do very often. What the button is really all about is the click event.

You connect to the button's click event just as you would with any other element. All you need to do is define a function that you want to execute when the button is clicked (say, buttonClick()) and then register a click event listener with the addEventListener() method.

TRY IT OUT Counting Button Clicks

In the following example, you use the methods described previously to record how often a button has been clicked.

```
<!DOCTYPE html>

<html lang="en">
<head>
    <title>Chapter 11: Example 2</title>
</head>
<body>
    <form action="" name="form1">
        <input type="button" name="myButton" value="Button clicked 0 times" />
    </form>

    <script>
        var myButton = document.form1.myButton;
        var numberOfClicks = 0;

        function myButtonClick() {
            numberOfClicks++;
            myButton.value = "Button clicked " + numberOfClicks + " times";
        }

        myButton.addEventListener("click", myButtonClick);
    </script>
</body>
</html>
```

Save this page as ch11_example2.html. If you load this page into your browser, you will see a button with "Button clicked 0 times" on it. If you repeatedly press this button, you will see the number of button clicks recorded on the text of the button.

You start the script block by defining two variables called myButton and numberOfClicks. The former holds a reference to the <input/> element object. You record the number of times the button has been clicked in the latter and use this information to update the button's text.

The other piece of code in the script block is the definition of the function `myButtonClick()`. This function handles the `<input/>` element's `click` event:

```
myButton.addEventListener("click", myButtonClick);
```

This element is for a `Button` element called `myButton` and is contained within a form called `form1`:

```
<form action="" name="form1">
    <input type="button" name="myButton" value="Button clicked 0 times" />
</form>
```

Let's look at the `myButtonClick()` function a little more closely. First, the function increments the value of the variable `numberOfClicks` by one:

```
function myButtonClick() {
    numberOfClicks++;
```

Next, you update the text on the button face using the `Button` object's `value` property:

```
    myButton.value = "Button clicked " + numberOfClicks + " times";
}
```

The function in this example is specific to this form and button, rather than a generic function you'll use in other situations. Therefore, the code in this example directly refers to a button using the `myButton` variable.

TRY IT OUT   mouseup and mousedown Events

Two less commonly used events supported by the `Button` object are the `mousedown` and `mouseup` events. You can see these two events in action in the next example.

```
<!DOCTYPE html>

<html lang="en">
<head>
    <title>Chapter 11: Example 3</title>
</head>
<body>
    <form action="" name="form1">
        <input type="button" name="myButton" value="Mouse goes up" />
    </form>

    <script>
        var myButton = document.form1.myButton;

        function myButtonMouseup() {
            myButton.value = "Mouse Goes Up";
        }

        function myButtonMousedown() {
```

```
          myButton.value = "Mouse Goes Down";
    }

    myButton.addEventListener("mousedown", myButtonMousedown);
    myButton.addEventListener("mouseup", myButtonMouseup);
  </script>
 </body>
</html>
```

Save this page as ch11_example3.html and load it into your browser. If you click the button with your left mouse button and keep it held down, you'll see the text on the button change to "Mouse Goes Down." As soon as you release the button, the text changes to "Mouse Goes Up."

In the body of the page, you define a button called myButton within a form called form1:

```
<form action="" name="form1">
    <input type="button" name="myButton" value="Mouse goes up" />
</form>
```

Your JavaScript code retrieves this Button object from the document and stores it in the myButton variable, and you register event listeners for the mouseup and mousedown events.

The myButtonMouseup() and myButtonMousedown() functions handle those events, respectively. Each function consists of just a single line of code, in which you use the value property of the Button object to change the text that is displayed on the button's face.

An important point to note is that events like mouseup and mousedown are triggered only when the mouse pointer is actually over the element in question. For example, if you click and hold down the mouse button over your button, then move the mouse away from the button before releasing the mouse button, you'll find that the mouseup event does not fire and the text on the button's face does not change. In this instance it would be the document object's mouseup event that would fire, if you'd connected any code to it.

Don't forget that, like all form element objects, the Button object also has the focus and blur events, though they are rarely used in the context of buttons.

Two additional button types are the Submit and Reset buttons. You define these buttons just as you do a standard button, except that the type attribute of the <input> tag is set to submit or reset rather than to button. For example, the Submit and Reset buttons in Figure 11-4 were created using the following code:

```
<input type="submit" value="Submit" name="submit1" />
<input type="reset" value="Reset" name="reset1" />
```

These buttons have special purposes, which are not related to script.

When the Submit button is clicked, the form data from the form that the button is inside gets sent to the server automatically, without the need for any script.

When the Reset button is clicked, all the elements in a form are cleared and returned to their default values (the values they had when the page was first loaded).

The Submit and Reset buttons have corresponding objects called `Submit` and `Reset`, which have exactly the same properties, methods, and events as a standard `Button` object.

Text Elements

The standard text elements enable users to enter a single line of text. This information can then be used in JavaScript code or submitted to a server for server-side processing.

The Text Box

A text box is created by means of the `<input/>` element, much as the button is, but with the `type` attribute set to `text`. Again, you can choose not to include the `value` attribute, but if you do, this value will appear inside the text box when the page is loaded.

In the following example the `<input/>` element has two additional attributes, `size` and `maxlength`. The `size` attribute determines how many characters wide the text box is, and `maxlength` determines the maximum number of characters the user can enter in the box. Both attributes are optional and use defaults determined by the browser.

For example, to create a text box 10 characters wide, with a maximum character length of 15, and initially containing the words `Hello World`, your `<input/>` element would be as follows:

```
<input type="text" name="myTextBox" size="10" maxlength="15" value="Hello World" />
```

The object that this element creates has a `value` property, which you can use in your scripts to set or read the text contained inside the text box. In addition to the common properties and methods discussed earlier, the object representing the text box also has the `select()` method, which selects or highlights all the text inside the text box. This may be used if the user has entered an invalid value, and you can set the `focus` to the text box and select the text inside it. This then puts the user's cursor in the right place to correct the data and makes it very clear to the user where the invalid data is. The `value` property always returns a string data type, even if number characters are being entered. If you use the value as a number, JavaScript normally does a conversion from a string data type to a number data type for you, but this is not always the case. For example, JavaScript won't do the conversion if the operation you're performing is valid for a string. If you have a form with two text boxes and you add the values returned from these, JavaScript concatenates rather than adds the two values, so 1 plus 1 will be 11 and not 2. To fix this, you need to convert all the values involved to a numerical data type, for example by using `parseInt()` or `parseFloat()` or `Number()`. However, if you subtract the two values, an operation only valid for numbers, JavaScript says "Aha, this can only be done with numbers, so I'll convert the values to a number data type." Therefore, 1 minus 1 will be returned as 0 without your having to use `parseInt()` or `parseFloat()`. This is a tricky bug to spot, so it's best to get into the habit of converting explicitly to avoid problems later.

In addition to the common events, such as `focus` and `blur`, the text box has the `change`, `select`, `keydown`, `keypress`, and `keyup` events.

The `select` event fires when the user selects some text in the text box.

More useful is the `change` event, which fires when the element loses focus if (and only if) the value inside the text box is different from the value it had when it got the focus. This enables you to do things like validity checks that occur only if something has changed.

You can use the readonly attribute of the <input/> element, or the corresponding readOnly property, to prevent the contents from being changed:

```
<input type="text" name="txtReadonly" value="Look but don't change"
    readonly="readonly">
```

The keypress, keydown, and keyup events fire, as their names suggest, when the user presses a key, when the user presses a key down, and when a key that is pressed down is let back up, respectively.

TRY IT OUT A Simple Form with Validation

Let's put all the information on text boxes and buttons together into an example. In this example, you have a simple form consisting of two text boxes and a button. The top text box is for the users' name, and the second is for their age. You do various validity checks. You check the validity of the age text box when it loses focus. However, the name and age text boxes are only checked to see if they are empty when the button is clicked. This example does not work properly on Firefox; we'll discuss this shortly.

```
<!DOCTYPE html>

<html lang="en">
<head>
    <title>Chapter 11: Example 4</title>
</head>
<body>
    <form action="" name="form1">
        Please enter the following details:
        <p>
            Name:
            <input type="text" name="txtName" />
        </p>
        <p>
            Age:
            <input type="text" name="txtAge" size="3" maxlength="3" />
        </p>
        <p>
            <input type="button" value="Check details" name="btnCheckForm">
        </p>
    </form>

    <script>
        var myForm = document.form1;

        function btnCheckFormClick(e) {
            var txtName = myForm.txtName;
            var txtAge = myForm.txtAge;

            if (txtAge.value == "" || txtName.value == "") {
                alert("Please complete all of the form");

                if (txtName.value == "") {
                    txtName.focus();
                } else {
                    txtAge.focus();
```

```
                }
            } else {
                alert("Thanks for completing the form " + txtName.value);
            }
        }

        function txtAgeBlur(e) {
            var target = e.target;

            if (isNaN(target.value)) {
                alert("Please enter a valid age");
                target.focus();
                target.select();
            }
        }

        function txtNameChange(e) {
            alert("Hi " + e.target.value);
        }

        myForm.txtName.addEventListener("change", txtNameChange);
        myForm.txtAge.addEventListener("blur", txtAgeBlur);
        myForm.btnCheckForm.addEventListener("click", btnCheckFormClick);
    </script>
  </body>
</html>
```

After you've entered the text, save the file as `ch11_example4.html` and load it into your web browser.

In the text box shown in Figure 11-5, type your name. When you leave the text box, you'll see `Hi yourname` appear in an `alert` box.

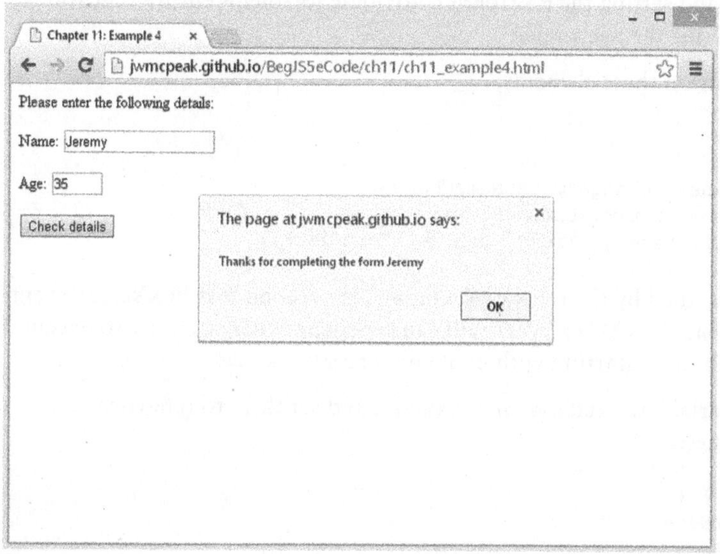

FIGURE 11-5

Enter an invalid value into the age text box, such as aaaa, and when you try to leave the box, it'll tell you of the error and send you back to correct it.

Finally, click the Check Details button and both text boxes will be checked to see that you have completed them. If either is empty, you'll get a message telling you to complete the whole form, and it'll send you back to the box that's empty.

If everything is filled in correctly, you'll get a message thanking you, as shown in Figure 11-5.

Within the body of the page, you create the HTML elements that define your form. Inside your form, which is called form1, you create three form elements with the names txtName, txtAge, and btnCheckForm:

```
<form action="" name="form1">
    Please enter the following details:
    <p>
        Name:
        <input type="text" name="txtName" />
    </p>
    <p>
        Age:
        <input type="text" name="txtAge" size="3" maxlength="3" />
    </p>
    <p>
        <input type="button" value="Check details"
                name="btnCheckForm">
    </p>
</form>
```

You'll see that for the second text box (the txtAge text box), you have included the size and maxlength attributes inside the <input/> element. Setting the size attribute to 3 gives the user an idea of how much text you are expecting, and setting the maxlength attribute to 3 helps ensure that you don't get overly large numbers entered for the age value.

You register listeners for various events on these elements:

```
var myForm = document.form1;

myForm.txtName.addEventListener("change", txtNameChange);
myForm.txtAge.addEventListener("blur", txtAgeBlur);
myForm.btnCheckForm.addEventListener("click", btnCheckFormClick);
```

The first text box's change event is handled by the txtNameChange(), the second text box's blur event is handled by txtAgeBlur(), and the button's click event will cause btnCheckFormClick() to execute. Let's look at each of these functions in turn, starting with btnCheckFormClick().

The first thing you do is define two variables, txtName and txtAge, and set them to reference <input/> elements with the same names:

```
function btnCheckFormClick(e) {
    var txtName = myForm.txtName;
    var txtAge = myForm.txtAge;
```

These are convenience variables, thus reducing the size of your code (you don't have to type `myForm`
`.txtName` every time you reference the `txtName` object). It makes your code more readable and
therefore easier to debug, and it saves typing.

After getting the reference to the `<input/>` element objects, you then use it in an `if` statement to check
whether the value in the text box named `txtAge` or the text box named `txtName` actually contains any
text:

```
if (txtAge.value == "" || txtName.value == "") {
    alert("Please complete all of the form");

    if (txtName.value == "") {
        txtName.focus();
    } else {
        txtAge.focus();
    }
}
```

If you do find an incomplete form, you alert the user. Then in an inner `if` statement, you check which
text box was not filled in. You set the focus to the offending text box, so that the user can start filling it
in straightaway without having to move the focus to it herself. It also lets the user know which text box
your program requires her to fill in. To avoid annoying your users, make sure that text in the page tells
them which fields are required.

If the original outer `if` statement finds that the form is complete, it lets the user know with a thank-you
message:

```
else {
    alert("Thanks for completing the form " + txtName.value);
}
}
```

In this sort of situation, it's probably more likely that you'll submit the form to the server than to let
the user know with a thank-you message. You can do this using the `Form` object's `submit()` method or
using a normal Submit button.

The next of the three functions is `txtAgeBlur()`, which handles the blur event of the `txtAge` text
box. This function's purpose is to check that the string value the user entered into the age box actually
consists of numeric characters:

```
function txtAgeBlur(e) {
    var target = e.target;
```

At the start of the function, you retrieve the target of the event (the `txtAge` text box) and store it in the
`target` variable. You could use `myForm.txtAge` to reference the same `txtAge` text box, but using the
`Event` object's `target` property is a better solution. The `txtAgeBlur()` function works only with the
element that received the blur event. As such, using the `Event` object's `target` property gives you a
generalized function that doesn't depend on any external variables, such as `myForm`. Plus, it's less typing.

The following `if` statement checks to see whether what has been entered in the `txtAge` text box can
be converted to a number. You use the `isNaN()` function to do this for you. If the value in the `txtAge`

text box is not a number, it tells the user and sets the focus back to the text box by calling the `focus()` method. Additionally, this time you highlight the text by using the `select()` method. This makes it even clearer to the users what they need to fix. It also allows them to rectify the problem without needing to delete text first.

```
if (isNaN(target.value)) {
    alert("Please enter a valid age");
    target.focus();
    target.select();
}
}
```

You could go further and check that the number inside the text box is actually a valid age—for example, 191 is not a valid age, nor is 255 likely to be. You just need to add another `if` statement to check for these possibilities.

This function handles the `blur` event of the `txtAge` text box, but why didn't you use the `change` event, with its advantage that it only rechecks the value when the value has actually been changed? The `change` event would not fire if the box was empty both before focus was passed to it and after focus was passed away from it. However, leaving the checking of the form completion until just before the form is submitted is probably best because some users prefer to fill in information out of order and come back to some form elements later.

The final function is for the `txtName` text box's `change` event. Its use here is a little flippant and intended primarily as an example of the `change` event:

```
function txtNameChange(e) {
    alert("Hi " + e.target.value);
}
```

When the `change` event fires (when focus is passed away from the name text box and its contents have changed), you take the value of the event target (again, making use of the `target` property) and put it into an `alert` box. It simply says `Hi yourname`.

Problems with Firefox and the blur Event

The previous example will fail with Firefox if you enter a name in the name text box and then an invalid age into the age box (for example, if you enter abc and then click the Check Form button). With other browsers the `blur` event fires and displays an `alert` box if the age is invalid, but the button's `click` event doesn't fire. However, in Firefox, both events fire with the result that the invalid age alert is hidden by the "form completed successfully" `alert` box.

In addition, if you enter an invalid age and then switch to a different program altogether, the "invalid age" alert box appears, which is annoying for the user. It could be that the user was opening up another program to check the details.

Although this is a fine example, it is not great for the real world. A better option would be to check the form when it's finally submitted and not while the user is entering data. Or, alternatively, you can check the data as it is entered but not use an `alert` box to display errors. Instead you could write out a warning in red next to the erroneous input control, informing the user of the invalid data, and then also get your code to check the form when it's submitted.

The Password Text Box

The only real purpose of the password box is to enable users to type in a password on a page and to have the password characters hidden, so that no one can look over the user's shoulder and discover his or her password. However, this protection is visual only. When sent to the server, the text in the password is sent as plaintext—there is no encryption or any attempt at hiding the text (unless the page is served over a secure connection from the server).

Defining a password box is identical to defining a text box, except that the type attribute is password:

```
<input name="password1" type="password" />
```

This form element creates an `<input/>` element object and has the same properties, methods, and events as normal text boxes.

The Hidden Text Box

The hidden text box can hold text and numbers just like a normal text box, with the difference being that it's not visible to the user. A hidden element? It may sound as useful as an invisible painting, but in fact it proves to be very useful.

To define a hidden text box, you use the following HTML:

```
<input type="hidden" name="myHiddenElement" />
```

The hidden text box creates yet another `<input/>` element object, and it can be manipulated in JavaScript like any other object—although, you can actually set its value only through its HTML definition or through JavaScript. As with a normal text box, its value is submitted to the server when the user submits the form.

So why are hidden text boxes useful? Imagine you have a lot of information that you need to obtain from the user, but to avoid having a page stuffed full of elements and looking like the control panel of the space shuttle, you decide to obtain the information over more than one page. The problem is, how do you keep a record of what was entered in previous pages? Easy—you use hidden text boxes and put the values in there. Then, in the final page, all the information is submitted to the server— it's just that some of it is hidden.

The textarea Element

The `<textarea/>` element allows multi-line input of text. Other than this, it acts very much like the text box element.

However, unlike the text box, the `<textarea/>` element has its own tag, the `<textarea>` tag, and it creates an HTMLTextAreaElement object. It also has two additional attributes: cols and rows. The cols attribute defines how many characters wide the text area will be, and the rows attribute defines how many character rows there will be. You set the text inside the element by putting

it between the start and closing tags, rather than by using the value attribute. So if you want a
<textarea/> element 40 characters wide by 20 rows deep with initial text Hello World on the first
line and Line 2 on the second line, you define it as follows:

```
<textarea name="myTextArea" cols="40" rows="20">Hello World
Line 2
</textarea>
```

Another attribute of the <textarea/> element is the wrap attribute, which determines what happens
when the user types to the end of a line. The default value for this is soft, so the user does not have
to press Return at the end of a line, though this can vary from browser to browser. To turn wrapping
on, you can use one of two values: soft and hard. As far as client-side processing goes, both do the
same thing: They switch wrapping on. However, when you come to server-side processing, they do
make a difference in terms of which information is sent to the server when the form is posted.

If you set the wrap attribute on by setting it to soft, wrapping will occur on the client side, but
the carriage returns won't be posted to the server, just the text. If the wrap attribute is set to hard,
any carriage returns caused by wrapping will be converted to hard returns—it will be as if the
user had pressed the Enter key, and these returns will be sent to the server. Also, you need to be
aware that the carriage-return character is determined by the operating system that the browser is
running on—for example, in Windows a carriage return is \r\n, on UNIX, UNIX-like systems, and
Mac OS X, a carriage return is \n. To turn off wrapping client-side, set wrap to off.

> **NOTE** The \n character is the universal line feed character. If you are
> formatting raw text output and need a new line, \n works in every browser on
> every operating system.

The object created by the <textarea/> element has the same properties, methods, and events as the
text box object you saw previously, except that the text area doesn't have the maxlength attribute.
Note that there is a value property even though the <textarea/> element does not have a value
attribute. The value property simply returns the text between the <textarea> and </textarea>
tags. The events supported by the <textarea/> element object include the keydown, keypress,
keyup, and change event handlers.

TRY IT OUT Event Watching

To help demonstrate how the keydown, keypress, keyup, and change events work (in particular, the
order in which they fire), you'll create an example that tells you what events are firing:

```
<!DOCTYPE html>

<html lang="en">
<head>
    <title>Chapter 11: Example 5</title>
</head>
<body>
    <form action="" name="form1">
```

```
            <textarea rows="15" cols="40" name="textarea1"></textarea>

            <textarea rows="15" cols="40" name="textarea2"></textarea>
            <br />
            <input type="button" value="Clear event textarea" name="button1" />
        </form>

        <script>
            var myForm = document.form1;
            var textArea1 = myForm.textarea1;
            var textArea2 = myForm.textarea2;
            var btnClear = myForm.button1;

            function displayEvent(e) {
                var message = textArea2.value;
                message = message + e.type + "\n";
                textArea2.value = message;
            }

            function clearEventLog(e) {
                textArea2.value = "";
            }

            textArea1.addEventListener("change", displayEvent);
            textArea1.addEventListener("keydown", displayEvent);
            textArea1.addEventListener("keypress", displayEvent);
            textArea1.addEventListener("keyup", displayEvent);
            btnClear.addEventListener("click", clearEventLog);
        </script>
    </body>
</html>
```

Save this page as ch11_example5.html. Load the page into your browser, and see what happens when you type any letter into the first text area box. You should see the events being fired listed in the second text area box (keydown, keypress, and keyup), as shown in Figure 11-6. When you click outside the first text area box, you'll see the change event fire.

Experiment with the example to see what events fire and when.

Within a form called form1 in the body of the page, you define two text areas and a button. The first text area is the one whose events you are going to monitor:

```
<form action="" name="form1">
    <textarea rows="15" cols="40" name="textarea1"></textarea>
```

Next, you have an empty text area the same size as the first:

```
    <textarea rows="15" cols="40" name="textarea2"></textarea>
```

Finally, you have your button:

```
        <input type="button" value="Clear event textarea" name="button1" />
    </form>
```

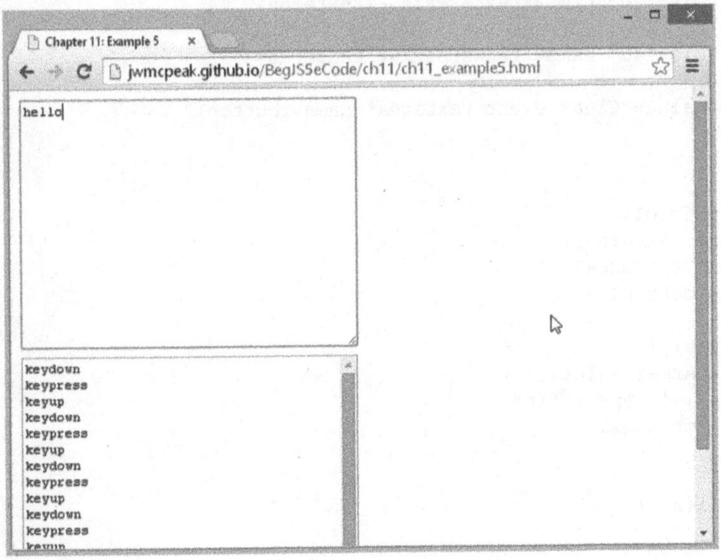

FIGURE 11-6

You'll register event listeners for the textarea1 and button1 elements in your JavaScript code. But first, you need to retrieve those element objects from the document. You do this very simply by using the form hierarchy:

```
var myForm = document.form1;
var textArea1 = myForm.textarea1;
var textArea2 = myForm.textarea2;
var btnClear = myForm.button1;
```

You start by creating the myForm variable to contain the <form/> element object, and then you use that variable to retrieve the other form elements. Now that you have the element objects, registering event listeners is as easy as calling the addEventListener() method:

```
textArea1.addEventListener("change", displayEvent);
textArea1.addEventListener("keydown", displayEvent);
textArea1.addEventListener("keypress", displayEvent);
textArea1.addEventListener("keyup", displayEvent);
btnClear.addEventListener("click", clearEventLog);
```

On the first <textarea/> element (textArea1), you listen for the change, keydown, keypress, and keyup events, using the displayEvent() function as the handling function. For the button, you listen for the click event with the clearEventLog() function.

The latter function is the simplest, so let's look at that first:

```
function clearEventLog(e) {
    textArea2.value = "";
}
```

The purpose of `clearEventLog()` is to clear the contents of the second `<textarea/>` element, and it achieves this by setting the `<textarea/>` element's `value` property to an empty string (`""`).

Now let's look at the `displayEvent()` function. It adds the name of the event that occurred to the text already contained in the second text area:

```
function displayEvent(e) {
    var message = textArea2.value;
    message = message + e.type + "\n";
```

You first retrieve the `<textarea/>` element's value and store it in the `message` variable. You then append the name of the event as well as a new line to the message. Putting each event name on a separate line makes it much easier to read and follow.

Then finally, you assign the new message to the text area's `value` property:

```
    textArea2.value = message;
}
```

Check Boxes and Radio Buttons

The discussions of check boxes and radio buttons are together because their objects have identical properties, methods, and events. A check box enables the user to check and uncheck it. It is similar to the paper surveys you may get where you are asked to "check the boxes that apply to you." Radio buttons are basically a group of check boxes where only one can be checked at a time. Of course, they also look different, and their group nature means that they are treated differently.

Creating check boxes and radio buttons requires our old friend the `<input/>` element. Its `type` attribute is set to `"checkbox"` or `"radio"` to determine which box or button is created. To set a check box or a radio button to be checked when the page is loaded, you simply insert the attribute `checked` into the `<input>` tag and assign its value as `checked`. This is handy if you want to set a default option like, for example, those "Check this box if you want our junk mail" forms you often see on the Net, which are usually checked by default, forcing you to uncheck them. So to create a check box that is already checked, your `<input>` tag will be the following:

```
<input type="checkbox" name="chkDVD" checked="checked" value="DVD" />
```

To create a checked radio button, the `<input>` tag would be as follows:

```
<input type="radio" name="radCPUSpeed" checked="checked" value="1 GHz" />
```

As previously mentioned, radio buttons are group elements. In fact, there is little point in putting just one on a page, because the user won't be able to choose between any alternative boxes.

To create a group of radio buttons, you simply give each radio button the same name. This creates an array of radio buttons going by that name that you can access, as you would with any array, using its index.

For example, to create a group of three radio buttons, your HTML would be as follows:

```
<input type="radio" name="radCPUSpeed" checked="checked" value="800 mhz" />
<input type="radio" name="radCPUSpeed" value="1 ghz" />
<input type="radio" name="radCPUSpeed" value="1.5 ghz" />
```

You can put as many groups of radio buttons in a form as you want, by just giving each group its own unique name. Note that you have only used one checked attribute, because only one of the radio buttons in the group can be checked. If you had used the checked attribute in more than one of the radio buttons, only the last of these would have actually been checked.

Using the value attribute of the check box and radio button elements is not the same as with previous elements you've looked at. It tells you nothing about the user's interaction with an element because it's predefined in your HTML or by your JavaScript. Whether a check box or radio button is checked or not, it still returns the same value.

Each check box has an associated Checkbox object, and each radio button in a group has a separate Radio object. As mentioned earlier, with radio buttons of the same name you can access each Radio object in a group by treating the group of radio buttons as an array, with the name of the array being the name of the radio buttons in the group. As with any array, you have the length property, which will tell you how many radio buttons are in the group.

> **NOTE** There actually aren't objects called Checkbox and Radio. All <input /> elements create an object of type HtmlInputElement. But for the sake of clarity, this text uses Checkbox and Radio to make explanations easier to follow and understand.

For determining whether a user has actually checked or unchecked a check box, you need to use the checked property of the Checkbox object. This property returns true if the check box is currently checked and false if not.

Radio buttons are slightly different. Because radio buttons with the same name are grouped together, you need to test each Radio object in the group in turn to see if it has been checked. Only one of the radio buttons in a group can be checked, so if you check another one in the group, the previously checked one will become unchecked, and the new one will be checked in its place.

Both Checkbox and Radio have the click, focus, and blur events, and these operate identically to the other elements, although they can also be used to cancel the default action, such as clicking the check box or radio button.

Scripting check box and radio buttons usually automatically adds extra stuff to your code—namely loops because you are working with multiple, near-identical elements. The next example demonstrates this.

TRY IT OUT Check Boxes and Radio Buttons

Let's look at an example that makes use of all the properties, methods, and events we have just discussed. The example is a simple form that enables a user to build a computer system. Perhaps it could be used in an e-commerce situation, to sell computers with the exact specifications determined by the customer.

```
<!DOCTYPE html>

<html lang="en">
<head>
    <title>Chapter 11: Example 6</title>
</head>
<body>
    <form action="" name="form1">
        <p>
            Tick all of the components you want included on your computer
        </p>
        <p>
            <label for="chkDVD">DVD-ROM</label>
            <input type="checkbox" id="chkDVD" name="chkDVD" value="DVD-ROM" />
        </p>
        <p>
            <label for="chkBluRay">Blu-ray</label>
            <input type="checkbox" id="chkBluRay" name="chkBluRay"
                value="Blu-ray" />
        </p>

        <p>
            Select the processor speed you require
        </p>
        <p>
            <input type="radio" name="radCpuSpeed" checked="checked"
                value="3.2 ghz" />
            <label>3.2 GHz</label>

            <input type="radio" name="radCpuSpeed" value="3.7 ghz" />
            <label>3.7 GHz</label>

            <input type="radio" name="radCpuSpeed" value="4.0 ghz" />
            <label>4.0 GHz</label>
        </p>

        <input type="button" value="Check form" name="btnCheck" />
    </form>

    <script>
        var myForm = document.form1;

        function getSelectedSpeedValue() {
            var radios = myForm.radCpuSpeed;

            for (var index = 0; index < radios.length; index++) {
                if (radios[index].checked) {
                    return radios[index].value;
                }
            }

            return "";
```

```
        }

        function findIndexOfSpeed(radio) {
            var radios = myForm.radCpuSpeed;

            for (var index = 0; index < radios.length; index++) {
                if (radios[index] == radio) {
                    return index;
                }
            }

            return -1;
        }

        function radCpuSpeedClick(e) {
            var radIndex = findIndexOfSpeed(e.target);

            if (radIndex == 1) {
                e.preventDefault();
                alert("Sorry that processor speed is currently unavailable");

                // to fix an issue with IE
                myForm.radCpuSpeed[0].checked = true;
            }
        }

        function btnCheckClick() {
            var numberOfControls = myForm.length;
            var compSpec = "Your chosen processor speed is ";
            compSpec = compSpec + getSelectedSpeedValue();
            compSpec = compSpec + "\nWith the following additional components:\n";

            for (var index = 0; index < numberOfControls; index++) {
                var element = myForm[index];
                if (element.type == "checkbox") {
                    if (element.checked) {
                        compSpec = compSpec + element.value + "\n";
                    }
                }
            }

            alert(compSpec);
        }

        for (var index = 0; index < myForm.radCpuSpeed.length; index++) {
            myForm.radCpuSpeed[index].addEventListener("click", radCpuSpeedClick);
        }

        myForm.btnCheck.addEventListener("click", btnCheckClick);
    </script>
</body>
</html>
```

Save the page as ch11_example6.html and load it into your web browser. You should see a form like the one shown in Figure 11-7.

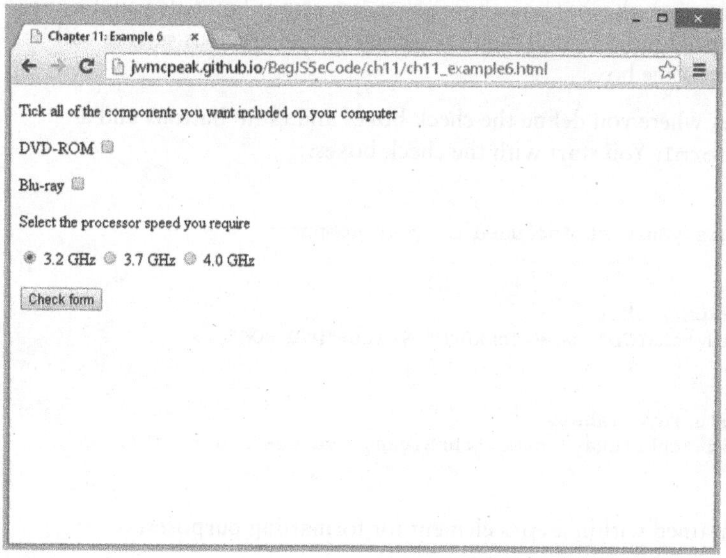

FIGURE 11-7

Check some of the check boxes, change the processor speed, and click the Check Form button. A message box appears and lists the components and processor speed you selected. For example, if you select a DVD-ROM and a 4.0 GHz processor speed, you will see something like what is shown in Figure 11-8.

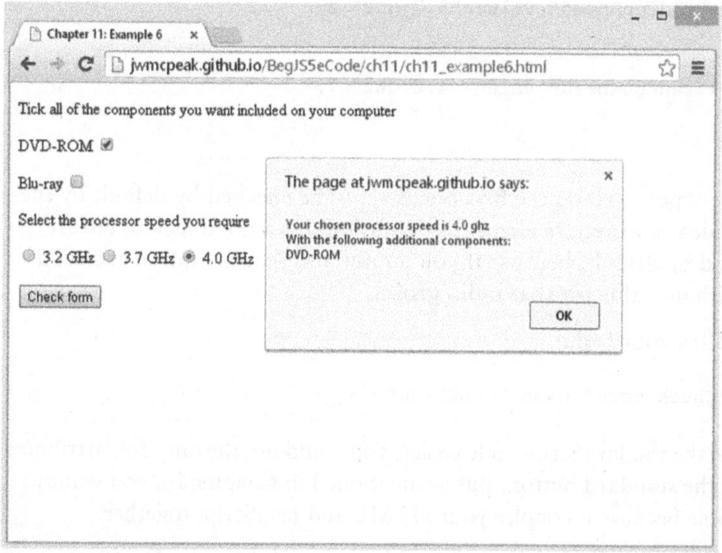

FIGURE 11-8

Note that the 3.7 GHz processor is out of stock, so if you choose that, a message box tells you it's out of stock, and the 3.2 GHz processor speed radio button won't be selected. The previous setting will be restored when the user dismisses the message box.

Let's first look at the body of the page, where you define the check boxes and radio buttons and a standard button inside a form called form1. You start with the check boxes:

```
<p>
    Tick all of the components you want included on your computer
</p>
<p>
    <label for="chkDVD">DVD-ROM</label>
    <input type="checkbox" id="chkDVD" name="chkDVD" value="DVD-ROM" />
</p>
<p>
    <label for="chkBluRay">Blu-ray</label>
    <input type="checkbox" id="chkBluRay" name="chkBluRay" value="Blu-ray" />
</p>
```

Each check box has a label and is contained within a `<p/>` element for formatting purposes.

Next come the radio buttons for selecting the required CPU speed. Again, each has a label, but unlike the check boxes, these radio buttons are contained within a single `<p/>` element:

```
<p>
    Select the processor speed you require
</p>
<p>
    <input type="radio" name="radCpuSpeed" checked="checked"
           value="3.2 ghz" />
    <label>3.2 GHz</label>

    <input type="radio" name="radCpuSpeed" value="3.7 ghz" />
    <label>3.7 GHz</label>

    <input type="radio" name="radCpuSpeed" value="4.0 ghz" />
    <label>4.0 GHz</label>
</p>
```

The radio button group name is radCpuSpeed. Here, the first one is set to be checked by default by the inclusion of the checked attribute inside the `<input/>` element's definition. It's a good idea to ensure that you have one radio button checked by default, because if you do not and the user doesn't select a button, the form will be submitted with no value for that radio group.

Next, the standard button that completes your form:

```
<input type="button" value="Check form" name="btnCheck" />
```

Before proceeding further, a note: To make the JavaScript code easier, you could use the onclick attributes on each of the radio buttons as well as the standard button. But as mentioned in Chapter 10, you want to avoid those attributes as much as possible because it couples your HTML and JavaScript together.

Two functions are used to handle the click events for the standard button and the radio buttons: btnCheckClick() and radCpuSpeedClick(), respectively. And before we look at these functions, you first need to register the `click` event listeners on their respective elements. As in previous examples, first create a variable called `myForm` to reference the form in the document:

```
var myForm = document.form1;
```

Now, register the `click` event listener on your radio buttons. Unfortunately, there's no magical command that says "use this function to handle all the radio buttons' `click` events." So, you'll have to call `addEventListener()` on every `Radio` object. This isn't as difficult as it sounds; a `for` loop will help you:

```
for (var index = 0; index < myForm.radCpuSpeed.length; index++) {
    myForm.radCpuSpeed[index].addEventListener("click", radCpuSpeedClick);
}
```

This `for` loop is fairly straightforward except for one thing: `myForm.radCpuSpeed`. What you are doing here is using the collection for the `radCpuSpeed` radio group. Each element in the collection actually contains an object, namely each of your three `Radio` objects. Therefore, you're looping over the `Radio` objects in the `radCpuSpeed` radio group, retrieving the `Radio` object at the given index, and calling its `addEventListener()` method.

Next, register the event listener for the form's standard button:

```
myForm.btnCheck.addEventListener("click", btnCheckClick);
```

Now let's look at the `radCpuSpeedClick()` function, the function that executes when the radio buttons are clicked. The first thing this function needs to do is to find the index of the event target in the `radCpuSpeed` radio group:

```
function radCpuSpeedClick(e) {
    var radIndex = findIndexOfSpeed(e.target);
```

You do this by calling the `findIndexOfSpeed()` helper function. We'll look at this function later, but for now, just know that it finds the index of the supplied `Radio` object in the `myForm.radCpuSpeed` collection.

The default action of clicking a radio button is to check the radio button. If you prevent the default action from occurring, the radio button will not be checked. As an example of this in action, you have an `if` statement on the next line. If the radio button's index value is `1` (that is, if the user checked the box for a 3.7 GHz processor), you tell the user that it's out of stock and cancel the clicking action by calling the `Event` object's `preventDefault()` method:

```
if (radIndex == 1) {
    e.preventDefault();
    alert("Sorry that processor speed is currently unavailable");
```

As previously mentioned, canceling the clicking action results in the radio button not being checked. In such a situation, all browsers (except for IE) recheck the previously checked radio button. IE, however, removes all checks from the radio group. To rectify this, you reset the radio group:

```
        // to fix an issue with IE
        myForm.radCpuSpeed[0].checked = true;
    }
}
```

You once again use the `myForm.radCpuSpeed` collection, retrieve the `Radio` object at index 0, and set its `checked` property to `true`. Let's take a moment and look at the `findIndexOfSpeed()` helper method. It accepts a `Radio` object as an argument, and it searches the `myForm.radCpuSpeed` collection for the given `Radio` object.

The first line of the function creates a variable called `radios`, and it contains a reference to the `myForm.radCpuSpeed` collection. This is to make typing and reading a bit easier:

```
function findIndexOfSpeed(radio) {
    var radios = myForm.radCpuSpeed;
```

Next, you want to loop through the `radios` collection and determine if each `Radio` object in the collection is the same `Radio` object in the radio variable:

```
for (var index = 0; index < radios.length; index++) {
    if (radios[index] == radio) {
        return index;
    }
}

return -1;
}
```

If you find a match, you return the value of the `index` variable. If the loop exits without finding a match, you return -1. This behavior is consistent with the `String` object's `indexOf()` method. Consistency is a very good thing!

The next function, `btnCheckClick()`, executes when the standard button's `click` event fires. In a real e-commerce situation, this button would be the place where you'd check your form and then submit it to the server for processing. Here you use the form to show a message box confirming which boxes you have checked (as if you didn't already know)!

At the top you declare two local variables to use in the function. The variable `numberOfControls` is set to the form's `length` property, which is the number of elements on the form. The variable `compSpec` is used to build the string that you'll display in a message box:

```
function btnCheckClick() {
    var numberOfControls = myForm.length;
    var compSpec = "Your chosen processor speed is ";
```

In the following line, you add the value of the radio button the user has selected to your message string:

```
compSpec = compSpec + findSelectedSpeedValue();
compSpec = compSpec + "\nWith the following additional components:\n";
```

You use yet another helper function called `getSelectedSpeedValue()`. As its name implies, it gets the value of the selected `Radio` object. You'll look at its code later.

Next, you loop through the form's elements:

```
for (var index = 0; index < numberOfControls; index++) {
    var element = myForm[index];
```

```
            if (element.type == "checkbox") {
                if (element.checked) {
                    compSpec = compSpec + element.value + "\n";
                }
            }
        }

        alert(compSpec);
}
```

It's here that you loop through each element on the form using `myForm[controlIndex]`, which returns a reference to the element object stored at the `controlIndex` index position.

You'll see that in this example the `element` variable is set to reference the object stored in the `myForm` collection at the index position stored in variable `controlIndex`. Again, this is for convenient shorthand purposes; now to use that particular object's properties or methods, you just type `element`, a period, and then the method or property name, making your code easier to read and debug, which also saves on typing.

You only want to see which check boxes have been checked, so you use the `type` property, which every HTML form element object has, to see what element type you are dealing with. If the `type` is `checkbox`, you go ahead and see if it's a checked check box. If so, you append its value to the message string in `compSpec`. If it is not a check box, it can be safely ignored.

Finally, you use the `alert()` method to display the contents of your message string.

The last function is `getSelectedSpeedValue()`. It doesn't accept any arguments, although you could generalize this function to accept a collection of `Radio` objects. Doing so would allow you to reuse the function in multiple projects.

But to get back to the actual code, the first statement of the function creates a `radios` variable that contains a reference to the `myForm.radCpuSpeed` collection:

```
function getSelectedSpeedValue() {
    var radios = myForm.radCpuSpeed;
```

Next, you want to find the selected `Radio` object and retrieve its value. You can do this with yet another `for` loop:

```
    for (var index = 0; index < radios.length; index++) {
        if (radios[index].checked) {
            return radios[index].value;
        }
    }

    return "";
}
```

The logic is straightforward: Loop through the `radios` collection and check each `Radio` object's `checked` property. If it's `true`, return the value of that `Radio` object, but if the loop exits without finding a `checked` `Radio` object, you return an empty string.

Selection Boxes

Although they look quite different, the drop-down list and the list boxes are actually both elements created with the `<select>` tag, and strictly speaking they are both select elements. The select element has one or more options in a list that you can select from; each of these options is defined by means of one or more `<option/>` elements inside the opening and closing `<select>` tags.

The `size` attribute of the `<select/>` element is used to specify how many of the options are visible to the user.

For example, to create a list box five rows deep and populate it with seven options, your HTML would look like this:

```
<select name="theDay" size="5">
    <option value="0" selected="selected">Monday</option>
    <option value="1">Tuesday</option>
    <option value="2">Wednesday</option>
    <option value="3">Thursday</option>
    <option value="4">Friday</option>
    <option value="5">Saturday</option>
    <option value="6">Sunday</option>
</select>
```

Notice that the `<option/>` element for Monday also contains the attribute `selected`; this will make this option selected by default when the page is loaded. The values of the options have been defined as numbers, but text would be equally valid.

If you want this to be a drop-down list, you just need to change the `size` attribute in the `<select/>` element to `1`, and presto, it's a drop-down list.

If you want to let the user choose more than one item from a list at once, you simply need to add the `multiple` attribute to the `<select/>` definition.

The `<select/>` element creates an `HTMLSelectElement` object (hereby known as `Select`). This object has an `options` collection property, which is made up of `HtmlOptionElement` (hereby known as `Option`) objects, one for each `<option/>` element inside the `<select/>` element associated with the `Select` object. For instance, in the preceding example, if the `<select/>` element was contained in a form called `theForm` with the following:

```
document.theForm.theDay.options[0]
```

you would access the option created for Monday.

How can you tell which option has been selected by the user? Easy: you use the `Select` object's `selectedIndex` property. You can use the index value returned by this property to access the selected option using the `options` collection.

The `Option` object also has `index`, `text`, and `value` properties. The `index` property returns the index position of that option in the `options` collection. The `text` property is what's displayed in the list, and the `value` property is the value defined for the option, which would be posted to the server if the form were submitted.

If you want to find out how many options are in a select element, you can use the `length` property of either the `Select` object itself or of its `options` collection property.

Let's see how you could loop through the `options` for the preceding select box:

```
var theDayElement = document.theForm.theDay;
document.write("There are " + theDayElement.length + "options<br />");

for (var index = 0; index < theDayElement.length; index++) {
    document.write("Option text is " +
        theDayElement.options[index].text);
    document.write(" and its value is ");
    document.write(theDayElement.options[index].value);
    document.write("<br />");
}
```

First, you set the variable `theDayElement` to reference the `Select` object. Then you write the number of options to the page, in this case 7.

Next you use a `for` loop to loop through the `options` collection, displaying the text of each option, such as `Monday`, `Tuesday`, and so on, and its value, such as 0, 1, and so on. If you create a page based on this code, it must be placed after the `<select/>` element's definition.

It's also possible to add options to a select element after the page has finished loading. You look at how to do this next.

Adding and Removing Options

To add a new option to a select element, you simply create a new `Option` object using the `new` operator and then insert it into the `options` collection of the `Select` object at an empty index position.

When you create a new `Option` object, you have two parameters to pass. The first is the text you want to appear in the list, and the second is the value to be assigned to the option:

```
var myNewOption = new Option("TheText","TheValue");
```

You then simply assign this `Option` object to an empty array element. For example:

```
theDayElement.options[0] = myNewOption;
```

If you want to remove an option, you simply set that part of the `options` collection to `null`. For example, to remove the element you just inserted, you need the following:

```
theDayElement.options[0] = null;
```

When you remove an `Option` object from the `options` collection, the collection is reordered so that the array index value of each of the options above the removed one has its index value decremented by one.

When you insert a new option at a certain index position, be aware that it will overwrite any `Option` object that is already there.

TRY IT OUT Adding and Removing List Options

In this Try It Out, you use the list-of-days example you saw previously to demonstrate adding and removing list options.

```
<!DOCTYPE html>

<html lang="en">
<head>
    <title>Chapter 11: Example 7</title>
</head>
<body>
    <form action="" name="theForm">
        <select name="theDay" size="5">
            <option value="0" selected="selected">Monday</option>
            <option value="1">Tuesday</option>
            <option value="2">Wednesday</option>
            <option value="3">Thursday</option>
            <option value="4">Friday</option>
            <option value="5">Saturday</option>
            <option value="6">Sunday</option>
        </select>
        <br />
        <input type="button" value="Remove Wednesday" name="btnRemoveWed" />
        <input type="button" value="Add Wednesday" name="btnAddWed" />
        <br />
    </form>

    <script>
        var theForm = document.theForm;

        function btnRemoveWedClick() {
            var options = theForm.theDay.options;

            if (options[2].text == "Wednesday") {
                options[2] = null;
            } else {
                alert("There is no Wednesday here!");
            }
        }

        function btnAddWedClick() {
            var options = theForm.theDay.options;

            if (options[2].text != "Wednesday") {
                var lastOption = new Option();
                options[options.length] = lastOption;

                for (var index = options.length - 1; index > 2; index--) {
                    var currentOption = options[index];
                    var previousOption = options[index - 1];

                    currentOption.text = previousOption.text;
                    currentOption.value = previousOption.value;
```

```
            }
                var option = new Option("Wednesday", 2);
                options[2] = option;
            } else {
                alert("Do you want to have TWO Wednesdays?");
            }
        }

        theForm.btnRemoveWed.addEventListener("click", btnRemoveWedClick);
        theForm.btnAddWed.addEventListener("click", btnAddWedClick);
    </script>
</body>
</html>
```

Save this as ch11_example7.html. If you type the page in and load it into your browser, you should see the form shown in Figure 11-9. Click the Remove Wednesday button, and you'll see Wednesday disappear from the list. Add it back by clicking the Add Wednesday button. If you try to add a second Wednesday or remove a nonexistent Wednesday, you'll get a polite warning telling you that you can't do that.

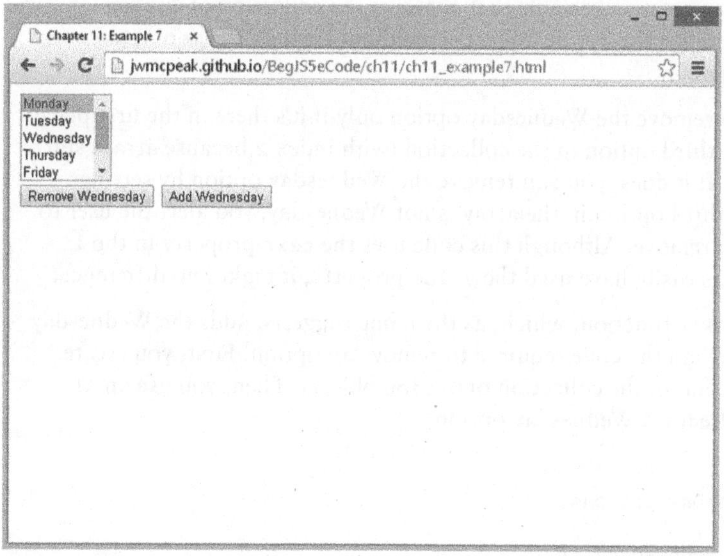

FIGURE 11-9

Within the body of the page, you define a form with the name theForm. This contains the <select/> element, which includes day-of-the-week options that you have seen previously. The form also contains two buttons, as shown here:

```
<input type="button" value="Remove Wednesday" name="btnRemoveWed" />
<input type="button" value="Add Wednesday" name="btnAddWed" />
```

You want to execute JavaScript code when these buttons are clicked; therefore, you want to register click event listeners for each of the buttons. To make this a bit easier, you first create a variable called theForm, which contains the <form/> element object:

```
var theForm = document.theForm;
```

You use this variable to access the individual buttons and register their `click` event listeners:

```
theForm.btnRemoveWed.addEventListener("click", btnRemoveWedClick);
theForm.btnAddWed.addEventListener("click", btnAddWedClick);
```

The "remove" button executes the `btnRemoveWedClick()` function, and the "add" button executes `btnAddWedClick()`. You take a look at each of these functions in turn.

The first function, `btnRemoveWedClick()`, removes the Wednesday option:

```
function btnRemoveWedClick() {
    var options = theForm.theDay.options;

    if (options[2].text == "Wednesday") {
        options[2] = null;
    } else {
        alert("There is no Wednesday here!");
    }
}
```

The first thing you do in the function is create a variable that contains the collection of `Option` elements. This lets you repeatedly reference the option collection without typing `document.theForm.theDay.options`, or any variation thereof.

Next, a sanity check: You must try to remove the Wednesday option only if it's there in the first place! You make sure of this by seeing if the third option in the collection (with index 2 because arrays start at index 0) has the text `"Wednesday"`. If it does, you can remove the Wednesday option by setting that particular option to `null`. If the third option in the array is not Wednesday, you alert the user to the fact that there is no Wednesday to remove. Although this code uses the `text` property in the `if` statement's condition, you could just as easily have used the `value` property; it makes no difference.

Next you come to the `btnAddWedClick()` function, which, as the name suggests, adds the Wednesday option. This is slightly more complex than the code required to remove an option. First, you create another variable, called `options`, to contain the collection of `Option` objects. Then, you use an `if` statement to check that there is not already a Wednesday option:

```
function btnAddWedClick() {
    var options = theForm.theDay.options;

    if (options[2].text != "Wednesday") {
        var lastOption = new Option();
        options[options.length] = lastOption;

        for (var index = options.length - 1; index > 2; index--) {
            var currentOption = options[index];
            var previousOption = options[index - 1];

            currentOption.text = previousOption.text;
            currentOption.value = previousOption.value;
        }
```

If there is no Wednesday option, you then need to make space for the new Wednesday option to be inserted.

At this point, you have six options (the last element is as index 5), so next you create a new option with the variable name lastOption and assign it to the element at the end of the collection. This new element is assigned at index position 6 by using the length property of the options collection, which previously had no contents. You next assign the text and value properties of each of the Option objects from Thursday to Sunday to the Option at an index value higher by one in the options array, leaving a space in the options array at position 2 to put Wednesday in. This is the task for the for loop within the if statement.

Next, you create a new Option object by passing the text "Wednesday" and the value 2 to the Option constructor. The Option object is then inserted into the options collection at position 2, and presto, it appears in your select box.

```
        var option = new Option("Wednesday", 2);
        options[2] = option;
    }
```

You end the function by alerting the user to the fact that there is already a Wednesday option in the list, if the condition in the if statement is false:

```
    else {
        alert("Do you want to have TWO Wednesdays?");
    }
}
```

This example works in every browser; however, all modern browsers provide additional methods to make adding and removing options easier.

Adding New Options with Standard Methods

In particular, the Select object you are interested in has additional add() and remove() methods, which add and remove options. These make life a little simpler.

Before you add an option, you need to create it. You do this just as before, using the new operator.

The Select object's add() method enables you to insert an Option object that you have created and accepts two parameters. The first parameter is the Option object you want to add. The second parameter is the Option object you want to place the new Option object before. However, in IE7 (or IE8 non-standards mode), the second parameter is the index position at which you want to add the option. In all browsers, you can pass null as the second parameter, and the added Option object will be added at the end of the options collection.

The add() method won't overwrite any Option object already at that position, but instead will simply move the Option objects up in the collection to make space. This is basically the same as what you had to code into the btnAddWedClick() function using your for loop.

Using the add() method, you can rewrite the btnAddWedClick() function in ch11_example7.html to look like this:

```
function btnAddWedClick() {
    var days = theForm.theDay;
```

```
        var options = days.options;

    if (options[2].text != "Wednesday") {
        var option = new Option("Wednesday", 2);
        var thursdayOption = options[2];

        try {
            days.add(option, thursdayOption);
        }
        catch (error) {
            days.add(option, 2);
        }
    } else {
        alert("Do you want to have TWO Wednesdays?");
    }
}
```

In IE7 (or IE8 in non-standards mode), the browser will throw an error if you pass an `Option` object as the second parameter. So use a `try...catch` statement to catch the error and pass a number to the second argument, as this code shows.

The `Select` object's `remove()` method accepts just one parameter, namely the index of the option you want removed. When an option is removed, the options at higher index positions are moved down in the collection to fill the gap.

Using the `remove()` method, you can rewrite the `btnRemoveWedClick()` function in `ch11_example7.html` to look like this:

```
function btnRemoveWedClick() {
    var days = theForm.theDay;

    if (days.options[2].text == "Wednesday") {
        days.remove(2);
    } else {
        alert("There is no Wednesday here!");
    }
}
```

Modify the previous example and save it as `ch11_example8.html` before loading it into your browser. You'll see that it works just as the previous version did.

Select Element Events

Select elements have three events: `blur`, `focus`, and `change`. You've seen all these events before. You saw the `change` event with the text box element, where it fired when focus was moved away from the text box *and* the value in the text box had changed. Here it fires when the user changes which option in the list is selected.

TRY IT OUT World Time Converter

Let's take a look at an example that uses the `change` event. The World Time Converter lets you calculate the time in different countries:

```html
<!DOCTYPE html>

<html lang="en">
<head>
    <title>Chapter 11: Example 9</title>
</head>
<body>
    <div>Local Time is <span id="spanLocalTime"></span></div>
    <div id="divCityTime"></div>

    <form name="form1">
        <select size="5" name="lstCity">
            <option value="60" selected>Berlin
            <option value="330">Bombay
            <option value="0">London
            <option value="180">Moscow
            <option value="-300">New York
            <option value="60">Paris
            <option value="-480">San Francisco
            <option value="600">Sydney
        </select>
        <p>
            <input type="checkbox" id="chkDst" name="chkDst" />

            <label for="chkDst">Adjust city time for Daylight Savings</label>
        </p>
    </form>


    <script>
        var myForm = document.form1;

        function updateTimeZone() {
            var lstCity = myForm.lstCity;
            var selectedOption = lstCity.options[lstCity.selectedIndex];
            var offset = selectedOption.value;
            var selectedCity = selectedOption.text;

            var dstAdjust = 0;

            if (myForm.chkDst.checked) {
                dstAdjust = 60;
            }

            updateOutput(selectedCity, offset, dstAdjust);
        }

        function updateOutput(selectedCity, offset, dstAdjust) {
            var now = new Date();

            document.getElementById("spanLocalTime")
                .innerHTML = now.toLocaleString();

            now.setMinutes(now.getMinutes() + now.getTimezoneOffset() +
```

```
                        parseInt(offset, 10) + dstAdjust);

                var resultsText = selectedCity + " time is " +
                    now.toLocaleString();

                document.getElementById("divCityTime").innerHTML = resultsText;
            }

            myForm.lstCity.addEventListener("change", updateTimeZone);
            myForm.chkDst.addEventListener("click", updateTimeZone);

            updateTimeZone();
        </script>
    </body>
</html>
```

Save this as ch11_example9.html. Open the page in your browser.

The form layout looks something like the one shown in Figure 11-10. Whenever the user clicks a city in the list, her local time and the equivalent time in the selected city are shown. In the example shown in Figure 11-10, the local region is set to Central Standard Time in the U.S., and the selected city is Berlin, with the daylight savings box checked.

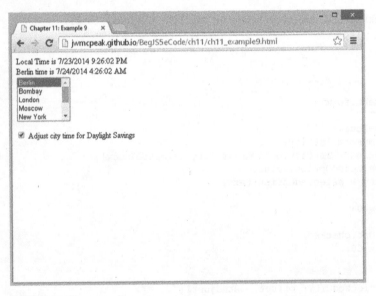

FIGURE 11-10

It's worth pointing out that this is just an example and not a totally foolproof one, because of the problems presented by daylight savings. Some locations don't have it, others do at fixed times of year, and yet others do but at varying times of the year. This makes it difficult to predict accurately when a country will have its daylight savings period. You have tried to solve this problem by adding a check box for the user to click if the city she chooses from the list is using daylight savings hours (which you assume will put the time in the city forward by one hour).

In addition, don't forget that some users may not even have their regional settings set correctly—there's no easy way around this problem.

In the body of this page is a pair of <div/> elements used for output:

```
<div>Local Time is <span id="spanLocalTime"></span></div>
<div id="divCityTime"></div>
```

There's also a form in which you've defined a list box using a <select> element:

```
<select size="5" name="lstCity">
    <option value="60" selected>Berlin
    <option value="330">Bombay
    <option value="0">London
    <option value="180">Moscow
    <option value="-300">New York
    <option value="60">Paris
    <option value="-480">San Francisco
    <option value="600">Sydney
</select>
```

Each of the options displays the city's name in the list box and has its value set to the difference in minutes between that city's time zone (in winter) and UTC. So London, which uses UTC, has a value of 0. Paris, which is an hour ahead of UTC, has a value of 60 (that is, 60 minutes). New York, which is five hours behind UTC, has a value of -300.

There's also a check box with an associated label:

```
<p>
    <input type="checkbox" id="chkDst" name="chkDst" />

    <label for="chkDst">Adjust city time for Daylight Savings</label>
</p>
```

Checking this check box will add an hour to a city's calculated time.

You'll register the change event listener of the <select/> element and the click event listener of the check box to call the updateTimeZone() function. As with previous versions, you create a global variable to provide easier access to the <form/> element object:

```
var myForm = document.form1;
```

Then you register the event listeners:

```
myForm.lstCity.addEventListener("change", updateTimeZone);
myForm.chkDst.addEventListener("click", updateTimeZone);
```

The function updateTimeZone() doesn't really update anything, but it does gather information and kick off the update process:

```
function updateTimeZone() {
    var lstCity = myForm.lstCity;
```

The first four statements of this function create four variables. The first, lstCity, contains a reference to the <select/> element object. You create this variable for convenience purposes—namely for the creation of the second variable: selectedOption:

```
var selectedOption = lstCity.options[lstCity.selectedIndex];
```

This selectedOption variable is retrieved by using the lstCity object's options property in conjunction with its selectedIndex property, and now that you have the selectedOption, you can easily get the information attached to the option:

```
var offset = selectedOption.value;
var selectedCity = selectedOption.text;
```

Next, you want to determine if the user checked the daylight savings check box:

```
var dstAdjust = 0;

if (myForm.chkDst.checked) {
    dstAdjust = 60;
}
```

You initialize the dstAdjust variable with 0. If the check box is checked, you modify dstAdjust to contain the value of 60. The value of 60 is for 60 minutes. As you have probably guessed, your time conversion calculation will be with minute values.

In the final part of updateTimeZone(), you call the updateTime() function, passing the values contained within the selectedCity, offset, and dstAdjust variables:

```
    updateTime(selectedCity, offset, dstAdjust);
}
```

In the function updateTime(), you write the current local time and the equivalent time in the selected city to the output elements.

You start at the top of the function by creating a new Date object, which is stored in the variable now. The Date object will be initialized to the current local time:

```
function updateOutput(selectedCity, offset, dstAdjust) {
    var now = new Date();
```

Next, you output the local time to the <span/> element with an id of spanLocalTime:

```
document.getElementById("spanLocalTime").innerHTML = now.toLocaleString();
```

You use the Date object's toLocaleString() method to format the date and time in your region's format.

You saw in Chapter 7 that if you set the value of a Date object's individual parts (such as hours, minutes, and seconds) to a value beyond their normal range, JavaScript assumes you want to adjust the date, hours, or minutes to take this into account. For example, if you set the hours to 36, JavaScript simply changes the hours to 12 and adds one day to the date stored inside the Date object. You use this to your benefit in the following line:

```
now.setMinutes(now.getMinutes() + now.getTimezoneOffset() +
    parseInt(offset, 10) + dstAdjust);
```

Let's break down this line to see how it works. Suppose that you're in New York, with the local summer time of 5:11, and you want to know what time it is in Berlin. How does your line of code calculate this?

First, you get the minutes of the current local time; it's 5:11, so now.getMinutes() returns 11.

Then you get the difference, in minutes, between the user's local time and UTC using now.getTimezoneOffset(). If you are in New York, which is different from UTC by 4 hours during the summer, this is 240 minutes.

Then you get the integer value of the time difference between the standard winter time in the selected city and UTC time, which is stored in offset. You've used parseInt() here because it's one of the few situations where JavaScript gets confused and assumes you want to join two strings together rather than treat the values as numbers and add them together. Remember that you got offset from an HTML element's value, and that an HTML element's values are strings, even when they hold characters that are digits. Because you want the time in Berlin, which is 60 minutes different from UTC time, this value will be 60.

Finally, you add the value of dstAdjust. Because it's summer where you are and Berlin uses daylight savings hours, this value is 60.

So you have the following:

```
11 + 240 + 60 + 60 = 371
```

Therefore, now.setMinutes() is setting the minutes to 371. Clearly, there's no such thing as 371 minutes past the hour, so instead JavaScript assumes you mean 6 hours and 11 minutes after 5:00, that being 11:11—the time in Berlin that you wanted.

Finally, the updateTime() function creates the resultsText variable and then writes the results to the divCityTime:

```
var resultsText = selectedCity + " time is " +
    now.toLocaleString();

document.getElementById("divCityTime").innerHTML = resultsText;
}
```

HTML5 FORM OBJECT PROPERTIES AND METHODS

HTML4 was finalized in 1997, and it wasn't until 2012 that the web community saw a push for HTML5. Needless to say, HTML hadn't seen a significant update until the introduction of HTML5. So for fifteen years, web developers have worked with form controls that grossly don't meet developers' and users' needs. Thankfully, that changes with HTML5.

One thing you've done throughout this chapter is respond to various form controls' `change`, `click`, `focus`, `blur`, and `keypress` events (among others). All of these events can be used in conjunction with one another so that you can respond to any user input, but that requires a lot of extra code.

A better solution would be to use the `input` event introduced in HTML5. This new event fires when the value of an element changes. That means you can listen for the `input` event on a `<form/>` object and process its data as any field is updated.

The target of the `input` event is the element that changed. You use the `input` event later in this chapter.

New Input Types

HTML5 introduces a slew of new types for `<input/>` elements, and the following table lists them, their descriptions, and a description of their output (the control's `value` if known). In all cases, the value is a string object.

TYPE	DESCRIPTION	VALUE
color	A control for specifying a color. The `value` is the color in hexadecimal format.	A hexadecimal value of the number (`#ff00ff`).
date	Used for entering the date (year, month, and day).	The date in `yyyy-mm-dd` format (`2014-07-14`).
datetime	Allows for entering the date and time based on UTC.	Not yet supported.
email	A field for editing an e-mail address. The value is automatically validated.	The text input into the field (even if invalid e-mail).
month	A control for entering month and year; no time zone.	The date in `yyyy-mm` format (`2014-07`).
number	Creates a control for numeric input, but does not prohibit alpha-character input.	The numeric data input into the field, or an empty string if not a number.
range	Creates a native slider for imprecise numeric input.	The value of the slider.
search	A single-line text entry control.	The text input into the field. Line breaks are removed.
tel	Creates a control for telephone entry.	The text input into the field. Line breaks are removed.
time	Allows time input with no time zone.	The time in 24-hour format (15:37 for 03:37PM).
url	A control for editing absolute URLs.	The text input into the field. Line breaks and leading/trailing whitespace are removed.

week	Creates a control for entering a date consisting of a week-year number and a week number with no time zone.	The year and week number (2014-W29).

Unfortunately, some of the new input types are not supported by any browser, and some are only supported by a few. Many of the supported input types exhibit inconsistent behavior between browsers. In short, if you plan on using any of these new input types, be sure to test your page in all modern browsers.

HTML5 also brings several new attributes to `<input/>` elements, all of which are accessible as properties of the element object. The following table lists just some of these attributes.

TYPE	DESCRIPTION
autocomplete	Specifies that the value of the control can be automatically completed by the browser.
autofocus	Determines if the control should have focus when the page loads.
form	The ID of the associated form. If specified, the control can be placed anywhere in the document. If not specified, the control can only reside within the form.
maxLength	Specifies the maximum number of characters the user can enter for text, email, search, password, tel, and url types.
pattern	A regular expression that the control's value is checked against.
placeholder	Displays a hint to the user of what can be entered in the field.
required	Specifies that the user must fill in a value for the field before submitting the form.

In addition to these properties, HTML5 specifies three unique properties/attributes for the range type:

➤ min: The minimum value of the slider

➤ max: The maximum value of the slider

➤ step: The increment between values

TRY IT OUT   New Input Types

Let's look at an example of the number and range input types, as well as the input event. Open your text editor and type the following:

```
<!DOCTYPE html>

<html lang="en">
<head>
    <title>Chapter 11: Example 10</title>
</head>
```

```
<body>
    <form name="form1">
        <p>
            <label for="minValue">Min: </label>
            <input type="number" id="minValue" name="minValue" />
        </p>
        <p>
            <label for="maxValue">Max: </label>
            <input type="number" id="maxValue" name="maxValue" />
        </p>
        <p>
            <label for="stepValue">Step: </label>
            <input type="number" id="stepValue" name="stepValue" />
        </p>
        <p>
            <input type="range" id="slider" name="slider" />
        </p>
    </form>
    <div id="output"></div>

    <script>
        var myForm = document.form1;
        var output = document.getElementById("output");

        function formInputChange() {
            var slider = myForm.slider;

            slider.min = parseFloat(myForm.minValue.value);
            slider.max = parseFloat(myForm.maxValue.value);
            slider.step = parseFloat(myForm.stepValue.value);

            output.innerHTML = slider.value;
        }

        myForm.addEventListener("input", formInputChange);
    </script>
</body>
</html>
```

Save this as ch11_example10.html.

When you open this page in a modern browser, you will see three text boxes and one slider. The three text boxes enable you to edit the minimum, maximum, and step of the slider. Providing any input to any of the form fields updates the min, max, and step properties of the slider, as well as displays the value of the slider in a <div/> element.

There is one exception: In IE, changing the value of the slider does not cause the input event to fire.

Let's first look at the form's HTML:

```
<form name="form1">
    <p>
        <label for="minValue">Min: </label>
        <input type="number" id="minValue" name="minValue" />
    </p>
```

```
<p>
    <label for="maxValue">Max: </label>
    <input type="number" id="maxValue" name="maxValue" />
</p>
<p>
    <label for="stepValue">Step: </label>
    <input type="number" id="stepValue" name="stepValue" />
</p>
```

You start with three `<input/>` elements of type `number`. Their purpose is to allow you to specify the minimum, maximum, and step values of the fourth `<input/>` element:

```
<p>
    <input type="range" id="slider" name="slider" />
</p>
</form>
```

This is a `range` `<input/>` element, and there are no attributes other than `type`, `id`, and `name`.

Outside of the form is a `<div/>` element with an `id` of `output`:

```
<div id="output"></div>
```

As you input data in the form, the contents of this `<div/>` element change with the value of the `range` `<input/>` element.

Now for the JavaScript. The first two lines of JavaScript code reach into the DOM and grab references to two elements:

```
var myForm = document.form1;
var output = document.getElementById("output");
```

The first is a reference to the `<form/>` element, and the second is the `<div id="output"/>` element.

To make this example work, you listen for the `myForm` object's `input` event. So, next you call `myForm.addEventListener()` to register the listener:

```
myForm.addEventListener("input", formInputChange);
```

The `formInputChange()` function executes when the `input` event fires, and in its first line of code, you create a variable called `slider` to contain the `range` `<input/>` element:

```
function formInputChange() {
    var slider = myForm.slider;
```

This is for convenience purposes because every statement in this function will reference the `slider` element in some way.

Next, you want to modify the slider's `min`, `max`, and `step` properties with the data entered into the form:

```
slider.min = parseFloat(myForm.minValue.value);
slider.max = parseFloat(myForm.maxValue.value);
slider.step = parseFloat(myForm.stepValue.value);
```

Remember that an `<input/>` element's value is string data—even if that string contains a number. Therefore, you need to convert the string into a numeric value. The `parseFloat()` function should be used here because floating-point numbers are valid values for a range's `min`, `max`, and `step` properties.

Finally, you display `slider`'s value.

```
output.innerHTML = slider.value;
}
```

New Elements

HTML5 also introduces three new form controls:

➤ `<output/>` is used to display the result of a calculation.

➤ `<meter/>` is a graphical display of a value.

➤ `<progress/>` represents the completion progress of a task.

The `<output/>` element is more of a traditional form control in that it has to be associated with a form; it can reside within a form or you can provide a form's `id` as the value of its `form` attribute.

The `<meter/>` and `<progress/>` elements, however, have no such requirement. They can appear anywhere within the document without any form association.

The `<output/>` Element

The `<output/>` element represents the result of a particular calculation or user action. No graphics or styling are associated with the element; it simply displays text (although you can apply styling with CSS).

At the heart of the `<output/>` element is its `value` property. Like a typical form control, the `value` property lets you get and set the value of the control, and setting the `value` visually updates the control to display whatever value you assigned to the property. But unlike typical form controls, the `<output/>` element does not have a `value` attribute. The value of the element is instead represented by a text node between the opening and closing `<ouput>` tags. For example:

```
<output name="result" id="result" for="field1 field2">10</output>
```

IE11 and below do not officially support the `<output/>` element, and setting the `value` property will result in an error. You might work around this issue by still using the `<output/>` element and settings its "value" with `innerHTML`. However, this workaround is not standard and is not recommended.

Finally, the `<output/>` element should be associated with fields involved in the result of calculations that the `<output/>` displays. You do this with the familiar `for` attribute. In the previous HTML, the `<output/>` element is associated with `field1` and `field2`.

TRY IT OUT Using the <output/> Element

In this exercise, you modify Example 10 and use the <output/> element to display the range's value. Feel free to copy and paste Example 10 and modify the highlighted lines of code:

```html
<!DOCTYPE html>

<html lang="en">
<head>
    <title>Chapter 11: Example 11</title>
</head>
<body>
    <form id="form1" name="form1">
        <p>
            <label for="minValue">Min: </label>
            <input type="number" id="minValue" name="minValue" />
        </p>
        <p>
            <label for="maxValue">Max: </label>
            <input type="number" id="maxValue" name="maxValue" />
        </p>
        <p>
            <label for="stepValue">Step: </label>
            <input type="number" id="stepValue" name="stepValue" />
        </p>
        <p>
            <input type="range" id="slider" name="slider" />
        </p>
    </form>
    <output id="result" name="result" form="form1" for="slider"></output>

    <script>
        var myForm = document.form1;
        var output = myForm.result;

        function formInputChange() {
            var slider = myForm.slider;

            slider.min = parseFloat(myForm.minValue.value);
            slider.max = parseFloat(myForm.maxValue.value);
            slider.step = parseFloat(myForm.stepValue.value);

            result.value = slider.value;
        }

        myForm.addEventListener("input", formInputChange);
    </script>
</body>
</html>
```

Save this as ch11_example11.html.

Because you're using standard <output/> code, you will need to open this page in Chrome, Firefox, or Opera.

Let's focus only on the lines that changed. First, you add an id attribute to the <form/> element:

```
<form id="form1" name="form1">
```

This addition is only necessary because you define the <output/> element outside of the form:

```
<output id="result" name="result" form="form1" for="slider"></output>
```

You define the <output/> element by setting its id and name attributes to result, the form attribute to form1, and the for attribute to slider. The latter isn't absolutely necessary for this example to work, but the for attribute exists so that you can write semantic markup. By setting for to slider, you (and readers of your code) know that the <output/> element displays the value related to the range field.

The next change is the second line of JavaScript code. Instead of retrieving a <div/> element, you grab a reference to your new <output/> element:

```
var output = myForm.result;
```

Notice the code: myForm.result. Even though the <output/> element is not inside the form, it is still associated with the form because of the for attribute. Therefore, you can walk the Form object hierarchy to reference the <output/> element.

The final change is the last statement of the formInputChange() function:

```
result.value = slider.value;
```

You set the <output/> element's value property to the value of slider; thus, updating the information displayed in the page.

The <meter/> and <progress/> Elements

As mentioned earlier, the <meter/> and <progress/> form controls are rather unique in that they can be used anywhere within a page. It might seem strange to call them "form controls" when they don't have to be used within a form—they don't even accept user input! Nevertheless, they're categorized as such.

At first glance, these elements look similar, but they, in fact, serve two different purposes and have a different set of attributes and properties.

The <meter/> element is used to graphically display an individual value within a particular range. For example, the RPMs of a vehicle's engine, the heat of a CPU, or disk usage indicators are perfect examples of what the <meter/> element is used for.

The <meter/> element consists of an opening and closing tag, and you can specify the low, optimum, and high sections of the meter. These are ranges, mostly for semantic purposes, that affect the meter's color. You can also set the min and max of possible values, as well as the value of the meter:

```
<meter min="0" max="150" low="40" optimum="75"
       high="100" value="80">80 Units of Something</meter>
```

These six attributes map to properties of the same names. If a browser doesn't support the `<meter/>` element, the text between the opening and closing tag is displayed in the browser.

> **NOTE** *IE9, IE10, and IE11 do not support the `<meter/>` element.*

The `<progress/>` element represents the completion progress of a task, and as with the preceding new elements, it consists of an opening and closing tag:

```
<progress max="100" value="40">40% done with what you're doing</progress>
```

It also has a max attribute that maps to the element object's max property, and the control's value is contained within the value attribute/property. Like `<meter/>`, the text between the opening and closing tags is displayed if the browser doesn't support the `<progress/>` element.

TRY IT OUT   The `<meter/>` and `<progress/>` Elements

Let's use the `<meter/>` and `<progress/>` elements in an example. Open your text editor and type the following:

```
<!DOCTYPE html>

<html lang="en">
<head>
    <title>Chapter 11: Example 12</title>
</head>
<body>
    <h2>Highway Speed Tracker</h2>
    <form id="form1" name="form1">
        <p>
            <label for="driverName">Driver Name: </label>
            <input type="text" id="driverName" name="driverName" />
        </p>
        <p>
            <label for="speed">Speed (Miles/Hour): </label>
            <input type="number" id="speed" name="speed" />
            <meter id="speedMeter" value="0" low="55" optimum="75"
                high="90" max="120"></meter>
        </p>
        <p>
            <label for="vehicle">Vehicle Type: </label>
            <input type="text" id="vehicle" name="vehicle" />
        </p>
    </form>
    <p>
        Form Completion Progress:
        <progress id="completionProgress" max="3" value="0"></progress>
    </p>

    <script>
        var myForm = document.form1;
```

```
            var completionProgress = document.getElementById("completionProgress");
            var speedMeter = document.getElementById("speedMeter");

            function countFieldData() {
                var count = 0;

                for (var index = 0; index < myForm.length; index++) {
                    var element = myForm[index];

                    if (element.value) {
                        count++;
                    }
                }

                return count;
            }

            function formInputChange() {
                completionProgress.value = countFieldData();

                speedMeter.value = myForm.speed.value;
            }

            myForm.addEventListener("input", formInputChange);
        </script>
    </body>
</html>
```

Save this as ch11_example12.html. Open the page in your browser (including IE—this example mostly works in IE9, IE10, and IE11), and you'll see a form with three fields: a driver's name, the driver's speed, and the type of vehicle the driver drove. As you fill out the form, you'll notice a few things going on.

First, the progress bar below the form changes in value. This indicates your progress in filling out the form. When all fields have a value, you're done! Second, you'll notice the meter next to the Speed field updates to visually represent the data from that field.

Now let's look at the HTML. In the body of the page, you define a form with three <input/> elements. The first is a normal text box for the driver's name:

```
<form id="form1" name="form1">
    <p>
        <label for="driverName">Driver Name: </label>
        <input type="text" id="driverName" name="driverName" />
    </p>
```

The next field is a number field for inputting the driver's speed:

```
    <p>
        <label for="speed">Speed (Miles/Hour): </label>
        <input type="number" id="speed" name="speed" />
        <meter id="speedMeter" value="0" low="55" optimum="75"
               high="90" max="120"></meter>
    </p>
```

Here, you also define a `<meter/>` element with an `id` of `speedMeter`. This meter is supposed to visually represent highway speed in miles per hour. In such cases, 55MPH is slow, 75MPH is optimum/standard, and 90MPH is high. The maximum value this meter can display is 120.

The last field is another text box for the driver's vehicle:

```
<p>
    <label for="vehicle">Vehicle Type: </label>
    <input type="text" id="vehicle" name="vehicle" />
</p>
```

Then after the form, you define a `<progress/>` element:

```
<p>
    Form Completion Progress:
    <progress id="completionProgress" max="3" value="0"></progress>
</p>
```

This is to track the user's progress in filling out the form. It has an `id` of `completionProgress` and has a maximum value of 3 because it contains three fields.

Of course, the HTML by itself isn't very interesting; so, let's look at the JavaScript. You first retrieve three elements from the document: the `<form/>`, `<progress/>`, and `<meter/>` elements.

```
var myForm = document.form1;
var completionProgress = document.getElementById("completionProgress");
var speedMeter = document.getElementById("speedMeter");
```

To retrieve the `<progress/>` and `<meter/>` elements, you use `document.getElementById()` because although these two elements are considered form controls, you cannot access them through the form hierarchy (which admittedly can be a little confusing).

Once again, the form's `input` event provides the magic for this example; so, you register its listener:

```
myForm.addEventListener("input", formInputChange);
```

The `formInputChange()` function is rather simple; it updates the values of both the `<progress/>` and `<meter/>` elements:

```
function formInputChange() {
    completionProgress.value = countFieldData();

    speedMeter.value = myForm.speed.value;
}
```

The value for `speedMeter` comes from the `speed` field in the form, but a little more work is needed to set the value for `completionProgress`.

You create a helper function called `countFieldData()`. Its job is straightforward: Examine the elements within the form and determine if they have a value. It's not a foolproof solution for determining if the user has completed the form, but it works for this example.

First, you define a counter variable to count how many fields have a value. You call this variable count:

```
function countFieldData() {
    var count = 0;
```

Now you need to check the value property of every element in the form. You could write code explicitly for this form, or you can take a more generic approach and loop through the form's elements. Let's do the latter:

```
for (var index = 0; index < myForm.length; index++) {
    var element = myForm[index];

    if (element.value) {
        count++;
    }
}
```

Using a for loop, you iterate over the myForm object/collection to retrieve each form control and check if it has a value. If the element has a value, you increment the count variable.

After the loop exits, you return the value of the count variable:

```
    return count;
}
```

SUMMARY

In this chapter, you looked at how to add a user interface onto your JavaScript so that you can interact with your users and acquire information from them. This chapter covered the following:

➤ The HTML form is where you place elements making up the interface in a page.

➤ Each HTML form groups together a set of HTML elements. When a form is submitted to a server for processing, all the data in that form is sent to the server. You can have multiple forms on a page, but only the information in one form can be sent to the server.

➤ A form is created with the opening tag <form> and ends with the close tag </form>. All the elements you want included in that form are placed in between the open and close <form> tags. The <form/> element has various attributes—for client-side scripting, the name attribute is the important one. You can access forms with either their name attribute or their ID attribute.

➤ Each <form> element creates a Form object, which is contained within the document object. To access a form named myForm, you write document.myForm. The document object also has a forms property, which is a collection containing every form inside the document. The first form in the page is document.forms[0], the second is document.forms[1], and so on. The length property of the forms property (document.forms.length) tells you how many forms are on the page.

➤ Having discussed forms, we then went on to look at the different types of HTML elements that can be placed inside forms, how to create them, and how they are used in JavaScript.

➤ The objects associated with the form elements have a number of properties, methods, and events that are common to them all. They all have the name property, which you can use to reference them in your JavaScript. They also all have the form property, which provides a reference to the Form object in which that element is contained. The type property returns a text string telling you what type of element this is; types include text, button, and radio.

➤ You also saw that the methods focus() and blur(), and the events focus and blur, are available to every form element object. Such an element is said to receive the focus when it becomes the active element in the form, either because the user has selected that element or because you used the focus() method. However an element got the focus, its focus event will fire. When another element is set as the currently active element, the previous element is said to lose its focus, or to blur. Again, loss of focus can be the result of the user selecting another element or the use of the blur() method; either way, when it happens the blur event fires. You saw that the firing of focus and blur can, if used carefully, be a good place to check things like the validity of data entered by a user into an element.

➤ All elements return a value, which is the string data assigned to that element. The meaning of the value depends on the element; for a text box, it is the value inside the text box, and for a button, it's the text displayed on its face.

➤ Having discussed the common features of elements, we then looked at each of the more commonly used elements in turn, starting with the button element.

➤ The button element's purpose in life is to be clicked by the user, where that clicking fires some script you have written. You can capture the clicking by connecting to the button's click event. A button is created by means of the <input/> element with the type attribute set to button. The value attribute determines what text appears on the button's face. Two variations on a button are the submit and reset buttons. In addition to acting as buttons, they also provide a special service not linked to code. The submit button automatically submits the form to the server; the reset button clears the form back to its default state when loaded in the page.

➤ The text element allows the user to enter a single line of plaintext. A text box is created by means of the <input/> element with the type attribute set to text. You can set how many characters the user can enter and how wide the text box is with the maxlength and size attributes, respectively, of the <input/> element. The text box has an associated object called Text, which has the additional events select and change. The select event fires when the user selects text in the box, and the more useful change event fires when the element loses focus and its contents have changed since the element gained the focus. The firing of the change event is a good place to do validation of what the user has just entered. If she entered illegal values, such as letters when you wanted numbers, you can let her know and send her back to correct her mistake. A variation on the text box is the password box, which is almost identical to the text box except that the values typed into it are hidden and shown as asterisks. Additionally, the text box also has the keydown, keypress, and keyup events.

➤ The next element you looked at was the text area, which is similar to the text box except that it allows multiple lines of text to be entered. This element is created with the open tag `<textarea>` and closed with the `</textarea>` tag, the width and height in characters of the text box being determined by the `cols` and `rows` attributes, respectively. The `wrap` attribute determines whether the text area wraps text that reaches the end of a line and whether that wrapping is sent when the contents are posted to the server. If this attribute is left out, or set to `off`, no wrapping occurs; if set to `soft`, it causes wrapping client-side, but is not sent to the server when the form is sent; if set to `hard`, it causes wrapping client-side and is sent to the server. The associated `Textarea` object has virtually the same properties, methods, and events as a `Text` object.

➤ You then looked at the check box and radio button elements together. Essentially they are the same type of element, except that the radio button is a grouped element, meaning that only one in a group can be checked at once. Checking another one causes the previously checked button to be unchecked. Both elements are created with the `<input/>` element, the `type` attribute being `checkbox` or `radio`. If `checked` is put inside the `<input>` tag, that element will be checked when the page is loaded. Creating radio buttons with the same name creates a radio button group. The name of a radio button actually refers to an array, and each element within that array is a radio button defined on the form to be within that group. These elements have associated objects called `Checkbox` and `Radio`. Using the `checked` property of these objects, you can find out whether a check box or radio button is currently checked. Both objects also have the `click` event in addition to the common events `focus` and `blur`.

➤ Next in your look at elements were the drop-down list and list boxes. Both, in fact, are the same select element, with the `size` attribute determining whether it's a drop-down or list box. The `<select>` tag creates these elements, the `size` attribute determining how many list items are visible at once. If a `size` of 1 is given, a drop-down box rather than a list box is created. Each item in a select element is defined by the `<option/>` element, or added to later by means of the `Select` object's `options` collection property, which is an array-like structure containing each `Option` object for that element. However, adding options after the page is loaded differs slightly between standards-compliant browsers and old-IE. The `Select` object's `selectedIndex` property tells you which option is selected; you can then use that value to access the appropriate option in the `options` collection and use the `Option` object's `value` property. The `Option` object also has the `text` and `index` properties, `text` being the displayed text in the list and `index` being its position in the `Select` object's `options` collection property. You can loop through the `options` collection, finding out its length from the `Select` object's `length` property. The `Select` object has the `change` event, which fires when the user selects another item from the list.

➤ You then looked at HTML5's new elements and input types, as well as the `input` event. You learned how to write JavaScript code to manipulate the `<output/>`, `<meter/>`, and `<progress/>` elements and modify their output when users input data in a form.

In the next chapter, you look at JavaScript Object Notation (JSON), a data format that lets you store JavaScript objects and arrays as string data.

EXERCISES

You can find suggested solutions to these questions in Appendix A.

1. Using the code from the temperature converter example you saw in Chapter 2, create a user interface for it and connect it to the existing code so that the user can enter a value in degrees Fahrenheit and convert it to centigrade.

2. Create a user interface that allows users to pick the computer system of their dreams, similar in principle to the e-commerce sites selling computers over the Internet. For example, they could be given a choice of processor type, speed, memory, and hard drive size, and the option to add additional components like a DVD-ROM drive, a sound card, and so on. As the users change their selections, the price of the system should update automatically and notify them of the cost of the system as they specified it, either by using an `alert` box or by updating the contents of a text box.

12

JSON

WHAT YOU WILL LEARN IN THIS CHAPTER:

➤ Discovering the limitations of using XML with JavaScript

➤ Recognizing the differences between JavaScript and JSON

➤ Serializing objects using the built-in JSON object

➤ Parsing JSON back into actual objects and values you can use in your pages

WROX.COM CODE DOWNLOADS FOR THIS CHAPTER

You can find the wrox.com code downloads for this chapter at `http://www.wiley.com/go/BeginningJavaScript5E` on the Download Code tab. You can also view all of the examples and related files at `http://beginningjs.com`.

If you aren't already, start thinking of a web page as a program. It does, after all, have all the trappings of a traditional program. It has a user interface, and it can process data with JavaScript. But as you well know, traditional programs can do more; they can store data as well as transmit data to other computers and systems. In the coming chapters, you learn that you can do the same things in a web page—all thanks to JavaScript.

But as you soon learn, you can't just store objects and arrays as they are; instead, you need to *serialize* them. Serialization is the process of translating an object into a string representation of that object. Once an object is serialized, the string representation of that object can then be stored in a more permanent storage facility or transmitted to another computer.

Serialization translates only the structure and pertinent information of an object—that is, only the properties are present in a serialized object. But once you need to work with the object within JavaScript, you can *deserialize* it, converting it back into a native JavaScript object.

The serialization format that web developers overwhelmingly embrace is called JavaScript Object Notation, or JSON (pronounced like the name: Jason). It is a subset of the JavaScript language; as such, it's easy to read, it's concise, and most importantly, it's easy to serialize to and deserialize from.

But the web hasn't always used JSON for serializing JavaScript objects. So before we look at the JSON format, let's look at what web developers used to use.

XML

There was a time when the web development community embraced XML for just about everything. Web services used it to communicate with one another and other computers, and JavaScript developers used it to communicate with the web application's server.

XML is a human-readable language thanks to its declarative syntax. It's not necessary for humans to read XML data, but being able to read and decipher the XML can be useful. Consider the following XML document as an example:

```
<person>
    <firstName>John</firstName>
    <lastName>Doe</lastName>
    <age>30</age>
</person>
```

Despite being a simple document, you know that this XML represents an individual person named John Doe who is 30 years old. You could catch and fix errors that may occur in your application as it generates the preceding XML-formatted data.

XML is also machine-readable, and it was a known commodity when developers started using it. Every modern programming language had the tools and capabilities for reading, parsing, and creating XML-formatted data, and so using XML to communicate between computer systems and applications seemed like a good idea.

But XML has its drawbacks. For one, XML's declarative syntax adds a lot of extra cruft to the data. Look again at the XML describing a person named John Doe:

```
<person>
    <firstName>John</firstName>
    <lastName>Doe</lastName>
    <age>30</age>
</person>
```

This simple XML is 101 bytes. That's not large by today's standards, but remember that this is just an example. This is information that a computer would send over the Internet to another computer.

First, the opening and closing <person> tags surround the actual data. Of course, the outer <person/> element exists for organizational purposes, but it is 17 bytes—16 percent of the entire payload. Other formats will still have some way to organize the document's real information (the first and last name), but they would be smaller in size.

Next, opening and closing tags surround both the first and last name. Naturally, there needs to be some way to organize that data, but yet, this XML uses 55 bytes to denote the first name, last name, and the age.

Another of XML's issues is the code necessary for reading, parsing, and generating XML data. Yes, most modern programming languages can handle XML, but it requires a lot of code—code that usually has to be rewritten for specific XML formats. For example, the following code is one way you could read the previous XML and parse it into an object called person:

```
var personElement = document.querySelector("person");
var firstName = personElement.querySelector("firstName").innerHTML;
var lastName = personElement.querySelector("lastName").innerHTML;
var age = personElement.querySelector("age").innerHTML;

var person = {
    firstName : firstName,
    lastName: lastName,
    age: age
};
```

This code demonstrates a straightforward approach to parsing the John Doe XML. It first retrieves the <person/> element using document.querySelector(). It then retrieves the <firstName/>, <lastName/>, and <age/> elements and stores their respective contents in the firstName, lastName, and age variables. Finally, it creates the person object and assigns the appropriate data to its properties. This code isn't complex, but as you might suspect, it wouldn't work for XML-formatted data with different element names and structures. Naturally, documents with more complex structures require much more code.

But parsing XML into a JavaScript object is only half of the story. Before you can send data from JavaScript to the server, you have to serialize the JavaScript object. Serializing a JavaScript object to XML-formatted data is not a trivial task. Like parsing, the same code usually doesn't work for different data structures. Plus, developers must ensure their generated XML data is well-formed.

Around 2007 and 2008, the web community thankfully adopted a different data format for storing and transmitting JavaScript data.

JSON

In 2006, Douglas Crockford wrote the JavaScript Object Notation specification. JSON is a subset of the JavaScript language, and it uses several of JavaScript's syntactical patterns for organizing and structuring data. As such, it is does a very good job of representing objects and their data (it's so good that other languages use JSON, too). It's extremely easy to parse JSON into JavaScript objects and to serialize objects into JSON. In today's modern browsers, it only takes one line of code!

As you soon see, JSON looks a lot like JavaScript's object and array literals. It's easy to confuse JSON and JavaScript as being the same thing, but it's important to understand the difference between the two. JavaScript is a programming language; JSON is a data format.

JSON lets you represent three types of data: simple values, objects, and arrays.

Simple Values

You can represent simple values like strings, numbers, booleans, and `null`. For example, the following line is valid JSON:

```
"JavaScript"
```

This JSON represents the string value of `"JavaScript"`, and it looks exactly like a normal JavaScript string. But there's a big difference between strings in JavaScript and JSON; JSON strings must use double quotes. Thus, the following is invalid JSON:

```
'JavaScript'
```

Numeric data is represented by what appears to be number literals, like this:

```
10
```

This is valid JSON representing the number 10. Similarly, boolean values and `null` look like JavaScript literals, too:

```
true
```

```
null
```

Objects

Objects in JSON are represented with what looks like JavaScript's object literal notation. For example, the following is a JavaScript object that represents the same person from earlier:

```
var person = {
    firstName: "John",
    lastName: "Doe",
    age: 30
};
```

The JSON representation of this object looks similar. Here is the same object represented in JSON:

```
{
    "firstName": "John",
    "lastName": "Doe",
    "age": 30
}
```

A few noticeable differences exist between the JavaScript and JSON representations of this object. First, JSON doesn't have the `person` variable name. Remember that JSON is a data format, not a language. It has no variables, functions, or methods. It simply defines the structure and data of an object.

The second difference is the object's property names. Notice that they are surrounded by double quotes. In JSON, an object's property names are strings, and the values of those properties follow the rules specified in the previous section. Double quotes surround the string values of `"John"` and `"Doe"`, and the number `30` appears as a literal value.

The final difference is the lack of a trailing semicolon after the closing curly brace. This isn't a JavaScript statement, and thus, the semicolon is not needed.

The size of this JSON data structure is 69 bytes. That's 68 percent of the 101 bytes of the equivalent XML.

Like JavaScript objects, JSON objects can be simple or complex. The data structure representing John Doe is rather simple, but you can easily add complexity by incorporating his address:

```
{
    "firstName": "John",
    "lastName": "Doe",
    "age": 30,
    "address": {
        "numberAndStreet": "123 Someplace",
        "city": "Somewhere",
        "state": "Elsewhere"
    }
}
```

This adds an `address` property to the main object, and its value is another object that contains John's mailing address.

Arrays

Like objects, arrays in JSON are similar to JavaScript's array literal notation. The following line of code is an array literal in JavaScript:

```
var values = ["John", 30, false, null];
```

The same array looks like this in JSON:

```
["John", 30, false, null]
```

Again, notice the JSON array does not have the `values` variable, nor does it have the trailing semicolon. And like objects, arrays are not limited to just simple values; they can contain complex objects, too:

```
[
    {
        "firstName": "John",
        "lastName": "Doe",
        "age": 30,
        "address": {
            "numberAndStreet": "123 Someplace",
            "city": "Somewhere",
            "state": "Elsewhere"
        }
    },
    {
        "firstName": "Jane",
        "lastName": "Doe",
```

```
        "age": 28,
        "address": {
            "numberAndStreet": "246 Someplace",
            "city": "Somewhere",
            "state": "Elsewhere"
        }
    }
]
```

This JSON array contains multiple objects that represent people and their addresses. The first is our familiar John Doe, and the second is his little sister, Jane, who lives down the street. JSON data structures can be as simple or complex as you need them to be.

Serializing Into JSON

It's extremely easy to serialize JavaScript objects into JSON. JavaScript has an aptly named JSON object that you use to parse JSON data and serialize JavaScript objects. All major browsers support this JSON object. Older browsers, such as IE7 and below, can use Crockford's JSON implementation (https://github.com/douglascrockford/JSON-js) to achieve the same results.

To serialize a JavaScript object into JSON, you use the JSON object's stringify() method. It accepts any value, object, or array and serializes it into JSON. For example:

```
var person = {
    firstName: "John",
    lastName: "Doe",
    age: 30
};

var json = JSON.stringify(person);
```

This code serializes the person object with JSON.stringify() and stores it in the json variable. The resulting JSON-formatted data looks like this:

```
{"firstName":"John","lastName":"Doe","age":30}
```

All unnecessary whitespace is removed, giving you an optimized payload that you can then send to the web server or store elsewhere.

Parsing JSON

Parsing JSON into JavaScript objects is equally simple. The JSON object has a parse() method that parses the JSON and returns the resulting object. Using the json variable from the previous code:

```
var johnDoe = JSON.parse(json);
```

This code parses the JSON text contained in json and stores the resulting object in the johnDoe variable. And here's the wonderful thing—you can immediately use johnDoe and access its properties, such as:

```
var fullName = johnDoe.firstName + " " + johnDoe.lastName;
```

It's really no wonder why developers embraced JSON. It's easy to work with!

JSON is useful when you need to store an object, but the API you're working with only lets you store text. In Chapter 10, you learned that the native drag and drop API has a `dataTransfer` object that you can use to work with data during the drag-and-drop operation. But as you learned, it doesn't let you store objects, but you can store text. JSON is text, so you can serialize a JavaScript object at the beginning of the drag operation and parse the JSON when the drop event fires.

TRY IT OUT   Using JSON in Drag and Drop

This example uses `ch10_example21.html` as a basis. Feel free to copy and paste the code from that example and make the highlighted modifications. Otherwise, open your text editor and type the following:

```html
<!DOCTYPE html>

<html lang="en">
<head>
    <title>Chapter 12: Example 1</title>
    <style>
        [data-drop-target] {
            height: 400px;
            width: 200px;
            margin: 2px;
            background-color: gainsboro;
            float: left;
        }

        .drag-enter {
            border: 2px dashed #000;
        }

        .box {
            width: 200px;
            height: 200px;
        }

        .navy {
            background-color: navy;
        }

        .red {
            background-color: red;
        }
    </style>
</head>
<body>
    <div data-drop-target="true">
        <div id="box1" draggable="true" class="box navy"></div>
        <div id="box2" draggable="true" class="box red"></div>
    </div>
```

```
<div data-drop-target="true"></div>

<script>
    function handleDragStart(e) {
        var data = {
            elementId: this.id,
            message: "You moved an element!"
        };

        e.dataTransfer.setData("text", JSON.stringify(data));
    }

    function handleDragEnterLeave(e) {
        if (e.type == "dragenter") {
            this.className = "drag-enter";
        } else {
            this.className = "";
        }
    }

    function handleOverDrop(e) {
        e.preventDefault();

        if (e.type != "drop") {
            return;
        }

        var json = e.dataTransfer.getData("text");
        var data = JSON.parse(json);

        var draggedEl = document.getElementById(data.elementId);

        if (draggedEl.parentNode == this) {
            this.className = "";
            return;
        }

        draggedEl.parentNode.removeChild(draggedEl);

        this.appendChild(draggedEl);
        this.className = "";

        alert(data.message);
    }

    var draggable = document.querySelectorAll("[draggable]");
    var targets = document.querySelectorAll("[data-drop-target]");

    for (var i = 0; i < draggable.length; i++) {
        draggable[i].addEventListener("dragstart", handleDragStart);
    }

    for (i = 0; i < targets.length; i++) {
        targets[i].addEventListener("dragover", handleOverDrop);
        targets[i].addEventListener("drop", handleOverDrop);
```

```
            targets[i].addEventListener("dragenter", handleDragEnterLeave);
            targets[i].addEventListener("dragleave", handleDragEnterLeave);
        }
    </script>
</body>
</html>
```

Save this file as `ch12_example1.html`.

You need just a few changes to make this example different from `ch10_example21.html`. The first is in the `handleDragStart()` function:

```
function handleDragStart(e) {
    var data = {
        elementId: this.id,
        message: "You moved an element!"
    };
```

The new code creates an object called `data`. It has an `elementId` property to contain the element's `id` value, and a `message` property that contains arbitrary text. You want to use this object as the drag and drop's transfer data; so, you have to serialize it:

```
        e.dataTransfer.setData("text", JSON.stringify(data));
    }
```

You call the `JSON.stringify()` method to do just that, and the resulting JSON text is set as the transfer's data.

The remaining changes appear in the `handleOverDrop()` function. Its first few lines are the same:

```
function handleOverDrop(e) {
    e.preventDefault();

    if (e.type != "drop") {
        return;
    }
```

But the next two lines are new:

```
    var json = e.dataTransfer.getData("text");
    var data = JSON.parse(json);
```

You retrieve the transferred data with the `getData()` method and store it in the `json` variable. You then parse the JSON into a JavaScript object that you store in the `data` variable. You need to retrieve the dragged element object from the document. So, you use `data.elementId` and pass it to `document` `.getElementById()`:

```
    var draggedEl = document.getElementById(data.elementId);

    if (draggedEl.parentNode == this) {
        this.className = "";
        return;
```

```
    }

    draggedEl.parentNode.removeChild(draggedEl);

    this.appendChild(draggedEl);
    this.className = "";
```

After you remove the dragged element from its parent and append it to the drop target, you reach into your data object and alert its message to the user:

```
    alert(data.message);
  }
```

This technique of using JSON to store object data is useful in a variety of scenarios. In the next chapter, you use the same technique to store object data directly in the browser.

SUMMARY

In this chapter, you looked at JSON, a text format for storing and transmitting objects, arrays, and simple values. Let's look at some of the things discussed in this chapter:

➤ Serialization is the process of translating objects and values into a string representation of those objects and values.

➤ The web used to use XML for storing and transmitting JavaScript data, but JSON is now the format of choice.

➤ JSON is not JavaScript, but a subset of JavaScript. Its syntax looks similar, but key differences exist between the two. For one, JSON does not have variables or functions. It is simply a data format.

➤ JSON strings must be surrounded by double quotes. Single quotes result in an error.

➤ Numbers, booleans, and null appear as literal values in JSON.

➤ JSON objects look very much like JavaScript object literals except their properties are strings and there are no trailing semicolons.

➤ JSON arrays are almost identical to JavaScript array literals, but they do not have a trailing semicolon.

➤ You serialize JavaScript objects, arrays, and values using the JSON object's stringify() method.

➤ You parse JSON text into a JavaScript object or value using JSON.parse().

In the next chapter, you look at how to store data in and for the browser using local storage and cookies.

EXERCISES

You can find a suggested solution to this question in Appendix A.

1. The code for alerting a single message in Example 1 isn't very exciting. Modify the code to display a random message from a set of three possible messages.

Data Storage

WHAT YOU WILL LEARN IN THIS CHAPTER:

➤ Storing data on the user's computer is possible with cookies and web storage

➤ Creating cookies is relatively straightforward, but reading them is complex

➤ Using web storage is easy

WROX.COM CODE DOWNLOADS FOR THIS CHAPTER

You can find the wrox.com code downloads for this chapter at http://www.wiley.com/go/BeginningJavaScript5E on the Download Code tab. You can also view all of the examples and related files at http://beginningjs.com.

Our goal as website programmers should be to make the website experience as easy and pleasant for the user as possible. Clearly, well-designed pages with easily navigable layouts are central to this, but they're not the whole story. You can go one step further by learning about your users and using information gained about them to personalize the website.

For example, imagine a user, whose name you asked on the first visit, returns to your website. You could welcome her back to the website by greeting her by name. Another good example is given by a website, such as Amazon's, that incorporates the one-click purchasing system. By already knowing the user's purchasing details, such as credit-card number and delivery address, you can allow the user to go from viewing a book to buying it in just one click, making the likelihood of the user purchasing it that much greater. Also, based on information, such as the previous purchases and browsing patterns of the user, it's possible to make book suggestions.

Such personalization requires that information about users be stored somewhere in between their visits to the website. Accessing the user's local filesystem from a web application is pretty much off limits because of security restrictions included in browsers. However, you, as a website developer, can store small amounts of information in a special place on the user's local disk, using what is called a *cookie*, and in the browser using HTML5's Web Storage.

BAKING YOUR FIRST COOKIE

The key to cookies is the `document` object's `cookie` property. Using this property, you can create and retrieve cookie data from within your JavaScript code.

You can set a cookie by setting `document.cookie` to a *cookie string*. You'll be looking in detail at how this cookie string is made up later in the chapter, but let's first create a simple example of a cookie and see where the information is stored on the user's computer.

A Fresh-Baked Cookie

The following code sets a cookie with the `UserName` set as `Paul` and an expiration date of 28 December, 2020:

```
<!DOCTYPE html>

<html lang="en">
<head>
    <title>Fresh-Baked Cookie</title>
    <script>
        document.cookie =
            "UserName=Paul;expires=Tue, 28 Dec 2020 00:00:00;";
    </script>
</head>
<body>
    <p>This page just created a cookie</p>
</body>

</html>
```

Save the page as `freshbakedcookie.html`. You'll see how the code works as you learn the parts of a cookie string, but first let's see what happens when a cookie is created.

How you view cookies without using code varies with the browser you are using.

Viewing Cookies in Internet Explorer

In this section, you see how to look at the cookies that are already stored by Internet Explorer (IE) on your computer. You then load the cookie-creating page you just created with the preceding code to see what effect this has. Follow these steps:

1. First, you need to open IE. The examples in this chapter use IE 11, so if you're using an earlier version of IE you may find the screenshots and menus in slightly different places.

2. Before you view the cookies, first clear the temporary Internet file folder for the browser, because this will make it easier to view the cookies that your browser has stored. Click the Gear icon and choose the Internet Options menu item, which is shown in Figure 13-1.

    You are presented with the Internet Options dialog box shown in Figure 13-2.

Internet Options ? ×

General | Security | Privacy | Content | Connections | Programs | Advanced

Home page

To create home page tabs, type each address on its own line.

http://www.google.com/

| Use current | Use default | Use new tab |

Startup

○ Start with tabs from the last session
⦿ Start with home page

Tabs

Change how webpages are displayed in tabs.   [Tabs]

Browsing history

Delete temporary files, history, cookies, saved passwords, and web form information.

☐ Delete browsing history on exit

[Delete...]   [Settings]

Appearance

[Colors] [Languages] [Fonts] [Accessibility]

[OK]   [Cancel]   [Apply]

Print   ▸
File   ▸
Zoom (100%)   ▸
Safety   ▸

Add site to Apps
View downloads   Ctrl+J
Manage add-ons
F12 Developer Tools
Go to pinned sites
Compatibility View settings

Report website problems

Internet options

About Internet Explorer

FIGURE 13-1   **FIGURE 13-2**

3. Click the Delete button under Browsing History. Another dialog box appears, as shown in Figure 13-3.

4. Make sure to select the tick boxes next to "Temporary Internet files and website files" and "Cookies and website data" and then click the Delete button. You now have a nice clean cache, which makes it easy to see when you create a cookie.

5. You can now close the dialog box and return to the main Internet Options dialog box.

Let's have a look at the cookies you have currently residing on your machine.

6. From the Internet Options dialog box, click the Settings button next to the Delete button grouped under Browsing History. You should see the dialog box shown in Figure 13-4.

7. Now click the View Files button, and a list of all the temporary pages and cookie files on your computer is displayed. If you followed the previous instructions and deleted all temporary Internet files, there should be nothing listed, as shown in Figure 13-5.

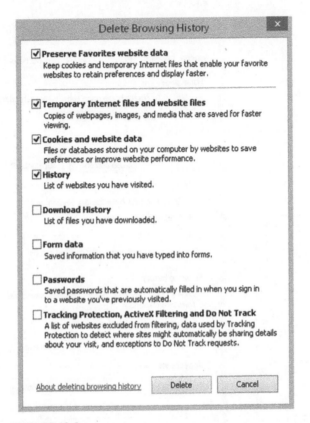

FIGURE 13-3

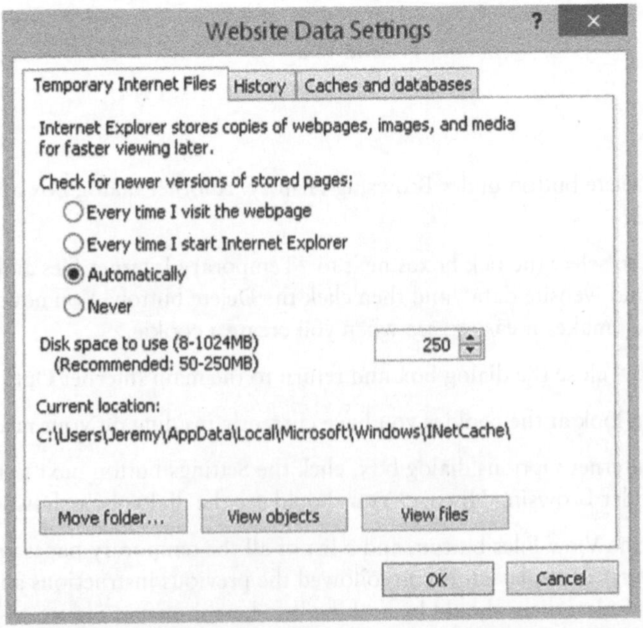

FIGURE 13-4

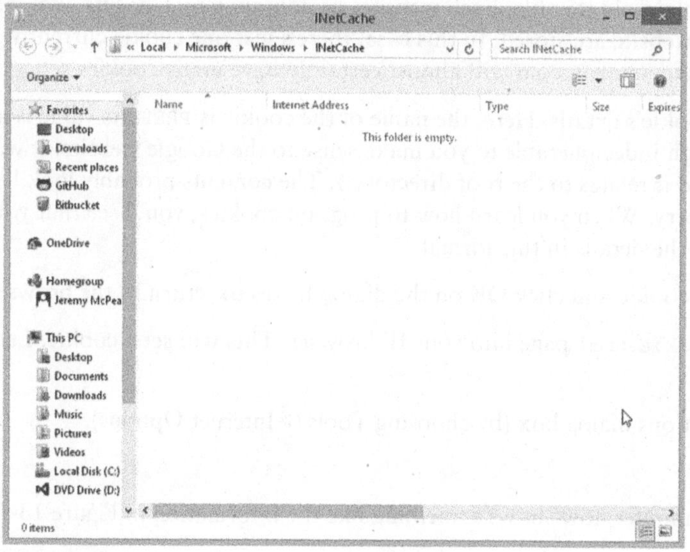

FIGURE 13-5

The actual cookies, their names, and their values may look slightly different depending on your computer's operating system.

You can examine the contents of the cookies by double-clicking them. Note that you may get a warning about the potential security risk of opening a text file, although you are fairly safe with cookies because they are simply text files. In Figure 13-6 you can see the contents of the cookie file named google set by the search engine Google.

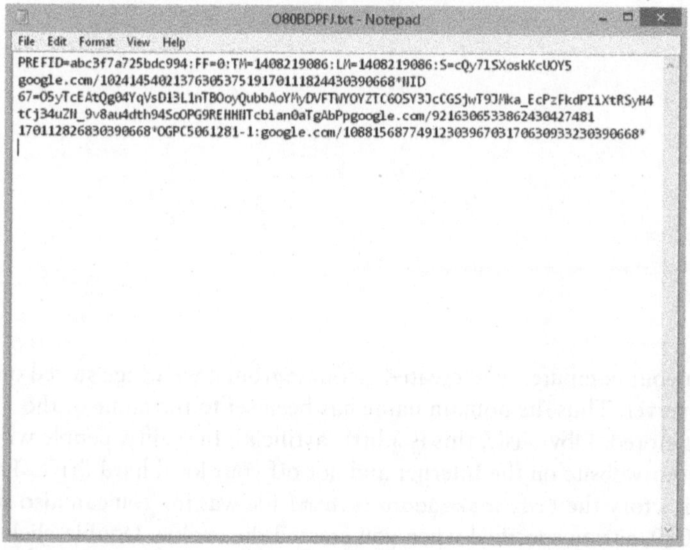

FIGURE 13-6

As you can see, a cookie is just a plain old text file. Each website, or *domain name*, has its own text file where all the cookies for that website are stored. In this case, there's just one cookie currently stored for google.com. Domains like amazon.com will almost certainly have many cookies set.

In Figure 13-6, you can see the cookie's details. Here, the name of the cookie is PREF; its value is a series of characters, which although indecipherable to you make sense to the Google website. It was set by the domain google.com, and it relates to the root directory /. The contents probably look like a mess of characters, but don't worry. When you learn how to program cookies, you'll see that you don't need to worry about setting the details in this format.

After you have finished, close the cookie and click OK on the dialog boxes to return to the browser.

Now let's load the `freshbakedcookie.html` page into your IE browser. This will set a cookie. Let's see how it has changed things:

1. Return to the Internet Options dialog box (by choosing Tools ⇨ Internet Options).

2. Click the Settings button.

3. Click View Files. Your computer now shows something like the information in Figure 13-7.

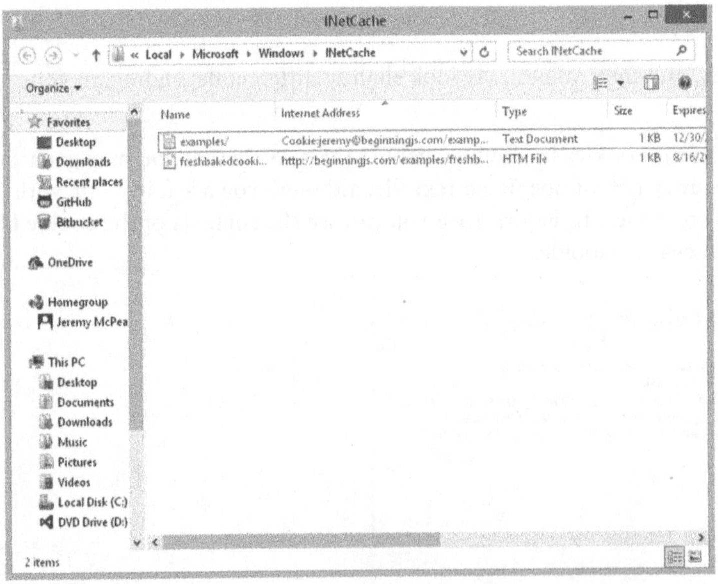

FIGURE 13-7

If you loaded the HTML file from your computer, you created a cookie from a web page stored on the local hard drive rather than a server. Thus, its domain name has been set to the name of the directory in which the web page is stored. Obviously, this is a little artificial. In reality, people will be loading your web pages from your website on the Internet and not off your local hard drive. The Internet address is based on the directory the `freshbakedcookie.html` file was in. You can also see that it expires on December 31, 2020, as you specified when you created the cookie. Double-click the cookie to view its contents, which look like those in Figure 13-8.

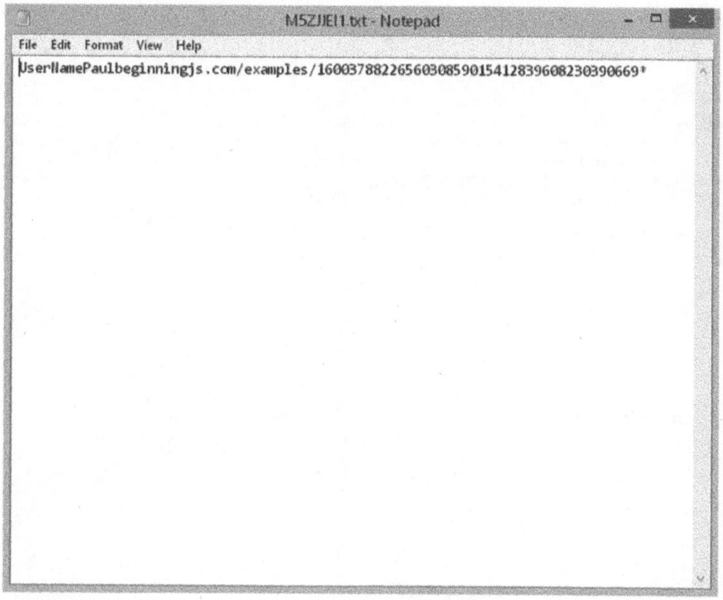

FIGURE 13-8

You can see the name you gave to the cookie at the left, UserName, its value, Paul, and also the directory it's applicable to. The expiration date is there as well; it's just not in an easily recognizable form. Note that you may sometimes need to close the browser and reopen it before you see the cookie file.

Viewing Cookies in Firefox

There is no sharing of cookies between browsers, so the cookies stored when you visited websites using IE won't be available to Firefox and vice versa. The examples in this section use Firefox 31.

Firefox keeps its cookies in a totally different place from IE, and the contents are viewed by a different means. To view cookies in Firefox:

1. Click the "Hamburger" icon and choose Options as shown in Figure 13-9.

2. Select the Privacy option.

3. Click the "remove individual cookies" link and you should see the dialog box shown in Figure 13-10.

4. Click Close to get back to the browser, and load freshbakedcookie.html.

FIGURE 13-9

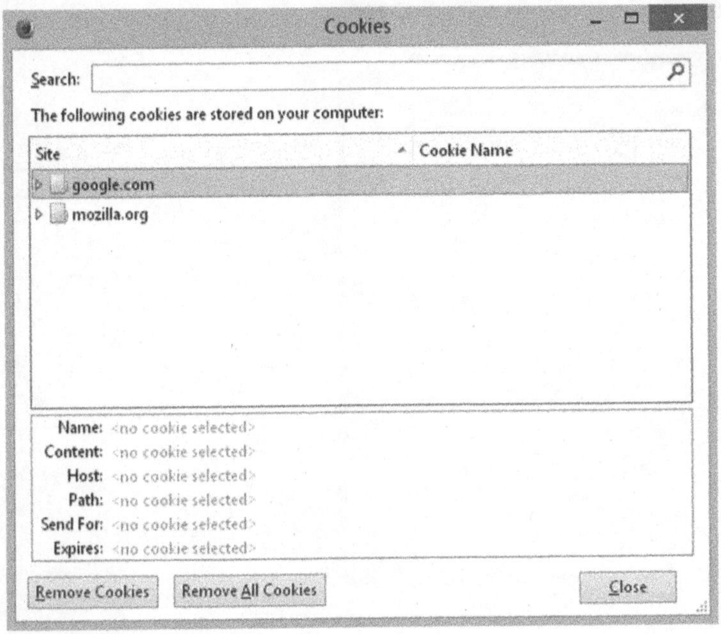

FIGURE 13-10

5. Repeat the process you followed previously to get to the Cookie Manager, and you should find that the UserName cookie has been added to the box. If loaded from your PC and not the Internet, the cookie will have a blank web address. The expanded cookie details are shown in Figure 13-11.

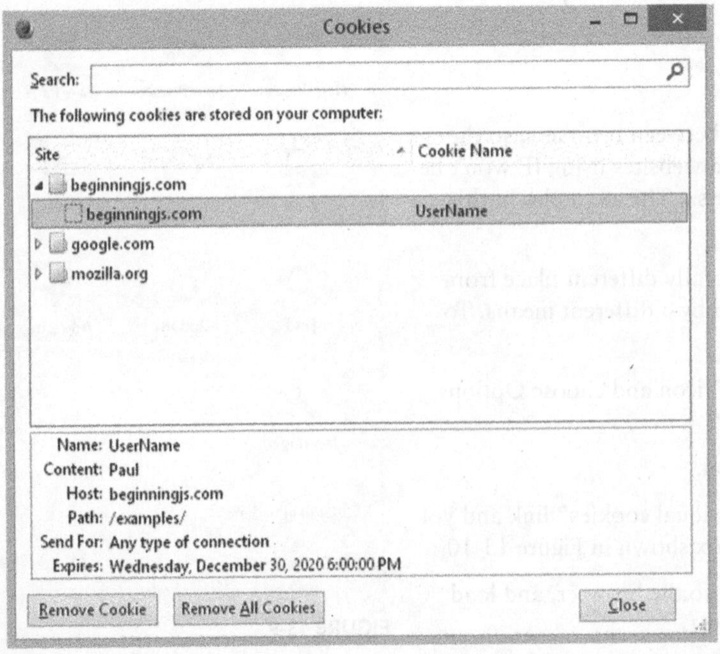

FIGURE 13-11

Note that buttons are provided at the bottom of the Cookie Manager to remove the selected cookie or all of the cookies that are stored.

Viewing Cookies in Chrome

When it comes to cookies, Chrome is somewhat similar to Firefox in that you view and manage them through the browser:

1. Click the "Hamburger" icon and choose Settings as shown in Figure 13-12.

2. In the "Search settings" box, type `cookies`. You'll see Chrome change the Settings page to look something like Figure 13-13. Click the "Content settings" button.

3. In the "Content settings" window, click the "All cookies and site data..." button. A new window pops up that lets you manage your cookies (Figure 13-14).

4. Load `freshbakedcookie.html` in a new tab or window.

5. Go back to the Settings page and click the Refresh icon. You'll now see an entry for the new cookie as shown in Figure 13-15.

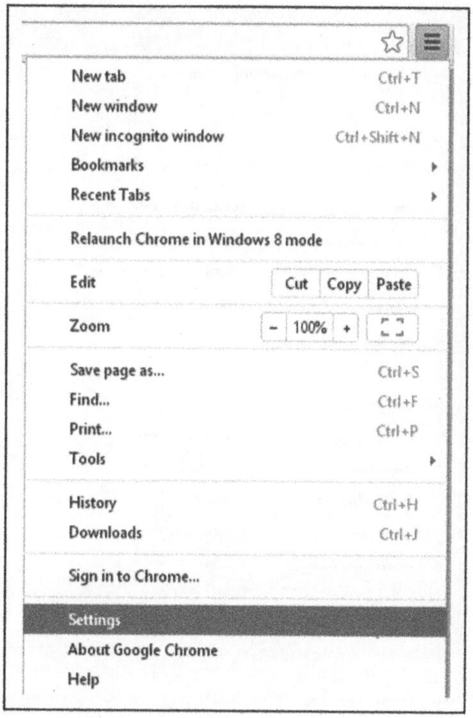

FIGURE 13-12

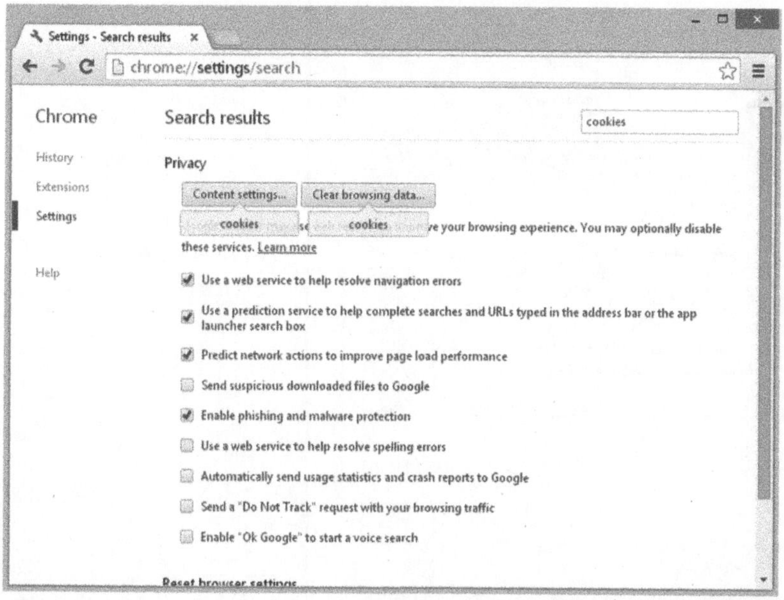

FIGURE 13-13

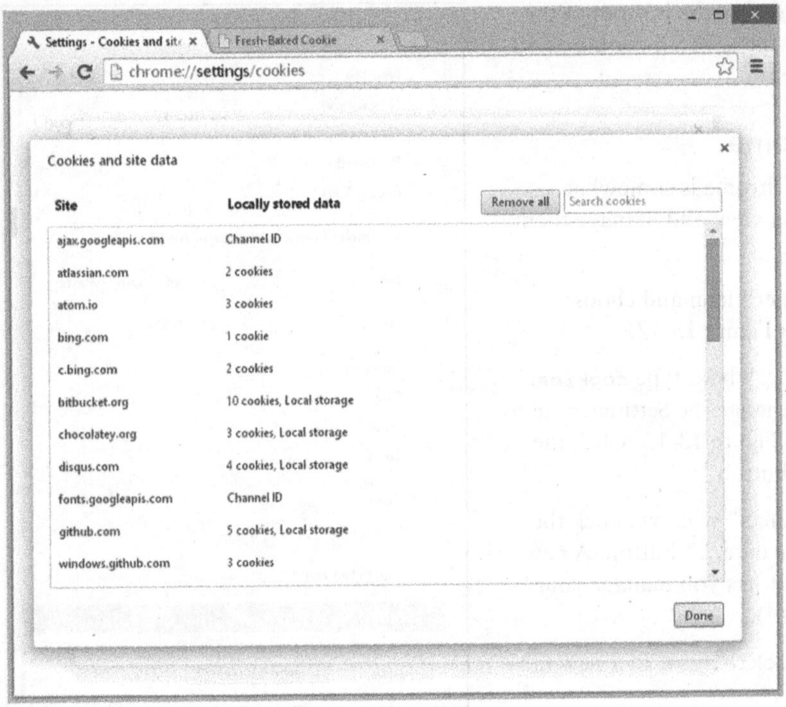

FIGURE 13-14

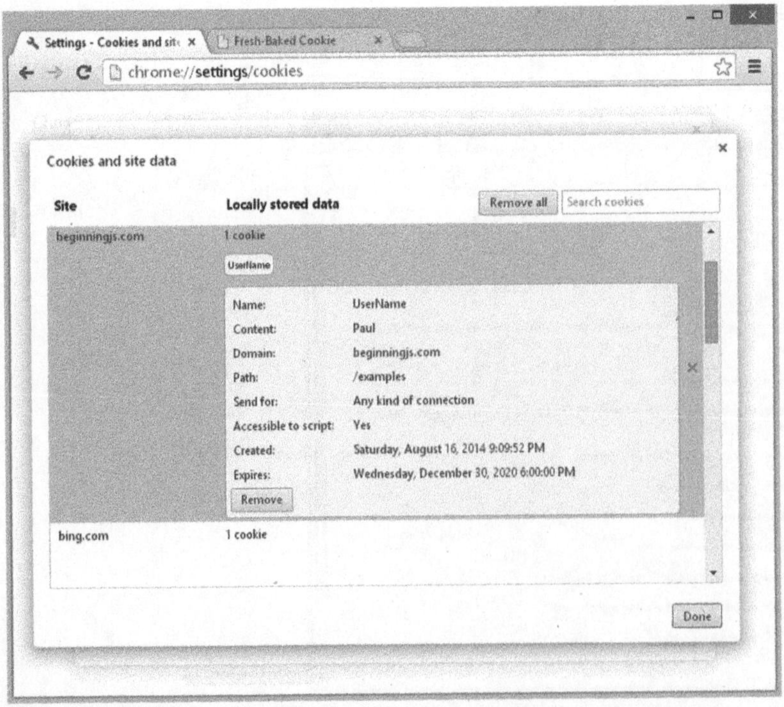

FIGURE 13-15

Now that you've seen how to view cookies manually, let's look at how you create them and read them using code. You start by looking at each of the parts that make up a cookie string.

The Cookie String

When you are creating a cookie, you can set six parts: `name`, `value`, `expires`, `path`, `domain`, and `secure`, although the latter four of these are optional. You'll now look at each of these in turn.

name and value

The first part of the cookie string consists of the name and value of the cookie. The name is used so that you can reference the cookie later, and the value is the information part of the cookie.

This name/value part of the cookie string is compulsory; it sort of defeats the point of the cookie if you don't store a name or value, because storing information is what cookies are all about. You should make sure that this part comes first in the cookie string.

The value for the cookie is a primitive string, although the string can hold number characters if it is numerical data that you want to store. If you are storing text, certain characters, such as semicolons, cannot be used inside the value, unless you use a special encoding, which you'll see later. In the case of semicolons, this is because they are used to separate the different parts of the cookie within the cookie string.

In the following line of code, you set a cookie with the name `UserName` and the value `Paul`:

```
document.cookie = "UserName=Paul;";
```

This cookie has a very limited *lifespan*, which is the length of time the information will continue to exist. If you don't set an expiration date, a cookie will expire when the user closes the browser. The next time the user opens the browser the cookie will be gone. This is fine if you just want to store information for the life of a user *session*, which is a single visit by the user to your website. However, if you want to ensure that your cookie is available for longer, you must set its expiration date, which you look at next.

expires

If you want a cookie to exist for longer than just a single user session, you need to set an expiration date using the second part of the cookie string, `expires`, as follows:

```
document.cookie = "UserName=Paul;expires=Tue, 28 Dec 2020 00:00:00 GMT; ";
```

The cookie set by the previous line of code will remain available for future use right up until December 28, 2020.

> **NOTE** *The format of the expiration date is very important. It should be the same format the cookie is given by the* `toUTCString()` *method.*

In practice, you'll probably use the Date object to get the current date, and then set a cookie to expire three or six months after this date. Otherwise, you're going to need to rewrite your pages on December 28, 2020.

For example, you could write the following:

```
var expire = new Date();
expire.setMonth(expire.getMonth() + 6);
document.cookie = "UserName=Paul;expires=" + expire.toUTCString() + ";";
```

This will create a new cookie called UserName with the value of Paul, which will expire six months from the current date. Note that other factors can cause a cookie to expire before its expiration date, such as the user deleting the cookie or the upper cookie limit being reached.

path

You'll find that 99 percent of the time you will only need to set the name, value, and expires parts of a cookie. However, at times the other three parts, such as the path part that you are looking at in this section, need to be set. The final two parts, domain and secure, are for advanced use beyond the scope of a beginners' book, but you'll look at them briefly just for completeness.

You're probably used to the idea of there being directories on your hard drive. Rather than storing everything on your computer in one place on the hard drive, you divide it into these directories. For example, you might keep your word-processing files in My Documents, your image files in My Images, and so on. You probably also subdivide your directories, so under My Images you might have subdirectories called My Family and My Holiday.

Well, web servers use the same principle. Rather than putting the whole website into one web directory, it's common and indeed sensible to divide it into various different directories. For example, if you visit the Wrox website at www.wrox.com and then click one of the book categories, you'll find that the path to the page navigated to is now www.wrox.com/Books/.

This is all very interesting, but why is it relevant to cookies?

The problem is that cookies are specific not only to a particular web domain, such as www.wrox.com, but also to a particular path on that domain. For example, if a page in www.wrox.com/Books/ sets a cookie, only pages in that directory or its subdirectories will be able to read and change the cookie. If a page in www.wrox.com/academic/ tried to read the cookie, it would fail. Why are cookies restricted like this?

Take the common example of free web space. A lot of companies on the web enable you to sign up for free web space. Usually everyone who signs up for this web space has a site at the same domain. For example, Bob's website might be at www.freespace.com/members/bob/. Belinda might have hers at www.freespace.com/members/belinda. If cookies could be retrieved and changed regardless of the path, then any cookies set on Bob's website could be viewed by Belinda and vice versa. This is clearly something neither of them would be happy about. Not only is there a security problem, but if, unknown to each other, they both have a cookie named MyHotCookie, there would be problems with each of them setting and retrieving the same cookie. When you think how many users a free web space provider often has, you can see that there is potential for chaos.

Okay, so now you know that cookies are specific to a certain path, but what if you want to view your cookies from two different paths on your server? Say, for example, you have an online store at `www.mywebsite.com/mystore/` but you subdivide the store into subdirectories, such as `/Books` and `/Games`. Now let's imagine that your checkout is in the directory `www.mywebsite.com/mystore/Checkout`. Any cookies set in the `/Books` and `/Games` directories won't be visible to each other or pages in the `/Checkout` directory. To get around this you can either set cookies only in the `/mystore` directory (because these can be read by that directory and any of its subdirectories), or you can use the `path` part of the cookie string to specify that the path of the cookie is `/mystore` even if it's being set in the `/Games` or `/Books` or `/Checkout` subdirectories.

For example, you could do this like so:

```
document.cookie = "UserName=Paul;expires=Tue, 28 Dec 2020 00:00:00" +
";path=/mystore;";
```

Now, even if the cookie is set by a page in the directory `/Books`, it will still be accessible to files in the `/mystore` directory and its subdirectories, such as `/Checkout` and `/Games`.

If you want to specify that the cookie is available to all subdirectories of the domain it is set in, you can specify a `path` of the root directory using the `/` character:

```
document.cookie = "UserName=Paul;expires=Tue, 28 Dec 2020 00:00:00;path=/;";
```

Now, the cookie will be available to all directories on the domain it is set from. If the website is just one of many at that domain, it's best not to do this because everyone else will also have access to your cookie information.

It's important to note that although Windows computers don't have case-sensitive directory names, many other operating systems do. For example, if your website is on a Unix- or Linux-based server, the `path` property will be case-sensitive.

domain

The fourth part of the cookie string is the `domain`. An example of a domain is `wrox.com` or `beginningjs.com`. Like the `path` part of the cookie string, the `domain` part is optional and it's unlikely that you'll find yourself using it very often.

By default, cookies are available only to pages in the domain in which they were set. For example, if you have your first website running on a server with the domain `mypersonalwebsite.mydomain.com` and you have a second website running under `mybusinesswebsite.mydomain.com`, a cookie set in one website will not be available to pages accessed under the other domain name, and vice versa. Most of the time, this is exactly what you want, but if it is not, you can use the `domain` part of the cookie string to specify that a cookie is available to all subdomains of the specified domain. For example, the following sets a cookie that can be shared across both subdomains:

```
document.cookie = "UserName=Paul;expires=Tue, 28 Dec 2020 00:00:00;path=/" +
";domain=mydomain.com;";
```

Note that the domain must be the same. You can't share `www.someoneelsesdomain.com` with `www.mydomain.com`.

secure

The final part of the cookie string is the `secure` part. This is simply a boolean value; if it's set to `true` the cookie will be sent only to a web server that tries to retrieve it using a secure channel. The default value, which is `false`, means the cookie will always be sent, regardless of the security. This is only applicable where you have set up a server with SSL (Secure Sockets Layer).

CREATING A COOKIE

To make life easier for yourself, you'll write a function that enables you to create a new cookie and set certain of its attributes with more ease. This is the first of a number of useful functions you'll create and add to a separate .js file so you can easily reuse the code in your future projects. You'll look at the code first and create an example using it shortly. First create a file called cookiefunctions.js and add the following to it:

```
function setCookie(name, value, path, expires) {
    value = escape(value);

    if (!expires) {
        var now = new Date();
        now.setMonth(now.getMonth() + 6);
        expires = now.toUTCString();
    }

    if (path) {
        path = ";Path=" + path;
    }

    document.cookie = name + "=" + value + ";expires=" + expires + path;
}
```

The `secure` and `domain` parts of the cookie string are unlikely to be needed, so you allow just the `name`, `value`, `expires`, and `path` parts of a cookie to be set by the function. If you don't want to set a path or expiration date, you can omit them or pass empty strings for those parameters. If no path is specified, the current directory and its subdirectories will be the path. If no expiration date is set, you just assume a date six months from now.

The first line of the function introduces the `escape()` function, which you've not seen before:

```
value = escape(value);
```

When we talked about setting the value of a cookie, we mentioned that certain characters cannot be used directly, such as a semicolon. (This also applies to the name of the cookie.) To get around this problem, you can use the built-in `escape()` and `unescape()` functions. The `escape()` function converts characters that are not text or numbers into the hexadecimal equivalent of their character in the Latin-1 character set, preceded by a `%` character.

For example, a space has the hexadecimal value 20, and the semicolon the value 3B. So the following code produces the output shown in Figure 13-16:

```
alert(escape("2001 a space odyssey;"));
```

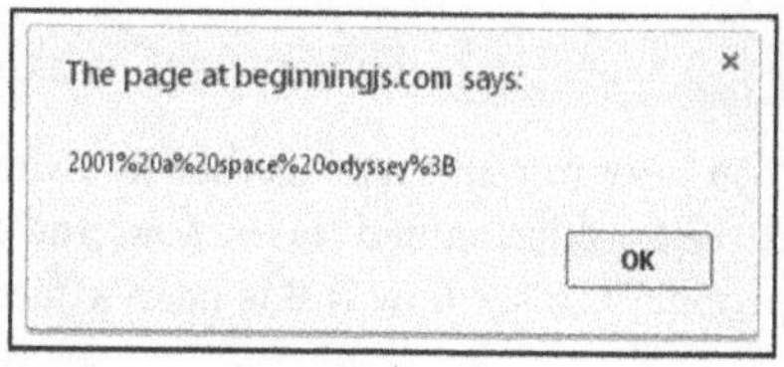

The page at beginningjs.com says:

2001%20a%20space%20odyssey%3B

OK

FIGURE 13-16

You can see that each space has been converted to %20, the % indicating that it represents an escape or special character rather than an actual character, and that 20 is the ASCII value of the actual character. The semicolon has been converted to %3B, as you'd expect.

As you see later, when retrieving cookie values you can use the unescape() function to convert from the encoded version to plaintext.

Back to your function; next you have an if statement:

```
if (!expires) {
    var now = new Date();
    now.setMonth(now.getMonth() + 6);
    expires = now.toUTCString();
}
```

This deals with the situation in which the expires parameter does not contain a usable value (either by omitting it or passing an empty string ""). Because most of the time you want a cookie to last longer than the session it's created in, you set a default value for expires that is six months after the current date.

Next, if a value has been passed to the function for the path parameter, you need to add that value when you create the cookie. You simply put "path=" in front of any value that has been passed in the path parameter:

```
if (path) {
    path = ";Path=" + path;
}
```

Finally, on the last line you actually create the cookie, putting together the name, cvalue, expires, and path parts of the string:

```
document.cookie = name + "=" + value + ";expires=" + expires + path;
```

You'll be using the setCookie() function whenever you want to create a new cookie because it makes setting a cookie easier than having to remember all the parts you want to set. More important, it can be used to set the expiration date to a date six months ahead of the current date.

For example, to use the function and set a cookie with default values for expires and path, you just type the following:

```
setCookie("cookieName","cookieValue");
```

TRY IT OUT Using setCookie()

You now put all this together in a simple example in which you use your `setCookie()` function to set three cookies named `Name`, `Age`, and `FirstVisit`. You then display what is in the `document.cookie` property to see how it has been affected.

Open your text editor and type the following:

```
<!DOCTYPE html>

<html lang="en">
<head>
    <title>Chapter 13: Example 1</title>
</head>
<body>
    <script src="cookiefunctions.js"></script>
    <script>
        setCookie("Name", "Bob");
        setCookie("Age", "101");
        setCookie("FirstVisit", "10 May 2007");

        alert(document.cookie);
    </script>
</body>
</html>
```

Save the example as `ch13_example1.html` and load it into a web browser.

You'll see the `alert` box shown in Figure 13-17. Note that all three cookies are displayed as name/value pairs separated from the others by semicolons, and also that the expiration date is not displayed. If you had set the path parameter, this also would not have been displayed. The `UserName` cookie from a previous example is also displayed.

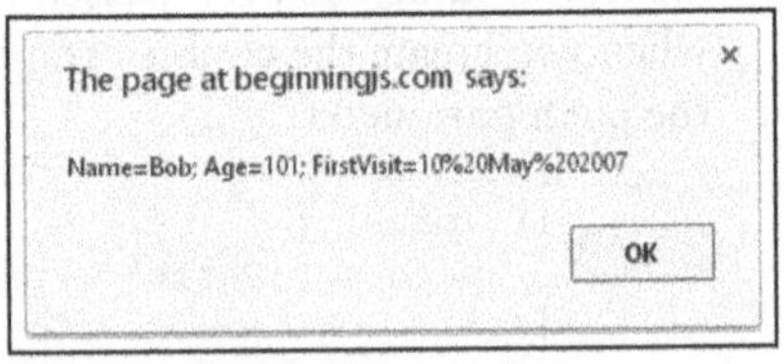

The page at beginningjs.com says:

Name=Bob; Age=101; FirstVisit=10%20May%202007

OK

FIGURE 13-17

You already know how the `setCookie()` function works, so let's look at the three lines that use the function to create three new cookies:

```
setCookie("Name", "Bob");
setCookie("Age", "101");
setCookie("FirstVisit", "10 May 2007");
```

It is all fairly simple. The first parameter is the name that you'll give the cookie. (You see shortly how you can retrieve a value of a cookie based on the name you gave it.) It's important that the names you use be only alphanumeric characters, with no spaces, punctuation, or special characters. Although you can use cookie names with these characters, doing so is more complex and best avoided. Next you have the value you want to give the cookie. The third parameter is the path, and the fourth parameter is the date on which you want the cookie to expire.

For example, take the first line where you use the `setCookie()` function. Here you are setting a cookie that will be named `Name` and have the value `Bob`. You don't want to set the `path` or `expires` parts, so you omit those parameters.

The remaining two lines in the previous code snippet set the cookies named `Age` and `FirstVisit` and set their values to `101` and `10 May 2007`, respectively.

If you did want to set the path and the expiration date, how might you change your code?

Well, imagine that you want the path to be `/MyStore` and the expiration date to be one year in the future. Then you can use the `setCookie()` function in the following way:

```
var expires = new Date();
expires.setMonth(expires.getMonth() + 12);
setCookie("Name","Bob","/MyStore", expires.toUTCString());
```

First, you create a new `Date` object, and by passing no parameter to its constructor, you let it initialize itself to the current date. In the next line, you add 12 months to that date. When setting the cookie using `setCookie()` you pass "/MyStore" as the path and `expires.toUTCString()` as the expires parameter.

What about the situation in which you've created your cookie, say, one named `Name` with a value of `Bob`, and you want to change its value? To do this, you can simply set the same cookie again, but with the new value. To change the cookie named `Name` from a value of `Bob` to a value of `Bobby`, you'd need the following code:

```
setCookie("Name","Bobby");
```

What if you want to delete an existing cookie? Well, that's easy. Just make it expire by changing its value and setting its expiration date to a date in the past, as in the following example:

```
setCookie("Name","","","Mon, 1 Jan 1990 00:00:00");
```

GETTING A COOKIE'S VALUE

In the preceding example, you used `document.cookie` to retrieve a string containing information about the cookies that have been set. However, this string has two limitations:

➤ The cookies are retrieved in name/value pairs, with each individual cookie separated by a semicolon. The expires, path, domain, and secure parts of the cookie are not available to you and cannot be retrieved.

➤ The `cookie` property enables you to retrieve only *all* the cookies set for a particular path and, when they are hosted on a web server, that web server. So, for example, there's no simple way of just getting the value of a cookie with the name `Age`. To do this you'll have to use the string manipulation techniques you learned in previous chapters to cut the information you want out of the returned string.

A lot of different ways exist to get the value of an individual cookie, but the way you'll use has the advantage of working with all cookie-enabled browsers. You use the following function, which you need to add to your `cookiefunctions.js` file:

```
function getCookieValue(name) {
    var value = document.cookie;
    var cookieStartsAt = value.indexOf(" " + name + "=");

    if (cookieStartsAt == -1) {
        cookieStartsAt = value.indexOf(name + "=");
    }

    if (cookieStartsAt == -1) {
        value = null;
    } else {
        cookieStartsAt = value.indexOf("=", cookieStartsAt) + 1;

        var cookieEndsAt = value.indexOf(";", cookieStartsAt);

        if (cookieEndsAt == -1) {
            cookieEndsAt = value.length;
        }

        value = unescape(value.substring(cookieStartsAt,
            cookieEndsAt));
    }

    return value;
}
```

The first task of the function is to get the `document.cookie` string and store it in the `value` variable:

```
var value = document.cookie;
```

Next, you need to find out where the cookie with the name passed as a parameter to the function is within the `value` string. You use the `indexOf()` method of the `String` object to find this information, as shown in the following line:

```
var cookieStartsAt = value.indexOf(" " + name + "=");
```

The method will return either the character position where the individual cookie is found or -1 if no such name, and therefore no such cookie, exists. You search on `" " + name + "="` so that you don't inadvertently find cookie names or values containing the name that you require. For example, if you have xFoo, Foo, and yFoo as cookie names, a search for Foo without a space in front would match xFoo first, which is not what you want!

If `cookieStartsAt` is -1, the cookie either does not exist or it's at the very beginning of the cookie string so there is no space in front of its name. To see which of these is true, you do another search, this time with no space:

```
if (cookieStartsAt == -1) {
    cookieStartsAt = value.indexOf(name + "=");
}
```

In the next `if` statement, you check to see whether the cookie has been found. If it hasn't, you set the value variable to `null`:

```
if (cookieStartsAt == -1) {
    value = null;
}
```

If the cookie has been found, you get the value of the cookie you want from the `document`
`.cookie` string in an `else` statement. You do this by finding the start and the end of the value part of that cookie. The start will be immediately after the equals sign following the name. So in the following line, you find the equals sign following the name of the cookie in the string by starting the `indexOf()` search for an `equals` sign from the character at which the cookie name/value pair starts:

```
else {
    cookieStartsAt = value.indexOf("=", cookieStartsAt) + 1;
```

You then add one to this value to move past the equals sign.

The end of the cookie value will either be at the next semicolon or at the end of the string, whichever comes first. You do a search for a semicolon, starting from the `cookieStartsAt` index, in the next line:

```
var cookieEndsAt = value.indexOf(";", cookieStartsAt);
```

If the cookie you are after is the last one in the string, there will be no semicolon and the `cookieEndsAt` variable will be `-1` for no match. In this case you know the end of the cookie value must be the end of the string, so you set the variable `cookieEndsAt` to the length of the string:

```
if (cookieEndsAt == -1) {
    cookieEndsAt = value.length;
}
```

You then get the cookie's value using the `substring()` method to cut the value that you want out of the main string. Because you have encoded the string with the `escape()` function, you need to unescape it to get the real value, hence the use of the `unescape()` function:

```
value = unescape(value.substring(cookieStartsAt,
    cookieEndsAt));
```

Finally, you return the value of the cookie to the calling function:

```
return value;
```

TRY IT OUT   What's New?

Now you know how to create and retrieve cookies. Let's use this knowledge in an example in which you check to see if any changes have been made to a website since the user last visited it.

You'll be creating two pages for this example. The first is the main page for a website; the second is the page with details of new additions and changes to the website. A link to the second page will appear on the first page only if the user has visited the page before (that is, if a cookie exists) but has not visited since the page was last updated.

Let's create the first page:

```
<!DOCTYPE html>

<html lang="en">
<head>
    <title>Chapter 13: Example 2a</title>
</head>
<body>
    <h1>Welcome to Example 2a</h1>

    <div id="whatsNew"></div>

    <script src="cookiefunctions.js"></script>
    <script>
        var lastUpdated = new Date("Tue, 28 Dec 2020");
        var lastVisit = getCookieValue("LastVisit");

        if (lastVisit) {
            lastVisit = new Date(lastVisit);

            if (lastVisit < lastUpdated) {
                document.getElementById("whatsNew").innerHTML =
                    "<a href='ch13_example2b.html'>What's New?</a>";
            }
        }

        var now = new Date();
        setCookie("LastVisit", now.toUTCString());
    </script>
</body>
</html>
```

Save this page as ch13_example2a.html. Note that it uses the two functions, setCookie() and getCookieValue(), that you created earlier.

Next, you just create a simple page to link to for the What's New? details:

```
<!DOCTYPE html>

<html lang="en">
<head>
    <title>Chapter 13: Example 2b</title>
</head>
<body>
    <h1>Welcome to Example 2b</h1>

    <h3>Here's what's new!</h3>
</body>
</html>
```

Save this page as ch13_example2b.html.

Load `ch13_example2a.html` into a browser. The first time you go to the main page, there will be nothing but a heading saying "Welcome to Example 2a." Obviously, if this were a real website, it would have a bit more than that, but it suffices for this example. However, refresh the page and suddenly you'll see the page shown in Figure 13-18.

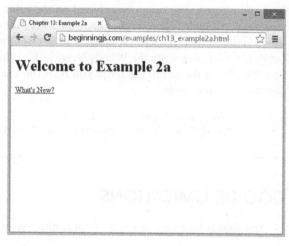

If you click the link, you're taken to the `ch13_example2b.html` page detailing all the things added to the website since you last visited. Obviously, nothing has actually changed in your example website between you loading the page and then refreshing it. You got around this for testing purposes by setting the date when the website last changed, stored in variable `lastUpdated`, to a date in the future (here, December 28, 2020).

FIGURE 13-18

The `ch13_example2b.html` page is just a simple HTML page with no script, so you will confine your attention to `ch13_example2a.html`. In the script block, you declare the variable `lastUpdated`:

```
var lastUpdated = new Date("Tue, 28 Dec 2020");
```

Whenever you make a change to the website, this variable needs to be changed. It's currently set to `Tue, 28 Dec 2020`, just to make sure you see the What's New? link when you refresh the page. A better alternative for live pages would be the `document.lastModified` property, which returns the date on which the page was last changed.

Next, you get the date of the user's last visit from the `LastVisit` cookie using the `getCookieValue()` function:

```
var lastVisit = getCookieValue("LastVisit");
```

If it's falsy, the user has either never been here before, or it has been six or more months since the last visit and the cookie has expired. Either way, you won't put the What's New? link up because everything is new if the user is a first-time visitor, and a lot has probably changed in the last six months—more than what your What's New? page will detail.

If `lastVisit` has a value, you need to check whether the user visited the site before it was last updated, and if so to direct the user to a page that shows what is new. You do this within the `if` statement:

```
if (lastVisit) {
    lastVisit = new Date(lastVisit);

    if (lastVisit < lastUpdated) {
        document.getElementById("whatsNew").innerHTML =
            "<a href='ch13_example2b.html'>What's New?</a>";
    }
}
```

You first create a new `Date` object based on the value of `lastVisit` and store that back into the `lastVisit` variable. Then, in the condition of the inner `if` statement, you compare the date of the user's last visit with the date on which you last updated the website. If things have changed since the user's last visit, you write the What's New? link to the page, so the user can click it and find out what's new. Finally, at the end of the script you reset the `LastVisit` cookie to today's date and time using the `setCookie()` function:

```
var now = new Date();
setCookie("LastVisit", nowDate.toUTCString());
```

COOKIE LIMITATIONS

You should be aware of a number of limitations when using cookies.

A User May Disable Cookies

The first limitation is that although all modern browsers support cookies, the user may have disabled them. In Firefox you can do this by selecting the Options menu, followed by the Privacy tab and the Cookies tab. In IE you select Internet Options on the gear menu. Select the Privacy tab and you can change the level with the scroll control. And in Chrome, choose the Settings option from the gear menu, search for cookies, and click "Content settings." Most users have session cookies enabled by default. Session cookies are cookies that last for as long as the user is browsing your website. After he's closed the browser the cookie will be cleared. More permanent cookies are also normally enabled by default. However, third-party cookies, those from a third-party site, are usually disabled. These are the cookies used for tracking people from site to site and hence the ones that raise the most privacy concerns.

Both the functions that you've made for creating and getting cookies will cause no errors when cookies are disabled, but of course the value of any cookie set will be `null` and you need to make sure your code can cope with this.

You could set a default action for when cookies are disabled. In the previous example, if cookies are disabled, the What's New? link will never appear.

Alternatively, you can let the user know that your website needs cookies to function by putting a message to that effect in the web page.

Another tactic is to actively check to see whether cookies are enabled and, if not, to take some action to cope with this, such as by directing the user to a page with less functionality that does not need cookies. How do you check to see if cookies are enabled?

In the following script, you set a test cookie and then read back its value. If the value is `null`, you know cookies are disabled:

```
setCookie("TestCookie","Yes");
if (!getCookieValue("TestCookie")) {
    alert("This website requires cookies to function");
}
```

Number and Information Limitation

A second limitation is on the number of cookies you can set on the user's computer for your website and how much information can be stored in each. In older browsers, for each domain, it was common that you could store only up to 20 cookies, and each *cookie pair*—that is, the name and value of the cookie combined—must not be more than 4,096 characters (4KB) in size. It's also important to be aware that all browsers do set some upper limit for the number of cookies stored. When that limit is reached, older cookies, regardless of expiration date, are often deleted. Some modern browsers have a 50-cookie limit, though this may vary.

To get around the cookie limits, you can store more than one piece of information per cookie. This example uses multiple cookies:

```
setCookie("Name", "Karen")
setCookie("Age", "44");
setCookie("LastVisit", "10 Jan 2001");
```

You could combine this information into one cookie, with each detail separated by a semicolon:

```
setCookie("UserDetails", "Karen;44;10 Jan 2001");
```

Because the setCookie() function escapes the value of the cookie, there is no confusion between the semicolons separating pieces of data in the value of the cookie, and the semicolons separating the parts of the cookie. When you get the cookie value back using getCookieValue(), you just split it into its constituent parts; however, you must remember the order you stored it in:

```
var cookieValues = getCookieValue("UserDetails");
cookieValues = cookieValues.split(";");
alert("Name = " + cookieValues[0]);
alert("Age = " + cookieValues[1]);
alert("Last Visit = " + cookieValues[2]);
```

Now you have acquired three pieces of information and still have 19 cookies left in the jar. This approach, however, is less than ideal, and you learn how to store data using newer technologies later in this chapter.

COOKIE SECURITY AND IE

IE6 introduced a new security policy for cookies based on the P3P an initiative set up by the World Wide Web Consortium (W3C). The general aim of P3P is to reassure users who are worried that cookies are being used to obtain personal information about their browsing habits. In IE you can select the Gear menu ⇨ Internet Options and click the Privacy tab to see where you can set the level of privacy with regards to cookies (see Figure 13-19). You have to strike a balance between setting it so high that no website will work and so low that your browsing habits and potentially personal data may be recorded.

Generally, by default session cookies—cookies that last for only as long as the user is browsing your website—are allowed. As soon as the user closes the browser, the session ends. However, if you want cookies to outlast the user's visit to your website, you need to create a privacy policy in line with the P3P recommendations. This sounds a little complex, and certainly the fine details of the policy can be. Because of this complexity, very few implementations of P3P exist. But many groups are working to make it easier for people to use.

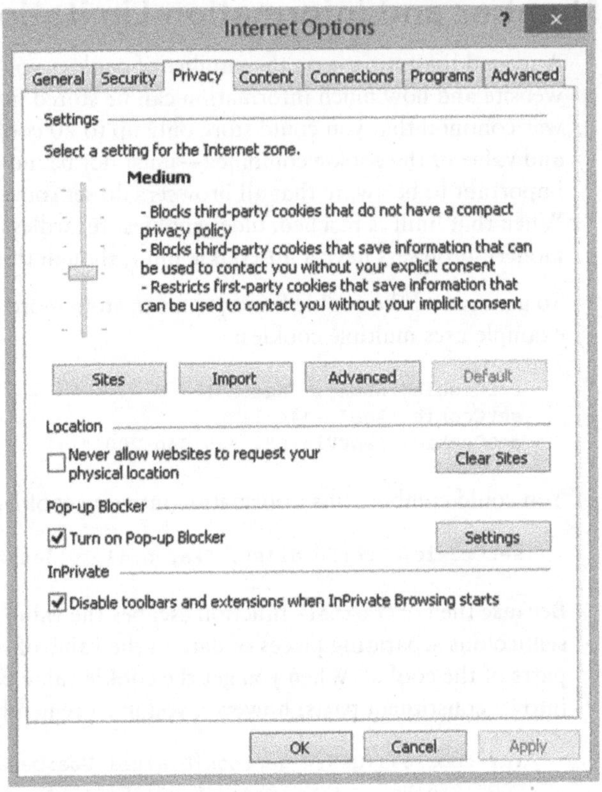

WEB STORAGE

Cookies are a useful tool that web developers can take advantage of to store data on the user's computer. But cookies are a tool designed for a different time, and thus, a different Web. Although they served a specific purpose (and did so reasonably well), their limitations are not ideal for modern JavaScript development:

FIGURE 13-19

➤ The first issue is the application programming interface (API). To write and read cookies, you use the document.cookie property. Writing a cookie is relatively straightforward, but reading a specific cookie requires a lot of code. You wrote two helper functions to make writing and reading cookies easier, but ideally, you shouldn't have to.

➤ Cookies are not a browser feature, but a feature of HTTP. As such, the browser sends them to the server on every request. This is useful for applications that live on the server, but it's unnecessary for JavaScript that runs in the browser.

➤ The browser limits the amount of cookies it stores and the size they can be. As mentioned earlier, this can be anywhere from 20 to 50 cookies for each domain, and each cookie cannot exceed 4KB.

➤ Cookies are shared between both the browser and the server. If your server application needs 30 cookies (120KB) to function, that at best leaves you with 20 cookies (80KB). You're out of luck if you need more.

➤ They can expire. Although you can control this by setting and maintaining an expiration date, it's simpler to not have one.

HTML5 introduced a new feature called *web storage*, and it solves each of cookies' aforementioned problems. Since its introduction, web storage has been moved out of the HTML5 specification and into its own (which is named Web Storage). It consists of two components: *session storage* and *local storage*. As you may have guessed, session storage is temporary storage that is cleared when the user closes the browser (like a cookie without an expiration date). But in most cases, you want to store data that persists between visits, and that is local storage's purpose. Other noteworthy features of web storage are:

➤ It stays within the browser and is not transmitted to the server. It is storage for JavaScript developers.

➤ It provides significantly more storage space. Chrome and Firefox support 5MB per domain. IE supports 10MB.

➤ The data stored in local storage never expires; it remains until you or the user deletes it.

> **NOTE** *This section focuses on local storage, but you can apply the same concepts to session storage.*

The data stored in web storage is associated with a unique name. In technical terms, we refer to this name as a *key*, and the data associated with a key is referred to as the *value*. Together, we refer to the key and its value as a key/value pair.

You access local storage using the `localStorage` object (session storage is accessed through `sessionStorage`), and it makes it easy to set, get, and remove data.

Setting Data

The `localStorage` object exposes a method called `setItem()`, and its purpose is to set a value associated with a given key. It's very simple to use, as shown here:

```
localStorage.setItem("userName", "Paul");
```

The first argument passed to `setItem()` is the key; the second is the value associated with that key. In the case of this code, the value of `Paul` is stored in local storage and is associated with the key of `userName`.

You can also set data using the more traditional `object.propertyName` syntax, like so:

```
localStorage.userName = "Paul";
```

The result of this code is identical to the previous `setItem()` example; the value of `Paul` is set for the key of `userName`.

If the results are identical, why use `setItem()`? The answer is that you don't have to unless your key is an invalid JavaScript identifier. For example, let's say you want to use the key `user name`. That's impossible to use as a property name:

```
localStorage.user name = "Paul"; // invalid!
```

But you can use `"user name"` as a key with the `setItem()` method:

```
localStorage.setItem("user name", "Paul");
```

In most cases, you won't use `setItem()`, but it is there to use if and when you need to.

Getting Data

Retrieving data from local storage is just as straightforward as setting it. With the getItem() method, you supply the key for which you want the value of:

```
var name = localStorage.getItem("userName");
```

This code uses the getItem() method to retrieve the value associated with the "userName" key and assigns that value to the name variable. In the case of the example from the previous section, name would contain "Paul".

You can also use the key as localStorage's property if it is a valid identifier:

```
var name = localStorage.userName;
```

This code also gets the value of Paul and assigns it to the name variable.

A word of note: Keys are case-sensitive. That may seem obvious if you are using object .propertyName syntax, but the rule applies to setItem() and getItem(). For example:

```
localStorage.setItem("userName", "Paul");

var name = localStorage.getItem("UserName"); // null
```

This code set a key of userName with a value of Paul. It then tries to retrieve a value with the key of UserName. Because of the uppercase U, UserName and userName are two different keys. We haven't set a value with UserName, so getItem() returns null.

Removing Data

Eventually, you will want to remove some data that you stored in local storage, and you can do that with the removeItem() method. Simply provide the key you want to remove, and the key/value pair will be deleted from local storage. For example:

```
localStorage.removeItem("userName");
```

This code deletes the userName/Paul key/value pair from local storage. If the key is a valid JavaScript identifier, you can also use object.propertyName syntax to do the same thing, like so:

```
localStorage.userName = null;
```

Here, you assign the value of null to the userName key/property, thus removing the key/value pair from local storage.

If your goal is to remove all keys and values from local storage, you can use the clear() method, like this:

```
localStorage.clear(); // no more key/value pairs
```

Storing Data as Strings

It's important to note that web storage is a string-only data store. This means that keys and their values can only be strings. If you try to store some other type of value (like a number) or object, it is converted to a string and stored as a string. For example, let's say you want to store the user's age in local storage. You can easily do so like this:

```
localStorage.age = 35;
```

As you rightly suspect, this creates a key/value pair of age/35. But 35 was converted to a string before it was stored in local storage. Therefore, when you retrieve the value associated with the age key, you have the string of 35:

```
var age = localStorage.age;

alert(typeof age); // string
```

This means that to use age in any mathematic calculations, you need to convert it to a number. That's easy enough to fix:

```
var age = parseInt(localStorage.age, 10);
```

But what about more complex objects? Consider the following object as an example:

```
var johnDoe = {
    firstName: "John",
    lastName: "Doe",
    age: 35
};
```

This johnDoe object represents an individual person named John Doe, and he is 35 years old. We want to save this object in local storage, so we assign it as the value to the person key, like this:

```
localStorage.person = johnDoe;
```

But there's a problem here: The person object cannot be reasonably converted into a string.

When you assign a value or object to a key, its toString() method is automatically called to convert it to a string. For primitive types like Number and Boolean, we get the string representation of that value. But by default, an object's toString() method returns "[object Object]". Therefore in the preceding example, the string "[object Object]" is stored in localStorage.person:

```
var savedPerson = localStorage.person;
alert(typeof savedPerson); // string
alert(savedPerson); "[object Object]"
```

This sounds like a huge limitation (and it is!), but we can serialize objects into JSON and parse them back into actual objects. Therefore, we can write this:

```
localStorage.person = JSON.stringify(johnDoe);

var savedPerson = JSON.parse(localStorage.person);
```

This code serializes the johnDoe object and stores the resulting JSON with the person key. Then, when you need to retrieve and use that information, you deserialize the JSON using JSON.parse() and assign the resulting object to the savedPerson variable. Now we can store just about anything we need to in local storage, and we have a ton of space to store it in!

TRY IT OUT   What's New? Now with Local Storage

Let's rewrite Example 2 using local storage. Feel free to copy and paste the contents of
ch13_example2a.html and ch13_example2b.html as the basis for the new files.

Let's create the first page:

```
<!DOCTYPE html>

<html lang="en">
<head>
    <title>Chapter 13: Example 3a</title>
</head>
<body>
    <h1>Welcome to Example 3a</h1>

    <div id="whatsNew"></div>

    <script>
        var lastUpdated = new Date("Tue, 28 Dec 2020");
        var lastVisit = localStorage.lastVisit;

        if (lastVisit) {
            lastVisit = new Date(lastVisit);

            if (lastVisit < lastUpdated) {
                document.getElementById("whatsNew").innerHTML =
                    "<a href='ch13_example3b.html'>What's New?</a>";
            }
        }

        localStorage.lastVisit = new Date();
    </script>
</body>
</html>
```

Save this page as ch13_example3a.html. Next, create a simple page to link to for the What's New?
details:

```
<!DOCTYPE html>

<html lang="en">
<head>
    <title>Chapter 13: Example 3b</title>
</head>
<body>
    <h1>Welcome to Example 3b</h1>

    <h3>Here's what's new!</h3>
</body>
</html>
```

Save this page as ch13_example3b.html.

Load `ch13_example3a.html` into a browser. This page behaves exactly like Example 2a. The first time you go to the main page, there will be nothing but a heading saying "Welcome to Example 3a." Refreshing the page displays the "What's New?" link in the page. Clicking this link takes you to `ch13_example3b.html`.

As before, we'll focus on the JavaScript contained within `ch13_example3b.html`.

First, you declare the `lastUpdated` variable:

```
var lastUpdated = new Date("Tue, 28 Dec 2020");
```

Next, you get the date of the user's last visit from local storage with the `lastVisit` key:

```
var lastVisit = localStorage.lastVisit;
```

This assigns one of two values to the `lastVisit` variable. If this is the user's first visit to the page, the `localStorage.lastVisit` key won't exist and returns `null` to `lastVisit`. In which case, you won't display the What's New? link in the document.

The second possible value of `lastVisit` is a string representation of the date the user last visited the page. In this situation, you need to check whether the user visited the site before it was last updated and direct the user to the What's New? page if so:

```
if (lastVisit) {
    lastVisit = new Date(lastVisit);

    if (lastVisit < lastUpdated) {
        document.getElementById("whatsNew").innerHTML =
            "<a href='ch13_example3b.html'>What's New?</a>";
    }
}
```

Remember that the data stored in local storage is strings; so, you create a new `Date` object based on the value of `lastVisit` and store it in the `lastVisit` variable. Then, if `lastVisit` is less than `lastUpdated`, you display the What's New? link in the document.

In the final line of code, you reset the value of the `localState.lastVisit` key:

```
localStorage.lastVisit = new Date();
```

Viewing Web Storage Content

Like cookies, you can also view the data stored in web storage, but doing so requires you to use the features found in each browser's development tools. You learn about the development tools found in Internet Explorer, Chrome, and Firefox in Chapter 18, but viewing the web storage content in Chrome is straightforward. Simply press F12 to bring up the development tools and click the Resources tab. Figure 13-20 shows you the local storage for the `beginningjs.com` domain.

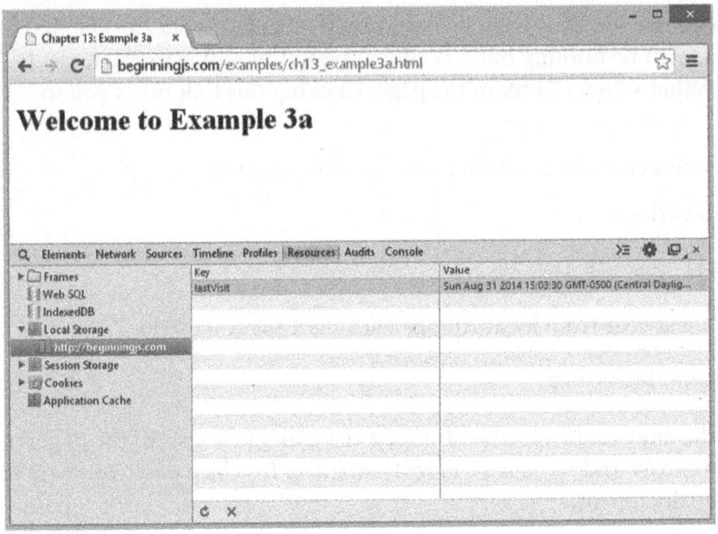

FIGURE 13-20

You can only view the web storage of the domain of the page currently loaded in a given tab; you cannot view one domain's web storage from another domain.

SUMMARY

In this chapter, you looked at how you can store information on the user's computer and use this information to personalize the website. In particular, you found the following:

➤ The key to cookies is the `document` object's `cookie` property.

➤ Creating a cookie simply involves setting the `document.cookie` property. Cookies have six different parts you can set. These are the name, the value, when it expires, the path it is available on, the domain it's available on, and finally whether it should be sent only over secure connections.

➤ Although setting a new cookie is fairly easy, you found that retrieving its value actually gets all the cookies for that domain and path, and that you need to split up the cookie name/value pairs to get a specific cookie using `String` object methods.

➤ Cookies have a number of limitations. First, the user can set the browser to disable cookies; and second, you are limited to 50 cookies per domain in IE7+ and Firefox and a maximum of 4,096 characters per cookie name/value pair.

➤ Web storage is a new key/value pair data store that replaces the need for cookies for JavaScript developers. Though it was originally introduced with HTML5, it is now its own specification.

➤ Setting, getting, and removing data from web storage is simple. You can either use `localStorage`'s `getItem()`, `setItem()`, and `removeItem()` methods, or you can assign and use properties on `localStorage` itself.

➤ The data stored in web storage is converted to strings. So, you have to convert the data back into its appropriate data type in order to effectively use it. This is easily done thanks to various functions like `parseInt()`, `Date`'s constructor, and `JSON.parse()`.

EXERCISES

You can find suggested solutions to these questions in Appendix A.

1. Using local storage, create a page that keeps track of how many times the page has been visited by the user in the last month.

2. Use local storage to load a different advertisement every time a user visits a web page.

14

Ajax

WHAT YOU WILL LEARN IN THIS CHAPTER:

➤ Making HTTP requests with the `XMLHttpRequest` object

➤ Writing a custom Ajax module

➤ Working with older Ajax techniques to preserve usability

WROX.COM CODE DOWNLOADS FOR THIS CHAPTER

You can find the wrox.com code downloads for this chapter at `http://www.wiley.com/go/BeginningJavaScript5E` on the Download Code tab. You can also view all of the examples and related files at `http://beginningjs.com`.

Since its inception, the Internet has used a transaction-like communication model; a browser sends a request to a server, which sends a response back to the browser, which (re)loads the page. This is typical HTTP communication, and it was designed to be this way. But this model is rather cumbersome for developers, because it requires web applications to consist of several pages. The resulting user experience becomes disjointed and interrupted due to these separate page loads.

In the early 2000s, a movement began to look for and develop new techniques to enhance the user's experience; to make web applications behave more like conventional applications. These new techniques offered the performance and usability usually associated with conventional desktop applications. It wasn't long before developers began to refine these processes to offer richer functionality to the user.

At the heart of this movement was one language: JavaScript, and its ability to make HTTP requests transparent to the user.

WHAT IS AJAX?

Essentially, *Ajax* allows client-side JavaScript to request and receive data from a server without refreshing the web page. This technique enables the developer to create an application that is uninterrupted, making only portions of the page reload with new data.

The term Ajax was originally coined by Jesse James Garrett in 2005. He wrote an article entitled "Ajax: A New Approach to Web Applications" (`www.adaptivepath.com/publications/essays/archives/000385.php`). In it, Garrett states that the interactivity gap between web and desktop applications is becoming smaller, and he cites applications such as Google Maps and Google Suggest as proof of this. The term originally stood for Asynchronous JavaScript + XML (XML was the format in which the browser and server communicated with each other). Today, Ajax simply refers to the pattern of using JavaScript to send and receive data from the web server without reloading the entire page.

Although the term Ajax was derived in 2005, the underlying methodology was used years before. Early Ajax techniques consisted of using hidden frames/iframes, dynamically adding `<script/>` elements to the document, and/or using JavaScript to send HTTP requests to the server; the latter has become quite popular in the past few years. These new techniques refresh only portions of a page, both cutting the size of data sent to the browser and making the web page feel more like a conventional application.

What Can It Do?

Ajax opened the doors for advanced web applications—ones that mimic desktop applications in form and in function. A variety of commercial websites employ the use of Ajax. These sites look and behave more like desktop applications than websites. The most notable Ajax-enabled web applications come from the search giant Google: Google Maps and Google Suggest.

Google Maps

Designed to compete with existing commercial mapping sites (and using images from its Google Earth), Google Maps (`http://maps.google.com`) uses Ajax to dynamically add map images to the web page. When you enter a location, the main page does not reload at all; the images are dynamically loaded in the map area. Google Maps also enables you to drag the map to a new location, and once again, the map images are dynamically added to the map area (see Figure 14-1).

Google Suggest

The now commonplace Google Suggest is another Google innovation that employs the use of Ajax. Upon first glance, it appears to be a normal Google search page. When you start typing, however, a drop-down box displays suggestions for search terms that might interest you. Under the suggested word or phrase is the number of results the search term returns (see Figure 14-2).

Browser Support

In the early years of Ajax, browser support was mixed. Every browser supported the basics in some way, but support differed from browser to browser. Today, Ajax is a just another normal part of JavaScript development, and today's modern browsers unquestionably support Ajax.

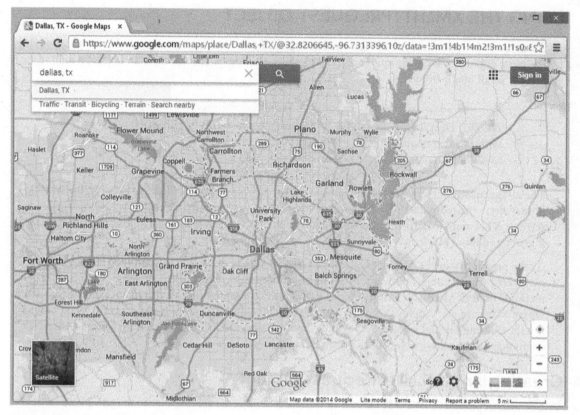

FIGURE 14-1

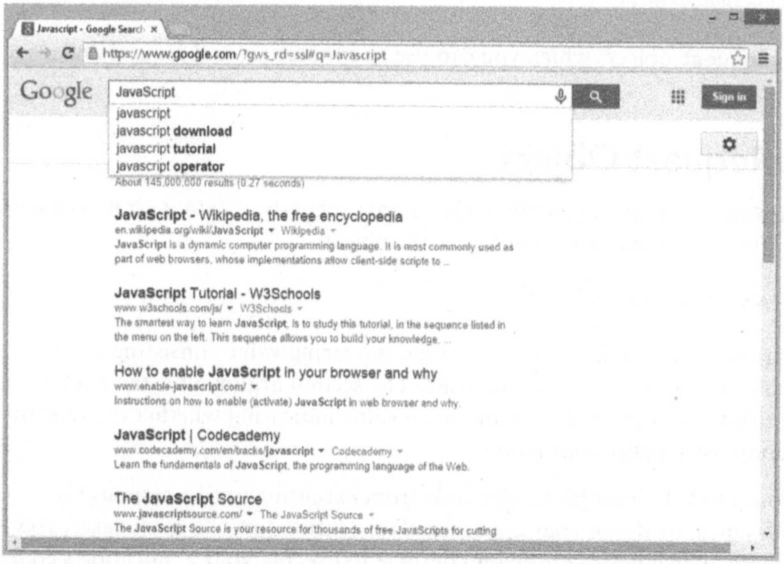

FIGURE 14-2

USING THE XMLHTTPREQUEST OBJECT

As stated before, you can create Ajax-enabled applications in a variety of ways. However, probably the most popular Ajax technique incorporates the JavaScript `XMLHttpRequest` object, which is present in all major browsers.

> **NOTE** *Despite its name, you can retrieve other types of data, like plaintext, with `XMLHttpRequest`.*

The `XMLHttpRequest` object originated as a Microsoft component, called `XmlHttp`, in the MSXML library first released with IE 5. It offered developers an easy way to open HTTP connections and retrieve XML data. Microsoft improved the component with each new version of MSXML, making it faster and more efficient.

As the popularity of the Microsoft `XMLHttpRequest` object grew, Mozilla decided to include its own version of the object with Firefox. The Mozilla version maintained the same properties and methods used in Microsoft's ActiveX component, making cross-browser usage possible. Soon after, Opera Software and Apple copied the Mozilla implementation, and Google naturally implemented it with Chrome's initial release. As for Internet Explorer, `XMLHttpRequest` is no longer an ActiveX component but a native object in the browser.

Creating an XMLHttpRequest Object

The `XMLHttpRequest` object is located in the `window` object. Creating an `XMLHttpRequest` object is as simple as calling its constructor:

```
var request = new XMLHttpRequest();
```

This line creates an `XMLHttpRequest` object, which you can use to connect to, and request and receive data from, a server.

Using the XMLHttpRequest Object

Once you create the `XMLHttpRequest` object, you are ready to start requesting data with it. The first step in this process is to call the `open()` method to initialize the object:

```
request.open(requestType, url, async);
```

This method accepts three arguments. The first, `requestType`, is a string value consisting of the type of request to make. The value can be either GET or POST. The second argument is the URL to send the request to, and the third is an optional `true` or `false` value indicating whether the request should be made in asynchronous or synchronous mode.

Requests made in synchronous mode halt all JavaScript code from executing until a response is received from the server. This can slow down your application's execution time. In most cases, you want to use asynchronous mode, which lets the browser continue to execute your application's code while the `XMLHttpRequest` object awaits a response from the server. Asynchronous mode is the default behavior of `XMLHttpRequest`, so you can usually omit the third argument to `open()`.

> **NOTE** In the past, it was considered best practice to pass true as the third argument.

The next step is to send the request; do this with the `send()` method. This method accepts one argument, which is a string that contains the request body to send along with the request. `GET` requests do not contain any information, so pass `null` as the argument:

```
var request = new XMLHttpRequest();
request.open("GET", "http://localhost/myTextFile.txt", false);
request.send(null);
```

This code makes a `GET` request to retrieve a file called `myTextFile.txt` in synchronous mode. Calling the `send()` method sends the request to the server.

> **WARNING** The send() method requires an argument to be passed, even if it is null.

Each `XMLHttpRequest` object has a `status` property. This property contains the HTTP status code sent with the server's response. The server returns a status of `200` for a successful request, and one of `404` if it cannot find the requested file. With this in mind, consider the following example:

```
var request = new XMLHttpRequest();
request.open("GET", "http://localhost/myTextFile.txt", false);
request.send(null);

var status = request.status;

if (status == 200) {
    alert("The text file was found!");
} else if (status == 404) {
    alert("The text file could not be found!");
} else {
    alert("The server returned a status code of " + status);
}
```

This code checks the status property to determine what message to display to the user. If successful (a status of 200), an `alert` box tells the user the request file exists. If the file doesn't exist (status 404), the user sees a message stating that the server cannot find the file. Finally, an `alert` box tells the user the status code if it equals something other than 200 or 404.

Many different HTTP status codes exist, and checking for every code is not feasible. Most of the time, you should only be concerned with whether your request is successful. Therefore, you can cut the previous code down to this:

```
var request = new XMLHttpRequest();
request.open("GET", "http://localhost/myTextFile.txt", false);
```

```
request.send(null);

var status = request.status;

if (status == 200) {
    alert("The text file was found!");
} else {
    alert("The server returned a status code of " + status);
}
```

This code performs the same basic function, but it only checks for a status code of 200 and sends a generic message to alert the user for other status codes.

Asynchronous Requests

The previous code samples demonstrate the simplicity of synchronous requests. Asynchronous requests, on the other hand, add some complexity to your code because you have to handle the readystatechange event. In asynchronous requests, the XMLHttpRequest object exposes a readyState property, which holds a numeric value; each value refers to a specific state in a request's life span, as follows:

➤ 0: The object has been created, but the open() method hasn't been called.

➤ 1: The open() method has been called, but the request hasn't been sent.

➤ 2: The request has been sent; headers and status are received and available.

➤ 3: A response has been received from the server.

➤ 4: The requested data has been fully received.

The readystatechange event fires every time the readyState property changes, calling the onreadystatechange event handler. The fourth and final state is the most important; it lets you know that the request completed.

> **NOTE** It is important to note that even if the request was successful, you may not have the information you wanted. An error may have occurred on the server's end of the request (a 404, 500, or some other error). Therefore, you still need to check the status code of the request.

Code to handle the readystatechange event could look like this:

```
var request = new XMLHttpRequest();

function reqReadyStateChange() {
    if (request.readyState == 4) {
        var status = request.status;

        if (status == 200) {
            alert(request.responseText);
```

```
        } else {
            alert("The server returned a status code of " + status);
        }
    }
}

request.open("GET", "http://localhost/myTextFile.txt");
request.onreadystatechange = reqReadyStateChange;

request.send(null);
```

This code first defines the `reqReadyStateChange()` function, which handles the `readystatechange` event. It first checks if the request completed by comparing `readyState` to 4. The function then checks the request's status to ensure the server returned the requested data. Once these two criteria are met, the code alerts the value of the `responseText` property (the actual requested data in plaintext format). Note the `open()` method's call; the third argument is omitted. This makes the `XMLHttpRequest` object request data asynchronously.

The benefits of using asynchronous communication are well worth the added complexity of the `readystatechange` event, because the browser can continue to load the page and execute your other JavaScript code while the request object sends and receives data. Perhaps a user-defined module that wraps an `XMLHttpRequest` object could make asynchronous requests easier to use and manage.

> **NOTE** An `XMLHttpRequest` object also has a property called `responseXML`, which attempts to load the received data into an HTML DOM (whereas `responseText` returns plaintext).

CREATING A SIMPLE AJAX MODULE

The concept of code reuse is important in programming; it is the reason why functions are defined to perform specific, common, and repetitive tasks. Chapter 5 introduced you to the object-oriented construct of code reuse: reference types. These constructs contain properties that contain data and/ or methods that perform actions with that data.

In this section, you write your own Ajax module called `HttpRequest`, thereby making asynchronous requests easier to make and manage. Before getting into writing this module, let's go over the properties and methods the `HttpRequest` reference type exposes.

Planning the HttpRequest Module

There's only one piece of information that you need to keep track of: the underlying `XMLHttpRequest` object. Therefore, this module will have only one property, `request`, which contains the underlying `XMLHttpRequest` object.

The `HttpRequest` exposes a single method called `send()`. Its purpose is to send the request to the server.

Now let's begin to write the module.

The HttpRequest Constructor

A reference type's constructor defines its properties and performs any logic needed to function properly:

```
function HttpRequest(url, callback) {
    this.request = new XMLHttpRequest();

    //more code here
}
```

The constructor accepts two arguments. The first, url, is the URL the XMLHttpRequest object will request. The second, callback, is a callback function; it will be called when the server's response is received (when the request's readyState is 4 and its status is 200). The first line of the constructor initializes the request property, assigning an XMLHttpRequest object to it.

With the request property created and ready to use, you prepare to send the request:

```
function HttpRequest(url, callback) {
    this.request = new XMLHttpRequest();
    this.request.open("GET", url);

    function reqReadyStateChange() {
        //more code here
    }

    this.request.onreadystatechange = reqReadyStateChange;
}
```

The first line of the new code uses the XMLHttpRequest object's open() method to initialize the request object. Set the request type to GET, and use the url parameter to specify the URL you want to request. Because you omit open()'s third argument, you set the request object to use asynchronous mode.

The next few lines define the reqReadyStateChange() function. Defining a function within a function may seem weird, but it is perfectly legal to do so. This inner function cannot be accessed outside the containing function (the constructor in this case), but it has access to the variables and parameters of the containing constructor function. As its name implies, the reqReadyStateChange() function handles the request object's readystatechange event, and you bind it to do so by assigning it to the onreadystatechange event handler:

```
function HttpRequest(url, callback) {
    this.request = new XMLHttpRequest();
    this.request.open("GET", url);

    var tempRequest = this.request;

    function reqReadyStateChange() {
        if (tempRequest.readyState == 4) {
            if (tempRequest.status == 200) {
                callback(tempRequest.responseText);
            } else {
                alert("An error occurred trying to contact the server.");
            }
        }
```

```
        }
    }

    this.request.onreadystatechange = reqReadyStateChange;
}
```

The new lines of code may once again look a little strange, but it's actually a pattern you'll often see when looking at other people's code. The first new line creates the `tempRequest` variable. This variable is a pointer to the current object's `request` property, and it's used within the `reqReadyStateChange()` function. This is a technique to get around scoping issues. Ideally, you would use `this.request` inside the `reqReadyStateChange()` function. However, the `this` keyword points to the `reqReadyStateChange()` function instead of to the `XMLHttpRequest` object, which would cause the code to not function properly. So when you see `tempRequest`, think `this.request`.

Inside the `reqReadyStateChange()` function, you see the following line:

```
callback(tempRequest.responseText);
```

This line calls the callback function specified by the constructor's `callback` parameter, and you pass the `responseText` property to this function. This allows the callback function to use the information received from the server.

Creating the send() Method

There is one method in this reference type, and it enables you to send the request to the server. Sending a request to the server involves the `XMLHttpRequest` object's `send()` method. This `send()` is similar, with the difference being that it doesn't accept arguments:

```
HttpRequest.prototype.send = function () {
    this.request.send(null);
};
```

This version of `send()` is simple in that all you do is call the `XMLHttpRequest` object's `send()` method and pass it `null`.

The Full Code

Now that the code's been covered, open your text editor and type the following:

```
function HttpRequest(url, callback) {
    this.request = new XMLHttpRequest();
    this.request.open("GET", url);

    var tempRequest = this.request;

    function reqReadyStateChange() {
        if (tempRequest.readyState == 4) {
            if (tempRequest.status == 200) {
                callback(tempRequest.responseText);
            } else {
                alert("An error occurred trying to contact the server.");
            }
```

```
        }
    }

    this.request.onreadystatechange = reqReadyStateChange;
}

HttpRequest.prototype.send = function () {
    this.request.send(null);
};
```

Save this file as `httprequest.js`. You'll use it later in the chapter.

The goal of this module was to make asynchronous requests easier to use, so let's look at a brief code-only example and see if that goal was accomplished.

The first thing you need is a function to handle the data received from the request; this function gets passed to the `HttpRequest` constructor:

```
function handleData(text) {
    alert(text);
}
```

This code defines a function called `handleData()` that accepts one argument called `text`. When executed, the function merely alerts the data passed to it. Now create an `HttpRequest` object and send the request:

```
var request = new HttpRequest(
        "http://localhost/myTextFile.txt", handleData);

request.send();
```

Pass the text file's location and a pointer of the `handleData()` function to the constructor, and send the request with the `send()` method. The `handleData()` function is called in the event of a successful request.

This module encapsulates the code related to asynchronous `XMLHttpRequest` requests nicely. You don't have to worry about creating the request object, handling the `readystatechange` event, or checking the request's `status`; the `HttpRequest` module does it all for you.

VALIDATING FORM FIELDS WITH AJAX

You've probably seen it many times: registering as a new user on a website's forum or signing up for web-based e-mail, only to find that your desired username is taken. Of course, you don't find this out until after you've filled out the entire form, submitted it, and watched the page reload with new data (not to mention that you've lost some of the data you entered). As you can attest, form validation can be a frustrating experience. Thankfully, Ajax can soften this experience by sending data to the server before submitting the form—allowing the server to validate the data, and letting the user know the outcome of the validation without reloading the page!

In this section, you create a form that uses Ajax techniques to validate form fields. It's possible to approach building such a form in a variety of ways; the easiest of which to implement provides a link that initiates an HTTP request to the server application to check whether the user's desired information is available to use.

The form you build resembles typical forms used today; it will contain the following fields:

> **Username (validated):** The field where the user types his or her desired username

> **Email (validated):** The field where the user types his or her e-mail

> **Password (not validated):** The field where the user types his or her password

> **Verify Password (not validated):** The field where the user verifies his or her password

Note that the Password and Verify Password fields are just for show in this example. Verifying a password is certainly something the server application can do; however, it is far more efficient to let JavaScript perform that verification. Doing so adds more complexity to this example, and we want to keep this as simple as possible to help you get a grasp of using Ajax.

Next to the Username and Email fields will be a hyperlink that calls a JavaScript function to query the server with your HttpRequest module from the previous section.

As mentioned earlier, Ajax is communication between the browser and server. So this example needs a simple server application to validate the form fields. PHP programming is beyond the scope of this book. However, we should discuss how to request data from the PHP application, as well as look at the response the application sends back to JavaScript.

Requesting Information

The PHP application looks for one of two arguments in the query string: username and email.

To check the availability of a username, use the username argument. The URL to do this looks like the following:

```
http://localhost/formvalidator.php?username=[usernameToSearchFor]
```

When searching for a username, replace [usernameToSearchFor] with the actual name.

Searching for an e-mail follows the same pattern. The e-mail URL looks like this, where you replace [emailToSearchFor] with the actual name:

```
http://localhost/formvalidator.php?email=[emailToSearchFor]
```

The Received Data

A successful request results in a simple JSON structure that defines two members called searchTerm and available, like this:

```
{
    "searchTerm": "jmcpeak",
    "available" : true
}
```

As its name implies, the searchTerm item contains the string used in the username or e-mail search. The available item is a boolean value. If true, the requested username and/or e-mail is available for use. If false, the username and/or e-mail is in use and therefore not available.

Before You Begin

This is a live-code Ajax example; therefore, your system must meet a few requirements if you want to run this example from your computer.

A Web Server

First, you need a web server. If you are using Windows, you have Microsoft's web server software, Internet Information Services (IIS), freely available to you. To install it on Windows, open Programs and Features in the Control Panel and click Turn Windows features on or off. Figure 14-3 shows the Windows Features dialog box in Windows 8.

Expand Internet Information Services and check the features you want to install. You must check World Wide Web Services (Figure 14-4). You may need your operating system's installation CD to complete the installation.

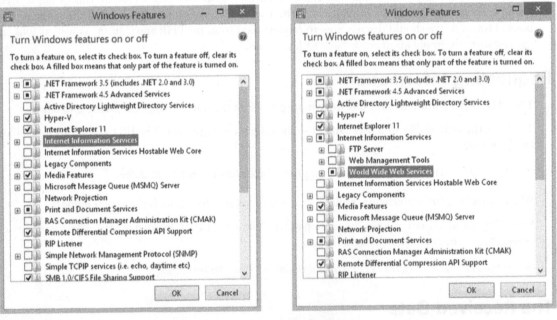

FIGURE 14-3   **FIGURE 14-4**

If you use another operating system, or you want to use another web server application, you can install Apache HTTP Server (www.apache.org). This is an open source web server and can run on a variety of operating systems, such as Linux, Unix, and Windows, to list only a few. Most websites run on Apache, so don't feel nervous about installing it on your computer. It is extremely stable.

If you do choose to use Apache, don't download and install it just yet; there are different versions of Apache. Instead, download PHP first because PHP's website gives you accurate information on which Apache version you should download and install.

PHP

PHP is a popular open source server-side scripting language and must be installed on your computer if you want to run PHP scripts. You can download PHP in a variety of forms (binaries, Windows installation wizards, and source code) at www.php.net. The PHP code used in this example was written in PHP 5.

TRY IT OUT XMLHttpRequest Smart Form

In this Try It Out, you will use Ajax to validate form fields. Open your text editor and type the following:

```html
<!DOCTYPE html>

<html lang="en">
<head>
    <title>Chapter 14: Example 1</title>
    <style>
        .fieldname {
            text-align: right;
        }

        .submit {
            text-align: right;
        }
    </style>
</head>
<body>
    <form>
        <table>
            <tr>
                <td class="fieldname">
                    Username:
                </td>
                <td>
                    <input type="text" id="username" />
                </td>
                <td>
                    <a id="usernameAvailability" href="#">Check Availability</a>
                </td>
            </tr>
            <tr>
                <td class="fieldname">
                    Email:
                </td>
                <td>
                    <input type="text" id="email" />
                </td>
                <td>
                    <a id="emailAvailability" href="#">Check Availability</a>
                </td>
            </tr>
            <tr>
                <td class="fieldname">
```

```
                    Password:
                </td>
                <td>
                    <input type="text" id="password" />
                </td>
                <td />
            </tr>
            <tr>
                <td class="fieldname">
                    Verify Password:
                </td>
                <td>
                    <input type="text" id="password2" />
                </td>
                <td />
            </tr>
            <tr>
                <td colspan="2" class="submit">
                    <input type="submit" value="Submit" />
                </td>
                <td />
            </tr>
        </table>
    </form>
    <script src="httprequest.js"></script>
    <script>
        function checkUsername(e) {
            e.preventDefault();

            var userValue = document.getElementById("username").value;

            if (!userValue) {
                alert("Please enter a user name to check!");
                return;
            }

            var url = "ch14_formvalidator.php?username=" + userValue;

            var request = new HttpRequest(url, handleResponse);
            request.send();
        }

        function checkEmail(e) {
            e.preventDefault();

            var emailValue = document.getElementById("email").value;

            if (!emailValue) {
                alert("Please enter an email address to check!");
                return;
            }

            var url = "ch14_formvalidator.php?email=" + emailValue;

            var request = new HttpRequest(url, handleResponse);
```

```
            request.send();
        }

        function handleResponse(responseText) {
            var response = JSON.parse(responseText);

            if (response.available) {
                alert(response.searchTerm + " is available!");
            } else {
                alert("We're sorry, but " + response.searchTerm +
                    " is not available.");
            }
        }

        document.getElementById("usernameAvailability")
                .addEventListener("click", checkUsername);

        document.getElementById("emailAvailability")
                .addEventListener("click", checkEmail);
    </script>
</body>

</html>
```

Save this file in your web server's root directory. If you're using IIS for your web server, save it as `c:\inetpub\wwwroot\ch14_example1.html`. If you're using Apache, you'll want to save it inside the `htdocs` folder: `path_to_htdocs\htdocs\ch14_example1.html`.

You also need to place `httprequest.js` (the `HttpRequest` module) and the `ch14_formvalidator.php` file (from the code download) into the same directory as `ch14_example1.html`.

Now open your browser and navigate to `http://localhost/ch14_formvalidator.php`. If everything is working properly, you should see the text "PHP is working correctly. Congratulations!" as in Figure 14-5.

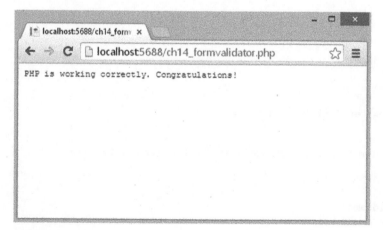

FIGURE 14-5

Now point your browser to http://localhost/ ch14_example1.html, and you should see something like Figure 14-6.

Type **jmcpeak** into the Username field and click the Check Availability link next to it. You'll see an alert box like the one shown in Figure 14-7.

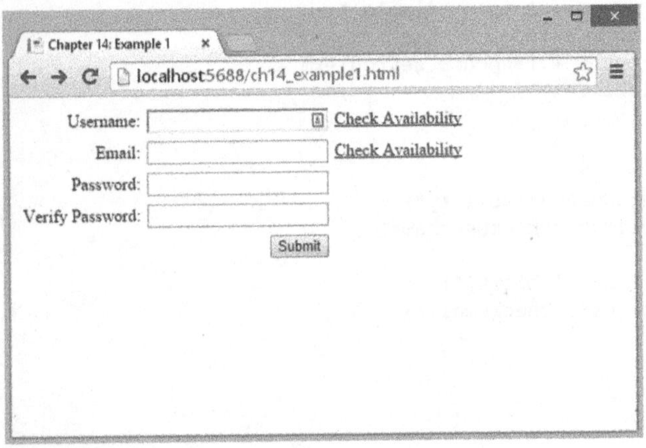

FIGURE 14-6

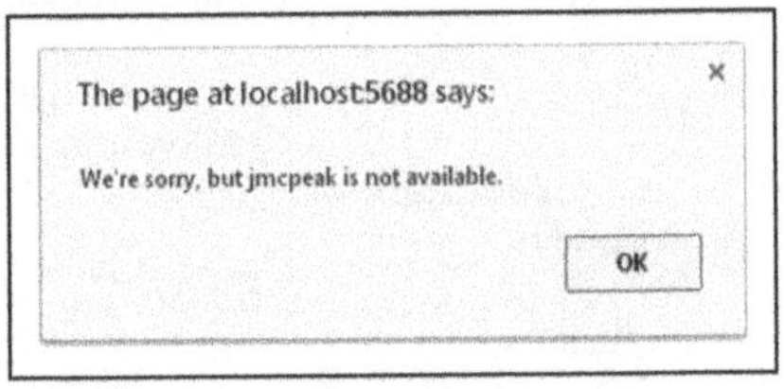

FIGURE 14-7

Now type **someone@xyz.com** in the e-mail field and click the Check Availability link next to it. Again, you'll be greeted with an alert box stating that the e-mail's already in use. Now input your own username and e-mail into these fields and click the appropriate links. Chances are an alert box will tell you that your username and/or e-mail is available (the usernames jmcpeak and pwilton and the e-mails someone@xyz.com and someone@zyx.com are the only ones used by the application).

The body of this HTML page contains a simple form whose fields are contained within a table. Each form field exists in its own row. The first two rows contain the fields you're most interested in: the Username and Email fields:

```
<form>
    <table>
        <tr>
            <td class="fieldname">
                Username:
            </td>
            <td>
                <input type="text" id="username" />
            </td>
            <td>
                <a id="usernameAvailability" href="#">Check Availability</a>
            </td>
        </tr>
        <tr>
            <td class="fieldname">
                Email:
            </td>
            <td>
```

```
                    <input type="text" id="email" />
                </td>
                <td>
                    <a id="emailAvailability" href="#">Check Availability</a>
                </td>
            </tr>
            <!-- HTML to be continued later -->
```

The first column contains text identifiers for the fields. The second column contains the `<input/>` elements themselves. Each of these tags has an id attribute: `username` for the Username field and `email` for the Email field. This enables you to easily find the `<input/>` elements and get the text entered into them.

The third column contains an `<a/>` element. These hyperlinks exist for the sole purpose of kicking off Ajax requests. As such, they have a hash (#) in their `href` attributes, thus preventing the browser from navigating to a different page (to be considered a valid, clickable hyperlink, an `<a/>` element must have an `href` value). Each of these links has an id attribute that you'll use later in your JavaScript code.

The remaining three rows in the table contain two password fields and the Submit button (the smart form currently does not use these fields):

```
            <!-- HTML continued from earlier -->
            <tr>
                <td class="fieldname">
                    Password:
                </td>
                <td>
                    <input type="text" id="password" />
                </td>
                <td />
            </tr>
            <tr>
                <td class="fieldname">
                    Verify Password:
                </td>
                <td>
                    <input type="text" id="password2" />
                </td>
                <td />
            </tr>
            <tr>
                <td colspan="2" class="submit">
                    <input type="submit" value="Submit" />
                </td>
                <td />
            </tr>
        </table>
    </form>
```

The CSS in this HTML page consists of only a couple of CSS rules:

```
.fieldname {
    text-align: right;
```

```
    }

    .submit {
        text-align: right;
    }
```

These rules align the fields to give the form a clean and unified look.

As stated earlier, the hyperlinks are key to the Ajax functionality, because they call JavaScript functions when clicked. The first function, checkUsername(), retrieves the text the user entered into the Username field and issues an HTTP request to the server.

This function executes because the user clicked a link. Therefore, you want to prevent the browser from navigating to the URL specified in its href attribute. Even though the URL is the hash (#), you still want to call preventDefault():

```
    function checkUsername(e) {
        e.preventDefault();

        var userValue = document.getElementById("username").value;
```

Use the document.getElementById() method to find the <input id="FileName_username"/> element and use its value property to retrieve the text typed into the text box. You then check to see if the user typed any text:

```
        if (!userValue) {
            alert("Please enter a user name to check!");
            return;
        }
```

If the text box is empty, the function alerts the user to input a username and stops the function from further processing. The application would make unnecessary requests to the server if the code didn't do this.

Next construct the URL to make the request to the PHP application and assign it to the url variable. Then create an HttpRequest object by passing the URL and the handleResponse() callback function to the constructor, and send the request by calling send():

```
        var url = "ch14_formvalidator.php?username=" + userValue;

        var request = new HttpRequest(url, handleResponse);
        request.send();
    }
```

You look at the handleResponse() function later. For now, let's examine the checkEmail() function.

Checking the e-mail address availability is almost identical to the username process. The checkEmail() function retrieves the text typed in the Email field and sends that information to the server application:

```
    function checkEmail(e) {
        e.preventDefault();

        var emailValue = document.getElementById("email").value;

        if (!emailValue) {
```

```
                  alert("Please enter an email address to check!");
                  return;
          }

          var url = "ch14_formvalidator.php?email=" + emailValue;

          var request = new HttpRequest(url, handleResponse);
          request.send();
      }
```

This function also uses `handleResponse()` to handle the server's response. The `handleResponse()` function executes when the `HttpRequest` object receives a complete response from the server. This function uses the requested information to tell the user whether the username or e-mail address is available. Remember, the response from the server is JSON-formatted data. So, you need to first parse the data into a JavaScript object:

```
      function handleResponse(responseText) {
          var response = JSON.parse(responseText);
```

The server's response is parsed into an object that is stored in the `response` variable. You then use this object's `available` property to display the appropriate message to the user:

```
      if (response.available) {
          alert(response.searchTerm + " is available!");
      } else {
          alert("We're sorry, but " + response.searchTerm + " is not available.");
      }
  }
```

If `available` is `true`, the function tells the user that his desired username or e-mail address is okay to use. If not, the `alert` box says that the user's desired username or e-mail address is taken.

Finally, you need to set up the event listeners for your two links:

```
  document.getElementById("usernameAvailability")
          .addEventListener("click", checkUsername);

  document.getElementById("emailAvailability")
          .addEventListener("click", checkEmail);
```

You do this by simply retrieving the `<a/>` elements by their respective `id` values and listening for the `click` event.

THINGS TO WATCH OUT FOR

Using JavaScript to communicate between server and client adds tremendous power to the language's abilities. However, this power does not come without its share of caveats. The two most important issues are security and usability.

Security Issues

Security is a hot topic in today's Internet, and as a web developer you must consider the security restrictions placed on Ajax. Knowing the security issues surrounding Ajax can save you development and debugging time.

The Same-Origin Policy

Since the early days of Netscape Navigator 2.0, JavaScript cannot access scripts or documents from a different origin. This is a security measure that browser makers adhere to; otherwise, malicious coders could execute code wherever they wanted. The same-origin policy dictates that two pages are of the same origin only if the protocol (HTTP), port (the default is 80), and host are the same.

Consider the following two pages:

➤   Page 1 is located at `http://www.site.com/folder/mypage1.htm`.

➤   Page 2 is located at `http://www.site.com/folder10/mypage2.htm`.

According to the same-origin policy, these two pages are of the same origin. They share the same host (`www.site.com`), use the same protocol (HTTP), and are accessed on the same port (none is specified; therefore, they both use 80). Because they are of the same origin, JavaScript on one page can access the other page.

Now consider the next two pages:

➤   Page 1 is located at `http://www.site.com/folder/mypage1.htm`.

➤   Page 2 is located at `https://www.site.com/folder/mypage2.htm`.

These two pages are not of the same origin. The host is the same, but their protocols and ports are different. Page 1 uses HTTP (port 80), whereas Page 2 uses HTTPS (port 443). This difference, though slight, is enough to give the two pages two separate origins. Therefore, JavaScript on one of these pages cannot access the other page.

So what does this have to do with Ajax? Everything, because a large part of Ajax is JavaScript. For example, because of this policy, an `XMLHttpRequest` object cannot retrieve any file or document from a different origin by default. There is, however, a legitimate need for cross-origin requests, and the W3C responded with the Cross-Origin Resource Sharing (CORS) specification.

CORS

The CORS specification defines how browsers and servers communicate with one another when sending requests across origins. For CORS to work, the browser must send a custom HTTP header called `Origin` that contains the protocol, domain name, and port of the page making the request. For example, if the JavaScript on the page `http://www.abc.com/xyz.html` used `XMLHttpRequest` to issue a request to `http://beginningjs.com`, the `Origin` header would look like this:

```
Origin: http://www.abc.com
```

When the server responds to a CORS request, it must also send a custom header called `Access-Control-Allow-Origin`, and it must contain the same origin specified in the request's `Origin` header. Continuing from the previous example, the server's response must contain the following `Access-Control-Allow-Origin` header for CORS to work:

```
Access-Control-Allow-Origin: http://www.abc.com
```

If this header is missing, or if the origins don't match, the browser doesn't process the request.

Alternatively, the server can include the `Access-Control-Allow-Origin` header with a value of `*`, signifying that all origins are accepted. This is primarily used by publicly available web services.

> **NOTE** These custom headers are automatically handled by the browser. You do not need to set your own `Origin` header, and you do not have to manually check the `Access-Control-Allow-Origin`.

Usability Concerns

Ajax breaks the mold of traditional web applications and pages. It enables developers to build applications that behave in a more conventional, non-"webbish" way. This, however, is also a drawback, because the Internet has been around for many, many years, and users are accustomed to traditional web pages.

Therefore, it is up to developers to ensure that users can use their web pages, and use them as they expect to, without causing frustration.

The Browser's Back Button

One of the advantages of `XMLHttpRequest` is its ease of use. You simply create the object, send the request, and await the server's response. Unfortunately, this object does have a downside: Most browsers do not log a history of requests made with the object. Therefore, `XMLHttpRequest` essentially breaks the browser's Back button. This might be a desired side-effect for some Ajax-enabled applications or components, but it can cause serious usability problems for the user.

Creating a Back/Forward-Capable Form with an IFrame

It's possible to avoid breaking the browser's navigational buttons by using an older but reliable Ajax technique: using hidden frames/iframes to facilitate client-server communication. You must use two frames for this method to work properly. One must be hidden, and one must be visible.

> **NOTE** Note that when you are using an iframe, the document that contains the iframe is the visible frame.

The hidden-frame technique consists of a four-step process:

1. The user initiates a JavaScript call to the hidden frame by clicking a link in the visible frame or performing some other type of user interaction. This call is usually nothing more

complicated that redirecting the hidden frame to a different web page. This redirection automatically triggers the second step.

2. The request is sent to the server, which processes the data.

3. The server sends its response (a web page) back to the hidden frame.

4. The browser loads the web page in the hidden frame and executes any JavaScript code to contact the visible frame.

The example in this section is based on the form validator built earlier in the chapter, but you'll use a hidden iframe to facilitate the communication between the browser and the server instead of an XMLHttpRequest object. Before getting into the code, you should first know about the data received from the server.

The Server Response

You expected a JSON data structure as the server's response when using XMLHttpRequest to get data from the server. The response in this example is different and must consist of two things:

➤ The data, which must be in HTML format

➤ A mechanism to contact the parent document when the iframe receives the HTML response

The following code is an example of the response HTML page:

```
<!DOCTYPE html>

<html lang="en">
<head>
    <title>Returned Data</title>
</head>
<body>
    <script>
        //more code here
    </script>
</body>
</html>
```

This simple HTML page contains a single <script/> element in the body of the document. The JavaScript code contained in this script block is generated by the PHP application, calling handleResponse() in the visible frame and passing it the expected JSON.

The JSON data structure has a new member: the value field. It contains the username or e-mail that was sent in the request. Therefore, the following HTML document is a valid response from the PHP application:

```
<!DOCTYPE html>

<html lang="en">
<head>
    <title>Returned Data</title>
</head>
<body>
```

```
        <script>
            top.handleResponse('{"available":false, "value":"jmcpeak"}');
        </script>
    </body>
</html>
```

The HTML page calls the `handleResponse()` function in the parent window and passes the JSON structure signifying that the username or e-mail address is available. With the response in this format, you can keep a good portion of the JavaScript code identical to Example 1.

TRY IT OUT | Iframe Smart Form

The code for this revised smart form is very similar to the code used previously with the `XMLHttpRequest` example. There are, however, a few changes. Open up your text editor and type the following:

```
<!DOCTYPE html>
<html lang="en">
<head>
    <title>Chapter 14: Example 2</title>
    <style>
        .fieldname {
            text-align: right;
        }

        .submit {
            text-align: right;
        }

        #hiddenFrame {
            display: none;
        }
    </style>
</head>
<body>
    <form>
        <table>
            <tr>
                <td class="fieldname">
                    Username:
                </td>
                <td>
                    <input type="text" id="username" />
                </td>
                <td>
                    <a id="usernameAvailability" href="#">Check Availability</a>
                </td>
            </tr>
            <tr>
                <td class="fieldname">
                    Email:
                </td>
                <td>
                    <input type="text" id="email" />
```

```
                    </td>
                    <td>
                        <a id="emailAvailability" href="#">Check Availability</a>
                    </td>
                </tr>
                <tr>
                    <td class="fieldname">
                        Password:
                    </td>
                    <td>
                        <input type="text" id="password" />
                    </td>
                    <td></td>
                </tr>
                <tr>
                    <td class="fieldname">
                        Verify Password:
                    </td>
                    <td>
                        <input type="text" id="password2" />
                    </td>
                    <td></td>
                </tr>
                <tr>
                    <td colspan="2" class="submit">
                        <input type="submit" value="Submit" />
                    </td>
                    <td></td>
                </tr>
            </table>
        </form>
        <iframe src="about:blank" id="hiddenFrame" name="hiddenFrame"></iframe>
        <script>
            function checkUsername(e) {
                e.preventDefault();

                var userValue = document.getElementById("username").value;

                if (!userValue) {
                    alert("Please enter a user name to check!");
                    return;
                }

                var url = "ch14_iframevalidator.php?username=" + userValue;

                frames["hiddenFrame"].location = url;
            }

            function checkEmail(e) {
                e.preventDefault();

                var emailValue = document.getElementById("email").value;

                if (!emailValue) {
                    alert("Please enter an email address to check!");
```

```
                return;
            }

            var url = "ch14_iframevalidator.php?email=" + emailValue;

            frames["hiddenFrame"].location = url;
        }

        function handleResponse(responseText) {
            var response = JSON.parse(responseText);

            if (response.available) {
                alert(response.searchTerm + " is available!");
            } else {
                alert("We're sorry, but " + response.searchTerm +
                    " is not available.");
            }
        }

        document.getElementById("usernameAvailability")
            .addEventListener("click", checkUsername);

        document.getElementById("emailAvailability")
            .addEventListener("click", checkEmail);
    </script>
</body>
</html>
```

Save this file as ch14_example2.html, and save it in your web server's root directory. Also locate the ch14_iframevalidator.php file from the code download and place it in the same directory.

Open your web browser and navigate to http://localhost/ch14_example2.html. You should see a page similar to Example 1.

Check for three usernames and e-mail addresses. After you clear the final alert box, click the browser's Back button a few times. You'll notice that it is cycling through the information you previously entered. The text in the text box will not change; however, the alert box will display the names and e-mails you entered. You can do the same thing with the Forward button.

The HTML in the body of the page remains unchanged except for the addition of the <iframe/> tag after the closing <form/> tag:

```
<iframe src="about:blank" id="hiddenFrame" name="hiddenFrame" />
```

This frame is initialized to have a blank HTML page loaded. Its name and id attributes contain the value of hiddenFrame. You use the value of the name attribute later to retrieve this frame from the frames collection in the BOM. Next, you set the CSS for the frame:

```
#hiddenFrame {
    display: none;
}
```

This rule contains one style declaration to hide the iframe from view.

> **NOTE** *Hiding an iframe through CSS enables you to easily show it if you need to debug the server-side application.*

Next up, the JavaScript:

```
function checkUsername(e) {
    e.preventDefault();

    var userValue = document.getElementById("username").value;

    if (!userValue) {
        alert("Please enter a user name to check!");
        return;
    }

    var url = "ch14_iframevalidator.php?username=" + userValue;

    frames["hiddenFrame"].location = url;
}
```

This `checkUsername()` function is almost identical to Example 1. The value of the `url` variable is changed to the new ch14_iframvalidator.php file. The actual request is made by accessing the `<iframe/>` element using the `frames` collection and setting its `location` property to the new URL.

The `checkEmail()` function has the same modifications:

```
function checkEmail(e) {
    e.preventDefault();

    var emailValue = document.getElementById("email").value;

    if (!emailValue) {
        alert("Please enter an email address to check!");
        return;
    }

    var url = "ch14_iframevalidator.php?email=" + emailValue;

    frames["hiddenFrame"].location = url;
}
```

As before, the `checkEmail()` function retrieves the text box's value and checks to see if the user entered data. It then constructs the URL using ch14_iframevalidator.php and loads the URL into the `<iframe/>`.

Dealing with Delays

The web browser is just like any other conventional application in that user interface (UI) cues tell the user that something is going on. For example, when a user clicks a link, the throbber animation may run or the cursor might change to display a "busy" animation.

This is another area in which Ajax solutions, and XMLHttpRequest specifically, miss the mark. However, this problem is simple to overcome: Simply add UI elements to tell the user something is going on and remove them when the action is completed. Consider the following code:

```
function requestComplete(responseText) {

    //do something with the data here

    document.getElementById("divLoading").style.display = "none";
}

var myRequest = new HttpRequest("http://localhost/myfile.txt",
                                requestComplete);

//show that we're loading
document.getElementById("divLoading").style.display = "block";

myRequest.send();
```

This code uses the HttpRequest module to request a text file. Before sending the request, it retrieves an HTML element in the document with an id of divLoading. This <div/> element tells the user that data is loading. The code then hides the element when the request completes, thus letting the user know that the process completed.

Offering this information to your users lets them know the application is doing something. Without such visual cues, users are left to wonder if the application is working on whatever they requested.

Degrade Gracefully When Ajax Fails

In a perfect world, the code you write would work every time it runs. Unfortunately, you have to face the fact that many times Ajax-enabled web pages will not use the Ajax-enabled goodness because a user turned off JavaScript in his browser.

The only real answer to this problem is to build an old-fashioned web page with old-fashioned forms, links, and other HTML elements. Then, using JavaScript, you can disable the default behavior of those HTML elements and add Ajax functionality. Consider this hyperlink as an example:

```
<a href="http://www.wrox.com" title="Wrox Publishing">Wrox Publishing</a>
```

This is a normal, run-of-the-mill hyperlink. When the user clicks it, the browser will take him to http://www.wrox.com. By using JavaScript, you of course can prevent this behavior by using the Event object's preventDefault() method. Simply register a click event handler for the <a/> element and call preventDefault(). Both Examples 1 and 2 demonstrated this technique.

As a rule of thumb, build your web page first and add Ajax later.

SUMMARY

This chapter introduced you to Ajax, and it barely scratched the surface of Ajax and its many uses:

➤ You looked at the XMLHttpRequest object, and learned how to make both synchronous and asynchronous requests to the server and how to use the onreadystatechange event handler.

➤ You built your own Ajax module to make asynchronous HTTP requests easier for you to code.

➤ You used your new Ajax module in a smarter form, one that checks usernames and e-mails to see if they are already in use.

➤ You saw how XMLHttpRequest breaks the browser's Back and Forward buttons, and addressed this problem by rebuilding the same form using a hidden iframe to make requests.

➤ You looked at some of the downsides to Ajax, including the security issues and the gotchas.

EXERCISES

You can find suggested solutions for these questions in Appendix A.

1. Extend the HttpRequest module to include synchronous requests in addition to the asynchronous requests the module already makes. You'll have to make some adjustments to your code to incorporate this functionality. (Hint: Create an async property for the module.)

2. It was mentioned earlier in the chapter that you could modify the smart form to not use hyperlinks. Change the form that uses the HttpRequest module so that the Username and Email fields are checked when the user submits the form. Listen for the form's submit event and cancel the submission if a username or e-mail is taken.

15

HTML5 Media

WHAT YOU WILL LEARN IN THIS CHAPTER:

➤ Playing audio and video natively in modern web browsers

➤ Writing a custom control UI for media playback

➤ Synchronizing your UI with the browser's native controls

➤ Parsing JSON back into actual objects and values you can use in your pages

WROX.COM CODE DOWNLOADS FOR THIS CHAPTER

You can find the wrox.com code downloads for this chapter at http://www.wiley.com/go/ BeginningJavaScript5E on the Download Code tab. You can also view all of the examples and related files at http://beginningjs.com.

At its inception, the Internet was a text delivery system. Whereas the first HTML specification described the `<img>` tag for embedding images within a document, HTTP and HTML were designed primarily for transmitting and displaying text (hence, Hyper-*Text*).

In the late 1990s, personal computers were finding their way into more households, and ordinary people were able to access the web. Naturally, people wanted more from the web, and browser makers accommodated this by designing their browsers to use plug-ins, third-party applications that were designed to do things browsers normally didn't, such as playing video and audio.

Plug-ins solved a particular problem, but they weren't without their faults—the largest being the need for so many of them. A wide variety of music and video formats were available, and certain plug-ins would only play certain formats. Stability was also an issue because a malfunctioning plug-in could crash the browser.

Then in 2005, some enterprising folks created YouTube, a video-sharing website. Instead of relying on QuickTime or Windows Media Player, YouTube's videos were served to users as

Macromedia/Adobe Flash files. This was advantageous because of Flash's ubiquity; Macromedia/Adobe had Flash plug-ins for every major browser and operating system. Soon thereafter, websites started using Flash for delivering their video and audio content to users, and everything was right in the world. Or was it?

Many people believe the browser should have the built-in capability for playing video and audio. So the people developing the HTML5 specification included two new tags, `<video>` and `<audio>`, for that express purpose. And although it's wonderful that, after so many years, browsers finally have the built-in capability of playing media, issues still exist that we developers have to deal with. But first, let's take a brief look at these new tags and how they work within the browser.

A PRIMER

Before we begin, the video used in this chapter is called Big Buck Bunny, and it is Creative Commons-licensed as an open movie. Because of its size, you will not find the video in the code download. You can, however, download Big Buck Bunny in a variety of formats at http://www.bigbuckbunny.org.

It's also worth noting that video and audio are very similar; in fact, the primary difference between the two elements is that `<audio/>` elements have no playback area for visual content. Although this discussion focuses primarily on video, the same concepts can be applied to audio.

Before HTML5, embedding video within a web page was cumbersome because it required you to use no less than three elements for the video to work in all browsers. With HTML5, however, all you need is the `<video/>` element:

```
<video src="bbb.mp4"></video>
```

The `<video/>` element's src attribute contains the location of the video file. In this case, the browser will attempt to load the bbb.mp4 file that is in the same directory as the page.

Of course, older browsers do not support the `<video/>` element, and as such, they will simply ignore the `<video/>` element. You can, however, add some content inside the `<video/>` element like this:

```
<video src="bbb.mp4">
    <a href="bbb.mp4">Download this video.</a>
</video>
```

Browsers that support native video will not display the link, but browsers that do not support native video will, as shown in Figure 15-1.

In most cases, you won't use the src attribute in your HTML. Instead, you'll define a `<source/>` element inside `<video/>`, like this:

```
<video>
    <source src="bbb.mp4" />
    <a href="bbb.mp4">Download this video.</a>
</video>
```

FIGURE 15-1

The reason is fairly simple: Different browsers support different formats. This is the primary issue we face with native video support. For example, Figure 15-2 shows IE11 with a page that contains the previous code.

The video is in H.264 format, which is supported by IE11 and Chrome. Firefox, at the time of this writing, has partial support, and viewing the same page gives you Figure 15-3.

FIGURE 15-2

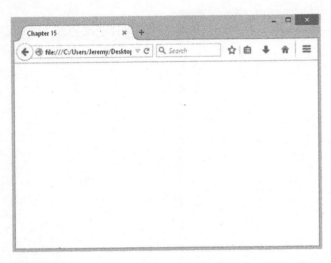

FIGURE 15-3

Bupkis. But you can skirt around this issue by providing the same video in different formats. Firefox has complete support for WebM, and you can accommodate other WebM-supporting browsers by adding another <source/> element, like this:

```
<video>
    <source src="bbb.mp4" />
    <source src="bbb.webm" />
    <a href="bbb.mp4">Download this video.</a>
</video>
```

Browsers will read each source in the order in which it appears in the HTML. They download the video's metadata to determine which video to load, and they load the first video that it supports. Chrome supports both H.264 and WebM; so, if Chrome were to load a page with this code, it would load the .mp4 file.

You can prevent the browser from downloading a video's metadata by providing the MIME type for each <source/> element. You do this with the type attribute, as shown here:

```
<video>
    <source src="bbb.mp4" type="video/mp4" />
    <source src="bbb.webm" type="video/webm" />
    <a href="bbb.mp4">Download this video.</a>
</video>
```

You can also provide the codec information in the type attribute to allow the browser to make more intelligent decisions like this:

```
<video>
    <source src="bbb.mp4"
            type='video/mp4; codecs="avc1.4D401E, mp4a.40.2"' />

    <source src="bbb.webm" type'video/webm; codecs="vp8.0, vorbis"' />
```

```
  <a href="bbb.mp4">Download this video.</a>
</video>
```

> **NOTE** It's beyond the scope of this book to provide an in-depth discussion on the various codecs used and the browsers that support them. So for the sake of simplicity, this chapter omits the type attribute altogether—along with the text-based fallback.

By default, videos do not display controls, but you can easily add the default controls by adding the controls attribute to the <video/> element:

```
<video controls>
```

You don't have to set controls to any value; its presence is enough to turn on the browser's default controls for the video.

You can also tell the browser to preload the video with the preload attribute:

```
<video controls preload>
```

This tells the browser to immediately start loading the video. Like the controls attribute, you don't have to set a value for preload.

By default, the browser uses the first frame of the video as the *poster* of the video, the initial visual representation of the video. You can use the poster attribute to display a custom image for the video's poster:

```
<video controls preload poster="bbb.jpg">
```

The poster attribute, as you might imagine, is specifically for <video/> elements, but you can add a few other attributes to the <video/> and <audio/> elements. Probably the most important, from a JavaScript perspective, is the id attribute. It is, after all, how you find specific media in the page so that you can script them.

SCRIPTING MEDIA

In the DOM, <video/> and <audio/> elements are HTMLMediaElement objects, and the HTML5 specification defines an API for working with these objects. But naturally, before you can use any of the methods, properties, or events of a media object, you need to first obtain one. You can retrieve an existing <video/> or <audio/> element in the page using any of the various methods for finding elements. For the sake of simplicity, assume there's a <video id="bbbVideo"> tag in the page. You could get it with the following code:

```
var video = document.getElementById("bbbVideo");
```

Or you can create one dynamically using `document.createElement()`, like this:

```
var video = document.createElement("video");
```

And once you have an `HTMLMediaElement` object, you can begin to program it with its robust API.

Methods

Media objects have just a handful of methods, and they're primarily used for controlling media playback, as shown in the following table.

METHOD NAME	DESCRIPTION
`canPlayType(mimeType)`	Determines the likelihood that the browser can play media of the provided MIME type and/or codec
`load()`	Begins to load the media from the server
`pause()`	Pauses the media playback
`play()`	Begins or continues the playback of the media

These are the methods defined by the HTML5 specification, but be aware that the various browsers can also implement their own methods in addition to these four. For example, Firefox adds many more methods to `HTMLMediaElement` objects. This book, however, does not cover them.

The `pause()` and `play()` methods are straightforward; you use them to pause and play the media, respectively:

```
video.play();
video.pause();
```

The other two methods are used when you want to load media dynamically. The `load()` method, obviously, tells the browser to load the specified media. The `canPlayType()` method, however, is a bit more involved because it doesn't return `true` or `false`. Instead, it returns a variety of values indicating the *likelihood* that the browser supports the given type. The possible values returned by `canPlayType()` are:

➤ `"probably"`: Indicates that the type appears to be playable

➤ `"maybe"`: It's impossible to tell if the type is playable without actually playing it.

➤ `""`: The media definitely cannot be played.

The `canPlayType()` and `load()` methods are only needed if you plan to load a video dynamically. Here's an example of how that code could look:

```
if (video.canPlayType("video/webm") == "probably") {
    video.src = "bbb.webm";
} else {
    video.src = "bbb.mp4";
```

```
        }

        video.load();
        video.play();
```

This code uses the `canPlayType()` method to determine if the browser supports the WebM format. If it does, the video's `src` property (which you learn more about in the next section) is set to the WebM version of the video. If WebM isn't supported, the browser's `src` is set to the MP4 version. Then, after the video is loaded with the `load()` method, the `play()` method plays the video.

TRY IT OUT Controlling Media Playback

Let's apply some of this newfound knowledge with a simple example. You write a web page that plays and pauses a video. Note that this example assumes you have two videos: `bbb.mp4` and `bbb.webm`. Open your text editor and type the following:

```
<!DOCTYPE html>

<html lang="en">
<head>
    <title>Chapter 15: Example 1</title>
</head>
    <body>
        <div>
            <button id="playbackController">Play</button>
        </div>
        <video id="bbbVideo">
            <source src="bbb.mp4" />
            <source src="bbb.webm" />
        </video>

        <script>
            function playbackClick(e) {
                var target = e.target;
                var video = document.getElementById("bbbVideo");

                if (target.innerHTML == "Play") {
                    video.play();
                    target.innerHTML = "Pause";
                } else {
                    video.pause();
                    target.innerHTML = "Play";
                }
            }

            document.getElementById("playbackController")
                    .addEventListener("click", playbackClick);
        </script>
    </body>
</html>
```

Save this file as `ch15_example1.html` and open it in your browser. You should see a button with the text Play and a video directly beneath it as shown in Figure 15-4.

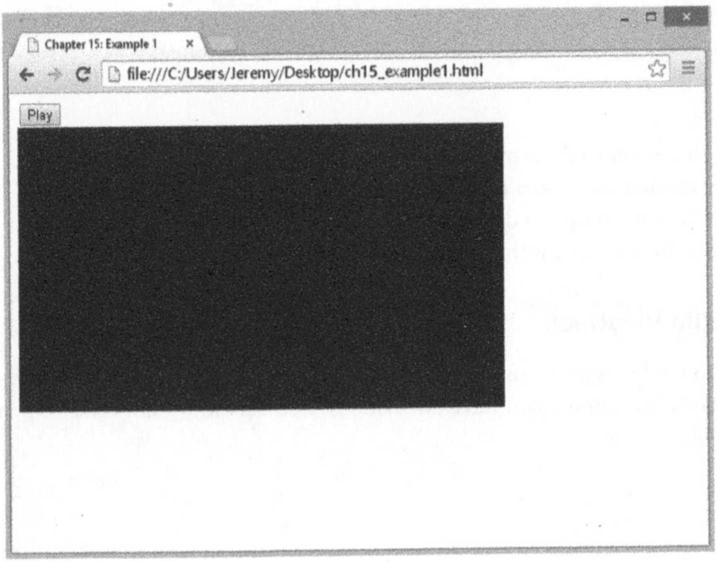

FIGURE 15-4

Clicking the button changes its text to Pause and starts playing the video. Clicking the button again changes the text back to Play and pauses the video.

In the body of the page, you have a `<button/>` element with the `id` of `playbackController`. As its ID implies, it is used for controlling the playback of the media, a video embedded with the `<video/>` element:

```
<video id="bbbVideo">
    <source src="bbb.mp4" />
    <source src="bbb.webm" />
</video>
```

The main portion of the JavaScript code is a function called `playbackClick()`, an event handler for the `<button/>`'s `click` event. The first two statements of this function create two variables called `target` and `video`:

```
function playbackClick(e) {
    var target = e.target;
    var video = document.getElementById("bbbVideo");
```

The `target` variable is the event target (the button), and `video` contains a reference to the `<video/>` element object.

Next you determine whether you need to play or pause the video, and you do that by checking the text of the `<button/>` element:

```
if (target.innerHTML == "Play") {
    video.play();
```

```
        target.innerHTML = "Pause";
   }
```

If it's Play, you want to play the video. You do so by using the `HTMLMediaElement` object's `play()` method, and you change the button's text to read Pause.

If the result of this `if` statement is `false`, you can assume that you want to pause the video:

```
   else {
      video.pause();
      target.innerHTML = "Play";
   }
}
```

So, in the `else` statement, you use the media object's `pause()` method and change the button's text back to Play.

Of course, this function won't execute itself, so you register a `click` event listener on the `<button/>` object:

```
document.getElementById("playbackController")
        .addEventListener("click", playbackClick);
```

This example works, but it's not an ideal solution for controlling media. Specifically, you shouldn't rely upon the text of an element to determine if you should play or pause. You can better control media by incorporating some of the many properties defined by the HTML5 specification.

Properties

Although the HTML5 specification defines just a few methods for media objects, it defines *a lot* of properties. You won't find a complete list of properties in this section, but Appendix C lists all of them.

Most of the `HTMLMediaElement`'s properties are for querying and/or modifying the state of the media; others, like `controls` and `poster` (the latter for video) are cosmetic.

The following table lists a few of the properties and their descriptions.

PROPERTY NAME	DESCRIPTION
autoplay	Gets or sets the `autoplay` HTML attribute, indicating whether playback should automatically begin as soon as enough media is available
controls	Reflects the `controls` HTML attribute
currentTime	Gets the current playback time. Setting this property seeks the media to the new time.
duration	Gets the length of the media in seconds; zero if no media is available. Returns NaN if the duration cannot be determined

continues

(continued)

PROPERTY NAME	DESCRIPTION
ended	Indicates whether the media element has ended playback
loop	Reflects the loop HTML attribute. Indicates whether the media element should start over when playback reaches the end
muted	Gets or sets whether the audio is muted
paused	Indicates whether the media is paused
playbackRate	Gets or sets the playback rate. 1.0 is normal speed.
poster	Gets or sets the poster HTML attribute
preload	Reflects the preload HTML element attribute
src	Gets or sets the src HTML attribute
volume	The audio volume. Valid values range from 0.0 (silent) to 1.0 (loudest).

Like the methods from the previous section, these properties are defined by the HTML5 specification, but some browser makers also implement their own proprietary properties. Also like the aforementioned methods, the majority of these properties are straightforward; their names do a pretty good job of describing what they're used for.

For example, the aptly named paused property can tell you if the media is paused, like this:

```
if (video.paused) {
    video.play();
} else {
    video.pause();
}
```

It's important to know that the default state of any media is paused. The browser only plays media when it's told to do so—either explicitly with the play() method or via the built-in controls, or implicitly with the autoplay property/HTML attribute.

You can use the muted property to not only tell you if the audio is muted, but to also mute the audio. For example:

```
if (video.muted) {
    video.muted = false;
} else {
    video.muted = true;
}
```

Or to write it in a more simplified manner:

```
video.muted = !video.muted;
```

This code achieves the same results as the previous example; it sets `video.muted` to the opposite of its current value.

The `src` property, however, is a bit different. It's clear that it sets the media of a `<video/>` or `<audio/>` element, but when you set the `src` of a media object, you have to load it explicitly with the `load()` method. Otherwise, whatever media is currently loaded by the browser will play when you call the `play()` method. Therefore, the following code does not correctly change and play the media of a media object:

```
// incorrect
video.src = "new_media.mp4";
video.play();
```

This code sets the `src` property, but it doesn't load the new media with the `load()` method. Therefore, when the video plays again, it still plays the media currently loaded by the browser. To fix this, you have to call `load()` before you call `play()`, like this:

```
video.src = "new_media.mp4";
video.load();
video.play();
```

TRY IT OUT   Controlling Media Playback II

Let's revisit Example 1 and improve it by taking advantage of some of the `HTMLMediaElement` object's properties. Open your text editor and type the following:

```
<!DOCTYPE html>

<html lang="en">
<head>
    <title>Chapter 15: Example 2</title>
</head>
    <body>
        <div>
            <button id="playbackController">Play</button>
            <button id="muteController">Mute</button>
        </div>
        <video id="bbbVideo">
            <source src="bbb.mp4" />
            <source src="bbb.webm" />
        </video>

        <script>
            function playbackClick(e) {
                var target = e.target;
                var video = document.getElementById("bbbVideo");

                if (video.paused) {
                    video.play();
                    target.innerHTML = "Pause";
                } else {
                    video.pause();
                    target.innerHTML = "Resume";
```

```
                }
            }

            function muteClick(e) {
                var target = e.target;
                var video = document.getElementById("bbbVideo");

                if (video.muted) {
                    video.muted = false;
                    target.innerHTML = "Mute";
                } else {
                    video.muted = true;
                    target.innerHTML = "Unmute";
                }

            }

            document.getElementById("playbackController")
                    .addEventListener("click", playbackClick);

            document.getElementById("muteController")
                    .addEventListener("click", muteClick);

        </script>
    </body>
</html>
```

Save this as ch15_example2.html and open it in your browser. You should now see two buttons: Play and Mute. Directly beneath these buttons is the video, as shown in Figure 15-5.

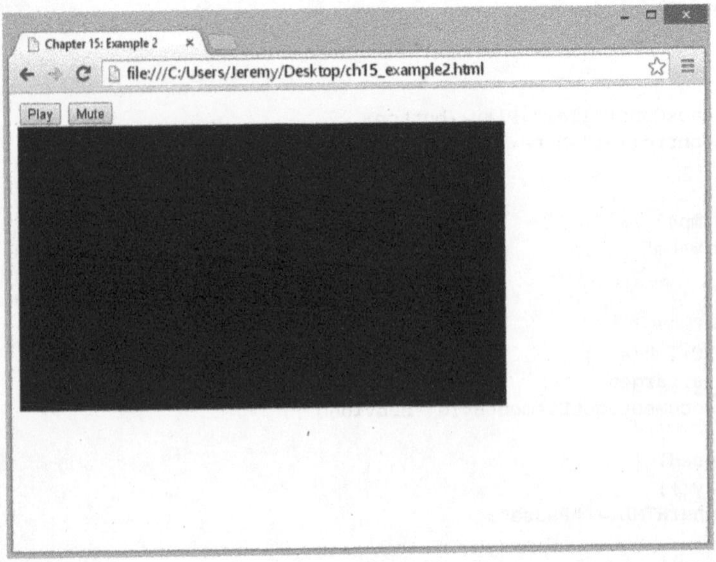

FIGURE 15-5

Start playing the video and click the Mute button. You'll notice that the audio is now muted and the button's text reads Unmute. Click the button again to unmute the audio.

Now click the Pause button. You'll notice that the video pauses and the button's text changes to Resume. Clicking the button again resumes the video.

This example is quite different from Example 1. Starting with the HTML, you added a new <button/> element:

```
<div>
    <button id="playbackController">Play</button>
    <button id="muteController">Mute</button>
</div>
```

It has an id of muteController and the text of Mute. As you already know, it's used for muting and unmuting the audio. You register the click event listener at the bottom of the code:

```
document.getElementById("muteController")
        .addEventListener("click", muteClick);
```

The function used to handle this event is called muteClick(). Its first two lines create the target and video variables—the former containing a reference to the <button/> element object, and the latter referencing the HTMLMediaElement object:

```
function muteClick(e) {
    var target = e.target;
    var video = document.getElementById("bbbVideo");
```

This function toggles the muted property of the media object, so you first need to check its current value with an if statement:

```
if (video.muted) {
    video.muted = false;
    target.innerHTML = "Mute";
}
```

If it's true, the audio is currently muted. So, you set video.muted to false and change the text of the button to Mute, thus unmuting the video.

But if muted is false, the else statement executes, muting the video:

```
    else {
      video.muted = true;
      target.innerHTML = "Unmute";
    }
}
```

You set the video's muted property to true to mute it, and then you change the button's text to Unmute.

The `playbackClick()` function is logically identical to `muteClick()`. After you set the target and video, you then determine whether you need to play or pause the video. You can accomplish this easily with the media object's `paused` property:

```
function playbackClick(e) {
    var target = e.target;
    var video = document.getElementById("bbbVideo");

    if (video.paused) {
        video.play();
        target.innerHTML = "Pause";
    }
}
```

If it's `true`, you call the `play()` method to either start or resume playback. If `paused` is `false`, you want to pause playback:

```
    else {
        video.pause();
        target.innerHTML = "Resume";
    }
}
```

You do so with the `pause()` method, and you change the button's text to Resume. The word "resume" was chosen to enhance the user's experience; people expect to resume from a paused state. You could have implemented something similar in Example 1, but because the video's state was determined by the text of a button, it would've required extra code to make it work.

Now, this example is a marked improvement over Example 1, but it still has an issue: Users can control the video through the context menu (Figure 15-6).

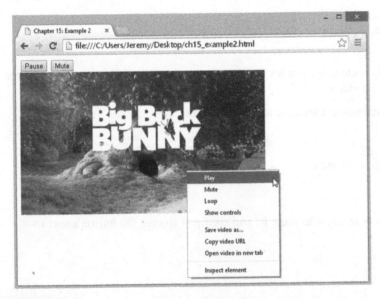

FIGURE 15-6

This in and of itself isn't exactly a problem; after all, the best user interfaces have redundancies. It becomes problem when your custom UI doesn't accurately portray the actual state of the media. Refer back to Figure 15-6. The context menu says Play whereas the custom Play/Pause button says Pause. Ideally, both the context menu and the custom UI should be in sync, and you can do that by listening for certain events.

Events

Events are the lifeblood of graphical applications, and media-based events are no exception. The folks behind the HTML5 specification did a very thorough job of defining the events web developers need to write robust media-driven pages and applications.

As you might suspect, there are a lot of events, and you can view the complete list in Appendix C. The following table, however, lists just a few.

EVENT NAME	DESCRIPTION
abort	Fires when playback is aborted
canplay	Sent when enough data is available to play the media
canplaythrough	Indicates that the entire media can be played through without interruption
durationchange	The media's metadata has changed, indicating a change in the media's duration.
ended	Fires when playback completes
error	Sent when an error occurs
loadstart	Downloading has begun.
pause	Fires when playback is paused
playing	Sent when the media starts or resumes playing
progress	Downloading is in progress.
ratechange	Fires when the playback speed changes
seeked	Seeking has ended.
seeking	Fires when playback is moved to a new position
timeupdate	The currentTime property has changed.
volumechange	Either the volume property or muted property has changed.

You register listeners for these events exactly like you would any other standard event: with addEventListener(). For example, you can execute code when the media is paused by listening for the pause event, like this:

```
function mediaPaused(e) {
    alert("You paused the video!");
}

video.addEventListener("pause", mediaPaused);
```

And just like any other type of event, you can register different event listeners using the same handler function:

```
function mediaPausedPlaying(e) {
    if (e.type == "pause") {
        alert("You paused the video!");
    } else {
        alert("You're playing the video!");
    }
}

video.addEventListener("pause", mediaPausedPlaying);
video.addEventListener("playing", mediaPausedPlaying);
```

This is advantageous if you need to execute the same or similar code for both events. In many (and perhaps most) cases, however, you'll more than likely want to define and use different functions for different events.

Listening for these "state change" events is ideal when coding your own custom controller UI. You want your UI to accurately reflect the state of the media, and the "state change" events fire only when the media's state changes. This, of course, makes them ideal for keeping a custom UI in sync with the built-in UI of the browser, as you see in the next example.

TRY IT OUT   Controlling Media Playback III

Let's use some of the events in the previous table to rewrite Example 2. The following code contains substantial changes, so you can use Example 2 as a starting point or type it all from scratch:

```
<!DOCTYPE html>

<html lang="en">
<head>
    <title>Chapter 15: Example 3</title>
</head>
<body>
    <div>
        <button id="playbackController">Play</button>
        <button id="muteController">Mute</button>
    </div>
    <video id="bbbVideo">
        <source src="bbb.mp4" />
        <source src="bbb.webm" />
    </video>

    <script>
        function pauseHandler(e) {
            playButton.innerHTML = "Resume";
        }

        function playingHandler(e) {
            playButton.innerHTML = "Pause";
```

```
        }

        function volumechangeHandler(e) {
            muteButton.innerHTML = video.muted ? "Unmute" : "Mute";
        }

        function playbackClick(e) {
            video.paused ? video.play() : video.pause();
        }

        function muteClick(e) {
            video.muted = !video.muted;
        }

        var video = document.getElementById("bbbVideo");
        var playButton = document.getElementById("playbackController");
        var muteButton = document.getElementById("muteController");

        video.addEventListener("pause", pauseHandler);
        video.addEventListener("playing", playingHandler);
        video.addEventListener("volumechange", volumechangeHandler);

        playButton.addEventListener("click", playbackClick);

        muteButton.addEventListener("click", muteClick);
    </script>
</body>
</html>
```

Save this as `ch15_example3.html` and open it in your browser. It will look exactly like Example 2. Each time you play, pause, mute, or unmute the video, be sure to open the media's context menu. Both the custom UI and the control options in the context menu will be in sync, as shown in Figure 15-7.

FIGURE 15-7

The HTML in this example is untouched from Example 2, so let's jump right to the code. Outside of any function, you define three variables for referencing the <video/> and two <button/> elements:

```
var video = document.getElementById("bbbVideo");
var playButton = document.getElementById("playbackController");
var muteButton = document.getElementById("muteController");
```

You'll use these variables throughout the various functions, but first, you register the event listeners.

For the <video/> element, you register pause, playing, and volumechange event listeners:

```
video.addEventListener("pause", pauseHandler);
video.addEventListener("playing", playingHandler);
video.addEventListener("volumechange", volumechangeHandler);
```

Each event listener uses a unique function—the pauseHandler() function handles the pause event, playingHandler() handles the playing event, and volumechangeHandler() handles the volumechange event. You could make the argument that the playing and pause event code is similar enough to use a single function, but keep it simple! Simple functions are happy functions.

And once again, the two <button/> elements register click events using the playbackClick() and muteClick() functions:

```
playButton.addEventListener("click", playbackClick);

muteButton.addEventListener("click", muteClick);
```

Each of the five functions in this example is reduced to a single responsibility. This is a good thing because it makes your code easier to manage and maintain (as well as find and fix errors if they occur). The first function is the pauseHandler() function, which as you know, handles the media's pause event:

```
function pauseHandler(e) {
    playButton.innerHTML = "Resume";
}
```

Its job is simple; change the text of the Play/Pause button to Resume when the pause event fires. This way, the button's text changes as the state of the video changes.

The next function is playingHandler(), the counterpart to the pauseHandler() function:

```
function playingHandler(e) {
    playButton.innerHTML = "Pause";
}
```

When the media plays, this function changes the Play/Pause button's text to Pause.

The volumechangeHandler() function is slightly more complicated because it fires for two types of events—when the volume changes and when the media is muted:

```
function volumechangeHandler(e) {
    muteButton.innerHTML = video.muted ? "Unmute" : "Mute";
}
```

Like the other media event handlers, `volumechangeHandler()` is responsible for changing the text of buttons in the UI. But to know which text value to use, you have to check the value of `video.muted`. You use the ternary operator here to reduce the code to a single line. You could use `if...else` if you wanted to:

```
if (video.muted) {
    muteButton.innerHTML = "Unmute";
} else {
    muteButton.innerHTML = "Mute";
}
```

This approach would be ideal if you needed to execute more code within the `if...else` statement, but in this case, the ternary approach might be better.

Next is the `playbackClick()` function, and it has changed significantly. Because the pause and playing event handlers are responsible for updating the UI, the `playbackClick()` function is only responsible for playing and pausing the media:

```
function playbackClick(e) {
    video.paused ? video.play() : video.pause();
}
```

Once again, you use the ternary operator to determine which method to execute. If `video.paused` is `true`, you call the `play()` method. Otherwise, you call `pause()`.

The `muteClick()` function has also been simplified because it is no longer responsible for updating the UI. It is solely responsible for muting and unmuting the media:

```
function muteClick(e) {
    video.muted = !video.muted;
}
```

You set the `muted` property to the opposite value. Therefore, if `muted` is `true`, it's set to `false`, and vice versa.

Native media is a feature that web developers have clamored for, for many years, and the first implementation (as specified by HTML5) is very robust and feature-filled. We unfortunately, however, still have to battle with the different browsers and the codecs they support. Hopefully, the web development community will see a unified set of codecs that are supported by all browsers.

Naturally, we've only scratched the surface of the native media API and what you can do with it. As with everything, experiment! The sky's the limit with such a robust and capable API.

SUMMARY

This chapter introduced you to the HTML5 video and audio API.

➤ You learned that HTML5 brings two new media elements: `<video/>` and `<audio/>`. It also defines a `<source/>` element to describe a media source.

➤ Unsurprisingly, different browsers support different video and audio formats and codecs, but you can address this issue by providing multiple sources. The browser is smart enough to know which one to load.

➤ Video and audio are programmatically identical—except video has a poster property. Both types of media are represented as HTMLMediaElement objects in the DOM.

➤ You learned how to play and pause media.

➤ You learned how to mute media and query the state of playback using the paused property.

➤ You learned how to register event listeners for the many media-based events, which allowed you to simplify your custom UI's code.

EXERCISES

You can find suggested solutions for these questions in Appendix A.

1. Being able to control playback is cool, but your custom UI needs to also control volume. Add an <input type="range" /> element to Example 3 to control the volume. Remember that the range of volume supported by media elements is 0.0 to 1.0. Look back at Chapter 11 if you need a refresher of the range input type. This unfortunately will not work in IE.

2. Add another range form control to Question 1's answer, and program it to seek the media. It should also update as the media plays. Use the durationchange event to set the slider's max value, and the timeupdate event to update the slider's value.

jQuery

JavaScript is essential to web development. And even though JavaScript development is relatively straightforward today, it was extremely challenging until early 2011 when Microsoft released the ninth version of Internet Explorer.

Let's rewind the clock to the year 2001. The first browser wars were coming to a close, and Microsoft sealed its overwhelming victory with IE6's release. A few months later the software giant released Windows XP, the longest-supported operating system in Microsoft's history, with IE6 as its default browser.

At first, Microsoft enjoyed its 85 percent market share, but as the years passed, growing pressure from Mozilla's Firefox spurred Microsoft to resume development on IE. In 2006, Microsoft released IE7. This new version included many bug fixes, as well as the implementation of new (and often nonstandard) features.

This was the beginning of a very challenging time for JavaScript developers. The problem with client-side development was the many different web browsers developers needed to support. Not only did developers have to support IE and Firefox, but developers had to support three major versions of IE (6, 7, and 8). Be it writing event-driven code or an Ajax application, somewhere down the line developers ran into the many incompatibilities between different browsers and versions.

Many professional developers found cross-browser development to be too time-consuming and cumbersome to deal with on a daily basis, so they set out to develop frameworks or libraries to aid in their cross-browser development. Some developers released their frameworks to the public, and a few of them gained quite a following. And much like the browser wars of old, eventually a victor emerged. Frameworks such as MooTools and Prototype were quite popular, but jQuery became the de facto standard.

jQuery, like most other frameworks, originated as an Ajax library to simplify client/server communication. Today, however, jQuery simplifies just about every common aspect of JavaScript development; DOM manipulation, Ajax, animation, and component development are much easier with jQuery. In this chapter, you look at jQuery and learn how to use it to simplify your JavaScript development.

Before beginning, a word of note: There is no doubt that jQuery adds benefit to your development time and process. But it is not a substitute for a solid understanding of the JavaScript language and the intricacies of the different browsers for which you have to develop. Frameworks and libraries come and go, but knowledge (and pure JavaScript) is forever.

GETTING jQUERY

Installing jQuery (or any framework for that matter) is very different from installing an application on your computer; there is no setup program, and the installation doesn't change any portion of your system. Basically, all you do is reference the jQuery JavaScript file in your web page.

Open your browser and go to http://jquery.com/download/. On this page, you'll find several links to different jQuery-related files. First, you'll see two versions of jQuery: 1.x and 2.x. The two versions are almost identical except that v1.x supports IE 6, 7, and 8 and v2.x does not.

Second, you'll need to choose the compressed or uncompressed version:

> **Compressed version:** This is *minified* (all comments and unnecessary white space are removed from the code files) to make their size as small as possible; doing so makes them faster to download when someone visits your web page. Unfortunately, the minification process makes the JavaScript code difficult to read if you open it in a text editor, but that's a reasonable trade-off in a production environment.

> **Uncompressed version:** This is not minified; it is simply normal JavaScript code files with their white space and comments intact. It's perfectly OK to use uncompressed JavaScript files. Because they are easier to read than compressed files, you can learn much from the gurus who design and develop these frameworks. However, if you plan to roll out a web page using

a framework, be sure to download and use the compressed version, because its file sizes are smaller and download faster.

> **NOTE** *The production version of jQuery 2.1.1 is provided in the code download from Wrox.*

You can obtain jQuery in one of two ways. First, simply download whichever version you prefer by right-clicking (or control-clicking on a Mac) the link, and save it in a location you can easily get to.

Alternatively, you can use jQuery's Content Delivery Network (CDN) to add jQuery to your web pages. This prevents you from having to download your own copy of jQuery, and it can also slightly increase the performance of your web pages.

Regardless of how you obtain jQuery, you add it to your pages just like any other external JavaScript file with the <script/> element:

```
<script src="jquery-2.1.1.min.js"></script>
<script src="//code.jquery.com/jquery-2.1.1.min.js"></script>
```

The only difference is the value of the src attribute. The first <script/> element in this example uses a local copy of jQuery 2.1.1, whereas the second uses jQuery's CDN. The examples in this chapter use a local copy of jQuery.

jQUERY'S API

jQuery is JavaScript, but it changes the way that you interact with the browser and document. Whether you're creating HTML elements and appending them to the page or making Ajax calls to the server, jQuery lets you do it in an easy fashion.

At the heart of jQuery is the jQuery() function, but in most cases, you won't write your code with jQuery(). Instead, you'll use an alias: the dollar function, $(). This can seem very weird at first, but it will become completely natural the more you use it.

You'll use the $() function for just about everything, including:

➤ Finding and selecting elements

➤ Creating, appending, and removing elements

➤ Wrapping normal DOM objects with jQuery objects

Selecting Elements

jQuery revolutionized the way developers find elements in the DOM: with CSS selectors. In fact, the querySelector() and querySelectorAll() methods discussed in Chapter 9 exist because of jQuery. To retrieve elements with jQuery, you use $() and pass it your CSS selector, like this:

```
var elements = $("a");
```

This code assigns a special object, called a jQuery object, that represents an array of all `<a/>` elements in the page to the elements variable.

jQuery was designed to make DOM manipulation easy, and because of this design philosophy, you can make changes to several elements at the same time. For example, imagine you built a web page with more than 100 links in the document, and one day you decide you want them to open in a new window by setting the target attribute to _blank. That's a tall task to take on, but it is something you can easily achieve with jQuery. Because you can retrieve all `<a/>` elements in the document by calling $("a"), you can call the attr() method, which gets or sets the value of an attribute, to set the target attribute. The following code does this:

```
elements.attr("target", "_blank");
```

Calling $("a") results in a jQuery object, but this object also doubles as an array. Any method you call on this particular jQuery object will perform the same operation on all elements in the array. By executing this line of code, you set the target attribute to _blank on every `<a/>` element in the page, and you didn't even have to use a loop!

Because jQuery objects are an array, you can use the length property to find out how many elements were selected with a CSS query:

```
var length = elements.length;
```

This information can be useful, but you usually won't need to know the length of a jQuery object. The most common use of an array's length property is for looping, and jQuery is designed to work with multiple elements at the same time. The methods you execute on a jQuery object have built-in loops; so, the length property is rarely used.

jQuery has a built-in CSS selector engine, and you can use just about any valid CSS selector to retrieve your desired elements—even if the browser doesn't support it. For example, IE6 does not support the parent > child CSS selector. If you have the unfortunate need to support that browser, jQuery can still select the appropriate elements with that selector. Consider the following HTML as an example:

```
<p>
    <div>Div 1</div>
    <div>Div 2</div>
    <span>Span 1</div>
</p>

<span>Span 2</span>
```

This HTML code defines a `<p/>` element that contains two `<div/>` elements and a `<span/>` element. Outside the `<p/>` element is another `<span/>` element. Let's say that you need the `<span/>` element inside the paragraph. You can easily select that element with the following:

```
var innerSpan = $("p > span");
```

This line of code uses the parent > child CSS selector syntax, and because jQuery has its own CSS selector engine, this code will work in every browser.

jQuery also lets you use multiple selectors in one function call. Simply delimit each selector with a comma as shown in the following code:

```
$("a, #myDiv, .myCssClass, p > span")
```

This code retrieves all <a/> elements, an element with an id of myDiv, elements with the CSS class myCssClass, and all <span/> children of <p/> elements. If you wanted to change the text's color of these elements to red, you could simply use the following code:

```
$("a, #myDiv, .myCssClass, p > span").attr("style", "color:red;");
```

This isn't the best way to change an element's style. In fact, jQuery provides you with many methods to alter an element's style.

> **NOTE** For a complete list of supported selectors, see `http://docs.jquery.com/Selectors`.

Changing Style

Changing an element's style requires you to either modify individual CSS properties or manipulate its CSS classes. jQuery makes it easy to do both. To change individual CSS properties, the jQuery object has a method called css(), and you can use this method in two ways.

First, you can pass two arguments to the css() method: the CSS property's name and its value. For example:

```
$("#myDiv").css("color", "red");
```

This code sets the color property to red, thus changing the element's text color to red. The property names you pass to the css() method can be in either style sheet format or in script format. That means if you want to change an element's background color, you can pass background-color or backgroundColor to the method, like this:

```
var allParagraphs = $("p");

allParagraphs.css("background-color", "yellow"); // correct!
allParagraphs.css("backgroundColor", "blue"); // correct, too!
```

This code changes the background color of every <p/> element in the page to yellow and then to blue.

> **NOTE** It's important to remember that jQuery's methods work with one or multiple elements. It doesn't matter how many elements are referenced by a jQuery object, a method like css() will change the style of every element in the object.

Many times, however, you need to change more than one CSS property. Although you can easily accomplish this by calling css() multiple times like this:

```
// don't do this
allParagraphs.css("color", "blue");
allParagraphs.css("background-color", "yellow");
```

a better solution would be to pass an object that contains the CSS properties and their values to the css() method. The following code calls css() once and achieves the same results:

```
allParagraphs.css({
    color: "blue",
    backgroundColor: "yellow"
});
```

Here, you pass an object that has color and backgroundColor properties to the css() method, and jQuery changes the element's or elements' text color to blue and background color to yellow.

Typically, though, if you want to change an element's style, it's better to change the element's CSS class instead of individual style properties.

Adding and Removing CSS Classes

The jQuery object exposes several methods to manipulate an element's className property; you can add, remove, and even toggle the classes that are applied to an element.

> **NOTE** Did you know you can assign multiple CSS classes to an element? Simply separate each class name with a space!

Let's assume that the following HTML is in one of your web pages:

```
<div id="content" class="class-one class-two">
    My div with two CSS classes!
</div>
```

This HTML defines a <div/> element with two CSS classes, class-one and class-two. You need to apply two more classes (class-three and class-four) to this element, and jQuery makes that very easy to do with the addClass() method. For example:

```
var content = $("#content");

content.addClass("class-three");
content.addClass("class-four");
```

This code first retrieves the <div/> element and then calls the addClass() method to add the desired classes. But you can simplify this code by using a technique called *method chaining*. Most jQuery methods return a jQuery object, so it's possible to call a method immediately after calling another method—essentially chaining the method calls as demonstrated with this code:

```
content.addClass("class-three").addClass("class-four");
```

This code achieves the same results as before but with fewer keystrokes.

> **NOTE** Most jQuery methods return a `jQuery` object, allowing you to immediately call methods one after another.

But you can simplify this code even more because you can pass both CSS class names to `addClass()`, like this:

```
content.addClass("class-three class-four");
```

You just have to separate the class names with a space.

The `removeClass()` method removes one or multiple classes:

```
content.removeClass("class-one");
```

This code uses the `removeClass()` method to remove the `class-one` class from the element. If you need to remove multiple classes, simply separate them with a space, like this:

```
content.removeClass("class-two class-four");
```

As you can see, the same concepts that let you add classes to an element apply to removing classes. But there's one very important difference: The arguments you pass to `removeClass()` are optional. If you do not pass any arguments to `removeClass()`, it will remove all classes from the element:

```
content.removeClass();
```

This code, therefore, removes all CSS classes from the element(s) represented by the `content` object.

Toggling Classes

Although the `addClass()` and `removeClass()` methods are certainly useful, sometimes you need to just toggle a class. In other words, you remove a class if it's present or add it if it's not. jQuery makes this easy with the aptly named `toggleClass()` method:

```
content.toggleClass("class-one");
```

This code first toggles the `class-one` class. If it is already applied to the element, jQuery removes `class-one`. Otherwise, it adds `class-one` to the element's class list.

This behavior is useful when you need to add or remove a specific class from the element. For example, the following code is vanilla JavaScript and DOM coding to add and remove a specific CSS class depending on the type of event:

```
var target = e.target;

if (e.type == "mouseover") {
    target.className = "class-one";
} else if (e.type == "mouseout") {
```

```
        eSrc.className = "";
}
```

You can greatly simplify this code by using the `toggleClass()` method, like this:

```
var target = $(e.target);

if (e.type == "mouseover" || e.type == "mouseout") {
    target.toggleClass("class-one");
}
```

Notice how the `$()` function is used in this code: It passes `e.target`, a DOM object, to `$()`. This can at first seem like a strange thing to do, but remember what we said earlier: `$()` is used for many things. One of those things is to *wrap* a normal DOM object with a jQuery object.

In technical terms, we call the resulting jQuery object a *wrapper object*. Wrapper objects are typically used to enhance the functionality of another object. With jQuery, you're wrapping a jQuery object around an element object, enabling you to use jQuery's API to manipulate the element. In the case of this code, you're wrapping a jQuery object around an element object so that you can use `toggleClass()` to toggle the `class-one` class.

Checking if a Class Exists

The last CSS class method is the `hasClass()` method, and it returns `true` or `false` depending on if an element has the specified CSS class. For example:

```
var hasClassOne = content.hasClass("class-one");
```

This code uses `hasClass()` to determine if the `class-one` is applied to `content`. If it is, `hasClassOne` is `true`. Otherwise, it's `false`.

Creating, Appending, and Removing Elements

Think back to Chapter 9 and how you create and append elements to the page. The following code will refresh your memory:

```
var a = document.createElement("a");

a.id = "myLink";
a.setAttribute("href", "http://jquery.com");
a.setAttribute("title", "jQuery's Website");

var text = document.createTextNode("Click to go to jQuery's website");

a.appendChild(text);
document.body.appendChild(a);
```

This code creates an `<a/>` element, assigns it an `id`, and sets the `href` and `title` attributes. It then creates a text node and assigns the object to the `text` variable. Finally, it appends the text node to the `<a/>` element and appends the `<a/>` element to the document's `<body/>` element. It goes without saying that creating elements with the DOM methods requires a lot of code.

Creating Elements

jQuery simplifies how you create elements with JavaScript. The following code shows you one way:

```
var a = $("<a/>").attr({
    id: "myLink",
    href: "http://jquery.com",
    title: "jQuery's Website"
}).text("Click here to go to jQuery's website");

$(document.body).append(a);
```

Let's break down this code to get a better understanding of what's taking place. First, this code calls $() and passes it the HTML to create. In this case, it's an <a/> element:

```
var a = $("<a/>")
```

Next, it chains the attr() method to set the <a/> element's attributes:

```
.attr({
    id: "myLink",
    href: "http://jquery.com",
    title: "jQuery's Website"
})
```

The attr() method is a lot like the css() method in that you can set an individual attribute by passing it the attribute's name and value, or you can set multiple attributes by passing an object that contains the attributes and their values.

The code then chains the text() method, setting the element's text:

```
.text("Click here to go to jQuery's website");
```

You can also create the same element by passing the entire HTML to $(), like this:

```
var a = $('<a href="http://jquery.com" title="jQuery\'s Website">' +
        "Click here to go to jQuery's website</a>");
```

This approach, however, can become less of a benefit and more of a hassle. Not only do you have to keep track of which type of quote you use where, but you might also have to escape quotes.

Appending Elements

The append() method is similar to the DOM appendChild() method in that it appends child nodes to the parent object. The similarities end there because jQuery's append() method is much more flexible than its DOM counterpart. The append() method can accept a DOM object, a jQuery object, or a string containing HTML or text content. Regardless of what you pass as the parameter to append(), it will append the content to the DOM object.

The previous code appends the jQuery-created <a/> element to the document's body, like this:

```
$(document.body).append(a);
```

Once again, the $() function wraps a jQuery object around the native document.body object to take advantage of jQuery's simple API.

Removing Elements

Removing elements from the DOM is also much easier with jQuery than with traditional DOM methods. With DOM methods, you need at least two element objects: the element you want to remove and its parent element.

As with everything thus far, jQuery simplifies this process. The only thing you need is the element that you want to remove. Simply call jQuery's remove() method, and it removes the element. For example:

```
$(".class-one").remove();
```

This code finds all elements that have the class-one CSS class and removes them from the document.

You can also completely empty, or remove all children of, an element with the aptly named empty() method. If you wanted to remove every element within the <body/>, you could use the following code:

```
$(document.body).empty();
```

Most DOM changes you'll make are in response to something the user did, whether moving the mouse over a particular element or clicking somewhere on the page. So naturally, you'll have to handle events at some point.

Handling Events

When jQuery was created, JavaScript developers had to contend with both the W3C standard and legacy IE event models. Although many developers wrote and used their own event utilities, the vast majority looked to third-party tools to make cross-browser code easier to write and maintain. jQuery was one such tool, and while standard support has gotten substantially better in all browsers, jQuery's event API, specifically the methods used to register event listeners, is still easier to use.

All jQuery objects expose a method called on() that you use to register event listeners for one or more events on the selected elements. Its most basic usage is very simple, as demonstrated here:

```
function elementClick(e) {
    alert("You clicked me!");
}

$(".class-one").on("click", elementClick);
```

This code registers a click event listener on all elements that have a class-one CSS class. Therefore, the elementClick() function executes when the user clicks any of these elements.

You can also register multiple event listeners with the same event handler function by passing multiple event names in the first argument. Simply separate each event name with a space, like this:

```
function eventHandler(e) {
    if (e.type == "click") {
        alert("You clicked me!");
```

```
        } else {
            alert("You double-clicked me!");
        }
    }

    $(".class-two").on("click dblclick", eventHandler);
```

This code registers event listeners for the click and dblclick events on all elements with a class-two CSS class. The code inside eventHandler() determines what event caused the function to execute and responds appropriately.

Although it can be useful to use a single function for handling multiple events, jQuery also lets you define multiple event listeners with different functions. Instead of passing two arguments to on() as shown in the previous examples, you pass an ordinary JavaScript object in which the properties are the event names, and their values are the functions that handle the events. For example:

```
function clickHandler(e) {
    alert("You clicked me!");
}

function dblclickHandler(e) {
    alert("You double-clicked me!");
}

$(".class-three").on({
    click: clickHandler,
    dblclick: dblclickHandler
});
```

This code registers click and dblclick event listeners for every element with the class-three CSS class; different functions handle the click and dblclick events.

Removing event listeners is equally simple with the off() method. Simply supply the same information you passed to on(). The following code removes the event listeners registered in the previous examples:

```
$(".class-one").off("click", elementClick);
$(".class-two").off("click dblclick", eventHandler);
$(".class-three").off({
    click: clickHandler,
    dblclick: dblclickHandler
});
```

You can also use the off() method to remove all event listeners for the selected elements by not passing any arguments to the method:

```
$(".class-four").off();
```

The jQuery Event Object

As you learned in Chapter 10, some big differences exist between the standard and legacy IE event models. Remember that jQuery was created to make cross-browser JavaScript easier to write and maintain. So when it came to events, John Resig, the creator of jQuery, decided to create his own `Event` object and base it on the standard DOM `Event` object. This means that you do not have to worry about supporting multiple event models; it's already done for you. All you have to do is write standard code inside your event handlers.

To demonstrate, you can write something like the following code, and it'll work in every browser:

```
function clickHandler(e) {
    e.preventDefault();

    alert(e.target.tagName + " clicked was clicked.");
}

$(".class-two").on("click", clickHandler);
```

> **NOTE** For a complete list of supported events, see jQuery's website at
> `http://docs.jquery.com/Events`.

Rewriting the Tab Strip with jQuery

You have learned how to retrieve elements in the DOM, change an element's style by adding and removing classes, add and remove elements from the page, and use events with jQuery.

Now you'll put this newfound knowledge to work by refactoring the toolbar from Chapter 10.

TRY IT OUT Revisiting the Tab Strip with jQuery

Open your text editor and type the following code:

```
<!DOCTYPE html>

<html lang="en">
<head>
    <title>Chapter 16: Example 1</title>
    <style>
        .tabStrip {
            background-color: #E4E2D5;
            padding: 3px;
            height: 22px;
        }

        .tabStrip div {
            float: left;
            font: 14px arial;
            cursor: pointer;
        }

        .tabStrip-tab {
            padding: 3px;
```

```
            }

            .tabStrip-tab-hover {
                border: 1px solid #316AC5;
                background-color: #C1D2EE;
                padding: 2px;
            }

            .tabStrip-tab-click {
                border: 1px solid #facc5a;
                background-color: #f9e391;
                padding: 2px;
            }
        </style>
    </head>
    <body>
        <div class="tabStrip">
            <div data-tab-number="1" class="tabStrip-tab">Tab 1</div>
            <div data-tab-number="2" class="tabStrip-tab">Tab 2</div>
            <div data-tab-number="3" class="tabStrip-tab">Tab 3</div>
        </div>
        <div id="descContainer"></div>

        <script src="jquery-2.1.1.min.js"></script>
        <script>
            function handleEvent(e) {
                var target = $(e.target);
                var type = e.type;

                if (type == "mouseover" || type == "mouseout") {
                    target.toggleClass("tabStrip-tab-hover");
                } else if (type == "click") {
                    target.addClass("tabStrip-tab-click");

                    var num = target.attr("data-tab-number");
                    showDescription(num);
                }
            }

            function showDescription(num) {
                var text = "Description for Tab " + num;

                $("#descContainer").text(text);
            }

            $(".tabStrip > div").on("mouseover mouseout click", handleEvent);
        </script>
    </body>
</html>
```

Save this as ch16_example1.html and open it in your browser and notice that its behavior is identical to that of ch10_example17.html.

If you compare this example with ch10_example17.html, you'll notice quite a few differences in the code's structure. Let's start with the very last line of code where you register the event listeners. Your tab strip needs to respond to the `mouseover`, `mouseout`, and `click` events on the `<div/>` elements inside of the tab strip. jQuery makes it extremely easy to register event listeners on these `<div/>` elements for the desired events:

```
$(".tabStrip > div").on("mouseover mouseout click", handleEvent);
```

This code selects all "tab elements" in the document with jQuery's `$()` function and uses the `on()` method to register the `mouseover`, `mouseout`, and `click` event listeners on those elements.

jQuery code aside, this approach is different from the original. Here, the event listeners are on the `<div/>` elements themselves as opposed to `document`. This will simplify the `handleEvent()` function. Let's look at that now.

The first two lines of `handleEvent()` do two things. The first line wraps a jQuery object around the event target, and the second gets the type of event that occurred:

```
function handleEvent(e) {
    var target = $(e.target);
    var type = e.type;
```

In the original version of this code, you used both the event type and the target's CSS class to determine which new CSS class you assigned to the element's `className` property. In this new version, you only need to know the event type. For `mouseover` and `mouseout` events, you simply toggle the `tabStrip-tab-hover` class:

```
if (type == "mouseover" || type == "mouseout") {
    target.toggleClass("tabStrip-tab-hover");
}
```

But for `click` events, your new code closely resembles the original's. First, you add the `tabStrip-tab-click` class to the element using jQuery's `addClass()` method:

```
else if (type == "click") {
    target.addClass("tabStrip-tab-click");

    var num = target.attr("data-tab-number");
    showDescription(num);
}
```

Then you get the value of the `data-tab-number` attribute. You could optionally use jQuery's `data()` method to do the same thing by passing it the attribute name without `data-`, like this: `data("tab-number")`.

Once you have the tab's number, you pass it on to `showDescription()`. This function did not change much; it simply uses jQuery's API to accomplish its task:

```
function showDescription(num) {
    var text = "Description for Tab " + num;

    $("#descContainer").text(text);
}
```

After you build the description text, you select the element serving as the description container and set its text using jQuery's text() method.

As you can see from this example, jQuery simplifies DOM manipulation and event handling. In this particular example, you wrote less JavaScript to attain the same results. That's well worth the time of learning jQuery, isn't it?

But that's not all; jQuery can do the same thing for your Ajax code.

Using jQuery for Ajax

In Chapter 14, you learned about Ajax and how asynchronous requests require you to write a lot of extra code. You wrote a simple utility to help alleviate the complexity of Ajax code, but jQuery can simplify Ajax even more.

Understanding the jQuery Function

The jQuery function ($()) is the doorway into all things jQuery, and you've used it quite a bit throughout this chapter. However, this function has other uses.

Functions are objects and they have a property called prototype. Like all other objects, you access a Function object's properties and methods using the object.property or object.method() syntax. Well, jQuery's $ function has many methods, and some of them are for making Ajax requests. One of them is the get() method, which is for making GET requests. The following code shows an example:

```
$.get("textFile.txt");
```

This code makes a GET request to the server for the textFile.txt file. But this code isn't very useful because it doesn't do anything with the server's response. So like the HttpRequest module you built in Chapter 14, the $.get() method lets you define a callback function that handles the response from the server:

```
function handleResponse(data) {
    alert(data);
}

$.get("textFile.txt", handleResponse);
```

This code defines a function called handleResponse() and passes it to $.get(). jQuery calls this function on a successful request and passes it the requested data (represented by the data parameter).

Remember the examples from Chapter 14? You created a form that checked if usernames and e-mail addresses were available using Ajax, and you sent those values to the server as parameters in the URL. For example, when you wanted to test a username, you used the username parameter, like this:

```
phpformvalidator.php?username=jmcpeak
```

With the $.get() method, you can do the same thing by passing an object containing the key/value pairs to the method. For example:

```
var parms = {
    username = "jmcpeak"
};

function handleResponse(json) {
    var obj = JSON.parse(json);

    // do something with obj
}

$.get("phpformvalidator.php", parms, handleResponse);
```

This code creates a new object called parms, and it has a username property with the value of jmcpeak. This object is passed to the $.get() method as the second argument, with the handleResponse() callback function passed as the third.

You can send as many parameters as you need; simply add them as properties to the parameter object.

Automatically Parsing JSON Data

In Chapter 14, the form validator PHP file returns the requested data in JSON format, and notice that the previous sample code expects JSON data and parses it with the JSON.parse() method. jQuery can eliminate this step and parse the response for you. Simply use the $.getJSON() method instead of $.get(). For example:

```
var parms = {
    username = "jmcpeak"
};

function handleResponse(obj) {
    // obj is already an object
}

$.getJSON("phpformvalidator.php", parms, handleResponse);
```

This code is almost identical to the previous example except for two things. First, this code uses $.getJSON() to issue a request to the PHP file. By doing so, you are expecting JSON-formatted data in the response, and jQuery will automatically parse it into a JavaScript object.

The second difference is inside the handleResponse() function. Because the response is automatically parsed, you don't have to call JSON.parse() in handleResponse().

The jqXHR Object

As you've seen in the previous sections, jQuery's get() and getJSON() methods do not actually return the data you requested; they rely upon a callback function that you provide and pass the requested data to it. But these methods do, in fact, return something useful: a special jqXHR object.

The `jqXHR` object is called a *deferred* object; it represents a task that hasn't yet completed. When you think about it, an asynchronous Ajax request is a deferred task because it doesn't immediately complete. After you make the initial request, you're left waiting for a response from the server.

jQuery's `jqXHR` object has many methods that represent different stages of a deferred task, but for the sake of this discussion, you'll look at only three. They are:

METHOD NAME	DESCRIPTION
`done()`	Executes when the deferred task successfully completes
`fail()`	Executes when the task fails
`always()`	Always executes, regardless if the task completed or failed

These methods let you add functions to what are called *callback queues*—collections of functions that serve as callbacks for a specified purpose. For example, the `done()` method lets you add functions to the "done" callback queue, and when the deferred action successfully completes, all of the functions in the "done" queue execute.

With this in mind, you can rewrite the previous code like this:

```
var parms = {
    username = "jmcpeak"
};

function handleResponse(obj) {
    // obj is already an object
}

var xhr = $.getJSON("phpformvalidator.php", parms);

xhr.done(handleResponse);
```

Notice that in this code, the `handleResponse()` function isn't passed to the `getJSON()` method; instead, it's added to the "done" queue by passing it to the `jqXHR` object's `done()` method. In most cases, you'd see this code written as follows:

```
$.getJSON("phpformvalidator.php", parms).done(handleResponse);
```

You can also chain these method calls to easily add multiple functions to the callback queues:

```
$.getJSON("phpformvalidator.php", parms)
        .done(handleResponse)
        .done(displaySuccessMessage)
        .fail(displayErrorMessage);
```

In this example, two functions, `handleResponse()` and `displaySuccessMessage()`, are added to the "done" queue; when the Ajax call successfully completes, both of these functions will execute. Additionally, this code adds the `displayErrorMessage()` function to the "fail" queue, and it executes if the Ajax request fails.

Using these callback queue methods does require you to write slightly more code, but they make your code's intentions absolutely clear. Plus, using them is generally accepted as a best practice, and you'll find them used in most modern jQuery-based code that you read.

Apply what you've learned and modify the form validator from ch14_example1.html. Open your text editor and type the following code:

```html
<!DOCTYPE html>

<html lang="en">
<head>
    <title>Chapter 16: Example 2</title>
    <style>
        .fieldname {
            text-align: right;
        }

        .submit {
            text-align: right;
        }
    </style>
</head>
<body>
    <form>
        <table>
            <tr>
                <td class="fieldname">
                    Username:
                </td>
                <td>
                    <input type="text" id="username" />
                </td>
                <td>
                    <a id="usernameAvailability" href="#">Check Availability</a>
                </td>
            </tr>
            <tr>
                <td class="fieldname">
                    Email:
                </td>
                <td>
                    <input type="text" id="email" />
                </td>
                <td>
                    <a id="emailAvailability" href="#">Check Availability</a>
                </td>
            </tr>
            <tr>
                <td class="fieldname">
                    Password:
                </td>
                <td>
```

```
                    <input type="text" id="password" />
                </td>
                <td />
            </tr>
            <tr>
                <td class="fieldname">
                    Verify Password:
                </td>
                <td>
                    <input type="text" id="password2" />
                </td>
                <td />
            </tr>
            <tr>
                <td colspan="2" class="submit">
                    <input type="submit" value="Submit" />
                </td>
                <td />
            </tr>
        </table>
    </form>
    <script src="jquery-2.1.1.min.js"></script>
    <script>
        function checkUsername(e) {
            e.preventDefault();

            var userValue = $("#username").val();

            if (!userValue) {
                alert("Please enter a user name to check!");
                return;
            }

            var parms = {
                username: userValue
            };

            $.getJSON("ch14_formvalidator.php", parms).done(handleResponse);
        }

        function checkEmail(e) {
            e.preventDefault();

            var emailValue = $("#email").val();

            if (!emailValue) {
                alert("Please enter an email address to check!");
                return;
            }

            var parms = {
                email: emailValue
            };

            $.getJSON("ch14_formvalidator.php", parms).done(handleResponse);
```

```
        }

        function handleResponse(response) {
            if (response.available) {
                alert(response.searchTerm + " is available!");
            } else {
                alert("We're sorry, but " + response.searchTerm +
                    " is not available.");
            }
        }

        $("#usernameAvailability").on("click", checkUsername);
        $("#emailAvailability").on("click", checkEmail);
    </script>
</body>

</html>
```

Save this as ch16_example2.html in your web server's root directory. Like the examples in Chapter 14, this file must be hosted on a web server in order to work correctly. Open your web browser to http://yourserver/ch16_example2.html. Type **jmcpeak** into the Username field and click the Check Availability link next to it. You'll see an alert box telling you the username is taken.

Now type **someone@xyz.com** in the Email field and click the Check Availability link next to it. Again, you'll be greeted with an alert box stating that the e-mail is already in use. Now input your own username and e-mail into these fields and click the appropriate links. Chances are an alert box will tell you that your username and/or e-mail is available (the usernames jmcpeak and pwilton and the e-mails someone@xyz.com and someone@zyx.com are the only ones used by the application).

The HTML and CSS in this example are identical to ch14_example1.html. So, let's dig into the JavaScript starting with the final two lines of code that set up the click event listeners on the Check Availability links. You could easily reuse the code from the original, but jQuery makes it a little easier to set up events:

```
$("#usernameAvailability").on("click", checkUsername);
$("#emailAvailability").on("click", checkEmail);
```

You select the elements by their ID and use jQuery's on() method to register the click event on those elements. Once again, checking the username value is the job of checkUsername(), and checkEmail() is responsible for checking the e-mail value.

The new checkUsername() function is somewhat similar to the original. You start by preventing the default behavior of the event by calling e.preventDefault():

```
function checkUsername(e) {
    e.preventDefault();
```

Next, you need to get the value of the appropriate <input/> element. You haven't learned how to retrieve the value of a form control with jQuery, but don't worry—it's very simple:

```
var userValue = $("#username").val();

if (!userValue) {
```

```
            alert("Please enter a user name to check!");
            return;
    }
```

You use $() to select the appropriate `<input/>` element and call the `val()` method. This retrieves the value of the form control and assigns it to the `userValue` variable.

After you validate the user's input, you're ready to start issuing a GET request to the server. First, you create an object to contain the information you want to send to the server:

```
        var parms = {
            username: userValue
        };
```

You call this object `parms` and populate it with the username property. As you learned earlier in this chapter, jQuery will add this property and its value to the query string.

Now, you can send the request using jQuery's `getJSON()` method:

```
        $.getJSON("ch14_formvalidator.php", parms).done(handleResponse);
    }
```

You add the `handleResponse()` function to the "done" queue, so that when the request successfully completes, an `alert` box will display the search results.

The new `checkEmail()` function is very similar to `checkUsername()`. The two main differences, of course, are the data you retrieve from the form and the data you send to the server:

```
    function checkEmail(e) {
        e.preventDefault();

        var emailValue = $("#email").val();

        if (!emailValue) {
            alert("Please enter an email address to check!");
            return;
        }

        var parms = {
            email: emailValue
        };

        $.getJSON("ch14_formvalidator.php", parms).done(handleResponse);
    }
```

The final function, `handleResponse()`, is mostly unchanged from the original version. Because jQuery's `getJSON()` method automatically parses the response into a JavaScript object, the new `handleResponse()` function simply uses the passed data as-is:

```
    function handleResponse(response) {
        if (response.available) {
            alert(response.searchTerm + " is available!");
        } else {
```

```
            alert("We're sorry, but " + response.searchTerm + " is not available.");
        }
    }
}
```

jQuery is an extensive framework, and adequately covering the topic in depth requires much more than this chapter can provide. Entire books are devoted to jQuery! However, the jQuery documentation is quite good, and you can view it at http://docs.jquery.com. jQuery's website also lists a variety of tutorials, so don't forget to check them out at http://docs.jquery.com/Tutorials.

SUMMARY

This chapter introduced you to jQuery, the most popular JavaScript library.

➤ You learned where and how to obtain jQuery and reference it in your pages.

➤ You also learned about jQuery's $() function, and how it is central to jQuery's functionality.

➤ jQuery popularized using CSS selectors to find elements within the DOM, and you learned how find elements with the $() function.

➤ You can change element styles with either the css() method, or by modifying the CSS classes with the addClass(), removeClass(), and toggleClass() methods.

➤ Cross-browser events can be a drag when dealing with older browser versions, but jQuery make registering event listeners and working with event data easy (and mostly standards compliant).

➤ jQuery also simplifies Ajax with its get() and getJSON() methods, and you learned that getJSON() automatically parses the response into a JavaScript object.

➤ You learned about deferred objects. You also learned about the "done," "fail," and "always" queues, and how you can chain them together to assign multiple handlers to the different queues.

EXERCISES

You can find suggested solutions for these questions in Appendix A.

1. Example 1 is based on Chapter 10's Example 17, and as you probably remember, you modified that example in response to one of Chapter 10's exercise questions. Modify this chapter's Example 1 so that only one tab is active at a time.

2. There is some repetitive code in Example 2. Refactor the code to reduce the duplication. Additionally, add a function to handle any errors that may occur with the request.

17

Other JavaScript Libraries

WHAT YOU WILL LEARN IN THIS CHAPTER:

➤ Using Modernizr to write feature-specific code

➤ Loading external resources for browsers that do not support certain features

➤ Using Prototype and MooTools to perform common tasks, such as DOM manipulation and Ajax requests

WROX.COM CODE DOWNLOADS FOR THIS CHAPTER

You can find the wrox.com code downloads for this chapter at http://www.wiley.com/go/BeginningJavaScript5E on the Download Code tab. You can also view all of the examples and related files at http://beginningjs.com.

jQuery is the most popular JavaScript library today. It's used on hundreds of thousands of websites, and yet it's not the only library JavaScript developers use. In fact, thousands of JavaScript libraries and utilities are available, and each one can typically be categorized into two groups: general and specialty.

The aim of general frameworks is to balance the differences between browsers by creating a new, unified API to perform general tasks like DOM manipulation and Ajax functionality (jQuery is a general framework). Specialty frameworks, on the other hand, focus on a specific ability, such as feature detection. So identify what it is you want to achieve and choose a framework based on that. For example, if you wanted to perform animations and only animations, the script.aculo.us framework (http://script.aculo.us/) could be a good choice for you.

This chapter looks at both general and specific frameworks. When deciding which framework to use, look at the framework's browser support, documentation, and community involvement.

The frameworks covered in this chapter are established, stable, popular, and compatible with every major modern browser (and even legacy versions of IE). You'll learn about:

➤ **Modernizr:** A library designed to detect HTML5 and CSS features supported by the browser. (http://modernizr.com/)

➤ **Prototype:** A framework that provides a simple API to perform web tasks. Although it offers ways of manipulating the DOM, Prototype's primary aim is to enhance the JavaScript language by providing class definition and inheritance. (http://www.prototypejs.org)

➤ **MooTools:** A framework that aims to be compact while offering a simple API to make common tasks easier. Like Prototype, MooTools also aims to enhance the JavaScript language—not just make DOM manipulation and Ajax easier. It also includes a lightweight effects component originally called moo.fx. (http://www.mootools.net)

These are just a tiny sampling of what is available for you to use in your web pages. Some other solutions not covered in this chapter are:

➤ **Yahoo! User Interface Framework (YUI):** A framework that ranges from basic JavaScript utilities to complete DHTML widgets. Yahoo! has a team devoted to developing YUI. (http://developer.yahoo.com/yui/)

➤ **Ext JS:** This framework started as an extension to the YUI. It offers customizable UI widgets for building rich Internet applications. (http://www.extjs.com)

➤ **Dojo:** A toolkit designed around a package system. The core functionality resembles that of any other framework (DOM manipulation, event normalization, DHTML widgets, and so on), but it provides and allows a way to add more functionality by adding more packages. (http://www.dojotoolkit.org)

➤ **MochiKit:** A framework that prides itself on its well-testedness (hundreds of tests according to the MochiKit site) and its compatibility with other JavaScript frameworks and libraries. (http://www.mochikit.com)

DIGGING INTO MODERNIZR

As you undoubtedly know from various previous chapters, JavaScript development is not utopia. It never has been, and realistically, it never will be simply due to the fact that multiple browsers exist (which is a good thing—don't get us wrong), and there is a certain disparity between the features those browsers implement. This is especially true as new features are developed and introduced to the browser. For example, HTML5 and CSS3 introduce many new features that some browsers haven't yet implemented. If you want to use any of these new features in your page or application, you have to ensure that the browser your visitor is using properly supports them. Otherwise, your page will break.

In Chapter 8, you learned how to write code that targets specific features through a process called feature detection, and although feature detection is a time-tested strategy, two problems exist:

➤ Some features can be difficult to detect.

➤ Different browsers may support what is essentially the same feature, but it may be implemented differently.

Modernizr fixes these problems by providing a unified API for detecting HTML5 and CSS features in the browser.

> **NOTE** Even though Modernizr offers many CSS-based features, this chapter focuses on Modernizr's JavaScript capabilities. If you are interested in its CSS capabilities, see `http://modernizr.com/docs/` for more information.

Getting Modernizr

Just like every other JavaScript library and framework, Modernizr is nothing more than a JavaScript file that you include within your page. It comes in two different flavors: development (uncompressed) and production (minified). In most cases, the production version is what you want to use in your page or application because it is smaller in size, but the development version could prove useful in certain situations where you need to debug your code along with Modernizr's (you learn about debugging in Chapter 18).

Modernizr also lets you pick and choose the tests you need to perform in your page or application (Figure 17-1). For example, if you only use localStorage or native drag and drop in your page, you can build a customized version of Modernizr that contains only the necessary code for testing the browser's support for those features.

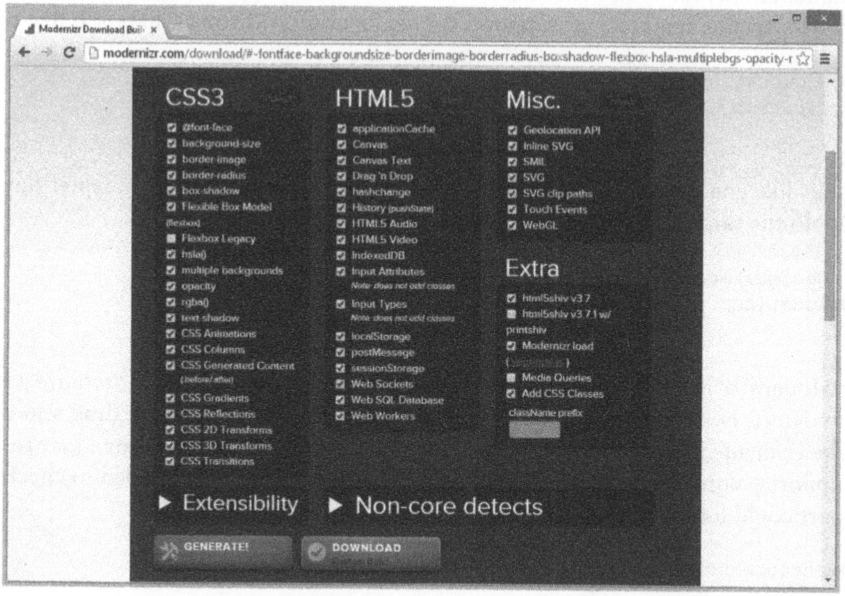

FIGURE 17-1

A feature that Modernizr includes by default is a utility called HTML5 Shiv. This utility is only for legacy versions of IE, and it enables you to style HTML5 elements that are not supported in versions prior to IE9. If you do not plan to target legacy IE, you can omit HTML5 Shiv in your customized build.

Modernizr's download experience varies depending on the version you want to download. The development version includes most tests by default (you can still customize the build if that's your thing), but the download page also has an easy-to-use Download button (as shown in Figure 17-1). Simply clicking the button downloads Modernizr to your computer, and you can save it wherever you need to.

The production version is just as simple to download. Most features are excluded by default, forcing you to pick the features that you need for your page or application. This is actually a good move by the Modernizr folks because you want a customized (and thus optimized) build for your specific needs. After you select your desired features and click the Generate button, the Download button appears.

> **NOTE** *For the sake of simplicity, you can find the full production version (v2.8.3) in the code download for this chapter. You can also download it at* `http://beginningjs.com/modernizr.js`*.*

Modernizr's developers suggest that, for best performance, you reference Modernizr's `<script/>` element inside the `<head/>` and after your style sheet references.

Modernizr's API

Modernizer has a straightforward API that revolves around a single object called `Modernizr`. It has a set of properties and methods that you use to determine if a browser supports a particular feature. For example, you can determine if a browser supports the geolocation API from Chapter 8 like this:

```
if (Modernizr.geolocation) {
    // use geolocation
}
```

At first glance, it looks like you haven't gained much by using Modernizr because in Chapter 8, you learned that you can do the same thing with the `navigator` object, like this:

```
if (navigator.geolocation) {
    // use geolocation
}
```

But remember that Modernizr is a library for detecting many features, even those that require a bit more involvement to detect. For example, the code for determining support for native drag and drop is more complex. The elements in browsers that support native drag and drop have a `draggable` attribute, or they support events like `dragstart` and `drop`. That means the code needed to check for drag and drop support could look like this:

```
var el = document.createElement("span");

if (typeof el.draggable != "undefined" ||
    (typeof el.ondragstart != "undefined" &&
     typeof el.ondrop != "undefined")) {

    // use native drag and drop
}
```

This code creates an arbitrary `<span/>` element and checks if it has a `draggable` property or `ondragstart` and `ondrop` properties. If any of these conditions are true, the browser supports drag and drop.

> **NOTE** The aforementioned test is written to accommodate IE8 because it supports native drag and drop, but it doesn't support the `draggable` attribute/property.

This code, however, is cumbersome to write and read. Modernizr simplifies it to:

```
if (Modernizr.draganddrop) {
    // use drag and drop
}
```

Here, you check the browser's support for drag and drop with Modernizr's `draganddrop` property, and you get the same results as the previous test.

Modernizr checks for a wide variety of HTML5 (and CSS3) features. The following table lists just a few:

HTML5 FEATURE	MODERNIZR PROPERTY
HTML5 Audio	`audio`
M4A Audio	`audio.m4a`
MP3 Audio	`audio.mp3`
OGG Audio	`audio.ogg`
WAV Audio	`audio.wav`
HTML5 Video	`video`
H.264 Video	`video.h264`
OGG Video	`video.ogg`
WebM Video	`video.webm`
Drag and Drop	`draganddrop`
Local Storage	`localstorage`
Geolocation	`geolocation`

In addition to the built-in tests, you can also extend Modernizr with your own tests.

Custom Tests

You can add your own tests to Modernizr with its `addTest()` method. The process is simple: simply call `Modernizr.addTest()`, pass it the name of your test, and pass the function that performs the test.

For example, it was mentioned earlier that although IE8 supports native drag and drop, it does not support the `draggable` attribute/property. You can extend Modernizr to test for this specific functionality like this:

```
Modernizr.addTest("draggable", function(){
    var span = document.createElement("span");
    return typeof span.draggable != "undefined"
});
```

This code adds a new test called `"draggable"`. Its function creates an arbitrary `<span/>` element and checks if it has a `draggable` property. In modern browsers, the `draggable` property defaults to `false`, but it is `undefined` in IE8. Therefore, when you use the test like this:

```
if (!Modernizr.draggable) {
    // code for IE8
}
```

you can run code for browsers that do not support the `draggable` attribute/property.

Sometimes, however, you don't want to use an `if` statement to run code for a specific browser (or a set of browsers). Instead, wouldn't it be nice if you could load an external JavaScript file for browsers that passed or failed a certain test? Modernizr can do that!

Loading Resources

Modernizr has an optional method called `load()` (you can omit it from your custom build), and it's used to load external JavaScript and CSS files based on the result of a test.

The `load()` method's basic usage is simple; you pass it an object that describes the test and resources you want to load. For example:

```
Modernizr.load({
    test: Modernizr.geolocation,
    nope: "geo-polyfill.js",
    yep: "geo.js"
});
```

This code calls `Modernizr.load()` and passes an object that has `test`, `nope`, and `yep` as properties (we'll call this a yepnope object). The `test` property contains the result of the test. If it passes, Modernizr loads the file assigned to the `yep` property (`geo.js` in this example). But if it fails, the file assigned to the `nope` property (`geo-polyfill.js`) is loaded instead.

> **NOTE** A polyfill is a third-party JavaScript component that replicates the standard API for older browsers.

The `yep` and `nope` properties are optional, so you can load only one resource if you need to. For example, the following code loads a JavaScript file only for browsers that do not support the `draggable` attribute/property:

```
Modernizr.load({
    test: Modernizr.draggable,
    nope: "draggable-polyfill.js"
});
```

This type of behavior is ideal in these situations. You don't want or need to load a polyfill for the `draggable` attribute/property for modern browsers, but you do for older browsers, like IE8, that do not support it.

Modernizr's `load()` method also lets you run multiple tests. Instead of passing a single yepnope object, you can pass an array of them, like this:

```
Modernizr.load([{
    test: Modernizr.draggable,
    nope: "draggable-polyfill.js"
},
{
    test: document.addEventListener,
    nope: "event-polyfill.js"
}]);
```

This code passes an array of two yepnope objects to the `load()` method. The first object is the same custom `draggable` test from the previous example. The second object checks if the browser supports the `document.addEventListener()` method; if it doesn't, Modernizr loads an event polyfill.

Modernizr loads external resources asynchronously. This means that the browser will continue to load the rest of the page while Modernizr downloads and executes the external resources. This can cause issues if your page relies on those resources; you have to ensure they are completely loaded before you attempt to use them.

You can avoid this type of issue by adding a `complete` property to your yepnope object. This property should contain a function, and it executes regardless of what happens when all (or even none) of the resources are finished loading. For example:

```
function init() {
    alert("Page initialization goes here!");
}

Modernizr.load([{
    test: Modernizr.draggable,
    nope: "draggable-polyfill.js"
},
{
    test: document.addEventListener,
    nope: "event-polyfill.js",
    complete: init
}]);
```

This new code adds two changes to the previous example. First, it defines a function called `init()`. This function would normally contain code to initialize the JavaScript used on the page (such as setting up event listeners).

The second change is the addition of the complete property to one of the yepnope objects. It's set to the aforementioned init() function, and it always executes—either when the resources are completely loaded, or immediately for browsers that do not need the resources.

TRY IT OUT   Revisiting Native Drag and Drop

As mentioned earlier in this section, IE8 supports native drag and drop, but it doesn't support the draggable attribute/property. In this example, you revisit ch10_example21.html and use Modernizr to load two polyfills: one to support draggable, and another to support the standard DOM event model.

These polyfills are written by Jeremy and are provided in the code download. They are event-polyfill.js and draggable-polyfill.js. Both are open source. Loading these polyfills will make this example work with minimal modifications to the existing code.

Open your text editor and type the following:

```html
<!DOCTYPE html>

<html lang="en">
<head>
    <title>Chapter 17: Example 1</title>
    <style>
        [data-drop-target] {
            height: 400px;
            width: 200px;
            margin: 2px;
            background-color: gainsboro;
            float: left;
        }

        .drag-enter {
            border: 2px dashed #000;
        }

        .box {
            width: 200px;
            height: 200px;
        }

        .navy {
            background-color: navy;
        }

        .red {
            background-color: red;
        }
    </style>
    <script src="modernizr.min.js"></script>
</head>
<body>
    <div data-drop-target="true">
        <div id="box1" draggable="true" class="box navy"></div>
        <div id="box2" draggable="true" class="box red"></div>
```

```
</div>
<div data-drop-target="true"></div>

<script>

    function handleDragStart(e) {
        e.dataTransfer.setData("text", this.id);
    }

    function handleDragEnterLeave(e) {
        if (e.type == "dragenter") {
            this.className = "drag-enter";
        } else {
            this.className = "";
        }
    }

    function handleOverDrop(e) {
        e.preventDefault();

        if (e.type != "drop") {
            return;
        }

        var draggedId = e.dataTransfer.getData("text");
        var draggedEl = document.getElementById(draggedId);

        if (draggedEl.parentNode == this) {
            this.className = "";
            return;
        }

        draggedEl.parentNode.removeChild(draggedEl);

        this.appendChild(draggedEl);
        this.className = "";
    }

    function init() {
        var draggable = document.querySelectorAll("[draggable]");
        var targets = document.querySelectorAll("[data-drop-target]");

        for (var i = 0; i < draggable.length; i++) {
            draggable[i].addEventListener("dragstart", handleDragStart);
        }

        for (i = 0; i < targets.length; i++) {
            targets[i].addEventListener("dragover", handleOverDrop);
            targets[i].addEventListener("drop", handleOverDrop);
            targets[i].addEventListener("dragenter", handleDragEnterLeave);
            targets[i].addEventListener("dragleave", handleDragEnterLeave);
        }
    }

    Modernizr.addTest('draggable', function () {
```

```
            var span = document.createElement("span");

            return typeof span.draggable != "undefined";
        });

        Modernizr.load([{
            test: Modernizr.draggable,
            nope: "draggable-polyfill.js"
        },
        {
            test: document.addEventListener,
            nope: "event-polyfill.js",
            complete: init
        }]);
    </script>

</body>
</html>
```

Save this as ch17_example1.html and load it into any browser (you can also view it
at http://beginningjs.com/examples/ch17_example1.html). You'll see that it behaves
exactly like ch10_example21.html, and if you can view it in IE8, you'll see that it works
there, too.

This code is almost identical to ch10_example21.html, so let's just go over the new/changed code.
First, you add a reference to Modernizr:

```
<script src="modernizr.min.js"></script>
```

As recommended by the folks at Modernizr, the <script/> element resides within the document's
<head/>.

The next change is the addition of the init() function. The function itself is new, but the code it
executes is the same initialization code from ch10_example21.html:

```
function init() {
    var draggable = document.querySelectorAll("[draggable]");
    var targets = document.querySelectorAll("[data-drop-target]");

    for (var i = 0; i < draggable.length; i++) {
        draggable[i].addEventListener("dragstart", handleDragStart);
    }

    for (i = 0; i < targets.length; i++) {
        targets[i].addEventListener("dragover", handleOverDrop);
        targets[i].addEventListener("drop", handleOverDrop);
        targets[i].addEventListener("dragenter", handleDragEnterLeave);
        targets[i].addEventListener("dragleave", handleDragEnterLeave);
    }
}
```

This code was wrapped within the init() function so that Modernizr can use it as the complete
callback function, therefore setting up the event listeners after the event-polyfill.js file has been
completely loaded. This is crucial because if the event polyfill isn't ready, the page will not work in IE8.

The final two additions are familiar to you; the first creates a custom Modernizr test called draggable:

```
Modernizr.addTest('draggable', function () {
    var span = document.createElement("span");

    return typeof span.draggable != "undefined";
});
```

The second calls Modernizr's `load()` method to load the necessary polyfills if they're needed:

```
Modernizr.load([{
    test: Modernizr.draggable,
    nope: "draggable-polyfill.js"
},
{
    test: document.addEventListener,
    nope: "event-polyfill.js",
    complete: init
}]);
```

We should admit that, in the case of this example, creating the custom draggable test is a bit overboard. You only use the test once, so it would be slightly more efficient to omit the custom test and write the first yepnope object like this:

```
{
    test: typeof document.createElement("span").draggable != "undefined",
    nope: "draggable-polyfill.js"
}
```

At the same time, this slightly more efficient version is a bit uglier. Ultimately, the choice is yours. In cases like this, however, many people create the custom test in a utility file because it could be reused in other projects.

DIVING INTO PROTOTYPE

jQuery is the most popular framework today, but that crown used to sit upon Prototype's head. Unlike jQuery, Prototype's focus is augmenting the way you program with JavaScript by providing classes and inheritance. It does, however, also provide a robust set of tools for working with the DOM and Ajax support.

Getting Prototype

Point your browser to Prototype's download page at http://prototypejs.org/download. Here, you'll be given the choice to download the latest stable version, or an older version. The examples in this book use the latest stable version at the time of this writing: v1.7.2.

> **NOTE** *The stable version of Prototype 1.7.2 is provided in the code download.*

No compressed versions of Prototype exist.

Testing Your Prototype Installation

The largest portion of the Prototype library is its DOM extensions. Like jQuery, it provides a variety of helpful utility functions to make DOM programming a bit easier; it even has its own $() function (unlike jQuery, Prototype doesn't have a special name for this function; it's simply called the dollar function):

```
var buttonObj = $("theButton");
```

Prototype's $() function only accepts element id attribute values or DOM element objects to select and add extra functionality to DOM objects. Prototype does have a function that allows you to use CSS selectors to select elements; you learn about that later.

Like jQuery, Prototype provides its own API for registering event listeners. It extends the Event object with a method called observe(), which is not unlike the evt.addListener() method you wrote in Chapter 10. For example:

```
function buttonClick() {
    alert("Hello, Prototype World!");
}

Event.observe(buttonObj, "click", buttonClick);
```

The Event.observe() method accepts three arguments: The first is the DOM or BOM object you want to register an event listener for, the second is the event name, and the third is the function to call when the event fires. You can use Event.observe() to register an event listener to any DOM or BOM object. You look at this method, and other ways to listen for events, later in this chapter.

Like jQuery, you can chain method calls together on wrapper objects created with the $() function. Prototype's method names, however, are a bit more verbose:

```
function buttonClick () {
    $(document.body).writeAttribute("bgColor", "yellow")
                    .insert("<h1>Hello, Prototype!</h1>");
}

Event.observe(buttonObj, "click", buttonClick);
```

The buttonClick() function now modifies the <body/> element by changing the background color to yellow and adding content to the page. Let's break down this statement.

First, you pass document.body to the $() function:

```
$(document.body)
```

This extends the standard <body/> element with Prototype's extension methods—one of which is the writeAttribute() method. As its name implies, it "writes" or sets an attribute on the element:

```
writeAttribute("bgColor", "yellow")
```

This sets the body's bgColor attribute to yellow. The writeAttribute() method returns the DOM object it was called on, the extended document.body object in this case. So you can call another extension method, called insert(), to set its content:

```
insert("<h1>Hello, Prototype!</h1>")
```

Let's use this as the basis for a file to test your Prototype installation. Open your text editor and type the following:

```html
<!DOCTYPE html>

<html lang="en">
<head>
    <title>Chapter 17: Example 2</title>
</head>
<body>
    <button id="theButton">Click Me!</button>
    <script src="prototype.1.7.2.js"></script>
    <script>
        var buttonObj = $("theButton");

        function buttonClick() {
            $(document.body).writeAttribute("bgColor", "yellow")
                            .insert("<h1>Hello, Prototype!</h1>");
        }

        Event.observe(buttonObj, "click", buttonClick);
    </script>
</body>
</html>
```

Save this as ch17_example2.html and open it in your browser (http://beginningjs.com/examples/ch17_example2.html). You should see something like Figure 17-2. If you don't, make sure that the Prototype JavaScript file is in the same directory as the HTML file.

Retrieving Elements

Prototype's $() function is very different from jQuery's. If you remember from the previous chapter, jQuery's $() function creates a jQuery object that wraps itself around one or multiple DOM element objects. In contrast, Prototype's $() function returns the actual DOM object (much like document.getElementById()), but it also extends the element object with many new properties and methods:

```
var el = $("myDiv");
```

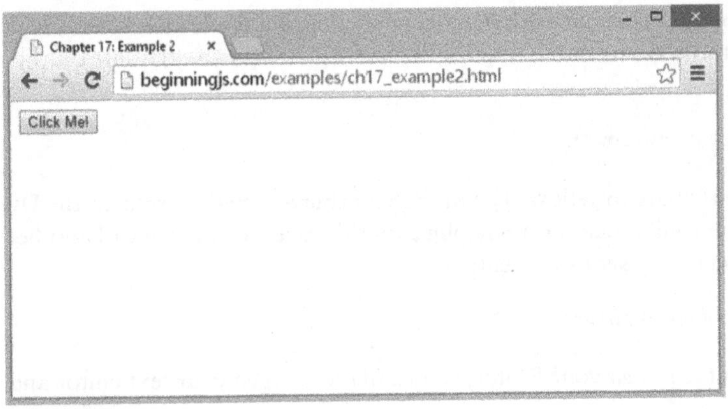

FIGURE 17-2

This code retrieves the element with an `id` of `myDiv`, and you can use this object just like you use any other element object. For example, the following code alerts the element's tag name with the `tagName` property:

```
alert(el.tagName);
```

You can also extend an element by passing the element's object to the dollar function. The following code passes the `document.body` object to the dollar function in order to extend it:

```
var body = $(document.body);
```

By doing this, you can use both native DOM methods and properties as well as Prototype's methods.

> **NOTE** *Prototype's dollar function returns* `null` *if the specified element cannot be found. This is unlike jQuery's* `$()` *function because Prototype returns an extended DOM element object; even though it is extended, it is still a DOM element object.*

Selecting Elements with CSS Selectors

As mentioned before, Prototype's dollar function does not select elements based upon CSS selectors; it only accepts element `id` values and element objects. Prototype does, however, have another function that behaves similarly to the jQuery function: the `$$()` function.

You can use the `$$()` function to locate and retrieve elements that match the provided CSS selector. For example, the following code retrieves all `<div/>` elements in the page and returns them in an array:

```
var divEls = $$("div");
```

The `$$()` function always returns an array—even if you use an `id` selector. One downside to `$$()` is that it returns an array of extended elements; so if you want to perform an operation on every element in the array, you have to iterate over the array with either a loop or an iterative `Array` method (from Chapter 5).

Performing an Operation on Elements Selected with $$()

Because `$$()` returns an array, you can use the `Array` methods to perform iterative operations. For example, the following code uses the `forEach()` method to insert content into each element in the array:

```
function insertText(element) {
    element.insert("This text inserted using the forEach() method.");
}

$$("div").forEach(insertText);
```

You can also use multiple CSS selectors to select elements with the `$$()` function. Instead of passing a single string that contains the multiple selectors, you pass each selector as an argument to the method, like this:

```
var elements = $$("#myDiv", "p > span, .class-one");
```

This code selects elements based upon two selectors: `#myDiv` and `p > span, .class-one`, and it returns an array that contains all of the extended element objects that match those selectors.

> **NOTE** For more information on the CSS selectors supported in Prototype, see
> `http://prototypejs.org/doc/latest/dom/dollar-dollar/`.

Manipulating Style

Prototype gives you several methods you can use to change an element's style. The most basic is the `setStyle()` method, which sets individual style properties. To use `setStyle()`, you create an object that contains the CSS properties and values that you want to set. For example, the following code sets an element's foreground and background colors:

```
var styles = {
    color: "red",
    backgroundColor: "blue"
};

$("myDiv").setStyle(styles);
```

As you know from previous chapters, changing an element's style in this manner is usually undesirable. A better solution is to manipulate the CSS classes applied to an element, and Prototype gives you four easy-to-use methods to do just that.

The first method, `addClassName()`, adds a CSS class to the element. The following code adds the `class-one` CSS class to the element:

```
$("myDiv").addClassName("class-one");
```

The second method, `removeClassName()`, removes the specified class from the element. The following code removes the `class-two` CSS class from the element:

```
$("myDiv").removeClassName("class-two");
```

Next is the `toggleClassName()` method, and it toggles the specified class. The following code toggles the `class-three` CSS class. If it is already applied to the element, the class is removed. Otherwise, it is applied to the element:

```
$("myDiv").toggleClassName("class-three");
```

The final method, `hasClassName()`, checks if the specified class is applied to the element:

```
$("myDiv").toggleClassName("class-three");
```

Naturally, if the class exists, the `toggleClassName()` method returns `true`. Otherwise, it returns `false`.

These CSS methods are very similar to jQuery's CSS class manipulation methods, but Prototype's methods for creating and inserting elements differ greatly from jQuery's methods. Removing elements, however, is very similar to jQuery.

Creating, Inserting, and Removing Elements

Prototype makes it easy to manipulate the DOM because it extends the `Element` object. Let's start by creating elements.

Creating an Element

Prototype adds a constructor for the `Element` object, and it accepts two arguments: the element's tag name and an object containing attributes and their values. The following code creates an `<a/>` element and populates its `id` and `href` attributes:

```
var attributes = {
    id = "myLink",
    href = "http://prototypejs.org"
};

var a = new Element("a", attributes);
```

The first few lines of this code create an object called `attributes` and define its `id` and `href` properties. They then create an `<a/>` element by using the `Element` object's constructor, passing `"a"` as the first argument and the `attributes` object as the second.

Adding Content

Prototype extends element objects with two methods for adding content: `insert()` and `update()`. The aptly named `insert()` method inserts new content at the end of the element. The following code inserts the a object from the previous example into the document's body:

```
$(document.body).insert(a);
```

The update() method *replaces* all existing content within the element. The following code updates the document's body with the a object, thereby replacing the existing content with the <a/> element:

```
$(document.body).update(a);
```

It's important to remember the distinction between the two methods; otherwise, you may experience unexpected results in your web page.

Removing an Element

Prototype makes it easy to remove an element from the DOM; simply call the remove() method on the element object you want to remove, like this:

```
a.remove();
```

Using Events

When you extend an Element object with the $() function, you gain access to its observe() method. Like the native addEventListener() method, this registers an event listener for a DOM element, and it accepts two arguments: the event name and the function to call when the event fires. For example, the following code registers a click event listener that executes the divClick() function:

```
function divClick(event) {
    // do something
}

$("myDiv").observe("click", divClick);
```

And as you saw earlier, you can also use the Event.observe() method. The following code achieves the same results using Event.observe():

```
function divClick(event) {
    // do something
}

Event.observe("myDiv", "click", divClick);
```

This code is slightly different from the first time you saw Event.observe() because the first argument, in this case, is a string. You can pass the id of an element or a DOM/BOM object as the first argument to Event.observe(). This method is particularly useful for objects like window. You cannot call $(window).observe() because the browser will throw an error. Instead, you have to use Event.observe().

Prototype doesn't emulate the W3C DOM event model. Instead, it extends the event objects of legacy-IE and standards-compliant browsers to give you a set of utility methods to work with event data.

For example, the element() method returns the event target (the srcElement property for legacy-IE, and the target property for W3C DOM browsers). The following code uses the `element()` method to retrieve the target of the `click` event and toggles the `class-one` CSS class:

```
function divClick(e) {
    var target = e.element();
    target.toggleClassName("class-one");
}

$("myDiv").observe("click", divClick);
```

The element returned by the `element()` method is already extended with Prototype's methods; so, there's no need to pass it to `$()` to get the extra functionality.

Rewriting the Tab Strip with Prototype

You now know how to retrieve and manipulate elements, add and remove elements, and register event listeners with Prototype. Let's adapt the jQuery version of the tab strip from `ch16_example2.html`.

TRY IT OUT Revisiting the Toolbar with Prototype

Open your text editor and type the following:

```
<!DOCTYPE html>

<html lang="en">
<head>
    <title>Chapter 17: Example 3</title>
    <style>
        .tabStrip {
            background-color: #E4E2D5;
            padding: 3px;
            height: 22px;
        }

        .tabStrip div {
            float: left;
            font: 14px arial;
            cursor: pointer;
        }

        .tabStrip-tab {
            padding: 3px;
        }

        .tabStrip-tab-hover {
            border: 1px solid #316AC5;
            background-color: #C1D2EE;
            padding: 2px;
        }

        .tabStrip-tab-click {
            border: 1px solid #facc5a;
            background-color: #f9e391;
```

```
                    padding: 2px;
            }
        </style>

    </head>
    <body>
        <div class="tabStrip">
            <div data-tab-number="1" class="tabStrip-tab">Tab 1</div>
            <div data-tab-number="2" class="tabStrip-tab">Tab 2</div>
            <div data-tab-number="3" class="tabStrip-tab">Tab 3</div>
        </div>
        <div id="descContainer"></div>

        <script src="prototype.1.7.2.js"></script>
        <script>
            function handleEvent(e) {
                var target = e.element();
                var type = e.type;

                if (type == "mouseover" || type == "mouseout") {
                    target.toggleClassName("tabStrip-tab-hover");
                } else if (type == "click") {
                    target.addClassName("tabStrip-tab-click");

                    var num = target.getAttribute("data-tab-number");
                    showDescription(num);
                }
            }

            function showDescription(num) {
                var text = "Description for Tab " + num;

                $("descContainer").update(text);
            }

            $$(".tabStrip > div").forEach(function(element) {
                element.observe("mouseover", handleEvent);
                element.observe("mouseout", handleEvent);
                element.observe("click", handleEvent);
            });
        </script>
    </body>
</html>
```

Save this file as `ch17_example3.html` and load it into your browser (http://beginningjs.com/ examples/ch17_example3.html). You'll notice it behaves the same as the other tab strip scripts.

Because the CSS and markup remains unchanged in the jQuery version, let's focus on the JavaScript that changed—starting with the `handleEvent()` function:

```
function handleEvent(e) {
    var target = e.element();
```

Here, you get the event target using the `element()` extension method and assign it to the `target` variable.

Next, you determine the type of event that took place. You first check for `mouseover` and `mouseout` events:

```
if (type == "mouseover" || type == "mouseout") {
    target.toggleClassName("tabStrip-tab-hover");
```

If either of these events takes place, you want to toggle the `tabStrip-tab-hover` CSS class. For `mouseover` events, this CSS class is applied to the target element, and for `mouseout`, the class is removed.

Now you need to determine if the `click` event fired:

```
} else if (type == "click") {
    target.addClassName("tabStrip-tab-click");
```

If so, you add the `tabStrip-tab-click` CSS class to the target element to change its style to that of a clicked tab. Then, you need to get the tab's number from the element's `data-tab-number` attribute:

```
    var num = target.getAttribute("data-tab-number");
    showDescription(num);
}
}
```

You use the native `getAttribute()` method to retrieve that attribute's value and pass it to `showDescription()`.

As you know, the `showDescription()` function adds the tab's description to the page.

```
function showDescription(num) {
    var text = "Description for Tab " + num;

    $("descContainer").update(text);
}
```

Here, you select the element representing the description container and replace its contents with the `update()` method.

The final bit of code sets up the event listeners for the tab elements. Using the `$$()` function, you retrieve them using the `.tabStrip > div` selector:

```
$$(".tabStrip > div").forEach(function (element) {
    element.observe("mouseover", handleEvent);
    element.observe("mouseout", handleEvent);
    element.observe("click", handleEvent);
});
```

You use the `Array` object's `forEach()` method to iterate over the array returned by `$$()`. The function you pass to `forEach()` is responsible for registering the `mouseover`, `mouseout`, and `click` event listeners on each element, and you register those events using the `observe()` extension method.

Prototype isn't just about DOM manipulation and language enhancement. It, too, provides you with Ajax capabilities that are easy to learn and use.

Using Ajax Support

Unfortunately, Prototype's Ajax support isn't as straightforward as jQuery's. Prototype's Ajax functionality centers on its Ajax object, which contains a variety of methods you can use to make Ajax calls. This object is much like the jQuery object in that you do not create an instance of Ajax; you use the methods made available by the object itself.

At the heart of the Ajax object is the Ajax.Request() constructor. It accepts two arguments: the URL and an object containing a set of options that the Ajax object uses when making a request. The options object can contain a variety of option properties to alter the behavior of Ajax.Request(). The following table describes just a few of them.

OPTION	DESCRIPTION
asynchronous	Determines whether or not the XMLHttpRequest object makes the request in asynchronous mode. The default is true.
method	The HTTP method used for the request. The default is "post". "get" is another valid value.
onSuccess	A callback function invoked when the request completes successfully
onFailure	A callback function invoked when the request completes, but results in an error status code
parameters	Either a string containing the parameters to send with the request, or an object containing the parameters and their values

> **NOTE** For a complete list of options, visit the Prototype documentation at http://prototypejs.org/doc/latest/ajax/.

Making a request with Prototype looks something like the following code:

```
function requestSuccess(transport) {
    alert(transport.responseText);
}

function requestFailed(transport) {
    alert("An error occurred! HTTP status code is " + transport.status);
}

var options = {
    method: "get",
    onSuccess: requestSuccess,
    onFailure: requestFailed
};

new Ajax.Request("someTextFile.txt", options);
```

The first few lines of code define the requestSuccess() and requestFailed() functions. These functions accept a parameter called transport—a special object that contains the server's response (more on this later).

After the function definitions, you create an options object that contains properties for the HTTP method option, the onSuccess option, and the onFailure option. Then, you finally make the request for the someTextFile.txt file, passing the options object to the Ajax.Request() constructor (don't forget the new keyword!).

If you need to send parameters with your request, you'll have to do a bit more preparation before calling new Ajax.Request(). Like jQuery, you can create an object to contain the parameter names and values. For example, if you need to send a parameter called username with your request, you can do something like this:

```
var parms = {
    username: "jmcpeak"
};

options.parameters = parms;
```

When you send the request by creating a new Ajax.Request object, the parameters are added to the URL before the request is sent to the server.

All callback functions are passed a parameter containing an Ajax.Response object, an object that wraps around the native XMLHttpRequest object. It contains a variety of useful properties for working with the server's response. It emulates the basic properties of XMLHttpRequest, such as readyState, responseText, responseXML, and status. But it also exposes a few convenience properties, as outlined in the following table.

PROPERTY NAME	PURPOSE
request	The Ajax.Request object used to make the request
responseJSON	A parsed JSON structure if the response's Content-Type header is application/json
statusText	The HTTP status text sent by the server
transport	The native XMLHttpRequest object used to make the request

Now that you've been given a crash course in Prototype's Ajax functionality, let's modify the Ajax Form Validator.

TRY IT OUT Revisiting the Form Validator with Prototype

Open your text editor and type the following:

```
<!DOCTYPE html>

<html lang="en">
<head>
    <title>Chapter 17: Example 4</title>
```

```html
    <style>
        .fieldname {
            text-align: right;
        }

        .submit {
            text-align: right;
        }
    </style>
</head>
<body>
    <form>
        <table>
            <tr>
                <td class="fieldname">
                    Username:
                </td>
                <td>
                    <input type="text" id="username" />
                </td>
                <td>
                    <a id="usernameAvailability" href="#">Check Availability</a>
                </td>
            </tr>
            <tr>
                <td class="fieldname">
                    Email:
                </td>
                <td>
                    <input type="text" id="email" />
                </td>
                <td>
                    <a id="emailAvailability" href="#">Check Availability</a>
                </td>
            </tr>
            <tr>
                <td class="fieldname">
                    Password:
                </td>
                <td>
                    <input type="text" id="password" />
                </td>
                <td />
            </tr>
            <tr>
                <td class="fieldname">
                    Verify Password:
                </td>
                <td>
                    <input type="text" id="password2" />
                </td>
                <td />
            </tr>
            <tr>
                <td colspan="2" class="submit">
```

```
                    <input type="submit" value="Submit" />
                </td>
                <td />
            </tr>
        </table>
    </form>
    <script src="prototype.1.7.2.js"></script>
    <script>
        function checkUsername(e) {
            e.preventDefault();

            var userValue = $("username").value;

            if (!userValue) {
                alert("Please enter a user name to check!");
                return;
            }

            var options = {
                method: "get",
                onSuccess: handleResponse,
                parameters: {
                    username: userValue
                }
            };

            new Ajax.Request("ch14_formvalidator.php", options);
        }

        function checkEmail(e) {
            e.preventDefault();

            var emailValue = $("email").value;

            if (!emailValue) {
                alert("Please enter an email address to check!");
                return;
            }

            var options = {
                method: "get",
                onSuccess: handleResponse,
                parameters: {
                    email: emailValue
                }
            };

            new Ajax.Request("ch14_formvalidator.php", options);
        }

        function handleResponse(transport) {
            var response = transport.responseJSON;

            if (response.available) {
                alert(response.searchTerm + " is available!");
```

```
                } else {
                    alert("We're sorry, but " + response.searchTerm +
                        " is not available.");
                }
            }

            $("usernameAvailability").observe("click", checkUsername);
            $("emailAvailability").observe("click", checkEmail);
        </script>
    </body>

    </html>
```

Save this as ch17_example4.html in your web server's root directory, because this file must be hosted on a web server to work correctly. Point your browser to http://yourserver/ch17_example4.html and test out the form.

This page works exactly like the previous versions. Let's start examining this version with the checkUsername() function. As you know, this function is responsible for gathering the user input and sending it to the server.

To get the user's input, you retrieve the appropriate <input/> element and get its value:

```
function checkUsername(e) {
    e.preventDefault();

    var userValue = $("username").value;
```

You could use the native document.getElementById() method to retrieve the <input/> element, but Prototype's $() function is much easier to type. It returns an extended Element object, but you use the standard value property to retrieve the element's value.

Next, you check the user input to ensure you have workable data:

```
    if (!userValue) {
        alert("Please enter a user name to check!");
        return;
    }
```

If the function makes it past this if statement, you need to assemble the options object that you pass to the Ajax.Request() constructor:

```
    var options = {
        method: "get",
        onSuccess: handleResponse,
        parameters: {
            username: userValue
        }
    };
```

This options object has the required method and onSuccess properties, and you also include the parameters—setting username to the value obtained from the form.

Now you're ready to send the request. So, you call the `Ajax.Request()` constructor and pass it the URL and `options` object.

As the last step in this function, you call the `Ajax.Request()` constructor, prepended by the new keyword, and pass the URL to `formvalidator.php` and the `options` object:

```
    new Ajax.Request("ch14_formvalidator.php", options);
}
```

The `checkEmail()` function is almost identical to `checkUsername()`. First, you retrieve the e-mail address from the form and validate it:

```
function checkEmail(e) {
    e.preventDefault();

    var emailValue = $("email").value;

    if (!emailValue) {
        alert("Please enter an email address to check!");
        return;
    }
```

Next, you build the `options` object:

```
    var options = {
        method: "get",
        onSuccess: handleResponse,
        parameters: {
            email: emailValue
        }
    };
```

Once again, you provide the obligatory `method` and `onSuccess` properties, as well as the `parameters` object. You set the `email` parameter property to the e-mail address from the form.

Then, you issue the request by calling the `Ajax.Request()` constructor:

```
    new Ajax.Request("ch14_formvalidator.php", options);
}
```

The `handleResponse()` function is not left untouched, but the change is subtle:

```
function handleResponse(transport) {
    var response = transport.responseJSON;

    if (response.available) {
        alert(response.searchTerm + " is available!");
    } else {
        alert("We're sorry, but " + response.searchTerm + " is not available.");
    }
}
```

This new version uses Prototype's `responseJSON` property to get the parsed JSON. You can use this property because `ch14_formvalidator.php`'s `Content-Type` header is set to `application/json`. If it was any other value, like `text/plain`, then `responseJSON` would be `null`, and you would have to use `responseText` in conjunction with `JSON.parse()`, like this:

```
var response = JSON.parse(transport.responseText);
```

The final two lines of code in this example register the click event listeners on the two `<a/>` elements:

```
$("usernameAvailability").observe("click", checkUsername);
$("emailAvailability").observe("click", checkEmail);
```

You retrieve the elements using Prototype's `$()` function, and then you use `observe()` to register the event listeners.

Prototype is a powerful framework that provides a rich set of utilities to change the way you write JavaScript. But a simple section such as this is far too small to cover the framework adequately. For further information on Prototype and the utility it offers, see the API documentation at `http://api.prototypejs.org/` and the tutorials at `http://prototypejs.org/learn/`.

DELVING INTO MOOTOOLS

At first glance, MooTools looks identical to Prototype, and rightly so. MooTools was first developed to work with Prototype, so you shouldn't be surprised to see some striking similarities between the two.

However, MooTools is more of a cross between jQuery and Prototype as far as DOM manipulation is concerned. Like Prototype, MooTools' goal is to augment the way you write JavaScript, providing tools to write classes and inherit from them. Also like Prototype, MooTools adds in a rich set of extensions to make DOM manipulation easier, and you'll find that selecting DOM objects in MooTools is exactly the same as Prototype. But as you'll see in the following sections, the extension method names and the way in which you use them is reminiscent of jQuery.

Getting MooTools

You can download MooTools in two ways: You can download the core, or you can customize your own build. The MooTools' core contains everything you need to perform common DOM and Ajax operations, but if you don't need the full power of core, you can pick and choose which pieces you need for your page or application.

Regardless of the version you want, you can download both at `http://mootools.net/core/builder`. Additionally, you can choose to download the compressed or uncompressed JavaScript file. The code download includes the compressed core of version 1.5.1.

Testing Your MooTools' Installation

As we mentioned earlier, many similarities exist between MooTools and Prototype; so, testing your MooTools' installation will look very similar to the Prototype test.

MooTools has a $() function, just like Prototype's:

```
var buttonObj = $("theButton");
```

It accepts either a string containing an element's id or a DOM element and returns the DOM object with an extended set of methods and properties. One such method is the addEvent() method which, as you probably deduced, registers an event listener.

The addEvent() method accepts two arguments: the event name and the function. So, you can register an event listener like this:

```
function buttonClick() {
    alert("You clicked the button!");
}

buttonObj.addEvent("click", buttonClick);
```

MooTools' extension methods provide a variety of methods and properties for manipulating elements in the page. Most of the methods are chainable, therefore allowing you to perform multiple operations with less code. For example:

```
function buttonClick() {
    $(document.body).setProperty("bgColor", "yellow")
                    .appendHTML("<h1>Hello, MooTools!</h1>");
}

buttonObj.addEvent("click", buttonClick);
```

You can set an element's attributes with the setProperty() method, as demonstrated in this code. This method returns the element object, so you can then immediately append content to the element by calling the appendHTML() method.

Use this code to test your MooTools' installation. Open your text editor and type the following:

```
<!DOCTYPE html>

<html lang="en">
<head>
    <title>Chapter 17: Example 5</title>
</head>
<body>
    <button id="theButton">Click Me!</button>
    <script src="mootools-core-1.5.1-compressed.js"></script>
    <script>
        var buttonObj = $("theButton");

        function buttonClick() {
            $(document.body).setProperty("bgColor", "yellow")
                            .appendHTML("<h1>Hello, MooTools!</h1>");
        }

        buttonObj.addEvent("click", buttonClick);
```

```
      </script>
    </body>
  </html>
```

Save this as ch17_example5.html and load it in your browser. When you click the button, the background color should change to yellow, and "Hello, MooTools!" should display in the page. If not, make sure the MooTools' JavaScript file is located in the same directory as your HTML page.

Finding Elements

Earlier, we mentioned that MooTools' $() function is similar to Prototype's. Well, let's clear it up now; they are exactly the same. They find the element object in the DOM and extend it, albeit with different methods that you'll see in the following sections. For example, the following code finds an element with an id of myDiv, extends it with MooTools' methods and properties, and returns it:

```
var element = $("myDiv");
```

With this object, you can use MooTools' extension methods as well as the native DOM methods and properties:

```
var tagName = element.tagName; // standard DOM
element.appendHTML("New Content"); // extension
```

If an element with the given id does not exist, $() returns null.

You can also pass a DOM object to the $() function to extend it as well:

```
var body = $(document.body);
```

Selecting Elements with CSS Selectors

MooTools has the $$() function to select elements with CSS selectors, and you can pass multiple CSS selectors to retrieve a wide variety of elements. Like Prototype, you pass each selector as an argument to the function:

```
var classOne = $$(".class-one");
var multiple = $$("div", ".class-one", "p > div")
```

The $$() function returns an array of extended DOM element objects. This is where MooTools and Prototype start to differ because while both frameworks extend the Array object returned by $$(), MooTools adds extension methods that manipulate the elements within the array.

Performing Operations on Elements

MooTools' $$() is a cross between jQuery's $() and Prototype's $$() in that it returns an array of extended element objects (like Prototype), but you can use a variety of methods to work with those elements without having to manually iterate the array. For example, you can change the style of all elements within an array by calling the setStyle() method, like this:

```
$$("div", ".class-one").setStyle("color", "red");
```

This code selects multiple types of elements and sets their text color to red. Contrast that with Prototype:

```
// Prototype
function changeColor(item) {
    var styles {
        color: "red"
    };

    item.setStyle(styles);
}

$$("div", ".class-one").forEach(changeColor);
```

Note that you could use this technique in MooTools. In fact, you want to do so when performing multiple operations to the same set of elements. Remember that methods like MooTools' setStyle() and jQuery's css() are iterative; they loop over the array. Chaining iterative methods together means you are executing multiple loops, which is inefficient.

Changing Style

The previous MooTools' code example introduced you to the setStyle() method. It accepts two arguments: the first is the CSS property, and the second is its value. Like jQuery, you can use the CSS property used in a style sheet or the camel-case version used in script:

```
$("myDiv").setStyle("background-color", "red"); // valid
$("myDiv").setStyle("backgroundColor", "red"); // valid, too
```

Both lines of this code set the element's background color to red; so you can use either property name to set individual style properties.

MooTools also has a setStyles() method for changing multiple CSS properties. To use this method, pass an object that contains the CSS properties and values, like this:

```
$("myDiv").setStyles({
    backgroundColor: "red",
    color: "blue"
});
```

This is, of course, not the ideal way to change an element's style. So, MooTools adds the addClass(), removeClass(), toggleClass(), and hasClass() extension methods to DOM element objects.

The addClass() and removeClass() methods do just what their names imply. They add or remove the specified class to or from the element:

```
var div = $("myDiv");

div.addClass("class-one");
div.removeClass("class-two");
```

The toggleClass() method, naturally, toggles a class.

```
div.toggleClass("class-three");
```

This code toggles the `class-three` CSS class. If the element already has the class, it is removed from the element. Otherwise, it is added.

The `hasClass()` method returns `true` or `false` depending on whether or not the element has the CSS class:

```
div.hasClass("class-four");
```

This code returns `false` because the `class-four` CSS class isn't applied to the element.

Of course, changing an element's style isn't the only DOM-related things MooTools can do; you can also create, insert, and remove elements from the DOM.

Creating, Inserting, and Removing Elements

Like Prototype, MooTools lets you create elements with the `Element` constructor:

```
var attributes = {
    id: "myLink",
    href: "mootools.net"
};

var a = new Element("a", attributes);
```

When you call the constructor, you pass the tag name and an object containing your desired attributes. The preceding code creates a new `<a/>` element and populates its `id` and `href` properties. You can then set its content with the `appendText()` or `appendHTML()` methods:

```
a.appendText("Go to MooTools' Website");
```

MooTools also adds a `set()` extension method that lets you set the value of a proprietary "property." These are not properties in the sense of a JavaScript property using `object.propertyName` syntax; instead, they're more of a virtual property. For example, there is an `html` property that sets the HTML of an element, and you set this property with the `set()` method, like this:

```
a.set("html", "Go to MooTool's Website");
```

This is essentially the same as using the native `innerHTML` property, and in most cases, you'd want to use `innerHTML`.

When you're ready to add the element to the page, use the `adopt()` method:

```
$(document.body).adopt(a);
```

This code appends the newly created `<a/>` element to the page's `<body/>` element with the `adopt()` method. Note that this doesn't replace existing content; it simply adds new content to the page. If you need to empty an element of its children, call the `empty()` method:

```
$(document.body).empty();
```

You can also remove an individual element with the `dispose()` method:

```
a.dispose();
```

Using Events

As you know, the `$()` function returns an extended element object. One of the extension methods is the `addEvent()` method, which registers an event listener:

```
function divClick(e) {
    alert("You clicked me!");
}

$("myDiv").addEvent("click", divClick);
```

The `addEvent()` method accepts two arguments: the event name and the function to execute when the event fires.

You can also register multiple event listeners with the `addEvents()` method. Instead of passing a single event name and function, you pass an object that contains the event names as properties and the functions as values. For example, the following code registers event handlers for the `mouseover` and `mouseout` events on an element:

```
function eventHandler(e) {
    // do something with the event here
}

var handlers = {
    mouseover: eventHandler,
    mouseout:  eventHandler
};

$("myDiv").addEvents(handlers);
```

When an event fires, MooTools passes its own event object (of type `DOMEvent`) to the event-handling function. This object has a hybrid set of properties and methods: Some are proprietary but most are standards-compliant. The following table lists some of the properties available with MooTools' `Event` object.

PROPERTY	DESCRIPTION
`page.x`	The horizontal position of the mouse relative to the browser window
`page.y`	The vertical position of the mouse relative to the browser window
`client.x`	The horizontal position of the mouse relative to the client area
`client.y`	The vertical position of the mouse relative to the client area
`target`	The extended event target
`relatedTarget`	The extended element related to the event target
`type`	The type of event that called the event handler

NOTE Visit http://mootools.net/core/docs/1.5.1/Types/DOMEvent *for a complete list of properties of MooTools'* DOMEvent *object.*

For example, the following code registers a click event listener on an element with an id of myDiv:

```
function divClick(e) {
    var target = e.target.addClass("class-one");

    alert("You clicked at X:" + e.client.x + " Y:" + e.client.y);
}

$("myDiv").addEvent("click", divClick);
```

When the click event fires, MooTools passes its own event object to divClick(). The first line of the function calls the addClass() method, adding the class-one CSS class to the element.

The addClass() method returns an extended element object, letting you both add the CSS class and assign the target variable with the extended event target. You then use an alert box to display the mouse pointer's coordinates by using the client.x and client.y properties.

Rewriting the Tab Strip with MooTools

Now that you've had a crash course in MooTools, let's rewrite the tab strip!

TRY IT OUT Revisiting the Toolbar with MooTools

Open your text editor and type the following:

```
<!DOCTYPE html>

<html lang="en">
<head>
    <title>Chapter 17: Example 6</title>
    <style>
        .tabStrip {
            background-color: #E4E2D5;
            padding: 3px;
            height: 22px;
        }

        .tabStrip div {
            float: left;
            font: 14px arial;
            cursor: pointer;
        }

        .tabStrip-tab {
            padding: 3px;
        }

        .tabStrip-tab-hover {
```

```
            border: 1px solid #316AC5;
            background-color: #C1D2EE;
            padding: 2px;
        }

        .tabStrip-tab-click {
            border: 1px solid #facc5a;
            background-color: #f9e391;
            padding: 2px;
        }
    </style>

</head>
<body>
    <div class="tabStrip">
        <div data-tab-number="1" class="tabStrip-tab">Tab 1</div>
        <div data-tab-number="2" class="tabStrip-tab">Tab 2</div>
        <div data-tab-number="3" class="tabStrip-tab">Tab 3</div>
    </div>
    <div id="descContainer"></div>

    <script src="mootools-core-1.5.1-compressed.js"></script>
    <script>
        function handleEvent(e) {
            var target = e.target;
            var type = e.type;

            if (type == "mouseover" || type == "mouseout") {
                target.toggleClass("tabStrip-tab-hover");
            } else if (type == "click") {
                target.addClass("tabStrip-tab-click");

                var num = target.getAttribute("data-tab-number");
                showDescription(num);
            }
        }

        function showDescription(num) {
            var text = "Description for Tab " + num;

            $("descContainer").set("html", text);
        }

        $$(".tabStrip > div").addEvents({
            mouseover: handleEvent,
            mouseout: handleEvent,
            click: handleEvent
        });
    </script>
</body>
</html>
```

Save this file as ch17_example6.html, and open it in your browser (http://beginningjs.com/examples/ch17_example6.html is available, too). Notice that this page works just like all the other versions.

Let's jump right into the code, starting with the `handleEvent()` function:

```
function handleEvent(e) {
    var target = e.target;
    var type = e.type;
```

Everything is standards-compliant code until you get to the `if` statement; that's when you use MooTools' `toggleClass()` method in the case of mouseover and mouseout events:

```
if (type == "mouseover" || type == "mouseout") {
    target.toggleClass("tabStrip-tab-hover");
```

If it is one of these events, you add the `tabStrip-tab-hover` CSS class to the event target. But if the event is a `click` event, you need to do a few things. First, you add the `tabStrip-tab-click` CSS class to the element. Then, you get the value of the `data-tab-number` attribute because you'll need to pass that to the `showDescription()` function:

```
} else if (type == "click") {
    target.addClass("tabStrip-tab-click");

    var num = target.getAttribute("data-tab-number");
    showDescription(num);
    }
}
```

The `showDescription()` function changed very slightly; in fact, just one statement needs your attention:

```
function showDescription(num) {
    var text = "Description for Tab " + num;

    $("descContainer").set("html", text);
}
```

You need to change the content of the description container element. Now, you can do that in a variety of ways, and as we mentioned earlier, the native `innerHTML` property would be ideal. However, for the sake of this example, you use MooTools' `set()` method to set the virtual `html` property.

Finally, you register your listeners for the mouseover, mouseout, and click events:

```
$$(".tabStrip > div").addEvents({
    mouseover: handleEvent,
    mouseout: handleEvent,
    click: handleEvent
});
```

Here, you use MooTools' `$$()` method to select the `<div/>` elements within the tab strip. Then you use the `addEvents()` method to register the three event listeners. As an alternative, you could use the technique demonstrated in the Prototype example:

```
$$(".tabStrip > div").forEach(function(item) {
    item.addEvents({
```

```
            mouseover: handleEvent,
            mouseout: handleEvent,
            click: handleEvent
        });
    });
```

However, there's no real need to do so in this example. But this would be the best way if you needed to perform other processes on each element. That way, you iterate over the elements once as opposed to multiple times.

Ajax Support in MooTools

MooTools has three objects for making HTTP requests, each targeting a specific purpose:

➤ `Request`: Used for general requests

➤ `Request.HTML`: Used specifically for receiving HTML

➤ `Request.JSON`: Specifically used for receiving JSON

Each of these objects is similar to Prototype's `Ajax.Request`, in that you directly create them by calling their constructor functions with the `new` operator and passing an object that contains various options:

```
var request = new Request({
    method: "get",
    url: "someFile.txt",
    onSuccess: requestSuccess
});
```

This code creates a `Request` object that makes a GET request for `someFile.txt` and calls the `requestSuccess()` function on a successful request.

You can pass many more options to the constructor; the following table lists some of them.

OPTION	DESCRIPTION
async	Determines whether or not the `XMLHttpRequest` object makes the request in asynchronous mode. The default is `true`.
data	An object containing the key/value pairs to send with the request
method	The HTTP method used for the request. The default is `"post"`.
onSuccess	A callback function invoked when the request completes successfully
onFailure	A callback function invoked when the request completes, but results in an error status code
url	The URL to send the request to

NOTE *Visit* http://mootools.net/core/docs/1.5.1/Request/Request *for a complete list of options and callback functions.*

Unfortunately, creating a `Request` object doesn't automatically send the request; you must explicitly send it with the `send()` method:

```
request.send();
```

But to save some typing, you can chain the `send()` method to the `Request` constructor, like this:

```
var request = new Request({
    method: "get",
    url: "someFile.txt",
    onSuccess: requestSuccess
}).send();
```

You can also use one of the many aliases for `send()`. Their names mirror those of the different HTTP methods, and they send the request with the given method. For example, the `get()` method sends a GET request, `post()` sends POST, `put()` is a PUT request, and so on. Using an alias eliminates the need to specify the `method` option. For example:

```
var request = new Request({
    url: "someFile.txt",
    onSuccess: requestSuccess
});

request.get(); // sends the request as GET
request.post(); // sends as POST
```

You can send data with your request in two different ways. First, you can make it part of the `Request` object. This is useful if you need to send the same data with every request you make with a single `Request` object. To do this, you add a `data` property to the `options` object you pass to the constructor. An example of this is:

```
var request = new Request({
    url: "ch14_formvalidator.php",
    data: {
        username: userValue // assuming userValue is assigned a value
    },
    onSuccess: requestSuccess
});
```

The second approach decouples the data from the `Request` object so that you can reuse the same `Request` object for sending different data. To use this approach, you pass the data to the `send()`, or other alias, method like this:

```
var request = new Request({
    url: "ch14_formvalidator.php",
    onSuccess: requestSuccess
```

```
  })}.get({
     data: {
          username: userValue
     }
  });
```

The onSuccess callback function varies between the different types of requests. For ordinary Request objects, the onSuccess callback function is called with two arguments—the responseText and responseXML:

```
function requestSuccess(responseText, responseXML) {
    // do something with either supplied value
}
```

The responseText is the plain textual representation of the server's response. If the response is a valid XML document, the responseXML parameter is a DOM tree containing the parsed XML.

The onSuccess callback is a bit more complicated for Request.HTML objects:

```
function requestHTMLSuccess(responseTree, responseElements,
                            responseHTML, responseJavaScript) {
    // do something with the data
}
```

The four parameters are:

➤ responseTree: The node list of the response

➤ responseElements: An array containing the elements of the response

➤ responseHTML: The string content of the response

➤ responseJavaScript: The JavaScript of the response

The onSuccess callback for Request.JSON objects is much simpler than Request.HTML's:

```
function requestJSONSuccess(responseJSON, responseText) {
    // do something with the provided data
}
```

The responseJSON parameter is an object—the parsed JSON structure. So you won't need to call JSON.parse(). The responseText parameter is the plaintext JSON structure. Honestly, your authors don't know why you would need the responseText with Request.JSON, but it's there just in case you need it (we don't think you will).

Let's use MooTools' Ajax utilities to modify the form validator from the previous chapter one last time!

TRY IT OUT Revisiting the Form Validator with MooTools

Open your text editor and type the following:

```
<!DOCTYPE html>

<html lang="en">
<head>
    <title>Chapter 17: Example 7</title>
    <style>
        .fieldname {
            text-align: right;
        }

        .submit {
            text-align: right;
        }
    </style>
</head>
<body>
    <form>
        <table>
            <tr>
                <td class="fieldname">
                    Username:
                </td>
                <td>
                    <input type="text" id="username" />
                </td>
                <td>
                    <a id="usernameAvailability" href="#">Check Availability</a>
                </td>
            </tr>
            <tr>
                <td class="fieldname">
                    Email:
                </td>
                <td>
                    <input type="text" id="email" />
                </td>
                <td>
                    <a id="emailAvailability" href="#">Check Availability</a>
                </td>
            </tr>
            <tr>
                <td class="fieldname">
                    Password:
                </td>
                <td>
                    <input type="text" id="password" />
                </td>
                <td />
            </tr>
            <tr>
                <td class="fieldname">
                    Verify Password:
                </td>
                <td>
                    <input type="text" id="password2" />
                </td>
                <td />
```

```
            </tr>
            <tr>
                <td colspan="2" class="submit">
                    <input type="submit" value="Submit" />
                </td>
                <td />
            </tr>
        </table>
    </form>
    <script src="mootools-core-1.5.1-compressed.js"></script>
    <script>
        function checkUsername(e) {
            e.preventDefault();

            var userValue = $("username").value;

            if (!userValue) {
                alert("Please enter a user name to check!");
                return;
            }

            var options = {
                url: "ch14_formvalidator.php",
                data: {
                    username: userValue
                },
                onSuccess: handleResponse
            };

            new Request.JSON(options).get();
        }

        function checkEmail(e) {
            e.preventDefault();

            var emailValue = $("email").value;

            if (!emailValue) {
                alert("Please enter an email address to check!");
                return;
            }

            var options = {
                url: "ch14_formvalidator.php",
                data: {
                    email: emailValue
                },
                onSuccess: handleResponse
            };

            new Request.JSON(options).get();
        }

        function handleResponse(data, json) {
            if (data.available) {
```

```
                    alert(data.searchTerm + " is available!");
               } else {
                    alert("We're sorry, but " + data.searchTerm + " is not available.");
               }
          }

          $("usernameAvailability").addEvent("click", checkUsername);
          $("emailAvailability").addEvent("click", checkEmail);
     </script>
</body>

</html>
```

Save this file as ch17_example7.html, and save it in your web server's root directory. Open and point your browser to http://yourserver/ch17_example7.html and test it. You'll find that it behaves just as all the previous versions did.

This version is very similar to Example 4—the Prototype version. In fact, checkUsername() and checkEmail() are identical to Example 4 except for the request code. So let's just look at that, starting with checkUsername().

After you get and validate the user input for the username, you build your options object:

```
var options = {
    url: "ch14_formvalidator.php",
    data: {
        username: userValue
    },
    onSuccess: handleResponse
};
```

You set the url, data, and onSuccess properties and pass the object to the Request.JSON() constructor:

```
new Request.JSON(options).get();
```

And to save some typing, you chain the get() call to the Request.JSON constructor.

The code inside checkEmail() is unsurprisingly similar (at this point, what is about this example?). First, you build your options object:

```
var options = {
    url: "ch14_formvalidator.php",
    data: {
        email: emailValue
    },
    onSuccess: handleResponse
};
```

Then you send the request:

```
new Request.JSON(options).get();
```

The `handleResponse()` function also saw a few changes. Thanks to MooTools' built-in support for JSON, the function has been simplified:

```
function handleResponse(data, json) {
    if (data.available) {
        alert(data.searchTerm + " is available!");
    } else {
        alert("We're sorry, but " + data.searchTerm + " is not available.");
    }
}
```

The data passed to the first parameter, `data`, is already parsed into a JavaScript object. So you simply use it to check if the username or e-mail is available and display the correct information to the user.

Finally, you wire up the events:

```
$("usernameAvailability").addEvent("click", checkUsername);
$("emailAvailability").addEvent("click", checkEmail);
```

You find the `<a/>` elements in the document and register their `click` event listeners with MooTools' `addEvent()` method.

MooTools is a popular framework because it offers you utility similar to jQuery while maintaining aspects of traditional DOM programming. MooTools also has an animation/effects component, making it a well-rounded framework. This section can hardly do the framework justice, so make sure to visit the API documentation at `http://mootools.net/core/docs/`.

SUMMARY

This chapter introduced you into the rather large world of JavaScript frameworks and libraries.

➤ You learned that two types of libraries and frameworks exist: general and specific. You were also given a short list of the popular solutions available today.

➤ You learned where to obtain the files needed to use Modernizr, Prototype, and MooTools.

➤ You learned how Modernizr helps you write feature-specific code, and how to load external resources, like polyfills, for browsers that don't support certain features.

➤ You learned the basics of the Prototype framework—how to retrieve, create, and manipulate elements. You also learned how to register event listeners and send Ajax requests.

➤ You learned how to use MooTools to create, select, and modify elements, as well as wire up event listeners and make Ajax requests.

EXERCISES

You can find suggested solutions for these questions in Appendix A.

1. Modify the answer to Chapter 14's Question 2 using Prototype. Also add error reporting for when an error occurs with the Ajax request.

2. If you guessed that this question would be: "Change the answer to Chapter 14's Question 2 using MooTools, and add error reporting for when an error occurs with the Ajax request" then you won!! Your prize is… completing the exercise.

18

Common Mistakes, Debugging, and Error Handling

WHAT YOU WILL LEARN IN THIS CHAPTER:

➤ Spotting common mistakes that everyone makes—even pros!

➤ Handling runtime errors, or exceptions, with the try...catch statement

➤ Debugging JavaScript with the development tools of various browsers

WROX.COM CODE DOWNLOADS FOR THIS CHAPTER

You can find the wrox.com code downloads for this chapter at http://www.wiley.com/go/ BeginningJavaScript5E on the Download Code tab. You can also view all of the examples and related files at http://beginningjs.com.

Even a JavaScript guru makes mistakes, even if they are just annoying typos. In particular, when code expands to hundreds or thousands of lines, the chance of something going wrong becomes much greater. In proportion, the difficulty in finding these mistakes, or bugs, also increases. In this chapter you look at various techniques that will help you minimize the problems that arise from this situation.

You start by taking a look at the top seven JavaScript coding mistakes. After you know what they are, you'll be able to look out for them when writing code, hopefully, so that you won't make them so often!

Then you look at how you can cope with errors when they do happen, so that you prevent users from seeing your coding mistakes.

Finally, you look at the debugging tools in Microsoft's Internet Explorer (IE11), Firebug (an add-on for Firefox), Chrome's Web Inspector, and Opera's Dragonfly. You see how you can use these tools to step through your code and check the contents of variables while the code is running, a process that enables you to hunt for difficult bugs. You also take a briefer look at the debugging tools available for Firefox.

D'OH! I CAN'T BELIEVE I JUST DID THAT: SOME COMMON MISTAKES

Several common mistakes are made by programmers. Some of these you'll learn to avoid as you become more experienced, but others may haunt you forever!

Undefined Variables

JavaScript is actually very easygoing when it comes to defining your variables before assigning values to them. For example, the following will implicitly create the new global variable abc and assign it to the value 23:

```
abc = 23;
```

Although strictly speaking, you should define the variable explicitly with the var keyword like this:

```
var abc = 23;
```

Your choice of whether to use the var keyword to declare a variable has a consequence on the variable's scope; so it is always best to use the var keyword. If a variable is used before it has been defined, an error will arise. For example, the following code will cause the error shown in Figure 18-1 in IE11 if the variable abc has not been previously defined (explicitly or implicitly):

```
alert(abc);
```

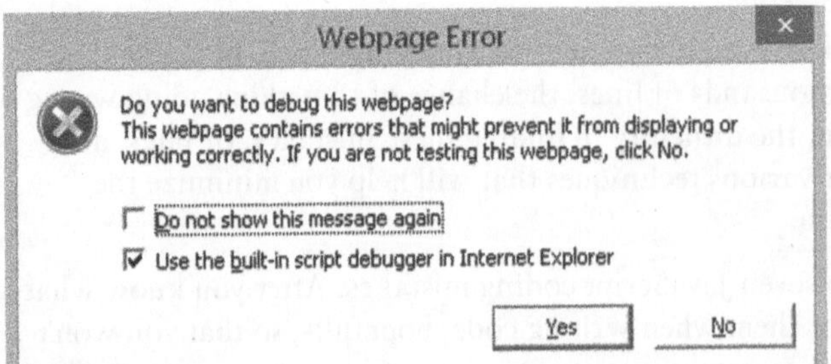

Webpage Error

[X] Do you want to debug this webpage?
This webpage contains errors that might prevent it from displaying or working correctly. If you are not testing this webpage, click No.

☐ Do not show this message again
☑ Use the built-in script debugger in Internet Explorer

[Yes]   [No]

Line: 8
Error: 'abc' is undefined

FIGURE 18-1

In other browsers, you'll need to look in the JavaScript console, which you can view by pressing Ctrl+Shift+J on your keyboard. You can also view the console by navigating through the browser's menu. You learn how to do this later.

In addition, you must remember that function definitions also have parameters, which if not declared correctly can lead to the same type of error.

Take a look at the following code:

```
function foo(parametrOne) {
    alert(parameterOne);
}
```

If you call this function, you get an error message similar to the one shown in Figure 18-2.

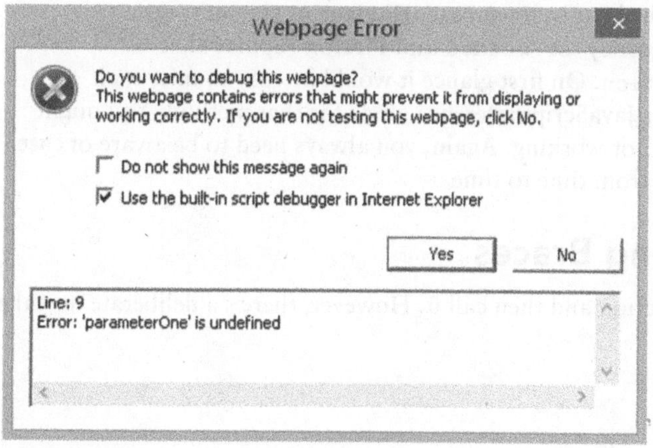

FIGURE 18-2

The error here is actually a simple typo in the function definition. The function's parameter should read parameterOne, not parametrOne. What can be confusing with this type of error is that although the browser tells us the error is on one line, the source of the error is on another line.

Case Sensitivity

This is a major source of errors, particularly because it can be difficult to spot at times.

For example, spot the three case errors in the following code:

```
var myName = "Jeremy";

If (myName == "jeremy") {
    alert(myName.toUppercase());
}
```

The first error is the if keyword; the code above has If rather than if. However, JavaScript won't tell us that the error is an incorrect use of case, but instead the browser will tell us Object expected or that If is not defined. Although error messages give us some idea of what's gone wrong, they often do so in an oblique way. In this case the browser thinks you are either trying to use an object called If or use an undefined function called If.

> **NOTE** *Different browsers use different wording when displaying errors. The overall meaning is the same, however, so you can identify what the problem is.*

Okay, with that error cleared up, you come to the next error, not one of JavaScript syntax, but a logic error. Remember that Jeremy does not equal jeremy in JavaScript, so myName == "jeremy" is false, even though it's quite likely that you didn't care whether the word is Jeremy or jeremy. This type of error will result in no error message at all because it is valid JavaScript; your only clue is that your code will not execute as you'd planned.

The third fault is with the toUpperCase() method of the String object. The previous code uses toUppercase, with the C in lowercase. IE gives us the message Object doesn't support this property or method and Firefox reports that myName.toUppercase is not a function. On first glance it would be easy to miss such a small mistake and start checking your JavaScript reference guide for that method. You might wonder why it's there, but your code is not working. Again, you always need to be aware of case, something that even experts get wrong from time to time.

Incorrect Number of Closing Braces

In the following code, you define a function and then call it. However, there's a deliberate mistake. See if you can spot where it is:

```
function myFunction()
{
var x = 1;
var y = 2;
if (x <= y)
{
if (x == y)
{
alert("x equals y");
}
}
myFunction();
```

This is why formatting your code is important—you'll have a much easier time spotting errors such as this:

```
function myFunction() {
    var x = 1;
    var y = 2;
    if (x <= y) {
        if (x == y) {
            alert("x equals y");
        }
    }

myFunction();
```

Now you can see that the ending curly brace of the function is missing. When you have a lot of `if`, `for`, or `do while` statements, it's easy to have too many or too few closing braces. This type of problem is much easier to spot with formatted code.

Incorrect Number of Closing Parentheses

Similarly, not having the correct number of closing parentheses can be problematic. Take a look at the following code:

```
if (myVariable + 12) / myOtherVariable < myString.length)
```

Spot the mistake? The problem is the missing parenthesis at the beginning of the condition. You want `myVariable + 12` to be calculated before the division by `myOtherVariable` is calculated, so quite rightly you know you need to put it in parentheses:

```
(myVariable + 12) / myOtherVariable
```

However, the `if` statement's condition must also be in parentheses. Not only is the initial parenthesis missing, but there is one more closing parenthesis than opening parentheses. Like curly braces, each opening parenthesis must have a closing parenthesis. The following code is correct:

```
if ((myVariable + 12) / myOtherVariable < myString.length)
```

It's very easy to miss a parenthesis or have one too many when you have many opening and closing parentheses.

Using Equals (=) Rather than Equality (==)

The equality operator is a commonly confused operator. Consider the following code:

```
var myNumber = 99;

if (myNumber = 101) {
    alert("myNumber is 101");
} else {
    alert("myNumber is " + myNumber);
}
```

At first glance, you'd expect that the code inside the `else` statement would execute, telling us that the number in `myNumber` is 99. It won't. This code makes the classic mistake of using the assignment operator (=) instead of the equality operator (==). Hence, instead of comparing `myNumber` with 101, this code sets `myNumber` to equal 101.

What makes things even trickier is that JavaScript does not report this as an error; it's valid JavaScript! The only indication that something isn't correct is that your code doesn't work. Assigning a variable a value in an `if` statement may look like an error, but it's perfectly legal.

When embedded in a large chunk of code, a mistake like this is easily overlooked. Just remember it's worth checking for this error the next time your program doesn't do what you expect. Debugging your code can help easily spot this type of error. You learn how to debug your code later in this chapter.

Using a Method as a Property and Vice Versa

Another common error is where either you forget to put parentheses after a method with no parameters, or you use a property and do put parentheses after it.

When calling a method, you must always have parentheses following its name; otherwise, JavaScript thinks that it must be a pointer to the method or a property. For example, examine the following code:

```
var nowDate = new Date();
alert(nowDate.getMonth);
```

The first line creates a Date object, and the second line uses its getMonth property. But you know that Date objects do not have a getMonth property; it's supposed to be a method. Now, this is valid JavaScript because you can pass a function pointer—which is what nowDate.getMonth is—to another function, and as such, the browser will not have any issues executing this code. And in many cases, you want to do that (like when registering event listeners). But chances are very good that we intended to call getMonth(). Therefore, the following is the corrected code:

```
var nowDate = new Date();
alert(nowDate.getMonth());
```

> **NOTE** To perhaps confuse the issue: technically, JavaScript doesn't have methods. What we think of as methods are actually functions assigned to an object's properties. But it's generally accepted to use the term method to describe such properties.

Similarly, another common mistake is to type parentheses after a property, making JavaScript think that you are trying to use a method of that object:

```
var myString = "Hello, World!";
alert(myString.length());
```

The second line uses the length property as a method, and JavaScript will attempt to treat it as one. When this code executes, you will see an error because length cannot be called as a method. This code should have been written like this:

```
var myString = new String("Hello");
alert(myString.length);
```

Missing Plus Signs During Concatenation

Ordinarily, string concatenation is a straightforward process, but it can become confusing when working with many variables and values. For example, there's a deliberate concatenation mistake in the following code. Spot it:

```
var myName = "Jeremy";
var myString = "Hello";
```

```
var myOtherString = "World";

myString = myName + " said " + myString + " " myOtherString;

alert(myString);
```

There should be a + operator between " " and `myOtherString` in the final line of code.

Although easy to spot in just a few lines, this kind of mistake can be more difficult to spot in large chunks of code. Also, the error message this type of mistake causes can be misleading. Load this code into a browser and you you'll be told `Error : Expected ';'` by IE, `Missing ; before statement` by Firefox, and `SyntaxError: Unexpected identifier` in Chrome. It's surprising how often this error crops up.

These most common mistakes are errors caused by the programmer. Other types of errors, called *runtime errors*, occur when your code executes in the browser, and they aren't necessarily caused by a typo or a missing curly brace or parenthesis. Runtime errors can still be planned for, as you see in the next section.

ERROR HANDLING

When writing your programs, you want to be informed of every error. However, the last things you want the user to see are error messages when you finally deploy the code to a web server for the whole world to access. Of course, writing bug-free code would be a good start, but keep the following points in mind:

➤ Conditions beyond your control can lead to errors. A good example of this is when you are relying on Ajax to talk to the web server, and something happens to the user's network connection.

➤ Murphy's Law states that anything that can go wrong will go wrong!

Preventing Errors

The best way to handle errors is to stop them from occurring in the first place. That seems like stating the obvious, but you should do a number of things if you want error-free pages:

➤ Thoroughly check pages in as many browsers as possible. This is easier said than done on some operating systems. The alternative is for you to decide which browsers you want to support for your web page, and then verify that your code works in them.

➤ Validate your data. If users can enter dud data that will cause your program to fail, then they will. Make sure that a text box has data entered into it if your code fails when the text box is empty. If you need a whole number, make sure that the user entered one. Is the date the user just entered valid? Is the e-mail address `mind your own business` the user just entered likely to be valid? No, so you must check that it is in the format `something@something.something`.

Okay, so let's say you carefully checked your pages and there is not a syntax or logic error in sight. You added data validation that confirms that everything the user enters is in a valid format. Things can still go wrong, and problems may arise that you can do nothing about. Here's a real-world example of something that can still go wrong.

One professional created an online message board that relies on a small Java applet to enable the transfer of data to and from the server without reloading the page (this was before Ajax). He checked the code and everything was fine, and it continued to work fine after launching the board, except that in about five percent of cases the Java applet initialized but then caused an error due to the user being behind a particular type of firewall (a firewall is a means of stopping intruders from getting into a local computer network, and many block Java applets because of Java's security issues). It's impossible to determine whether a user is behind a certain type of firewall, so there is nothing that can be done in that sort of exceptional circumstance. Or is there?

In fact, JavaScript includes something called the `try...catch` statement. This enables you to try to run your code; if it fails, the error is caught by the `catch` clause and can be dealt with as you wish. For the message board, this professional used a `try...catch` clause to catch the Java applet's failure and redirected the user to a more basic page that still displayed messages, but without using the applet.

The try...catch Statements

The `try...catch` statements work as a pair; you can't have one without the other. You use the `try` statement to define a block of code that you want to try to execute, and use the `catch` statement to define a block of code that executes when an exception occurs in the `try` statement. The term *exception* is key here; it means a circumstance that is extraordinary and unpredictable. Compare that with an *error*, which is something in the code that has been written incorrectly. If no exception occurs, the code inside the `catch` statement never executes. The `catch` statement also enables you to get the contents of the exception message that would have been shown to the user had you not caught it first.

Let's create a simple example of a `try...catch` clause:

```
<!DOCTYPE html>

<html lang="en">
<head>
    <title>Chapter 18: Example 1</title>
</head>
<body>
    <script>
        try {
            alert("This is code inside the try clause");
            alert("No Errors so catch code will not execute");
        } catch (exception) {
            alert("The error is " + exception.message);
        }
    </script>
</body>
</html>
```

Save this as `ch18_example1a.html` and open it in your browser.

This code defines the `try` statement, and as with all other blocks of code, you mark out the `try` block by enclosing it in curly braces.

Immediately following the `try` block is the `catch` statement, and notice that it includes `exception` inside a set of parentheses. This `exception` is simply a variable name, and it stores an object that contains information about any exception that may occur inside the try code block. We'll call this object the *exception object*. Although the word exception is used here, you can use any valid variable name. For example, catch(ex) would be fine.

The exception object contains several properties that provide information about the exception that occurred, but the most commonly used properties are name and message. The aptly named name property contains the name of the error type, and the message property contains the error message the user would normally see.

Back to the code at hand, within the catch block is the code that executes when an exception occurs. In this case, the code within the try block will not throw an exception, and so the code inside the catch block will never execute.

But let's insert a deliberate error. Change the highlighted line in the following code:

```
try {
    alert("This is code inside the try clause");
    ablert("No Errors so catch code will not execute");
} catch (exception) {
    alert("The error is " + exception.message);
}
```

Save the document as ch18_example1b.html and open it in your browser.

The browser will start executing this code as normal. It will execute the first call to alert()inside the try block and display the message to the user. However, the call to ablert() will cause an exception. The browser will stop executing the try block, and instead will start executing the catch block. You'll see a message similar to "The error is ablert is not defined."

Let's change this code once again to introduce a different error. As before, modify the highlighted line in the following code:

```
try {
    alert("This is code inside the try clause");
    alert('This code won't work');
} catch (exception) {
    alert("The error is " + exception.message);
}
```

Save this as ch18_example1c.html and open it in your browser. You will not see any alert box because this code contains a syntax error; the functions and methods are valid, but you have an invalid character. The single quote in the word won't has ended the string value being passed to alert().

Before executing any code, the JavaScript engine goes through all the code and checks for syntax errors, or code that breaches JavaScript's rules. If the engine finds a syntax error, the browser deals with it as usual; your try clause never runs and therefore cannot handle syntax errors.

Throwing Errors

You can use the throw statement to create your own runtime exceptions. Why create a statement to generate an exception, when a bit of bad coding will do the same?

Throwing errors can be very useful for indicating problems such as invalid user input. Rather than using lots of if...else statements, you can check the validity of user input, then use throw to stop code execution in its tracks and cause the error-catching code in the catch block of code to take over. In the catch clause, you can determine whether the error is based on user input, in which case you can notify the user what went wrong and how to correct it. Alternatively, if it's an unexpected error, you can handle it more gracefully than with lots of JavaScript errors.

You can throw anything; from a simple string or number to an object. In most cases, however, you'll throw an object. To use throw, type **throw** and include the object after it. For example, if you are validating a set of form fields, your exception object could contain not only the message, but the id of the element that has invalid data. An example could look like this:

```
throw {
    message : "Please type a valid email address",
    elementId : "txtEmail"
};
```

The objects you throw should include at least a message property; most error-handling code will be looking for it.

TRY IT OUT   try...catch and Throwing Errors

In this example you modify ch16_example2.html to use the try...catch and throw statements to validate the e-mail and username fields. Feel free to use ch16_example2.html as a basis for this new file. For your convenience, the following code listing highlights the key changes:

```
<!DOCTYPE html>

<html lang="en">
<head>
    <title>Chapter 18: Example 2</title>
    <style>
        .fieldname {
            text-align: right;
        }

        .submit {
            text-align: right;
        }
    </style>
</head>
<body>
    <form>
        <table>
            <tr>
                <td class="fieldname">
                    Username:
                </td>
                <td>
                    <input type="text" id="username" />
```

```
                    </td>
                    <td>
                        <a id="usernameAvailability" href="#">Check Availability</a>
                    </td>
                </tr>
                <tr>
                    <td class="fieldname">
                        Email:
                    </td>
                    <td>
                        <input type="text" id="email" />
                    </td>
                    <td>
                        <a id="emailAvailability" href="#">Check Availability</a>
                    </td>
                </tr>
                <tr>
                    <td class="fieldname">
                        Password:
                    </td>
                    <td>
                        <input type="text" id="password" />
                    </td>
                    <td />
                </tr>
                <tr>
                    <td class="fieldname">
                        Verify Password:
                    </td>
                    <td>
                        <input type="text" id="password2" />
                    </td>
                    <td />
                </tr>
                <tr>
                    <td colspan="2" class="submit">
                        <input type="submit" value="Submit" />
                    </td>
                    <td />
                </tr>
            </table>
    </form>
    <script src="jquery-2.1.1.min.js"></script>
    <script>
        function checkUsername(e) {
            e.preventDefault();

            var userValue = $("#username").val();

            try {
                if (!userValue) {
                    throw {
                        message: "Please enter a user name to check!"
                    };
```

```
            }

            var parms = {
                username: userValue
            };

            $.getJSON("ch14_formvalidator.php", parms).done(handleResponse);
        } catch (ex) {
            alert(ex.message);
        }
    }

    function checkEmail(e) {
        e.preventDefault();

        var emailValue = $("#email").val();

        try {
            if (!emailValue) {
                throw {
                    message: "Please enter an email address to check!"
                };
            }

            var parms = {
                email: emailValue
            };

            $.getJSON("ch14_formvalidator.php", parms).done(handleResponse);
        } catch (ex) {
            alert(ex.message);
        }
    }

    function handleResponse(response) {
        if (response.available) {
            alert(response.searchTerm + " is available!");
        } else {
            alert("We're sorry, but " + response.searchTerm +
                " is not available.");
        }
    }

    $("#usernameAvailability").on("click", checkUsername);
    $("#emailAvailability").on("click", checkEmail);
    </script>
</body>

</html>
```

Remember that this example relies upon Ajax in order to work; so, be sure to save this page as ch18_example2.html in your web server's root. In case you haven't set up a web server yet, see Chapter 14 for more information.

You know how this example works, so we'll focus only on the highlighted code.

Let's first look at the checkUsername() function. It has been rewritten to use the try...catch and throw statements for validating the username <input/> element, and the majority of this function's code resides within the try block:

```
try {
    if (!userValue) {
        throw {
            message: "Please enter a user name to check!"
        };
    }

    var parms = {
        username: userValue
    };

    $.getJSON("ch14_formvalidator.php", parms).done(handleResponse);
}
```

Before you make the Ajax request, you first ensure the user provided a value to the username field. If userValue is blank, you throw a new object detailing the cause of the exception with its message property. This causes the JavaScript engine to stop executing code in this try block and starts executing the catch block:

```
catch (ex) {
    alert(ex.message);
}
```

Here, you simply alert the exception's message property, displaying the "Please enter a user name to check!" message to the user.

Naturally, the changes made to the checkEmail() function are almost identical to checkUsername():

```
try {
    if (!emailValue) {
        throw {
            message: "Please enter an email address to check!"
        };
    }

    var parms = {
        email: emailValue
    };

    $.getJSON("ch14_formvalidator.php", parms).done(handleResponse);
} catch (ex) {
    alert(ex.message);
}
```

Once again, the majority of the function code resides within a try code block. If the e-mail field validation fails, you throw an object containing the exception message and display that message in an alert box—the result of executing the code in the catch block.

Nested try...catch Statements

So far you've been using just one try...catch statement, but it's possible to include a try...catch statement inside another try statement. Indeed, you can go further and have a try...catch inside the try statement of this inner try...catch, or even another inside that, the limit being what it's actually sensible to do.

So why would you use nested try...catch statements? Well, you can deal with certain errors inside the inner try...catch statement. If, however, you're dealing with a more serious error, the inner catch clause could pass that error to the outer catch clause by throwing the error to it.

Here's an example:

```
try {
    try {
        ablurt("This code has an error");
    } catch(exception) {
        var name = exception.name;

        if (name == "TypeError" || name == "ReferenceError") {
            alert("Inner try...catch can deal with this error");
        } else {
            throw exception;
        }
    }
} catch(exception) {
    alert("The inner try...catch could not handle the exception.");
}
```

In this code you have two try...catch pairs, one nested inside the other.

The inner try statement contains a line of code that contains an error. The catch statement of the inner try...catch checks the value of the error's name. If the exception's name is either TypeError or ReferenceError, the inner try...catch deals with it by way of an alert box (see Appendix B for a full list of error types and their descriptions). Unfortunately, and unsurprisingly, the type of error thrown by the browser depends on the browser itself. In the preceding example, IE reports the error as a TypeError whereas the other browsers report it as a ReferenceError.

If the error caught by the inner catch statement is any other type of error, it is thrown up in the air again for the catch statement of the outer try...catch to deal with.

finally Clauses

The try...catch statement has a finally clause that defines a block of code that always executes—even if an exception wasn't thrown. The finally clause can't appear on its own; it must be after a try block, which the following code demonstrates:

```
try {
    ablurt("An exception will occur");
} catch(exception) {
    alert("Exception occurred");
} finally {
    alert("This line always executes");
}
```

The `finally` part is a good place to put any cleanup code that needs to execute regardless of any exceptions that previously occurred.

You've seen the top mistakes made by developers, and you've also seen how to handle errors in your code. Unfortunately, errors will still occur in your code, so let's take a look at one way to make remedying them easier by using a debugger.

DEBUGGING

JavaScript is traditionally looked upon as a difficult language to write and debug due to the lack of decent development tools. This, however, is no longer the case thanks to the tools made available through the browser: the debugging tools available for Internet Explorer, Firefox, Chrome, and Opera. With these tools, you can halt the execution of your script with breakpoints and then step through code line by line to see exactly what is happening.

You can also find out what data is being held in variables and execute statements on the fly. Without debuggers, the best you can do is use the `alert()` method in your code to show the state of variables at various points.

Debugging is generally universal across all browsers, and even languages. Some debugging tools may offer more features than others, but for the most part, the following concepts apply to any debugger:

➤   Breakpoints tell the debugger it should break, or pause code execution, at a certain point. You can set a breakpoint anywhere in your JavaScript code, and the debugger will halt code execution when it reaches the breakpoint.

➤   Watches enable you to specify variables that you want to inspect when your code pauses at a breakpoint.

➤   The call stack is a record of what functions and methods have been executed to the breakpoint.

➤   The console enables you to execute JavaScript commands in the context of the page and within the scope of the breakpoint. In addition, it catalogs all JavaScript errors found in the page.

➤   Stepping is the most common procedure in debugging. It enables you to execute one line of code at a time. You can step through code in three ways:

    ➤   Step Into executes the next line of code. If that line is a function call, the debugger executes the function and halts at the first line of the function.

    ➤   Step Over, like Step Into, executes the next line of code. If that line is a function, Step Over executes the entire function and halts at the first line outside the function.

    ➤   Step Out returns to the calling function when you are inside a called function. Step Out resumes the execution of code until the function returns. It then breaks at the return point of the function.

Before delving into the various debuggers, let's create a page you can debug:

```
<!DOCTYPE html>

<html lang="en">
<head>
    <title>Chapter 18: Example 3</title>
</head>
<body>
    <script>
        function writeTimesTable(timesTable) {
            var writeString;
            for (var counter = 1; counter < 12; counter++) {
                writeString = counter + " * " + timesTable + " = ";
                writeString = writeString + (timesTable * counter);
                writeString = writeString + "<br />";
                document.write(writeString);
            }
        }

        writeTimesTable(2);
    </script>
</body>

</html>
```

Save this as ch18_example3.html. You will need to open this file in each browser in order to debug it.

The next section walks you through the features and functionality of Chrome's JavaScript debugger. Because of the universal nature of debugging and debuggers, the sections for Internet Explorer, Firefox, and Safari will merely familiarize you with the UI for each browser's debugger and point out any differences.

Debugging in Chrome (and Opera)

Chrome and Opera use the same rendering and JavaScript engine, and as such, they also share the same development tools. For the sake of simplicity, this section focuses on Chrome, but keep in mind that Opera is exactly the same.

You can access Chrome's developer tools a couple of ways. You can click the "hamburger menu" in the top right-hand corner of the window and select More Tools ➤ Developers tools. You can also open them by pressing the F12 key.

> **NOTE** You'll find that F12 opens the developer tools in almost every browser.

By default, the Developer tools opens as a panel in Chrome (see Figure 18-3).

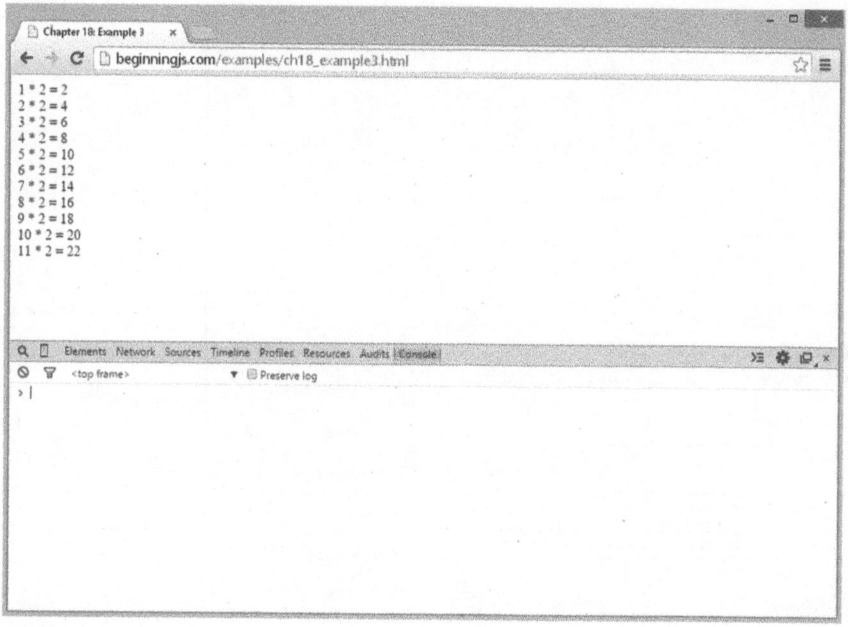

FIGURE 18-3

You can pop it out to its own window by clicking the icon next to the Close button.

Open `ch18_example3.html` (either from your computer or the web) in Chrome and open Chrome's developer tools.

The JavaScript debugger is contained in the Sources tab, and it is made up of three panels (Figure 18-4). The left panel contains the list of sources to choose from. You'll only see one source available in this chapter because there is only one file loaded by the browser. But if you load a page with multiple external JavaScript files, you'll find each of them listed in the left panel.

The center panel contains the source code of the selected file, and it's here that you'll set breakpoints and step through code. The code displayed in this panel is read-only; if you want to change it, you have to edit the file in your text editor and reload the page.

The right panel contains several different subpanels. In this chapter, we focus on Breakpoints, Scope Variables, Watch Expressions, and Call Stack:

➤ **Breakpoints:** Lists all breakpoints that you've created for the code in the current page

➤ **Scope Variables:** Lists the variables and their values in scope of the breakpoint

➤ **Watch Expressions:** Lists the "watches" that you specify. These are typically variables and/or expressions that you want to inspect at a breakpoint.

➤ **Call Stack:** Displays the call stack

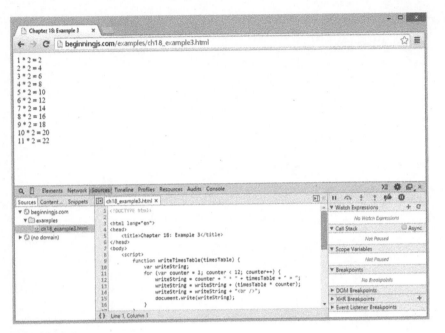

FIGURE 18-4

Setting Breakpoints

As mentioned earlier, breakpoints tell the debugger to pause code execution at a specific point in your code. This is useful when you want to inspect your code while it executes.

Creating breakpoints is straightforward. Simply left-click the line number, and Chrome highlights the line number with a blue tag icon. This highlight denotes a breakpoint in Chrome.

You can also hard-code a breakpoint by using the debugger keyword directly in your code (we'll use this a bit later).

Set a breakpoint on line 13:

```
writeString = writeString + (timesTable * counter);
```

Reload the page, and notice Chrome paused code execution at the newly created breakpoint. Chrome highlights the current line of code in blue. This line hasn't been executed yet.

Look at the Breakpoints in the right panel; it shows you the list of breakpoints (only one in this case). Each entry in the list consists of a checkbox to enable/disable the breakpoint, the filename and line number of the source file, and the source text of the breakpoint.

Now look at the Scope Variables.

Scope Variables and Watches

The Scope Variables pane displays variables and their values currently in scope at the current line. Figure 18-5 shows the contents of the Scope Variables pane at this breakpoint.

Notice that the `counter`, `timesTable`, and `writeString` variables are visible (as is `this`).

Now look at the Watch Expressions pane. There are currently no watch expressions, but you can add them by simply clicking the add icon (the plus sign). Type the variable name or expression you want to watch, and press the Enter key.

Go ahead and create a watch expression for `counter == 1`. You'll see your expression followed by a colon and the value of the expression. At this point in time, you should see the following as shown in Figure 18-6:

```
counter == 1: true
```

If the watch is in scope, the expression's value is displayed. If the variable is out of scope, you'll see "not available."

```
▼ Scope Variables
▼ Local
    counter: 1
  ▶ this: Window
    timesTable: 2
    writeString: "1 * 2 = "
▶ Global                    Window
```

FIGURE 18-5

```
▼ Watch Expressions          +  ↻
    counter == 1: true
```

FIGURE 18-6

Although this information is helpful when you want to see what exactly is going on in your code, it's not very helpful if you can't control code execution. It's impractical to set a breakpoint and reload the page multiple times just to advance to the next line, so we use a process called *stepping*.

Stepping through Code

Code stepping is controlled by four buttons in the upper-right of the developer tools (Figure 18-7).

➤ **Continue (shortcut key is F8):** Its function is to continue code execution until either the next breakpoint or the end of all code is reached.

➤ **Step Over (F10):** This executes the current line of code and moves to the next statement. However, if the statement is a function, it executes the function and steps to the next line after the function call.

FIGURE 18-7

➤ **Step Into (shortcut key is F11):** Executes the current line of code and moves to the next statement. If the current line is a function, it steps to the first line of the function.

➤ **Step Out (Shift-F11):** Returns to the calling function.

Let's do some stepping; follow these steps:

1. Step Into the code by clicking the icon or pressing F11. The debugger executes the currently highlighted line of code and moves to the next line.

2. Look at the value of `writeString` in the Scope Variables pane; it is `"1 * 2 = 2"`. As you can see, the values displayed in the Watch tab are updated in real time.

3. One nice feature of Chrome's developer tools is the page updates, if necessary, as you step through code. Click Step Into two more times to see this in action. Figure 18-8 shows the page updated while stepping through code.

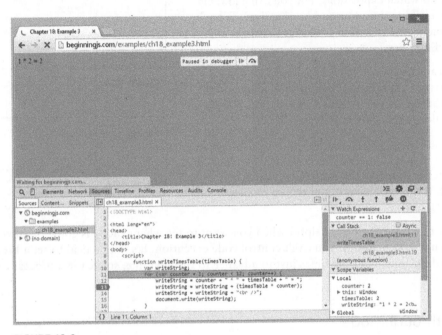

FIGURE 18-8

You may find that the function you stepped into is not the source of the bug, in which case you want to execute the remaining lines of code in the function so that you can continue stepping after the function. Do so by clicking the Step Out icon to step out of the code. However, if you're in a loop and the breakpoint is set inside the loop, you will not step out of the function until you iterate through the loop.

There may also be times when you have some buggy code that calls a number of functions. If you know that some of the functions are bug-free, you may want to just execute those functions instead of stepping into them. Use Step Over in these situations to execute the code within a function but without going through it line by line.

Alter your times-table code in ch18_example3.html as follows so you can use it for the three kinds of stepping:

```
<!DOCTYPE html>

<html lang="en">
<head>
    <title>Chapter 18: Example 4</title>
</head>
```

```
<body>
    <script>
        function writeTimesTable(timesTable) {
            var writeString;
            for (var counter = 1; counter < 12; counter++) {
                writeString = counter + " * " + timesTable + " = ";
                writeString = writeString + (timesTable * counter);
                writeString = writeString + "<br />";
                document.write(writeString);
            }
        }

        for (var timesTable = 1; timesTable <= 12; timesTable++) {
            document.write("<p>");
            writeTimesTable(timesTable);
            document.write("</p>");
        }
    </script>
</body>

</html>
```

Save this as `ch18_example4.html` and open it in your browser. The following instructions walk you through the process of stepping through code:

1. Set a breakpoint in line 19, the `for` loop in the body of the page, and reload the page.

2. Click the Step Into icon and code execution moves to the next statement. Now the first statement inside the `for` loop, `document.write("<p>")`, is up for execution.

3. When you click the Step Into icon again, it takes you to the next line (the first calling of the `writeTimesTable()` function).

4. You want to see what's happening inside that function, so click Step Into again to step into the function. Your screen should look similar to Figure 18-9.

5. Click the Step Into icon a few times to get the gist of the flow of execution of the function. In fact, stepping through code line by line can get a little tedious. So let's imagine you're happy with this function and want to run the rest of it.

6. Use Step Out to run the rest of the function's code. You're back to the original `for` loop, and the debugger is paused on line 22, as you can see from Figure 18-10.

7. Click the Step Into icon to execute `document.write()` (it won't be visible because it's a closing tag).

8. Click Step Into four more times. Execution continues through the condition and increments parts of the `for` loop, ending back at the line that calls `writeTimesTable()`.

9. You've already seen this code in action, so you want to step over this function. Well, no prizes for guessing that Step Over is what you need to do. Click the Step Over icon (or press the F10 key) and the function executes, but without stepping through it statement by statement. You should find yourself back at the `document.write("</p>")` line.

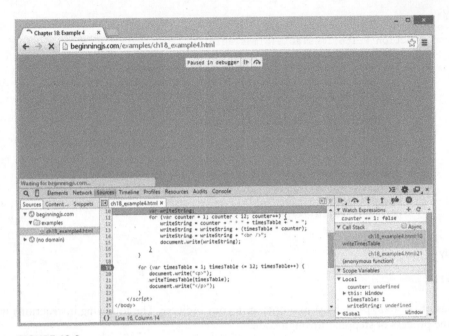

FIGURE 18-9

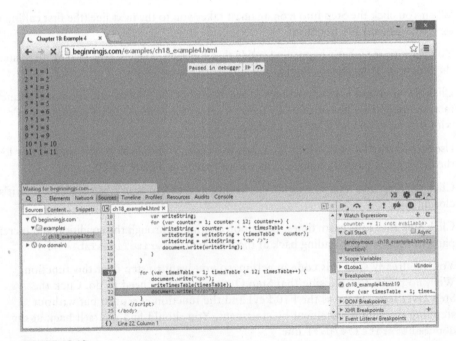

FIGURE 18-10

If you've finished debugging, you can run the rest of the code without stepping through each line by clicking the Continue icon (or pressing F8) on the toolbar. You should see a page of times tables from 1*1=1 to 11*12=132 in the browser.

The Console

While you're stepping through code and checking its flow of execution, it would be really useful to evaluate conditions and even to change things on the fly. You can do these things using the console.

Follow these steps:

1. Remove the previously set breakpoint by clicking it and set a new breakpoint at line 15:

    ```
    document.write(writeString);
    ```

2. Let's see how you can find out the value currently contained in the variable writeString. Reload the page. When the debugger stops at the breakpoint, click the Console tab and type the name of the variable you want to examine, in this case writeString. Press the Enter key. This causes the value contained in the variable to be printed below your command in the command window, as shown in Figure 18-11.

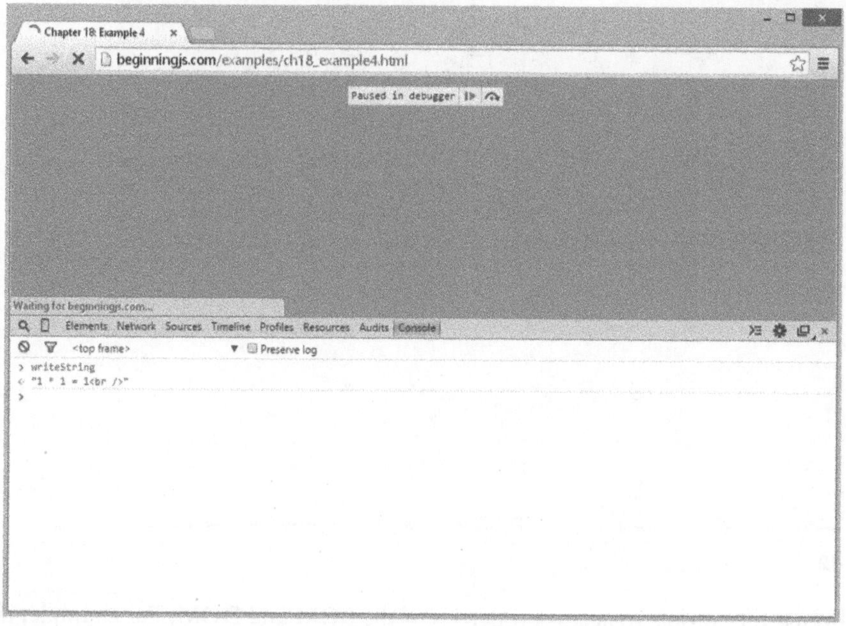

FIGURE 18-11

3. If you want to change a variable, you can write a line of JavaScript into the command window and press Enter. Try it with the following code:

    ```
    writeString = "Changed on the Fly<br />";
    ```

4. Click the Sources tab, remove the breakpoint, and then click the Continue icon. You see the results of your actions: Where the 1*1 times table result should be, the text you changed on the fly has been inserted.

> **NOTE** *This alteration does not change your actual HTML source file.*

The console can also evaluate conditions. Set a breakpoint on line 20 and reload the page. Leave execution stopped at the breakpoint, and Step Into the for loop's condition.

Go to the Console, type the following, and press Enter:

```
timesTable <= 12
```

Because this is the first time the loop has been run, as shown in Figure 18-12, timesTable is equal to 1 so the condition timesTable <= 12 evaluates to true.

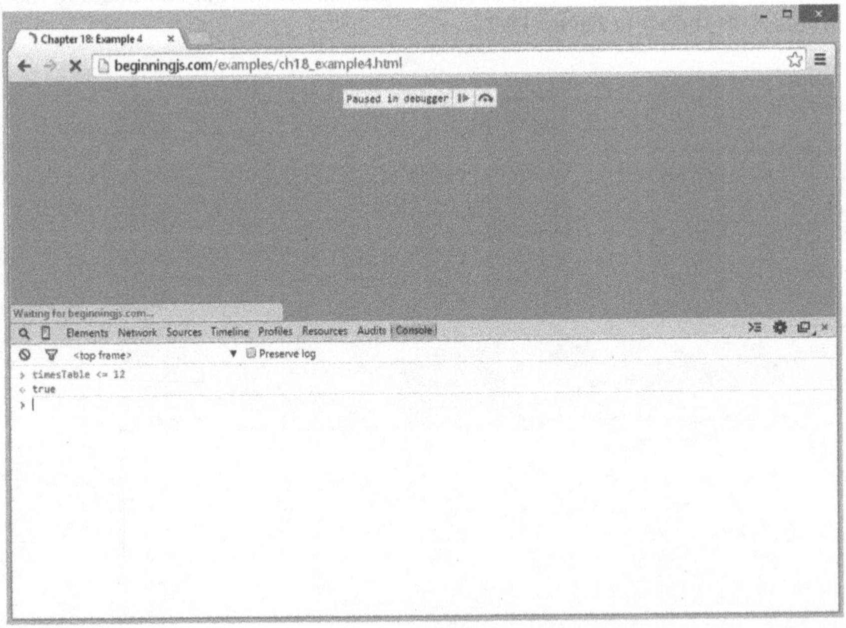

FIGURE 18-12

You can also use the console to access properties of the BOM and DOM. For example, if you type location.href into the console and press Enter, it will tell you the web page's URL.

> **NOTE** *You can evaluate any JavaScript in the console, and it executes within the scope of the page and/or breakpoint. This makes the console an extremely powerful tool.*

Call Stack Window

When you are single-stepping through the code, the call stack window keeps a running list of which functions have been called to get to the current point of execution in the code.

Let's create an example web page to demonstrate the call stack. Open your text editor and type the following:

```
<!DOCTYPE html>

<html lang="en">
<head>
    <title>Chapter 18: Example 5</title>
</head>
<body>
    <input type="button" value="Button" name="button1" id="button1" />

    <script>
        function firstCall() {
            secondCall();
        }

        function secondCall() {
            thirdCall();
        }

        function thirdCall() {
            //
        }

        function buttonClick() {
            debugger;
            firstCall();
        }

        document.getElementById("button1")
                .addEventListener("click", buttonClick);
    </script>
</body>

</html>
```

Save this file as ch18_example5.html and open it in Chrome. You'll see a page with a simple button. With the development tools open, click the button and examine the Call Stack pane. You should see something like Figure 18-13.

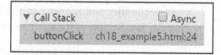

FIGURE 18-13

Chrome adds the function to the top of the call stack for every function call. It displays the name of the function, the file the function resides in, and the line number of the currently executing statement within the function. You can already see that the first function called was buttonClick(), it is inside ch18_example5.html, and the execution is at line 24.

Now Step Into twice, and you'll be taken inside the `firstCall()` function. Once again, examine the Call Stack pane, and you'll see something similar to Figure 18-14.

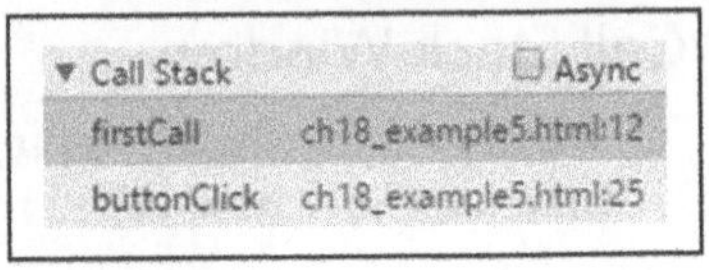

FIGURE 18-14

You can click each entry in the Call Stack pane to examine where the JavaScript engine is currently executing in each of the functions. If you click the `buttonClick` entry, the developer tools highlight line 25, the line inside of `buttonClick()` that is currently executing.

Now step into `secondCall()`, and another entry is added to the call stack. One more step takes you into `thirdCall()`, again with its name being added to the top of the call stack.

Step Into again, and as you leave the `thirdCall()` you will see that its corresponding entry is removed from the top of the call stack. Yet another step takes you out of `secondCall()`. Each additional step takes you out of a function and removes its name from the call stack, until eventually all the code has been executed.

This demo page was very simple to follow, but with complex pages, the call stack can prove very useful for tracking where you are, where you have been, and how you got there.

As mentioned earlier, most other developer tools for other browsers are similar to Chrome's developer tools in functionality, but as you'll soon see with IE11, the tools can look a bit different.

Debugging in Internet Explorer

Before version 8, developers had to download and install the Microsoft Script Debugger for any type of script debugging. Thankfully, Microsoft built a debugger into IE8, and every subsequent version includes a suite of tools to ease our lives.

You can access the debugger in a couple of ways, the easiest being to press the F12 key. However, you can also bring up the development tools by clicking the "gear" menu and choosing the F12 Developer Tools option.

By default, the F12 Developer Tools opens as a panel within the browser window (Figure 18-15), but as with Chrome's tools, you can pop it out with the icon next to the Close button.

As you can tell from Figure 18-15, IE's tools are laid out much differently than Chrome's. On the left-hand side, you see a list of icons. The two we are concerned with are the second and third icons: the console (Figure 18-16) and debugger (Figure 18-17), respectively.

As you can see in Figure 18-17, the debugger is made up of two panels. The left displays the source code of the file, and it uses a tabbed interface to display the source of multiple files. If multiple files contain JavaScript, you can open them in a new tab using the file selection button.

The right panel contains two subpanel tabs:

➤ **Watches:** Lists the variables/expressions and their values you specify to watch at the breakpoint. This also displays the variables in scope.

➤ **Breakpoints/Call Stack:** Lists all breakpoints that you've created for the code in the current page. You can click "Call Stack" to display the call stack.

Now load `ch18_example4.html`, and you'll see the times table in your web page.

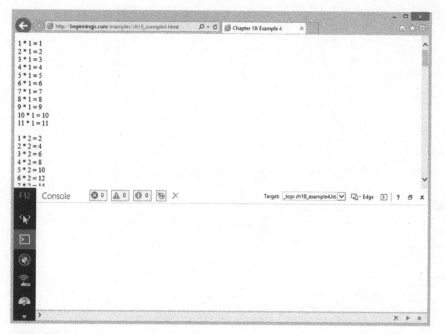

FIGURE 18-15

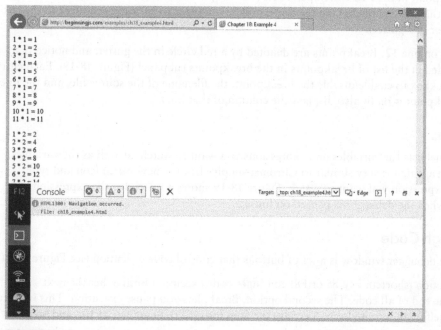

FIGURE 18-16

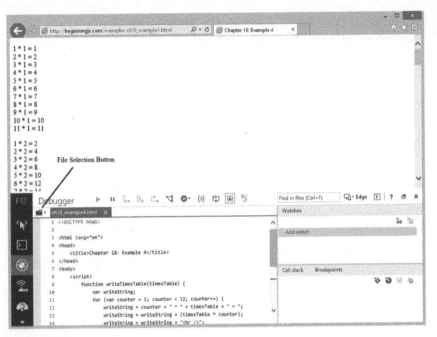

FIGURE 18-17

Setting Breakpoints

Creating a breakpoint in the F12 Developer Tools is as simple and straightforward as it is in Chrome, except that instead of clicking the line number, you want to click the gray area to the left of the line number (the gutter).

Set a breakpoint on line 12. Breakpoints are denoted by a red circle in the gutter, and notice that an entry was added in the list of breakpoints in the breakpoints subpanel (Figure 18-18). Each entry consists of a checkbox to enable/disable the breakpoint, the filename of the source file, and the line number the breakpoint is on (it also displays the column of that line).

Adding Watches

The Watches panel lists the variables and expressions you want to watch, as well as the variables in scope. Adding a watch is very similar to Chrome; simply click the new watch icon and type the variable or expression you want to watch. Figure 18-19 shows a watch for the expression `counter == 1` when the debugger is paused on line 12.

Stepping through Code

At the top of the debugger window is a set of buttons that control code execution (see Figure 18-20).

The Continue option (shortcut key F5 or F8) continues code execution until either the next breakpoint or the end of all code. The second option, Break, lets you pause execution. This is useful if you find yourself in an infinite loop. Next are the Step Into (F11), Step Over (F10), and Step Out (Shift+11) buttons.

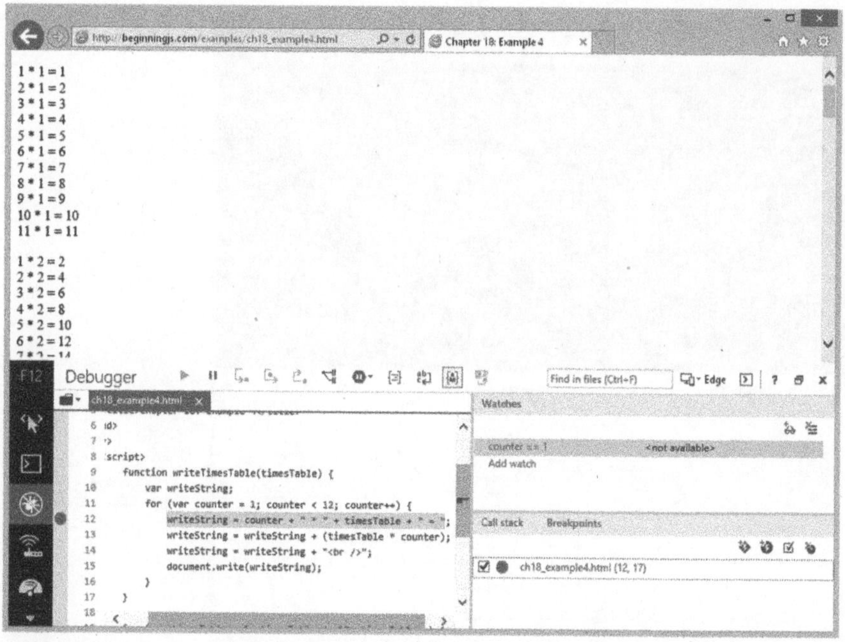

FIGURE 18-18

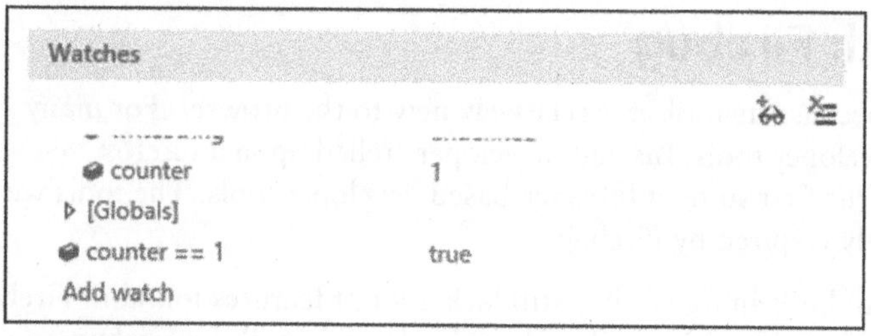

FIGURE 18-19

FIGURE 18-20

The F12 Developer Tools debugger denotes the current line by highlighting the line in yellow and adds a yellow arrow in the gutter. But unlike Chrome, stepping through code does not update the web page. The JavaScript executes, but you will not see the results until all code is executed.

The Console

The console logs JavaScript errors and enables you to execute code within the context of the line at which the debugger is stopped. Figure 18-21 shows the "Changed on the Fly" example.

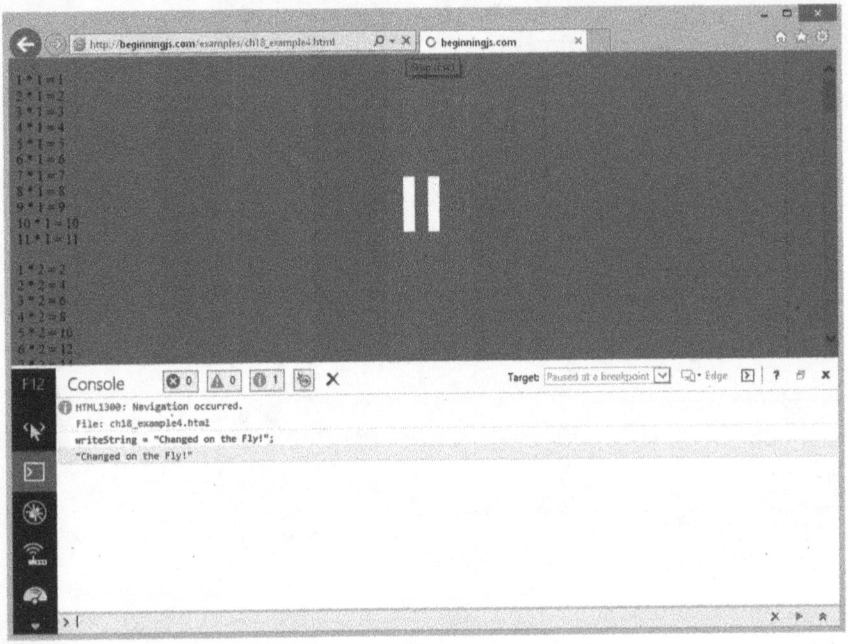

FIGURE 18-21

Debugging in Firefox with Firebug

Firefox's story is an interesting one because its toolset is relatively new to the browser. For many years, Firefox did not have native developer tools. Instead, developers relied upon a Firefox extension called Firebug, which was the first suite of browser-based developer tools. The tools we use in every browser today are directly inspired by Firebug.

Even though Firefox has its own set of built-in tools, they still lack a lot of features found in Firebug (and other browsers' tools). So for this section, you need to download and install the Firebug extension.

To install Firebug, open Firefox and go to http://www.getfirebug.com. Click the Install button on the web page and follow the instructions. In most cases, you will not need to restart Firefox.

You can access Firebug by clicking the Firebug icon in the toolbar (Figure 18-22). You can also access a dropdown menu by clicking the down arrow next to the Firebug icon to reveal additional settings. Many panels are disabled by default, so clicking on the Enable All Panels option is very useful.

The JavaScript debugger is contained in the Script tab, and it is made up of two panels. The left panel contains the source code, and the right panel contains three different views to choose from: Watch, Stack, and Breakpoints.

Setting Breakpoints

Creating breakpoints in Firebug is easy; simply left-click the line number or the gutter. Breakpoints are denoted by a red circle in the gutter.

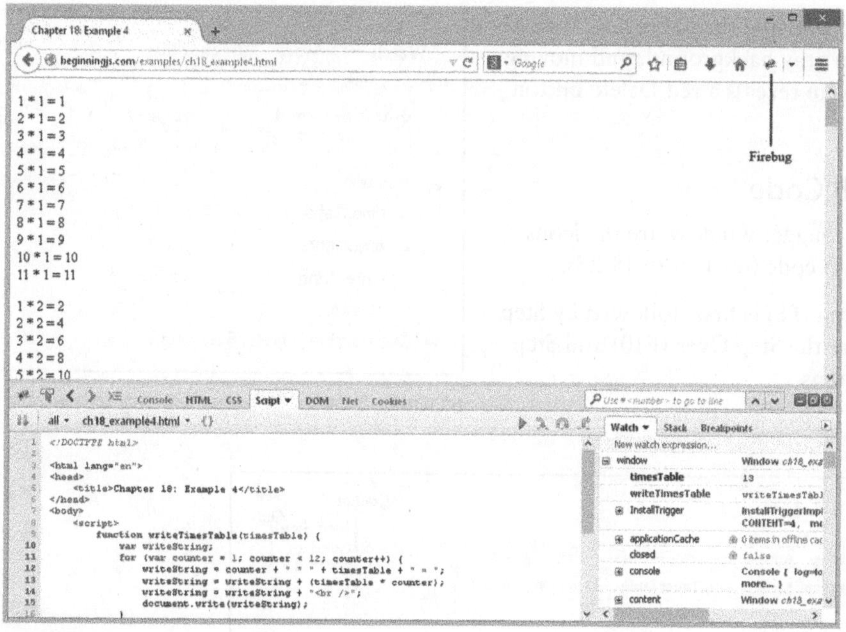

FIGURE 18-22

The Breakpoints tab in the right pane displays the list of breakpoints you have created, and it shows all the information you expect: the filename, the code at that breakpoint, and the line number. Figure 18-23 shows a breakpoint on line 12.

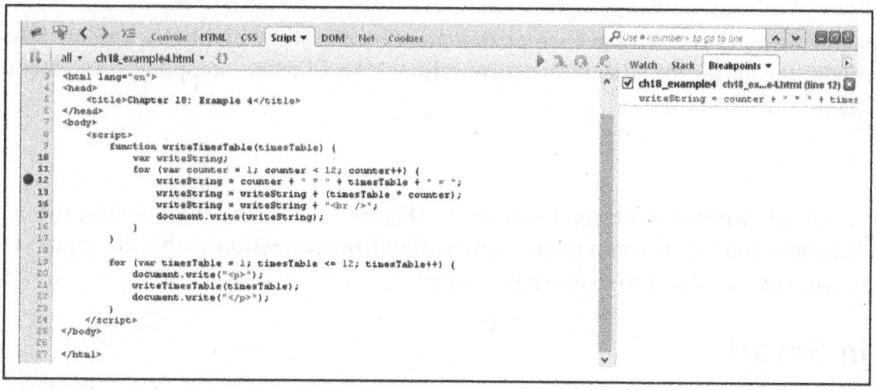

FIGURE 18-23

Now click the Watch tab.

Watches

The Watch tab displays variables and their values currently in scope at the current line, and you can add your own watch by clicking "New watch expression...," typing the variable or expression you want to watch, and pressing the Enter key. Watches that you add have a gray background, and moving your mouse over them reveals a red Delete button (Figure 18-24).

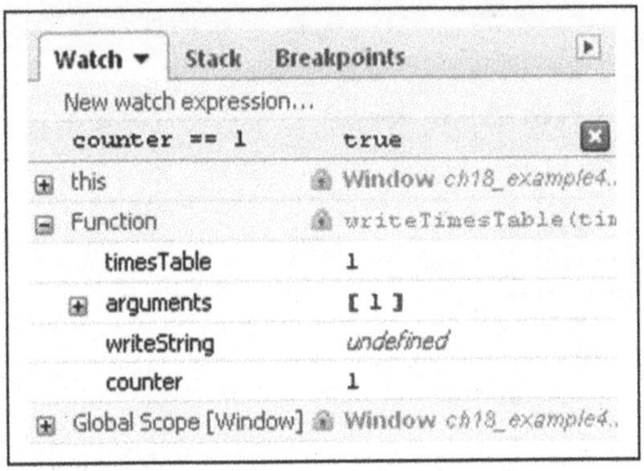

Stepping through Code

At the top of the debugger window are the icons for stepping through code (see Figure 18-25).

The Continue button (F8) is first, followed by Step Into (F11). Next are the Step Over (F10) and Step Out (Shift+11) buttons.

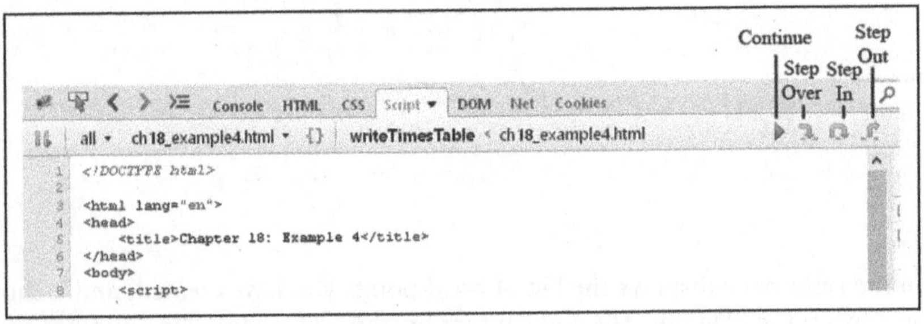

FIGURE 18-24

FIGURE 18-25

As you step through code, you can tell the current statement by its yellow highlight. Firebug also uses a yellow arrow in the gutter to indicate the current line. Like Chrome, stepping through code updates the web page.

The Console

Firebug provides a console window with the Console tab (Figure 18-26), and it works like the console found in Chrome and IE. You can inspect any variable or expression within the context of the scope or page, and you can use it to execute JavaScript.

Debugging in Safari

Safari's story is similar to IE's. Safari's rendering engine is called Webkit, and the folks that write and maintain Webkit built a separate tool, codenamed Drosera, that contained the tools similar to the other browsers. It was a separate download, and it required you to attach it to a specific Safari/Webkit window. Today, Safari includes a tool called Web Inspector, and it provides the functionality you would expect from a browser-based suite of tools.

Safari's Web Inspector is disabled by default. To enable it, follow these steps:

1. Click the Settings menu button and choose the Preferences option (see Figure 18-27).

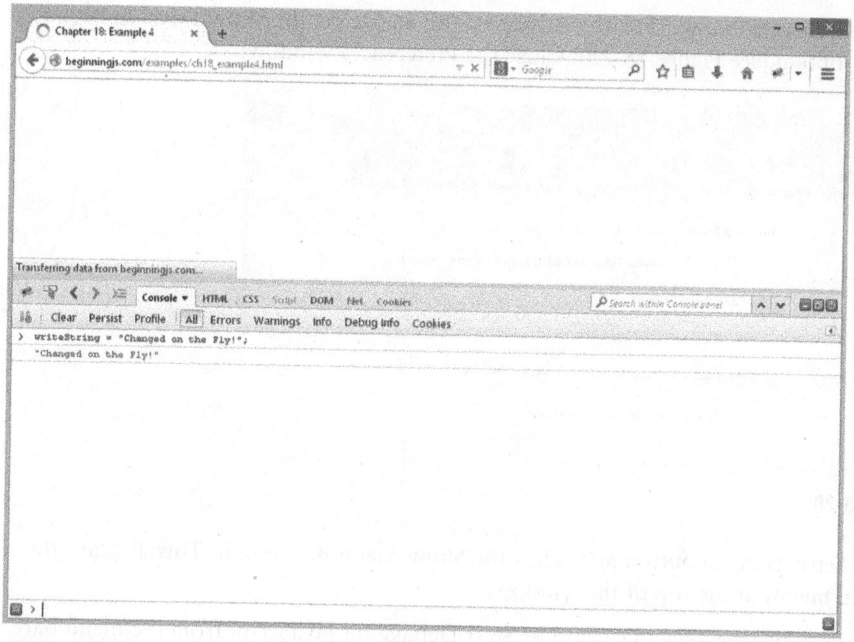

FIGURE 18-26

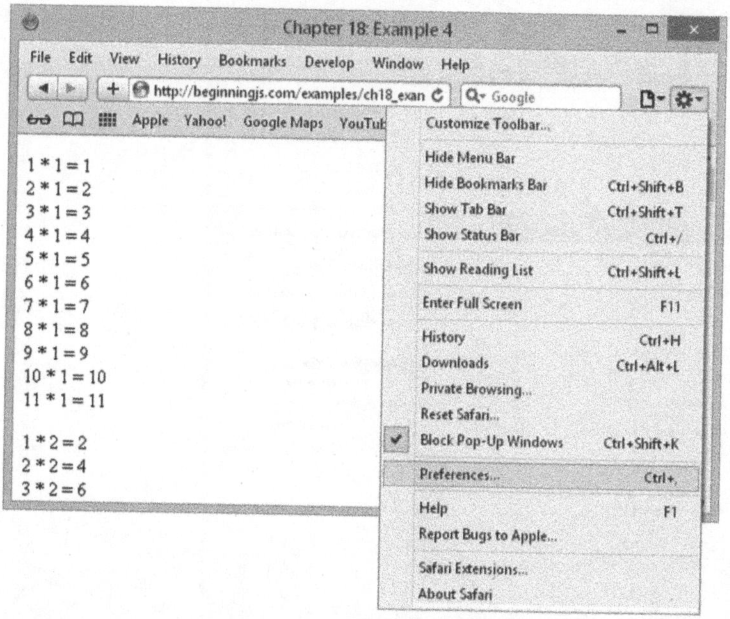

FIGURE 18-27

2. In the Preferences window, click the Advanced tab and select the Show Develop Menu in Menu Bar option (see Figure 18-28). Close the Preferences window.

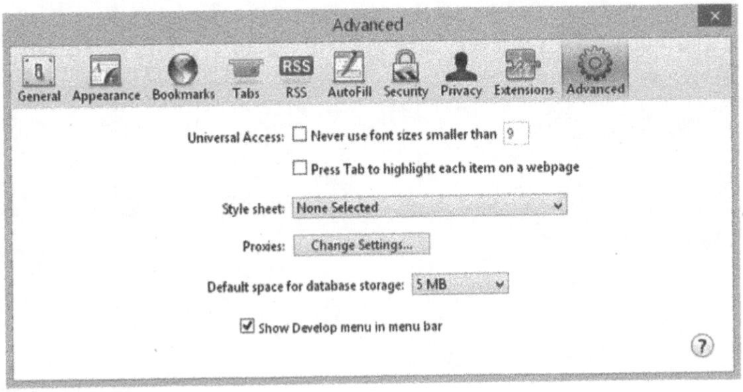

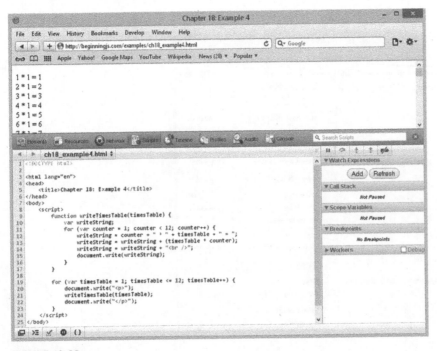

FIGURE 18-28

3. Click the Settings menu button and select the Show Menu Bar option. This displays the traditional menus at the top of the window.

4. To open the debugger, select Develop ➤ Start Debugging JavaScript from the menu bar.

Let's look at the window and identify the separate parts. Figure 18-29 shows the JavaScript debugger when it was first opened on the ch18_example4.html file.

FIGURE 18-29

Safari's Web Inspector looks a lot like Chrome's, doesn't it? That's because Chrome is built using a heavily modified version of WebKit. The Scripts tab is much like Chrome's Sources tab; you can see the code, watch expressions, call stack, scope variables, and breakpoints all at one time.

Setting Breakpoints

Creating a breakpoint follows the same procedure in Web Inspector as Chrome: Click the line number at which you want the debugger to break. Breakpoints in Web Inspector are denoted by the same blue tag used in Chrome. Create one on line 12. The breakpoints' subsection lists the breakpoints you create, and it displays the same information you expect it to.

Adding Watches

In earlier versions, Web Inspector did not allow you to add watches. But in Safari 5, you can create watches to inspect variables and expressions. Simply click the Add button to create your watch. Figure 18-30 shows the watch `counter == 1` when the debugger is paused on line 12.

FIGURE 18-30

To remove a watch, click the red X next to it.

Stepping through Code

The code-stepping buttons are at the top of the right panel and underneath the search box (see Figure 18-31).

These buttons perform the same functions as the other browser tools. You have the Continue button, followed by Step Over, then Step In, and finally Step Out.

Like Chrome and Firebug, Web Inspector updates the page as you step through code. So you can see the results as each line executes.

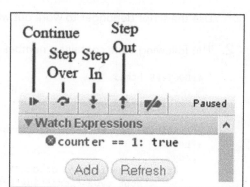

FIGURE 18-31

The Console

The console serves the same purpose as it does in the previous tools. You can check the value of a variable by typing the variable and pressing the Enter key. You can also execute code in the context of the current line of code. Try the "Changed on the Fly" example to see it in action.

SUMMARY

In this chapter you looked at the less exciting part of coding, namely bugs. In an ideal world you'd get things right the first time, every time, but in reality any code more than a few lines long is likely to suffer from bugs.

➤ You first looked at some of the more common errors, those made not just by JavaScript beginners, but also by experts with lots of experience.

➤ Some errors are not necessarily bugs in your code, but in fact exceptions to the normal circumstances that cause your code to fail. You saw that the `try...catch` statements are good for dealing with this sort of error, and that you can use the `catch` clause with the `throw` statement to deal with likely errors, such as those caused by user input. Finally, you saw that if you want a block of code to execute regardless of any error, you can use the `finally` clause.

➤ You looked at the debugging tools found in Chrome (and by extension Opera), Internet Explorer, Firebug for Firefox, and Safari. With these tools you can analyze code as it executes, which enables you to see its flow step by step, and to check variables and conditions. And although these debuggers have different interfaces, their principles are identical.

EXERCISES

You can find suggested solutions to these questions in Appendix A.

1. The example `ch18_example4.html` has a deliberate bug. For each times table it creates only multipliers with values from 1 to 11.

   Use the script debugger to work out why this is happening, and then correct the bug.

2. The following code contains a number of common errors. See if you can spot them:

```
<!DOCTYPE html>

<html lang="en">
<head>
    <title>Chapter 18: Question 2</title>
</head>
<body>
    <form name="form1" action="">
        <input type="text" id="text1" name="text1" />
        <br />
        CheckBox 1<input type="checkbox" id="checkbox2" name="checkbox2" />
        <br />
        CheckBox 1<input type="checkbox" id="checkbox1" name="checkbox1" />
        <br />
        <input type="text" id="text2" name="text2" />
        <p>
            <input type="submit" value="Submit" id="submit1" name="submit1" />
        </p>
    </form>

    <script>
        function checkForm(e) {
            var elementCount = 0;
            var theForm = document.form1;

            while(elementCount =<= theForm.length) {
```

```
                if (theForm.elements[elementcount].type == "text") {
                    if (theForm.elements[elementCount].value() = "")
                        alert("Please complete all form elements");
                    theForm.elements[elementCount].focus;
                    e.preventDefault();
                    break;
                }
            }
        }

        document.form1.addEventListener("submit", checkForm);
    </script>
</body>

</html>
```

A

Answers to Exercises

This appendix provides the answers to the questions you find at the end of each chapter in this book.

CHAPTER 2

Exercise 1 Question

Write a JavaScript program to convert degrees centigrade into degrees Fahrenheit, and to write the result to the page in a descriptive sentence. The JavaScript equation for Fahrenheit to centigrade is as follows:

```
degFahren = 9 / 5 * degCent + 32
```

Exercise 1 Solution

```html
<!DOCTYPE html>

<html lang="en">
<head>
    <title>Chapter 2: Question 1</title>
</head>
<body>
    <script>
        var degCent = prompt("Enter the degrees in centigrade", 0);
        var degFahren = 9 / 5 * degCent + 32;

        document.write(degCent + " degrees centigrade is " + degFahren +
            " degrees Fahrenheit");
    </script>
</body>
</html>
```

Save this as ch2_question1.html.

Exercise 2 Question

The following code uses the `prompt()` function to get two numbers from the user. It then adds those two numbers and writes the result to the page:

```
<!DOCTYPE html>

<html lang="en">
<head>
    <title>Chapter 2, Question 2</title>
</head>
<body>

<script>
    var firstNumber = prompt("Enter the first number","");
    var secondNumber = prompt("Enter the second number","");
    var theTotal = firstNumber + secondNumber;

    document.write(firstNumber + " added to " + secondNumber +
        " equals " + theTotal);
</script>
</body>
</html>
```

However, if you try out the code, you'll discover that it doesn't work. Why not? Change the code so that it does work.

Exercise 2 Solution

The data that the `prompt()` actually obtains is a string. So both `firstNumber` and `secondNumber` contain text that happens to be number characters. When you use the + symbol to add the two variables together, JavaScript assumes that because it's string data, you must want to concatenate the two and not sum them.

To make it explicit to JavaScript that you want to add the numbers, you need to convert the data to numbers using the `parseFloat()` function:

```
var firstNumber = parseFloat(prompt("Enter the first number",""));
var secondNumber = parseFloat(prompt("Enter the second number",""));
var theTotal = firstNumber + secondNumber;

document.write(firstNumber + " added to " + secondNumber + " equals " +
    theTotal);
```

Save this as `ch2_question2.html`.

Now the data returned by the `prompt()` function is converted to a floating-point number before being stored in the `firstNumber` and `secondNumber` variables. Then, when you do the addition that is stored in `theTotal`, JavaScript makes the correct assumption that, because both the variables are numbers, you must mean to add them up and not concatenate them.

The general rule is that where you have expressions with only numerical data, the + operator means "do addition." If there is any string data, the + means concatenate.

CHAPTER 3

Exercise 1 Question

A junior programmer comes to you with some code that appears not to work. Can you spot where he went wrong? Give him a hand and correct the mistakes.

```
var userAge = prompt("Please enter your age");

if (userAge = 0) {;
    alert("So you're a baby!");
} else if ( userAge < 0 | userAge > 200)
    alert("I think you may be lying about your age");
else {
    alert("That's a good age");
}
```

Exercise 1 Solution

Oh dear, our junior programmer is having a bad day! There are two mistakes on the line:

```
if (userAge = 0) {;
```

First, he has only one equals sign instead of two in the `if`'s condition, which means `userAge` will be assigned the value of 0 rather than `userAge` being compared to 0. The second fault is the semicolon at the end of the line—statements such as `if` and loops such as `for` and `while` don't require semicolons. The general rule is that if the statement has an associated block (that is, code in curly braces), no semicolon is needed. So the line should be:

```
if (userAge == 0) {
```

The next fault is with these lines:

```
else if ( userAge < 0 | userAge > 200)
    alert("I think you may be lying about your age");
else {
```

The junior programmer's condition is asking if `userAge` is less than 0 OR `userAge` is greater than 200. The correct operator for a boolean OR is | |, but the programmer has only used one |.

Exercise 2 Question

Using `document.write()`, write code that displays the results of the 12 times table. Its output should be the results of the calculations.

```
12 * 1 = 12
12 * 2 = 24
12 * 3 = 36
...
12 * 11 = 132
12 * 12 = 144
```

Exercise 2 Solution

```
<!DOCTYPE html>

<html lang="en">
<head>
    <title>Chapter 3: Question 2</title>
</head>
<body>
    <script>
        var timesTable = 12;

        for (var timesBy = 1; timesBy < 13; timesBy++) {
            document.write(timesTable + " * " +
                            timesBy + " = " +
                            timesBy * timesTable + "<br />");
        }
    </script>
</body>
</html>
```

Save this as ch3_question2.html.

You use a `for` loop to calculate from `1 * 12` up to `12 * 12`. The results are written to the page with `document.write()`. What's important to note here is the effect of the order of precedence; the concatenation operator (the `+`) has a lower order of precedence than the multiplication operator, `*`. This means that the `timesBy * timesTable` is done before the concatenation, which is the result you want. If this were not the case, you'd have to put the calculation in parentheses to raise its order of precedence.

CHAPTER 4

Exercise 1 Question

Change the code of Question 2 from Chapter 3 so that it's a function that takes as parameters the times table required and the values at which it should start and end. For example, you might try the four times table displayed starting with `4 * 4` and ending at `4 * 9`.

Exercise 1 Solution

```
<!DOCTYPE html>

<html lang="en">
<head>
    <title>Chapter 4: Question 1</title>
</head>
<body>
    <script>
        function writeTimesTable(timesTable, timesByStart, timesByEnd) {
            for (; timesByStart <= timesByEnd; timesByStart++) {
```

```
                    document.write(timesTable + " * " + timesByStart + " = " +
                        timesByStart * timesTable + "<br />");
                }
            }

            writeTimesTable(4, 4, 9);
        </script>
    </body>
</html>
```

Save this as `ch4_question1.html`.

You've declared your function, calling it `writeTimesTable()`, and given it three parameters. The first is the times table you want to write, the second is the start point, and the third is the number it should go up to.

You've modified your `for` loop. First you don't need to initialize any variables, so the initialization part is left blank—you still need to put a semicolon in, but there's no code before it. The `for` loop continues while the `timesByStart` parameter is less than or equal to the `timesByEnd` parameter. You can see that, as with a variable, you can modify parameters—in this case, `timesByStart` is incremented by one for each iteration through the loop.

The code to display the times table is much the same. For the function's code to be executed, you now actually need to call it, which you do in the line:

```
writeTimesTable(4, 4, 9);
```

This will write the 4 times table starting at 4 times 4 and ending at 9 times 4.

Exercise 2 Question

Modify the code of Question 1 to request the times table to be displayed from the user; the code should continue to request and display times tables until the user enters -1. Additionally, do a check to make sure that the user is entering a valid number; if the number is not valid, ask the user to re-enter it.

Exercise 2 Solution

```
<!DOCTYPE html>

<html lang="en">
<head>
    <title>Chapter 4: Question 2</title>
</head>
<body>
    <script>
        function writeTimesTable(timesTable, timesByStart, timesByEnd) {
            for (; timesByStart <= timesByEnd; timesByStart++) {
                document.write(timesTable + " * " + timesByStart + " = " +
                    timesByStart * timesTable + "<br />");
            }
```

```
        }

        var timesTable;

        while ((timesTable = prompt("Enter the times table", -1)) != -1) {
            while (isNaN(timesTable) == true) {
                timesTable = prompt(timesTable + " is not a " +
                                    "valid number, please retry", -1);
            }

            if (timesTable == -1) {
                break;
            }

            document.write("<br />The " + timesTable +
                        " times table<br />");
            writeTimesTable(timesTable, 1, 12);
        }
    </script>
  </body>
</html>
```

Save this as ch4_question2.html.

The function remains the same, so let's look at the new code. The first change from Question 1 is that you declare a variable, timesTable, and then initialize it in the condition of the first while loop. This may seem like a strange thing to do at first, but it does work. The code in parentheses inside the while loop's condition:

```
(timesTable = prompt("Enter the times table",-1))
```

is executed first because its order of precedence has been raised by the parentheses. This will return a value, and it is this value that is compared to -1. If it's not -1, then the while condition is true, and the body of the loop executes. Otherwise it's skipped over, and nothing else happens in this page.

In a second while loop nested inside the first, you check to see that the value the user has entered is actually a number using the function isNaN(). If it's not, you prompt the user to try again, and this will continue until a valid number is entered.

If the user had entered an invalid value initially, then in the second while loop, that user may have entered -1, so following the while is an if statement that checks to see if -1 has been entered. If it has, you break out of the while loop; otherwise the writeTimesTable() function is called.

CHAPTER 5

Exercise 1 Question

Using the Date type, calculate the date 12 months from now and write this into a web page.

Exercise 1 Solution

```
<!DOCTYPE html>

<html lang="en">
<head>
    <title>Chapter 5: Question 1</title>
</head>
<body>
    <script>
        var months = ["Jan", "Feb", "Mar", "Apr", "May", "Jun",
                      "Jul", "Aug", "Sep", "Oct", "Nov", "Dec"];

        var nowDate = new Date();

        nowDate.setMonth(nowDate.getMonth() + 12);
        document.write("Date 12 months ahead is " + nowDate.getDate());
        document.write(" " + months[nowDate.getMonth()]);
        document.write(" " + nowDate.getFullYear());
    </script>
</body>
</html>
```

Save this as ch5_question1.html.

Because the getMonth() method returns a number between 0 and 11 for the month rather than its name, an array called months has been created that stores the name of each month. You can use getMonth() to get the array index for the correct month name.

The variable nowDate is initialized to a new Date object. Because no initial value is specified, the new Date object will contain today's date.

To add 12 months to the current date you simply use setMonth(). You get the current month value with getMonth(), and then add 12 to it.

Finally you write the result out to the page.

Exercise 2 Question

Obtain a list of names from the user, storing each name entered in an array. Keep getting another name until the user enters nothing. Sort the names in ascending order and then write them out to the page, with each name on its own line.

Exercise 2 Solution

```
<!DOCTYPE html>

<html lang="en">
<head>
    <title>Chapter 5: Question 2</title>
</head>
<body>
    <script>
```

```
        var inputName = "";
        var namesArray = [];

        while ((inputName = prompt("Enter a name", "")) != "") {
            namesArray[namesArray.length] = inputName;
        }

        namesArray.sort();

        var namesList = namesArray.join("<br/>");
        document.write(namesList);
    </script>
    </body>
    </html>
```

Save this as ch5_question2.html.

First you declare two variables: inputName, which holds the name entered by the user, and namesArray, which holds an Array object that stores each of the names entered.

You use a while loop to keep getting another name from the user as long as the user hasn't left the prompt box blank. Note that the use of parentheses in the while condition is essential. By placing the following code inside parentheses, you ensure that this is executed first and that a name is obtained from the user and stored in the inputName variable:

```
(inputName = prompt("Enter a name",""))
```

Then you compare the value returned inside the parentheses—whatever was entered by the user—with an empty string (denoted by ""). If they are not equal—that is, if the user did enter a value, you loop around again.

Now, to sort the array into order, you use the sort() method of the Array object:

```
namesArray.sort();
```

Finally, to create a string containing all values contained in the array elements with each being on a new line, you use the HTML <br/> element and write the following:

```
var namesList = namesArray.join("<br/>")
document.write(namesList);
```

The code namesArray.join("<br/>") creates the string where a <br/> is between each element in the array. Finally, you write the string into the page with document.write().

Exercise 3 Question

Example 8 uses a function to create objects using literal notation. Modify this example to use the Person data type.

Exercise 3 Solution

```html
<!DOCTYPE html>

<html lang="en">
<head>
    <title>Chapter 5, Question 3</title>
</head>
<body>
    <script>
        function Person(firstName, lastName) {
            this.firstName = firstName;
            this.lastName = lastName;
        }

        Person.prototype.getFullName = function () {
            return this.firstName + " " + this.lastName;
        };

        Person.prototype.greet = function (person) {
            alert("Hello, " + person.getFullName() +
                    ". I'm " + this.getFullName());
        };

        var johnDoe = new Person("John", "Doe");
        var janeDoe = new Person("Jane", "Doe");

        johnDoe.greet(janeDoe);
    </script>
</body>
</html>
```

Save this as `ch5_question3.html`.

This is a simple matter of replacing the `createPerson()` function with the `Person` reference type you defined at the end of Chapter 5.

To create your `Person` objects, you use the new operator when calling the `Person` constructor function, passing in the first and last names of the people you want to represent.

CHAPTER 6

Exercise 1 Question

What problem does the following code solve?

```javascript
var myString = "This sentence has has a fault and and we need to fix it.";
var myRegExp = /(\b\w+\b) \1/g;
myString = myString.replace(myRegExp,"$1");
```

Now imagine that you change that code, so that you create the `RegExp` object like this:

```
var myRegExp = new RegExp("(\b\w+\b) \1");
```

Why would this not work, and how could you rectify the problem?

Exercise 1 Solution

The problem is that the sentence has "has has" and "and and" inside it, clearly a mistake. A lot of word processors have an autocorrect feature that fixes common mistakes like this, and what your regular expression does is mimic this feature.

So the erroneous `myString`:

"This sentence has has a fault and and we need to fix it."

will become:

"This sentence has a fault and we need to fix it."

Let's look at how the code works, starting with the regular expression:

```
/(\b\w+\b) \1/g;
```

By using parentheses, you have defined a group, so `(\b\w+\b)` is group 1. This group matches the pattern of a word boundary followed by one or more alphanumeric characters, that is, a–z, A–Z, 0–9, and _, followed by a word boundary. Following the group you have a space then `\1`. What `\1` means is match exactly the same characters as were matched in pattern group 1. So, for example, if group 1 matched "has," then `\1` will match "has" as well. It's important to note that `\1` will match the exact previous match by group 1. So when group 1 then matches the "and," the `\1` now matches "and" and not the "has" that was previously matched.

You use the group again in your `replace()` method; this time the group is specified using the `$` symbol, so `$1` matches group 1. It's this that causes the two matched "has" and "and" to be replaced by just one.

Turning to the second part of the question, how do you need to change the following code so that it works?

```
var myRegExp = new RegExp("(\b\w+\b) \1");
```

Easy; now you are using a string passed to the `RegExp` object's constructor, and you need to use two slashes (`\\`) rather than one when you mean a regular expression syntax character, like this:

```
var myRegExp = new RegExp("(\\b\\w+\\b) \\1","g");
```

Notice you've also passed a `g` to the second parameter to make it a global match.

Exercise 2 Question

Write a regular expression that finds all of the occurrences of the word "a" in the following sentence and replaces them with "the":

"a dog walked in off a street and ordered a finest beer"

The sentence should become:

"the dog walked in off the street and ordered the finest beer"

Exercise 2 Solution

```
<!DOCTYPE html>

<html lang="en">
<head>
    <title>Chapter 6: Question 2</title>
</head>
<body>
    <script>
        var myString = "a dog walked in off a street and " +
                        "ordered a finest beer";
        var myRegExp = /\ba\b/gi;

        myString = myString.replace(myRegExp, "the");
        alert(myString);
    </script>
</body>
</html>
```

Save this as ch6_question2.html.

With regular expressions, it's often not just what you want to match, but also what you don't want to match that is a problem. Here you want to match the letter a, so why not just write:

```
var myRegExp = /a/gi;
```

Well, that would work, but it would also replace the "a" in "walked," which you don't want. You want to replace the letter "a" but only where it's a word on its own and not inside another word. So when does a letter become a word? The answer is when it's between two word boundaries. The word boundary is represented by the regular expression special character \b so the regular expression becomes:

```
var myRegExp = /\ba\b/gi;
```

The gi at the end ensures a global, case-insensitive search.

Now with your regular expression created, you can use it in the replace() method's first parameter:

```
myString = myString.replace(myRegExp,"the");
```

Exercise 3 Question

Imagine you have a website with a message board. Write a regular expression that would remove barred words. (You can make up your own words!)

Exercise 3 Solution

```
<!DOCTYPE html>

<html lang="en">
```

```
<head>
    <title>Chapter 6: Question 3</title>
</head>
<body>
    <script>
        var myRegExp = /(sugar )?candy|choc(olate|oholic)?/gi;
        var myString = "Mmm, I love chocolate, I'm a chocoholic. " +
            "I love candy too, sweet, sugar candy";

        myString = myString.replace(myRegExp,"salad");
        alert(myString);
    </script>
</body>
</html>
```

Save this as ch6_question3.html.

For this example, pretend you're creating script for a board on a dieting site where text relating to candy is barred and will be replaced with a much healthier option, salad.

The barred words are

> ➤ chocolate

> ➤ choc

> ➤ chocoholic

> ➤ sugar candy

> ➤ candy

Let's examine the regular expression to remove the offending words:

1. Start with the two basic words, so to match "choc" or "candy," you use:

    candy|choc

2. Add the matching for "sugar candy." Because the "sugar" bit is optional, you group it by placing it in parentheses and adding the "?" after it. This means match the group zero times or one time:

    (sugar)?candy|choc

3. You need to add the optional "olate" and "oholic" end bits. You add these as a group after the "choc" word and again make the group optional. You can match either of the endings in the group by using the | character:

    (sugar)?candy|choc(olate|oholic)?/gi

4. You then declare it as:

    var myRegExp = /(sugar)?candy|choc(olate|oholic)?/gi

The gi at the end means the regular expression will find and replace words on a global, case-insensitive basis.

So, to sum up:

```
/(sugar )?candy|choc(olate|oholic)?/gi
```

Au: close up line space

reads as:

Either match zero or one occurrences of "sugar" followed by "candy." Or alternatively match "choc" followed by either one or zero occurrences of "olate" or match "choc" followed by zero or one occurrence of "oholic."

Finally, the following:

```
myString = myString.replace(myRegExp,"salad");
```

replaces the offending words with "salad" and sets myString to the new clean version:

```
"Mmm, I love salad, I'm a salad. I love salad too, sweet, salad."
```

CHAPTER 7

Exercise 1 Question

Create a page that gets the user's date of birth. Then, using that information, tell her on what day of the week she was born.

Exercise 1 Solution

```
<!DOCTYPE html>

<html lang="en">
<head>
    <title>Chapter 7: Question 1</title>
</head>
<body>
    <script>
        var days = ["Sunday", "Monday", "Tuesday", "Wednesday",
                    "Thursday", "Friday", "Saturday"];

        var year = prompt("Enter the four digit year you were born.");
        var month = prompt("Enter your birth month (1 - 12).");
        var date = prompt("Enter the day you were born.");

        var birthDate = new Date(year, month - 1, date);

        alert(days[birthDate.getDay()]);
    </script>
</body>
</html>
```

Save this as ch7_question1.html.

The solution is rather simple. You create a new Date object based on the year, month, and day entered by the user. Then you get the day of the week using the Date object's getDay() method. This returns a number, but by defining an array of days of the week to match this number, you can use the value of getDay() as the index to your days array.

Exercise 2 Question

Create a web page similar to Example 4, but make it display only the hour, minutes, and seconds.

Exercise 2 Solution

```
<!DOCTYPE html>

<html lang="en">
<head>
    <title>Chapter 7, Question 2</title>
</head>
<body>
    <div id="output"></div>
    <script>
        function updateTime() {
            var date = new Date();

            var value = date.getHours() + ":" +
                        date.getMinutes() + ":" +
                        date.getSeconds();

            document.getElementById("output").innerHTML = value;
        }

        setInterval(updateTime, 1000);
    </script>
</body>
</html>
```

Save this as ch7_question2.html.

Displaying only the hour, minutes, and seconds is an easy task; it just requires a little extra code. You modify the updateTime() function to first create a Date object to get the time information from.

```
var date = new Date();
```

Then you build a string in hh:mm:ss format:

```
var value = date.getHours() + ":" +
            date.getMinutes() + ":" +
            date.getSeconds();
```

Finally, you output that string to the page:

```
document.getElementById("output").innerHTML = value;
```

CHAPTER 8

Exercise 1 Question

Create two pages, one called `legacy.html` and the other called `modern.html`. Each page should have a heading telling you what page is loaded. For example:

```
<h2>Welcome to the Legacy page. You need to upgrade!</h2>
```

Using feature detection and the `location` object, send browsers that do not support geolocation to `legacy.html`; send browsers that do support geolocation to `modern.html`.

Exercise 1 Solution

The `modern.html` page is as follows:

```
<!DOCTYPE html>

<html lang="en">
<head>
    <title>Chapter 2: Question 1</title>
</head>
<body>
    <h2>Welcome to the Modern page!</h2>
    <script>
        if (!navigator.geolocation) {
            location.replace("legacy.html");
        }
    </script>
</body>
</html>
```

The `legacy.html` page is very similar:

```
<!DOCTYPE html>

<html lang="en">
<head>
    <title>Chapter 2: Question 1</title>
</head>
<body>
    <h2>Welcome to the Legacy page. You need to upgrade!</h2>
    <script>
        if (navigator.geolocation) {
            location.replace("modern.html");
        }
    </script>
</body>
</html>
```

These two pages are incredibly simple. Starting with the `legacy.html` page, you check if `navigator.geolocation` is a truthy value:

```
if (navigator.geolocation) {
    location.replace("modern.html");
}
```

If it is, you redirect the user to the `modern.html` page. Note that you use `replace()` rather than `href`, because you don't want the user to be able to click the browser's Back button. This way it's less easy to spot that a new page is being loaded.

The `modern.html` page is almost identical, except that in your `if` statement you check if `navigator.geolocation` is falsey:

```
if (!navigator.geolocation) {
    location.replace("legacy.html");
}
```

If so, you redirect to `legacy.html`.

Exercise 2 Question

Modify Example 3 to display one of the four images randomly. Hint: refer to Chapter 5 and the `Math.random()` method.

Exercise 2 Solution

```
<!DOCTYPE html>

<html lang="en">
<head>
    <title>Chapter 8, Question 2</title>
</head>
<body>
    <img src="" width="200" height="150" alt="My Image" />
    <script>
        function getRandomNumber(min, max) {
            return Math.floor(Math.random() * max) + min;
        }

        var myImages = [
            "usa.gif",
            "canada.gif",
            "jamaica.gif",
            "mexico.gif"
        ];

        var random = getRandomNumber(0, myImages.length);

        document.images[0].src = myImages[random];
    </script>
</body>
</html>
```

Save this as ch8_question2.html.

The key to this solution is getting a random number between 0 and the length of the myImages array, and writing a function to generate a random number would greatly help with that. So, you write a function called getRandomNumber():

```
function getRandomNumber(min, max) {
    return Math.floor(Math.random() * max) + min;
}
```

It generates a random number within the range of min and max. The algorithm was copied from Chapter 5.

Now you can use getRandomNumber() to generate a number for you, passing 0 as the min and the length of the array as the max:

```
var random = getRandomNumber(0, myImages.length);
```

You then use the random number to get the image:

```
document.images[0].src = myImages[random];
```

CHAPTER 9

Exercise 1 Question

Here's some HTML code that creates a table. Re-create this table using only JavaScript and the core DOM objects to generate the HTML. Test your code in all browsers available to you to make sure it works in them. Hint: Comment each line as you write it to keep track of where you are in the tree structure, and create a new variable for every element on the page (for example, not just one for each of the TD cells but nine variables).

```
<table>
    <tr>
        <td>Car</td>
        <td>Top Speed</td>
        <td>Price</td>
    </tr>
    <tr>
        <td>Chevrolet</td>
        <td>120mph</td>
        <td>$10,000</td>
    </tr>
    <tr>
        <td>Pontiac</td>
        <td>140mph</td>
        <td>$20,000</td>
    </tr>
</table>
```

Exercise 1 Solution

It seems a rather daunting example, but rather than being difficult, it is just a conjunction of two areas, one building a tree structure and the other navigating the tree structure. You start at the <body/> element and create a <table/> element. Now you can navigate to the new <table/> element you've created and create a new <tr/> element and carry on from there. It's a lengthy, repetitious, and tedious process, so that's why it's a good idea to comment your code to keep track of where you are.

```
<!DOCTYPE html>

<html lang="en">
<head>
    <title>Chapter 9: Question 1</title>
</head>
<body>
<script>
var tableElem = document.createElement("table");
var trElem1 = document.createElement("tr");
var trElem2 = document.createElement("tr");
var trElem3 = document.createElement("tr");
var tdElem1 = document.createElement("td");
var tdElem2 = document.createElement("td");
var tdElem3 = document.createElement("td");
var tdElem4 = document.createElement("td");
var tdElem5 = document.createElement("td");
var tdElem6 = document.createElement("td");
var tdElem7 = document.createElement("td");
var tdElem8 = document.createElement("td");
var tdElem9 = document.createElement("td");
var textNodeA1 = document.createTextNode("Car");
var textNodeA2 = document.createTextNode("Top Speed");
var textNodeA3 = document.createTextNode("Price");
var textNodeB1 = document.createTextNode("Chevrolet");
var textNodeB2 = document.createTextNode("120mph");
var textNodeB3 = document.createTextNode("$10,000");
var textNodeC1 = document.createTextNode("Pontiac");
var textNodeC2 = document.createTextNode("140mph");
var textNodeC3 = document.createTextNode("$14,000");

var docNavigate = document.body;   //Starts with body element

docNavigate.appendChild(tableElem);       //Adds the table element
docNavigate = docNavigate.lastChild;      //Moves to the table element
docNavigate.appendChild(trElem1);         //Adds the TR element
docNavigate = docNavigate.firstChild;     //Moves the TR element
docNavigate.appendChild(tdElem1);         //Adds the first TD element in the
                                          //  heading
docNavigate.appendChild(tdElem2);         //Adds the second TD element in the
                                          //  heading
docNavigate.appendChild(tdElem3);         //Adds the third TD element in the
                                          //  heading
docNavigate = docNavigate.firstChild;     //Moves to the first TD element
```

```
docNavigate.appendChild(textNodeA1);          //Adds the second text node
docNavigate = docNavigate.nextSibling;        //Moves to the next TD element
docNavigate.appendChild(textNodeA2);          //Adds the second text node
docNavigate = docNavigate.nextSibling;        //Moves to the next TD element
docNavigate.appendChild(textNodeA3);          //Adds the third text node
docNavigate = docNavigate.parentNode;         //Moves back to the TR element
docNavigate = docNavigate.parentNode;         //Moves back to the table element

docNavigate.appendChild(trElem2);             //Adds the second TR element
docNavigate = docNavigate.lastChild;          //Moves to the second TR element
docNavigate.appendChild(tdElem4);             //Adds the TD element
docNavigate.appendChild(tdElem5);             //Adds the TD element
docNavigate.appendChild(tdElem6);             //Adds the TD element
docNavigate = docNavigate.firstChild;         //Moves to the first TD element
docNavigate.appendChild(textNodeB1);          //Adds the first text node
docNavigate = docNavigate.nextSibling;        //Moves to the next TD element
docNavigate.appendChild(textNodeB2);          //Adds the second text node
docNavigate = docNavigate.nextSibling;        //Moves to the next TD element
docNavigate.appendChild(textNodeB3);          //Adds the third text node
docNavigate = docNavigate.parentNode;         //Moves back to the TR element
docNavigate = docNavigate.parentNode;         //Moves back to the table element

docNavigate.appendChild(trElem3);             //Adds the TR element
docNavigate = docNavigate.lastChild;          //Moves to the TR element
docNavigate.appendChild(tdElem7);             //Adds the TD element
docNavigate.appendChild(tdElem8);             //Adds the TD element
docNavigate.appendChild(tdElem9);             //Adds the TD element
docNavigate = docNavigate.firstChild;         //Moves to the TD element
docNavigate.appendChild(textNodeC1);          //Adds the first text node
docNavigate = docNavigate.nextSibling;        //Moves to the next TD element
docNavigate.appendChild(textNodeC2);          //Adds the second text node
docNavigate = docNavigate.nextSibling;        //Moves to the next TD element
docNavigate.appendChild(textNodeC3);          //Adds the third text node
</script>

</body>
</html>
```

Save this as `ch9_question1.html`.

Exercise 2 Question

Modify Example 6 so that the amount of pixels moved in either direction is controlled by a global variable. Call it `direction`. Remove the `switchDirection` variable, and change the code to use the new `direction` variable to determine when the animation should change directions.

Exercise 2 Solution

```
<!DOCTYPE html>

<html lang="en">
<head>
    <title>Chapter 9, Question 2</title>
```

```
        <style>
            #divAdvert {
                position: absolute;
                font: 12px Arial;
                top: 4px;
                left: 0px;
            }
        </style>
    </head>
    <body>
        <div id="divAdvert">
            Here is an advertisement.
        </div>

        <script>
            var direction = 2;

            function doAnimation() {
                var divAdvert = document.getElementById("divAdvert");
                var currentLeft = divAdvert.offsetLeft;

                if (currentLeft > 400 || currentLeft < 0) {
                    direction = -direction;
                }

                var newLocation = currentLeft + direction;

                divAdvert.style.left = newLocation + "px";
            }

            setInterval(doAnimation, 10);
        </script>
    </body>
</html>
```

Save this as ch9_question2.html.

This modification sounds complex at first, but it actually simplifies the doAnimation() function because one variable is responsible for:

➤ the amount of pixels moved

➤ the direction the element is moved

First, you remove the switchDirection variable and create a new one called direction, initializing it with the value of 2:

```
var direction = 2;
```

Then inside the doAnimation() function, you change the value of direction when the <div/> element reaches one of its bounds (0 pixels or 400 pixels):

```
if (currentLeft > 400 || currentLeft < 0) {
    direction = -direction;
}
```

The new `direction` value is simple; you simply make `direction` negative. So if `direction` is positive, it becomes negative. If `direction` is negative, it becomes positive (remember: a negative times a negative is a positive).

You then calculate the new left position and change the element's style:

```
var newLocation = currentLeft + direction;

divAdvert.style.left = newLocation + "px";
```

CHAPTER 10

Exercise 1 Question

Add a method to the event utility object called `isOldIE()` that returns a boolean value indicating whether or not the browser is old-IE.

Exercise 1 Solution

```
var evt = {
    addListener: function(obj, type, fn) {
        if (typeof obj.addEventListener != "undefined") {
            obj.addEventListener(type, fn);
        } else {
            obj.attachEvent("on" + type, fn);
        }
    },
    removeListener: function(obj, type, fn) {
        if (typeof obj.removeEventListener != "undefined") {
            obj.removeEventListener(type, fn);
        } else {
            obj.detachEvent("on" + type, fn);
        }
    },
    getTarget: function(e) {
        if (e.target) {
            return e.target;
        }

        return e.srcElement;
    },
    preventDefault : function(e) {
        if (e.preventDefault) {
            e.preventDefault();
        } else {
            e.returnValue = false;
        }
    },
    isOldIE: function() {
        return typeof document.addEventListener == "undefined";
    }
};
```

Save this as `ch10_question1.html`.

You have many ways to determine if the browser is an older version of Internet Explorer. Your author chose to check if `document.addEventListener()` is undefined. IE9+ supports the method, whereas IE8 and below do not.

Exercise 2 Question

Example 15 exhibits some behavior inconsistencies between standards-compliant browsers and old-IE. Remember that the event handlers execute in reverse order in old-IE. Modify this example to use the new `isOldIE()` method so that you can write specific code for old-IE and standards-compliant browsers (hint: you will call the `addListener()` method four times).

Exercise 2 Solution

```
<!DOCTYPE html>

<html lang="en">
<head>
    <title>Chapter 10: Question 2</title>
</head>
<body>
    <img id="img0" src="usa.gif" />
    <div id="status"></div>

    <script src="ch10_question1.js"></script>
    <script>
        var myImages = [
            "usa.gif",
            "canada.gif",
            "jamaica.gif",
            "mexico.gif"
        ];

        function changeImg(e) {
            var el = evt.getTarget(e);
            var newImgNumber = Math.round(Math.random() * 3);

            while (el.src.indexOf(myImages[newImgNumber]) != -1) {
                newImgNumber = Math.round(Math.random() * 3);
            }

            el.src = myImages[newImgNumber];
        }

        function updateStatus(e) {
            var el = evt.getTarget(e);
            var status = document.getElementById("status");

            status.innerHTML = "The image changed to " + el.src;

            if (el.src.indexOf("mexico") > -1) {
                evt.removeListener(el, "click", changeImg);
```

```
                        evt.removeListener(el, "click", updateStatus);
                }
        }

        var imgObj = document.getElementById("img0");

        if (evt.isOldIE()) {
            evt.addListener(imgObj, "click", updateStatus);
            evt.addListener(imgObj, "click", changeImg);
        } else {
            evt.addListener(imgObj, "click", changeImg);
            evt.addListener(imgObj, "click", updateStatus);
        }
    </script>
</body>
</html>
```

Save this as ch10_question2.html.

The majority of the code is identical to Example 15. The only difference is how you register the event listeners. With your new isOldIE() method, you can register the click event listeners in the correct order (for old-IE). For standards-compliant browsers, you register the event listeners in the same order as Example 15.

Exercise 3 Question

Example 17 had you write a cross-browser tab script, but as you probably noticed, it behaves peculiarly. The basic idea is there, but the tabs remain active as you click another tab. Modify the script so that only one tab is active at a time.

Exercise 3 Solution

Example 17 is incomplete because the script doesn't keep track of which tab is active. Probably the simplest way to add state recognition to the script is to add a global variable that keeps track of the tab that was last clicked. This particular solution uses this idea. Changed lines of code are highlighted.

```
<!DOCTYPE html>

<html lang="en">
<head>
    <title>Chapter 10: Question 3</title>
    <style>
        .tabStrip {
            background-color: #E4E2D5;
            padding: 3px;
            height: 22px;
        }

        .tabStrip div {
            float: left;
            font: 14px arial;
```

```
            cursor: pointer;
        }

        .tabStrip-tab {
            padding: 3px;
        }

        .tabStrip-tab-hover {
            border: 1px solid #316AC5;
            background-color: #C1D2EE;
            padding: 2px;
        }

        .tabStrip-tab-click {
            border: 1px solid #facc5a;
            background-color: #f9e391;
            padding: 2px;
        }
    </style>
</head>
<body>
    <div class="tabStrip">
        <div data-tab-number="1" class="tabStrip-tab">Tab 1</div>
        <div data-tab-number="2" class="tabStrip-tab">Tab 2</div>
        <div data-tab-number="3" class="tabStrip-tab">Tab 3</div>
    </div>
    <div id="descContainer"></div>

    <script src="ch10_question1.js"></script>
    <script>
        var activeTab = null;

        function handleEvent(e) {
            var target = evt.getTarget(e);

            switch (e.type) {
            case "mouseover":
                if (target.className == "tabStrip-tab") {
                    target.className = "tabStrip-tab-hover";
                }
                break;
            case "mouseout":
                if (target.className == "tabStrip-tab-hover") {
                    target.className = "tabStrip-tab";
                }
                break;
            case "click":
                if (target.className == "tabStrip-tab-hover") {

                    if (activeTab) {
                        activeTab.className = "tabStrip-tab";
                    }

                    var num = target.getAttribute("data-tab-number");

                    target.className = "tabStrip-tab-click";
```

```
                    showDescription(num);
                    activeTab = target;
                }
                break;
            }
        }
    }

    function showDescription(num) {
        var descContainer = document.getElementById("descContainer");

        var text = "Description for Tab " + num;

        descContainer.innerHTML = text;
    }

    evt.addListener(document, "mouseover", handleEvent);
    evt.addListener(document, "mouseout", handleEvent);
    evt.addListener(document, "click", handleEvent);
    </script>
</body>
</html>
```

Save this as ch10_question3.html.

This solution starts with a new global variable called activeTab. Its purpose is to contain a reference to the tab element that was last clicked, and you initialize it as null.

When you click a tab element, you first need to deactivate the currently active tab:

```
if (activeTab) {
    activeTab.className = "tabStrip-tab";
}
```

To do that, you first check if you have an active tab, and if so, you set its className property back to the original tabStrip-tab. Then after you activate the new tab, you assign it to the activeTab variable:

```
activeTab = target;
```

Simple, but effective.

CHAPTER 11

Exercise 1 Question

Using the code from the temperature converter example you saw in Chapter 2, create a user interface for it and connect it to the existing code so that the user can enter a value in degrees Fahrenheit and convert it to centigrade.

Exercise 1 Solution

```html
<!DOCTYPE html>

<html lang="en">
<head>
    <title>Chapter 11: Question 1</title>
</head>
<body>
    <form action="" name="form1">
        <p>
            <input type="text" name="txtCalcBox" value="0.0" />
        </p>
        <input type="button" value="Convert to centigrade"
                id="btnToCent" name="btnToCent" />
    </form>
    <script>
        function convertToCentigrade(degFahren) {
            var degCent = 5 / 9 * (degFahren - 32);

            return degCent;
        }

        function btnToCentClick() {
            var calcBox = document.form1.txtCalcBox;

            if (isNaN(calcBox.value) == true || calcBox.value == "") {
                calcBox.value = "Error Invalid Value";
            } else {
                calcBox.value = convertToCentigrade(calcBox.value);
            }
        }

        document.getElementById("btnToCent")
                .addEventListener("click", btnToCentClick);
    </script>
</body>
</html>
```

Save this as ch11_question1.html.

The interface part is simply a form containing a text box into which users enter the Fahrenheit value and a button they click to convert that value to centigrade. The button has a click event listener that executes btnToCentClick() when the event fires.

The first line of btnToCentClick() declares a variable and sets it to reference the object representing the text box:

```
var calcBox = document.form1.txtCalcBox;
```

Why do this? Well, in your code when you want to use document.form1.txtCalcBox, you can now just use the much shorter calcBox; it saves typing and keeps your code shorter and easier to read.

So:

```
alert(document.form1.txtCalcBox.value);
```

is the same as:

```
alert(calcBox.value);
```

In the remaining part of the function you do a sanity check—if what the user has entered is a number (that is, it is not NotANumber) and the text box does contain a value, you use the Fahrenheit-to-centigrade conversion function you saw in Chapter 2 to do the conversion, the results of which are used to set the text box's value.

Exercise 2 Question

Create a user interface that allows users to pick the computer system of their dreams, similar in principle to the e-commerce sites selling computers over the Internet. For example, they could be given a choice of processor type, speed, memory, and hard drive size, and the option to add additional components like a DVD-ROM drive, a sound card, and so on. As the users change their selections, the price of the system should update automatically and notify them of the cost of the system as they specified it, either by using an alert box or by updating the contents of a text box.

Exercise 2 Solution

```html
<!DOCTYPE html>

<html lang="en">
<head>
    <title>Chapter 11: Question 2</title>
</head>
<body>
    <form action="" name="form1">
        <p>
            Choose the components you want included on your computer
        </p>
        <p>
            <label for="cboProcessor">Processor</label>
            <select name="cboProcessor" id="cboProcessor">
                <option value="100">Dual-core 2GHz</option>
                <option value="101">Quad-core 2.4GHz</option>
                <option value="102">Eight-core 3GHz</option>
            </select>
        </p>
        <p>
            <label for="cboSsd">Solid-state Drive</label>
            <select name="cboSsd" id="cboSsd">
                <option value="200">250GB</option>
                <option value="201">512GB</option>
                <option value="202">1TB</option>
            </select>
        </p>
```

```
    <p>
        <label for="chkDVD">DVD-ROM</label>
        <input type="checkbox" id="chkDVD" name="chkDVD" value="300" />
    </p>
    <p>
        <label for="chkBluRay">Blu-ray</label>
        <input type="checkbox" id="chkBluRay" name="chkBluRay"
            value="301" />
    </p>
    <fieldset>
        <legend>Case</legend>
        <p>
            <label for="desktop">Desktop</label>
            <input type="radio" id="desktop"
                name="radCase" checked value="400" />
        </p>
        <p>
            <label for="minitower">Mini-tower</label>
            <input type="radio" id="minitower"
                name="radCase" value="401" />
        </p>
        <p>
            <label for="fulltower">Full-tower</label>
            <input type="radio" id="fulltower"
                name="radCase" value="402" />
        </p>
    </fieldset>

    <p>
        <input type="button" value="Update"
            id="btnUpdate" name="btnUpdate" />
    </p>
    <p>
        <label for="txtOrder">Order Summary:</label>
    </p>
    <p>
        <textarea rows="20" cols="35" id="txtOrder"
                name="txtOrder"></textarea>
    </p>
</form>
<script>
    var productDb = [];
    productDb[100] = 150;
    productDb[101] = 350;
    productDb[102] = 700;

    productDb[200] = 100;
    productDb[201] = 200;
    productDb[202] = 500;

    productDb[300] = 50;
    productDb[301] = 75;

    productDb[400] = 75;
    productDb[401] = 50;
```

```javascript
productDb[402] = 100;

function getDropDownInfo(element) {
    var selected = element[element.selectedIndex];

    return {
        text: selected.text,
        price: productDb[selected.value]
    };
}

function getCheckboxInfo(element) {
    return {
        checked: element.checked,
        price: productDb[element.value]
    };
}

function getRadioInfo(elements) {
    for (var i = 0; i < elements.length; i++) {
        if (!elements[i].checked) {
            continue;
        }

        var selected = elements[i];

        var label = document.querySelector(
                        "[for=" + selected.id + "]");

        return {
            text: label.innerHTML,
            price: productDb[selected.value]
        };
    }
}

function btnUpdateClick() {
    var total = 0;
    var orderDetails = "";
    var theForm = document.form1;

    var selectedProcessor = getDropDownInfo(theForm.cboProcessor);
    total = selectedProcessor.price;
    orderDetails = "Processor : " + selectedProcessor.text;
    orderDetails = orderDetails + " $" +
                    selectedProcessor.price + "\n";

    var selectedSsd = getDropDownInfo(theForm.cboSsd);
    total = total + selectedSsd.price;
    orderDetails = orderDetails + "Solid-state Drive : " +
                    selectedSsd.text;
    orderDetails = orderDetails + " $" + selectedSsd.price + "\n";

    var dvdInfo = getCheckboxInfo(theForm.chkDVD);
    if (dvdInfo.checked) {
```

```
                total = total + dvdInfo.price;

                orderDetails = orderDetails + "DVD-ROM : $" +
                    dvdInfo.price + "\n";
            }

            var bluRayInfo = getCheckboxInfo(theForm.chkBluRay);
            if (bluRayInfo.checked) {
                total = total + bluRayInfo.price;

                orderDetails = orderDetails + "Blu-ray : $" +
                    bluRayInfo.price + "\n";
            }

            var caseInfo = getRadioInfo(theForm.radCase);
            total = total + caseInfo.price;
            orderDetails = orderDetails + caseInfo.text + " : $" +
                    caseInfo.price;

            orderDetails = orderDetails + "\n\nTotal Order Cost is " +
                        "$" + total;

            theForm.txtOrder.value = orderDetails;
        }

        document.getElementById("btnUpdate")
                .addEventListener("click", btnUpdateClick);

        </script>




        </script>
    </body>
    </html>
```

Save this as ch11_question2.html.

This is just one of many ways to tackle this question—you may well have thought of a better way.

Here you are displaying the results of the user's selection as text in a textarea box, with each item and its cost displayed on separate lines and a final total at the end.

Each form element has a value set to hold a stock ID number. For example, a full tower case is stock ID 402. The actual cost of the item is held in an array called productDb. Why not just store the price in the value attribute of each form element? Well, this way is more flexible. Currently your array just holds price details for each item, but you could modify it that so it holds more data—for example price, description, number in stock, and so on. Also, if this form is posted to a server the values passed will be stock IDs, which you could then use for a lookup in a stock database. If the values were set to prices and the form was posted, you'd have no way of telling what the customer ordered—all you'd know is how much it all cost.

This solution includes an Update button which, when clicked, updates the order details in the textarea box. However, you may want to add event handlers to each form element and update when anything changes.

Turning to the function that actually displays the order summary, btnUpdateClick(), you can see that there is a lot of code, and although it looks complex, it's actually fairly simple. A lot of it is repeated with slight modification. It also relies upon several helper functions to pull various information from the selected form elements.

To save on typing and make the code a little more readable, this solution declares the theForm variable to contain the Form object After the variable's declaration, you then find out which processor has been selected and get its cost and text with the getDropDownInfo() function:

```
function getDropDownInfo(element) {
    var selected = element[element.selectedIndex];

    return {
        text: selected.text,
        price: productDb[selected.value]
    };
}
```

The selectedIndex property tells you which Option object inside the select control has been selected by the user. You return a new object that contains the selected Option's text and the price from the product database.

So to get the processor information, you pass theForm.cboProcessor to getDropDownInfo() and assign the resulting object to selectedProcessor. You then calculate the total and update the order details:

```
var selectedProcessor = getDropDownInfo(theForm.cboProcessor);
total = selectedProcessor.price;
orderDetails = "Processor : " + selectedProcessor.text;
orderDetails = orderDetails + " $" + selectedProcessor.price + "\n";
```

The same principle applies when you find the selected solid-state drive, so let's turn next to the check boxes for the optional extra items, looking first at the DVD-ROM check box:

```
var dvdInfo = getCheckboxInfo(theForm.chkDVD);
if (dvdInfo.checked) {
    total = total + dvdInfo.price;

    orderDetails = orderDetails + "DVD-ROM : $" +
        dvdInfo.price + "\n";
}
```

Again, you use a helper function—this one's called getCheckboxInfo()—to retrieve the information about the given check box:

```
function getCheckboxInfo(element) {
    return {
```

```
            checked: element.checked,
            price: productDb[element.value]
        };
    }
```

This returns a new object that tells you the price of the component, as well as if the check box is checked.

If the check box is checked, you add a DVD-ROM to the order details and update the running total. The same principle applies for the Blu-ray check box.

Finally, you have the computer's case. Because only one case type out of the options can be selected, you used a radio button group. Unfortunately, there is no selectedIndex for radio buttons as there is for check boxes, so you have to go through each radio button in turn and find out if it has been selected. The getRadioInfo() helper function does just that:

```
function getRadioInfo(elements) {
    for (var i = 0; i < elements.length; i++) {
        if (!elements[i].checked) {
            continue;
        }

        var selected = elements[i];

        var label = document.querySelector("[for=" + selected.id + "]");

        return {
            text: label.innerHTML,
            price: productDb[selected.value]
        };
    }
}
```

It loops through the radio button group and checks each radio button's checked property. If it's false, the loop iterates with the continue operator. But if the radio button is checked, you need to get the text associated with the label for the selected radio button and the component's price from the productDb array.

So, inside the btnUpdateClick() function, you can use this helper function to get everything you need to add the selected computer case to the total and description:

```
var caseInfo = getRadioInfo(theForm.radCase);
total = total + caseInfo.price;
orderDetails = orderDetails + caseInfo.text + " : $" +
        caseInfo.price;
```

Finally, set the textarea to the details of the system the user has selected:

```
orderDetails = orderDetails + "\n\nTotal Order Cost is " + total;
theForm.txtOrder.value = orderDetails;
```

CHAPTER 12

Exercise 1 Question

The code for alerting a single message in Example 1 isn't very exciting. Modify the code to display a random message from a set of three possible messages.

Exercise 1 Solution

```html
<!DOCTYPE html>

<html lang="en">
<head>
    <title>Chapter 12: Question 1</title>
    <style>
        [data-drop-target] {
            height: 400px;
            width: 200px;
            margin: 2px;
            background-color: gainsboro;
            float: left;
        }

        .drag-enter {
            border: 2px dashed #000;
        }

        .box {
            width: 200px;
            height: 200px;
        }

        .navy {
            background-color: navy;
        }

        .red {
            background-color: red;
        }
    </style>
</head>
<body>
    <div data-drop-target="true">
        <div id="box1" draggable="true" class="box navy"></div>
        <div id="box2" draggable="true" class="box red"></div>
    </div>
    <div data-drop-target="true"></div>

    <script>
        function getRandomMessage() {
            var messages = [
                "You moved an element!",
                "Moved and element, you have! Mmmmmmm?",
```

```
            "Element overboard!"
    ];

    return messages[Math.floor((Math.random() * 3) + 0)];
}

function handleDragStart(e) {
    var data = {
        elementId: this.id,
        message: getRandomMessage()
    };

    e.dataTransfer.setData("text", JSON.stringify(data));
}

function handleDragEnterLeave(e) {
    if (e.type == "dragenter") {
        this.className = "drag-enter";
    } else {
        this.className = "";
    }
}

function handleOverDrop(e) {
    e.preventDefault();

    if (e.type != "drop") {
        return;
    }

    var json = e.dataTransfer.getData("text");
    var data = JSON.parse(json);

    var draggedEl = document.getElementById(data.elementId);

    if (draggedEl.parentNode == this) {
        this.className = "";
        return;
    }

    draggedEl.parentNode.removeChild(draggedEl);

    this.appendChild(draggedEl);
    this.className = "";

    alert(data.message);
}

var draggable = document.querySelectorAll("[draggable]");
var targets = document.querySelectorAll("[data-drop-target]");

for (var i = 0; i < draggable.length; i++) {
    draggable[i].addEventListener("dragstart", handleDragStart);
```

```
        }

        for (i = 0; i < targets.length; i++) {
            targets[i].addEventListener("dragover", handleOverDrop);
            targets[i].addEventListener("drop", handleOverDrop);
            targets[i].addEventListener("dragenter", handleDragEnterLeave);
            targets[i].addEventListener("dragleave", handleDragEnterLeave);
        }
    </script>
</body>
</html>
```

Save this as `ch12_question1.html`.

This solution is rather simple. It introduces a new function called `getRandomMessage()`, which returns one of three messages:

```
function getRandomMessage() {
    var messages = [
        "You moved an element!",
        "Moved and element, you have! Mmmmmmm?",
        "Element overboard!"
    ];

    return messages[Math.floor((Math.random() * 3) + 0)];
}
```

And you use this function when you assign the `message` property to the data object in `handleDragStart()`:

```
var data = {
    elementId: this.id,
    message: getRandomMessage()
};
```

Sadly, this solution still doesn't add much excitement to the example. But some is better than none, right?

CHAPTER 13

Exercise 1 Question

Using local storage, create a page that keeps track of how many times the page has been visited by the user in the last month.

Exercise 1 Solution

```
<!DOCTYPE html>

<html lang="en">
<head>
    <title>Chapter 13: Question 1</title>
</head>
```

```
<body>
    <script>
        var pageViewCount = localStorage.getItem("pageViewCount");
        var pageFirstVisited = localStorage.getItem("pageFirstVisited");
        var now = new Date();

        if (pageViewCount == null) {
            pageViewCount = 0;
            pageFirstVisited = now.toUTCString();
        }

        var oneMonth = new Date(pageFirstVisited);
        oneMonth.setMonth(oneMonth.getMonth() + 1);

        if (now > oneMonth) {
            pageViewCount = 0;
            pageFirstVisited = now.toUTCString();
        }

        pageViewCount = parseInt(pageViewCount, 10) + 1;

        localStorage.setItem("pageViewCount", pageViewCount);
        localStorage.setItem("pageFirstVisited", pageFirstVisited);

        var output = "You've visited this page " + pageViewCount +
            " times since " + pageFirstVisited;

        document.write(output);
    </script>
</body>
</html>
```

Save this as ch13_question1.html.

The first two lines get two values from localStorage and store them in variables. The first holds the number of visits, the second the date the page was first visited. You also create a variable to contain the current date:

```
var pageViewCount = localStorage.getItem("pageViewCount");
var pageFirstVisited = localStorage.getItem("pageFirstVisited");
var now = new Date();
```

If the pageViewCount key does not exist in localStorage, the variable of the same name is null, and you'll need to initialize the pageViewcount and pageFirstVisited variables with 0 and the current date, respectively. Remember that localStorage contains only string data, so you use the Date object's toUTCString() method to convert the date to a string:

```
if (pageViewCount == null) {
    pageViewCount = 0;
    pageFirstVisited = now.toUTCString();
}
```

You're only tracking the number of visits within a month's time span. So, next you need a variable to contain a Date object one month from the first visit:

```
var oneMonth = new Date(pageFirstVisited);
oneMonth.setMonth(oneMonth.getMonth() + 1);
```

If the current date and time is later than oneMonth, it's time to reset the counter and visited variables:

```
if (now > oneMonth) {
    pageViewCount = 0;
    pageFirstVisited = now.toUTCString();
}
```

Then you increment the counter and store it and the first visit value in localStorage:

```
pageViewCount = parseInt(pageViewCount, 10) + 1;

localStorage.setItem("pageViewCount", pageViewCount);
localStorage.setItem("pageFirstVisited", pageFirstVisited);
```

Finally, write information to the page:

```
var output = "You've visited this page " + pageViewCount +
    " times since " + pageFirstVisited;

document.write(output);
```

Exercise 2 Question

Use cookies to load a different advertisement every time a user visits a web page.

Exercise 2 Solution

```
<!DOCTYPE html>

<html lang="en">
<head>
    <title>Chapter 13: Question 2</title>
</head>
<body>
    <script>
        var ads = [
            "Buy Product A! You won't be sorry!",
            "You need Product B! Buy buy buy!",
            "Don't buy Product A or B! Product C is the only option for you!"
        ];

        function getRandomNumber(min, max) {
            return Math.floor((Math.random() * max) + min);
```

```
        }

        var lastAdNumber = localStorage.getItem("lastAdNumber");
        var nextNumber = getRandomNumber(0, ads.length);

        if (lastAdNumber == null) {
            lastAdNumber = nextNumber;
        } else {
            lastAdNumber = parseInt(lastAdNumber, 10);
            while (lastAdNumber == nextNumber) {
                nextNumber = getRandomNumber(0, ads.length);
            }
        }

        localStorage.setItem("lastAdNumber", nextNumber);

        document.write(ads[nextNumber]);
    </script>
</body>
</html>
```

Save this as `ch13_question2.html`.

This solution is loosely based on similar questions in previous chapters where you have displayed random images or messages. In this case you display a different message in the page each time the user visits it; you'll never see the same message displayed two times in a row in the same browser.

You store the last number of the previously displayed ad in `localStorage` with the key `lastAdNumber`. So, you retrieve that value and generate the next number with a `getRandomNumber()` helper function (you know this algorithm):

```
var lastAdNumber = localStorage.getItem("lastAdNumber");
var nextNumber = getRandomNumber(0, ads.length);
```

If `lastAdNumber` is `null`, you can use the value in `nextNumber`:

```
if (lastAdNumber == null) {
    lastAdNumber = nextNumber;
}
```

But if `lastAdNumber` is not `null`, you need to generate a random number that is not `lastAdNumber`. So first, you convert `lastAdNumber` to a number with the `parseInt()` function:

```
else {
    lastAdNumber = parseInt(lastAdNumber, 10);
    while (lastAdNumber == nextNumber) {
        nextNumber = getRandomNumber(0, ads.length);
    }
}
```

Then you use a `while` loop to generate a unique random number. The loop iterates if `lastAdNumber` is equal to `nextNumber`, and it continues to do so until the next number is different than `lastAdNumber`.

Once you have a unique next number, you store it in `localStorage` and display the ad in the page:

```
localStorage.setItem("lastAdNumber", nextNumber);

document.write(ads[nextNumber]);
```

CHAPTER 14

Exercise 1 Question

Extend the HttpRequest module to include synchronous requests in addition to the asynchronous requests the module already makes. You'll have to make some adjustments to your code to incorporate this functionality. (Hint: Create an async property for the module.)

Exercise 1 Solution

```
function HttpRequest(url, callback) {
    this.url = url;
    this.callBack = callback;
    this.async = true;
    this.request = new XMLHttpRequest();
};

HttpRequest.prototype.send = function() {
    this.request.open("GET", this.url, this.async);

    if (this.async) {
        var tempRequest = this.request;
        var callback = this.callBack;

        function requestReadystatechange() {
            if (tempRequest.readyState == 4) {
                if (tempRequest.status == 200) {
                    callback(tempRequest.responseText);
                } else {
                    alert("An error occurred while attempting to " +
                        "contact the server.");
                }
            }
        }

        this.request.onreadystatechange = requestReadystatechange;
    }

    this.request.send(null);

    if (!this.async) {
        this.callBack(this.request.responseText);
    }
};
```

It's possible to add synchronous communication to your HttpRequest module in a variety of ways. The approach in this solution refactors the code to accommodate a new property called async, which contains either `true` or `false`. If it contains `true`, the underlying `XMLHttpRequest` object uses asynchronous communication to retrieve the file. If `false`, the module uses synchronous communication.

The first change made to the module is in the constructor itself. The original constructor initializes and readies the `XMLHttpRequest` object to send data. This will not do for this new version, however. Instead, the constructor merely initializes all the properties:

```
function HttpRequest(url, callback) {
    this.url = url;
    this.callBack = callback;
    this.async = true;
    this.request = new XMLHttpRequest();
};
```

You have three new properties here. The first, `url`, contains the URL that the `XMLHttpRequest` object should attempt to request from the server. The `callBack` property contains a reference to the callback function, and the `async` property determines the type of communication the `XMLHttpRequest` object uses. Setting `async` to `true` in the constructor gives the property a default value. Therefore, you can send the request in asynchronous mode without setting the property externally.

The new constructor and properties are actually desirable, because they enable you to reuse the same `HttpRequest` object for multiple requests. If you wanted to make a request to a different URL, all you would need to do is assign the `url` property a new value. The same can be said for the callback function as well.

The majority of changes to the module are in the `send()` method. It is here that the module decides whether to use asynchronous or synchronous communication. Both types of communication have very little in common when it comes to making a request; asynchronous communication uses the onreadystatechange event handler, and synchronous communication allows access to the `XMLHttpRequest` object's properties when the request is complete. Therefore, code branching is required:

```
HttpRequest.prototype.send = function() {
    this.request.open("GET", this.url, this.async);

    if (this.async) {
        //more code here
    }
    this.request.send(null);

    if (!this.async) {
        //more code here
    }
}
```

The first line of this method uses the `open()` method of the `XMLHttpRequest` object. The async property is used as the final parameter of the method. This determines whether or not the XHR object uses asynchronous communication. Next, an `if` statement tests to see if `this.async` is `true`; if it is, the asynchronous code will be placed in this `if` block. Next, the `XMLHttpRequest` object's `send()` method is called, sending the request to the server. The final `if` statement checks to see whether `this.async` is `false`. If it is, synchronous code is placed within the code block to execute.

```
HttpRequest.prototype.send = function() {
    this.request.open("GET", this.url, this.async);

    if (this.async) {
        var tempRequest = this.request;
        var callback = this.callBack;

        function requestReadystatechange() {
            if (tempRequest.readyState == 4) {
                if (tempRequest.status == 200) {
                    callback(tempRequest.responseText);
                } else {
                    alert("An error occurred while attempting to " +
                        "contact the server.");
                }
            }
        }

        this.request.onreadystatechange = requestReadystatechange;
    }

    this.request.send(null);

    if (!this.async) {
        this.callBack(this.request.responseText);
    }
};
```

This new code finishes off the method. Starting with the first `if` block, a new variable called `callback` is assigned the value of `this.callBack`. This is done for the same reasons as with the `tempRequest` variable—scoping issues—because `this` points to the `requestReadystatechange()` function instead of the `HttpRequest` object. Other than this change, the asynchronous code remains the same. The `requestReadystatechange()` function handles the `readystatechange` event and calls the callback function when the request is successful.

The second `if` block is much simpler. Because this code executes only if synchronous communication is desired, all you have to do is call the callback function and pass the `XMLHttpRequest` object's `responseText` property.

Using this newly refactored module is quite simple. The following code makes an asynchronous request for a fictitious text file called `test.txt`:

```
function requestCallback(responseText) {
    alert(responseText);
}

var http = new HttpRequest("test.txt", requestCallback);

http.send();
```

Nothing has really changed for asynchronous requests. This is the exact same code used earlier in the chapter. If you want to use synchronous communication, simply set `async` to `false`, like this:

```
function requestCallback(responseText) {
    alert(responseText);
}

var http = new HttpRequest("test.txt", requestCallback);

http.async = false;

http.send();
```

You now have an Ajax module that requests information in both asynchronous and synchronous communication!

Exercise 2 Question

It was mentioned earlier in the chapter that you could modify the smart forms to not use hyperlinks. Change the form that uses the `HttpRequest` module so that the Username and Email fields are checked when the user submits the form. Listen for the form's `submit` event and cancel the submission if a username or e-mail is taken.

Exercise 2 Solution

First, a disclaimer: Ideally, the service provided by `ch14_formvalidator.php` should allow you to check both the username and e-mail address with a single request. That would greatly simplify this solution. However, sometimes you need to make multiple requests, and each request is sometimes dependent upon the outcome of a previous request. This question and solution is meant to emulate that.

Additionally, issuing multiple (and linked) asynchronous operations is a rather complex ordeal—a condition referred to "callback hell." You'll get a taste of that in this solution.

```
<!DOCTYPE html>

<html lang="en">
<head>
    <title>Chapter 14: Question 2</title>
    <style>
        .fieldname {
            text-align: right;
        }

        .submit {
            text-align: right;
        }
    </style>
</head>
<body>
    <form name="theForm">
```

```
<table>
    <tr>
        <td class="fieldname">
            Username:
        </td>
        <td>
            <input type="text" id="username" />
        </td>
        <td>

        </td>
    </tr>
    <tr>
        <td class="fieldname">
            Email:
        </td>
        <td>
            <input type="text" id="email" />
        </td>
        <td>

        </td>
    </tr>
    <tr>
        <td class="fieldname">
            Password:
        </td>
        <td>
            <input type="text" id="password" />
        </td>
        <td />
    </tr>
    <tr>
        <td class="fieldname">
            Verify Password:
        </td>
        <td>
            <input type="text" id="password2" />
        </td>
        <td />
    </tr>
    <tr>
        <td colspan="2" class="submit">
            <input id="btnSubmit" type="submit" value="Submit" />
        </td>
        <td />
    </tr>
</table>
</form>
<script src="ch14_question1.js"></script>
<script>
    function btnSubmitClick(e) {
        e.preventDefault();

        checkUsername();
```

```
    }

function checkUsername() {
    var userValue = document.getElementById("username").value;

    if (!userValue) {
        alert("Please enter a user name to check!");
        return;
    }

    var url = "ch14_formvalidator.php?username=" + userValue;

    var request = new HttpRequest(url, handleUsernameResponse);
    request.send();
}

function checkEmail() {
    var emailValue = document.getElementById("email").value;

    if (!emailValue) {
        alert("Please enter an email address to check!");
        return;
    }

    var url = "ch14_formvalidator.php?email=" + emailValue;

    var request = new HttpRequest(url, handleEmailResponse);
    request.send();
}

function handleUsernameResponse(responseText) {
    var response = JSON.parse(responseText);

    if (!response.available) {
        alert("The username " + response.searchTerm +
                " is unavailable. Try another.");
        return;
    }

    checkEmail();
}

function handleEmailResponse(responseText) {
    var response = JSON.parse(responseText);

    if (!response.available) {
        alert("The email address " + response.searchTerm +
                " is unavailable. Try another.");
        return;
    }

    document.theForm.submit();
}

document.getElementById("btnSubmit")
        .addEventListener("click", btnSubmitClick);
```

```
        </script>
    </body>

    </html>
```

Save this as `ch14_question2.html`.

In the HTML, notice that the links for checking the username and e-mail address are gone. There is no need for them, because those values are checked when the user clicks the Submit button. The last statement of the JavaScript code registers that event listener:

```
document.getElementById("btnSubmit")
        .addEventListener("click", btnSubmitClick);
```

The function that handles the button's click event is called `btnSubmitClick()`. It's a simple function that kicks off the whole process:

```
function btnSubmitClick(e) {
    e.preventDefault();

    checkUsername();
}
```

Its first statement prevents the form from submitting. This is important because, due to the nature of asynchronous processes, `btnSubmitClick()` cannot be responsible for submitting the form. Therefore, another function will need to submit the form if both the username and e-mail address validate and are available.

The second statement calls `checkUsername()`, which is left mostly unchanged:

```
function checkUsername() {
    var userValue = document.getElementById("username").value;

    if (!userValue) {
        alert("Please enter a user name to check!");
        return;
    }

    var url = "ch14_formvalidator.php?username=" + userValue;

    var request = new HttpRequest(url, handleUsernameResponse);
    request.send();
}
```

In fact, the only change to this function is the callback passed to the `HttpRequest` constructor. It's a new callback function called `handleUsernameResponse()`, and it somewhat resembles the original `handleResponse()` function:

```
function handleUsernameResponse(responseText) {
    var response = JSON.parse(responseText);

    if (!response.available) {
        alert("The username " + response.searchTerm +
            " is unavailable. Try another.");
```

```
            return;
        }

        checkEmail();
    }
```

This function takes the response and parses it into a JavaScript object. If the username is not available, it displays the error message to the user and returns. Nothing else is processed when the username is unavailable, but if it is available, it calls `checkEmail()`:

```
function checkEmail() {
    var emailValue = document.getElementById("email").value;

    if (!emailValue) {
        alert("Please enter an email address to check!");
        return;
    }

    var url = "ch14_formvalidator.php?email=" + emailValue;

    var request = new HttpRequest(url, handleEmailResponse);
    request.send();
}
```

This function is also largely the same. The only difference is the callback function passed to the `HttpRequest` constructor; it's called `handleEmailResponse()`. It parses the request, and it is the last step in the process:

```
function handleEmailResponse(responseText) {
    var response = JSON.parse(responseText);

    if (!response.available) {
        alert("The email address " + response.searchTerm +
            " is unavailable. Try another.");
        return;
    }

    document.theForm.submit();
}
```

Once again, if the e-mail address is not available, this function displays the error message to the user and returns. But if the e-mail address is available, the form is finally submitted.

CHAPTER 15

Exercise 1 Question

Being able to control playback is cool, but your custom UI needs to also control volume. Add an `<input type="range" />` element to Example 3 to control the volume. Remember that the range of volume supported by media elements is 0.0 to 1.0. Look back at Chapter 11 if you need a refresher of the range input type. This unfortunately will not work in IE.

Exercise 1 Solution

```
<!DOCTYPE html>

<html lang="en">
<head>
    <title>Chapter 15: Question 1</title>
</head>
<body>
    <div>
        <button id="playbackController">Play</button>
        <button id="muteController">Mute</button>
        <input type="range" id="volumeController"
               min="0" max="1" step=".1" value="1"/>
    </div>
    <video id="bbbVideo">
        <source src="bbb.mp4" />
        <source src="bbb.webm" />
    </video>

    <script>
        function pauseHandler(e) {
            playButton.innerHTML = "Resume";
        }

        function playingHandler(e) {
            playButton.innerHTML = "Pause";
        }

        function volumechangeHandler(e) {
            muteButton.innerHTML = video.muted ? "Unmute" : "Mute";
        }

        function playbackClick(e) {
            video.paused ? video.play() : video.pause();
        }

        function muteClick(e) {
            video.muted = !video.muted;
        }

        function volumeInput(e) {
            video.volume = volumeSlider.value;
        }

        var video = document.getElementById("bbbVideo");
        var playButton = document.getElementById("playbackController");
        var muteButton = document.getElementById("muteController");
        var volumeSlider = document.getElementById("volumeController");

        video.addEventListener("pause", pauseHandler);
```

```
            video.addEventListener("playing", playingHandler);
            video.addEventListener("volumechange", volumechangeHandler);

            playButton.addEventListener("click", playbackClick);
            muteButton.addEventListener("click", muteClick);
            volumeSlider.addEventListener("input", volumeInput);
        </script>
    </body>
</html>
```

Save this as ch15_question1.html.

This solution is built on Example 3. The additions are highlighted for your convenience.

The volume will be controlled by an <input/> element:

```
<input type="range" id="volumeController"
       min="0" max="1" step=".1" value="1"/>
```

It's a range control, and it's set to a minimum value of 0, a maximum value of 1, and the step is .1. Its initial value is set to 1, meaning full volume.

In the JavaScript code, you retrieve this element and store it in the volumeSlider variable:

```
var volumeSlider = document.getElementById("volumeController");
```

And you register an input event listener:

```
volumeSlider.addEventListener("input", volumeInput);
```

The volumeInput() function handles this event, and it is responsible for setting the media's volume to the slider's corresponding value:

```
function volumeInput(e) {
    video.volume = volumeSlider.value;
}
```

Exercise 2 Question

Add another range form control to Question 1's answer, and program it to seek the media. It should also update as the media plays. Use the durationchange event to set the slider's max value, and the timeupdate event to update the slider's value.

Exercise 2 Solution

```
<!DOCTYPE html>

<html lang="en">
<head>
    <title>Chapter 15: Question 2</title>
</head>
<body>
    <div>
```

```
        <button id="playbackController">Play</button>
        <button id="muteController">Mute</button>
        <input type="range" id="volumeController"
               min="0" max="1" step=".1" value="1"/>
    </div>
    <video id="bbbVideo">
        <source src="bbb.mp4" />
        <source src="bbb.webm" />
    </video>
    <div>
        <input type="range" id="seekController"
               min="0" step="1" value="0" />
    </div>
    <script>
        function pauseHandler(e) {
            playButton.innerHTML = "Resume";
        }

        function playingHandler(e) {
            playButton.innerHTML = "Pause";
        }

        function volumechangeHandler(e) {
            muteButton.innerHTML = video.muted ? "Unmute" : "Mute";
        }

        function durationchangeHandler(e) {
            seekSlider.max = video.duration;
        }

        function timeupdateHandler(e) {
            seekSlider.value = video.currentTime;
        }

        function playbackClick(e) {
            video.paused ? video.play() : video.pause();
        }

        function muteClick(e) {
            video.muted = !video.muted;
        }

        function volumeInput(e) {
            video.volume = volumeSlider.value;
        }

        function seekInput(e) {
            video.currentTime = seekSlider.value;
        }


        var video = document.getElementById("bbbVideo");
        var playButton = document.getElementById("playbackController");
        var muteButton = document.getElementById("muteController");
        var volumeSlider = document.getElementById("volumeController");
```

```
            var seekSlider = document.getElementById("seekController");

            video.addEventListener("pause", pauseHandler);
            video.addEventListener("playing", playingHandler);
            video.addEventListener("volumechange", volumechangeHandler);
            video.addEventListener("durationchange", durationchangeHandler);
            video.addEventListener("timeupdate", timeupdateHandler);


            playButton.addEventListener("click", playbackClick);
            muteButton.addEventListener("click", muteClick);
            volumeSlider.addEventListener("input", volumeInput);
            seekSlider.addEventListener("input", seekInput);

        </script>
    </body>
    </html>
```

Save this as `ch15_question2.html`.

Once again, the changes are highlighted. You add another range control to the page:

```
<div>
    <input type="range" id="seekController"
           min="0" step="1" value="0" />
</div>
```

This one is called `seekController`. It is set to a minimum value of 0, a step of 1, and an initial value of 0. A maximum value is not set because you do not yet know the duration of the video. You will, however, when the media's `durationchange` event fires. You register a listener for this event; it calls the `durationchangeHandler()` function when it fires.

```
function durationchangeHandler(e) {
    seekSlider.max = video.duration;
}
```

It simply sets the slider's `max` property to the media's duration.

You also register a listener for the media's `timeupdate` event with the `timeupdateHandler()` function. You use this to update the slider's value when the media's current time changes:

```
function timeupdateHandler(e) {
    seekSlider.value = video.currentTime;
}
```

But you also want to control the media's seek with the slider, so you listen for the range control's input event:

```
function seekInput(e) {
    video.currentTime = seekSlider.value;
}
```

And you set the media's `currentTime` property to the slider's value.

CHAPTER 16

Exercise 1 Question

Example 1 is based on Chapter 10's Example 17, and as you probably remember, you modified that example in response to one of Chapter 10's exercise questions. Modify this chapter's Example 1 so that only one tab is active at a time.

Exercise 1 Solution

```
<!DOCTYPE html>

<html lang="en">
<head>
    <title>Chapter 16: Question 1</title>
    <style>
        .tabStrip {
            background-color: #E4E2D5;
            padding: 3px;
            height: 22px;
        }

            .tabStrip div {
                float: left;
                font: 14px arial;
                cursor: pointer;
            }

        .tabStrip-tab {
            padding: 3px;
        }

        .tabStrip-tab-hover {
            border: 1px solid #316AC5;
            background-color: #C1D2EE;
            padding: 2px;
        }

        .tabStrip-tab-click {
            border: 1px solid #facc5a;
            background-color: #f9e391;
            padding: 2px;
        }
    </style>
</head>
<body>
    <div class="tabStrip">
        <div data-tab-number="1" class="tabStrip-tab">Tab 1</div>
        <div data-tab-number="2" class="tabStrip-tab">Tab 2</div>
        <div data-tab-number="3" class="tabStrip-tab">Tab 3</div>
    </div>
```

```
<div id="descContainer"></div>

<script src="jquery-2.1.1.min.js"></script>
<script>
    var activeTab = null;

    function handleEvent(e) {
        var target = $(e.target);
        var type = e.type;

        if (type == "mouseover" || type == "mouseout") {
            target.toggleClass("tabStrip-tab-hover");
        } else if (type == "click") {

            if (activeTab) {
                activeTab.removeClass("tabStrip-tab-click");
            }

            target.addClass("tabStrip-tab-click");

            var num = target.attr("data-tab-number");
            showDescription(num);

            activeTab = target;
        }
    }

    function showDescription(num) {
        var text = "Description for Tab " + num;

        $("#descContainer").text(text);
    }

    $(".tabStrip > div").on("mouseover mouseout click", handleEvent);
</script>

</body>
</html>
```

Save this as ch16_question1.html.

The overall logic of this solution is identical to Chapter 10's Solution 3. You define a variable to track the active tab:

```
var activeTab = null;
```

Then when the user clicks one of the tabs, you remove the tabStrip-tab-click CSS class from the active tab (if one exists):

```
if (activeTab) {
    activeTab.removeClass("tabStrip-tab-click");
}
```

And then you set the current tab as the active tab:

```
activeTab = target;
```

Exercise 2 Question

There is some repetitive code in Example 2. Refactor the code to reduce the duplication. Additionally, add a function to handle any errors that may occur with the request.

Exercise 2 Solution

```
<!DOCTYPE html>

<html lang="en">
<head>
    <title>Chapter 16: Question 2</title>
    <style>
        .fieldname {
            text-align: right;
        }

        .submit {
            text-align: right;
        }
    </style>
</head>
<body>
    <form>
        <table>
            <tr>
                <td class="fieldname">
                    Username:
                </td>
                <td>
                    <input type="text" id="username" />
                </td>
                <td>
                    <a id="usernameAvailability" href="#">Check Availability</a>
                </td>
            </tr>
            <tr>
                <td class="fieldname">
                    Email:
                </td>
                <td>
                    <input type="text" id="email" />
                </td>
                <td>
                    <a id="emailAvailability" href="#">Check Availability</a>
                </td>
            </tr>
            <tr>
                <td class="fieldname">
                    Password:
                </td>
                <td>
                    <input type="text" id="password" />
                </td>
```

```
                <td />
            </tr>
            <tr>
                <td class="fieldname">
                    Verify Password:
                </td>
                <td>
                    <input type="text" id="password2" />
                </td>
                <td />
            </tr>
            <tr>
                <td colspan="2" class="submit">
                    <input type="submit" value="Submit" />
                </td>
                <td />
            </tr>
        </table>
    </form>
    <script src="jquery-2.1.1.min.js"></script>
    <script>
        function checkUsername(e) {
            e.preventDefault();

            var userValue = $("#username").val();

            if (!userValue) {
                alert("Please enter a user name to check!");
                return;
            }

            makeRequest({
                username: userValue
            });
        }

        function checkEmail(e) {
            e.preventDefault();

            var emailValue = $("#email").val();

            if (!emailValue) {
                alert("Please enter an email address to check!");
                return;
            }

            makeRequest({
                email: emailValue
            });
        }

        function makeRequest(parameters) {
            $.getJSON("ch14_formvalidator.php", parameters)
                .done(handleResponse)
                .fail(handleError);
```

```
        }

        function handleError() {
            alert("A network error occurred. Please try again " +
                "in a few moments.");
        }

        function handleResponse(response) {
            if (response.available) {
                alert(response.searchTerm + " is available!");
            } else {
                alert("We're sorry, but " + response.searchTerm +
                    " is not available.");
            }
        }

        $("#usernameAvailability").on("click", checkUsername);
        $("#emailAvailability").on("click", checkEmail);
    </script>
</body>

</html>
```

Save this as ch16_question2.html.

The main source of duplication is the code that makes the actual request:

```
$.getJSON("ch14_formvalidator.php", parms).done(handleResponse);
```

Although it's a single line of code, it can be moved into a separate function to make it easier to maintain. Plus, when you add a function for handling Ajax errors, you have to visit only one function as opposed to two.

First write a function that displays a message to the user when the Ajax request fails. Call it handleError():

```
function handleError() {
    alert("A network error occurred. Please try again " +
        "in a few moments.");
}
```

Now write a function that performs the Ajax request, and chain a fail() call to done():

```
function makeRequest(parameters) {
    $.getJSON("ch14_formvalidator.php", parameters)
        .done(handleResponse)
        .fail(handleError);
}
```

You can now use this makeRequest() function inside the checkUsername() function:

```
function checkUsername(e) {
    e.preventDefault();

    var userValue = $("#username").val();

    if (!userValue) {
        alert("Please enter a user name to check!");
        return;
    }

    makeRequest({
        username: userValue
    });
}
```

And the `checkEmail()` function:

```
function checkEmail(e) {
    e.preventDefault();

    var emailValue = $("#email").val();

    if (!emailValue) {
        alert("Please enter an email address to check!");
        return;
    }

    makeRequest({
        email: emailValue
    });
}
```

You can also eliminate the parms variable in both of the functions, as shown in this solution. Just pass the object literal directly to `makeRequest()` to make your code more concise.

CHAPTER 17

Exercise 1 Question

Modify the answer to Chapter 14's Question 2 using Prototype. Also add error reporting for when an error occurs with the Ajax request.

Exercise 1 Solution

```
<!DOCTYPE html>

<html lang="en">
<head>
    <title>Chapter 17: Question 1</title>
    <style>
        .fieldname {
            text-align: right;
```

```
                }
            .submit {
                text-align: right;
            }
        </style>
    </head>
    <body>
        <form name="theForm">
            <table>
                <tr>
                    <td class="fieldname">
                        Username:
                    </td>
                    <td>
                        <input type="text" id="username" />
                    </td>
                    <td></td>
                </tr>
                <tr>
                    <td class="fieldname">
                        Email:
                    </td>
                    <td>
                        <input type="text" id="email" />
                    </td>
                    <td></td>
                </tr>
                <tr>
                    <td class="fieldname">
                        Password:
                    </td>
                    <td>
                        <input type="text" id="password" />
                    </td>
                    <td />
                </tr>
                <tr>
                    <td class="fieldname">
                        Verify Password:
                    </td>
                    <td>
                        <input type="text" id="password2" />
                    </td>
                    <td />
                </tr>
                <tr>
                    <td colspan="2" class="submit">
                        <input id="btnSubmit" type="submit" value="Submit" />
                    </td>
                    <td />
                </tr>
            </table>
        </form>
        <script src="prototype.1.7.2.js"></script>
        <script>
            function btnSubmitClick(e) {
```

```
        e.preventDefault();

        checkUsername();
    }

function checkUsername() {
    var userValue = $("username").value;

    if (!userValue) {
        alert("Please enter a user name to check!");
        return;
    }

    var options = {
        method: "get",
        onSuccess: handleUsernameResponse,
        onFailure: handleError,
        parameters: {
            username: userValue
        }
    };

    new Ajax.Request("ch14_formvalidator.php", options);
}

function checkEmail() {
    var emailValue = $("email").value;

    if (!emailValue) {
        alert("Please enter an email address to check!");
        return;
    }

    var options = {
        method: "get",
        onSuccess: handleEmailResponse,
        onFailure: handleError,
        parameters: {
            email: emailValue
        }
    };

    new Ajax.Request("ch14_formvalidator.php", options);
}

function handleUsernameResponse(transport) {
    var response = transport.responseJSON;

    if (!response.available) {
        alert("The username " + response.searchTerm +
                " is unavailable. Try another.");
        return;
    }

    checkEmail();
```

```
            }

        function handleEmailResponse(transport) {
            var response = transport.responseJSON;

            if (!response.available) {
                alert("The email address " + response.searchTerm +
                        " is unavailable. Try another.");
                return;
            }

            document.theForm.submit();
        }

        function handleError() {
            alert("A network error occurred. Please try again " +
                    "in a few moments.");
        }

        $("btnSubmit").observe("click", btnSubmitClick);
    </script>
</body>

</html>
```

Save this as ch17_question1.html.

This solution is based on Chapter 14's Solution 2, but the code has changed to use Prototype's API. There's also a new function called handleError() for handling errors:

```
function handleError() {
    alert("A network error occurred. Please try " +
            "again in a few moments.");
}
```

This function is called handleError(), and it simply displays a message to the user. You'll assign this function to the onFailure option when you make your Ajax requests.

Making a request is many more lines of code due to Prototype's Ajax API:

```
var options = {
    method: "get",
    onSuccess: handleEmailResponse,
    onFailure: handleError,
    parameters: {
        email: emailValue
    }
};

new Ajax.Request("ch14_formvalidator.php", options);
```

This excerpt is taken from checkUsername(). You create your options object containing the method, onSuccess, onFailure, and parameters properties, and then you issue the request.

On a successful request, the `handleUsernameResponse()` and `handleEmailResponse()` functions execute. They no longer manually parse the JSON data into a JavaScript object; instead, they use the `responseJSON` property:

```
var response = transport.responseJSON;
```

And finally, you register the button's `click` event listener using the `observe()` method:

```
$("btnSubmit").observe("click", btnSubmitClick);
```

Exercise 2 Question

If you guessed that this question would be: "Change the answer to Chapter 14's Question 2 using MooTools, and add error reporting for when an error occurs with the Ajax request" then you won!! Your prize is…completing the exercise.

Exercise 2 Solution

```
<!DOCTYPE html>

<html lang="en">
<head>
    <title>Chapter 17: Question 2</title>
    <style>
        .fieldname {
            text-align: right;
        }

        .submit {
            text-align: right;
        }
    </style>
</head>
<body>
    <form name="theForm">
        <table>
            <tr>
                <td class="fieldname">
                    Username:
                </td>
                <td>
                    <input type="text" id="username" />
                </td>
                <td></td>
            </tr>
            <tr>
                <td class="fieldname">
                    Email:
                </td>
                <td>
                    <input type="text" id="email" />
                </td>
```

```
                <td></td>
            </tr>
            <tr>
                <td class="fieldname">
                    Password:
                </td>
                <td>
                    <input type="text" id="password" />
                </td>
                <td />
            </tr>
            <tr>
                <td class="fieldname">
                    Verify Password:
                </td>
                <td>
                    <input type="text" id="password2" />
                </td>
                <td />
            </tr>
            <tr>
                <td colspan="2" class="submit">
                    <input id="btnSubmit" type="submit" value="Submit" />
                </td>
                <td />
            </tr>
        </table>
</form>
<script src="mootools-core-1.5.1-compressed.js"></script>
<script>
    function btnSubmitClick(e) {
        e.preventDefault();

        checkUsername();
    }

    function checkUsername() {
        var userValue = $("username").value;

        if (!userValue) {
            alert("Please enter a user name to check!");
            return;
        }

        var options = {
            url: "ch14_formvalidator.php",
            data: {
                username: userValue
            },
            onSuccess: handleUsernameResponse,
            onFailure: handleError
```

```
        };

        new Request.JSON(options).get();


    }

    function checkEmail() {
        var emailValue = $("email").value;

        if (!emailValue) {
            alert("Please enter an email address to check!");
            return;
        }

        var options = {
            url: "ch14_formvalidator.php",
            data: {
                email: emailValue
            },
            onSuccess: handleEmailResponse,
            onFailure: handleError
        };

        new Request.JSON(options).get();

    }

    function handleUsernameResponse(response) {
        if (!response.available) {
            alert("The username " + response.searchTerm +
                    " is unavailable. Try another.");
            return;
        }

        checkEmail();
    }

    function handleEmailResponse(response) {
        if (!response.available) {
            alert("The email address " + response.searchTerm +
                    " is unavailable. Try another.");
            return;
        }

        document.theForm.submit();
    }

    function handleError() {
        alert("A network error occurred. Please try again " +
                "in a few moments.");
    }

    $("btnSubmit").addEvent("click", btnSubmitClick);
</script>
```

```
        </body>

        </html>
```

CHAPTER 18

Exercise 1 Question

The example `ch18_example4.html` has a deliberate bug. For each times table it creates only multipliers with values from 1 to 11.

Use the script debugger to work out why this is happening, and then correct the bug.

Exercise 1 Solution

The problem is with the code's logic rather than its syntax. Logic errors are much harder to spot and deal with because, unlike with syntax errors, the browser won't inform you that there's such and such error at line so and so but instead just fails to work as expected. The error is with this line:

```
for (var counter = 1; counter < 12; counter++)
```

You want the loop to go from 1 to 12 inclusive. Your `counter < 12` statement will be `true` up to and including 11 but will be `false` when the counter reaches 12; hence 12 gets left off. To correct this, you could change the code to the following:

```
for (var counter = 1; counter <= 12; counter++)
```

Exercise 2 Question

The following code contains a number of common errors. See if you can spot them:

```
<!DOCTYPE html>

<html lang="en">
<head>
    <title>Chapter 18: Question 2</title>
</head>
<body>
    <form name="form1" action="">
        <input type="text" id="text1" name="text1" />
        <br />
        CheckBox 1<input type="checkbox" id="checkbox2" name="checkbox2" />
        <br />
        CheckBox 1<input type="checkbox" id="checkbox1" name="checkbox1" />
        <br />
        <input type="text" id="text2" name="text2" />
        <p>
            <input type="submit" value="Submit" id="submit1"
                   name="submit1" />
        </p>
    </form>

    <script>
        function checkForm(e) {
```

```
                var elementCount = 0;
                var theForm = document.form1;

                while(elementCount =<= theForm.length) {
                    if (theForm.elements[elementcount].type == "text") {
                        if (theForm.elements[elementCount].value() = "")
                            alert("Please complete all form elements");
                        theForm.elements[elementCount].focus;
                        e.preventDefault();
                        break;
                    }
                }
            }

        document.form1.addEventListener("submit", checkForm);
    </script>
</body>

</html>
```

Exercise 2 Solution

The bug-free version looks like this:

```
<!DOCTYPE html>

<html lang="en">
<head>
    <title>Chapter 18: Question 2</title>
</head>
<body>
    <form name="form1" action="">
        <input type="text" id="text1" name="text1" />
        <br />
        CheckBox 1<input type="checkbox" id="checkbox2" name="checkbox2" />
        <br />
        CheckBox 1<input type="checkbox" id="checkbox1" name="checkbox1" />
        <br />
        <input type="text" id="text2" name="text2" />
        <p>
            <input type="submit" value="Submit" id="submit1"
                name="submit1" />
        </p>
    </form>

    <script>
        function checkForm(e) {
            var elementCount = 0;
            var theForm = document.form1;

            while(elementCount < theForm.length) {
                if (theForm.elements[elementCount].type == "text") {
                    if (theForm.elements[elementCount].value == "") {
                        alert("Please complete all form elements");
                        theForm.elements[elementCount].focus();
```

```
                              e.preventDefault();
                              break;
                    }
            }

            elementCount++;
          }
    }

      document.form1.addEventListener("submit", checkForm);
    </script>
  </body>

  </html>
```

Let's look at each error in turn. The first error is a logic error:

```
while(elementCount =< theForm.length)
```

Arrays start at 0 so the first `element` object is at index array 0, the second at 1, and so on. The last object has an index value of 4. However, `theForm.length` will return 5 because there are five elements in the form. So the `while` loop will continue until `elementCount` is less than or equal to 5, but because the last element has an index of 4, this is one past the limit. You should write either this:

```
while(elementCount < theForm.length)
```

or this:

```
while(elementCount <= theForm.length - 1)
```

Either is fine, though the first is shorter.

You come to your second error in the following line:

```
if (theForm.elements[elementcount].type == "text")
```

On a quick glance it looks fine, but it's JavaScript's strictness on case sensitivity that has caused the downfall. The variable name is `elementCount`, not `elementcount` with a lowercase c. So this line should read as follows:

```
if (theForm.elements[elementCount].type == "text")
```

The next line with an error is this:

```
if (theForm.elements[elementCount].value() = "")
```

This has two errors. First, `value` is a property and not a method, so there is no need for parentheses after it. Second, you have the all-time classic error of one equals sign instead of two. Remember that one equals sign means "Make it equal to," and two equals signs mean "Check if it is equal to." So with the changes, the line is:

```
if (theForm.elements[elementCount].value == "")
```

The next error is the failure to put your block of `if` code in curly braces. Even though JavaScript won't throw an error because the syntax is fine, the logic is not so fine, and you won't get the results you expect. With the braces, the `if` statement should be as follows:

```
if (theForm.elements[elementCount].value == "") {
    alert("Please complete all form elements")
    theForm.elements[elementCount].focus;
    formValid = false;
    break;
}
```

The penultimate error is in this line:

```
theForm.elements[elementCount].focus;
```

This time you have a method but with no parentheses after it. Even methods that have no parameters must have the empty parentheses after them if you intend to execute that method. So, corrected, the line is as follows:

```
theForm.elements[elementCount].focus();
```

Now you're almost done; there is just one more error. This time it's not something wrong with what's there, but rather something very important that should be there but is missing. What is it? It's this:

```
elementCount++;
```

This line should be in your `while` loop, otherwise `elementCount` will never go above `0` and the `while` loop's condition will always be `true`, resulting in the loop continuing forever: a classic infinite loop.

B

JavaScript Core Reference

This appendix outlines the syntax of all the JavaScript core language functions and objects with their properties and methods. If changes have occurred between versions, they have been noted.

BROWSER REFERENCE

The following table outlines which JavaScript version is in use and in which browser it is used. Note that earlier versions of Internet Explorer implemented Jscript, Microsoft's version of JavaScript. However, Jscript's features are relatively the same as JavaScript.

JAVASCRIPT VERSION	MOZILLA FIREFOX	INTERNET EXPLORER	CHROME	SAFARI	OPERA
1.0		3.0			
1.1					
1.2					
1.3		4.0			
1.4					
1.5	1.0	5.5, 6, 7, 8	1–10	3-5	6, 7, 8, 9
1.6	1.5				
1.7	2.0		28		
1.8	3.0				11.5
1.8.1	3.5				
1.8.2	3.6				
1.8.5	4	9	32	6	11.6

RESERVED WORDS

Various words and symbols are reserved by JavaScript. These words cannot be used as variable names, nor can the symbols be used within them. They are listed in the following table.

abstract	boolean	break
byte	case	catch
char	class	const
continue	debugger	default
delete	do	double
else	enum	export
extends	false	final
finally	float	for
function	goto	if
implements	import	in
instanceof	int	interface
let	long	native
new	null	package
private	protected	public
return	short	static
super	switch	synchronized
this	throw	throws
transient	true	try
typeof	var	void
volatile	while	with
-	!	~
%	/	*
>	<	=
&	^	|
+	?	

Other Identifiers to Avoid

It is best to avoid the use of the following identifiers as variable names.

JavaScript 1.0

abs acos anchor asin atan atan2 big blink bold ceil charAt comment cos Date E
escape eval exp fixed floor fontcolor fontsize getDate getDay getHours getMinutes
getMonth getSeconds getTime getTimezoneOffset getYear indexOf isNaN italics
lastIndexOf link log LOG10E LOG2E LN10 LN2 Math max min Object parse parseFloat
parseInt PI pow random round, setDate setHours setMinutes setMonth setSeconds
setTime setYear sin slice small sqrt SQRT1_2 SQRT2 strike String sub substr
substring sup tan toGMTString toLocaleString toLowerCase toUpperCase unescape UTC

JavaScript 1.1

caller className constructor java JavaArray JavaClass JavaObject JavaPackage
join length MAX_VALUE MIN_VALUE NaN NEGATIVE_INFINITY netscape Number POSITIVE_
INFINITY prototype reverse sort split sun toString valueOf

JavaScript 1.2

arity callee charCodeAt compile concat exec fromCharCode global ignoreCase index
input label lastIndex lastMatch lastParen leftContext match multiline Number
Packages pop push RegExp replace rightContext search shift slice splice source
String test unshift unwatch watch

JavaScript 1.3

apply call getFullYear getMilliseconds getUTCDate getUTCDay getUTCFullYear
getUTCHours getUTCMilliseconds getUTCMinutes getUTCMonth getUTCSeconds Infinity
isFinite NaN setFullYear setMilliseconds setUTCDate setUTCFullYear setUTCHours
setUTCMilliseconds setUTCMinutes setUTCMonth setUTCSeconds toSource toUTCString
undefined

JAVASCRIPT OPERATORS

The following sections list the various operators available to you in JavaScript.

Assignment Operators

Assignment operators allow you to assign a value to a variable. The following table lists the different
assignment operators you can use.

NAME	INTRODUCED	MEANING
Assignment	JavaScript 1.0	Sets variable `v1` to the value of variable `v2`. `var v1 = v2;`
Shorthand addition or Shorthand concatenation same as `v1 = v1 + v2`	JavaScript 1.0	`v1 += v2`
Shorthand subtraction same as `v1 = v1 - v2`	JavaScript 1.0	`v1 -= v2`
Shorthand multiplication same as `v1 = v1 * v2`	JavaScript 1.0	`v1 *= v2`
Shorthand division same as `v1 = v1 / v2`	JavaScript 1.0	`v1 /= v2`
Shorthand modulus same as `v1 = v1 % v2`	JavaScript 1.0	`v1 %= v2`
Shorthand left-shift same as `v1 = v1 << v2`	JavaScript 1.0	`v1 <<= v2`
Shorthand right-shift same as `v1 = v1 >> v2`	JavaScript 1.0	`v1 >>= v2`
Shorthand zero-fill right-shift same as `v1 = v1 >>> v2`	JavaScript 1.0	`v1 >>>= v2`
Shorthand AND same as `v1 = v1 & v2`	JavaScript 1.0	`v1 &= v2`
Shorthand XOR same as `v1 = v1 ^ v2`	JavaScript 1.0	`v1 ^= v2`
Shorthand OR same as `v1 = v1	v2`	JavaScript 1.0	`v1 |= v2`

Comparison Operators

Comparison operators allow you to compare one variable or value with another. Any comparison statement returns a boolean value.

NAME	INTRODUCED	MEANING
Equal	JavaScript 1.0	`v1 == v2` True if two operands are strictly equal or equal once cast to the same type.
Not equal	JavaScript 1.0	`v1 != v2` True if two operands are not strictly equal or not equal once cast to the same type.

Greater than	JavaScript 1.0	`v1 > v2` True if left-hand side (LHS) operand is greater than right-hand side (RHS) operand.
Greater than or equal to	JavaScript 1.0	`v1 >= v2` True if LHS operand is greater than or equal to RHS operand.
Less than	JavaScript 1.0	`v1 < v2` True if LHS operand is less than RHS operand.
Less than or equal to	JavaScript 1.0	`v1 <= v2` True if LHS operand is less than or equal to RHS operand.
Strictly equal	JavaScript 1.3	`v1 === v2` True if operands are equal and of the same type.
Not strictly equal	JavaScript 1.3	`v1 !== v2` True if operands are not strictly equal.

Arithmetic Operators

Arithmetic operators allow you to perform arithmetic operations between variables or values.

NAME	INTRODUCED	MEANING
Addition	JavaScript 1.0	`v1 + v2` Sum of `v1` and `v2`. (Concatenation of `v1` and `v2`, if either operand is a string.)
Subtraction	JavaScript 1.0	`v1 - v2` Difference between `v1` and `v2`.
Multiplication	JavaScript 1.0	`v1 * v2` Product of `v1` and `v2`.
Division	JavaScript 1.0	`v1 / v2` Quotient of `v2` into `v1`.
Modulus	JavaScript 1.0	`v1 % v2` Integer remainder of dividing `v1` by `v2`.

continues

(continued)

NAME	INTRODUCED	MEANING
Prefix increment	JavaScript 1.0	`++v1 * v2(v1 + 1) * v2` Note: `v1` will be left as `v1 + 1`.
Postfix increment	JavaScript 1.0	`v1++ * v2(v1 * v2)` `v1` is then incremented by 1.
Prefix decrement	JavaScript 1.0	`-- v1 * v2(v1 - 1) * v2` Note: `v1` is left as `v1 - 1`.
Postfix decrement	JavaScript 1.0	`v1 -- * v2(v1 * v2)` `v1` is then decremented by 1.

Bitwise Operators

Bitwise operators work by converting values in `v1` and `v2` to 32-bit binary numbers and then comparing the individual bits of these two binary numbers. The result is returned as a normal decimal number.

NAME	INTRODUCED	MEANING
Bitwise AND	JavaScript 1.0	`v1 & v2` The bitwise AND lines up the bits in each operand and performs an AND operation between the two bits in the same position. If both bits are 1, the resulting bit in this position of the returned number is 1. If either bit is 0, the resulting bit in this position of the returned number is 0.
Bitwise OR	JavaScript 1.0	`v1	v2` The bitwise OR lines up the bits in each operand and performs an OR operation between the two bits in the same position. If either bit is 1, the resulting bit in this position of the returned number is 1. If both bits are 0, the resulting bit in this position of the returned number is 0.
Bitwise XOR	JavaScript 1.0	`v1 ^ v2` The bitwise XOR lines up the bits in each operand and performs an XOR operation between the two bits in the same position. The resulting bit in this position is 1 only if one bit from both operands is 1. Otherwise, the resulting bit in this position of the returned number is 0.
Bitwise NOT	JavaScript 1.0	`v1 ~ v2` Inverts all the bits in the number.

Bitwise Shift Operators

These work by converting values in v1 to 32-bit binary numbers and then moving the bits in the number to the left or the right by the specified number of places.

NAME	INTRODUCED	MEANING
Left-shift	JavaScript 1.0	v1 << v2 Shifts v1 to the left by v2 places, filling the new gaps in with zeros.
Sign-propagating right-shift	JavaScript 1.4	v1 >> v2 Shifts v1 to the right by v2 places, ignoring the bits shifted off the number.
Zero-fill right-shift	JavaScript 1.0	v1 >>> v2 Shifts v1 to the right by v2 places, ignoring the bits shifted off the number and adding v2 zeros to the left of the number.

Logical Operators

These should return one of the boolean literals, true or false. However, this may not happen if v1 or v2 is neither a boolean value nor a value that easily converts to a boolean value, such as 0, 1, null, the empty string, or undefined.

NAME	INTRODUCED	MEANING
Logical AND	JavaScript 1.0	v1 && v2 Returns true if both v1 and v2 are true, or false otherwise. Will not evaluate v2 if v1 is false.
Logical OR	JavaScript 1.0	v1 || v2 Returns false if both v1 and v2 are false, or true if one operand is true. Will not evaluate v2 if v1 is true.
Logical NOT	JavaScript 1.0	!v1 Returns false if v1 is true, or true otherwise.

Object Operators

JavaScript provides a number of operators to work with objects. The following table lists them.

NAME	INTRODUCED	MEANING
`delete`	JavaScript 1.2	`delete obj` Deletes an object, one of its properties, or the element of an array at the specified index. Also deletes variables *not* declared with the `var` keyword.
`in`	JavaScript 1.4	`for (prop in somObj)` Returns `true` if `someObj` has the named property.
`instanceof`	JavaScript 1.4	`someObj instanceof ObjType` Returns `true` if `someObj` is of type `ObjType`; otherwise, returns `false`.
`new`	JavaScript 1.0	`new ObjType()` Creates a new instance of an object with type `ObjType`.
`this`	JavaScript 1.0	`this.property` Refers to the current object.

Miscellaneous Operators

The following table lists miscellaneous operators.

NAME	INTRODUCED	MEANING
Conditional operator	JavaScript 1.0	`(evalquery) ? v1 : v2` If `evalquery` is `true`, the operator returns `v1`; otherwise it returns `v2`.
Comma operator	JavaScript 1.0	`var v3 = (v1 + 2, v2 * 2)` Evaluates both operands while treating the two as one expression. Returns the value of the second operand. In this example, `v3` holds the resulting value of `v2 * 2`.
`typeof`	JavaScript 1.1	`typeof v1` Returns a string holding the type of `v1`, which is not evaluated.
`void`	JavaScript 1.1	`void(eval)` Evaluates `eval1` but does not return a value.

Operator Precedence

Does `1 + 2 * 3 = 1 + (2 * 3) = 7` or does it equal `(1 + 2) * 3 = 9`?

Operator precedence determines the order in which operators are evaluated. For example, the multiplicative operator (`*`) has a higher precedence than the additive operator (`+`). Therefore, the correct answer to the previous question is:

```
1 + (2 * 3)
```

The following table lists the operator precedence in JavaScript from highest to lowest. The third column explains whether to read 1+2+3+4 as ((1+2)+3)+4 (left to right) or 1+(2+(3+(4))) (right to left).

OPERATOR TYPE	OPERATORS	EVALUATION ORDER FOR LIKE ELEMENTS
Member	`. or []`	Left to right
Create instance	`new`	Right to left
Function call	`()`	Left to right
Increment	`++`	N/a
Decrement	`--`	N/a
Logical not	`!`	Right to left
Bitwise not	`~`	Right to left
Unary +	`+`	Right to left
Unary –	`-`	Right to left
Type of	`typeof`	Right to left
Void	`void`	Right to left
Delete	`delete`	Right to left
Multiplication	`*`	Left to right
Division	`/`	Left to right
Modulus	`%`	Left to right
Addition	`+`	Left to right
Subtraction	`-`	Left to right
Bitwise shift	`<<, >>, >>>`	Left to right
Relational	`<, <=, >, >=`	Left to right
In	`in`	Left to right
Instance of	`instanceof`	Left to right

continues

(continued)

OPERATOR TYPE	OPERATORS	EVALUATION ORDER FOR LIKE ELEMENTS
Equality	`==, !=, ===, !===`	Left to right
Bitwise AND	`&`	Left to right
Bitwise XOR	`^`	Left to right
Bitwise OR	`|`	Left to right
Logical AND	`&&`	Left to right
Logical OR	`||`	Left to right
Conditional	`?:`	Right to left
Assignment	`=, +=, -=, *=, /=, %=, <<=, >>=, >>>=, &=, ^=, |=`	Right to left
Comma	`,`	Left to right

JAVASCRIPT STATEMENTS

The following tables describe core JavaScript statements.

Block

JavaScript blocks start with an opening curly brace ({) and end with a closing curly brace (}). Block statements are meant to make the contained single statements execute together, such as the body of a function or a condition.

STATEMENT	INTRODUCED	DESCRIPTION
`{ }`	JavaScript 1.5	Used to group statements as delimited by the curly brackets.

Conditional

The following table lists conditional statements for JavaScript as well as the version in which they were introduced.

STATEMENT	INTRODUCED	DESCRIPTION
`if`	JavaScript 1.2	Executes a block of code if a specified condition is `true`.
`else`	JavaScript 1.2	The second half of an `if` statement. Executes a block of code if the result of the `if` statement is `false`.
`switch`	JavaScript 1.2	Specifies various blocks of statements to be executed depending on the value of the expression passed in as the argument.

Declarations

These keywords declare variables or functions in JavaScript code.

STATEMENT	INTRODUCED	DESCRIPTION
var	JavaScript 1.0	Used to declare a variable. Initializing it to a value is optional at the time of declaration.
function	JavaScript 1.0	Used to declare a function with the specified parameters, which can be strings, numbers, or objects. To return a value, the function must use the return statement.

Loop

Loops execute a block of code while a specified condition is true.

STATEMENT	INTRODUCED	DESCRIPTION
do...while	JavaScript 1.2	Executes the statements specified until the test condition after the while evaluates to false. The statements are executed at least once because the test condition is evaluated last.
for	JavaScript 1.0	Creates a loop controlled according to the three optional expressions enclosed in the parentheses after the for and separated by semicolons. The first of these three expressions is the initial-expression, the second is the test condition, and the third is the increment-expression.
for...in	JavaScript 1.0	Used to iterate over all the properties of an object using a variable. For each property the specified statements within the loop are executed.
while	JavaScript 1.0	Executes a block of statements if a test condition evaluates to true. The loop then repeats, testing the condition with each repeat, ceasing if the condition evaluates to false.
break	JavaScript 1.0	Used within a while or for loop to terminate the loop and transfer program control to the statement following the loop. Can also be used with a label to break to a particular program position outside of the loop.
label	JavaScript 1.2	An identifier that can be used with break or continue statements to indicate where the program should continue execution after the loop execution is stopped.

Execution Control Statements

Code execution is controlled in a variety of ways. In addition to the conditional and loop statements, the following statements also contribute to execution control.

STATEMENT	INTRODUCED	DESCRIPTION
`continue`	JavaScript 1.0	Used to stop execution of the block of statements in the current iteration of a `while` or `for` loop; execution of the loop continues with the next iteration.
`return`	JavaScript 1.0	Used to specify the value to be returned by a function.
`with`	JavaScript 1.0	Specifies the default object for a block of code.

Exception Handling Statements

Errors are a natural part of programming, and JavaScript provides you with the means to catch errors and handle them gracefully.

STATEMENT	INTRODUCED	DESCRIPTION
`Throw`	JavaScript 1.4	Throws a custom exception defined by the user.

`try...`
`catch...`
`finally`
	JavaScript 1.4	Executes the statements in the `try` block; if any exceptions occur, these are handled in the `catch` block. The `finally` block allows you to stipulate statements that will be executed after both the `try` and `catch` statements.

Other Statements

The following table lists other JavaScript statements and when they were introduced.

STATEMENT	INTRODUCED	DESCRIPTION
`// single line` `comment`	JavaScript 1.0	Single lines of notes that are ignored by the script engine and that can be used to explain the code.
`/* multi-line` `comment */`	JavaScript 1.0	Multiple lines of notes that are ignored by the script engine and that can be used to explain the code.

TOP-LEVEL PROPERTIES AND FUNCTIONS

These are core properties and functions, which are not associated with any lower-level object, although in the terminology used by ECMAScript and by Jscript, they are described as properties and methods of the global object.

The top-level properties were introduced in JavaScript 1.3, but in previous versions, Infinity and NaN existed as properties of the Number object.

Top-Level Properties

PROPERTY	INTRODUCED	DESCRIPTION
Infinity	JavaScript 1.3	Returns infinity.
NaN	JavaScript 1.3	Returns a value that is not a number.
undefined	JavaScript 1.3	Indicates that a value has not been assigned to a variable.

Top-Level Functions

FUNCTION	INTRODUCED	DESCRIPTION
decodeURI()	JavaScript 1.5	Used to decode a URI encoded with encodeURI().
decodeURIcomponent()	JavaScript 1.5	Used to decode a URI encoded with encodeURIComponent().
encodeURI()	JavaScript 1.5	Used to compose a new version of a complete URI, replacing each instance of certain characters. It is based on the UTF-8 encoding of the characters.
encodeURIComponent()	JavaScript 1.5	Used to compose a new version of a complete URI by replacing each instance of the specified character with escape sequences. Representation is via the UTF encoding of the characters.
escape()	JavaScript 1.0	Used to encode a string in the ISO Latin-1 character set; for example, to add to a URL.
eval()	JavaScript 1.0	Returns the result of the JavaScript code, which is passed in as a string parameter.
isFinite()	JavaScript 1.3	Indicates whether the argument is a finite number.
isNaN()	JavaScript 1.1	Indicates if the argument is not a number.
Number()	JavaScript 1.2	Converts an object to a number.
parseFloat()	JavaScript 1.0	Parses a string and returns it as a floating-point number.

continues

(continued)

FUNCTION	INTRODUCED	DESCRIPTION
`parseInt()`	JavaScript 1.0	Parses a string and returns it as an integer. An optional second parameter specifies the base of the number to be converted.
`String()`	JavaScript 1.2	Converts an object to a string.
`unescape()`	JavaScript 1.0	Returns the ASCII string for the specified hexadecimal encoding value.

JAVASCRIPT CORE OBJECTS

This section describes the objects available in the JavaScript core language and their methods and properties.

Array

The `Array` object represents an array of variables. It was introduced in JavaScript 1.1. An `Array` object can be created with the `Array` constructor:

```
var objArray = new Array(10);          // an array of 11 elements
var objArray = new Array("1", "2", "4"); // an array of 3 elements
```

Arrays can also be created using array literal syntax:

```
var objArray = [];
```

Literal syntax is the preferred method of creating an array.

Properties

PROPERTY	INTRODUCED	DESCRIPTION
`constructor`	JavaScript 1.1	Used to reference the constructor function for the object.
`length`	JavaScript 1.1	Returns the number of elements in the array.
`prototype`	JavaScript 1.1	Returns the prototype for the object, which can be used to extend the object's interface.

> **NOTE** Square brackets ([]) surrounding a parameter means that parameter is optional.

Methods

METHOD	INTRODUCED	DESCRIPTION
`concat(value1 [, value2,...])`	JavaScript 1.2	Concatenates two arrays and returns the new array thus formed.
`every(testFn(element, index, array))`	JavaScript 1.6	Iterates over the array, executing `testFn()` on every element. Returns `true` if all iterations return `true`. Otherwise, it returns `false`.
`filter(testFn(element, index, array))`	JavaScript 1.6	Iterates over the array, executing `testFn()` on every element. Returns a new array of elements that pass `testFn()`.
`foreach(fn(element, index, array))`	JavaScript 1.6	Iterates over the array, executing `fn()` on every element.
`indexOf(element [, startIndex])`	JavaScript 1.6	Returns an index of the specified element if found, or -1 if not found. Starts at `startIndex` if specified.
`join([separator])`	JavaScript 1.1	Joins all the elements of an array into a single string delimited by a separator if specified.
`lastIndexOf(element [, startIndex])`	JavaScript 1.6	Searches an array starting at the last element and moves backwards. Returns an index of the specified element if found, or -1 if not found. Starts at `startIndex` if specified.
`map(fn(element, index, array))`	JavaScript 1.6	Iterates over the array, executing `fn()` on every element. Returns a new array based on the outcome of `fn()`.
`pop()`	JavaScript 1.2	Pops the last element from the end of the array and returns that element.
`push(value1 [, value2, ...])`	JavaScript 1.2	Pushes one or more elements onto the end of the array and returns the new length of the array. The array's new `length` is returned.
`reverse()`	JavaScript 1.1	Reverses the order of the elements in the array, so the first element becomes the last and the last becomes the first.
`shift()`	JavaScript 1.2	Removes the first element from the beginning of the array and returns that element.
`slice(startIndex [, endIndex])`	JavaScript 1.2	Returns a slice of the array starting at the start index and ending at the element before the end index.

continues

(continued)

METHOD	INTRODUCED	DESCRIPTION
some(testFn(element, index, array))	JavaScript 1.6	Iterates over the array, executing testFn() on every element. Returns true if at least one result of testFn() is true.
sort([sortFn(a,b)])	JavaScript 1.1	Sorts the elements of the array. Executes sortFn() for sorting if it is provided.
splice(startIndex [, length, value1, ...)	JavaScript 1.2	Removes the amount of elements denoted by length starting at startIndex. Provided values replace the deleted elements. Returns the deleted elements.
toString()	JavaScript 1.1	Converts the Array object into a string.
unshift(value1 [, value2, ...])	JavaScript 1.2	Adds elements to the beginning of the array and returns the new length.
valueOf()	JavaScript 1.1	Returns the primitive value of the array.

Boolean

The Boolean object is used as a wrapper for a boolean value. It was introduced in JavaScript 1.1. It is created with the Boolean constructor, which takes as a parameter the initial value for the object (if this is not a boolean value, it will be converted into one).

Falsey values are null, undefined, "", and 0. All other values are considered truthy.

Properties

PROPERTY	INTRODUCED	DESCRIPTION
constructor	JavaScript 1.1	Specifies the function that creates an object's prototype.
prototype	JavaScript 1.1	Returns the prototype for the object, which can be used to extend the object's interface.

Methods

METHOD	INTRODUCED	DESCRIPTION
toString()	JavaScript 1.1	Converts the Boolean object into a string.
valueOf()	JavaScript 1.1	Returns the primitive value of the Boolean object.

Date

The Date object is used to represent a given date-time. It was introduced in JavaScript 1.0.

Properties

PROPERTY	INTRODUCED	DESCRIPTION
constructor	JavaScript 1.1	Used to reference the constructor function for the object.
prototype	JavaScript 1.1	Returns the prototype for the object, which can be used to extend the object's interface.

Methods

METHOD	INTRODUCED	DESCRIPTION
getDate()	JavaScript 1.0	Retrieves the date in the month from the Date object.
getDay()	JavaScript 1.0	Retrieves the day of the week from the Date object.
getFullYear()	JavaScript 1.3	Retrieves the full year from the Date object.
getHours()	JavaScript 1.0	Retrieves the hour of the day from the Date object.
getMilliseconds()	JavaScript 1.3	Retrieves the number of milliseconds from the Date object.
getMinutes()	JavaScript 1.0	Retrieves the number of minutes from the Date object.
getMonth()	JavaScript 1.0	Retrieves the month from the Date object.
getSeconds()	JavaScript 1.0	Retrieves the number of seconds from the Date object.
getTime()	JavaScript 1.0	Retrieves the number of milliseconds since January 1, 1970 00:00:00 from the Date object.
getTimezoneOffset()	JavaScript 1.0	Retrieves the difference in minutes between the local time zone and universal time (UTC).
getUTCDate()	JavaScript 1.3	Retrieves the date in the month from the Date object adjusted to universal time.
getUTCDay()	JavaScript 1.3	Retrieves the day of the week from the Date object adjusted to universal time.
getUTCFullYear()	JavaScript 1.3	Retrieves the year from the Date object adjusted to universal time.

continues

(continued)

METHOD	INTRODUCED	DESCRIPTION
`getUTCHours()`	JavaScript 1.3	Retrieves the hour of the day from the `Date` object adjusted to universal time.
`getUTCMilliseconds()`	JavaScript 1.3	Retrieves the number of milliseconds from the `Date` object adjusted to universal time.
`getUTCMinutes()`	JavaScript 1.3	Retrieves the number of minutes from the `Date` object adjusted to universal time.
`getUTCMonth()`	JavaScript 1.3	Retrieves the month from the `Date` object adjusted to universal time.
`getUTCSeconds()`	JavaScript 1.3	Retrieves the number of seconds from the `Date` object adjusted to universal time.
`getYear()`	JavaScript 1.0	Retrieves the year from the `Date` object.
`parse(dateString)`	JavaScript 1.0	Retrieves the number of milliseconds in a date since January 1, 1970 00:00:00, local time.
`setDate(dayOfMonth)`	JavaScript 1.0	Sets the date in the month for the `Date` object.
`setFullYear(year [, month, day])`	JavaScript 1.3	Sets the full year for the `Date` object.
`setHours(hours [, minutes, seconds, milliseconds])`	JavaScript 1.0	Sets the hour of the day for the `Date` object.
`setMilliseconds (milliseconds)`	JavaScript 1.3	Sets the number of milliseconds for the `Date` object.
`setMinutes(minutes [, seconds, milliseconds])`	JavaScript 1.0	Sets the number of minutes for the `Date` object.
`setMonth(month [, day])`	JavaScript 1.0	Sets the month for the `Date` object.
`setSeconds(seconds [, milliseconds])`	JavaScript 1.0	Sets the number of seconds for the `Date` object.
`setTime(milliseconds)`	JavaScript 1.0	Sets the time for the `Date` object according to the number of milliseconds since January 1, 1970 00:00:00.
`setUTCDate(dayOfMonth)`	JavaScript 1.3	Sets the date in the month for the `Date` object according to universal time.
`setUTCFullYear(year [, month, day])`	JavaScript 1.3	Sets the full year for the `Date` object according to universal time.

`setUTCHours(hours [, minutes, seconds, milliseconds])`	JavaScript 1.3	Sets the hour of the day for the `Date` object according to universal time.
`setUTCMilliseconds (milliseconds)`	JavaScript 1.3	Sets the number of milliseconds for the `Date` object according to universal time.
`setUTCMinutes(mintes [, seconds, milliseconds])`	JavaScript 1.3	Sets the number of minutes for the `Date` object according to universal time.
`setUTCMonth(month [, day])`	JavaScript 1.3	Sets the month for the `Date` object according to universal time.
`setUTCSeconds()`	JavaScript 1.3	Sets the number of seconds for the `Date` object according to universal time.
`setYear(year)`	JavaScript 1.0	Sets the year for the `Date` object. Deprecated in favor of `setFullYear()`.
`toGMTString()`	JavaScript 1.0	Converts the `Date` object to a string according to Greenwich Mean Time. Replaced by `toUTCString`.
`toLocaleString()`	JavaScript 1.0	Converts the `Date` object to a string according to the local time zone.
`toString()`	JavaScript 1.1	Converts the `Date` object into a string.
`toUTCString()`	JavaScript 1.3	Converts the `Date` object to a string according to universal time.
`UTC(year, month [, day, hours, minutes, seconds, milliseconds])`	JavaScript 1.0	Retrieves the number of milliseconds in a date since January 1, 1970 00:00:00, universal time.
`valueOf()`	JavaScript 1.1	Returns the primitive value of the `Date` object.

Function

Introduced in JavaScript 1.1, a `Function` object is created with the `Function` constructor.

Functions can be defined in a variety of ways. You can create a function using the following standard function statement:

```
function functionName() {
    // code here
}
```

You can also create an anonymous function and assign it to a variable. The following code demonstrates this approach:

```
var functionName = function() {
    // code here
};
```

The trailing semicolon is not a typo because this statement is an assignment operation, and all assignment operations should end with a semicolon.

Functions are objects, and thus they have a constructor. It's possible to create a function using the `Function` object's constructor as shown in the following code:

```
var functionName = new Function("arg1", "arg2", "return arg1 + arg2");
```

The first arguments to the constructor are the names of the function's parameters—you can add as many parameters as you need. The last parameter you pass to the constructor is the function's body. The previous code creates a function that accepts two arguments and returns their sum.

There are very few instances where you will use the `Function` constructor. It is preferred to define a function using the standard function statement or by creating an anonymous function and assigning it to a variable.

Properties

PROPERTY	INTRODUCED	DESCRIPTION
arguments	JavaScript 1.1	An array containing the parameters passed into the function.
arguments.length	JavaScript 1.1	Returns the number of parameters passed into the function.
constructor	JavaScript 1.1	Used to reference the constructor function for the object.
length	JavaScript 1.1	Returns the number of parameters expected by the function. This differs from `arguments.length`, which returns the number of parameters actually passed into the function.
prototype	JavaScript 1.1	Returns the prototype for the object, which can be used to extend the object's interface.

Methods

METHOD	INTRODUCED	DESCRIPTION
apply(thisObj, arguments)	JavaScript 1.3	Calls a function or method as if it belonged to `thisObj` and passes `arguments` to the function or method. `arguments` must be an array.

call(thisObj, arg1, ...)	JavaScript 1.3	Identical to apply(), except arguments are passed individually instead of in an array.
toString()	JavaScript 1.1	Converts the Function object into a string.
valueOf()	JavaScript 1.1	Returns the primitive value of the Function object.

JSON

The JSON object contains methods for parsing JavaScript Object Notation (JSON) into objects and serializing JavaScript objects into JSON. Introduced in JavaScript 1.8.5, the JSON object is a top-level object, which can be accessed without a constructor.

Methods

METHOD	INTRODUCED	DESCRIPTION
parse(json)	JavaScript 1.8.5	Transforms JSON into a JavaScript object or value.
stringify(obj)	JavaScript 1.8.5	Transforms a JavaScript object or value into JSON.

Math

The Math object provides methods and properties used for mathematical calculations. Introduced in JavaScript 1.0, the Math object is a top-level object, which can be accessed without a constructor.

Properties

PROPERTY	INTRODUCED	DESCRIPTION
E	JavaScript 1.0	Returns Euler's constant (the base of natural logarithms; approximately 2.718).
LN10	JavaScript 1.0	Returns the natural logarithm of 10 (approximately 2.302).
LN2	JavaScript 1.0	Returns the natural logarithm of 2 (approximately 0.693).
LOG10E	JavaScript 1.0	Returns the Base 10 logarithm of E (approximately 0.434).
LOG2E	JavaScript 1.0	Returns the Base 2 logarithm of E (approximately 1.442).
PI	JavaScript 1.0	Returns pi, the ratio of the circumference of a circle to its diameter (approximately 3.142).
SQRT1_2	JavaScript 1.0	Returns the square root of 1/2 (approximately 0.707).
SQRT2	JavaScript 1.0	Returns the square root of 2 (approximately 1.414).

Methods

METHOD	INTRODUCED	DESCRIPTION
`abs(x)`	JavaScript 1.0	Returns the absolute (positive) value of a number.
`acos(x)`	JavaScript 1.0	Returns the arccosine of a number (in radians).
`asin(x)`	JavaScript 1.0	Returns the arcsine of a number (in radians).
`atan(x)`	JavaScript 1.0	Returns the arctangent of a number (in radians).
`atan2(y, x)`	JavaScript 1.0	Returns the angle (in radians) between the x-axis and the position represented by the y and x coordinates passed in as parameters.
`ceil(x)`	JavaScript 1.0	Returns the value of a number rounded up to the nearest integer.
`cos(x)`	JavaScript 1.0	Returns the cosine of a number.
`exp(x)`	JavaScript 1.0	Returns E to the power of the argument passed in.
`floor(x)`	JavaScript 1.0	Returns the value of a number rounded down to the nearest integer.
`log(x)`	JavaScript 1.0	Returns the natural logarithm (base E) of a number.
`max(a, b)`	JavaScript 1.0	Returns the greater of two numbers passed in as parameters.
`min(a, b)`	JavaScript 1.0	Returns the lesser of two numbers passed in as parameters.
`pow(x, y)`	JavaScript 1.0	Returns the first parameter raised to the power of the second.
`random()`	JavaScript 1.1	Returns a pseudo-random number between 0 and 1.
`round(x)`	JavaScript 1.0	Returns the value of a number rounded up or down to the nearest integer.
`sin(x)`	JavaScript 1.0	Returns the sine of a number.
`sqrt(x)`	JavaScript 1.0	Returns the square root of a number.
`tan(x)`	JavaScript 1.0	Returns the tangent of a number.

Number

The `Number` object acts as a wrapper for primitive numeric values. Introduced in JavaScript 1.1, a `Number` object is created using the `Number` constructor with the initial value for the number passed in as a parameter.

Properties

PROPERTY	INTRODUCED	DESCRIPTION
constructor	JavaScript 1.1	Used to reference the constructor function for the object.
MAX_VALUE	JavaScript 1.1	Returns the largest number that can be represented in JavaScript (approximately 1.79E+308).
MIN_VALUE	JavaScript 1.1	Returns the smallest number that can be represented in JavaScript (5E–324).
NaN	JavaScript 1.1	Returns a value that is "not a number."
NEGATIVE_INFINITY	JavaScript 1.1	Returns a value representing negative infinity.
POSITIVE_INFINITY	JavaScript 1.1	Returns a value representing (positive) infinity.
prototype	JavaScript 1.1	Returns the prototype for the object, which can be used to extend the object's interface.

Methods

METHOD	INTRODUCED	DESCRIPTION
toExponential(fractionDigits)	JavaScript 1.5	Returns a string containing the exponent notation of a number. The parameter should be between 0 and 20 and determines the number of digits after the decimal.
toFixed([digits])	JavaScript 1.5	The format number for digits number of digits. The number is rounded up, and 0s are added after the decimal point to achieve the desired decimal length.
toPrecision([precision])	JavaScript 1.5	Returns a string representing the Number object to the specified precision.
toString()	JavaScript 1.1	Converts the Number object into a string.
valueOf()	JavaScript 1.1	Returns the primitive value of the Number object.

Object

`Object` is the primitive type for JavaScript objects, from which all other objects are descended (that is, all other objects inherit the methods and properties of the `Object` object). Introduced in JavaScript 1.0, you can create an `Object` object using the `Object` constructor as follows:

```
var obj = new Object();
```

You can also create an object using object literal notation like this:

```
var obj = {};
```

Literal notation is the preferred method of creating an object.

Properties

PROPERTY	INTRODUCED	DESCRIPTION
constructor	JavaScript 1.1	Used to reference the constructor function for the object.
prototype	JavaScript 1.1	Returns the prototype for the object, which can be used to extend the object's interface.

Methods

METHOD	INTRODUCED	DESCRIPTION
hasOwnProperty(propertyName)	JavaScript 1.5	Checks whether the specified property is inherited. Returns `true` if not inherited; `false` if inherited.
isPrototypeOf(obj)	JavaScript 1.5	Determines if the specified object is the prototype of another object.
propertyIsEnumerable(propertyName)	JavaScript 1.5	Determines if the specified property can be seen by a `for in` loop.
toString()	JavaScript 1.0	Converts the `Object` object into a string.
valueOf()	JavaScript 1.1	Returns the primitive value of the `Object` object.

RegExp

The RegExp object is used to find patterns within string values. RegExp objects can be created in two ways: using the RegExp constructor or a text literal. It was introduced in JavaScript 1.2.

Some of the properties in the following table have both long and short names. The short names are derived from the Perl programming language.

Properties

PROPERTY	INTRODUCED	DESCRIPTION
constructor	JavaScript 1.2	Used to reference the constructor function for the object.
global	JavaScript 1.2	Indicates whether all possible matches in the string are to be made, or only the first. Corresponds to the g flag.
ignoreCase	JavaScript 1.2	Indicates whether the match is to be case-insensitive. Corresponds to the i flag.
input	JavaScript 1.2	The string against which the regular expression is matched.
lastIndex	JavaScript 1.2	The position in the string from which the next match is to be started.
multiline	JavaScript 1.2	Indicates whether strings are to be searched across multiple lines. Corresponds with the m flag.
prototype	JavaScript 1.2	Returns the prototype for the object, which can be used to extend the object's interface.
source	JavaScript 1.2	The text of the pattern for the regular expression.

Methods

METHOD	INTRODUCED	DESCRIPTION
exec(stringToSearch)	JavaScript 1.2	Executes a search for a match in the string parameter passed in.
test(stringToMatch)	JavaScript 1.2	Tests for a match in the string parameter passed in.
toString()	JavaScript 1.2	Converts the RegExp object into a string.
valueOf()	JavaScript 1.2	Returns the primitive value of the RegExp object.

Special Characters Used in Regular Expressions

CHARACTER	EXAMPLES	FUNCTION
\	/n/ matches n;/\n/ matches a linefeed character;/^/ matches the start of a line; and/\^/ matches ^.	For characters that are by default treated as normal characters, the backslash indicates that the next character is to be interpreted with a special value. For characters that are usually treated as special characters, the backslash indicates that the next character is to be interpreted as a normal character.
^	/^A/ matches the first but not the second A in "A man called Adam."	Matches the start of a line or of the input.
$	/r$/ matches only the last r in "horror."	Matches the end of a line or of the input.
*	/ro*/ matches r in "right," ro in "wrong," and "roo" in "room."	Matches the preceding character zero or more times.
+	/1+/ matches 1 in "life," 11 in "still," and 111 in "stilllife."	Matches the preceding character one or more times. For example, /a+/ matches the a in "candy" and all the as in "caaaaaaandy."
?	/Smythe?/ matches "Smyth" and "Smythe."	Matches the preceding character once or zero times.
.	/.b/ matches the second but not the first ob in "blob."	Matches any character apart from the newline character.
(x)	/(Smythe?)/ matches "Smyth" and "Smythe" in "John Smyth and Rob Smythe" and allows the substrings to be retrieved as RegExp.$1 and RegExp.$2, respectively.	Matches x and remembers the match. The matched substring can be retrieved from the elements of the array that results from the match, or from the RegExp object's properties $1, $2 ... $9, or lastParen.
x|y	/Smith|Smythe/ matches "Smith" and "Smythe."	Matches either x or y (where x and y are blocks of characters).
{n}	/1{2}/ matches 11 in "still" and the first two 1s in "stilllife."	Matches exactly n instances of the preceding character (where n is a positive integer).

{n,}	/l{2,}/ matches ll in "still" and lll in "stilllife."	Matches n or more instances of the preceding character (where n is a positive integer).
{n,m}	/l{1,2}/ matches l in "life," ll in "still," and the first two ls in "stilllife."	Matches between n and m instances of the preceding character (where n and m are positive integers).
[xyz]	[ab] matches a and b; [a-c] matches a, b and c.	Matches any one of the characters in the square brackets. A range of characters in the alphabet can be matched using a hyphen.
[^xyz]	[^aeiouy] matches s in "easy"; [^a-y] matches z in "lazy."	Matches any character except those enclosed in the square brackets. A range of characters in the alphabet can be specified using a hyphen.
[\b]		Matches a backspace.
\b	/t\b/ matches the first t in "about time."	Matches a word boundary (for example, a space or the end of a line).
\B	/t\Bi/ matches ti in "it is time."	Matches when there is no word boundary in this position.
\cX	/\cA/ matches Ctrl+A.	Matches a control character.
\d	/IE\d/ matches IE4, IE5, etc.	Matches a digit character. This is identical to [0-9].
\D	/\D/ matches the decimal point in "3.142."	Matches any character that is not a digit. This is identical to [^0-9].
\f		Matches a form-feed character.
\n		Matches a line-feed character.
\r		Matches a carriage return character.
\s	/\s/ matches the space in "not now."	Matches any white space character, including space, tab, line-feed, etc. This is identical to [\f\n\r\t\v].
\S	/\S/ matches a in "a."	Matches any character other than a white space character. This is identical to [^ \f\n\r\t\v].

continues

(*continued*)

CHARACTER	EXAMPLES	FUNCTION
\t		Matches a tab character.
\v		Matches a vertical tab character.
\w	/\w/ matches 0 in "0?!" and 1 in "$1."	Matches any alphanumeric character or the underscore. This is identical to [A-Za-z0-9_].
\W	/\W/ matches $ in "$10million" and @ in "j_smith@wrox."	Matches any non-alphanumeric character (excluding the underscore). This is identical to [^A-Za-z0-9_].
()\n	/(Joh?n) and \1/ matches John and John in "John and John's friend" but does not match "John and Jon."	Matches the last substring that matched the nth match placed in parentheses and remembered (where n is a positive integer).
\octal\xhex	/\x25/ matches %.	Matches the character corresponding to the specified octal or hexadecimal escape value.

String

The `string` object is used to contain a string of characters. It was introduced in JavaScript 1.0. This must be distinguished from a string literal, but the methods and properties of the `String` object can also be accessed by a string literal, because a temporary object will be created when they are called.

The HTML methods in the last table are not part of any ECMAScript standard, but they have been part of the JavaScript language since version 1.0. They can be useful because they dynamically generate HTML.

Properties

Property	Introduced	Description
constructor	JavaScript 1.1	Used to reference the constructor function for the object.
length	JavaScript 1.0	Returns the number of characters in the string.
prototype	JavaScript 1.1	Returns the prototype for the object, which can be used to extend the object's interface.

Methods

METHOD	INTRODUCED	DESCRIPTION
`charAt(index)`	JavaScript 1.0	Returns the character at the specified position in the string.
`charCodeAt(index)`	JavaScript 1.2	Returns the Unicode value of the character at the specified position in the string.
`concat(value1, value2, ...)`	JavaScript 1.2	Concatenates the strings supplied as arguments and returns the string thus formed.
`fromCharCode(value1, value2, ...)`	JavaScript 1.2	Returns the string formed from the concatenation of the characters represented by the supplied Unicode values.
`indexOf(substr [, startIndex])`	JavaScript 1.0	Returns the position within the `String` object of the first match for the supplied substring. Returns `-1` if the substring is not found. Starts the search at `startIndex` if specified.
`lastIndexOf(substr [, startIndex])`	JavaScript 1.0	Returns the position within the `String` object of the last match for the supplied substring. Returns `-1` if the substring is not found. Starts the search at `startIndex` if specified.
`match(regexp)`	JavaScript 1.2	Searches the string for a match to the supplied pattern. Returns an array or `null` if not found.
`replace(regexp, newValue)`	JavaScript 1.2	Used to replace a substring that matches a regular expression with a new value.
`search(regexp)`	JavaScript 1.2	Searches for a match between a regular expression and the string. Returns the index of the match, or `-1` if not found.
`slice(startIndex [, endIndex])`	JavaScript 1.0	Returns a substring of the `String` object.
`split(delimiter)`	JavaScript 1.1	Splits a `String` object into an array of strings by separating the string into substrings.
`substr(startIndex [, length])`	JavaScript 1.0	Returns a substring of the characters from the given starting position and containing the specified number of characters.
`substring(startIndex [, endIndex])`	JavaScript 1.0	Returns a substring of the characters between two positions in the string. The character at `endIndex` is not included in the substring.
`toLowerCase()`	JavaScript 1.0	Returns the string converted to lowercase.
`toUpperCase()`	JavaScript 1.0	Returns the string converted to uppercase.

HTML Methods

METHOD	INTRODUCED	DESCRIPTION
anchor(name)	JavaScript 1.0	Returns the string surrounded by `<a>...</a>` tags with the `name` attribute assigned the passed parameter.
big()	JavaScript 1.0	Encloses the string in `<big>...</big>` tags.
blink()	JavaScript 1.0	Encloses the string in `<blink>...</blink>` tags.
bold()	JavaScript 1.0	Encloses the string in `<b>...</b>` tags.
fixed()	JavaScript 1.0	Encloses the string in `<tt>...</tt>` tags.
fontcolor(color)	JavaScript 1.0	Encloses the string in `<font>...</font>` tags with the `color` attribute assigned a parameter value.
fontsize(size)	JavaScript 1.0	Encloses the string in `<font>...</font>` tags with the `size` attribute assigned a parameter value.
italics()	JavaScript 1.0	Encloses the string in `<i>...</i>` tags.
link(url)	JavaScript 1.0	Encloses the string in `<a>...</a>` tags with the `href` attribute assigned a parameter value.
small()	JavaScript 1.0	Encloses the string in `<small>...</small>` tags.
strike()	JavaScript 1.0	Encloses the string in `<strike>...</strike>` tags.
sub()	JavaScript 1.0	Encloses the string in `<sub>...</sub>` tags.
sup()	JavaScript 1.0	Encloses the string in `<sup>...</sup>` tags and causes a string to be displayed as superscript.

C

W3C DOM Reference

Because JavaScript is primarily used to program the browser and add behavior to web pages, it's only natural to include a reference to the W3C DOM.

The following pages list the objects made available by the W3C DOM.

DOM CORE OBJECTS

This section describes and lists objects defined by the DOM standards—starting with the lowest level of DOM objects. All objects are in alphabetical order.

Low-Level DOM Objects

The DOM specification describes the Node, NodeList, and NamedNodeMap objects. These are the lowest-level objects in the DOM, and are the primary building blocks of higher-level objects.

Node

Defined in DOM Level 1, the Node object is the primary data type for the entire DOM. All objects in the DOM inherit from Node. There are 12 different types of Node objects; each type has an associated integer value. The following tables list the Node object's type values, properties, and methods.

Node Types

TYPE NAME	INTEGER VALUE	INTRODUCED	ASSOCIATED DATA TYPE
ELEMENT_NODE	1	Level 1	Element
ATTRIBUTE_NODE	2	Level 1	Attr
TEXT_NODE	3	Level 1	Text
CDATA_SECTION_NODE	4	Level 1	CDATASection
ENTITY_REFERENCE_NODE	5	Level 1	EntityReference
ENTITY_NODE	6	Level 1	Entity
PROCESSING_INSTRUCTION_NODE	7	Level 1	ProcessingInstruction
COMMENT_NODE	8	Level 1	Comment
DOCUMENT_NODE	9	Level 1	Document
DOCUMENT_TYPE_NODE	10	Level 1	DocumentType
DOCUMENT_FRAGMENT_NODE	11	Level 1	DocumentFragment
NOTATION_NODE	12	Level 1	Notation

Properties

PROPERTY NAME	DESCRIPTION	INTRODUCED
attributes	A NamedNodeMap containing the attributes of this node if it is an Element, or null otherwise.	Level 1
childNodes	A NodeList containing all children of this node.	Level 1
firstChild	Gets the first child of this node. Returns null if no child exists.	Level 1
lastChild	Gets the last child of this node. Returns null if no child exists.	Level 1
localName	Returns the local part of the node's qualified name (the part after the colon of the qualified name when namespaces are used). Used primarily in XML DOMs.	Level 2
namespaceURI	The namespace URI of the node, or null if not specified.	Level 2

`nextSibling`	Gets the node immediately following this node. Returns `null` if no following sibling exists.	Level 1
`nodeName`	Gets the name of this node.	Level 1
`nodeType`	An integer representing the type of this node. See previous table.	Level 1
`nodeValue`	Gets the value of this node, depending on the type.	Level 1
`ownerDocument`	Gets the `Document` object this node is contained in. If this node is a `Document` node, it returns `null`.	Level 1
`parentNode`	Gets the parent node of this node. Returns `null` for nodes that are currently not in the DOM tree.	Level 1
`prefix`	Returns the namespace prefix of this node, or `null` if not specified.	Level 2
`previousSibling`	Gets the node immediately before this node. Returns `null` if no previous sibling.	Level 1

Methods

METHOD NAME	DESCRIPTION	INTRODUCED
`appendChild(newChild)`	Adds the `newChild` to the end of the list of children.	Level 1
`cloneNode(deep)`	Returns a duplicate of the node. The returned node has no parent. If `deep` is `true`, this clones all nodes contained within the node.	Level 1
`hasAttributes()`	Returns a boolean value based on if the node has any attributes (if the node is an element).	Level 2
`hasChildNodes()`	Returns a boolean value based on whether the node has any child nodes.	Level 1
`insertBefore(newChild, refChild)`	Inserts the `newChild` node before the existing child referenced by `refChild`. If `refChild` is `null`, `newChild` is added at the end of the list of children.	Level 1
`removeChild(oldChild)`	Removes the specified child node and returns it.	Level 1
`replaceChild(newChild, oldChild)`	Replaces `oldChild` with `newChild` and returns `oldChild`.	Level 1

NodeList

The NodeList object is an ordered collection of nodes. The items contained in the NodeList are accessible via an index starting from 0.

A NodeList is a live snapshot of nodes. Any changes made to the nodes within the DOM are immediately reflected in every reference of the NodeList.

Properties

PROPERTY NAME	DESCRIPTION	INTRODUCED
length	The number of nodes in the list.	Level 1

Methods

METHOD NAME	DESCRIPTION	INTRODUCED
item(index)	Returns the item at the specified index. Returns null if the index is greater than or equal to the list's length.	Level 1

NamedNodeMap

Objects referred to as NamedNodeMaps represent collections of nodes that can be accessed by name. This object does not inherit from NodeList. An element's attribute list is an example of a NamedNodeMap.

Properties

PROPERTY NAME	DESCRIPTION	INTRODUCED
length	The number of nodes in the map.	Level 1

Methods

METHOD NAME	DESCRIPTION	INTRODUCED
getNamedItem(name)	Retrieves a node by the specified name.	Level 1
removeNamedItem(name)	Removes an item by the specified name.	Level 1
setNamedItem(node)	Adds a node to the list by using its nodeName property as its key.	Level 1

High-Level DOM Objects

These objects inherit Node and are the basis for even higher-level DOM objects as specified by the HTML DOM. These objects mirror the different node types.

The following objects are listed in alphabetical order. The `CDATASection`, `Comment`, `DocumentType`, `Entity`, `EntityReference`, `Notation`, and `ProcessingInstruction` objects are purposefully omitted from this section.

Attr

The `Attr` object represents an `Element` object's attribute. Even though `Attr` objects inherit from `Node`, they are not considered children of the element they describe, and thus are not part of the DOM tree. The `Node` properties of `parentNode`, `previousSibling`, and `nextSibling` return `null` for `Attr` objects.

Properties

PROPERTY NAME	DESCRIPTION	INTRODUCED
ownerElement	Returns the `Element` object the attribute is attached to.	Level 2
name	Returns the name of the attribute.	Level 1
value	Returns the value of the attribute.	Level 1

Document

The `Document` object represents the entire HTML or XML document. It is the root of the document tree. The `Document` is the container for all nodes within the document, and each `Node` object's `ownerDocument` property points to the `Document`.

Properties

PROPERTY NAME	DESCRIPTION	INTRODUCED
docType	The `DocType` object associated with this document. Returns `null` for HTML and XML documents without a document type declaration.	Level 1
documentElement	Returns the root element of the document. For HTML documents, the `documentElement` is the `<html/>` element.	Level 1
implementation	The `DOMImplementation` object associated with the `Document`.	Level 1

Methods

METHOD NAME	DESCRIPTION	INTRODUCED
createAttribute(name)	Returns a new `Attr` object with the specified name.	Level 1
createAttributeNS(namespaceURI, qualifiedName)	Returns an attribute with the given qualified name and namespace URI. Not for HTML DOMs.	Level 2

continues

(continued)

METHOD NAME	DESCRIPTION	INTRODUCED
`createComment(data)`	Returns a new `Comment` object with the specified data.	Level 1
`createCDATASection(data)`	Returns a new `CDATASection` object whose value is the specified data.	Level 1
`createDocumentFragment()`	Returns an empty `DocumentFragment` object.	Level 1
`createElement(tagName)`	Returns a new `Element` object with the specified tag name.	Level 1
`createElementNS(namespaceURI, qualifiedName)`	Returns an element of the specified qualified name and namespace URI. Not for HTML DOMs.	Level 2
`createTextNode(text)`	Returns a new `Text` object containing the specified text.	Level 1
`getElementById(elementId)`	Returns the `Element` with the specified ID value. Returns `null` if the element does not exist.	Level 2
`getElementsByTagName(tagName)`	Returns a `NodeList` of all `Element` objects with the specified tag name in the order in which they appear in the DOM tree.	Level 1
`getElementsByTagNameNS(namespaceURI, localName)`	Returns a `NodeList` of all elements with the specified local name and namespace URI. Elements returned are in the order they appear in the DOM.	Level 2
`importNode(importedNode, deep)`	Imports a node from another document. The source node is not altered or removed from its document. A copy of the source is created. If `deep` is `true`, all child nodes of the imported node are imported. If `false`, only the node is imported.	Level 2

DocumentFragment

The DocumentFragment object is a lightweight Document object. Its primary purpose is efficiency. Making many changes to the DOM tree, such as appending several nodes individually, is an expensive process. It is possible to append Node objects to a DocumentFragment object, which allows you to easily and efficiently insert all nodes contained within the DocumentFragment into the DOM tree.

The following code shows the use of a DocumentFragment:

```
var documentFragment = document.createDocumentFragment();

for (var i = 0; i < 1000; i++) {
    var element = document.createElement("div");
    var text = document.createTextNode("Here is test for div #" + i);

    element.setAttribute("id", i);

    documentFragment.appendChild(element);
}

document.body.appendChild(documentFragment);
```

Without the DocumentFragment object, this code would update the DOM tree 1,000 times, thus degrading performance. With the DocumentFragment object, the DOM tree is updated only once.

The DocumentFragment object inherits the Node object, and as such has Node's properties and methods. It does not have any other properties or methods.

Element

Elements are the majority of objects, other than text, that you will encounter in the DOM.

Properties

PROPERTY NAME	DESCRIPTION	INTRODUCED
tagName	Returns the name of the element. The same as Node.nodeName for this node type.	Level 1

Methods

METHOD NAME	DESCRIPTION	INTRODUCED
getAttribute(name)	Retrieves the attribute's value by the specified name.	Level 1
getAttributeNS(namespaceURI, localName)	Returns the Attr object by local name and namespace URI. Not for HTML DOMs.	Level 2

continues

(continued)

METHOD NAME	DESCRIPTION	INTRODUCED
`getAttributeNode(name)`	Returns the `Attr` object associated with the specified name. Returns `null` if no attribute by that name exists.	Level 1
`getElementsByTagName(tagName)`	Returns a `NodeList` of all descendant elements with the specified `tagName` in the order in which they appear in the tree.	Level 1
`getElementsByTagNameNS(namespaceURI, localName)`	Returns a `NodeList` of all the descendant `Element` objects with the specified local name and namespace URI. Not for HTML DOMs.	Level 2
`hasAttribute(name)`	Returns a boolean value based on whether or not the element has an attribute with the specified name.	Level 2
`hasAttributeNS(namespaceURI, localName)`	Returns a boolean value based on whether the `Element` has an attribute with the given local name and namespace URI. Not for HTML DOMs.	Level 2
`querySelector(selector)`	Retrieves the first child element that matches the specified selector.	Level 3
`querySelectorAll(selector)`	Retrieves all child elements that match the specified selector.	Level 3
`removeAttribute(name)`	Removes the attribute with the specified name.	Level 1
`removeAttributeNS(namespaceURI, localName)`	Removes an attribute specified by the local name and namespace URI. Not for HTML DOMs.	Level 2
`removeAttributeNode(oldAttr)`	Removes and returns the specified attribute.	Level 1
`setAttribute(name, value)`	Creates and adds a new attribute, or changes the value of an existing attribute. The value is a simple string.	Level 1

setAttributeNS(namespaceURI, qualifiedName, value)	Creates and adds a new attribute with the specified namespace URI, qualified name, and value.	Level 2
setAttributeNode(newAttr)	Adds the specified attribute to the element. Replaces the existing attribute with the same name if it exists.	Level 1
setAttributeNodeNS(newAttr)	Adds the specified attribute to the element.	Level 2

Text

The Text object represents text content of an Element or Attr object.

Methods

METHOD NAME	DESCRIPTION	INTRODUCED
splitText(indexOffset)	Breaks the Text node into two nodes at the specified offset. The new nodes stay in the DOM tree as siblings.	Level 1

HTML DOM OBJECTS

In order to adequately interface with the DOM, the W3C extends the DOM Level 1 and 2 specifications to describe objects, properties, and methods, specific to HTML documents.

Most of the objects you'll interface with as a front-end developer are contained in this section.

Miscellaneous Objects: The HTML Collection

The HTMLCollection object is a list of nodes, much like NodeList. It does not inherit from NodeList, but HTMLCollections are considered live, like NodeLists, and are automatically updated when changes are made to the document.

Properties

PROPERTY NAME	DESCRIPTION	INTRODUCED
length	Returns the number of elements in the collection.	Level 1

Methods

METHOD NAME	DESCRIPTION	INTRODUCED
`item(index)`	Returns the element at the specified index. Returns `null` if `index` is larger than the collection's length.	Level 1
`namedItem(name)`	Returns the element using a name. It first searches for an element with a matching `id` attribute value. If none are found, it searches for elements with a matching `name` attribute value.	Level 1

HTML Document Objects: The HTML Document

The `HTMLDocument` object is the root of HTML documents and contains the entire content.

Properties

PROPERTY NAME	DESCRIPTION	INTRODUCED
`anchors`	Returns an `HTMLCollection` of all `<a/>` elements in the document that have a value assigned to their `name` attribute.	Level 1
`applets`	Returns an `HTMLCollection` of all `<applet/>` elements and `<object/>` elements that include applets in the document.	Level 1
`body`	Returns the element that contains the document's content. Returns the `<body/>` element, or the outermost `<frameset/>` element depending on the document.	Level 1
`cookie`	Returns the cookies associated with the document. Returns an empty string if none.	Level 1
`domain`	Returns the domain name of the server that served the document. Returns `null` if the domain name cannot be identified.	Level 1
`forms`	Returns an `HTMLCollection` of all `<form/>` elements in the document.	Level 1
`images`	Returns an `HTMLCollection` object containing all `<img/>` elements in the document.	Level 1
`links`	Returns an `HTMLCollection` of all `<area/>` and `<a/>` elements (with an `href` value) in the document.	Level 1

referrer	Returns the URL of the page that linked to the page. Returns an empty string if the user navigated directly to the page.	Level 1
title	The title of the document as specified by the `<title/>` element in the document's `<head/>` element.	Level 1
URL	The complete URL of the document.	Level 1

Methods

METHOD NAME	DESCRIPTION	INTRODUCED
`close()`	Closes a document.	Level 1
`getElementById(elementId)`	Returns the element with the given `elementId` or `null` if no element could be found. Removed in DOM Level 2 and added to the `Document` object.	Level 1
`getElementsByName(name)`	Returns an `HTMLCollection` of elements with the specified `name` attribute value.	Level 1
`open()`	Opens a document for writing.	Level 1
`write()`	Writes a string of text to the document.	Level 1
`writeln()`	Writes a string of text to the document followed by a newline.	Level 1

HTML Element Objects

HTML element attributes are exposed as properties of the various HTML element objects. Their data type is determined by the attribute's type in the HTML 4.0 specification.

Other than `HTMLElement`, all HTML element objects are described here in alphabetical order. The following pages do not contain a complete list of HTML element object types. Instead, only the following element object types are listed:

- ➤ `HTMLAnchorElement`
- ➤ `HTMLBodyElement`
- ➤ `HTMLButtonElement`
- ➤ `HTMLDivElement`
- ➤ `HTMLFormElement`
- ➤ `HTMLFrameElement`

- ➤ HTMLFrameSetElement
- ➤ HTMLIFrameElement
- ➤ HTMLImageElement
- ➤ HTMLInputElement
- ➤ HTMLOptionElement
- ➤ HTMLParagraphElement
- ➤ HTMLSelectElement
- ➤ HTMLTableCellElement
- ➤ HTMLTableElement
- ➤ HTMLTableRowElement
- ➤ HTMLTableSectionElement
- ➤ HTMLTextAreaElement

HTMLElement

HTMLElement is the base object for all HTML elements, much like how Node is the base object for all DOM nodes. Therefore, all HTML elements have the following properties.

Properties

PROPERTY NAME	DESCRIPTION	INTRODUCED
className	Gets or sets the value of the element's class attribute.	Level 1
id	Gets or sets the value of the element's id attribute.	Level 1

HTMLAnchorElement

Represents the HTML <a/> element.

Properties

PROPERTY NAME	DESCRIPTION	INTRODUCED
accessKey	Gets or sets the value of the accessKey attribute.	Level 1
href	Gets or sets the value of the href attribute.	Level 1
name	Gets or sets the value of the name attribute.	Level 1
target	Gets or set the value of the target attribute.	Level 1

Methods

METHOD NAME	DESCRIPTION	INTRODUCED
blur()	Removes the keyboard focus from the element.	Level 1
focus()	Gives keyboard focus to the element.	Level 1

HTMLBodyElement

Represents the `<body/>` element.

Properties

PROPERTY NAME	DESCRIPTION	INTRODUCED
aLink	Deprecated. Gets or sets the value of the `alink` attribute.	Level 1
background	Deprecated. Gets or sets the value of the `background` attribute.	Level 1
bgColor	Deprecated. Gets or sets the value of the `bgColor` attribute.	Level 1
link	Deprecated. Gets or sets the value of the `link` attribute.	Level 1
text	Deprecated. Gets or sets the value of the `text` attribute.	Level 1
vLink	Deprecated. Gets or sets the value of the `vlink` attribute.	Level 1

HTMLButtonElement

Represents `<button/>` elements.

Properties

PROPERTY NAME	DESCRIPTION	INTRODUCED
accessKey	Gets or sets the value of the `accessKey` attribute.	Level 1
disabled	Gets or sets the value of the `disabled` attribute.	Level 1
form	Gets the `HTMLFormElement` object containing the button. Returns `null` if the button is not inside a form.	Level 1
name	Gets or sets the value of the `name` attribute.	Level 1
type	Gets the value of the `type` attribute.	Level 1
value	Gets or sets the value of the `value` attribute.	Level 1

HTMLDivElement

Represents the `<div/>` element.

Properties

PROPERTY NAME	DESCRIPTION	INTRODUCED
align	Deprecated. Gets or sets the value of the `align` attribute.	Level 1

HTMLFormElement

Represents the `<form/>` element.

Properties

PROPERTY NAME	DESCRIPTION	INTRODUCED
action	Gets or sets the value of the `action` attribute.	Level 1
elements	Returns an `HTMLCollection` object containing all form control elements in the form.	Level 1
enctype	Gets or sets the value of the `enctype` attribute.	Level 1
length	Returns the number of form controls within the form.	Level 1
method	Gets or sets the value of the `method` attribute.	Level 1
name	Gets or sets the value of the `name` attribute.	Level 1
target	Gets or sets the value of the `target` attribute.	Level 1

Methods

METHOD NAME	DESCRIPTION	INTRODUCED
reset()	Resets all form control elements contained within the form to their default values.	Level 1
submit()	Submits the form. Does not fire the `submit` event.	Level 1

HTMLFrameElement

Represents the `<frame/>` element.

Properties

PROPERTY NAME	DESCRIPTION	INTRODUCED
contentDocument	Gets the Document object for the frame. Returns null if one isn't available.	Level 2
frameBorder	Gets or sets the value of the frameBorder attribute.	Level 1
marginHeight	Gets or sets the value of the marginHeight attribute.	Level 1
marginWidth	Gets or sets the value of the marginWidth attribute.	Level 1
name	Gets or sets the value of the name attribute.	Level 1
noResize	Gets or sets the value of the noResize attribute.	Level 1
scrolling	Gets or sets the value of the scrolling attribute.	Level 1
src	Gets or sets the value of the src attribute.	Level 1

HTMLFrameSetElement

Represents the <frameset/> element.

Properties

PROPERTY NAME	DESCRIPTION	INTRODUCED
cols	Gets or sets the value of the cols attribute.	Level 1
rows	Gets or sets the value of the rows attribute.	Level 1

HTMLIFrameElement

Represents the <iframe/> element.

Properties

PROPERTY NAME	DESCRIPTION	INTRODUCED
align	Deprecated. Gets or sets the value of the align attribute.	Level 1
contentDocument	Gets the Document object of the frame. Returns null if one doesn't exist.	Level 2

continues

(continued)

PROPERTY NAME	DESCRIPTION	INTRODUCED
frameBorder	Gets or sets the value of the frameBorder attribute.	Level 1
height	Gets or sets the value of the height attribute.	Level 1
marginHeight	Gets or sets the value of the marginHeight attribute.	Level 1
marginWidth	Gets or sets the value of the marginWidth attribute.	Level 1
name	Gets or sets the value of the name attribute.	Level 1
noResize	Gets or sets the value of the noResize attribute.	Level 1
scrolling	Gets or sets the value of the scrolling attribute.	Level 1
src	Gets or sets the value of the src attribute.	Level 1
width	Gets or sets the value of the width attribute.	Level 1

HTMLImageElement

Represents the `<img/>` element.

Properties

PROPERTY NAME	DESCRIPTION	INTRODUCED
align	Deprecated. Gets or sets the value of the align attribute.	Level 1
alt	Gets or sets the value of the alt attribute.	Level 1
border	Deprecated. Gets or sets the value of the border attribute.	Level 1
height	Gets or sets the value of the height attribute.	Level 1
name	Gets or sets the value of the name attribute.	Level 1
src	Gets or sets the value of the src attribute.	Level 1
width	Gets or sets the value of the width attribute.	Level 1

HTMLInputElement

Represents the `<input/>` element.

Properties

PROPERTY NAME	DESCRIPTION	INTRODUCED
accessKey	Gets or sets the value of the accessKey attribute.	Level 1
align	Deprecated. Gets or sets the value of the align attribute.	Level 1
alt	Gets or sets the value of the alt attribute.	Level 1
checked	Used when type is checkbox or radio. Returns a boolean value depending on whether or not the checkbox or radio button is checked.	Level 1
defaultChecked	Used when type is checkbox or radio. Gets or sets the checked attribute. The value does not change when other checkboxes or radio buttons are checked.	Level 1
disabled	Gets or sets the value of the disabled attribute.	Level 1
form	Gets the HTMLFormElement object containing the `<input/>` element. Returns null if the element is not inside a form.	Level 1
maxLength	Gets or sets the value of the maxLength attribute.	Level 1
name	Gets or sets the value of the name attribute.	Level 1
readOnly	Used only if type is text or password. Gets or sets the value of the readonly attribute.	Level 1
size	Gets or sets the value of the size attribute.	Level 1
src	If type is image, this gets or sets the value of the src attribute.	Level 1
type	Gets the value of the type attribute.	Level 1
value	Gets or sets the value of the value attribute.	Level 1

Methods

METHOD NAME	DESCRIPTION	INTRODUCED
blur()	Removes keyboard focus from the element.	Level 1
click()	Simulates a mouse click for `<input/>` elements with `type` `button`, `checkbox`, `radio`, `reset`, and `submit`.	Level 1
focus()	Gives keyboard focus to the element.	Level 1
select()	Selects content of `<input/>` elements with `type` `text`, `password`, and `file`.	Level 1

HTMLOptionElement

Represents the `<option/>` element.

Properties

PROPERTY NAME	DESCRIPTION	INTRODUCED
defaultSelected	Gets or sets the `selected` attribute. The value of this property does not change as other `<option/>` elements in the `<select/>` element are selected.	Level 1
disabled	Gets or sets the value of the `disabled` attribute.	Level 1
form	Gets the `HTMLFormElement` object containing the `<option/>` element. Returns `null` if the element is not inside a form.	Level 1
index	Gets the index position of the `<option/>` element in its containing `<select/>` element. Starts at `0`.	Level 1
label	Gets or sets the value of the `label` attribute.	Level 1
selected	Returns a boolean value depending on whether or not the `<option/>` element is currently selected.	Level 1
text	Gets the text contained within the `<option/>` element.	Level 1
value	Gets or sets the value of the `value` attribute.	Level 1

HTMLOptionCollection

The `HTMLOptionCollection` object was introduced in DOM Level 2. It contains a list of `<option/>` elements.

PROPERTY NAME	DESCRIPTION	INTRODUCED
length	Gets the number of `<option/>` elements in the list.	Level 2

Methods

METHOD NAME	DESCRIPTION	INTRODUCED
item(index)	Retrieves the `<option/>` element at the specified index.	Level 2
namedItem(name)	Retrieves the `<option/>` element by the specified name. It first attempts to find an `<option/>` element with the specified id. If none can be found, it looks for `<option/>` elements with the specified name attribute.	Level 2

HTMLParagraphElement

Represents the `<p/>` element.

Properties

PROPERTY NAME	DESCRIPTION	INTRODUCED
align	Deprecated. Gets or sets the value of the align attribute.	Level 1

HTMLSelectElement

Represents the `<select/>` element.

Properties

PROPERTY NAME	DESCRIPTION	INTRODUCED
disabled	Gets or sets the value of the disabled attribute.	Level 1
form	Gets the `HTMLFormElement` object containing the `<select/>` element. Returns null if the element is not inside a form.	Level 1

continues

(continued)

PROPERTY NAME	DESCRIPTION	INTRODUCED
length	Returns the number of <option/> elements.	Level 1
multiple	Gets or sets the value of the multiple attribute.	Level 1
name	Gets or sets the value of the name attribute.	Level 1
options	Returns an HTMLOptionsCollection object containing the list of the <option/> elements.	Level 1
selectedIndex	Returns the index of the currently selected <option/> element. Returns -1 if nothing is selected and returns the first <option/> element selected if multiple items are selected.	Level 1
size	Gets or sets the value of the size attribute.	Level 1
type	Gets the value of the type attribute.	Level 1
value	Gets or sets the current form control's value.	Level 1

Methods

METHOD NAME	DESCRIPTION	INTRODUCED
add(element[, before])	Adds an <option/> element to the <select/> element. If before is null, then element is added at the end of the list.	Level 1
blur()	Removes keyboard focus from the elements.	Level 1
focus()	Gives keyboard focus to the element.	Level 1
remove(index)	Removes the <option/> element at the given index. Does nothing if index is out of range.	Level 1

HTMLTableCellElement

Represents the <td/> element.

Properties

PROPERTY NAME	DESCRIPTION	INTRODUCED
align	Deprecated. Gets or sets the value of the align attribute.	Level 1
bgColor	Deprecated. Gets or sets the value of the bgcolor attribute.	Level 1

cellIndex	The index of the cell in the row in DOM tree order.	Level 1
colSpan	Gets or sets the value of the colspan attribute.	Level 1
height	Deprecated. Gets or sets the value of the height attribute.	Level 1
noWrap	Deprecated. Gets or sets the value of the nowrap attribute.	Level 1
rowSpan	Gets or sets the value of the rowSpan attribute.	Level 1
vAlign	Gets or sets the value of the valign attribute.	Level 1
width	Deprecated. Gets or sets the value of the width attribute.	Level 1

HTMLTableElement

Represents the <table/> element.

Properties

PROPERTY NAME	DESCRIPTION	INTRODUCED
align	Deprecated. Gets or sets the value of the align attribute.	Level 1
bgColor	Deprecated. Gets or sets the value of the bgcolor attribute.	Level 1
border	Gets or sets the value of the border attribute.	Level 1
cellPadding	Gets or sets the value of the cellPadding attribute.	Level 1
cellSpacing	Gets or sets the value of the cellSpacing attribute.	Level 1
rows	Returns an HTMLCollection containing all rows in the table.	Level 1
tBodies	Returns an HTMLCollection of the defined <tbody/> element objects in the table.	Level 1
tFoot	Returns the table's <tfoot/> element object (HTMLTableSectionElement), or null if one doesn't exist.	Level 1

continues

(continued)

PROPERTY NAME	DESCRIPTION	INTRODUCED
tHead	Returns the table's `<thead/>` element object (`HTMLTableSectionElement`), or `null` if one doesn't exist.	Level 1
width	Gets or sets the value of the `width` attribute.	Level 1

Methods

METHOD NAME	DESCRIPTION	INTRODUCED
createTFoot()	Creates and returns a `<tfoot/>` element if one does not exist. Returns the existing `<tfoot/>` element if it exists.	Level 1
createTHead()	Creates and returns a `<thead/>` element if one does not exist. Returns the existing `<thead/>` element if it exists.	Level 1
deleteRow(index)	Deletes the row at the specified index.	Level 1
deleteTFoot()	Deletes the table's footer if one exists.	Level 1
deleteTHead()	Deletes the table's header if one exists.	Level 1
insertRow(index)	Inserts and returns a new row at the specified index. If `index` is -1 or equal to the number of rows, the new row is appended to the end of the row list.	Level 1

HTMLTableRowElement

Represents the `<tr/>` element.

Properties

PROPERTY NAME	DESCRIPTION	INTRODUCED
align	Deprecated. Gets or sets the value of the `align` attribute.	Level 1
bgColor	Deprecated. Gets or sets the value of the `bgcolor` attribute.	Level 1
cells	Returns an `HTMLCollection` containing the cells in the row.	Level 1

rowIndex	The index of the row in the table.	Level 1
sectionRowIndex	The index of the row relative to the section it belongs to (`<thead/>`, `<tfoot/>`, or `<tbody/>`).	Level 1
vAlign	Gets or sets the value of the `valign` attribute.	Level 1

Methods

METHOD NAME	DESCRIPTION	INTRODUCED
deleteCell(index)	Deletes the cell at the specified index.	Level 1
insertCell(index)	Inserts and returns an empty `<td/>` element. If index is -1 or equal to the number of cells in the row, the new cell is appended to the end of the list.	Level 1

HTMLTableSectionElement

Represents the `<thead/>`, `<tbody/>`, and `<tfoot/>` elements.

Properties

PROPERTY NAME	DESCRIPTION	INTRODUCED
align	Deprecated. Gets or sets the value of the `align` attribute.	Level 1
rows	Returns an `HTMLCollection` containing the rows of the section.	Level 1
vAlign	Gets or sets the value of the `valign` attribute.	Level 1

Methods

METHOD NAME	DESCRIPTION	INTRODUCED
deleteRow(index)	Deletes the row at the specified index relative to the section.	Level 1
insertRow(index)	Inserts and returns a new row into the section at the specified index (relative to the section). If index is -1 or equal to the number of rows, the row is appended to the end of the list.	Level 1

HTMLTextAreaElement

Represents the `<textarea/>` element.

Properties

PROPERTY NAME	DESCRIPTION	INTRODUCED
accessKey	Gets or sets the value of the `accessKey` attribute.	Level 1
cols	Gets or sets the value of the `cols` attribute.	Level 1
defaultValue	Gets or sets the contents of the element. The value does not change when the content changes.	Level 1
disabled	Gets or sets the value of the `disabled` attribute.	Level 1
form	Gets the `HTMLFormElement` object containing the `<textarea/>` element. Returns `null` if the element is not inside a form.	Level 1
name	Gets or sets the value of the `name` attribute.	Level 1
readOnly	Used only if `type` is `text` or `password`. Gets or sets the value of the `readonly` attribute.	Level 1
rows	Gets or sets the value of the `rows` attribute.	Level 1
type	Gets the value of the `type` attribute. Always set to `textarea`.	Level 1
value	Gets or sets the current value of the element.	Level 1

Methods

METHOD NAME	DESCRIPTION	INTRODUCED
blur()	Removes keyboard focus from the element.	Level 1
focus()	Gives keyboard focus to the element.	Level 1
select()	Selects the contents of the element.	Level 1

HTML Media Objects

The `HTMLMediaElement` object is the base type for both `<video/>` and `<audio/>` elements.

HTMLMediaElement

Properties

PROPERTY NAME	DESCRIPTION	INTRODUCED
autoplay	Reflects the autoplay attribute, and determines where playback should automatically begin as soon as enough media is available.	HTML5
buffered	Gets the ranges of the media source that the browser has buffered.	HTML5
controller	Gets or sets the media controller associated with the element; returns null if none is linked.	HTML5
controls	Gets or sets the controls attribute, determining if the browser's default controls are displayed.	HTML5
currentSrc	Gets the absolute URL of the media.	HTML5
currentTime	The current playback time in seconds. Setting seeks the media to the specified time.	HTML5
defaultMuted	Gets or sets the muted attribute. This does not affect the audio after playback starts. Use the muted property for that.	HTML5
defaultPlaybackRate	The speed of playback. 1.0 is normal.	HTML5
duration	Gets the length of the media in seconds.	HTML5
ended	Indicates whether the media element has ended playback.	HTML5
error	The most recent error; null if no error has occurred.	HTML5
loop	Gets or sets the loop attribute; indicates whether the media should start over when it reaches the end.	HTML5
mediaGroup	Gets or sets the mediagroup attribute.	HTML5
muted	Mutes or unmutes the audio.	HTML5
networkState	The current state of fetching the media over the network.	HTML5
paused	Indicates whether the media element is paused.	HTML5

continues

(continued)

PROPERTY NAME	DESCRIPTION	INTRODUCED
playbackRate	Gets or sets the current playback rate.	HTML5
played	Gets the ranges that the media source has played, if any.	HTML5
preload	Gets or sets the `preload` attribute.	HTML5
readyState	Gets the readiness of the media.	HTML5
seekable	Gets the time ranges that the user can seek.	HTML5
seeking	Indicates whether the media is in the process of seeking to a new position.	HTML5
src	Gets or sets the `src` attribute.	HTML5
volume	Gets or sets the volume of the audio. 0.0 (silent) to 1.0 (loudest)	HTML5

Methods

METHOD NAME	DESCRIPTION	INTRODUCED
canPlayType()	Determines the likelihood the browser can play the given media type.	HTML5
load()	Begins loading the media content from the server.	HTML5
pause()	Pauses the media playback.	HTML5
play()	Begins or resumes the media playback.	HTML5

HTMLAudioElement

The `<audio/>` element does not have any unique properties or methods from `HTMLMediaElement`.

HTMLVideoElement

The `<video/>` element has a few unique properties.

Properties

PROPERTY NAME	DESCRIPTION	INTRODUCED
height	Gets or sets the `height` attribute, determining the size of the display area.	HTML5

poster	Gets or sets the `poster` attribute, specifying the image to show while no video data is available.	HTML5
videoHeight	Gets the intrinsic height of the resource in CSS pixels.	HTML5
videoWidth	Gets the intrinsic width of the resource in CSS pixels.	HTML5
width	Gets or sets the `width` attribute, determine the size of the display area.	HTML5

DOM EVENT MODEL AND OBJECTS

The DOM event model was introduced in DOM Level 2. It describes an event system where every event has an event target. When an event reaches an event target, all registered event handlers on the event target are triggered for that specific event. The following objects are described by the DOM event model.

EventTarget

The `EventTarget` object is inherited by all `HTMLElement` objects in the DOM. This object provides the means for the registration and removal of event handlers on the event target.

Methods

METHOD NAME	DESCRIPTION
`addEventListener(type, listener, useCapture)`	Registers an event handler on an element. `type` is the event type to listen for, `listener` is the JavaScript function to call when the event is fired, and `useCapture` determines whether the event is captured or bubbles.
`removeEventListener(type, listener, useCapture)`	Removes a listener from the element.

Event

When an event fires, an `Event` object is passed to the event handler if one is specified. This object contains contextual information about an event.

Properties

PROPERTY NAME	DESCRIPTION	INTRODUCED
bubbles	Indicates whether or not the event is a bubbling event.	Level 2
cancelable	Indicates whether or not the event can have its default action prevented.	Level 2
currentTarget	Indicates the EventTarget whose listeners are currently being processed.	Level 2
target	Indicates the EventTarget object to which the event was originally fired.	Level 2
timeStamp	Specifies the time (in milliseconds) at which the event was fired.	Level 2
type	The name of the event (remember: this is the name without the on prefix).	Level 2

Methods

METHOD NAME	DESCRIPTION	INTRODUCED
preventDefault()	Cancels the event, preventing the default action from taking place, only if the event is cancelable.	Level 2
stopPropagation()	Prevents further propagation of an event.	Level 2

MouseEvent

The MouseEvent object provides specific information associated with mouse events. MouseEvent objects contain not only the following properties, but also the properties and methods of the Event object.

Valid mouse events are shown in the following table.

EVENT NAME	DESCRIPTION
click	Occurs when the mouse button is clicked over an element. A click is defined as a mousedown and mouseup over the same screen location.
mousedown	Occurs when the mouse button is pressed over an element.
mouseup	Occurs when the mouse button is released over an element.
mouseover	Occurs when the mouse pointer moves onto an element.
mousemove	Occurs when the mouse pointer moves while it is over the element.
mouseout	Occurs when the mouse pointer moves away from an element.

Properties

PROPERTY NAME	DESCRIPTION	INTRODUCED
altKey	Returns a boolean value indicating whether or not the Alt key was pressed during the event's firing.	Level 2
button	Indicates which mouse button was pressed, if applicable. The number 0 represents the left button, 1 indicates the middle button, and 2 indicates the right button. Left-hand-configured mice reverse the buttons (right is 0, middle is 1, and left is 2).	Level 2
clientX	The horizontal coordinate relative to the client area.	Level 2
clientY	The vertical coordinate relative to the client area.	Level 2
ctrlKey	Returns a boolean value indicating whether or not the Ctrl key was pressed when the event fired.	Level 2
relatedTarget	Indentifies a secondary EventTarget. Currently, this property is used with the mouseover event to indicate the EventTarget that the mouse pointer exited and with the mouseout event to indicate which EventTarget the pointer entered.	Level 2
screenX	The horizontal coordinate relative to the screen.	Level 2
screenY	The vertical coordinate relative to the screen.	Level 2
shiftKey	Returns a boolean value indicating whether or not the Shift key was pressed when the event fired.	Level 2

MISCELLANEOUS EVENTS

The following tables describe the events available in client-side JavaScript.

Mouse Events

EVENT	DESCRIPTION
click	Raised when the user clicks an HTML control.
dblclick	Raised when the user double-clicks an HTML control.
mousedown	Raised when the user presses a mouse button.

continues

(continued)

EVENT	DESCRIPTION
mousemove	Raised when the user moves the mouse pointer.
mouseout	Raised when the user moves the mouse pointer out from within an HTML control.
mouseover	Raised when the user moves the mouse pointer over an HTML control.
mouseup	Raised when the user releases the mouse button.

Keyboard Events

EVENT	DESCRIPTION
keydown	Raised when the user presses a key on the keyboard.
keypress	Raised when the user presses a key on the keyboard. This event will be raised continually until the user releases the key.
keyup	Raised when the user releases a key that had been pressed.

HTML Control Events

EVENT	DESCRIPTION
blur	Raised when an HTML control loses focus.
change	Raised when an HTML control loses focus and its value has changed.
focus	Raised when focus is set to the HTML control.
reset	Raised when the user resets a form.
select	Raised when the user selects text in an HTML control.
submit	Raised when the user submits a form.

Window Events

EVENT	DESCRIPTION
load	Raised when the window has completed loading.
resize	Raised when the user resizes the window.
unload	Executes JavaScript code when the user exits a document.

Media Events

EVENT	DESCRIPTION
abort	Raised when playback is aborted.
canplay	Sent when enough data is available that the media can be played.
canplaythrough	Fired when the entire media can be played without interruption.
durationchange	Raised when the metadata has changed.
emptied	Fires when the media has become empty.
ended	Sent when playback completes.
error	Sent when an error occurs.
loadeddata	The media's first frame has been loaded.
loadedmetadata	Fired when the media's metadata is loaded.
loadstart	Sent when downloading begins.
pause	Playback has been paused.
play	Playback begins after a pause.
playing	Raised when media begins to play.
progress	Indicates the progress of the media download.
ratechange	Fires when the playback rate changes.
seeked	Seeking has ended.
seeking	Playback is being moved to a new position.
stalled	Raised when the browser tries to download the media, but receives no data.
suspend	Sent when the loading of the media is suspended.
timeupdate	The media's currentTime has changed.
volumechange	Fires when the audio volume changes (both when volume is set and when muted).
waiting	Raised when playback is paused in order to download more data.

Other Events

EVENT	DESCRIPTION
abort	Raised when the user aborts loading an image.
error	Raised when an error occurs loading the page.

D

Latin-1 Character Set

This appendix contains the Latin-1 character set and the character codes in both decimal and hexadecimal formats. As explained in Chapter 2, the escape sequence \xNN, where NN is a hexadecimal character code from the Latin-1 character set shown here, can be used to represent characters that can't be typed directly in JavaScript.

DECIMAL CHARACTER CODE	HEXADECIMAL CHARACTER CODE	SYMBOL
32	20	Space
33	21	!
34	22	"
35	23	#
36	24	$
37	25	%
38	26	&
39	27	'
40	28	(
41	29	)
42	2A	*
43	2B	+
44	2C	,
45	2D	-

continues

(continued)

DECIMAL CHARACTER CODE	HEXADECIMAL CHARACTER CODE	SYMBOL
46	2E	.
47	2F	/
48	30	0
49	31	1
50	32	2
51	33	3
52	34	4
53	35	5
54	36	6
55	37	7
56	38	8
57	39	9
58	3A	:
59	3B	;
60	3C	<
61	3D	=
62	3E	>
63	3F	?
64	40	@
65	41	A
66	42	B
67	43	C
68	44	D
69	45	E
70	46	F
71	47	G
72	48	H

73	49	I
74	4A	J
75	4B	K
76	4C	L
77	4D	M
78	4E	N
79	4F	O
80	50	P
81	51	Q
82	52	R
83	53	S
84	54	T
85	55	U
86	56	V
87	57	W
88	58	X
89	59	Y
90	5A	Z
91	5B	[
92	5C	\
93	5D	]
94	5E	^
95	5F	_
96	60	`
97	61	a
98	62	b
99	63	c
100	64	d
101	65	e

continues

(continued)

DECIMAL CHARACTER CODE	HEXADECIMAL CHARACTER CODE	SYMBOL
102	66	f
103	67	g
104	68	h
105	69	i
106	6A	j
107	6B	k
108	6C	l
109	6D	m
110	6E	n
111	6F	o
112	70	p
113	71	q
114	72	r
115	73	s
116	74	t
117	75	u
118	76	v
119	77	w
120	78	x
121	79	y
122	7A	z
123	7B	{
124	7C	|
125	7D	}
126	7E	~
160	A0	Non-breaking space
161	A1	¡

162	A2	¢
163	A3	£
164	A4	¤
165	A5	¥
166	A6	¦
167	A7	§
168	A8	¨
169	A9	©
170	AA	ª
171	AB	«
172	AC	¬
173	AD	Soft hyphen
174	AE	®
175	AF	¯
176	B0	°
177	B1	±
178	B2	²
179	B3	³
180	B4	´
181	B5	µ
182	B6	¶
183	B7	·
184	B8	¸
185	B9	¹
186	BA	º
187	BB	»
188	BC	~QF
189	BD	~HF
190	BE	~TQF

continues

(continued)

DECIMAL CHARACTER CODE	HEXADECIMAL CHARACTER CODE	SYMBOL
191	BF	¿
192	C0	À
193	C1	Á
194	C2	Â
195	C3	Ã
196	C4	Ä
197	C5	Å
198	C6	Æ
199	C7	Ç
200	C8	È
201	C9	É
202	CA	Ê
203	CB	Ë
204	CC	Ì
205	CD	Í
206	CE	Î
207	CF	Ï
208	D0	Ð
209	D1	Ñ
210	D2	Ò
211	D3	Ó
212	D4	Ô
213	D5	Õ
214	D6	Ö
215	D7	∞
216	D8	Ø
217	D9	Ù

218	DA	Ú
219	DB	Û
220	DC	Ü
221	DD	Ý
222	DE	þ
223	DF	ß
224	E0	à
225	E1	á
226	E2	â
227	E3	ã
228	E4	ä
229	E5	å
230	E6	æ
231	E7	ç
232	E8	è
233	E9	é
234	EA	ê
235	EB	ë
236	EC	ì
237	ED	í
238	EE	î
239	EF	ï
240	F0	ð
241	F1	ñ
242	F2	ò
243	F3	ó
244	F4	ô
245	F5	õ
246	F6	ö

continues

(continued)

DECIMAL CHARACTER CODE	HEXADECIMAL CHARACTER CODE	SYMBOL
247	F7	÷
248	F8	ø
249	F9	ù
250	FA	ú
251	FB	û
252	FC	ü
253	FD	ý
254	FE	þ
255	FF	ÿ

INDEX